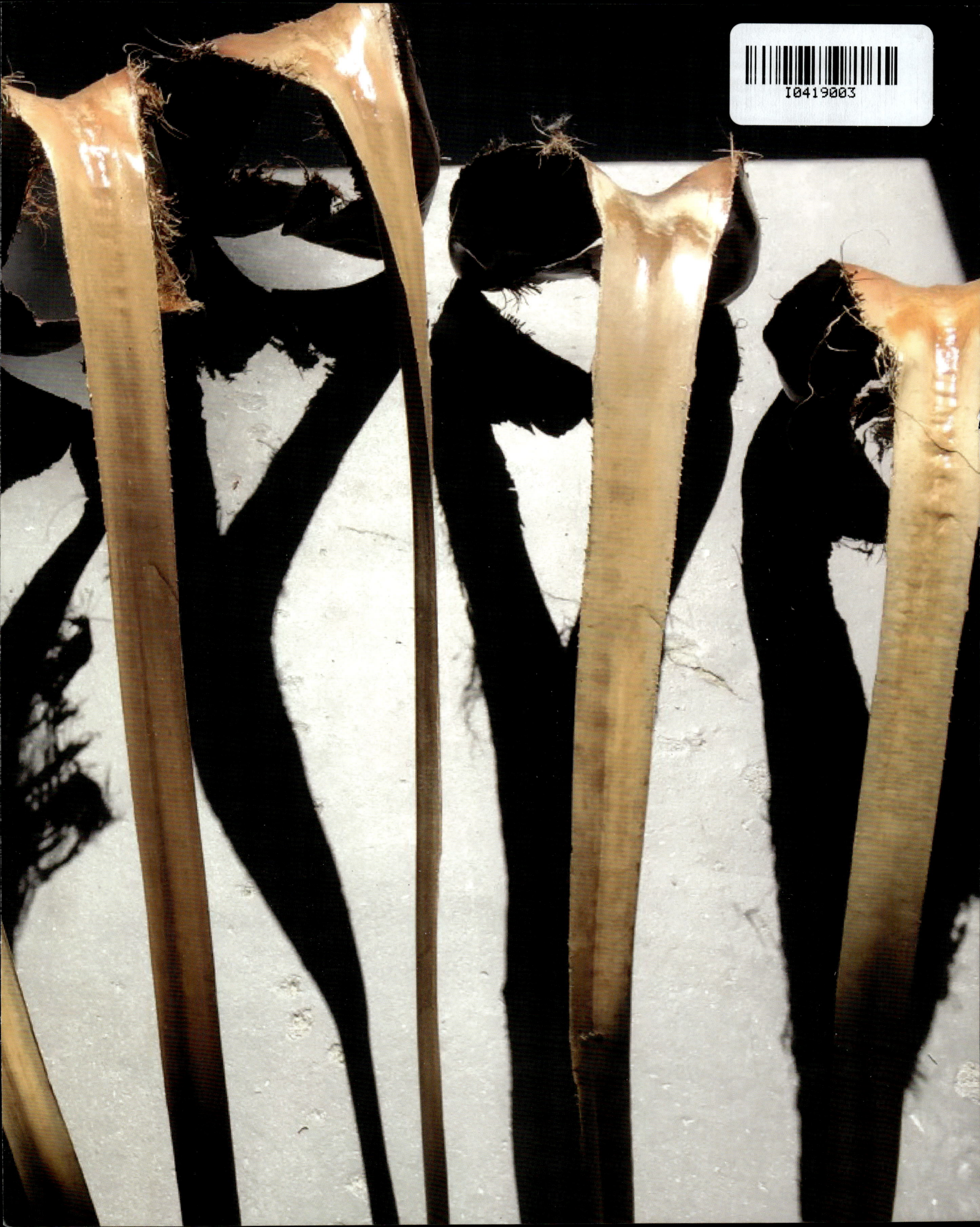

JAMES MACDONELL

RETROSPECTIVE 2004 - 2024

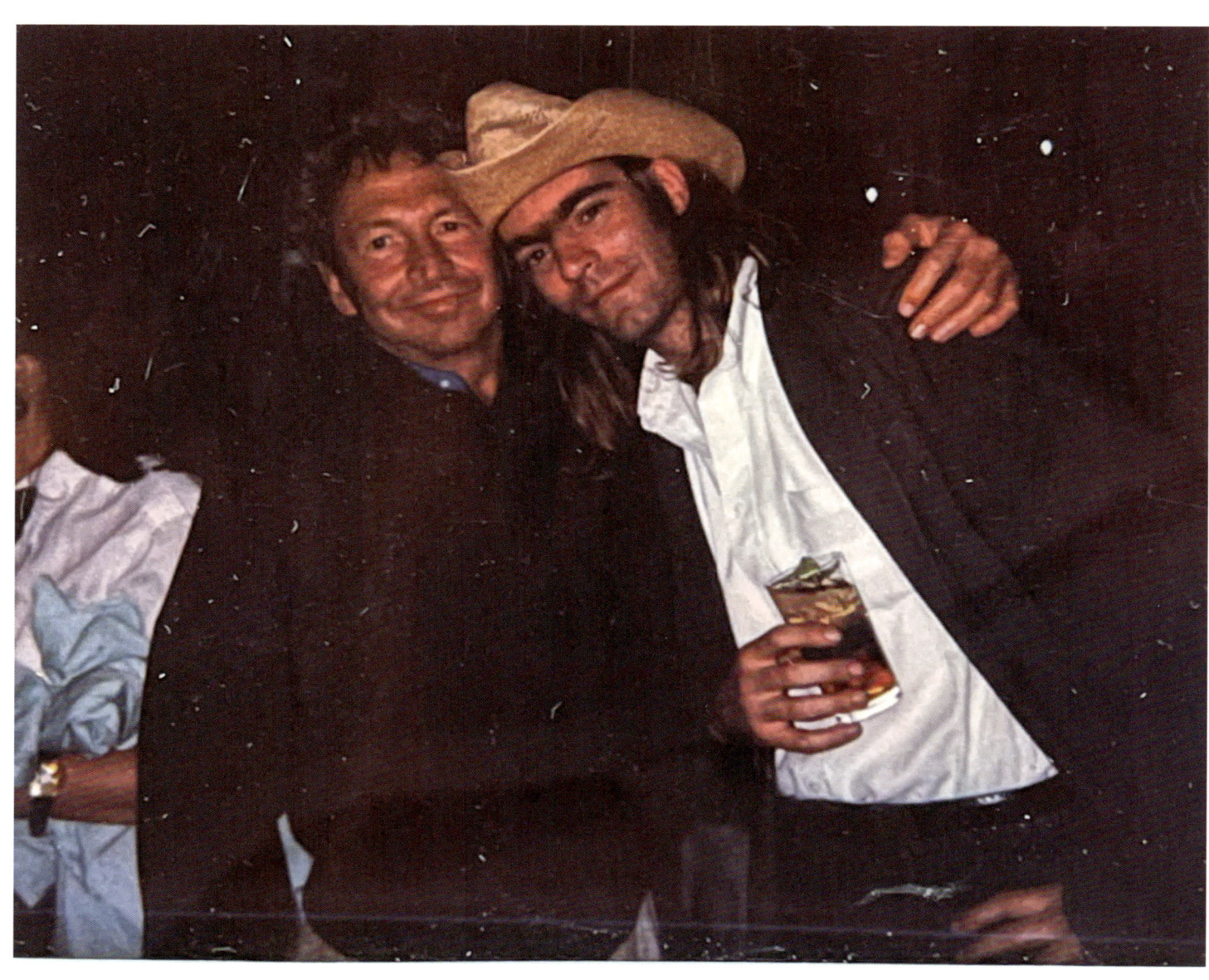

Robert Rauschenberg & James Macdonell, Lafayette, Louisiana (2005)

To Valerie and Mac,

For this life with which I am well pleased.

To Rick, Janet, Bob and Shannon,

For always being there
And keeping me connected to the things
That matter most.

The following artists have long been inspirational to me. Thanks to all of you for your kindness and acceptance along the way, for the sharing of your wisdom, for "keeping the channel open", for creating work that challenges us all to continually refine our processes and perspective, and to make beautiful the ways in which we see and interpret the world. Charlie Yoder, Al Taylor, Hisashika Takahashi, Larry B. Wright, Richard 'Dickie' Landry, Francis Pavy, Dawn DeDeaux, Mel Chin, Robert Wilson, Illigilli, Josef Beuys, Eva Hesse, Robert Tannen, and Robert Rauschenberg.

Special thanks to Master carpenter Wardell Joiner and technical consultant artist Matthew Foreman for their work in the printing and fabrication of many of the pieces presented here.

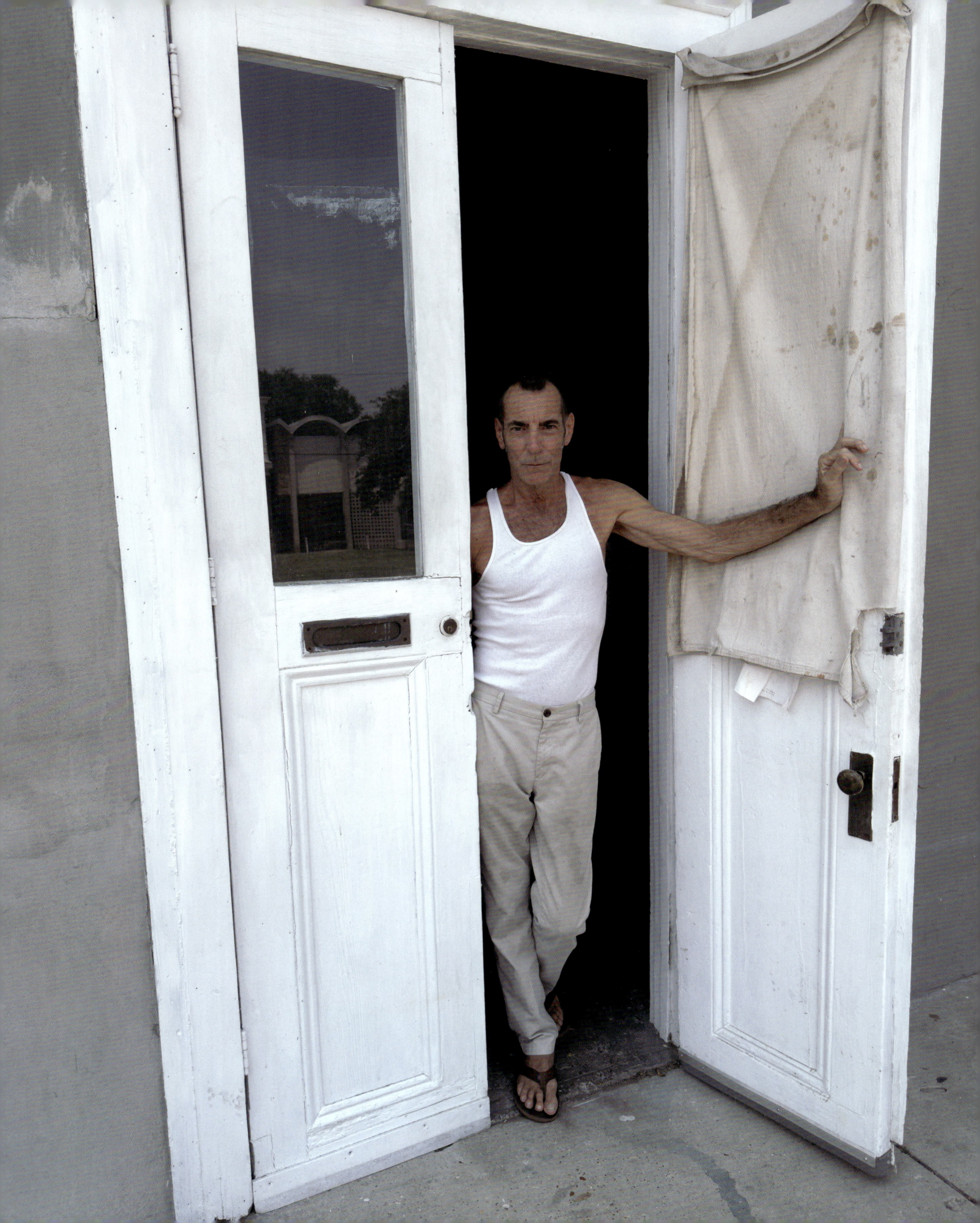

"A true artist realizes how little time they actually have. Thus, they are always filled with a sense of urgency. They understand completely the bargain they have made: that one's 'calling', one's 'great sense of purpose', requires a lifetime of risk and sacrifice; that the truth itself is no guarantor of success, and that their great reward may well be to labor in obscurity. Still, they remain. Undeterred. I can say only... trust your intuition, stay diligent, the world is full of wonders."

- JAMES MACDONELL

JAMES MACDONELL

RETROSPECTIVE 2004 - 2024

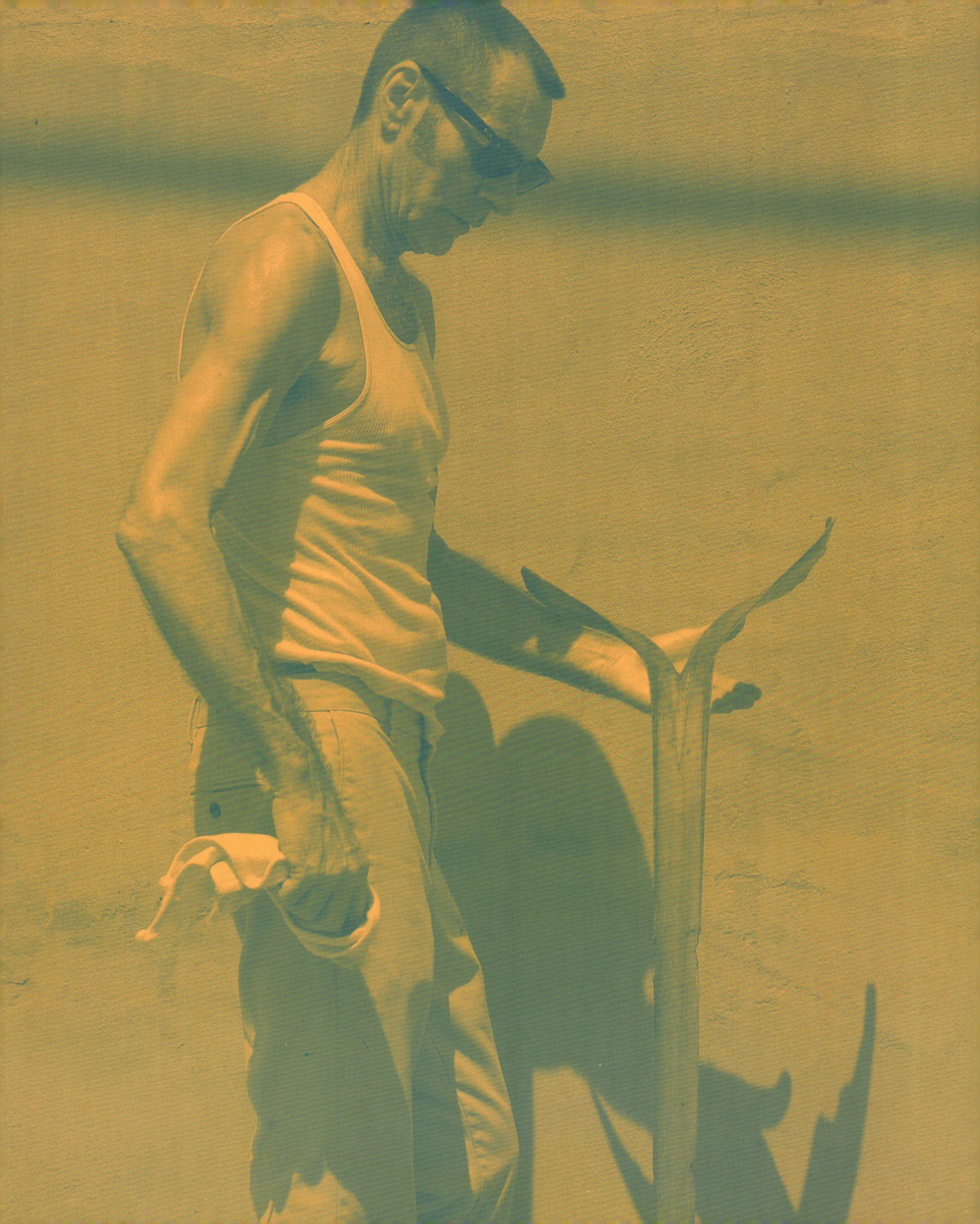

ASSEMBLAGE, SCULPTURE, COMBINES & FOUND OBJECTS

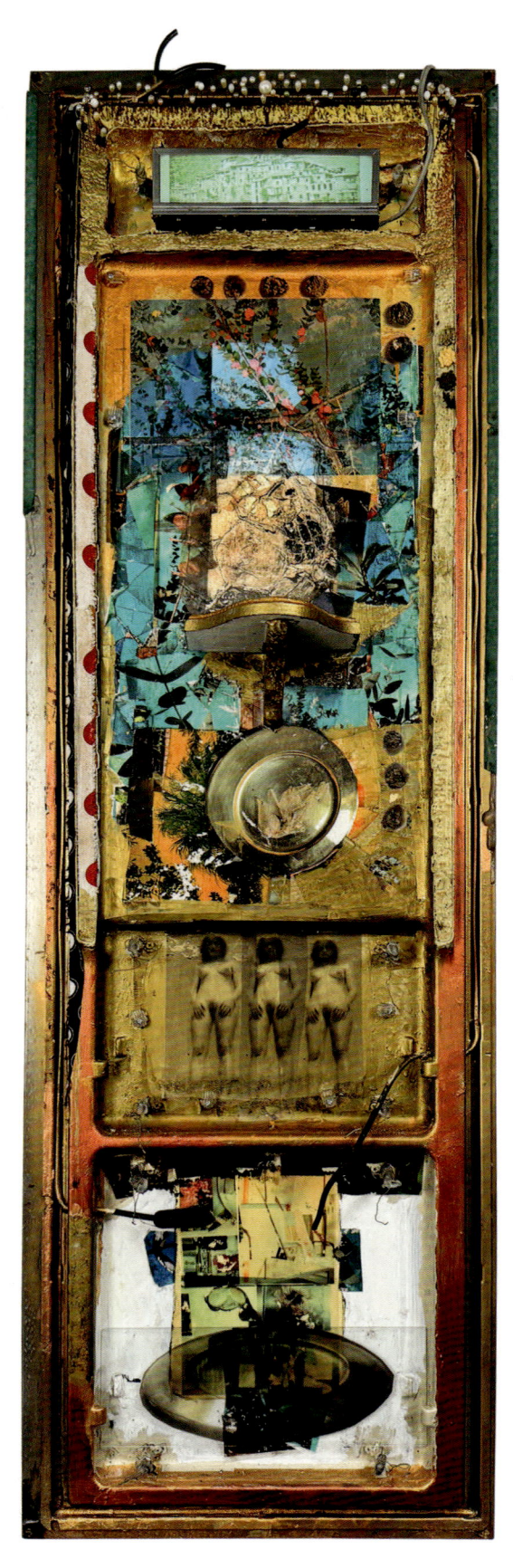

Surveyor
65 x 20 ½ x 10 inches
Mixed Media
2022

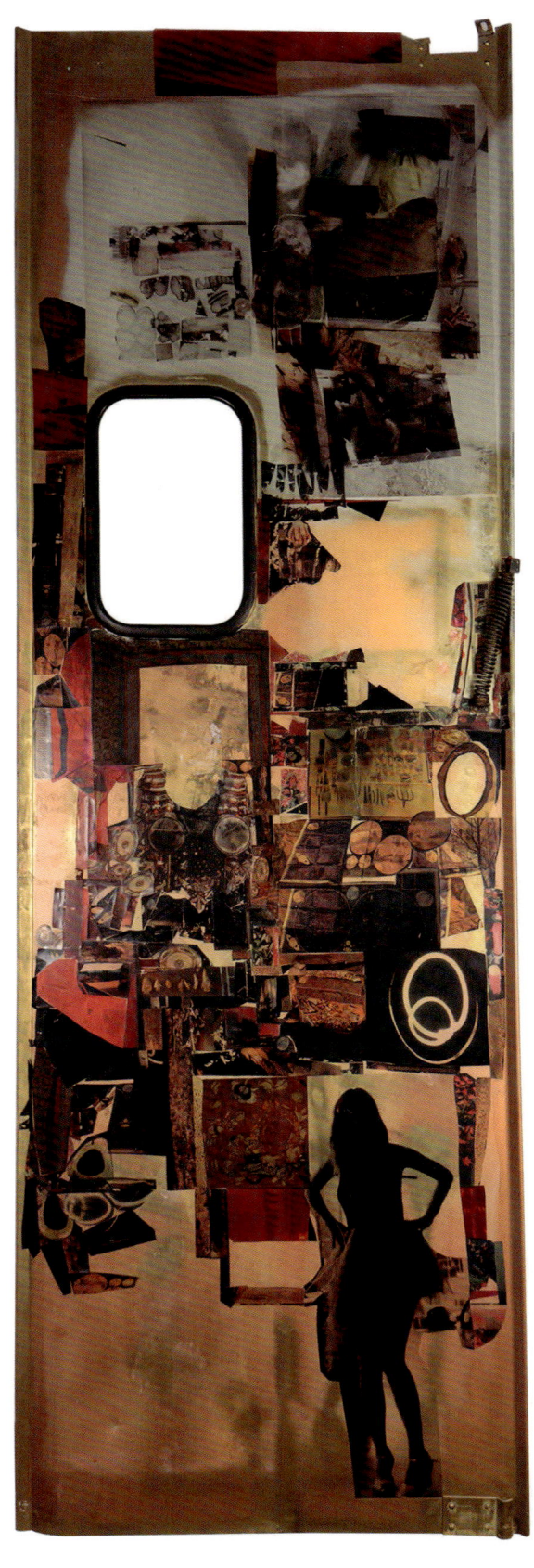

Kitchen Door
88 x 29 inches
Mixed Media
2016

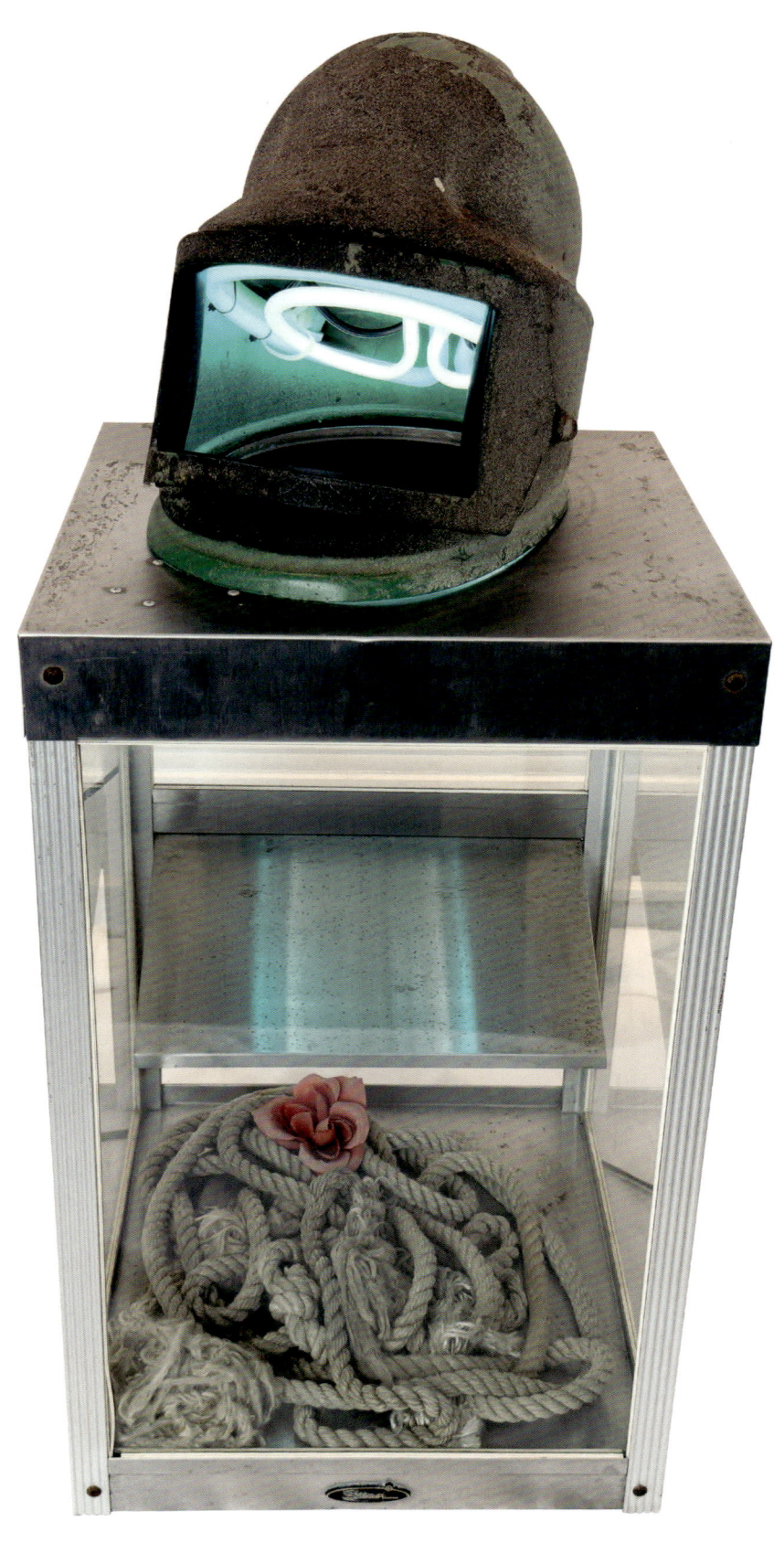

Headlamp
34 x 15 x 15 inches
Mixed Media
2011

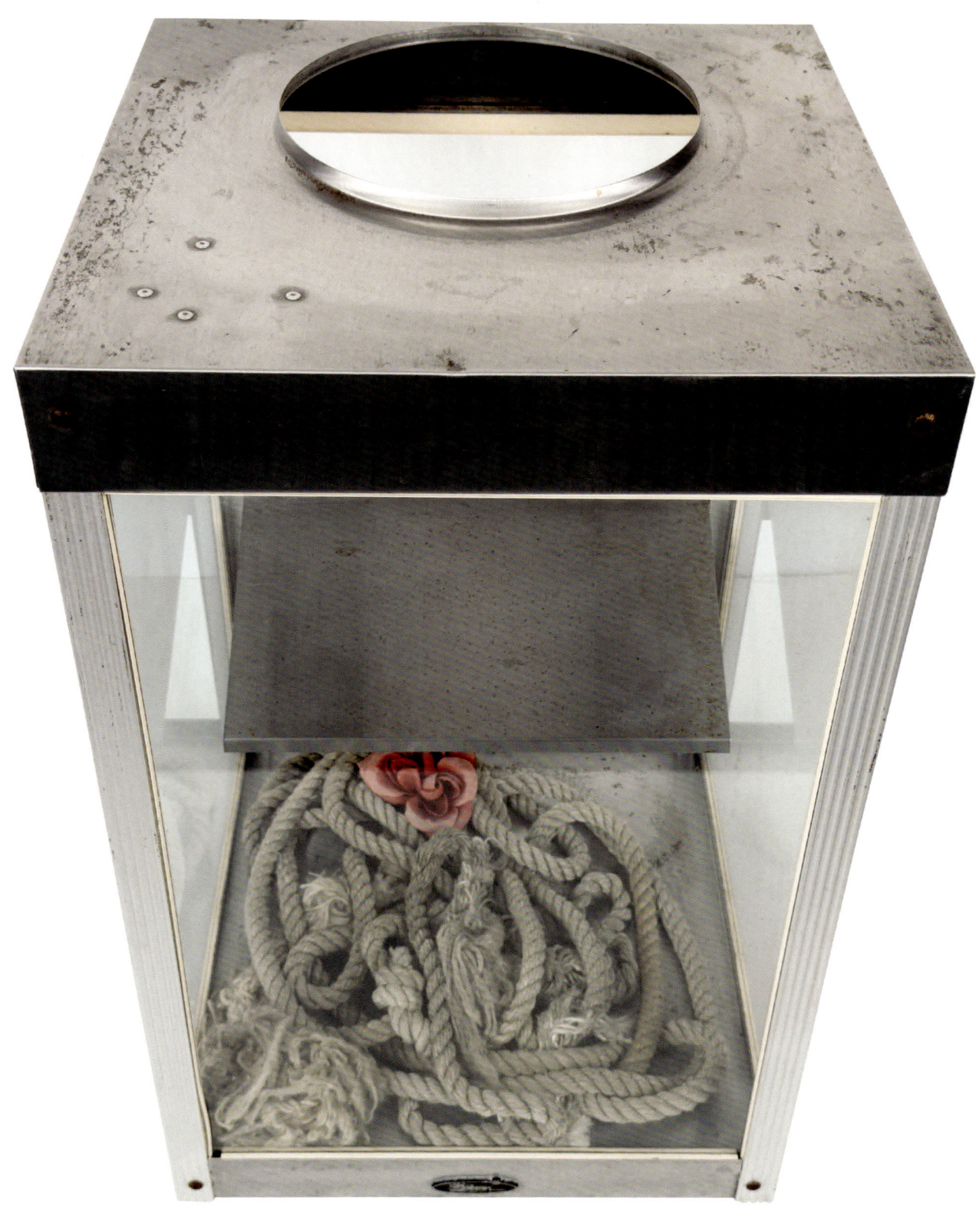

Headlamp (Detail)

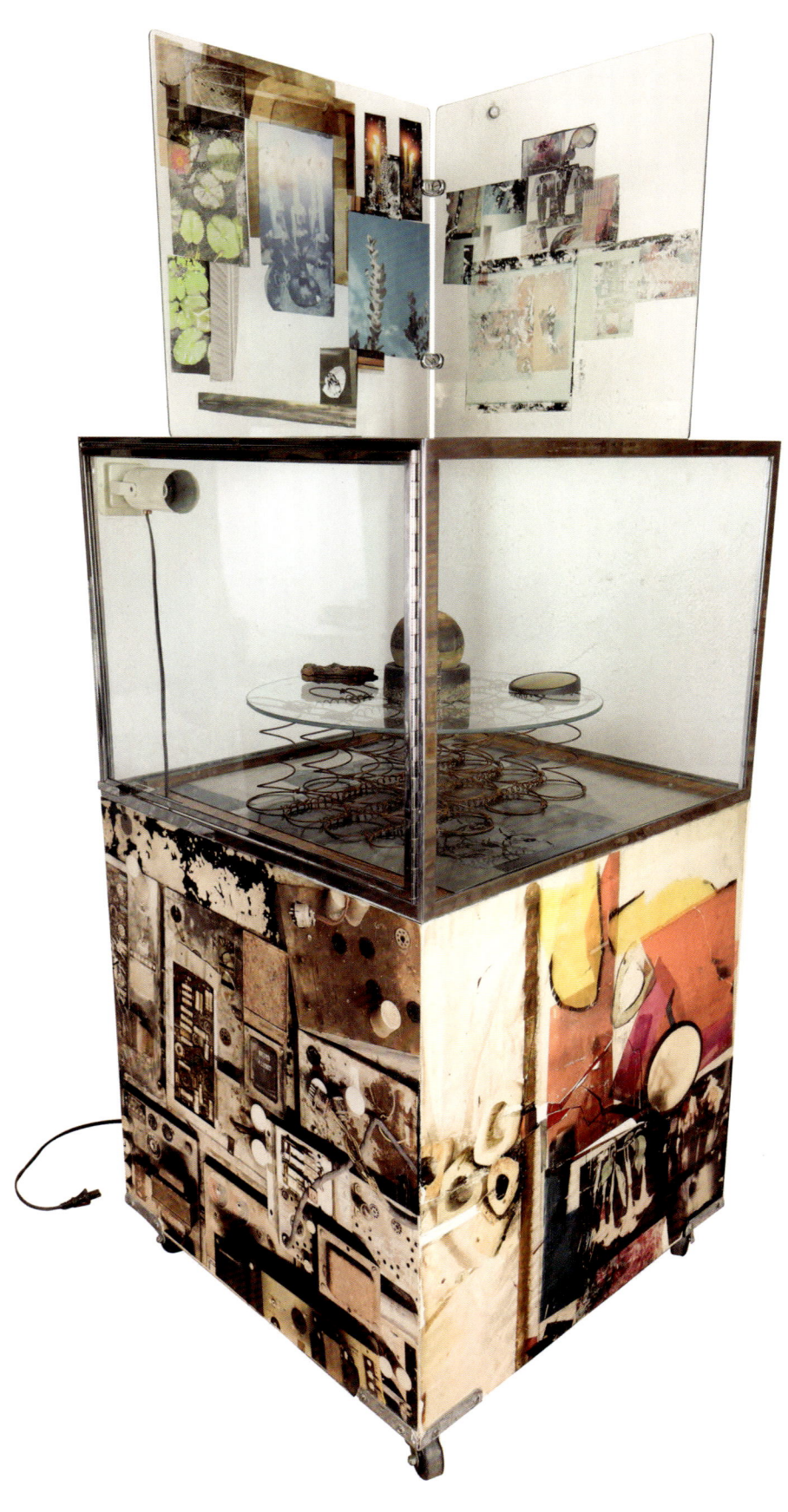

Ark (Front View)
64 x 24 x 24 inches
Mixed Media
2016

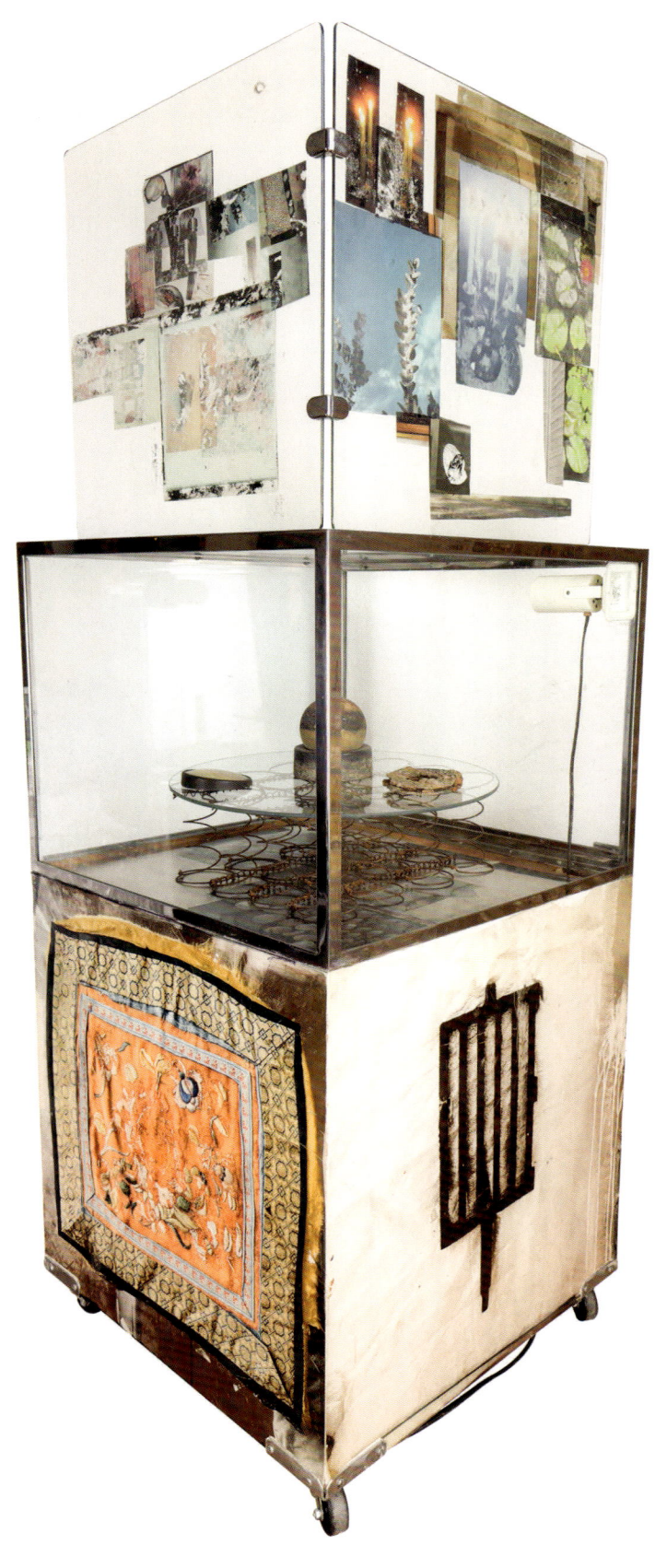

Ark (Back View)

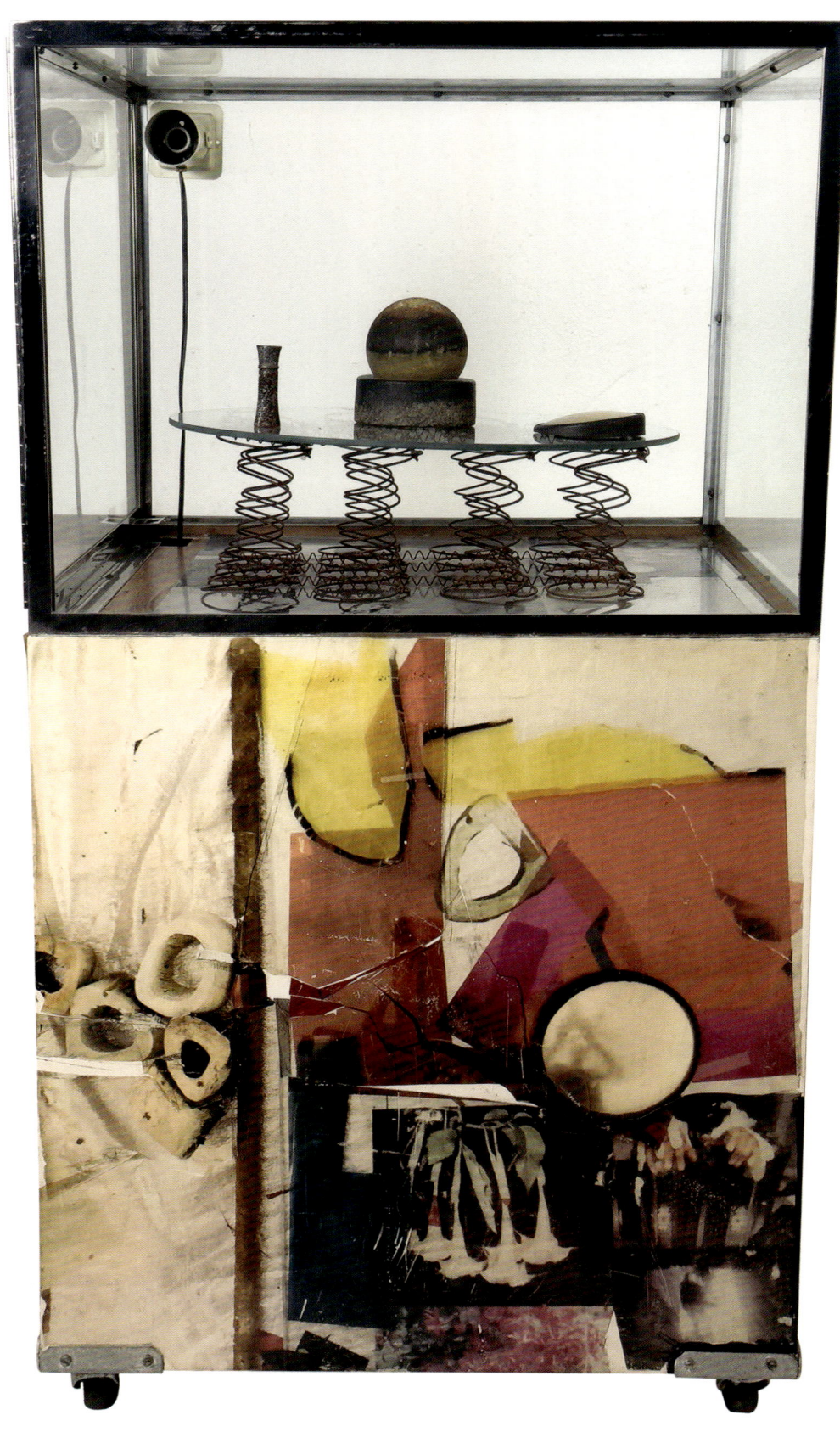

Ark (Side 1)

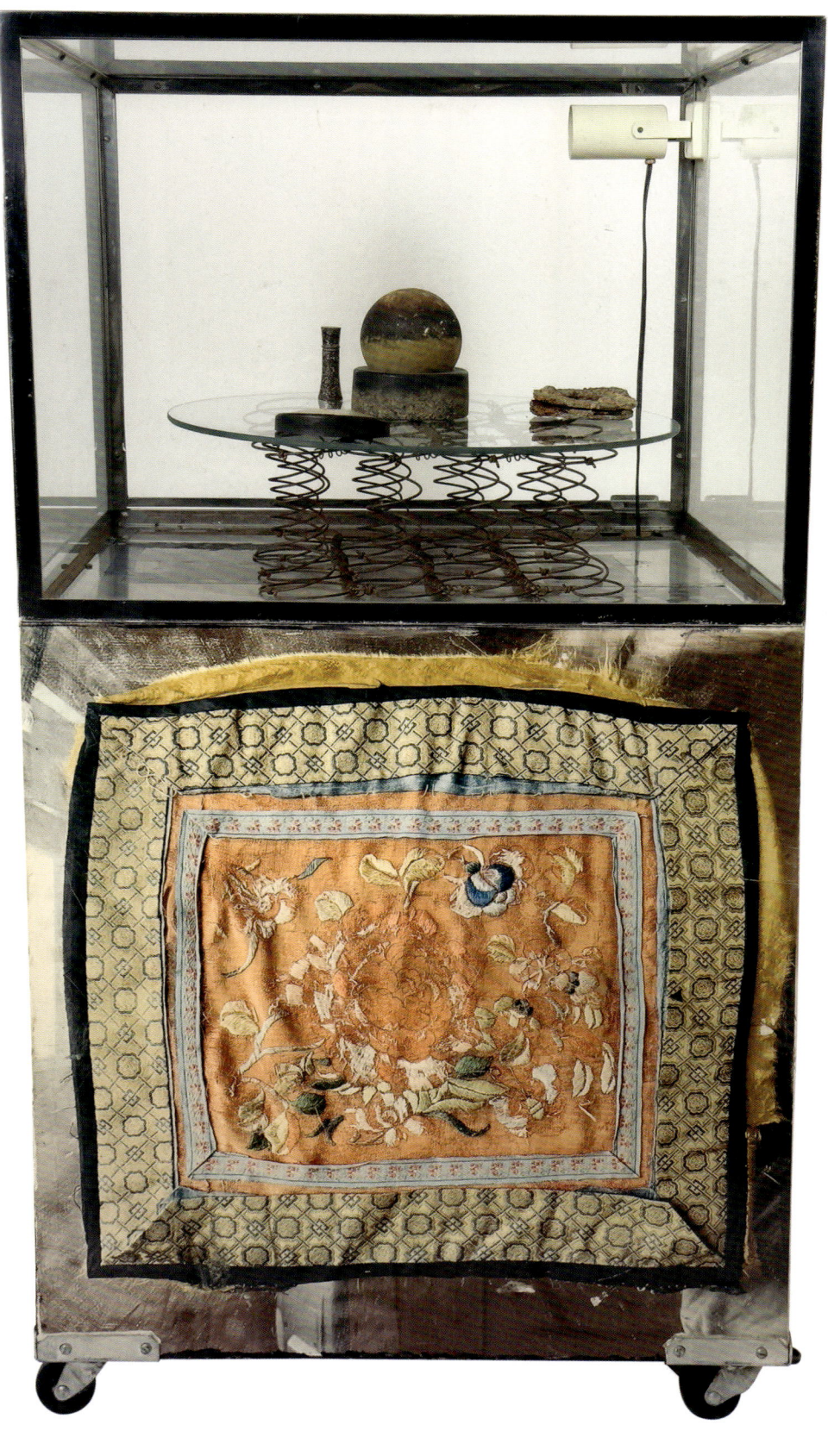

Ark (Side 2)

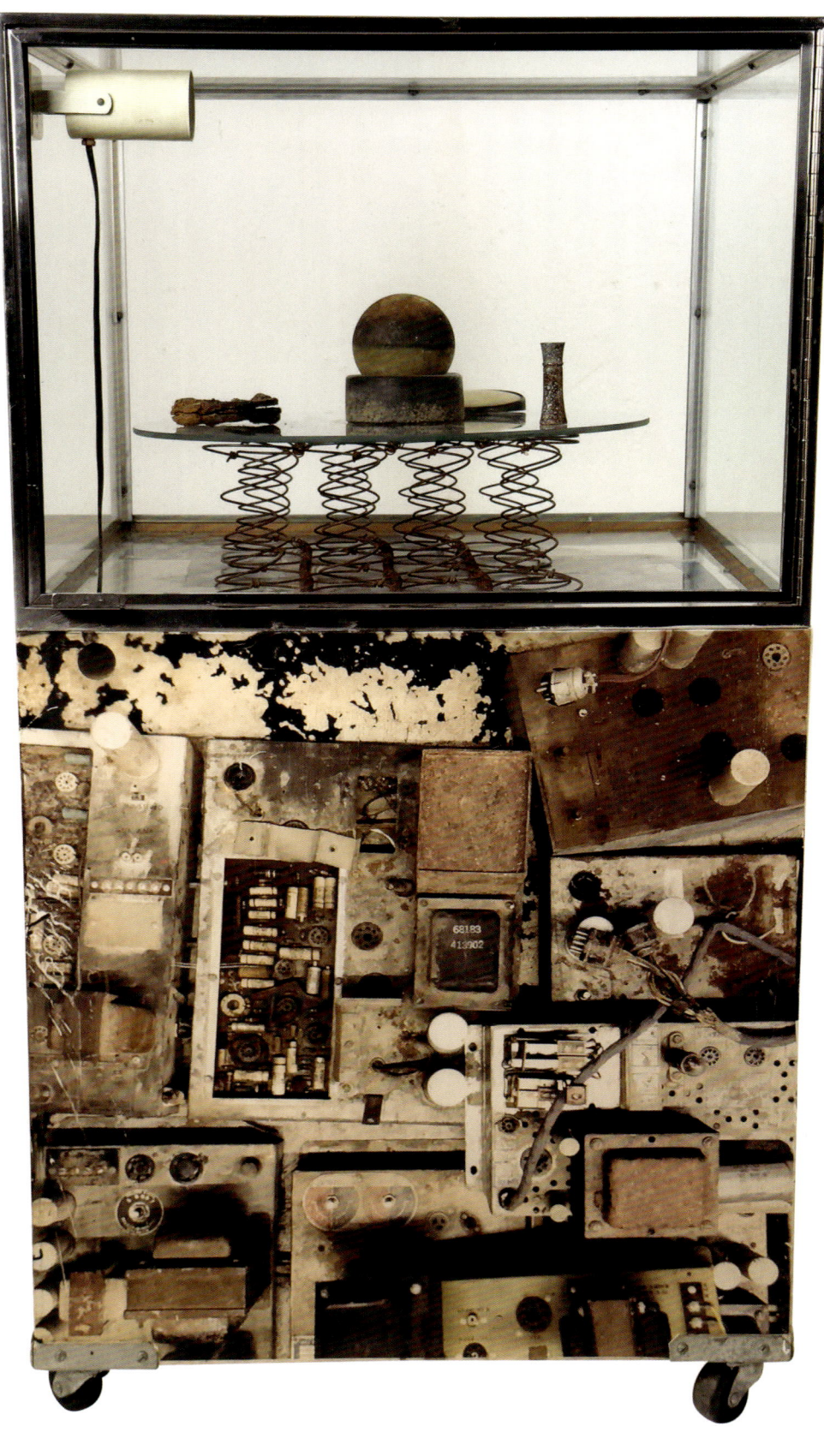

Ark (Side 3)

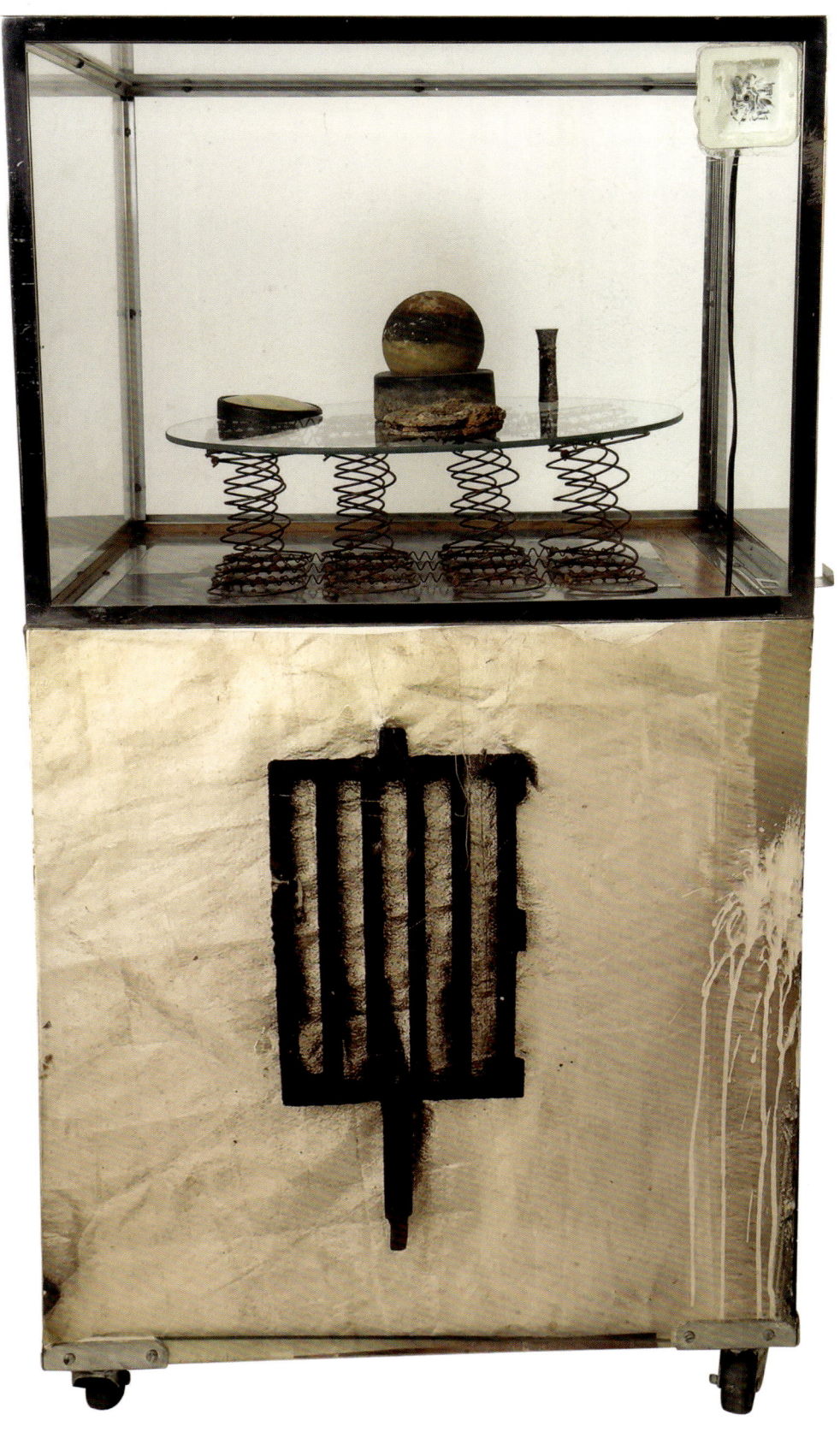

Ark (Side 4)

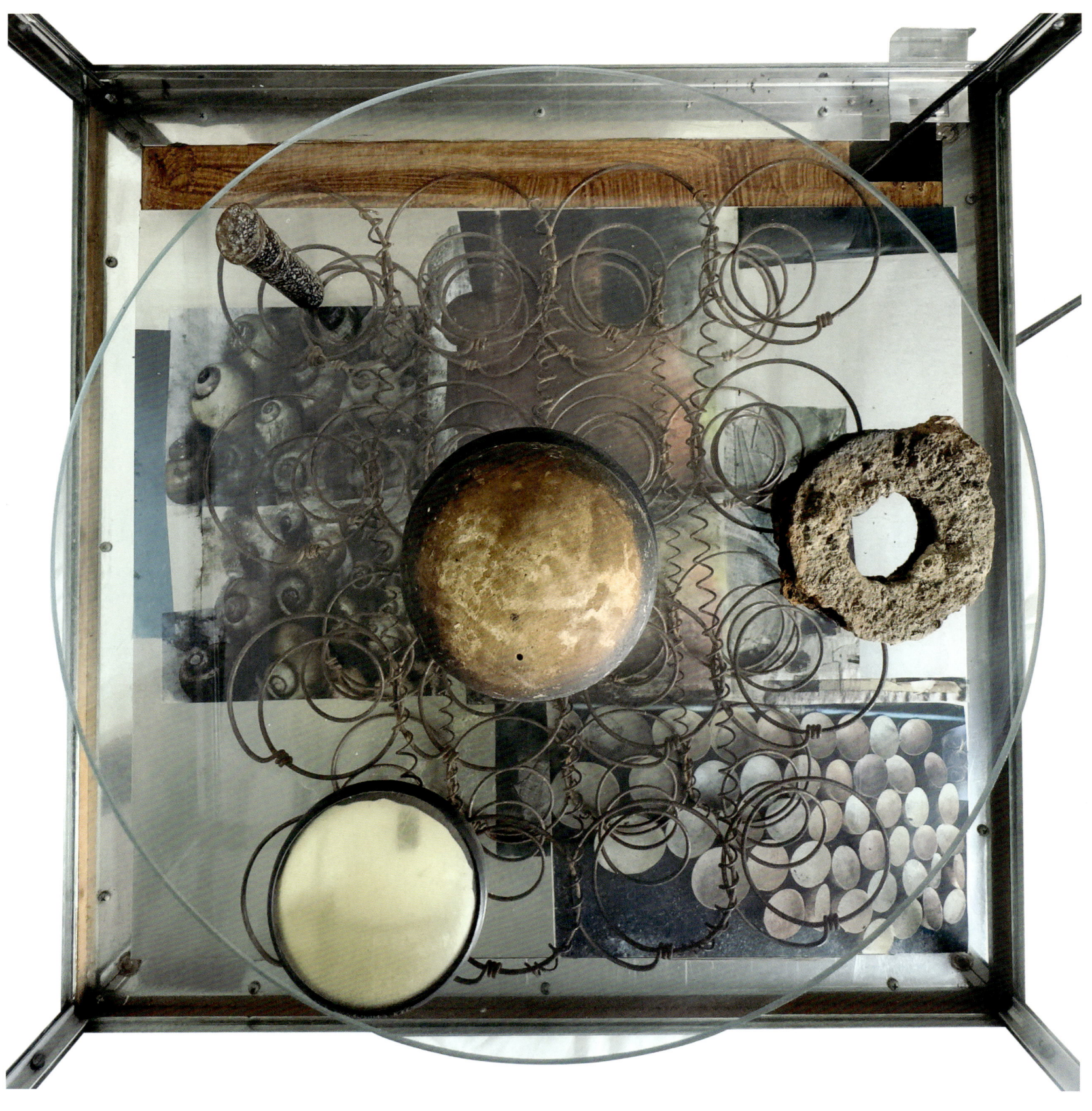

Ark (Detail Top View)

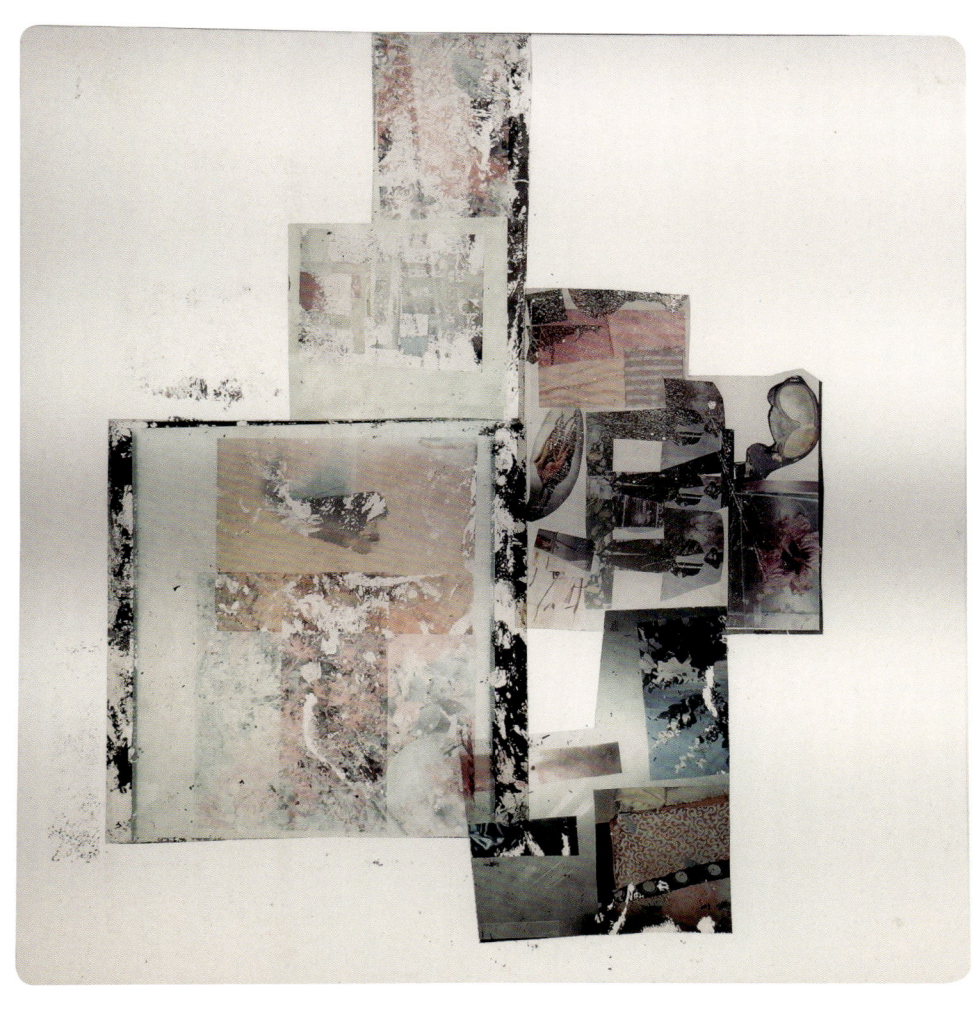

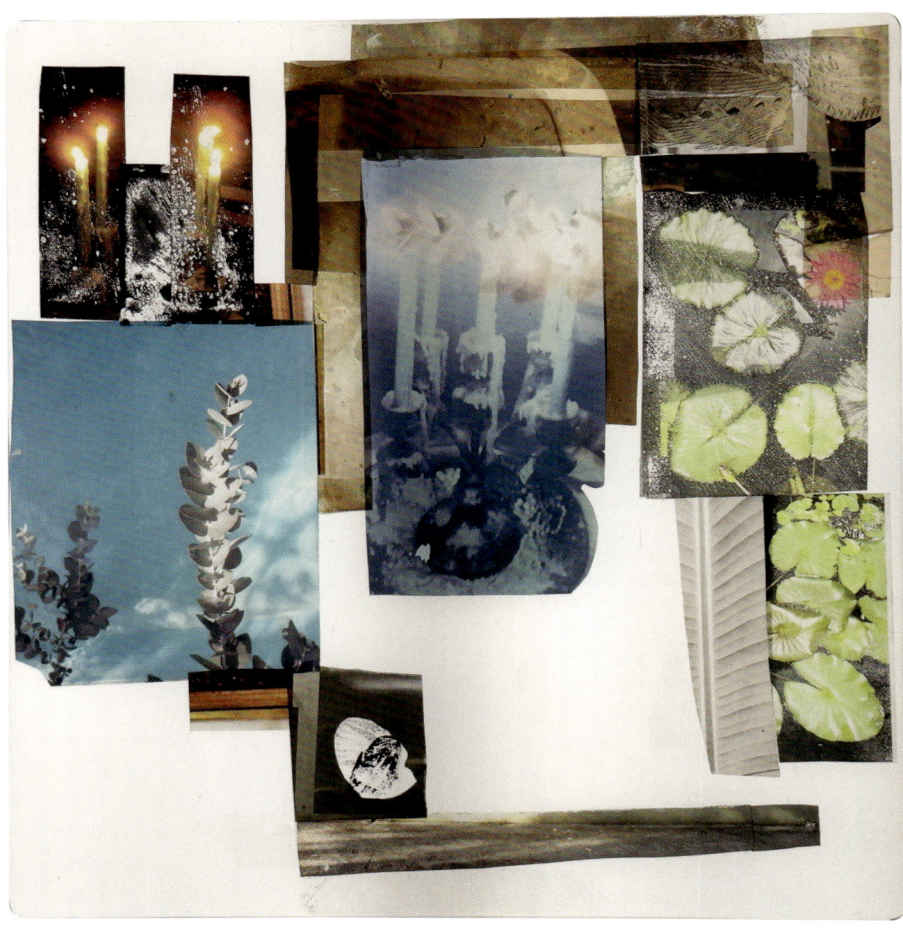

Ark (Detail Top Panels)

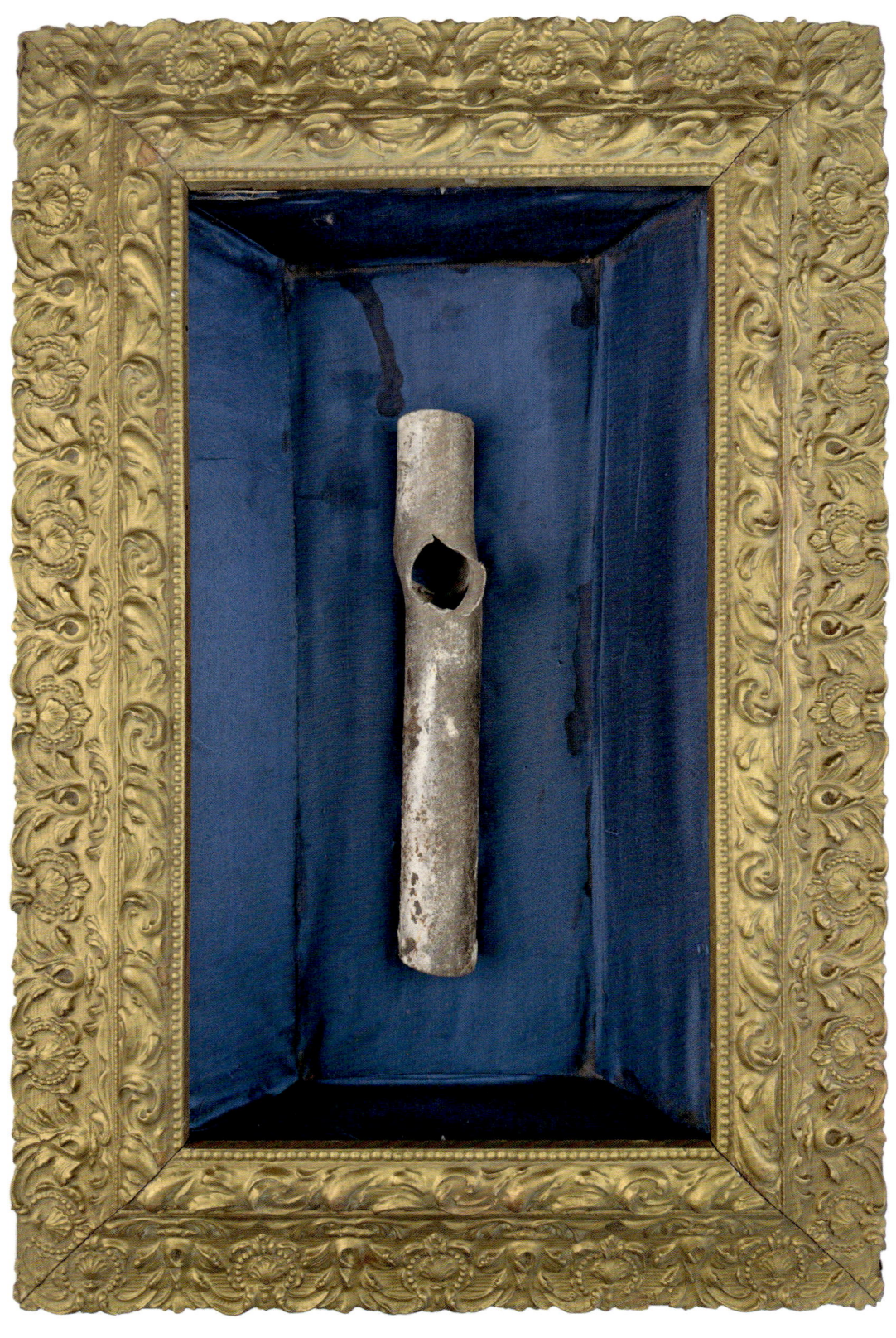

Plumb
25 ½ x 17 ½ x 4 inches
Pipe, Fabric and Wood Frame
2018

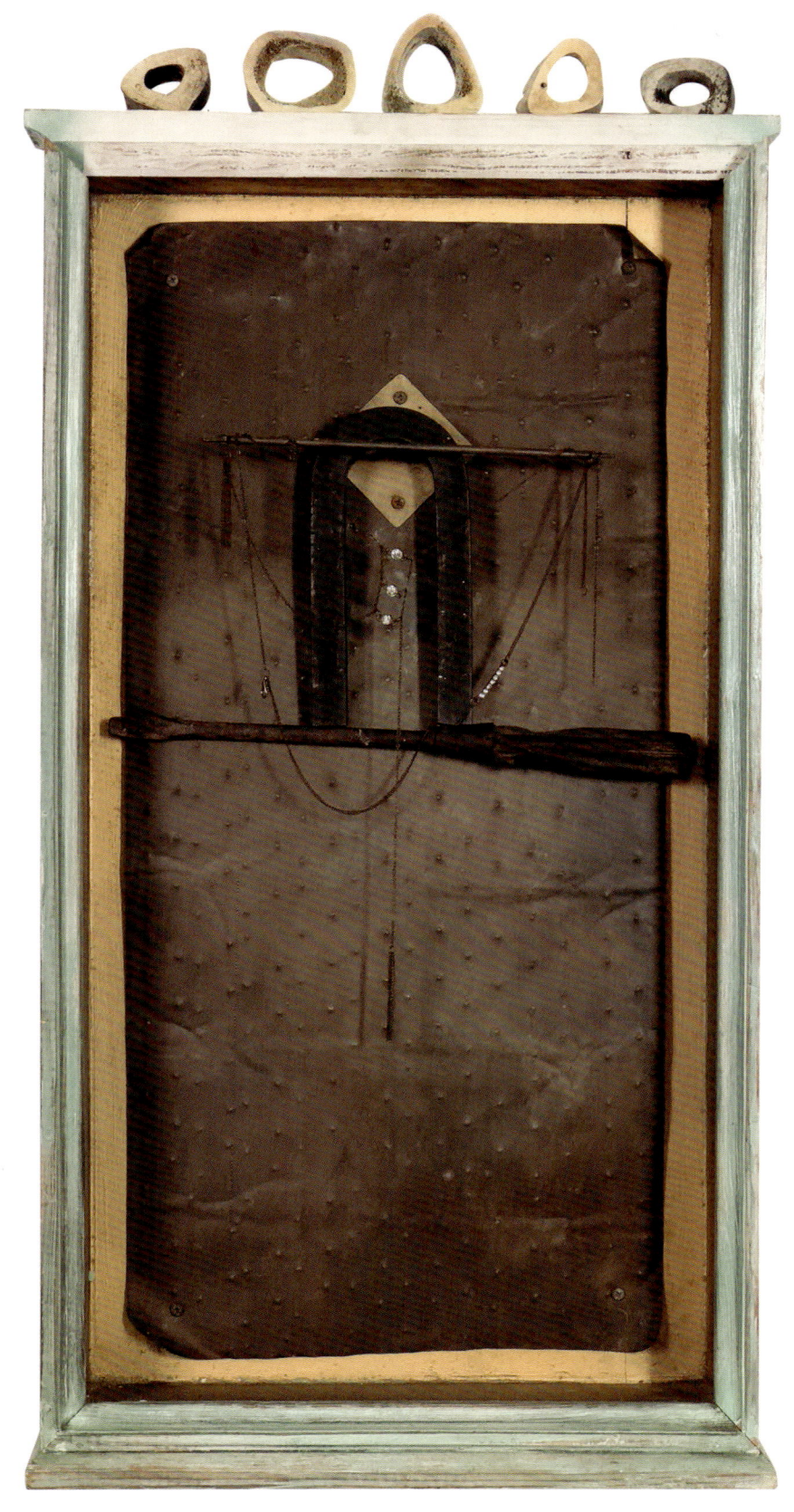

Toolbox
31 x 16 ½ x 5 inches
Metal, Wood, Stones and Bones
2018

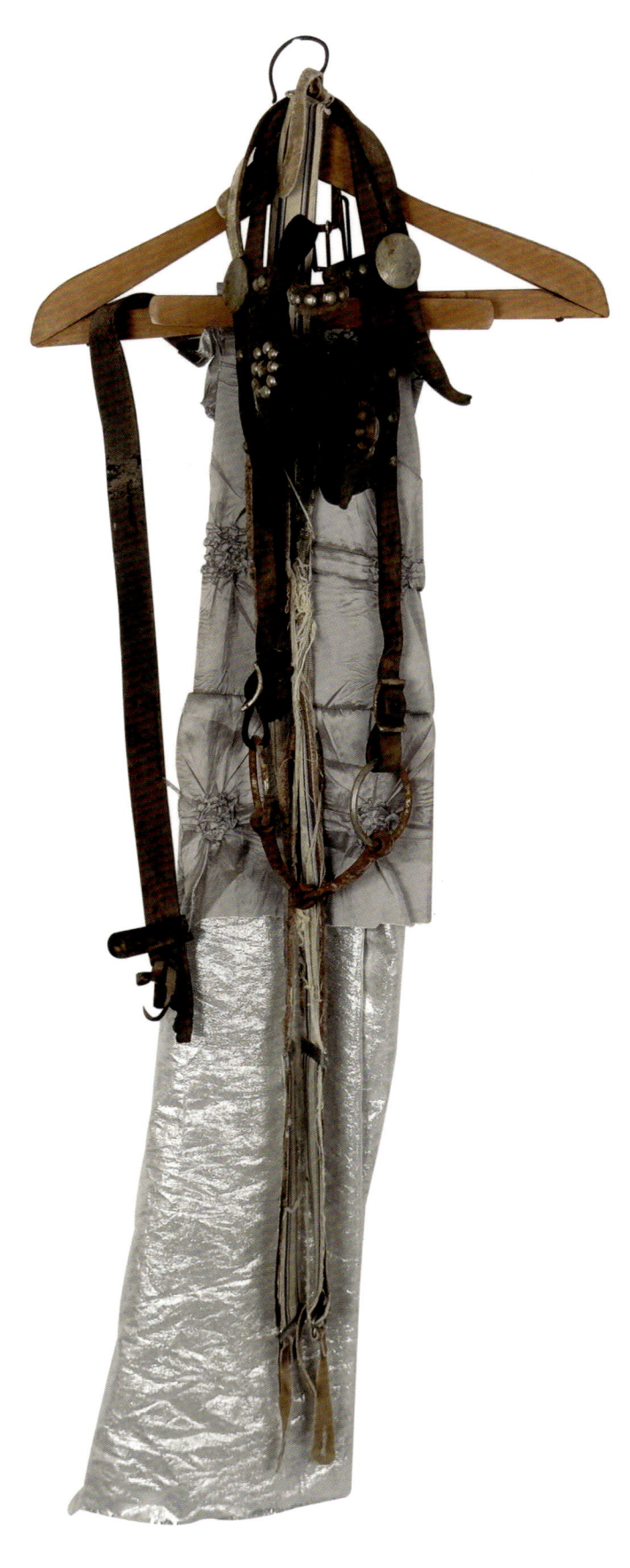

Hanger
46 x 17 inches
Mixed Media
2016

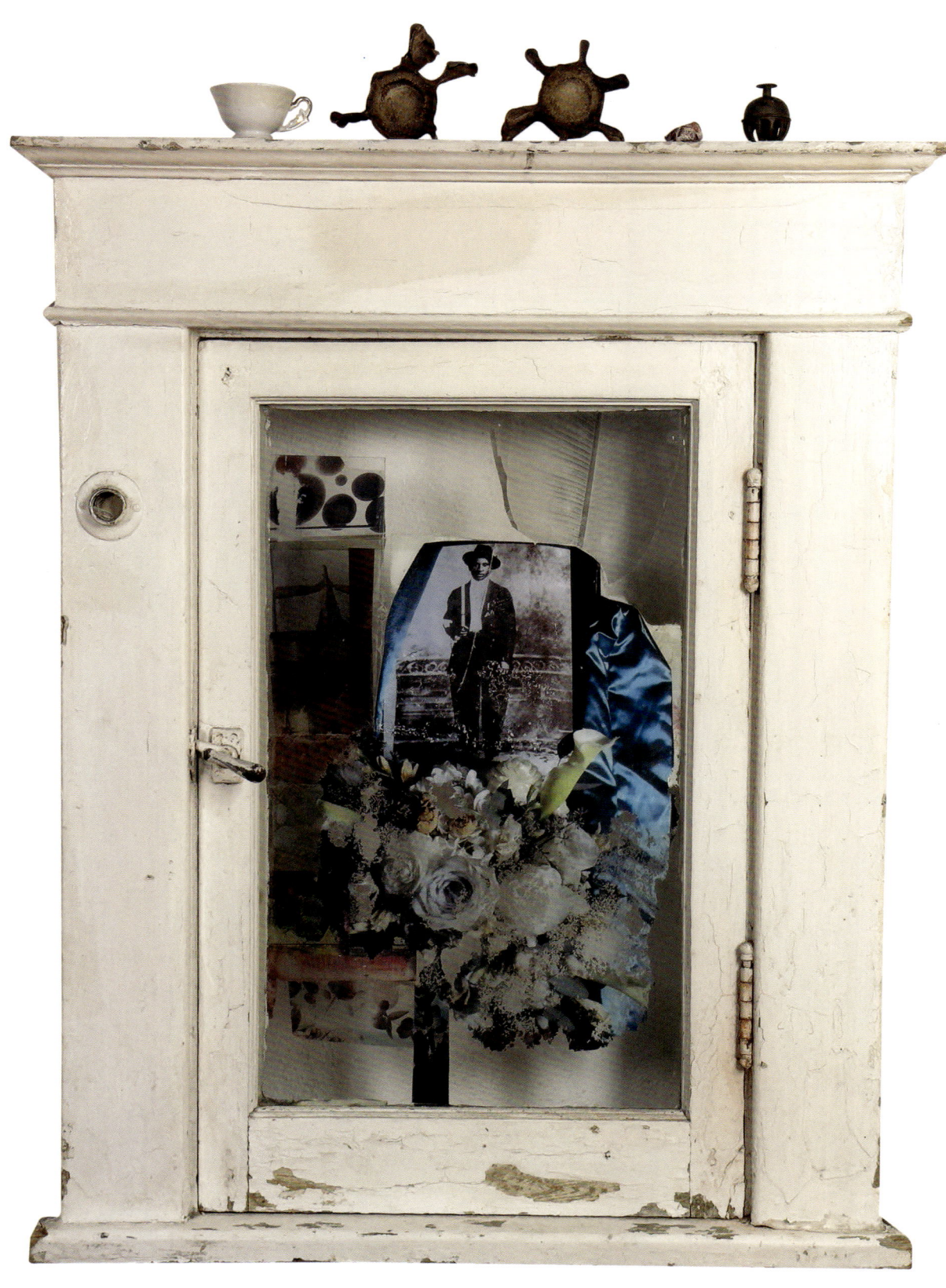

The Bandstand
44 x 32 inches
Mixed Media
2014

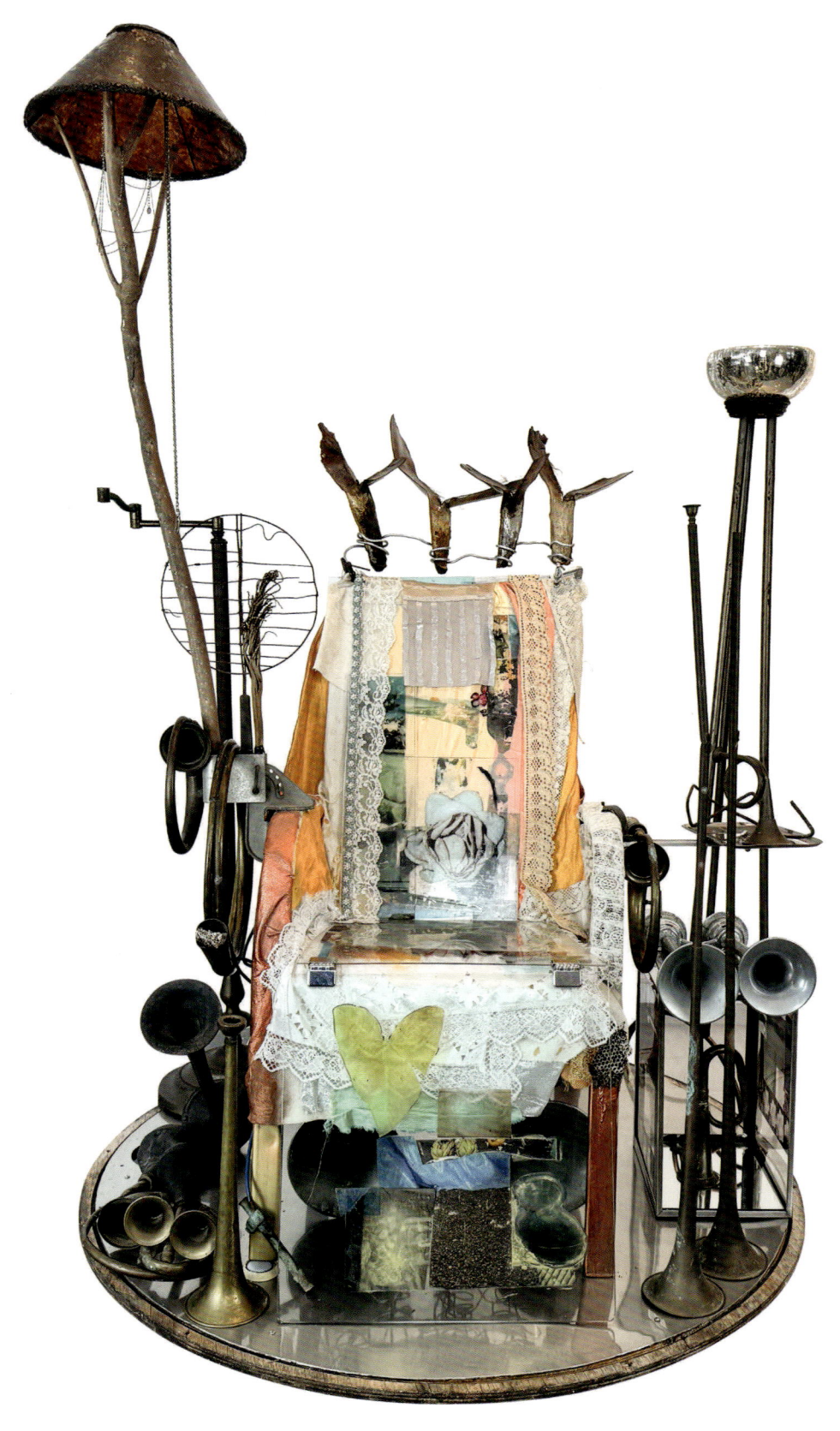

Chair
71 x 48 inches
Mixed Media
2024

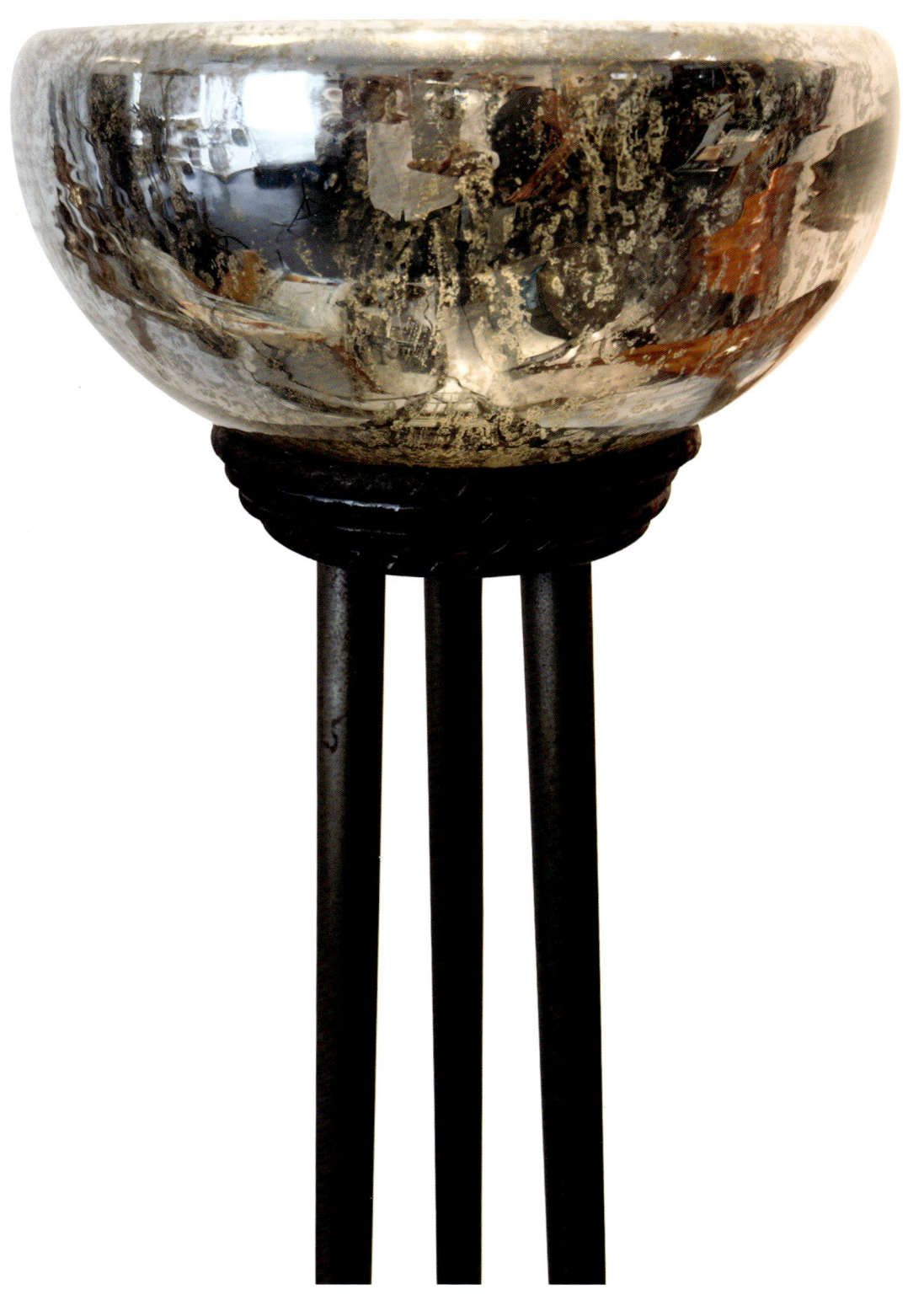

Chair (Detail)

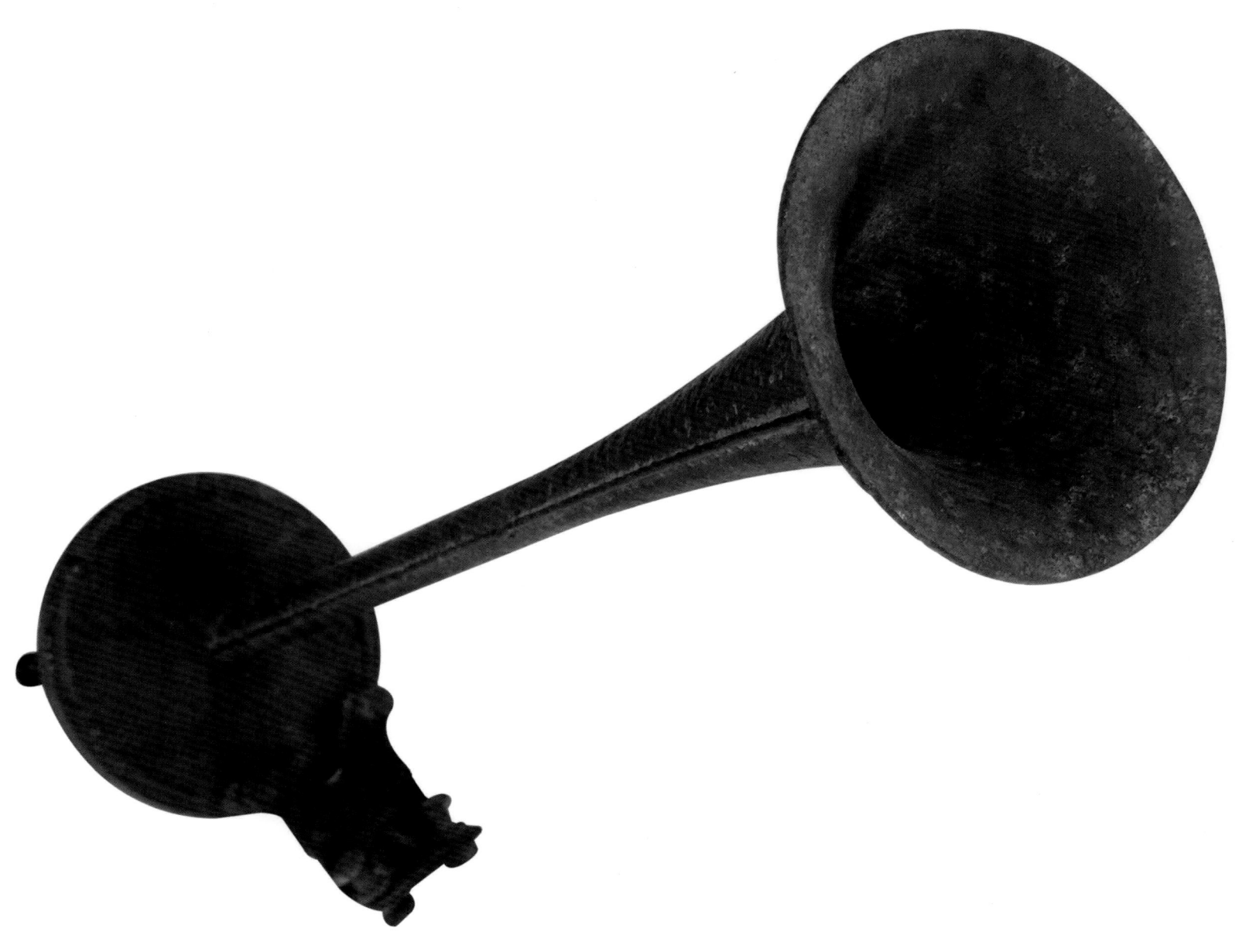

Chair (Detail)

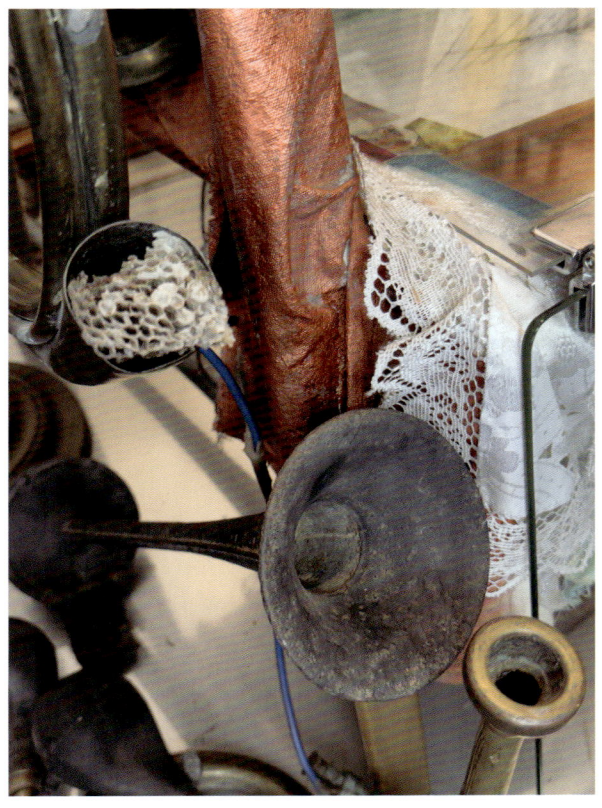
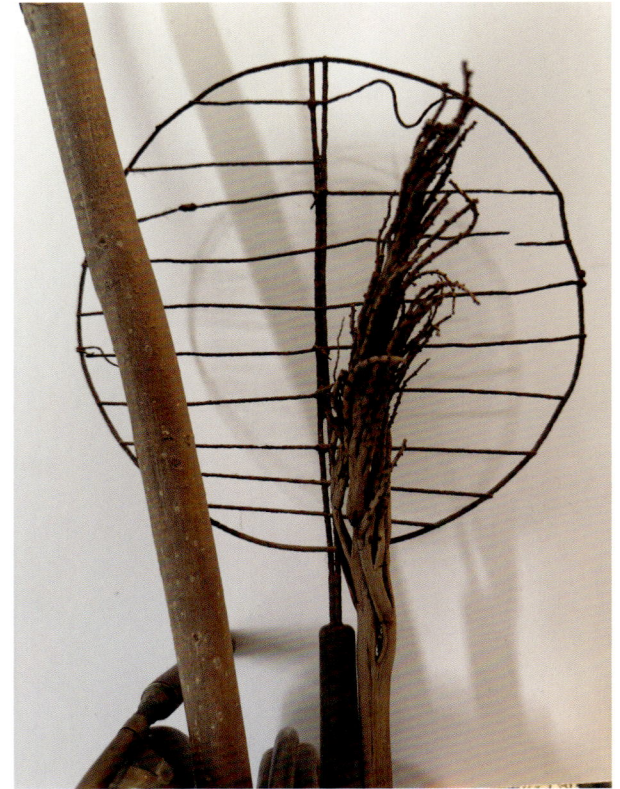
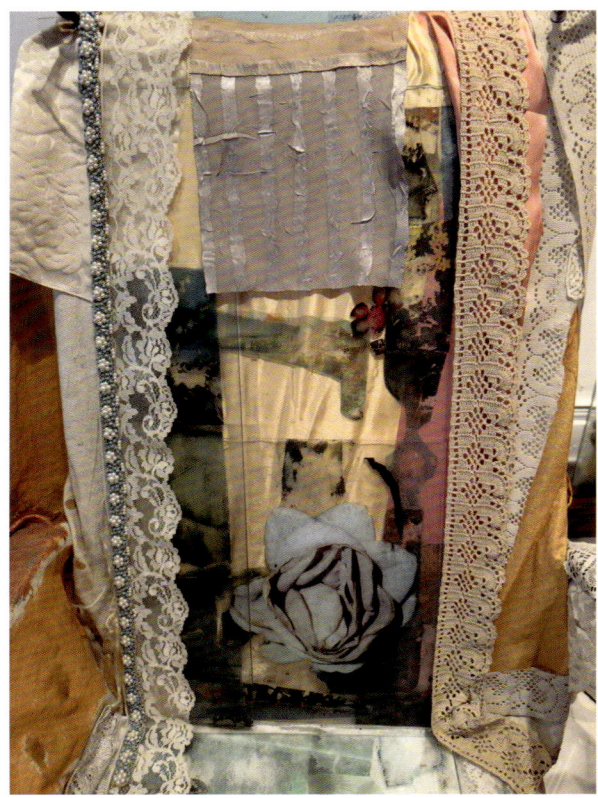
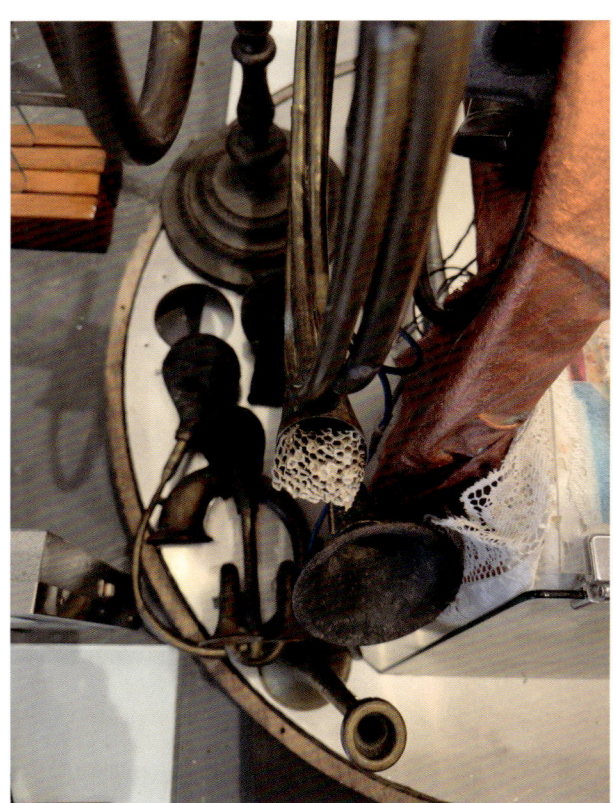

Chair (Details)

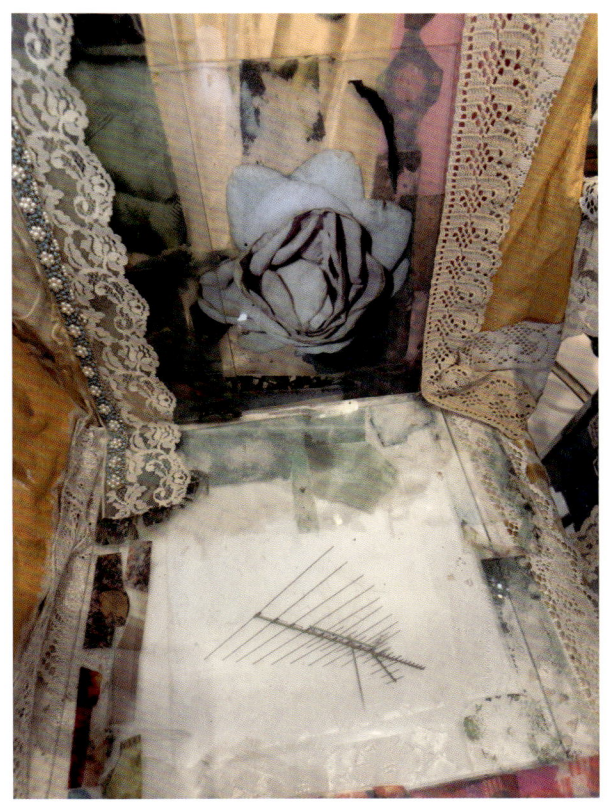
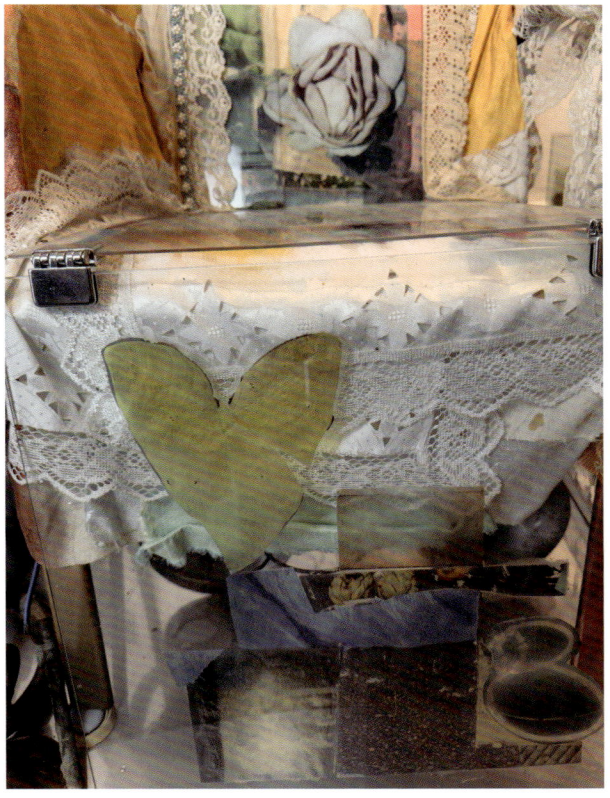
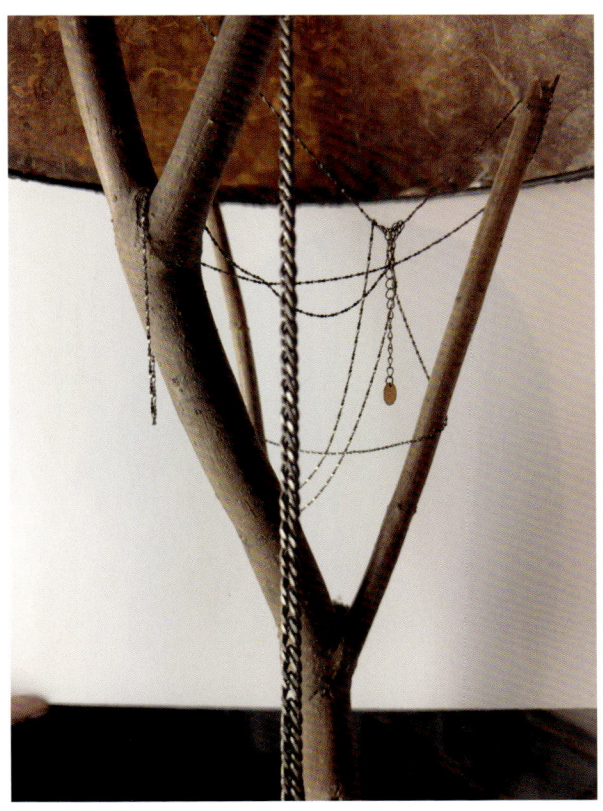
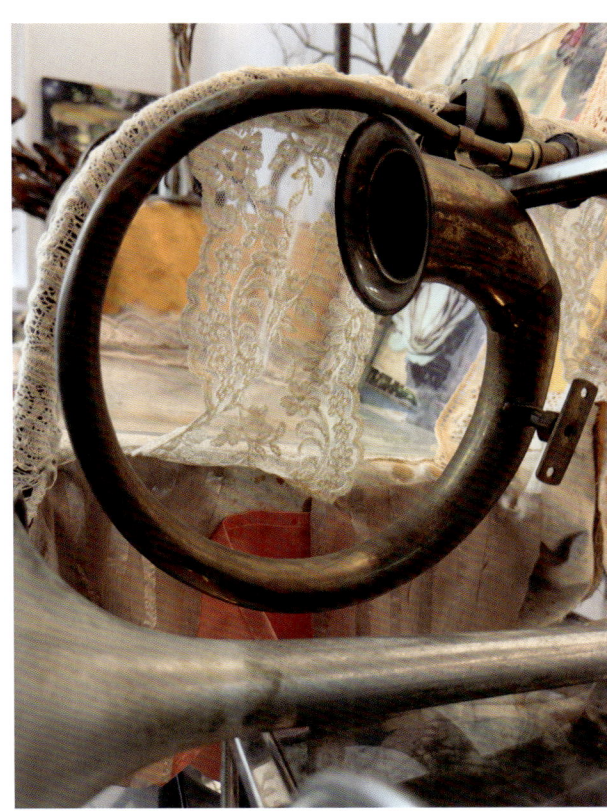

Chair (Details)

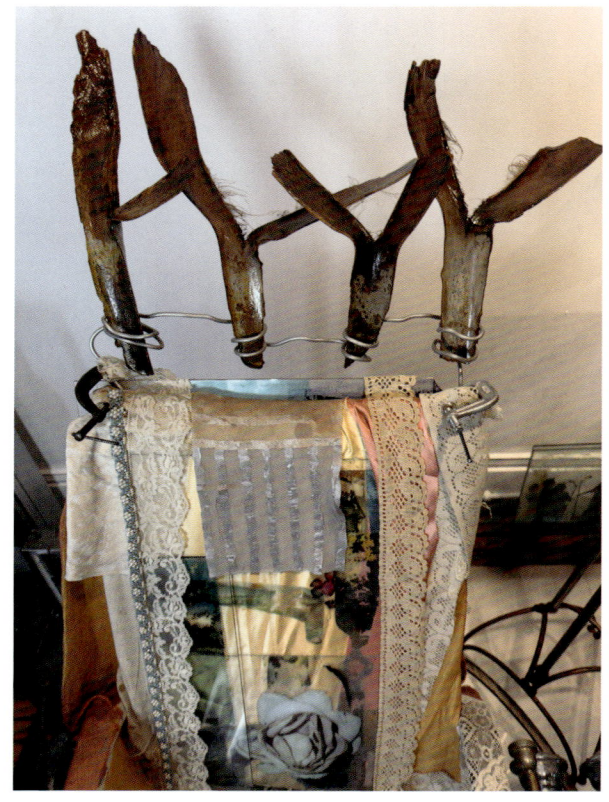
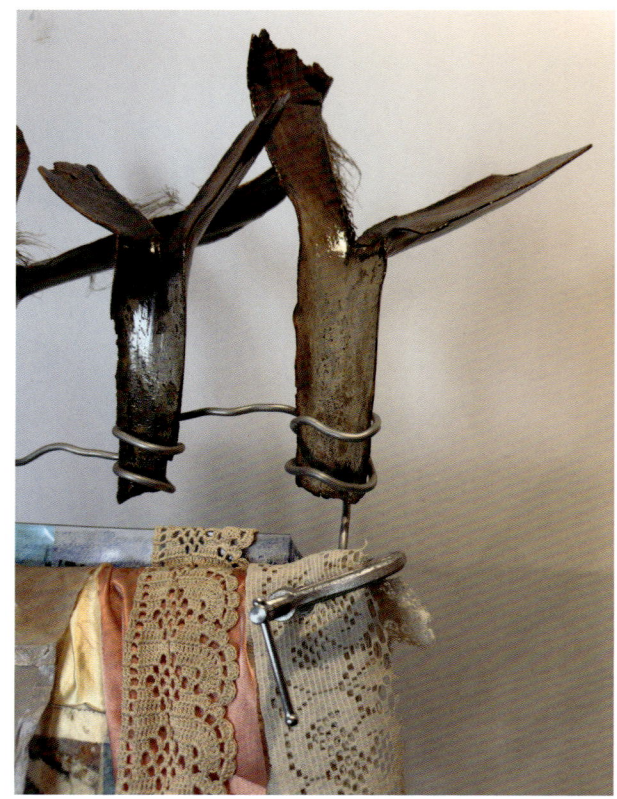
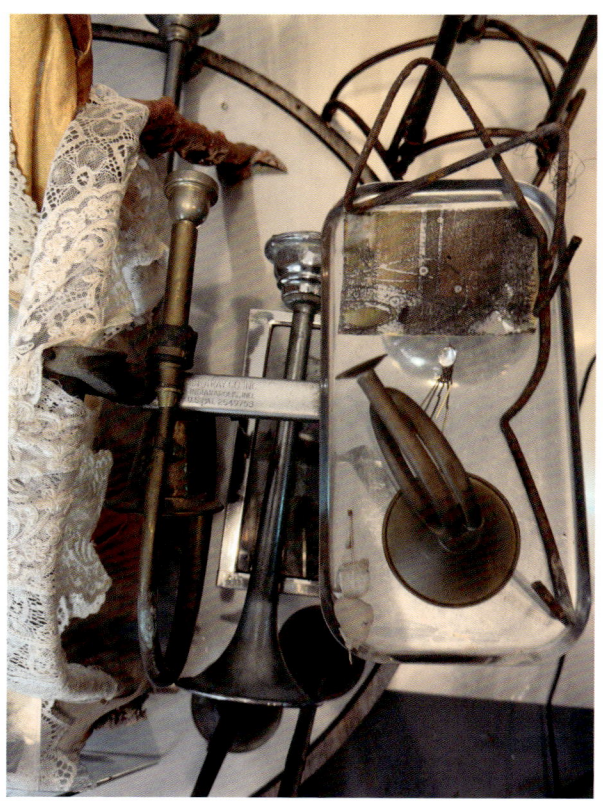
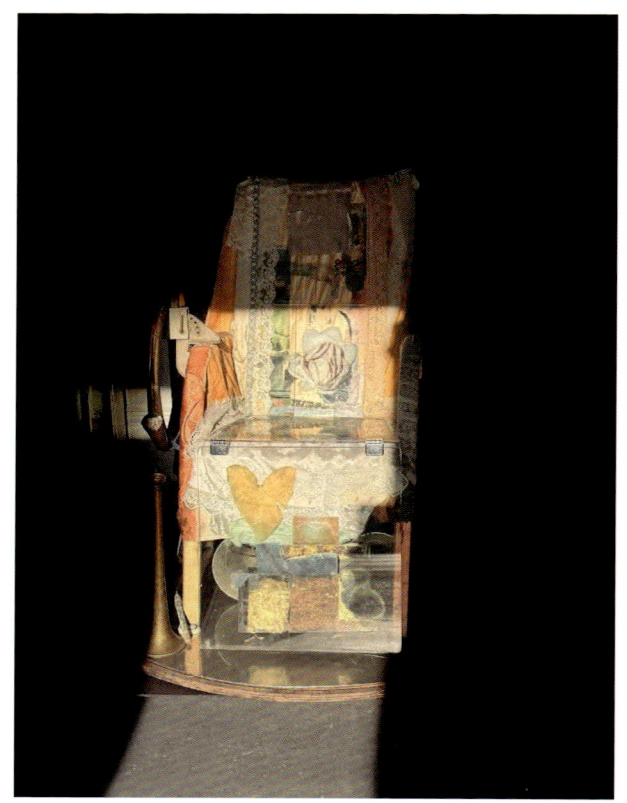

Chair (Details)

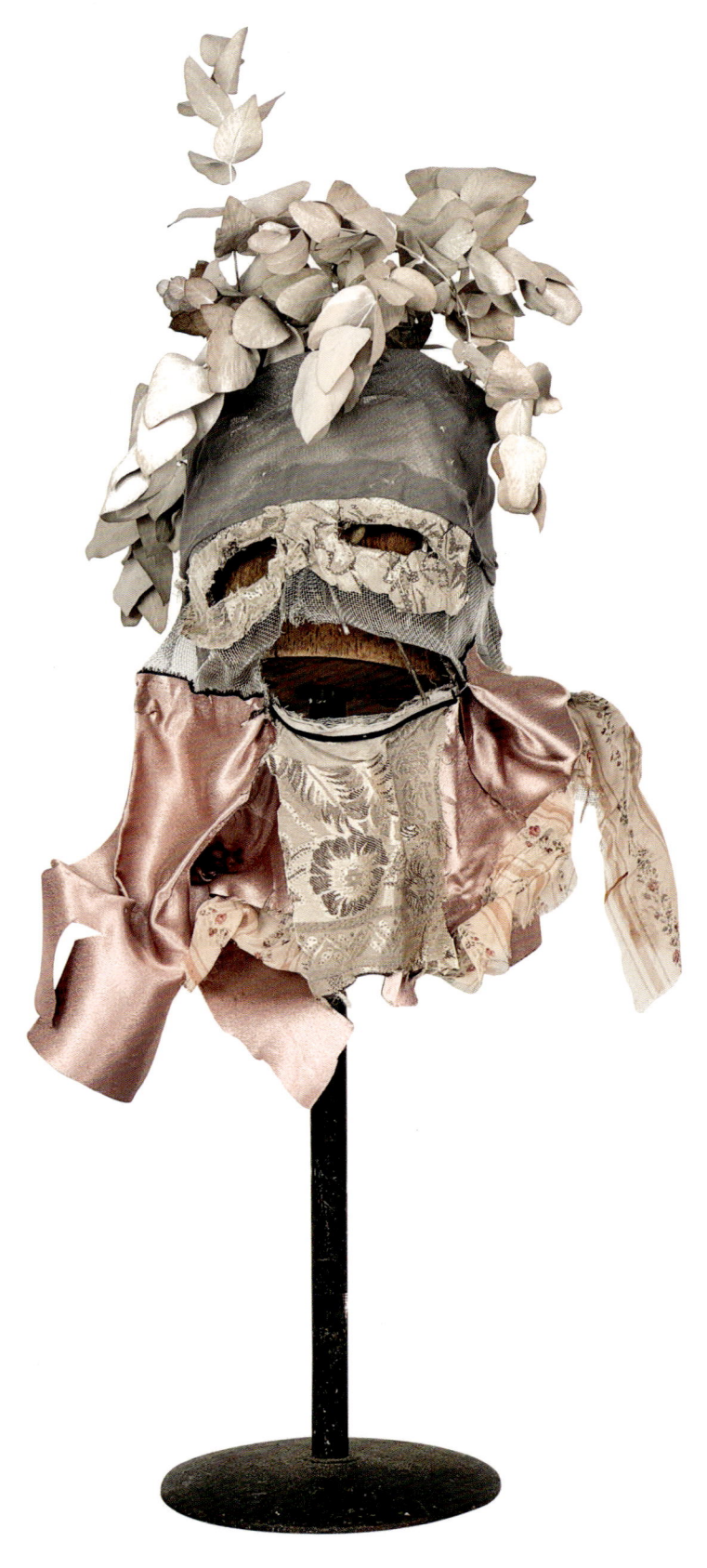

Masquer
36 x 18 inches
Mixed Media, Fabric, Screen, Eucalyptus
2017

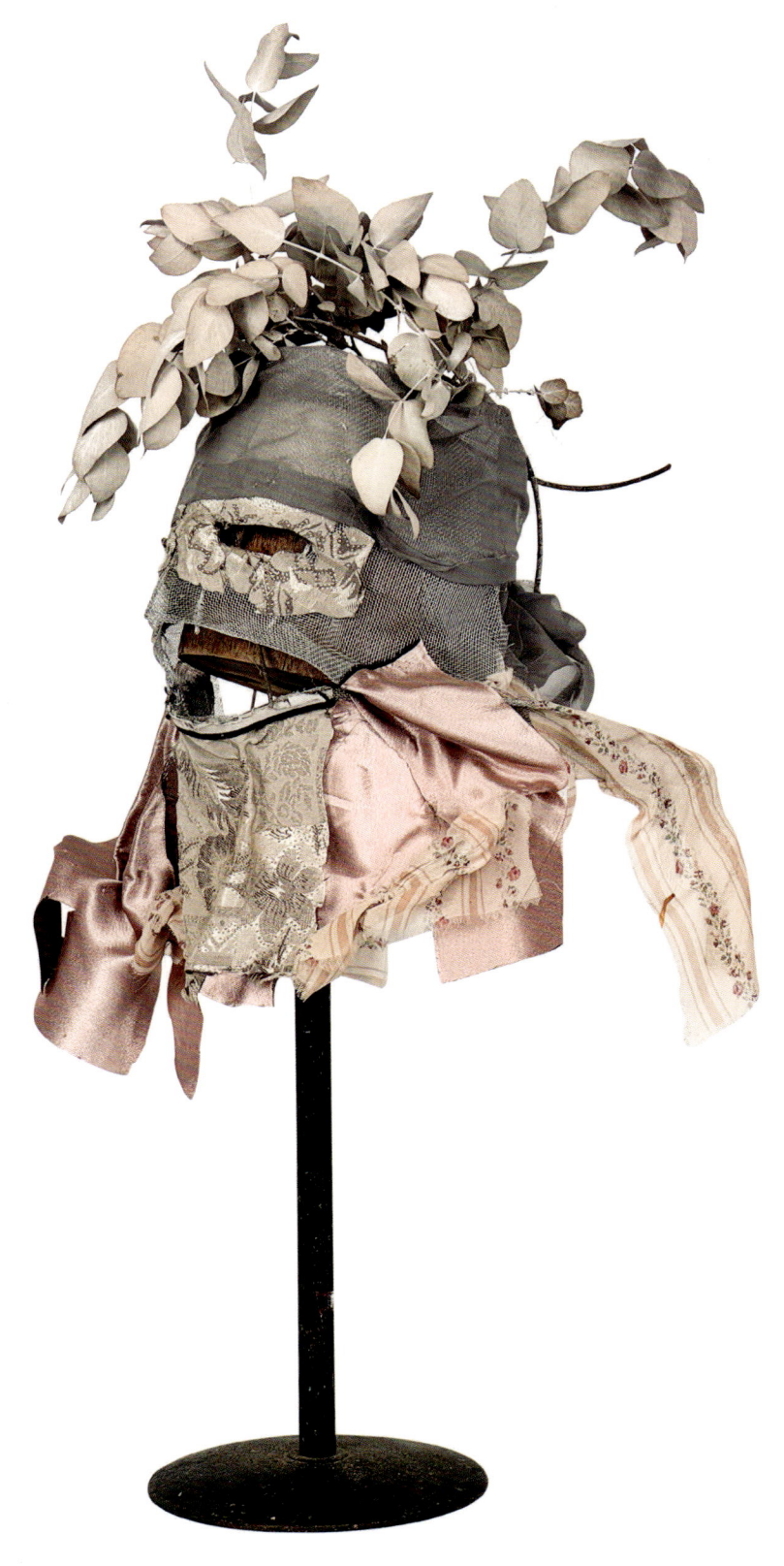

Masquer (Profile)

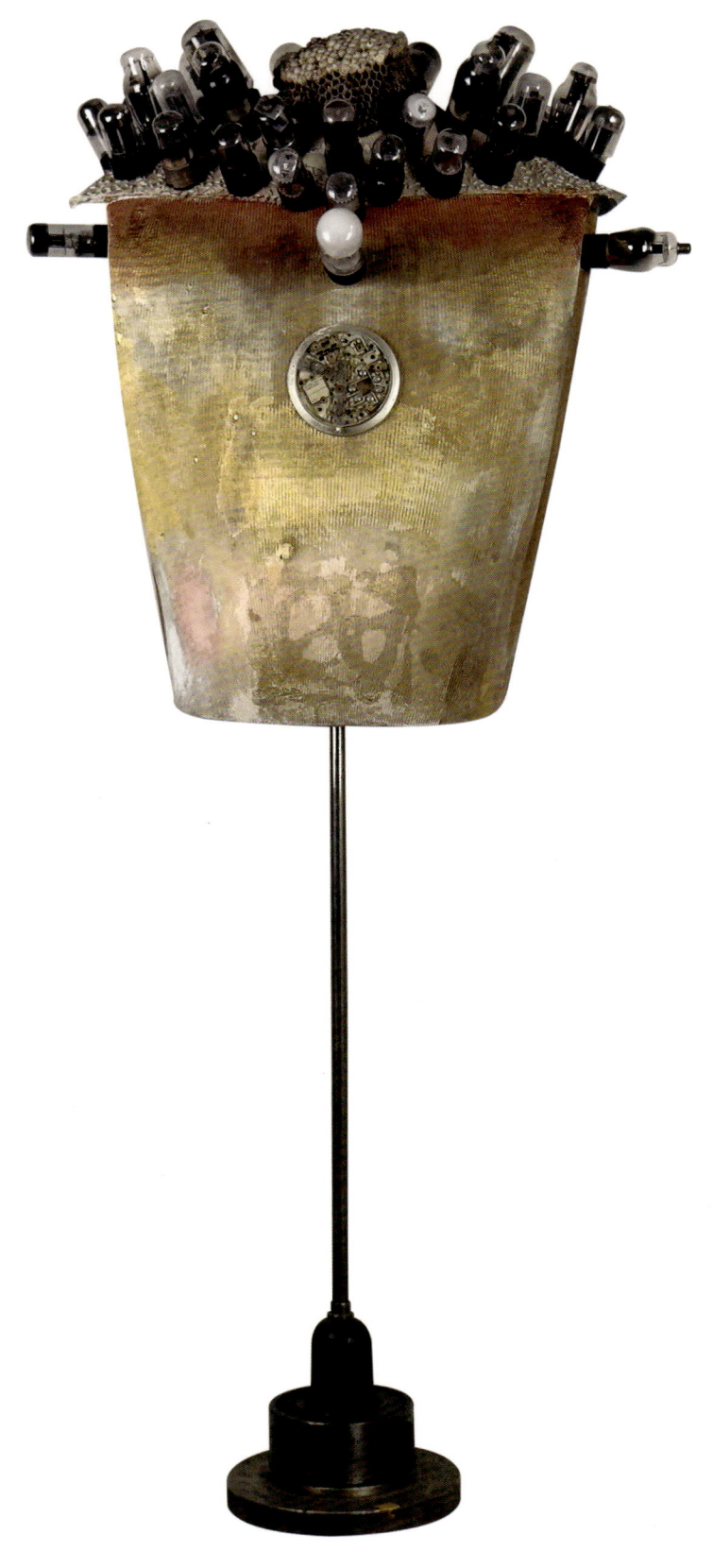

The Boatman
51 x 24 x 12 inches
Mixed Media
2016

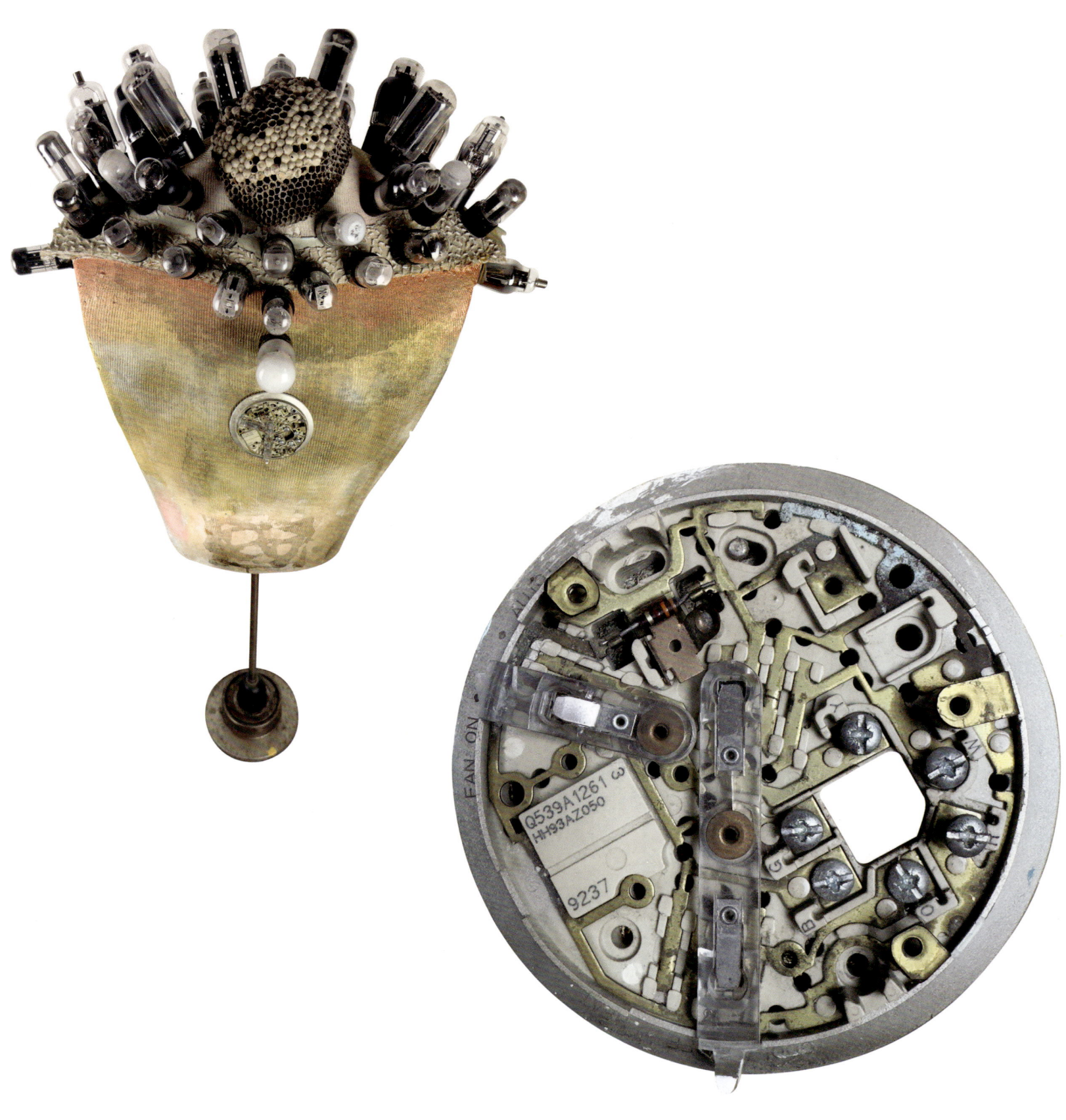

The Boatman (Details)

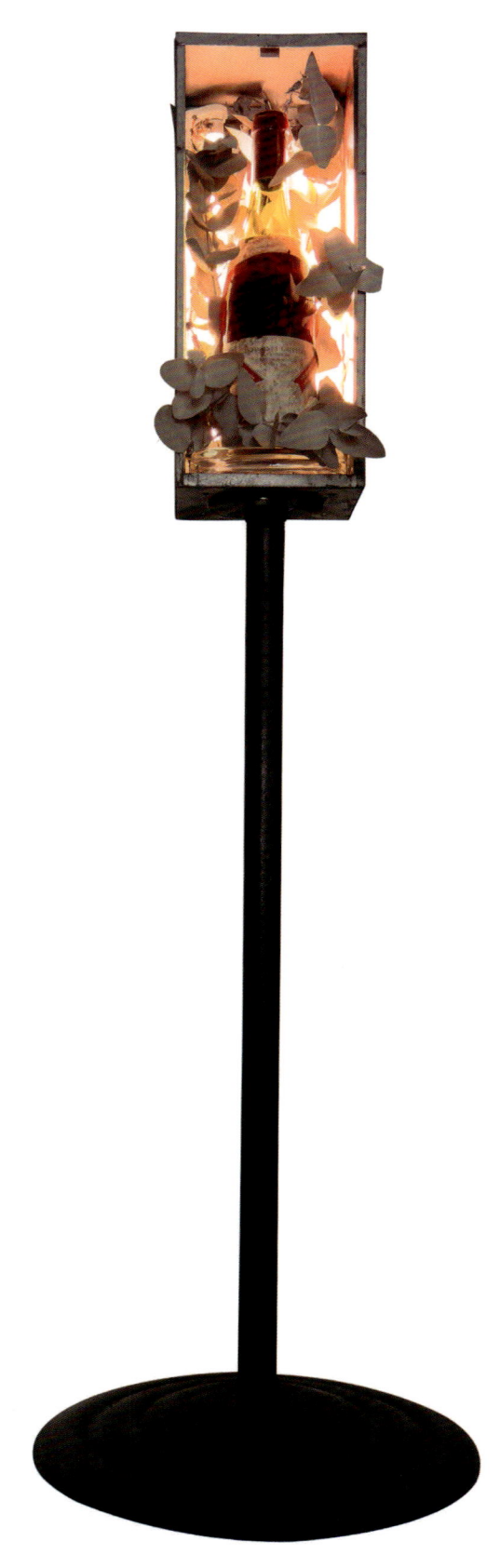

Mac's Clos Vougeot 1961
45 ½ x 6 x 5 w/ 15 in. base
Mixed Media w/ Lights
2016

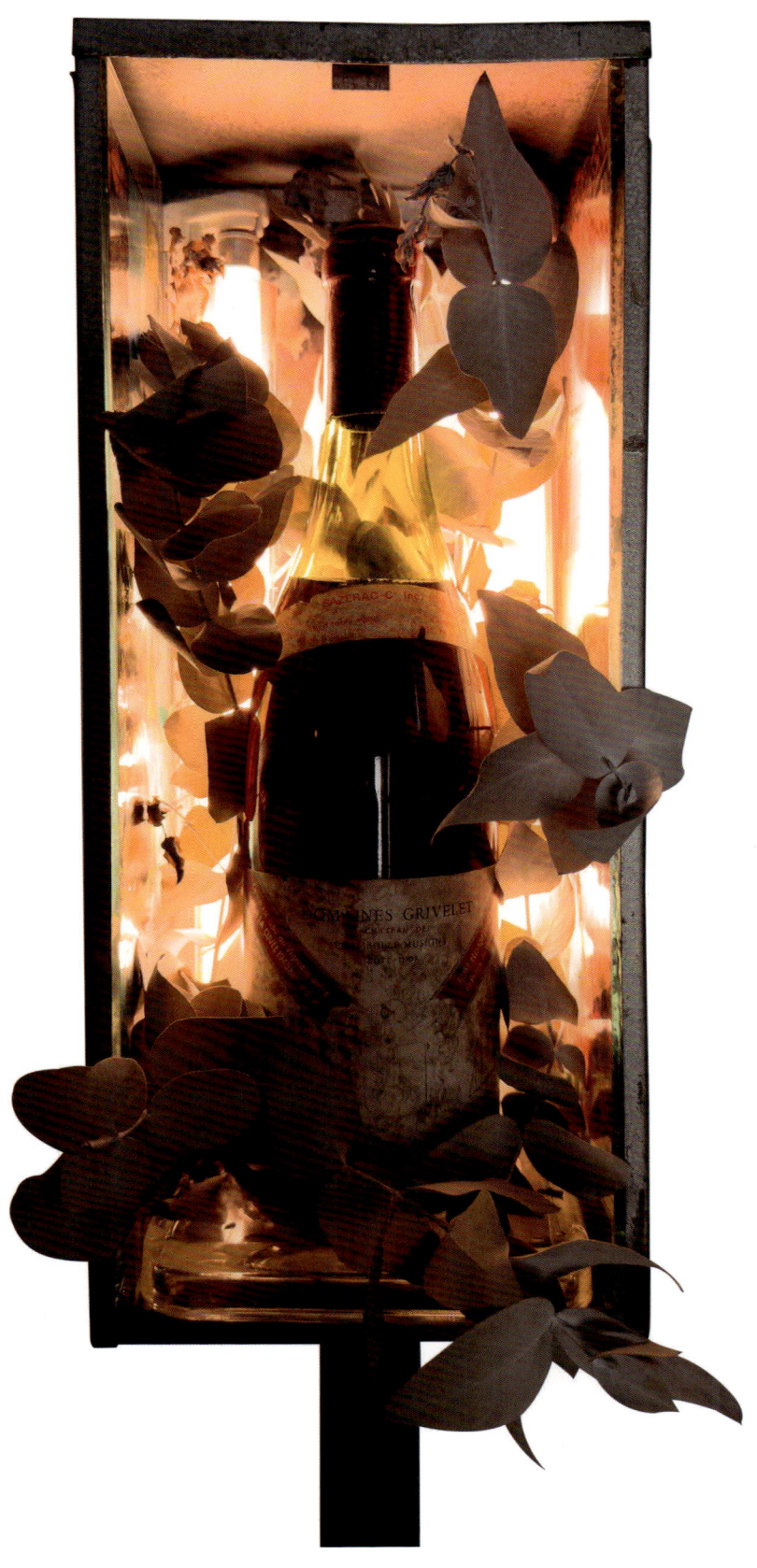

Mac's Clos Vougeot 1961 (Detail)

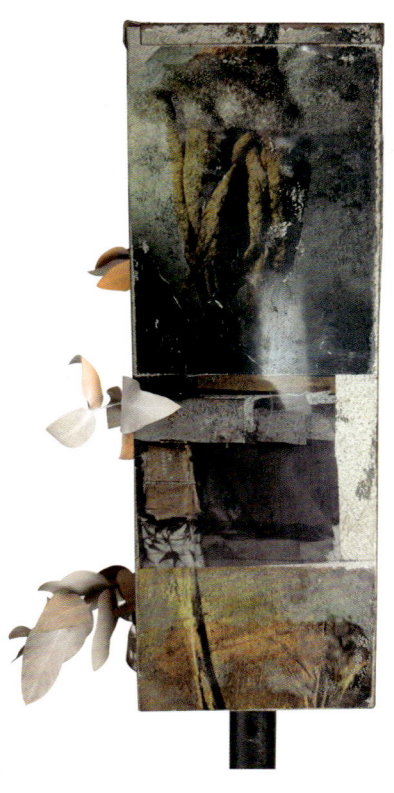

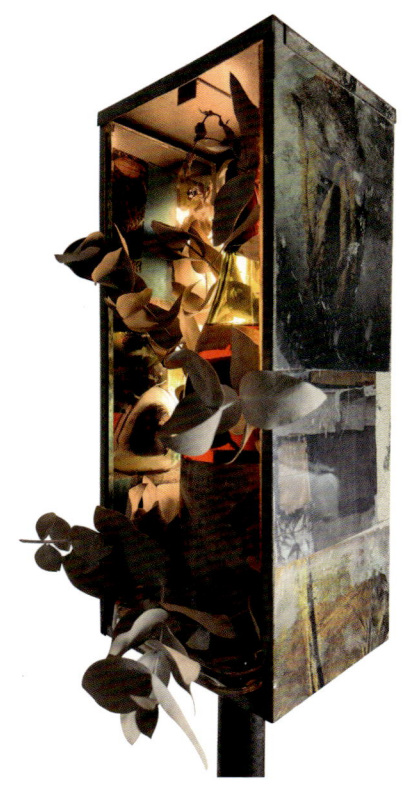

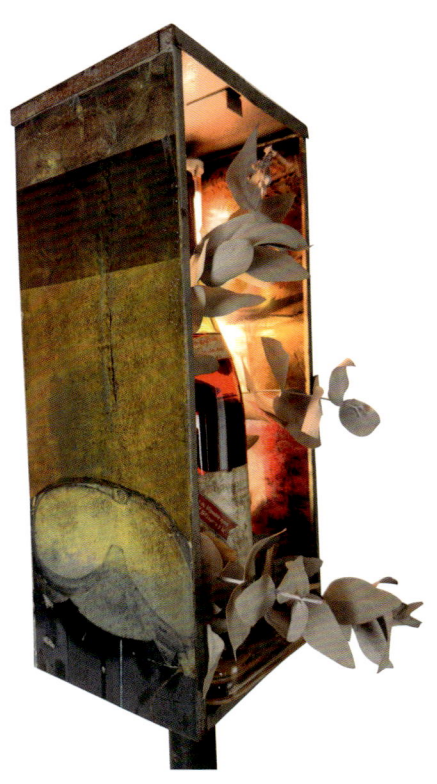

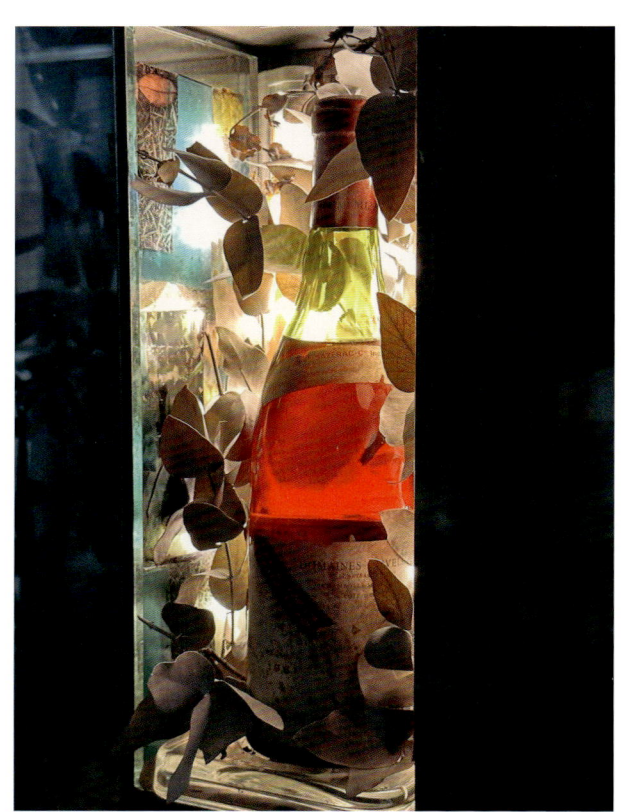

Mac's Clos Vougeot 1961 (Details)

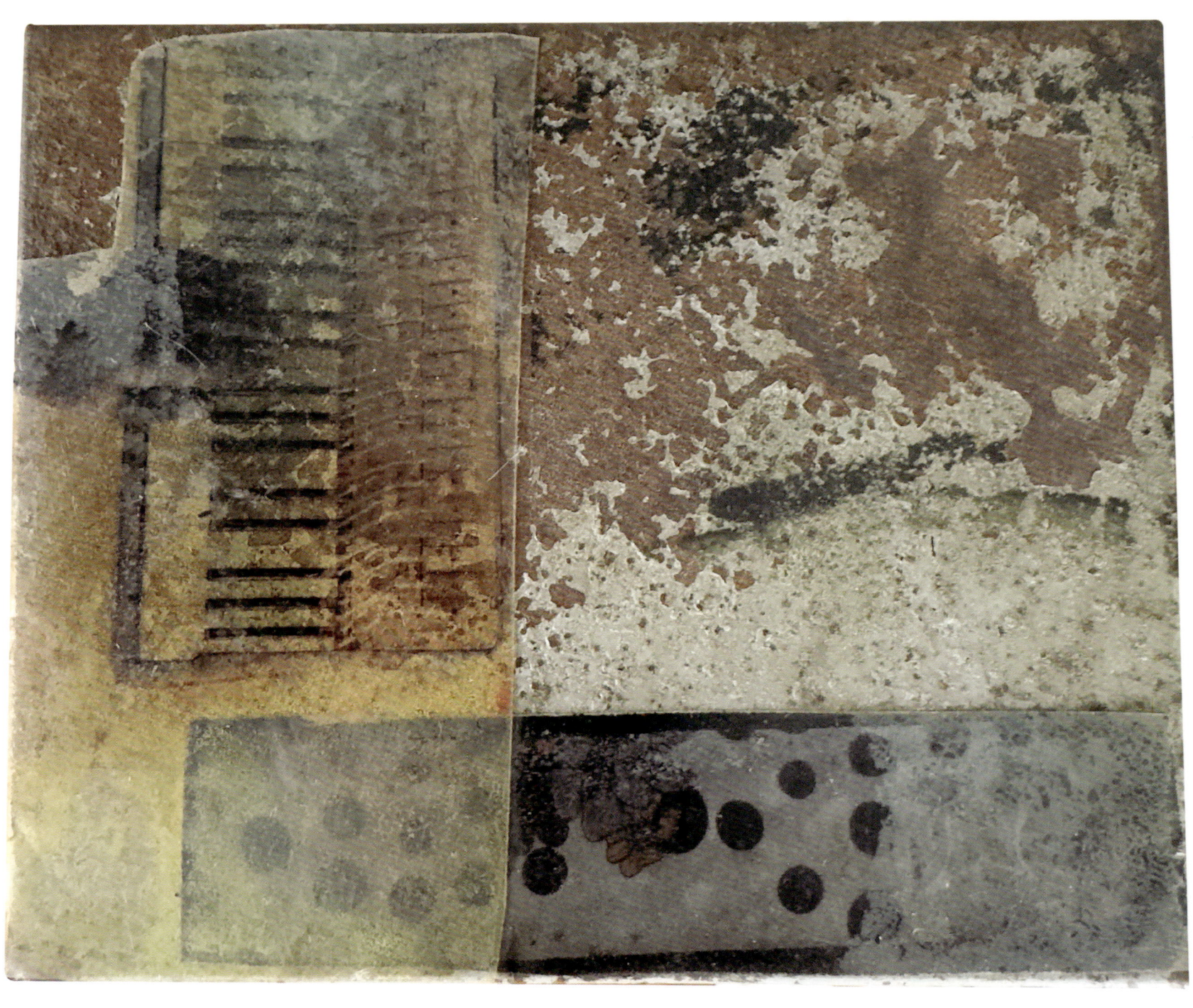

Mac's Clos Vougeot 1961 (Detail)

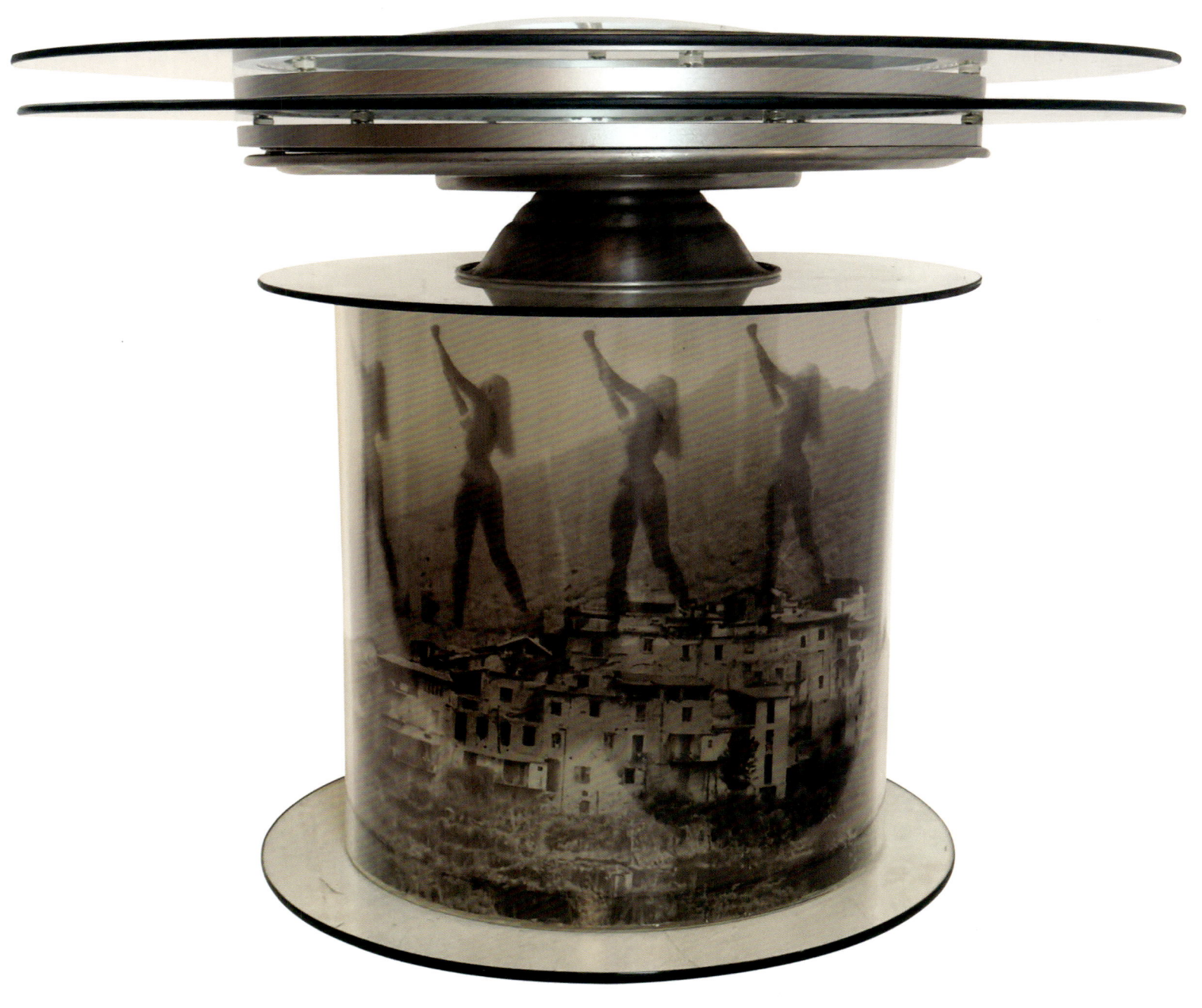

Prototype
23 ½ x 30 x 20 inches
Mixed Media, Glass and Metal
2024

46

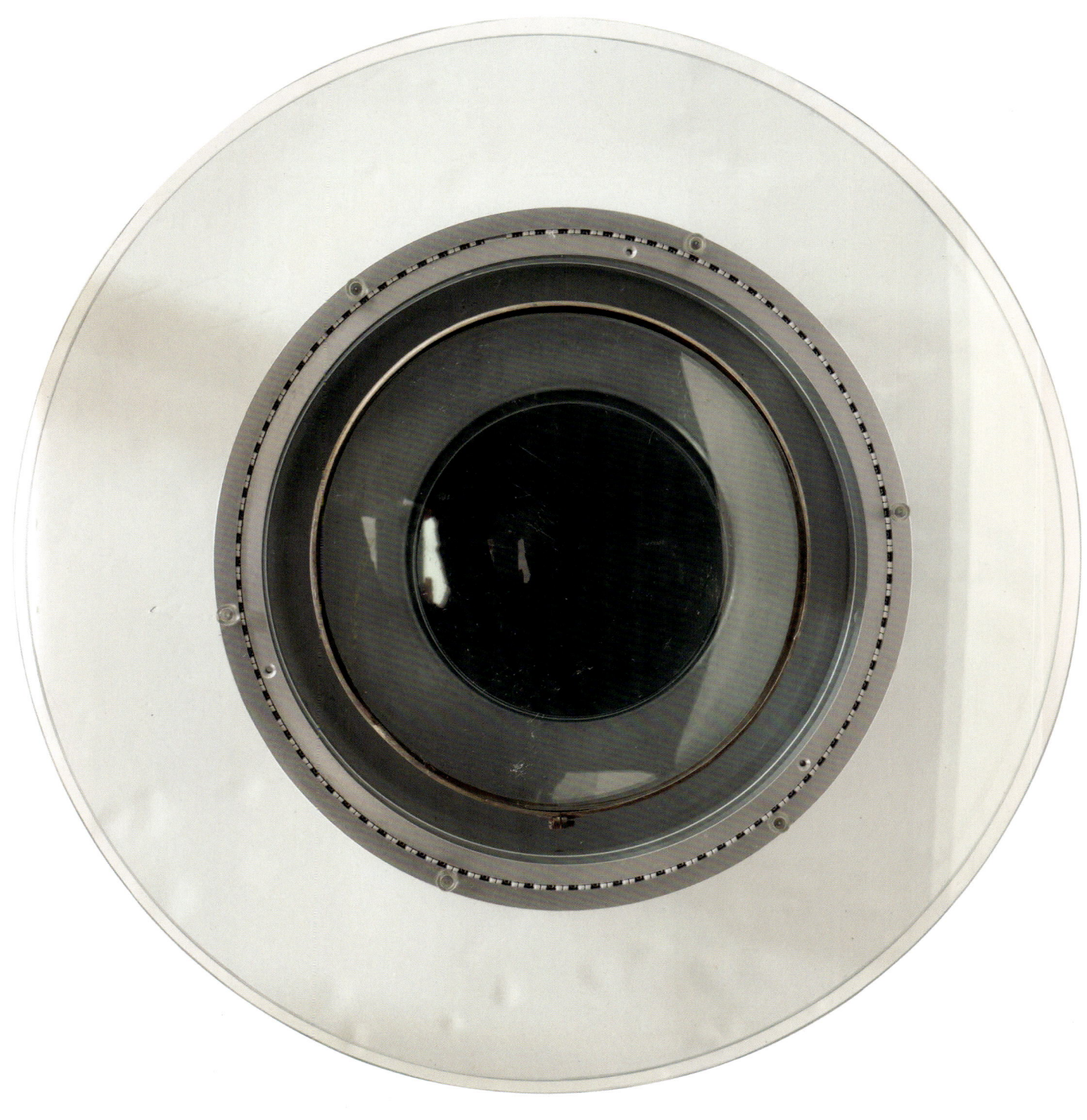

Prototype (Detail)

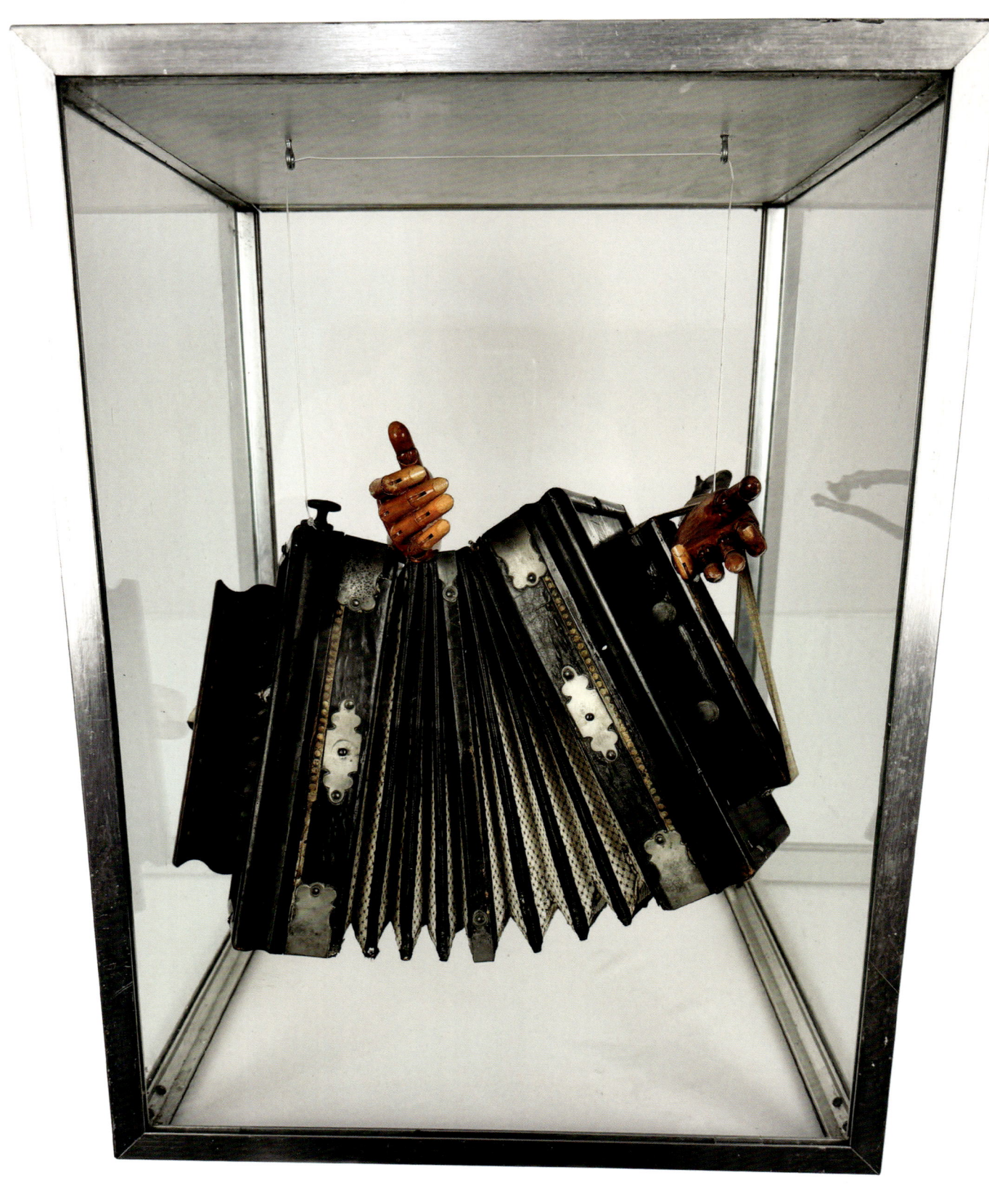

Lyric
24 x 18 x 18 inches
Mixed Media
2014

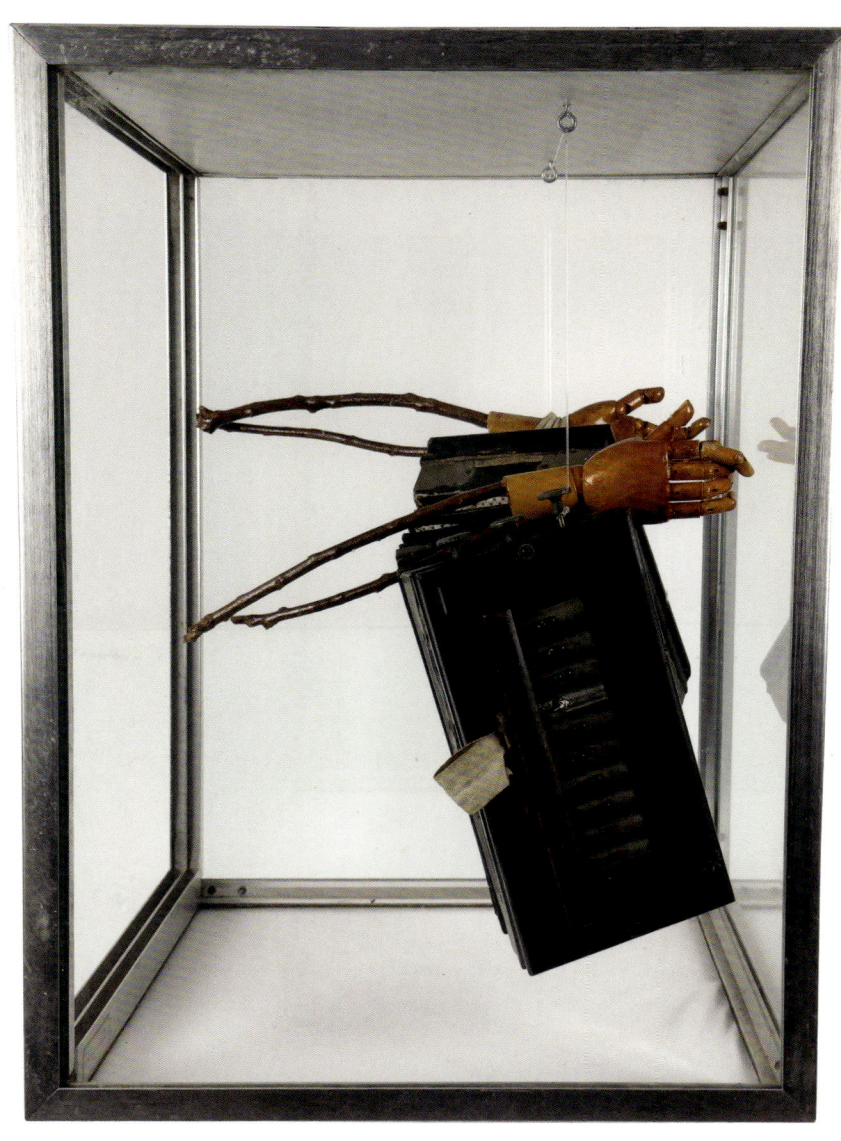
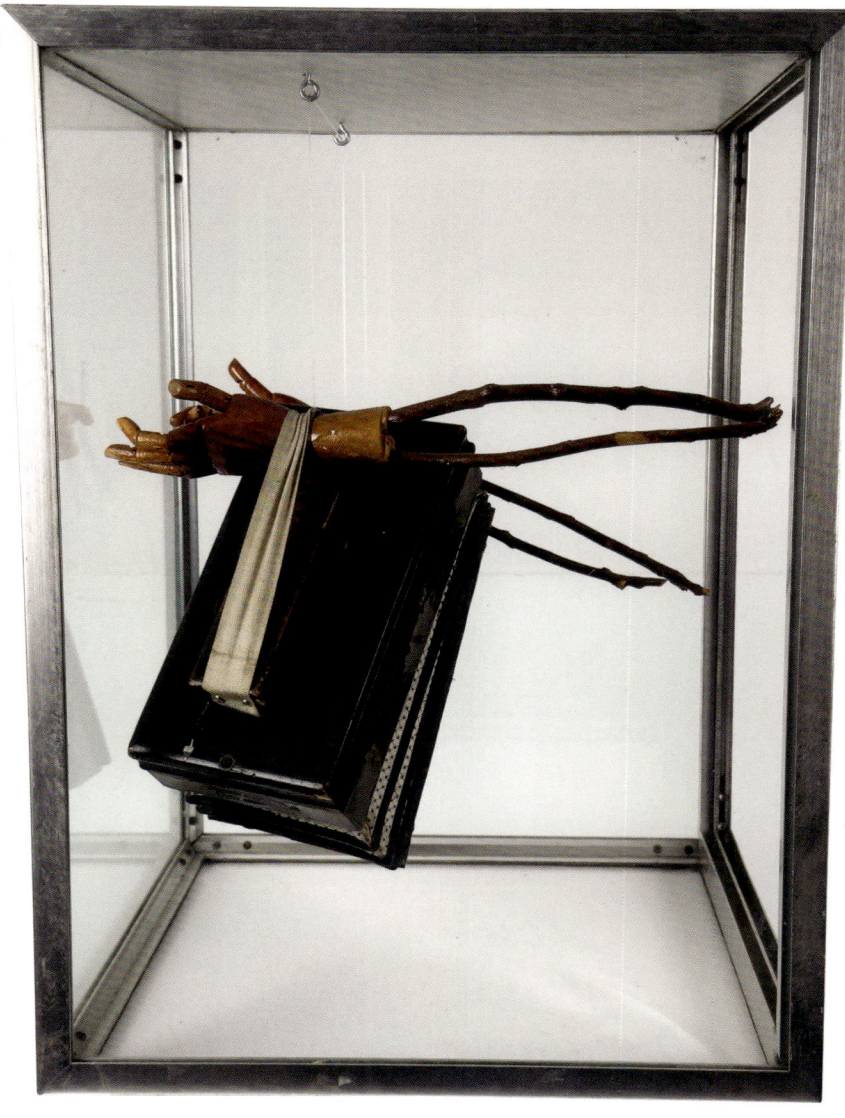

Lyric (Profiles)

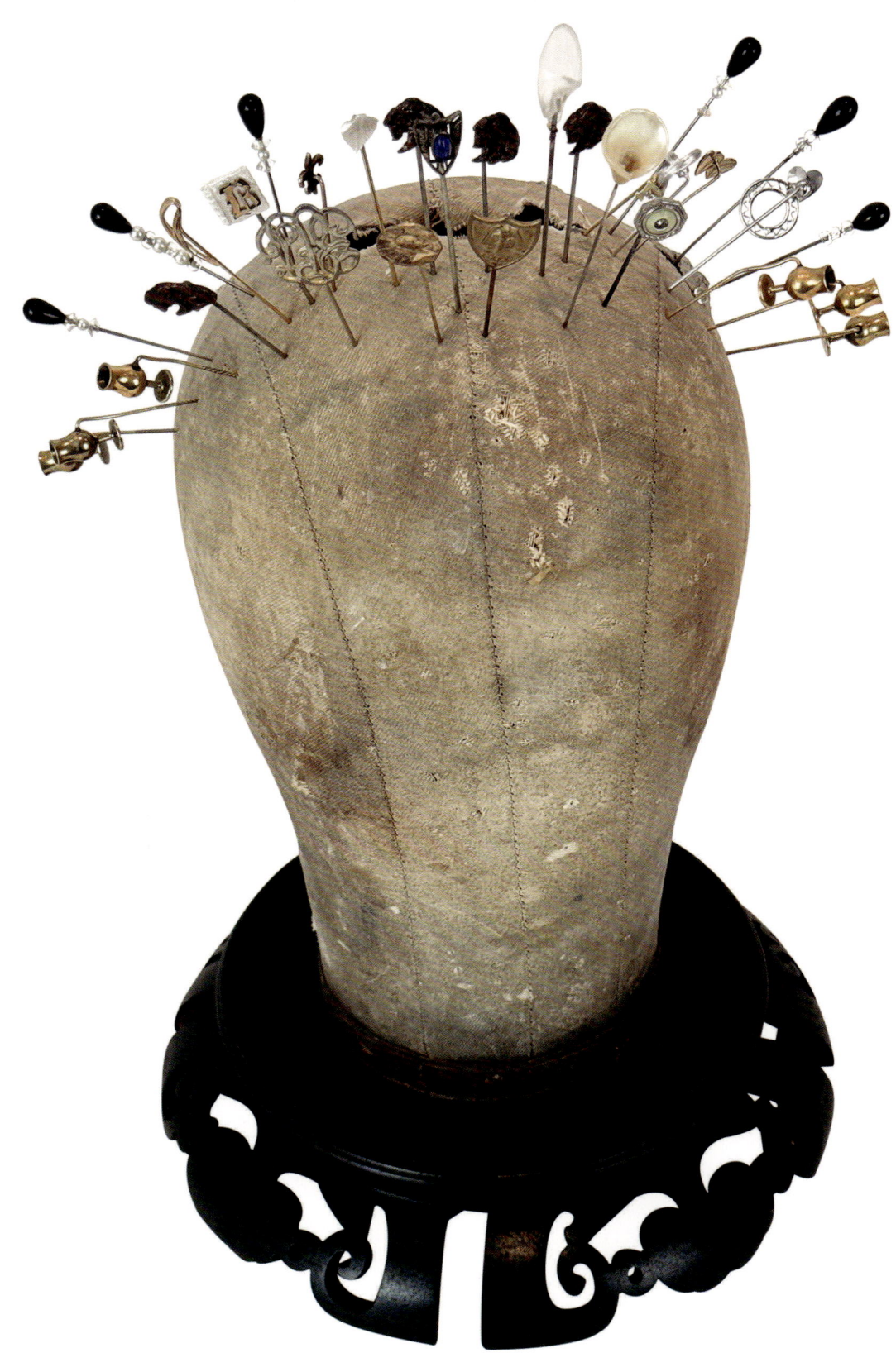

Cluster
14 x 9 x 8 inches
Mixed Media on Wooden Pedestal
2018

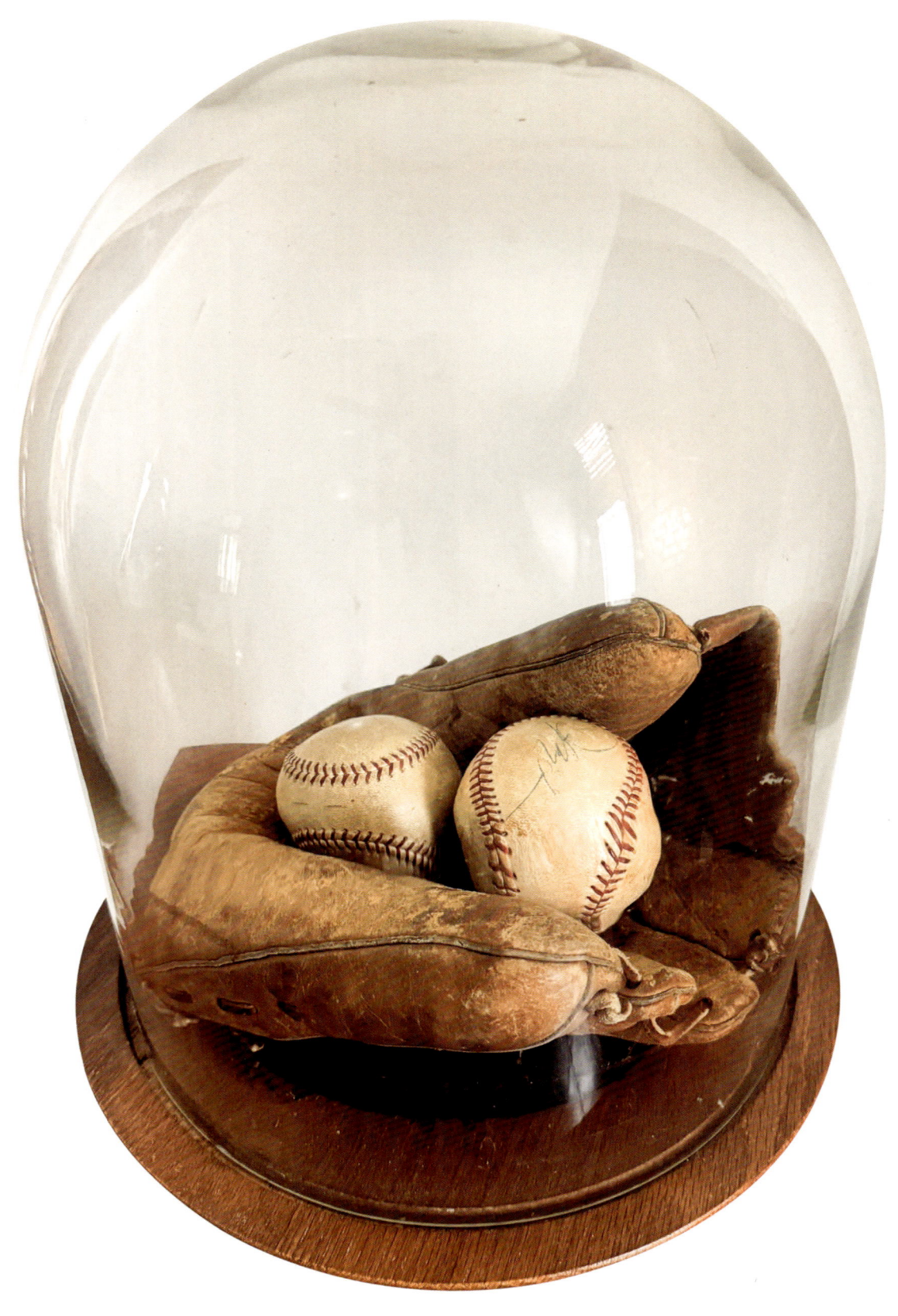

Shrine
12 x 10 inches
Leather Glove and Balls
2004

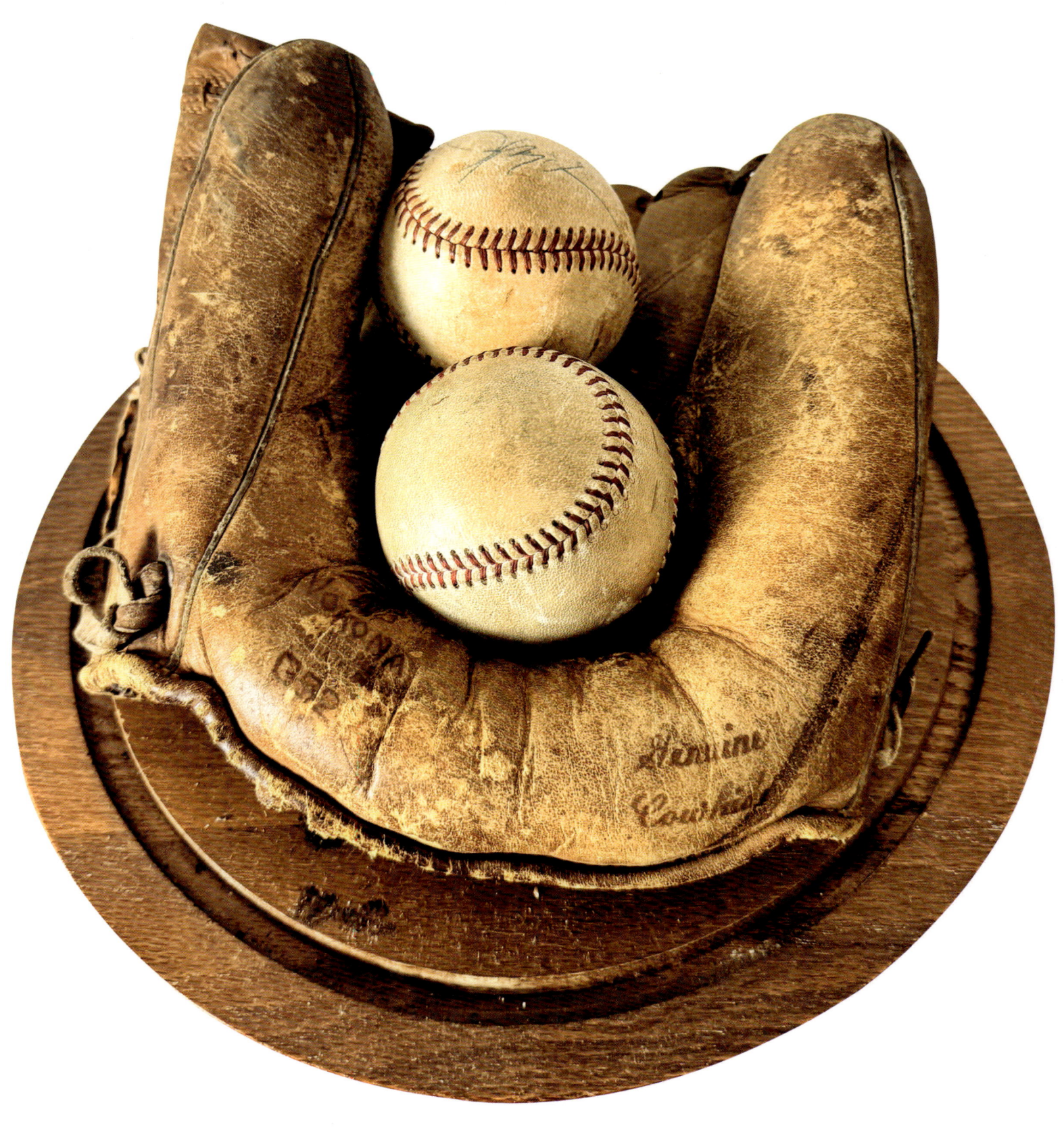

Shrine (Detail)

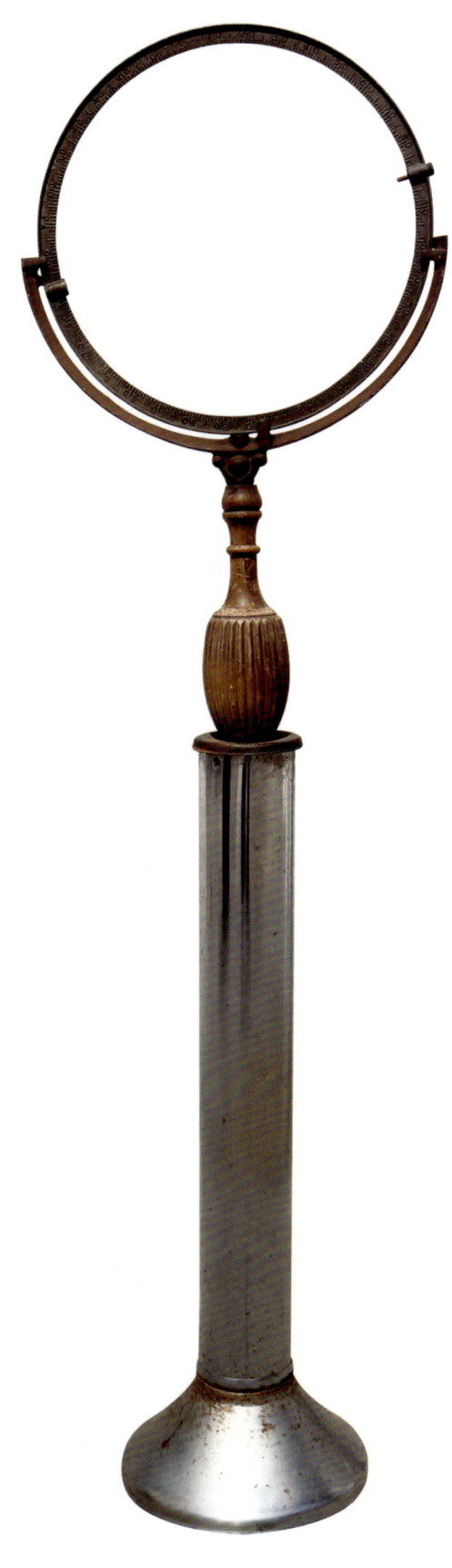

Compass
52 x 15 x 8 inches
Metal and Wood
2013

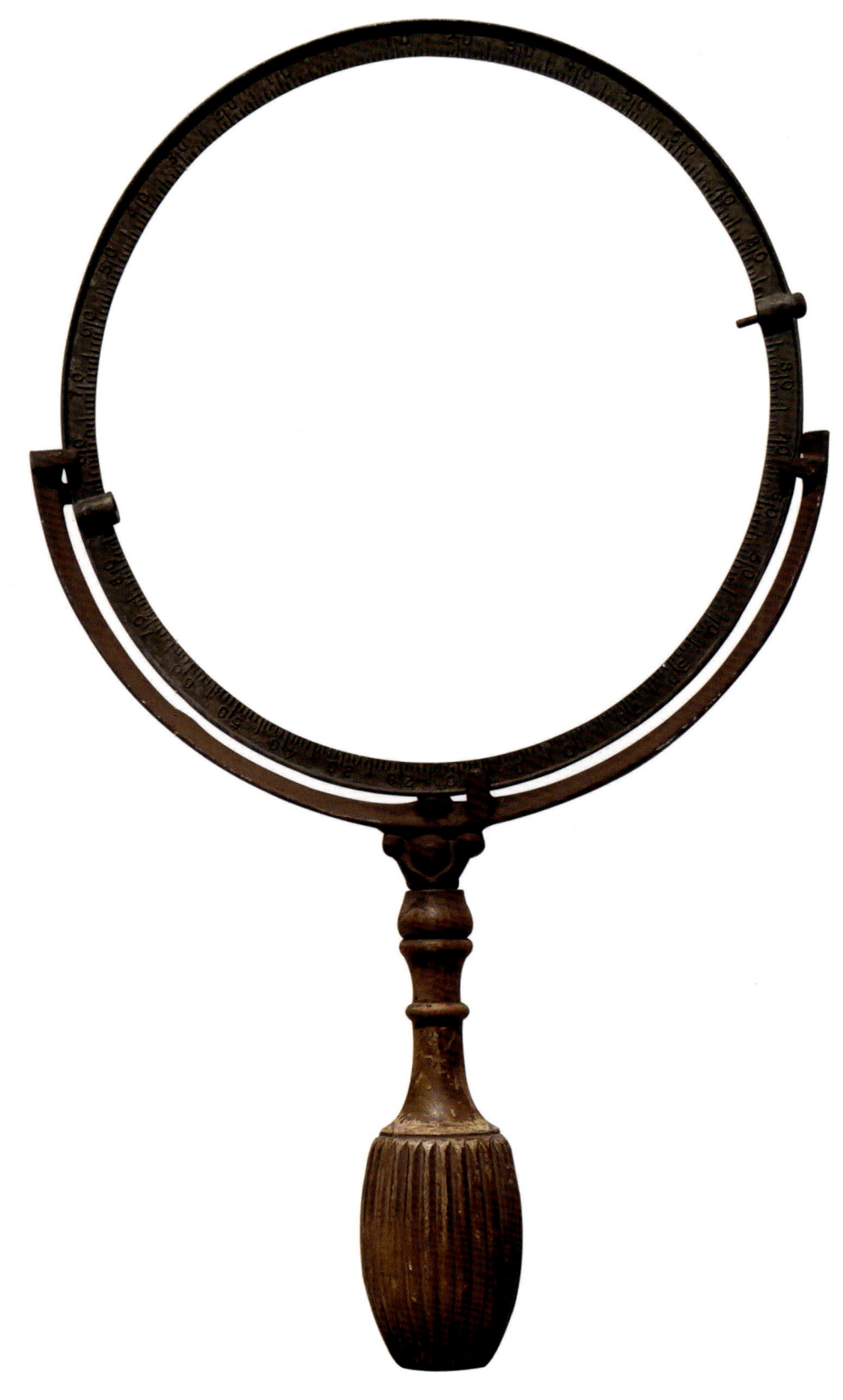

Compass (Detail)

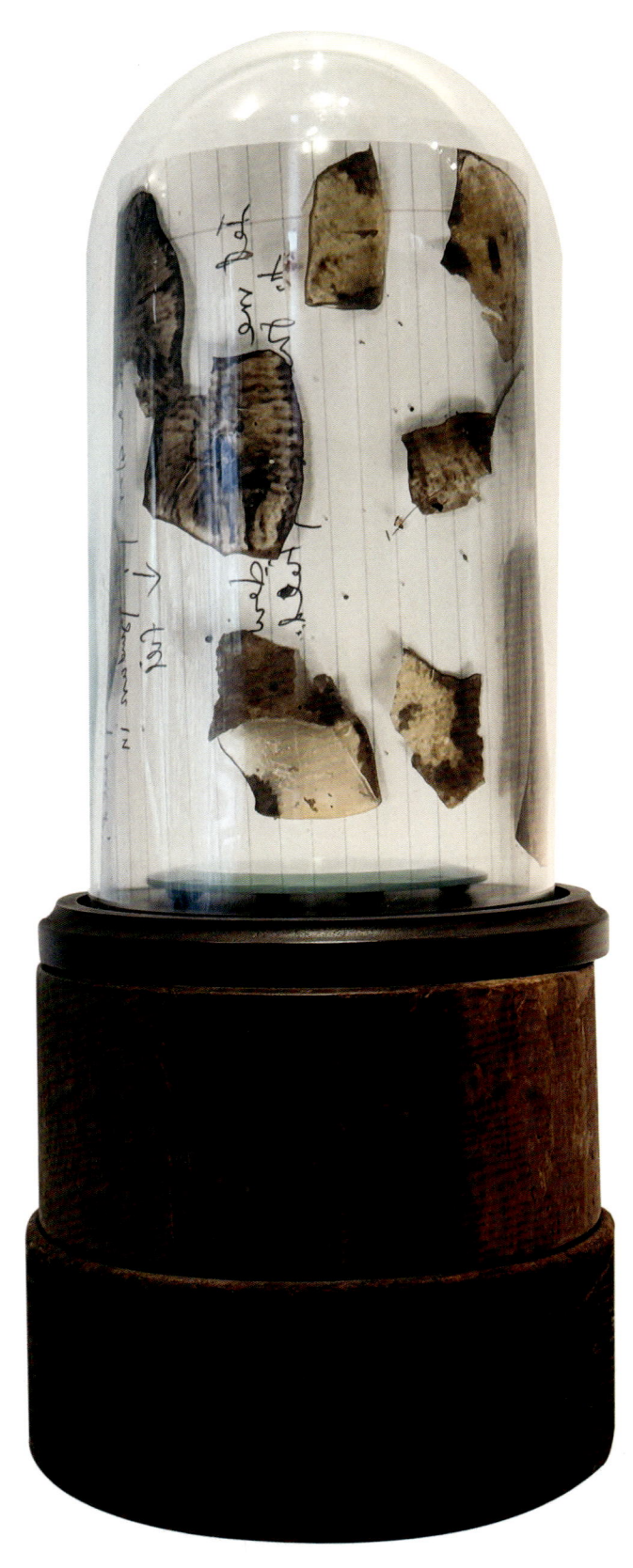

Dome Orbital
16 x 8 inches
Print Under Glass, Mirror, Hat Block
2018

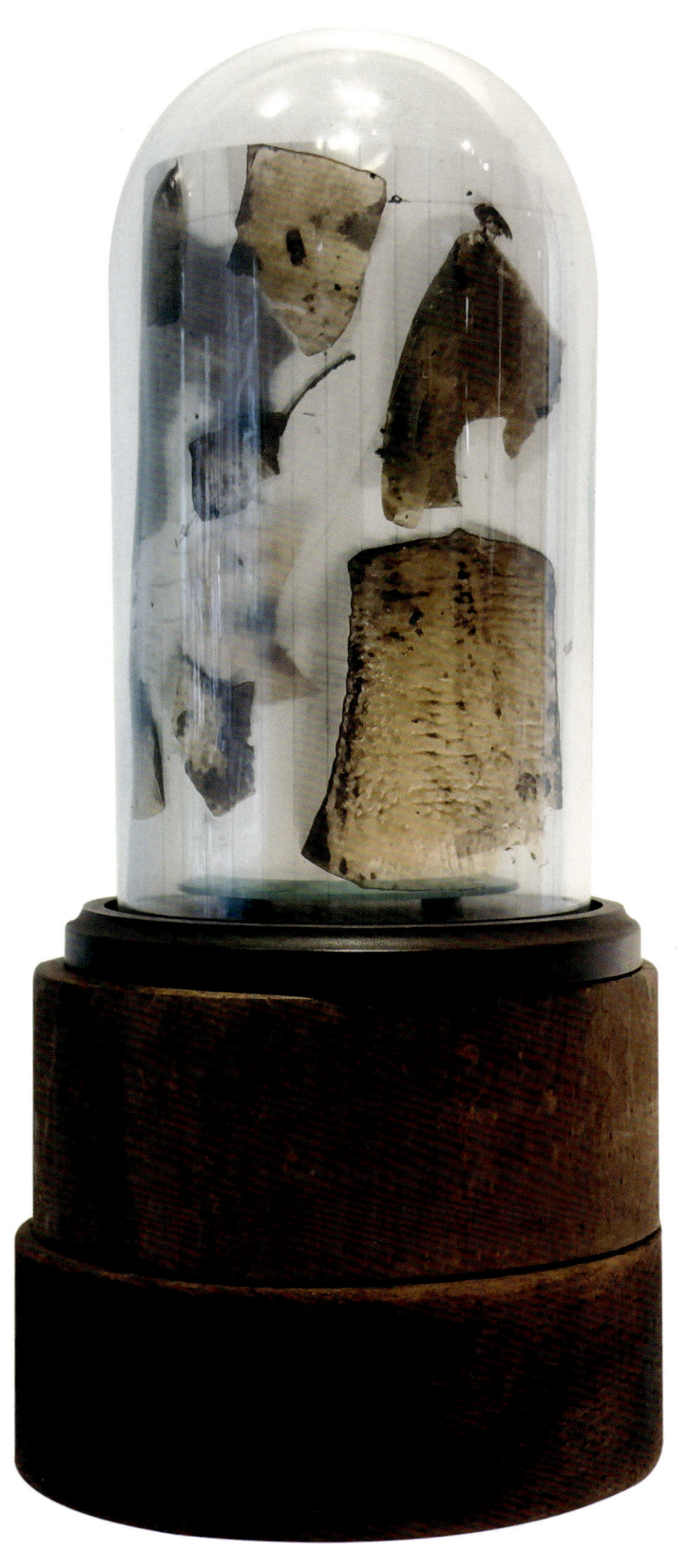

Dome Orbital (Alternate View)

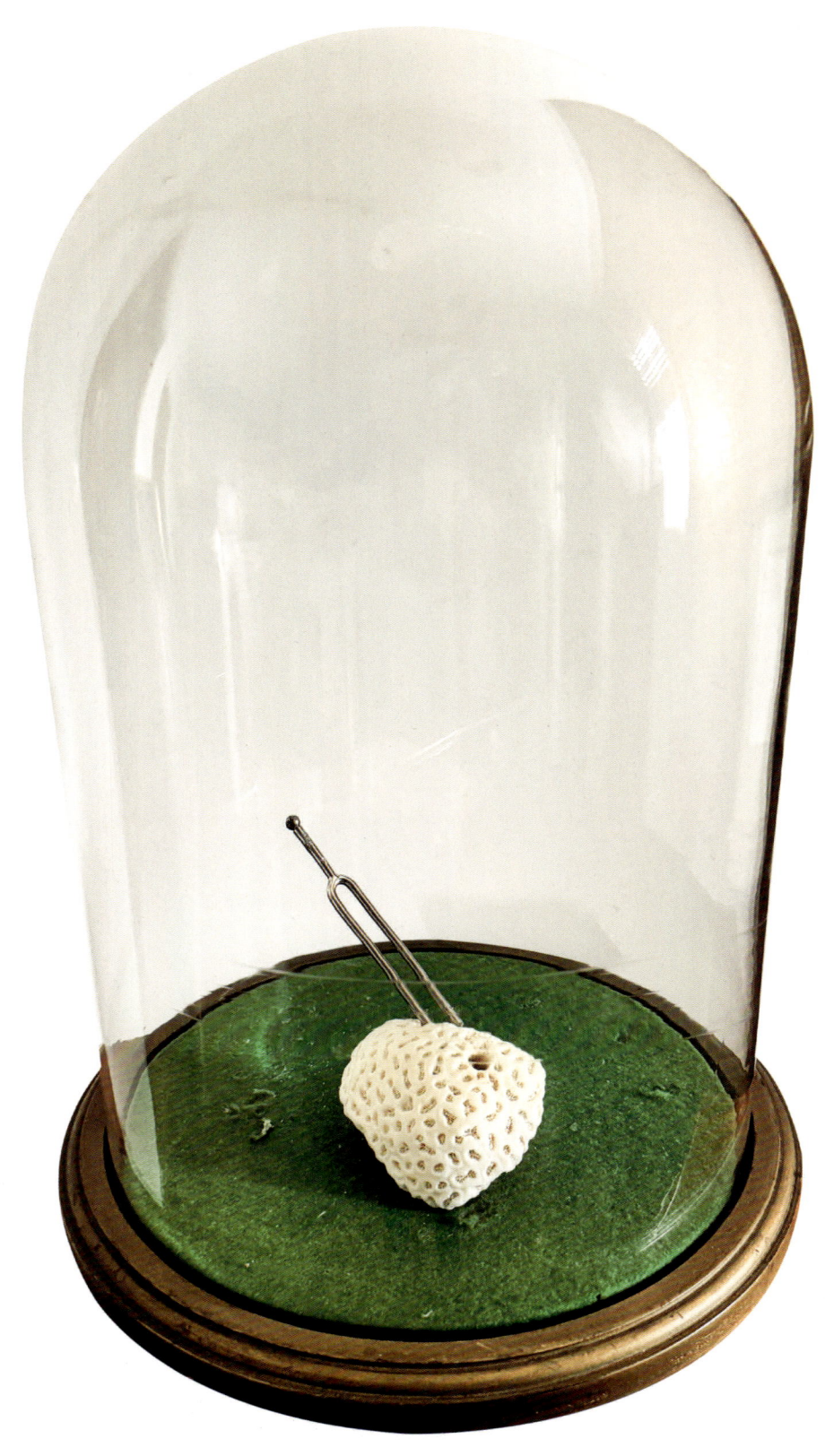

Tune
16 x 11 inches
Coral Rock w/ Tuning Fork
2004

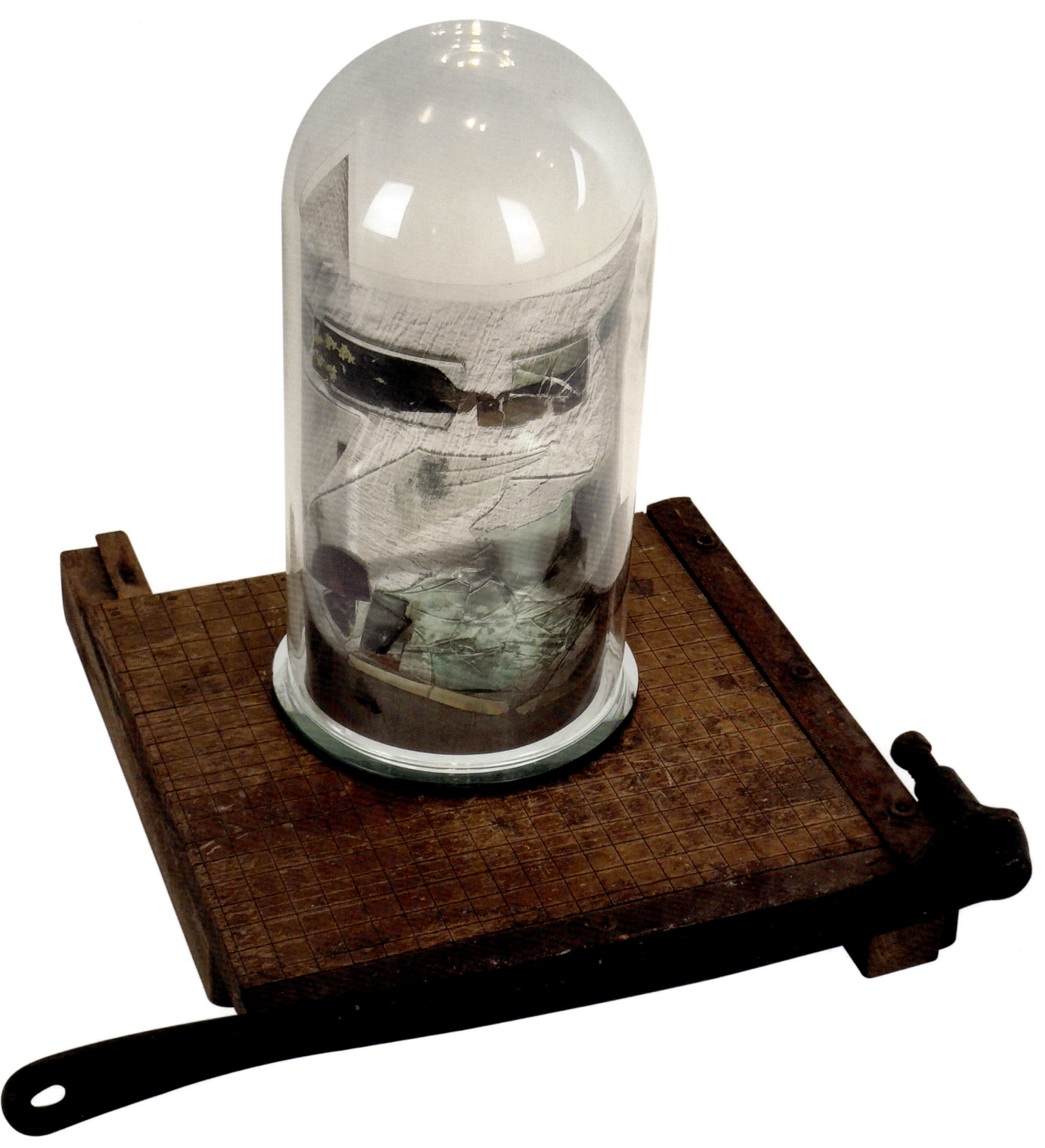

Dome Orbital 2
13 x 14 inches
Print Under Glass, Mirror, Paper Cutter
2018

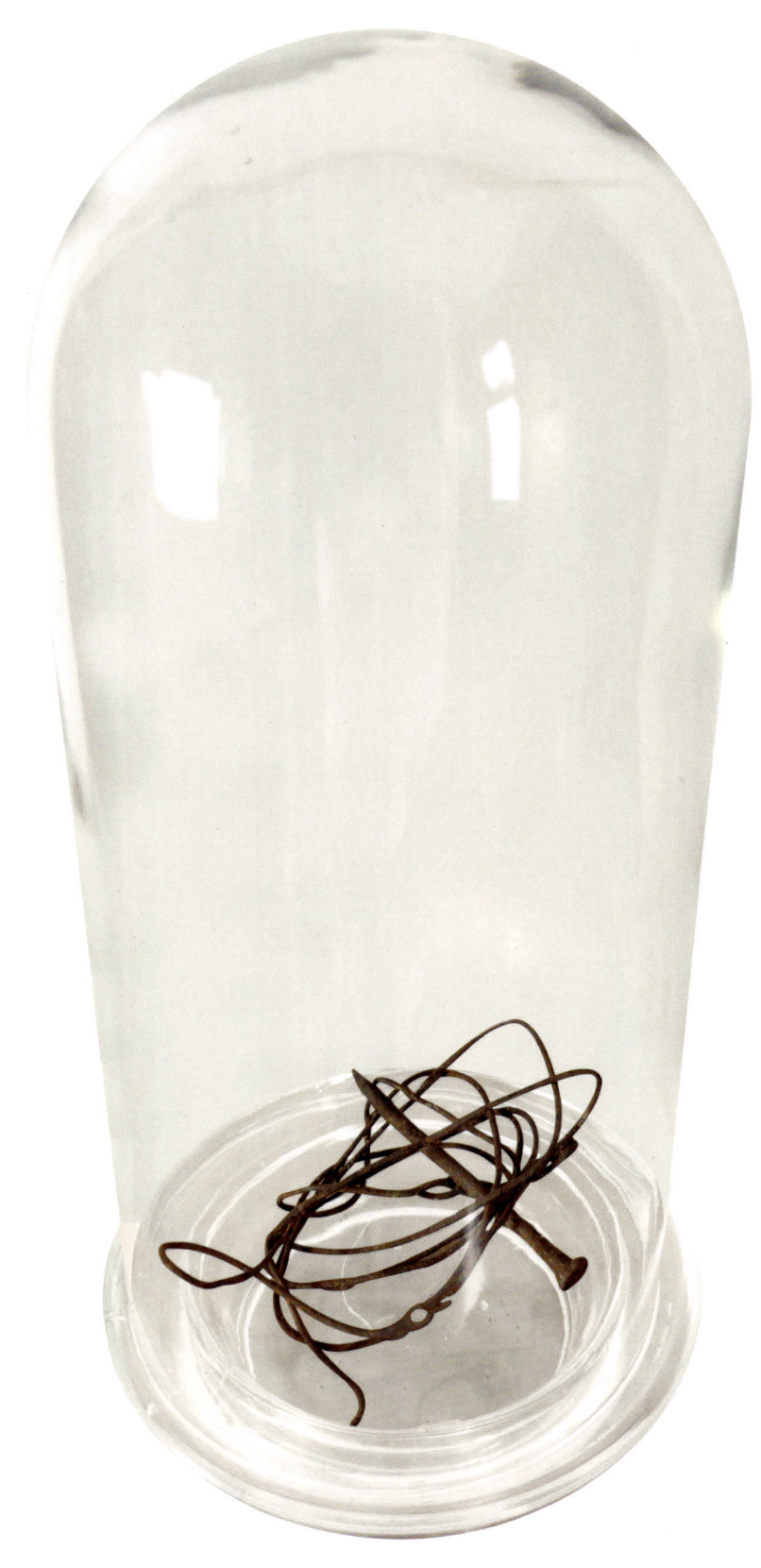

Souvenir from the Beach
14 ½ x 7 inches
Nail w/ Rusted Wire
2005

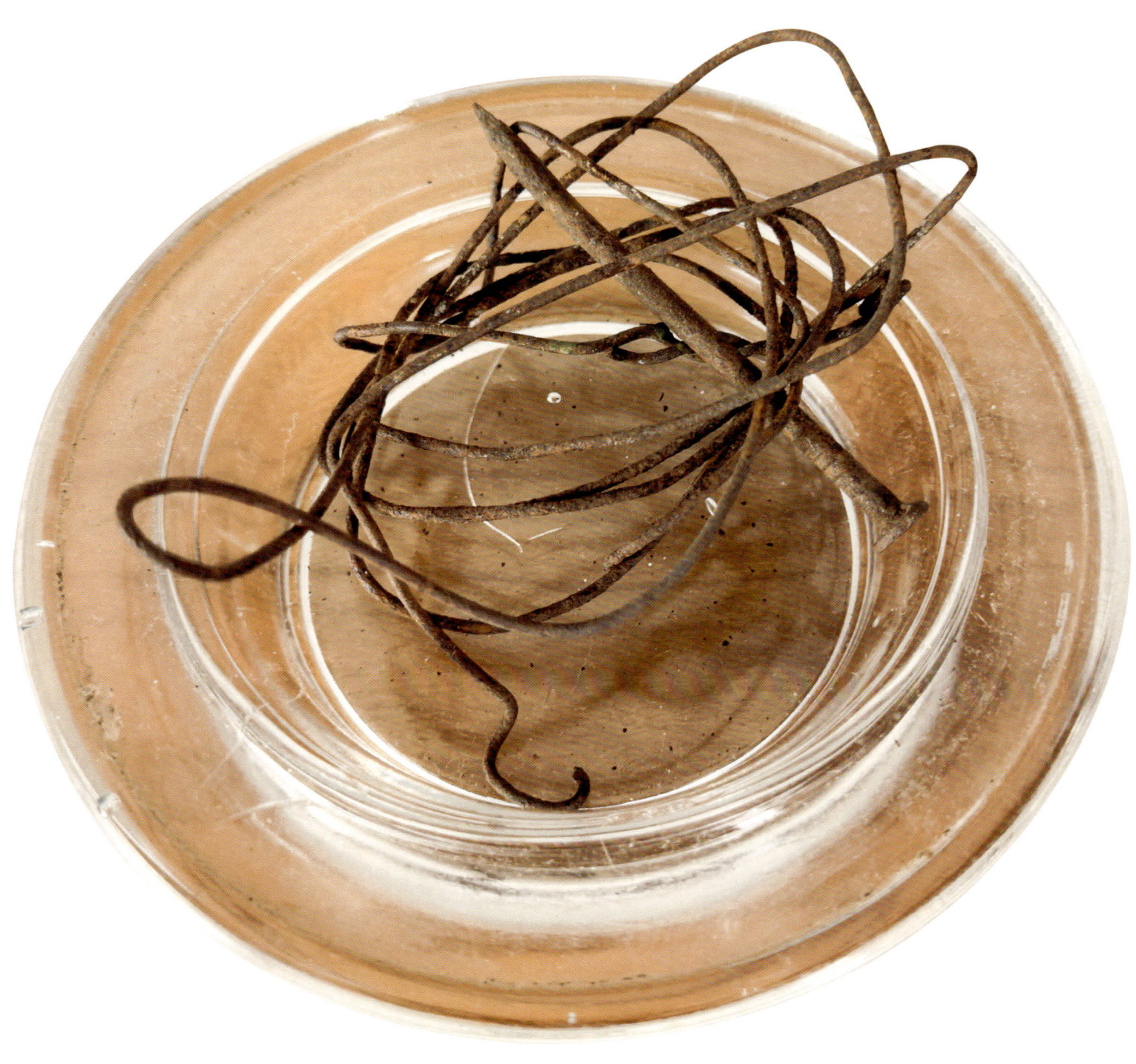

Souvenir from the Beach (Detail)

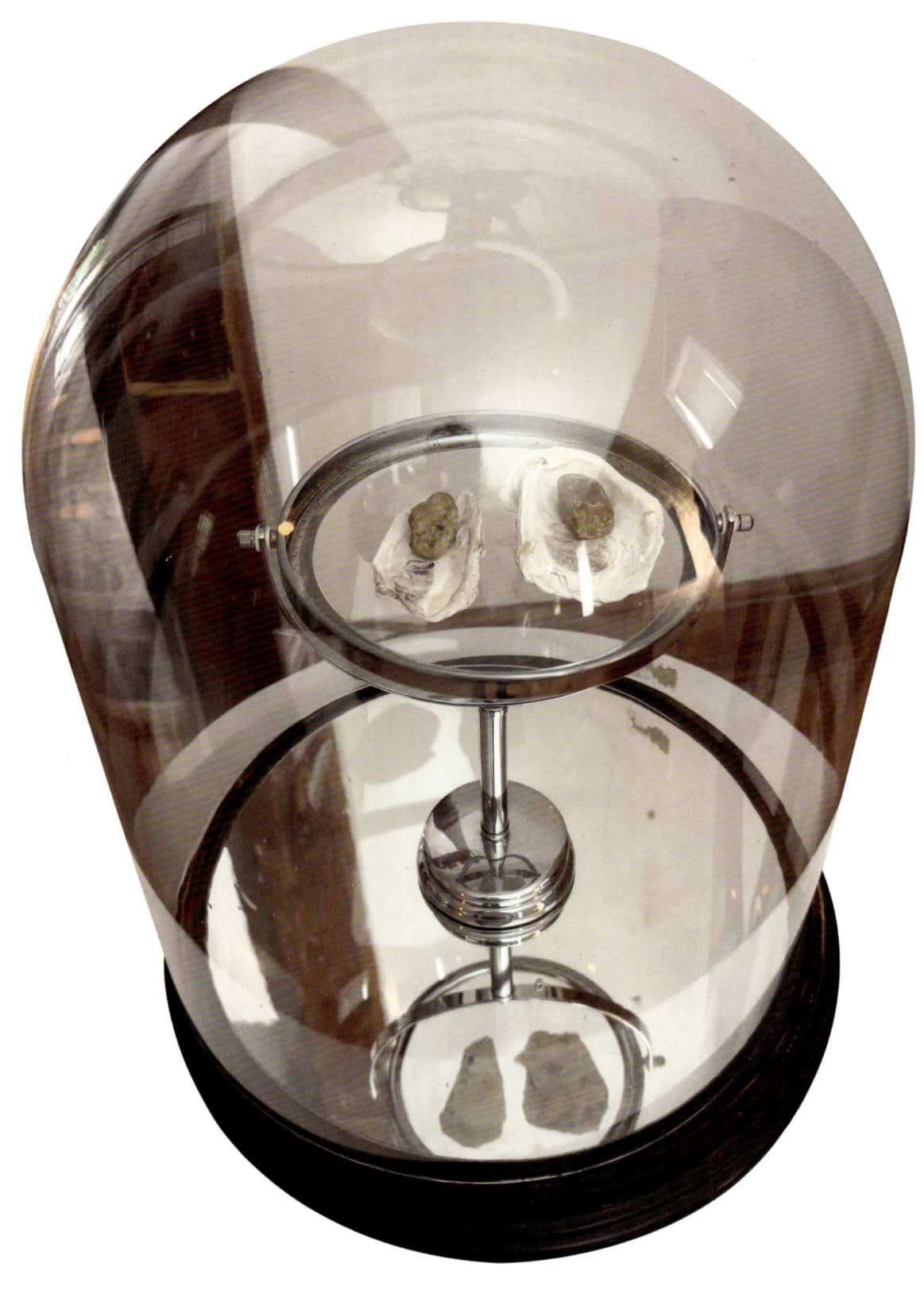

Prix Fixe
20 x 15 inches
Rocks, Shells, Glass, and Wood
2007

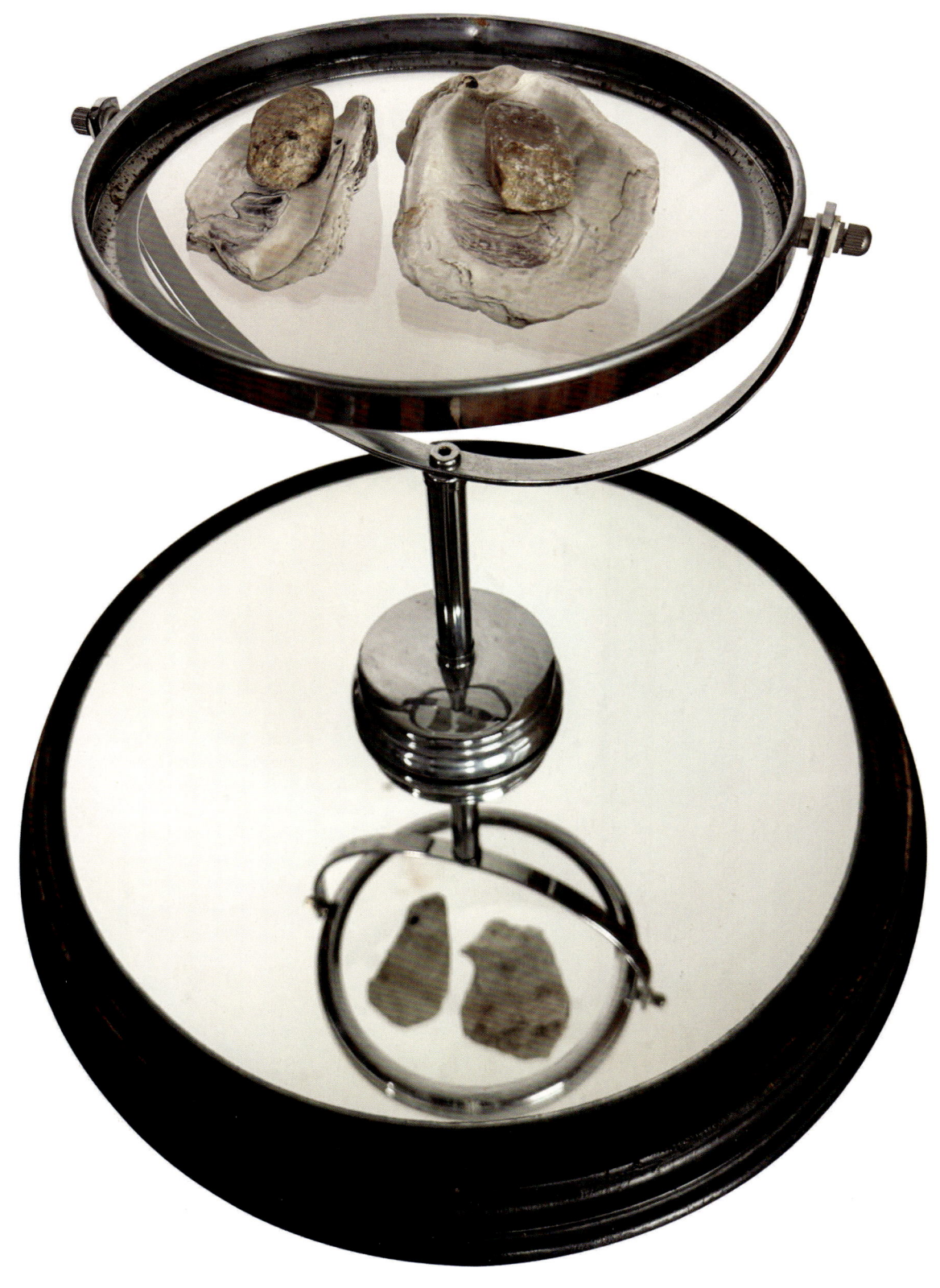

Prix Fixe (Detail)

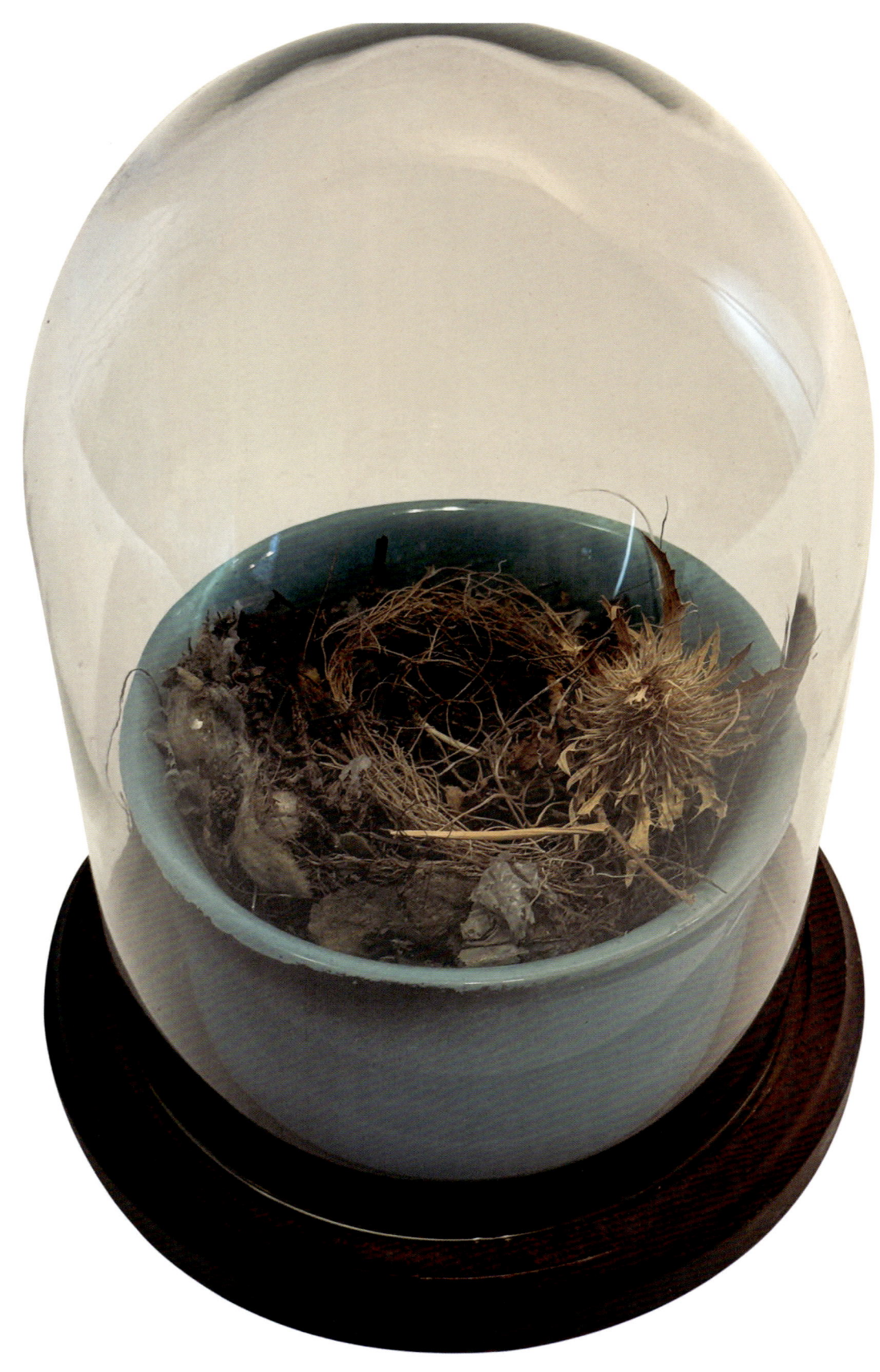

Nest
8 ½ x 6 ½ inches
Bird Nest w/ Ceramic Bowl and Glass Dome
2009

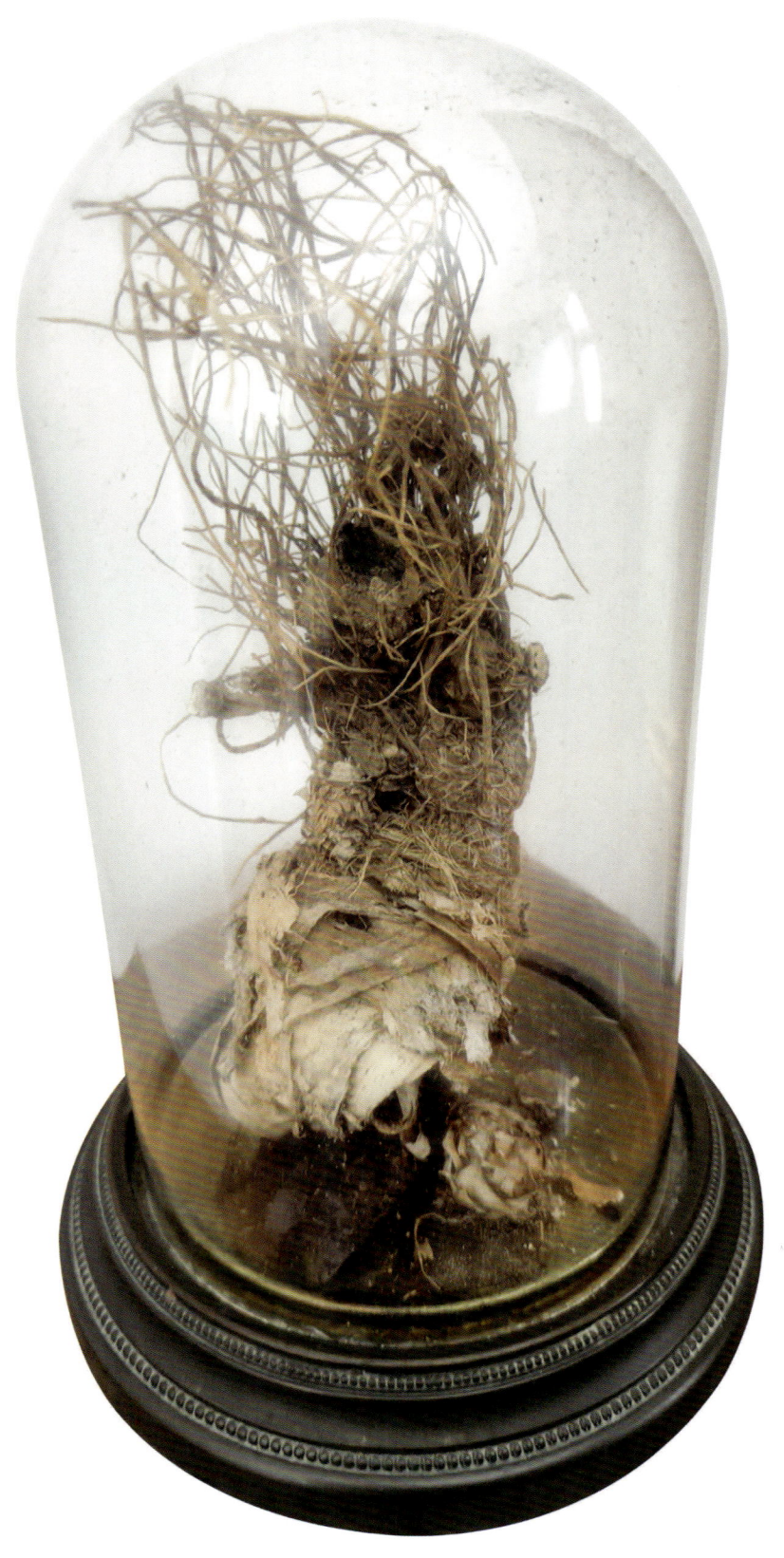

Silhouette
12 x 7 ½ inches
Root, Glass and Brass
2007

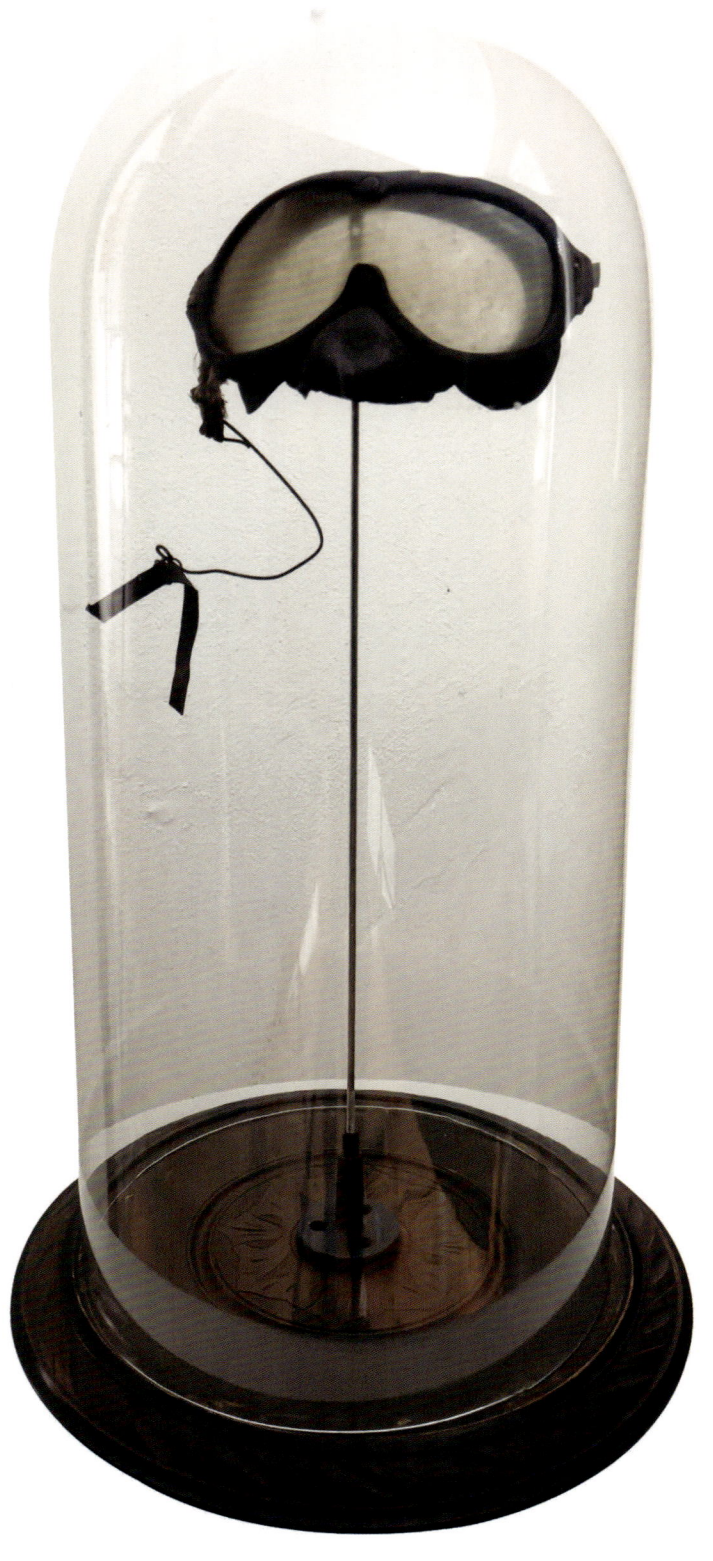

Visor
28 x 15 inches
Mask, Wire, Glass and Wood
2007

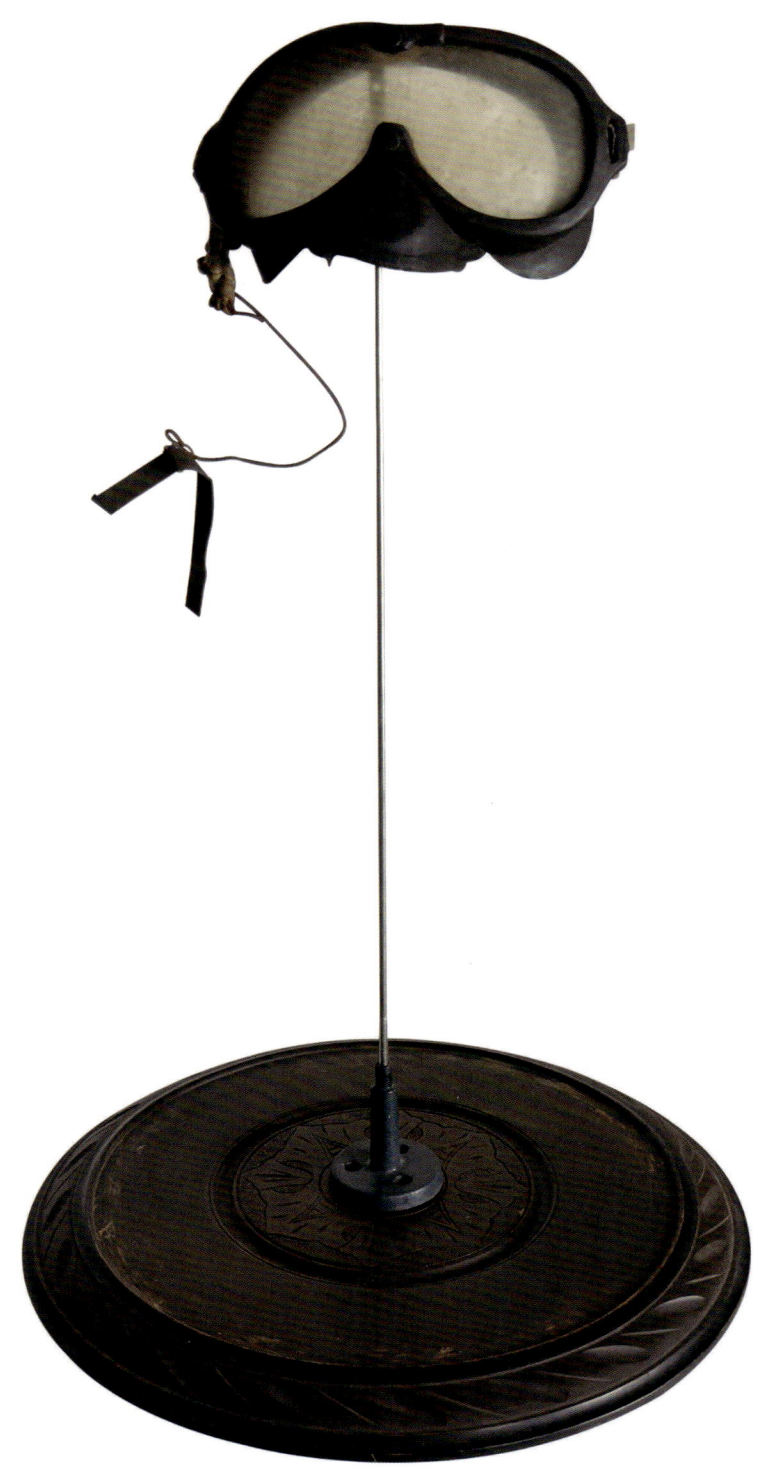

Visor (Detail)

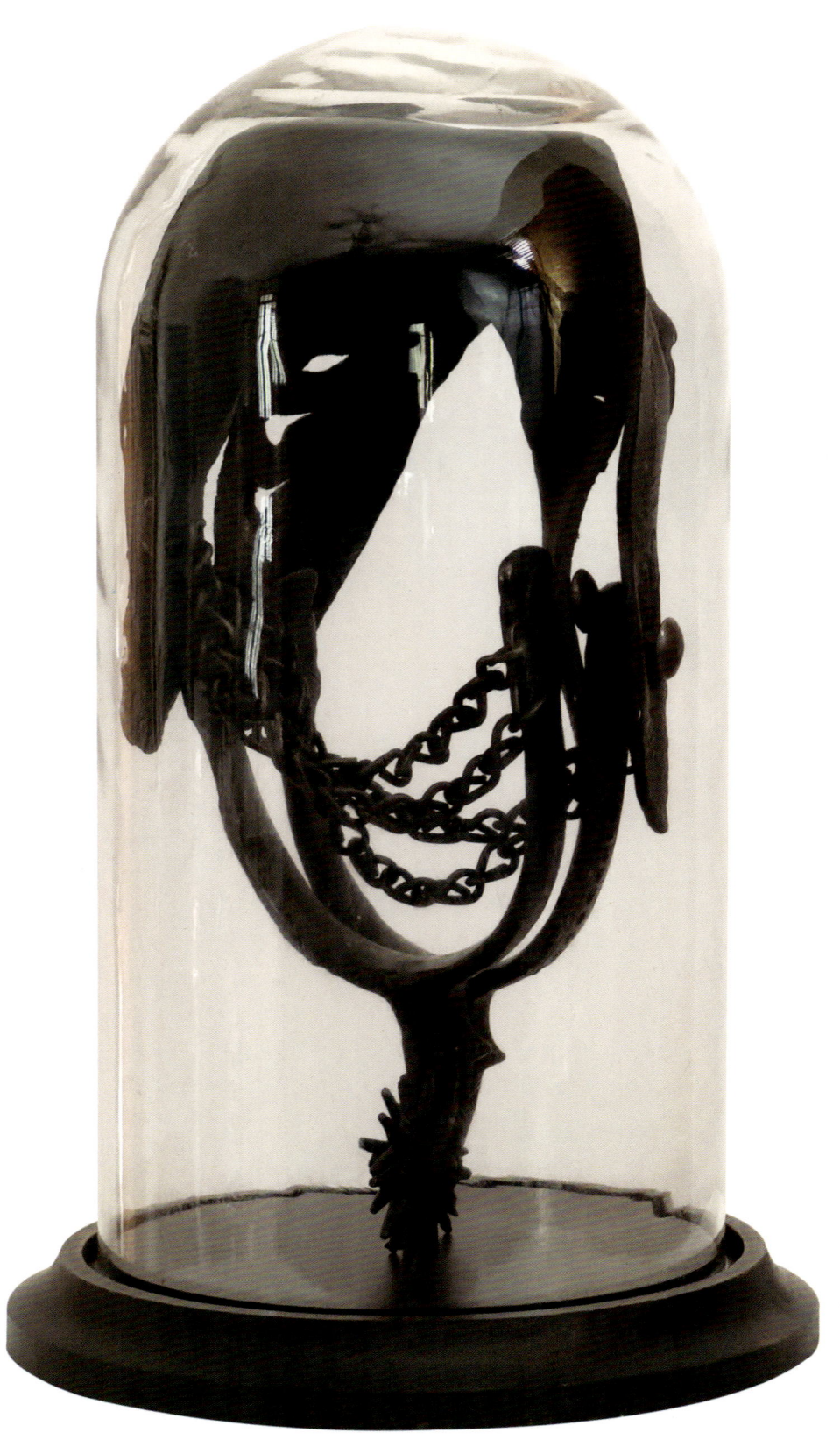

Spurs
12 x 5 ½ inches
Iron and Leather
2004

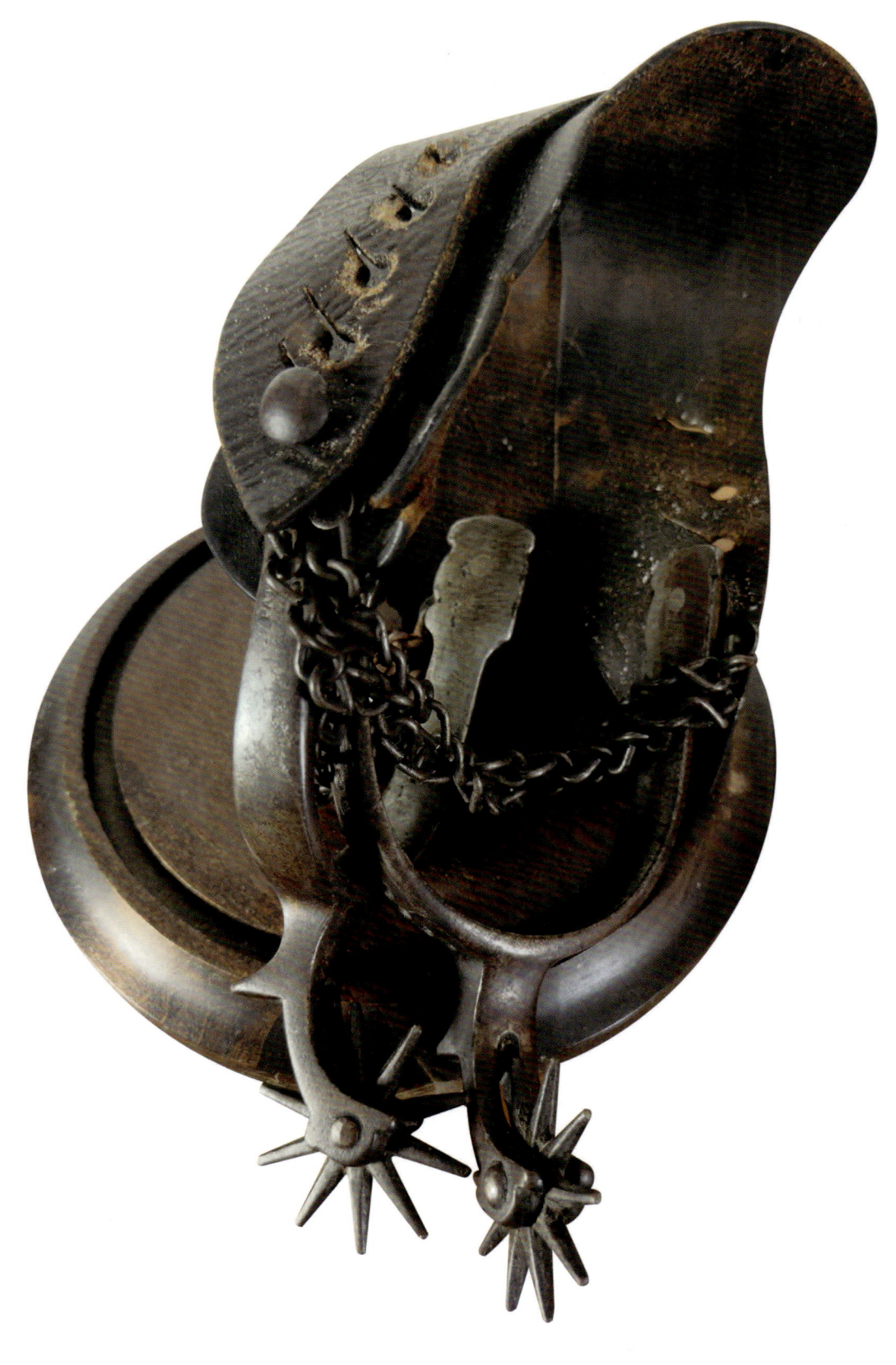

Spurs (Detail)

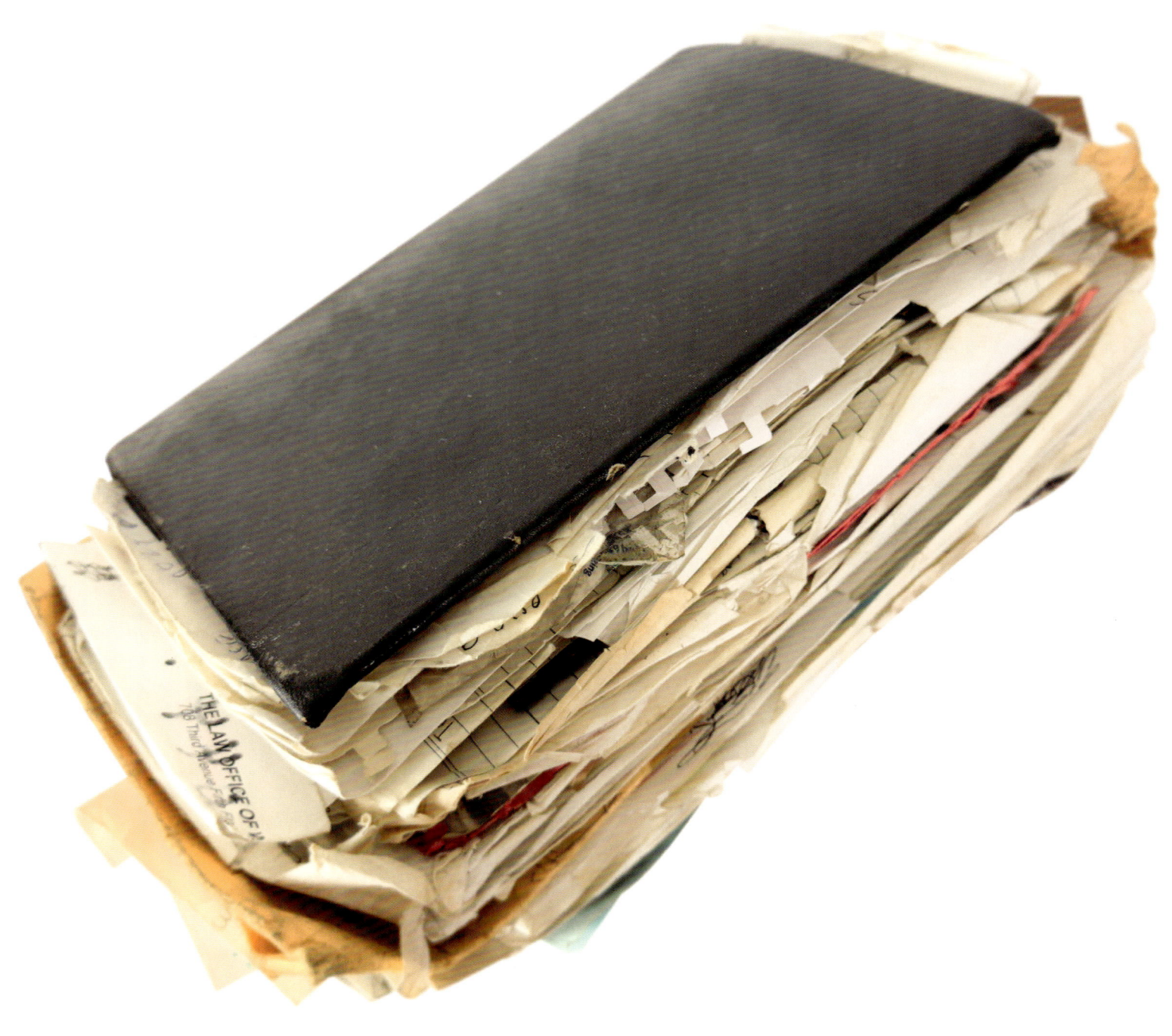

The Band's Phonebook
11 x 6 x 4 inches
Leather, Graphite, Ink on Paper
2004

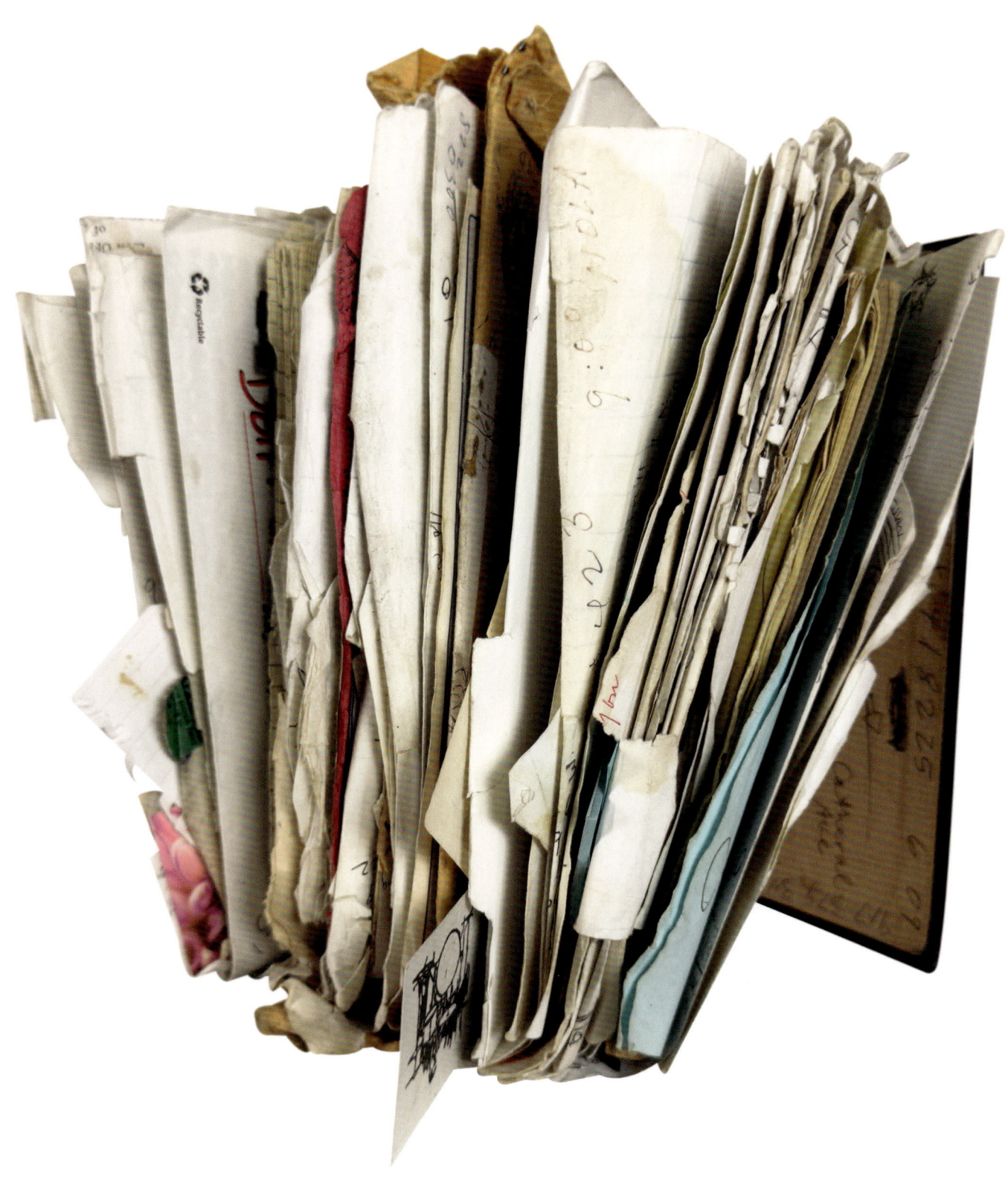

The Band's Phonebook (Detail)

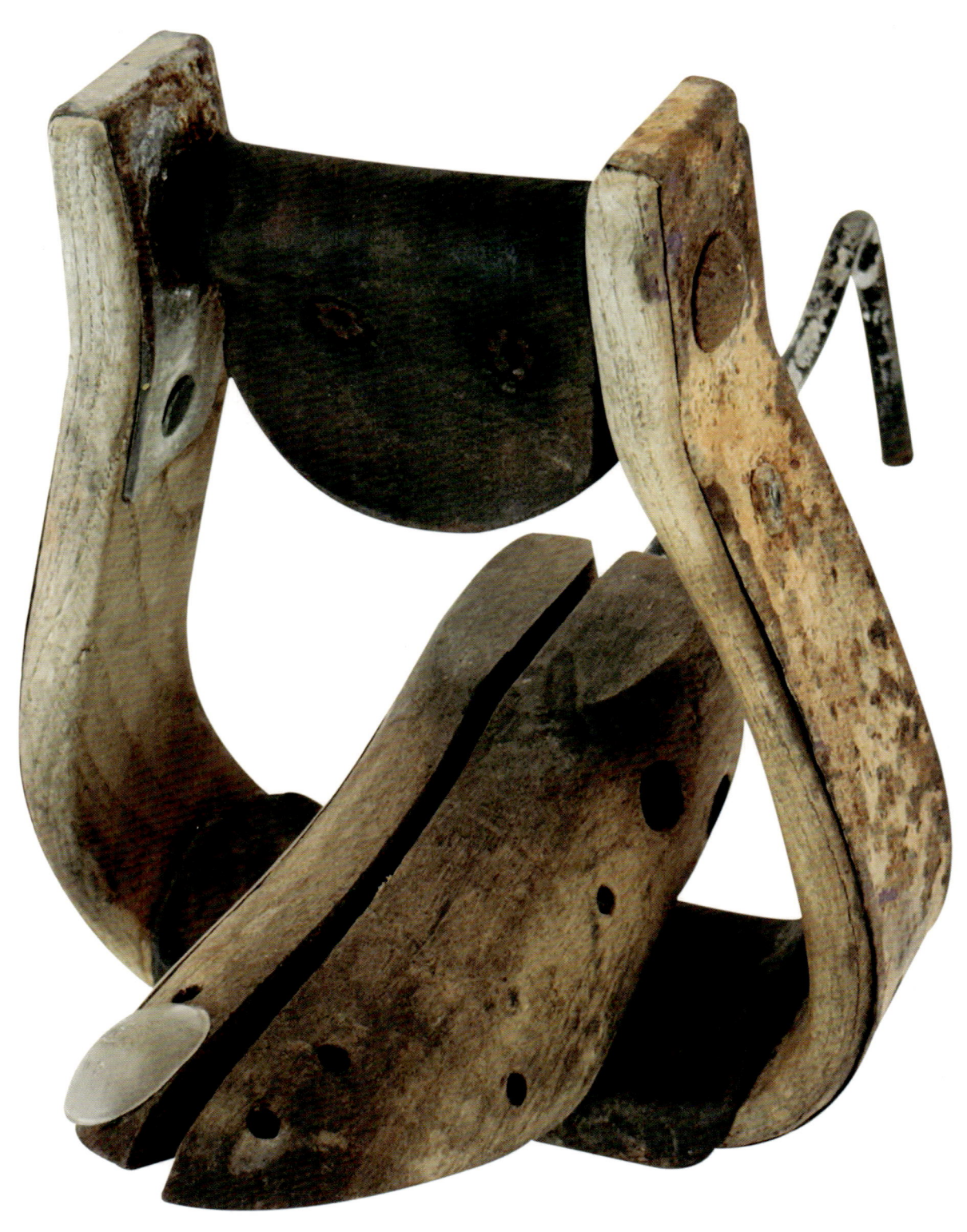

Hoofer
11 x 7 x 8 inches
Stirrup w/ Shoe Block
2010

72

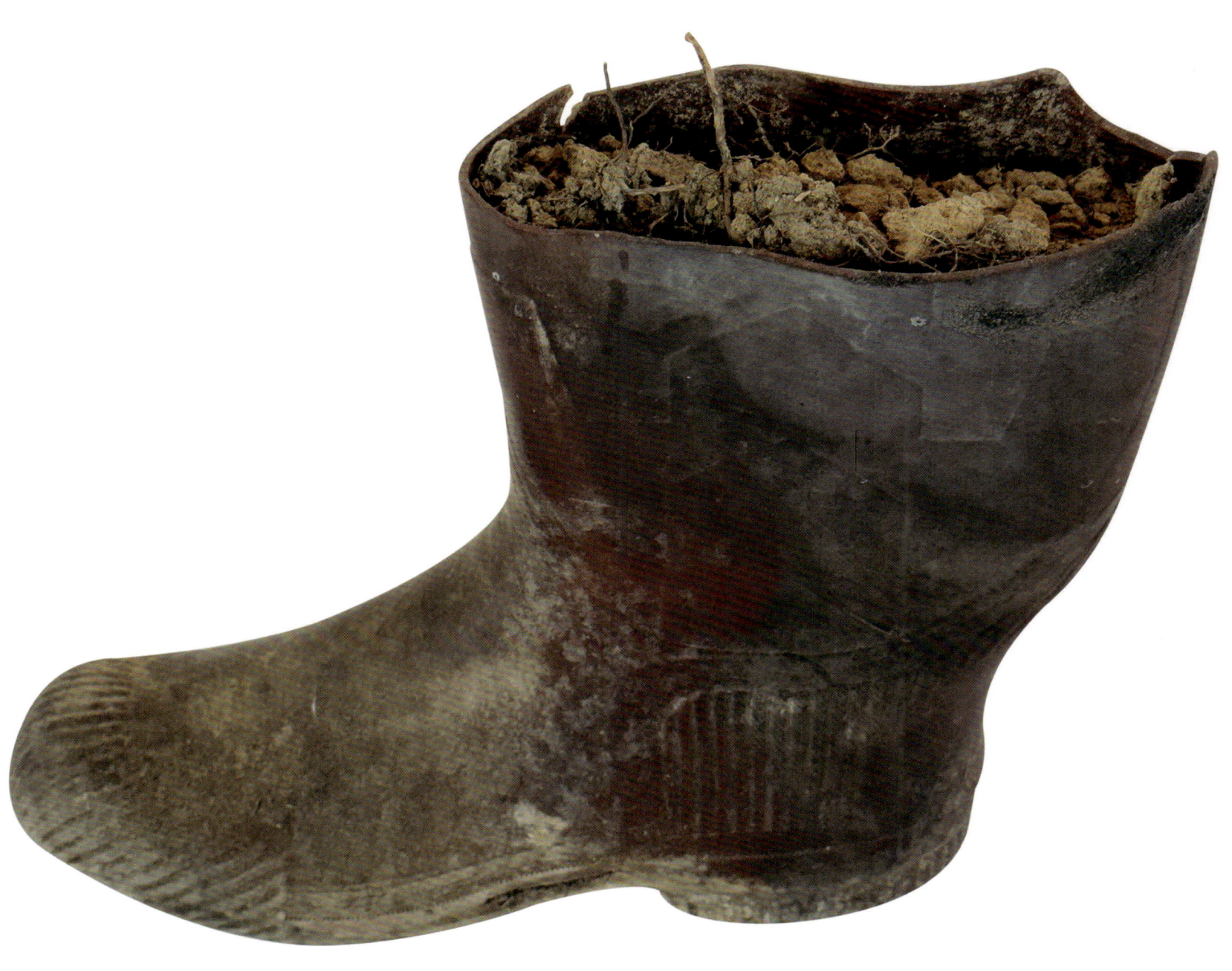

All That's Left of the Backhoe
9 x 9 inches
Rubber Boot w/ Dirt
2010

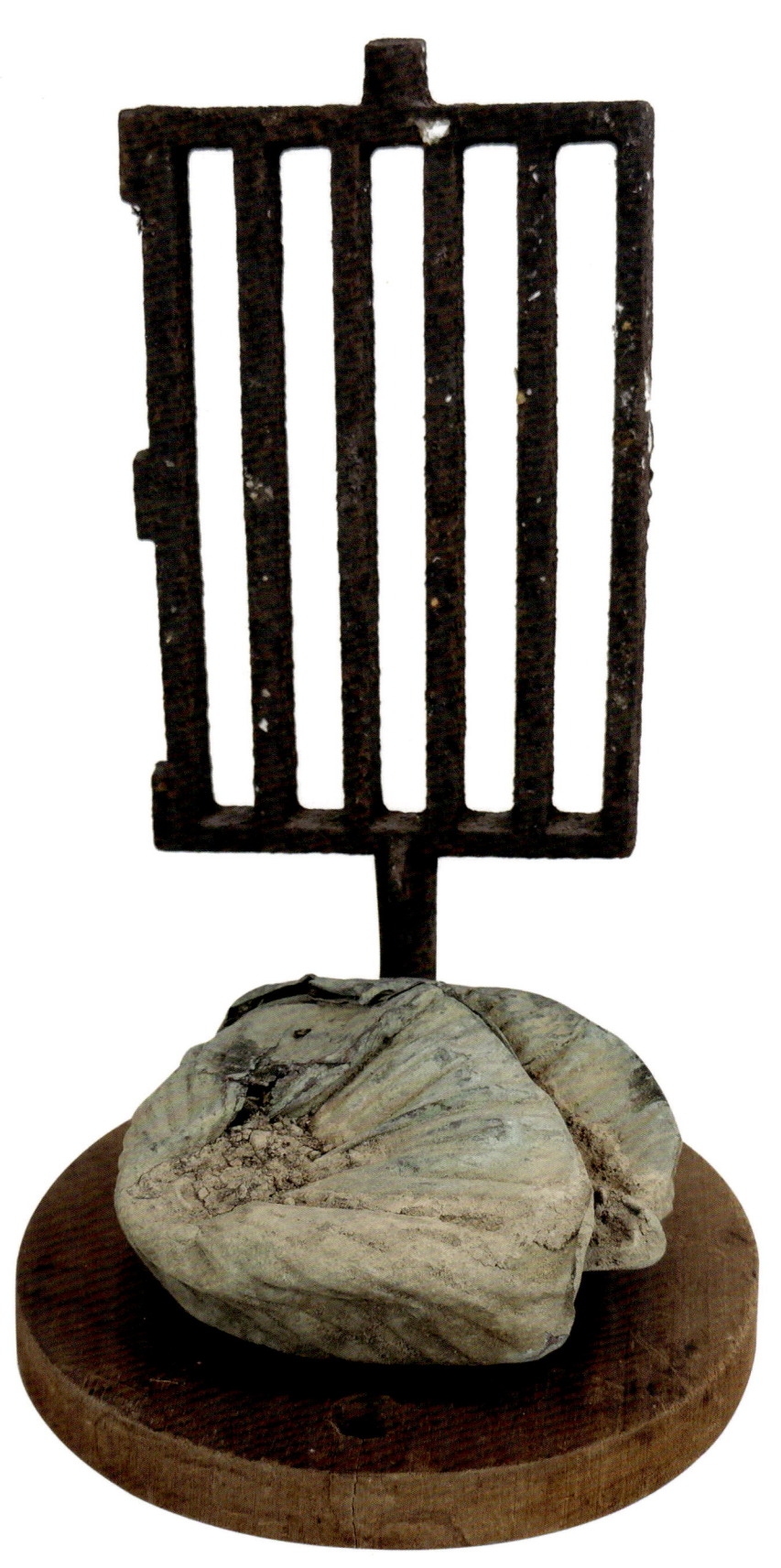

Eulogy
10 ½ x 8 inches
Metal, Wood and Cast Iron
2007

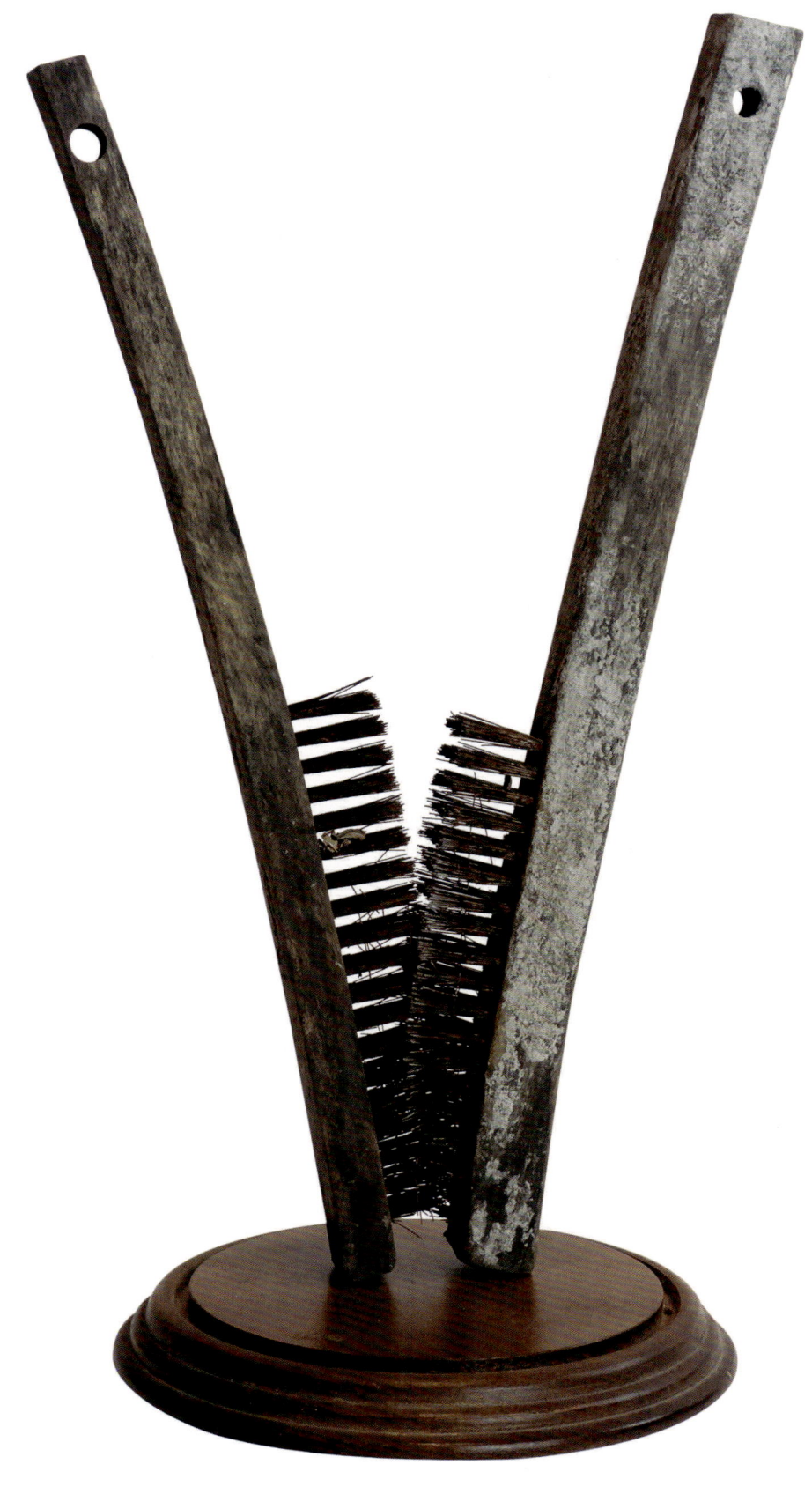

Crown
14 x 7 inches
Metal Brushes
2011

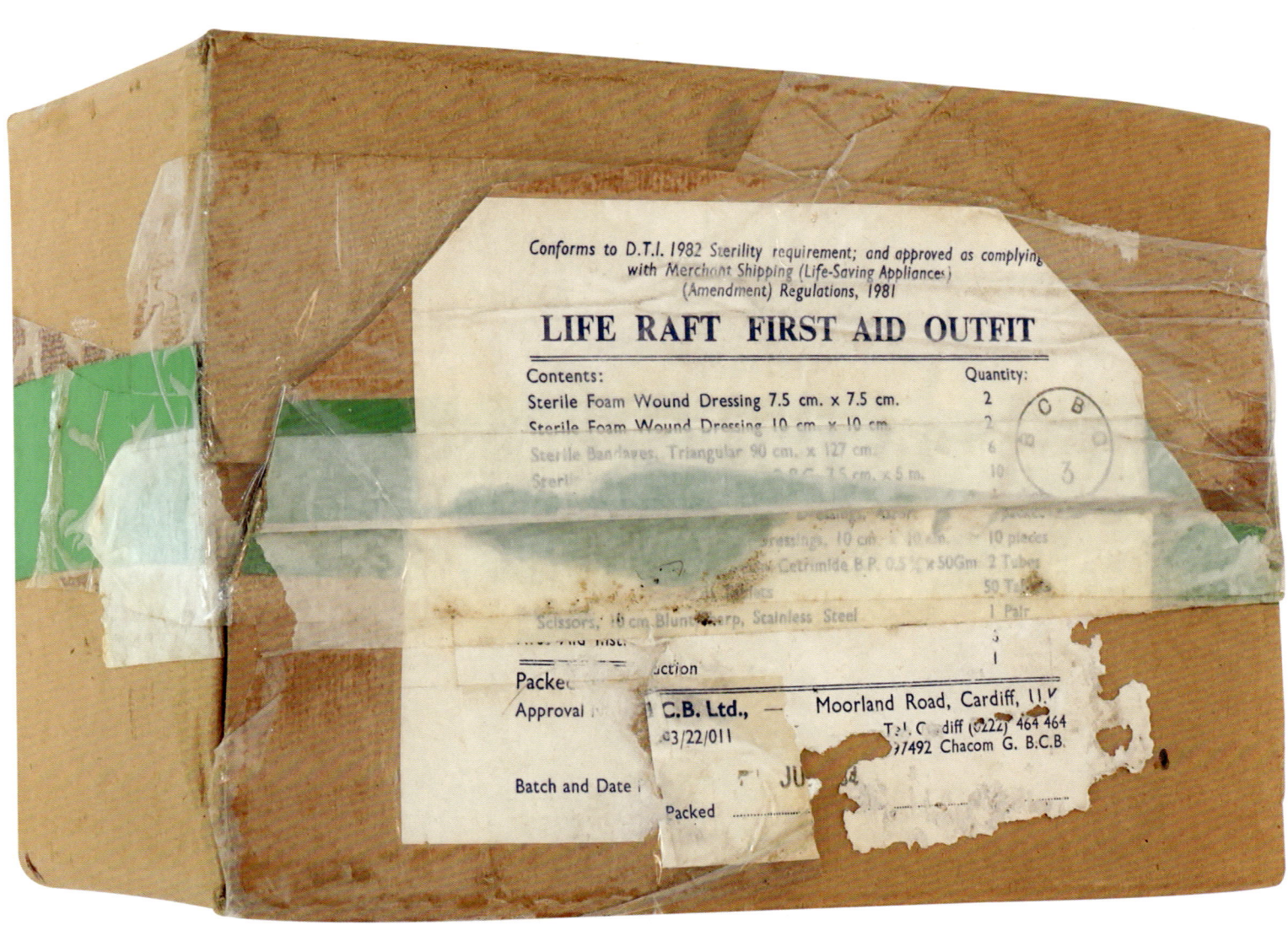

The label on the box reads:

Conforms to D.T.I. 1982 Sterility requirement; and approved as complying
with Merchant Shipping (Life-Saving Appliances)
(Amendment) Regulations, 1981

LIFE RAFT FIRST AID OUTFIT

Contents:	Quantity
Sterile Foam Wound Dressing 7.5 cm. x 7.5 cm.	2
Sterile Foam Wound Dressing 10 cm. x 10 cm.	2
Sterile Bandages, Triangular 90 cm. x 127 cm.	6
Steril... 7.5 cm. x 5 m.	10
...ressings, 10 cm. x 10 cm.	10 pieces
... Cetrimide B.P. 0.5% x 50Gm	2 Tubes
...les	50 Tablets
Scissors, 10 cm Blunt Sharp, Stainless Steel	1 Pair
...First Aid Instr...	1

Packed ...uction

Approval ... C.B. Ltd., — Moorland Road, Cardiff, U.K.
...03/22/011   Tel. Cardiff (0222) 464 464
                   ...7492 Chacom G. B.C.B.

Batch and Date ...   ...JU... Packed

Open In Case of Emergency
9 x 6 x 4 inches
Cardboard Box, Tape and Paper
1982

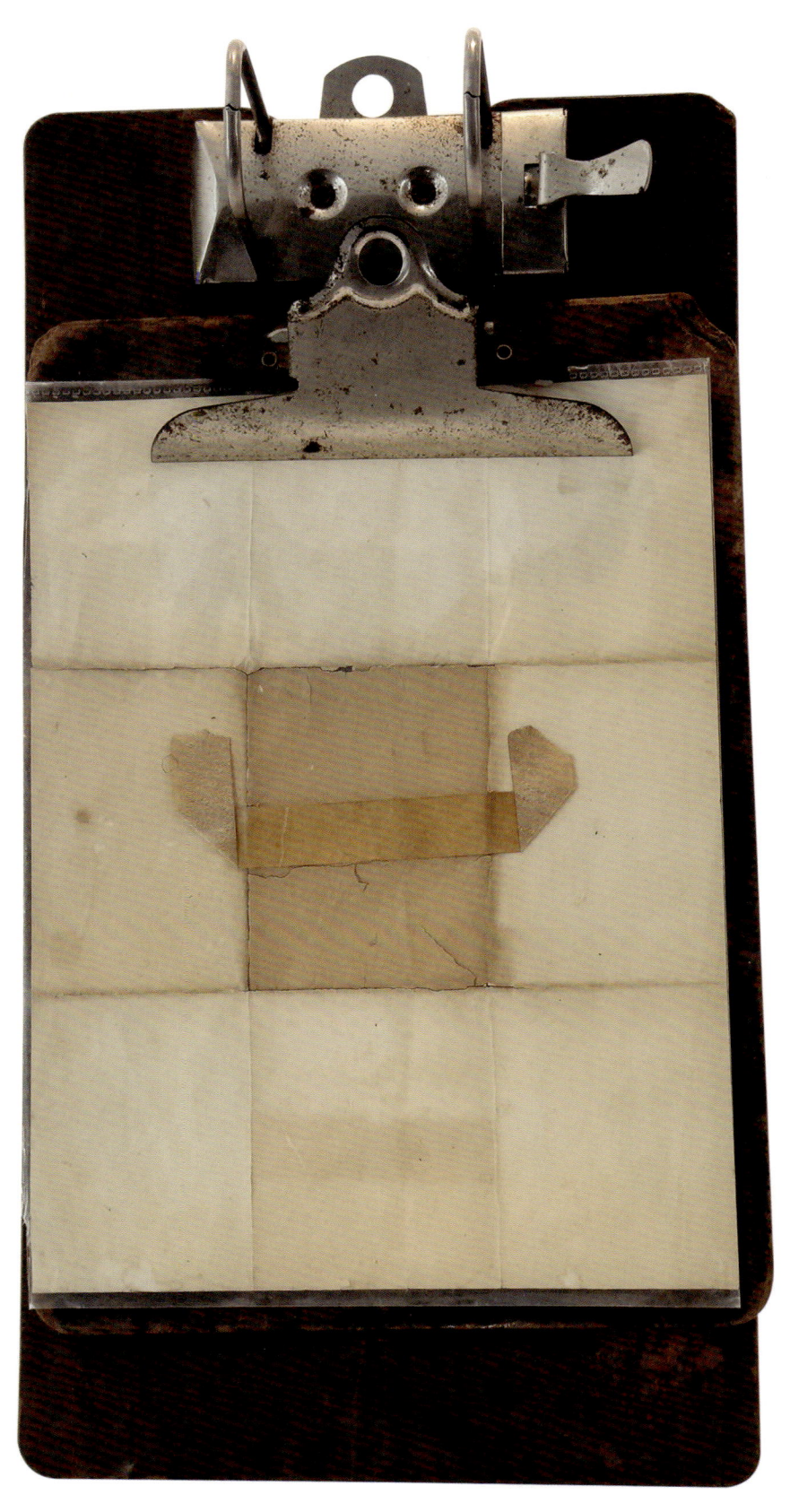

The Report
17 ½ x 9 inches
Paper, Board and Steel
2011

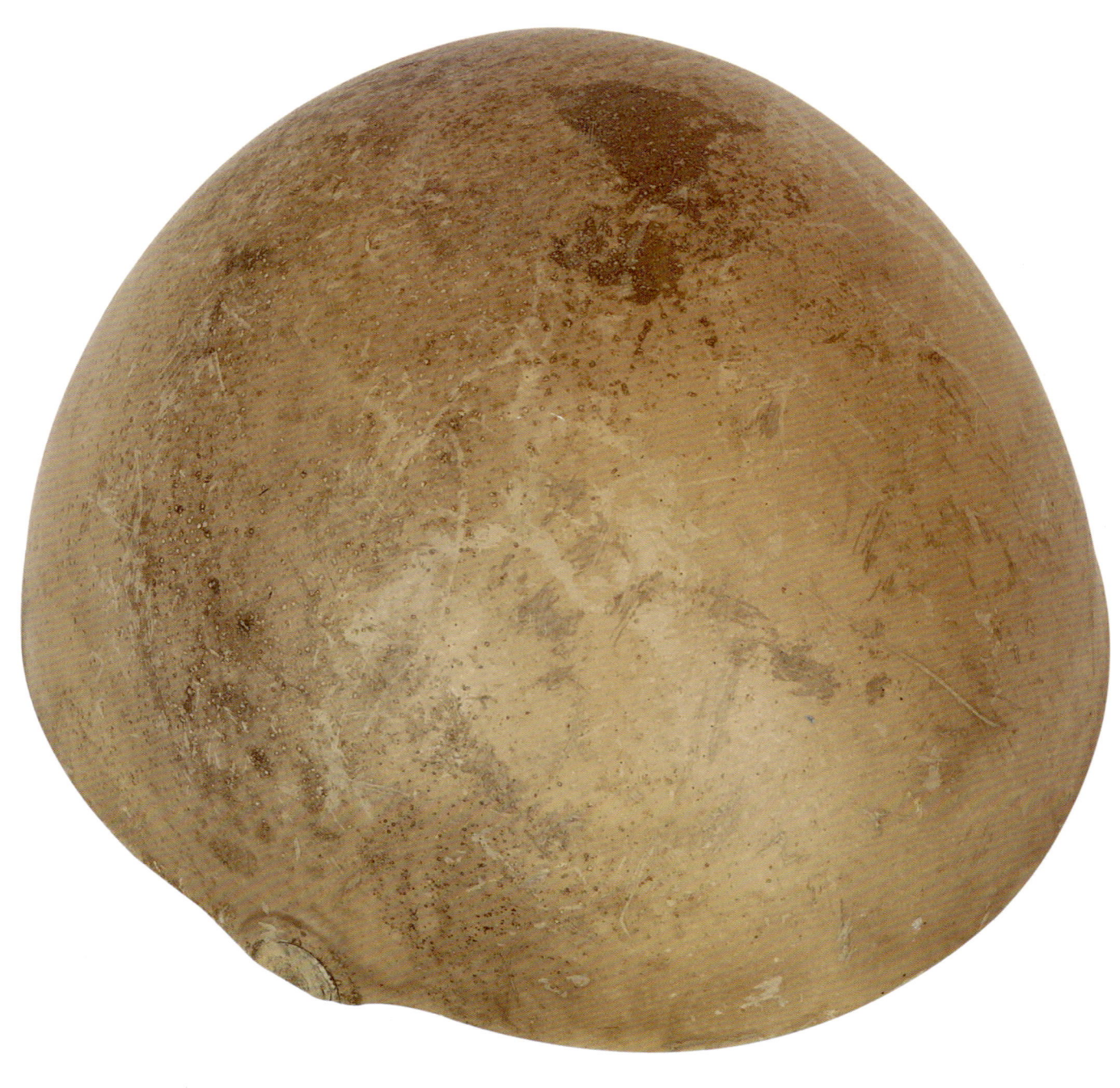

Bowl
8 x 5 inches
Sawed Gord
2009

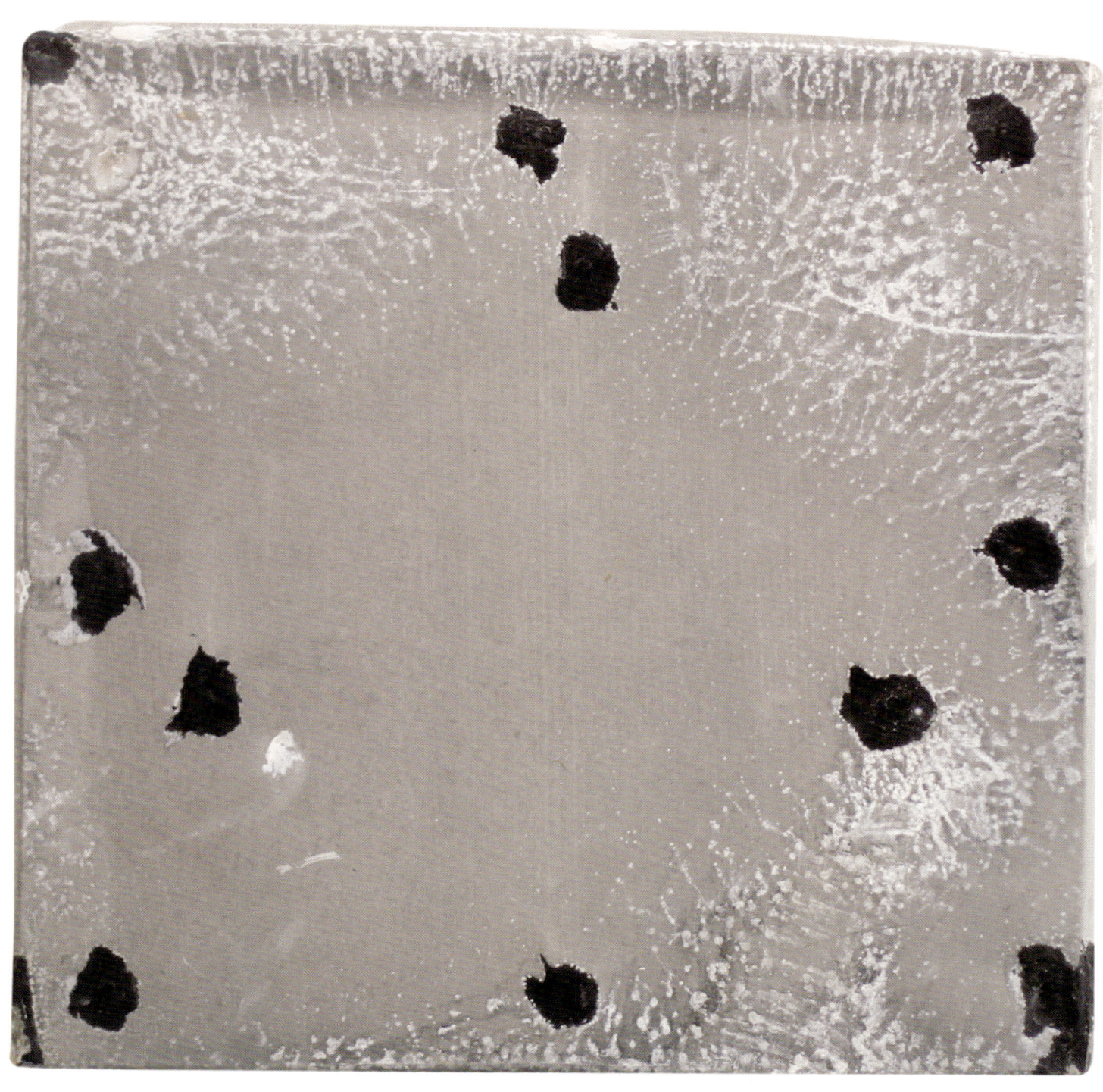

Hatch
26 x 24 x 3 inches
Galvanized Steel and Glue
2016

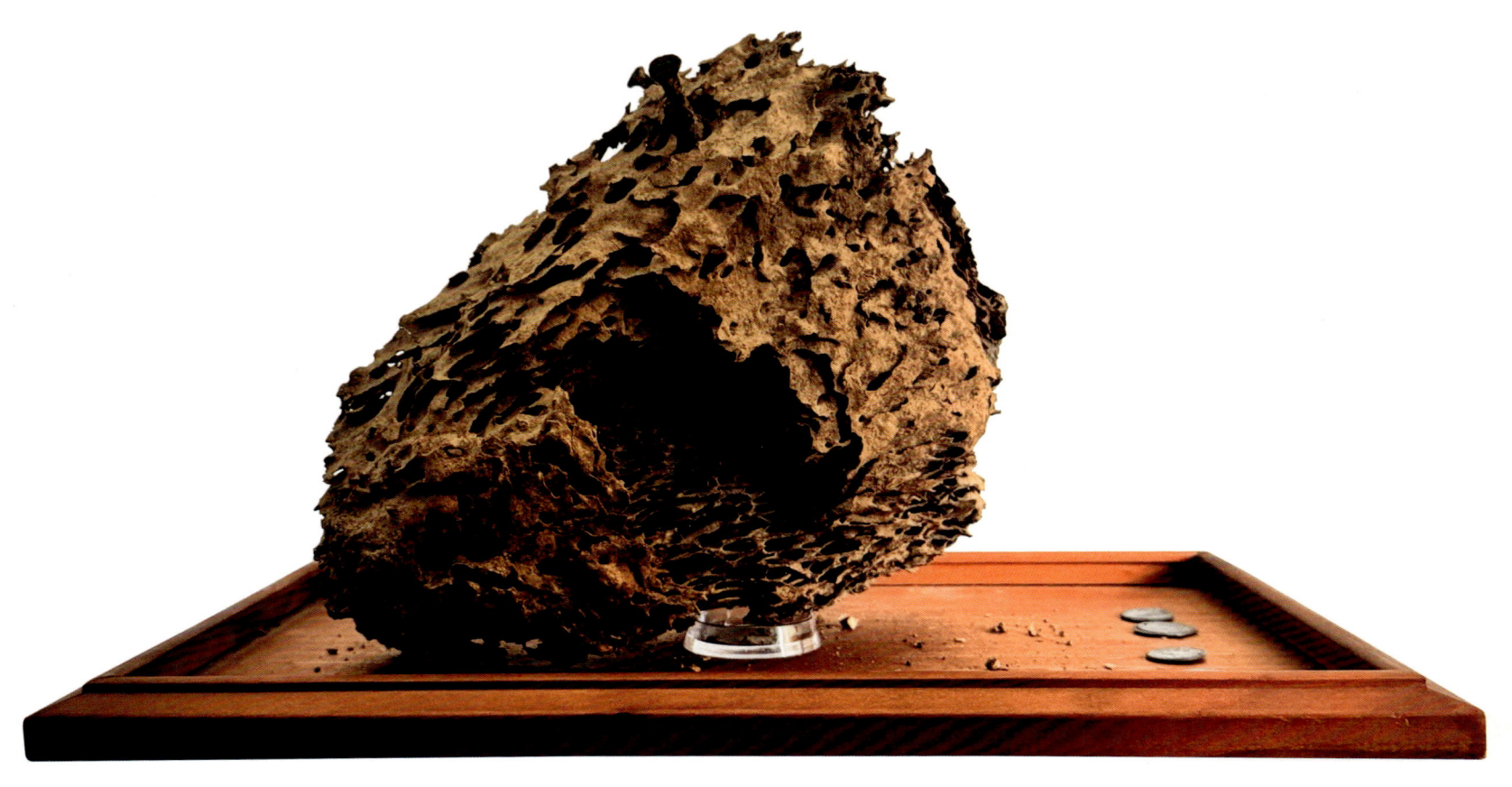

The Queen's Chamber
7 x 9 x 8 inches
Wood, Plastic and Metal
2005

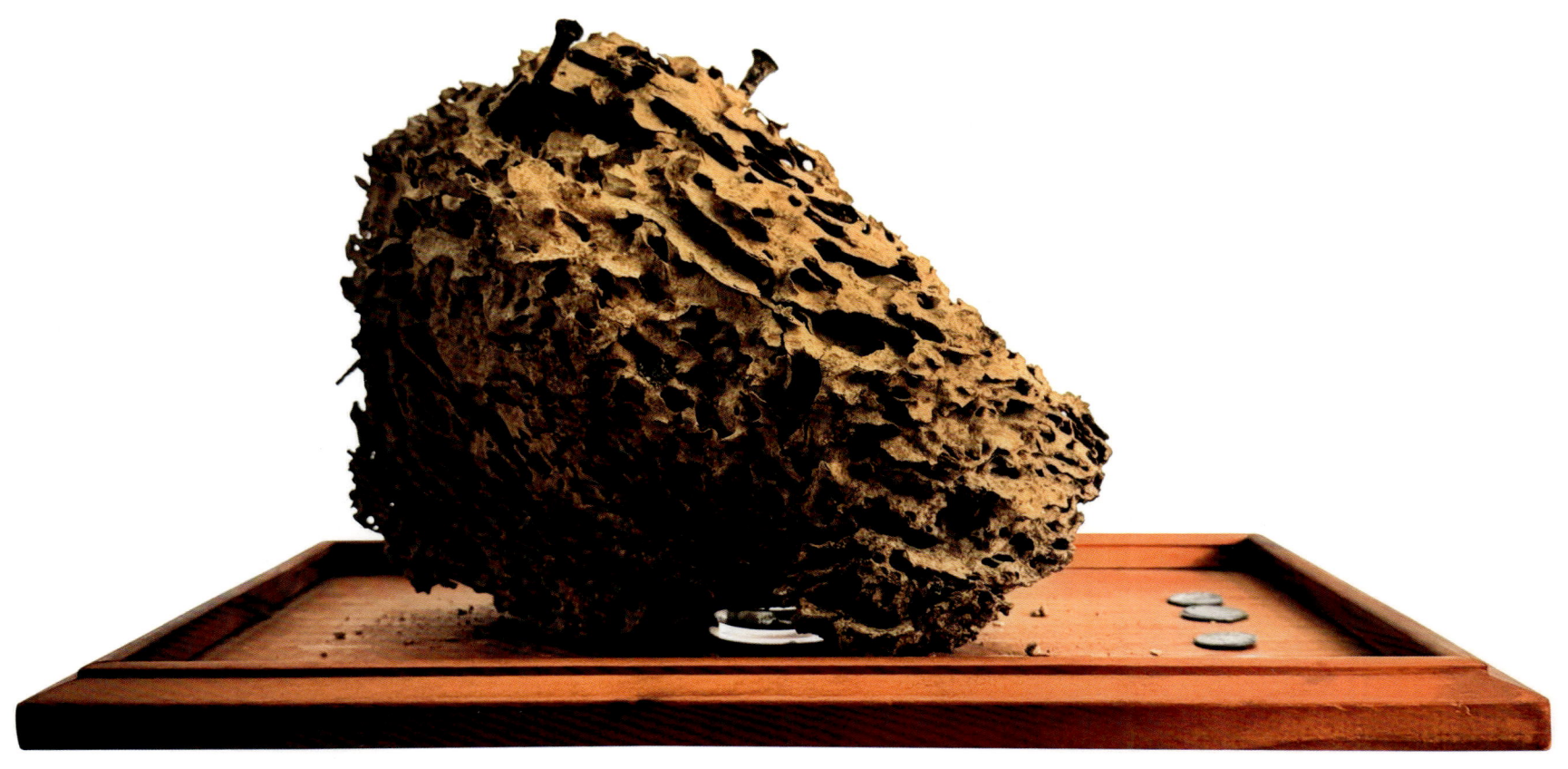

The Queen's Chamber (Alternate View)

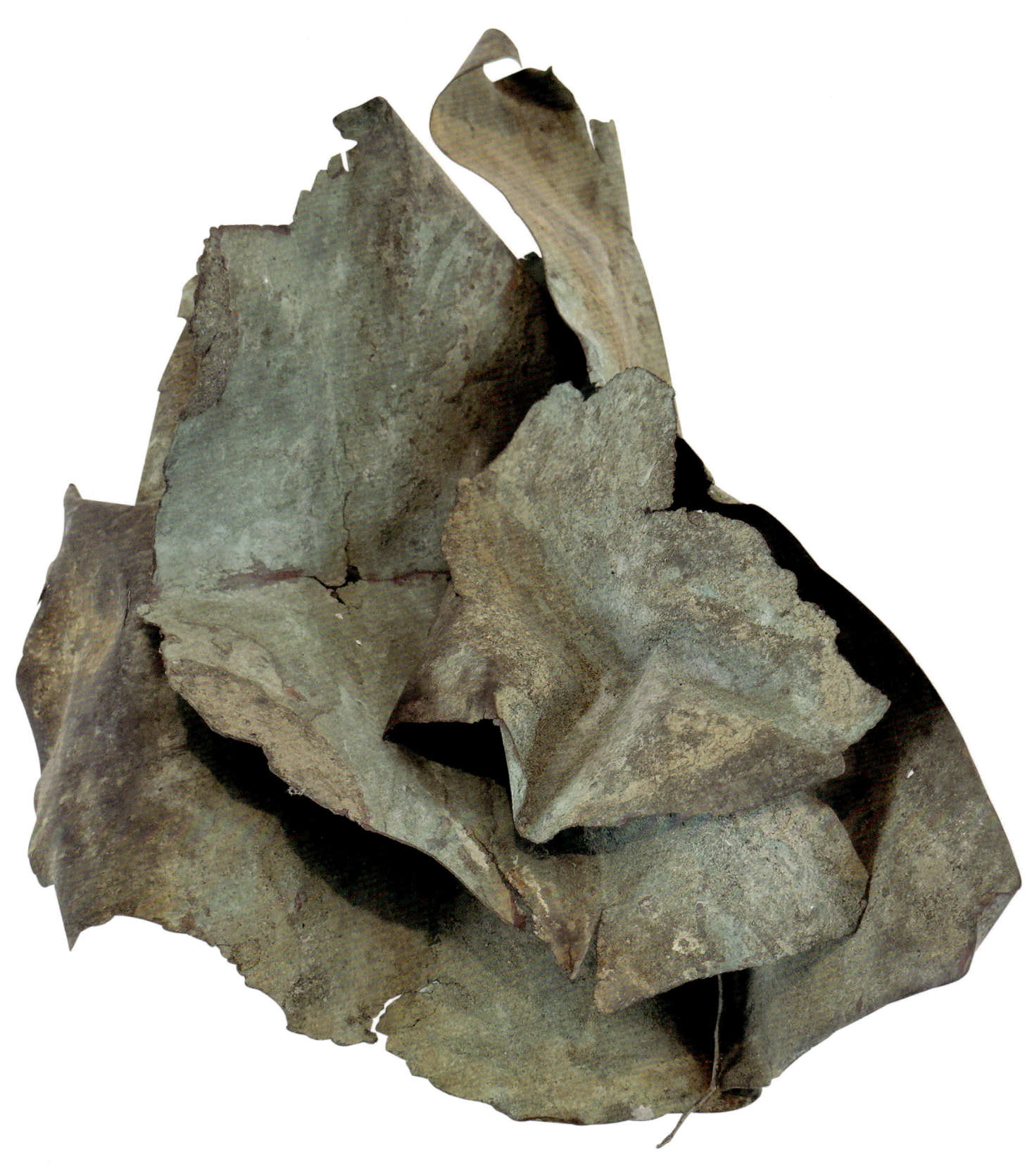

A Piece of the Riverbed
14 x 11 x 4 inches
Copper
2008

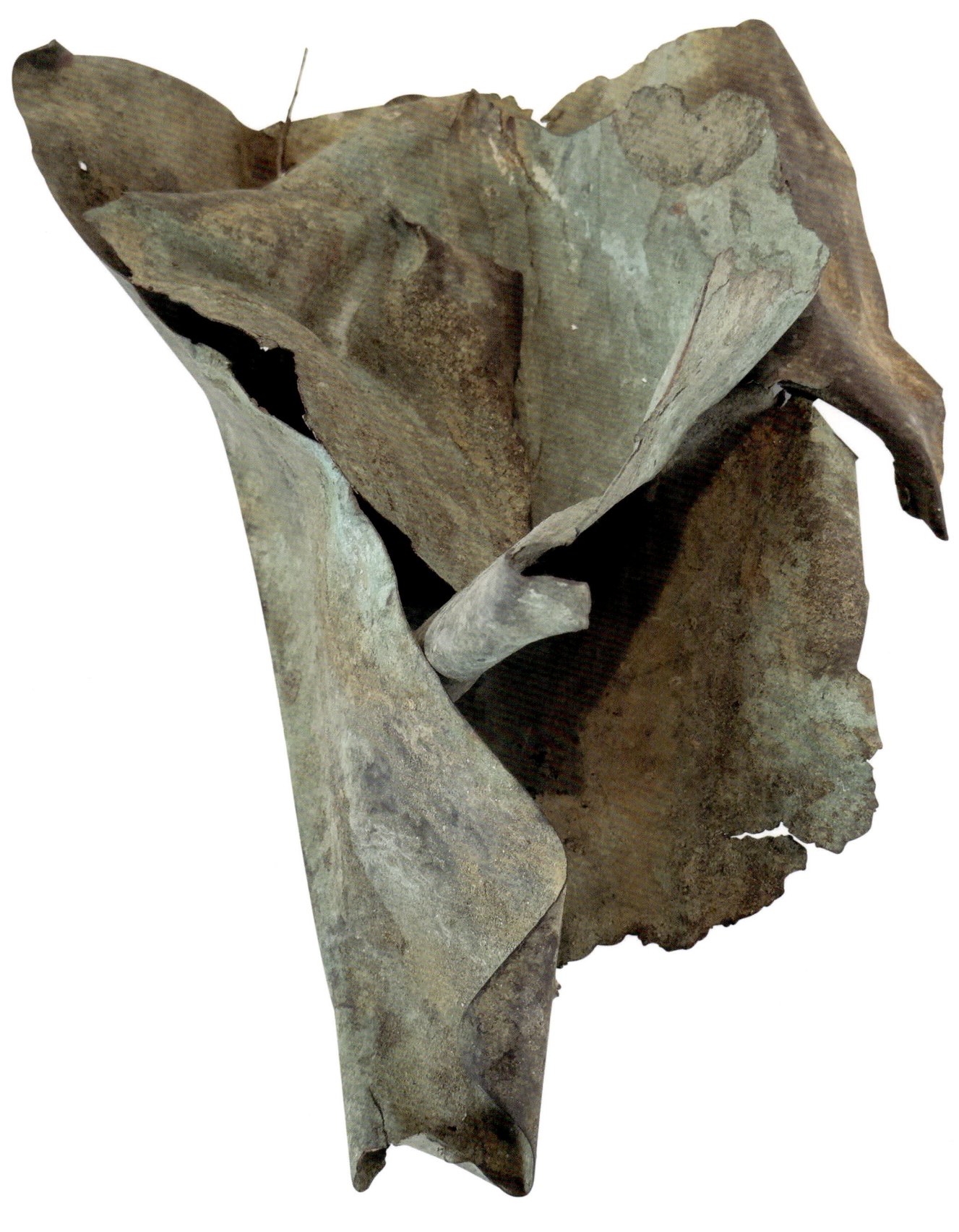

A Piece of the Riverbed (Alternate Profile View)

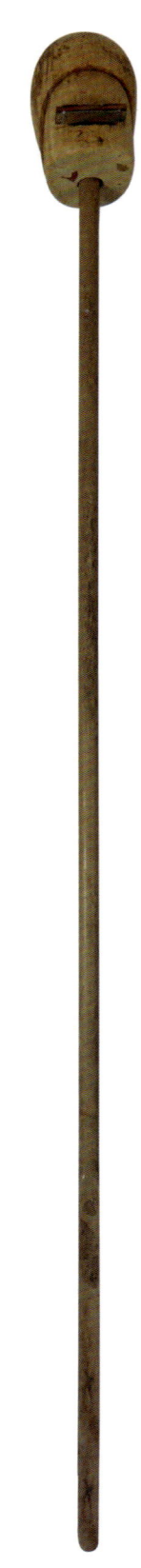

Busker
95 x 14 x 7 inches
Wood and Metal
2013

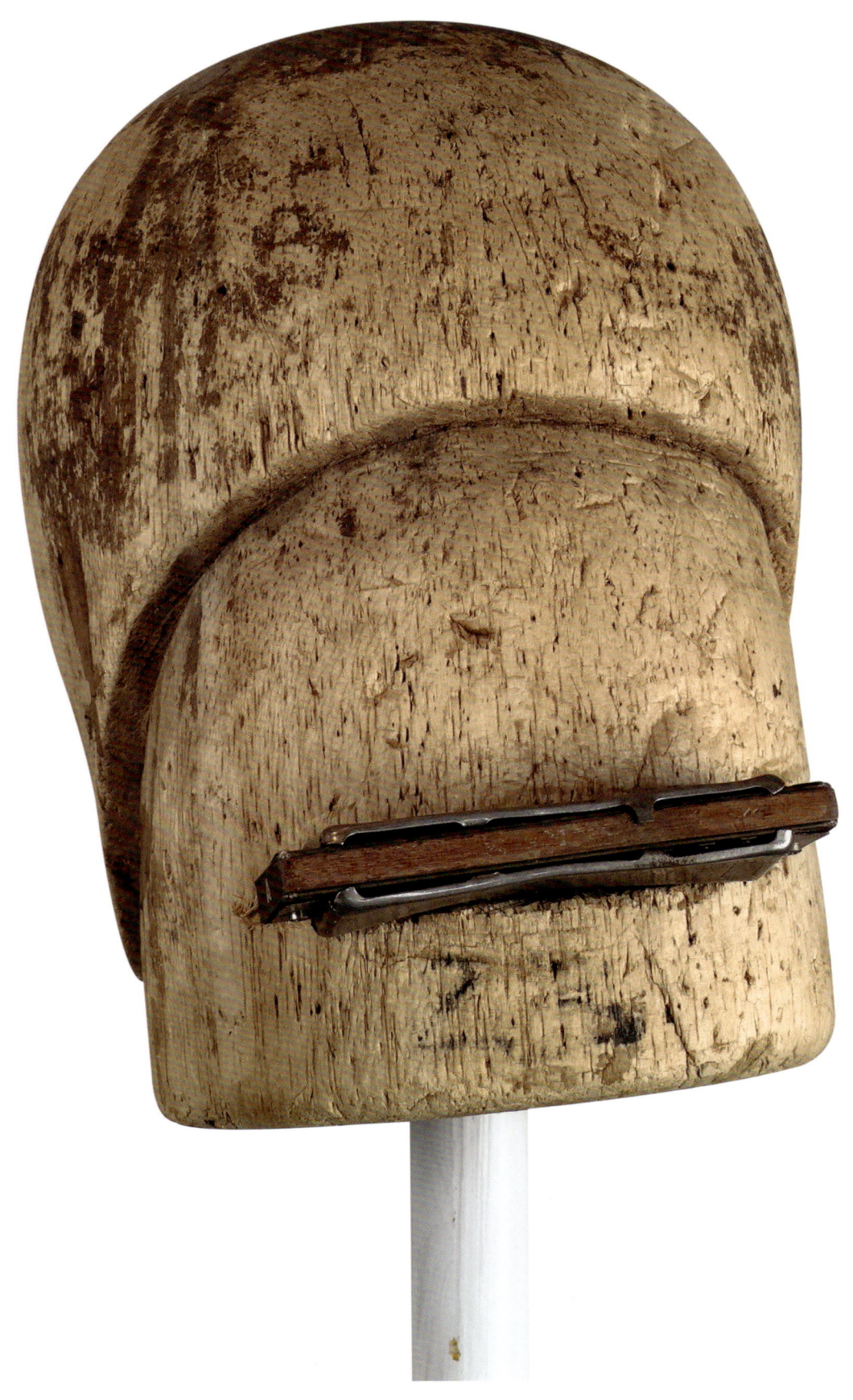

Busker (Detail)

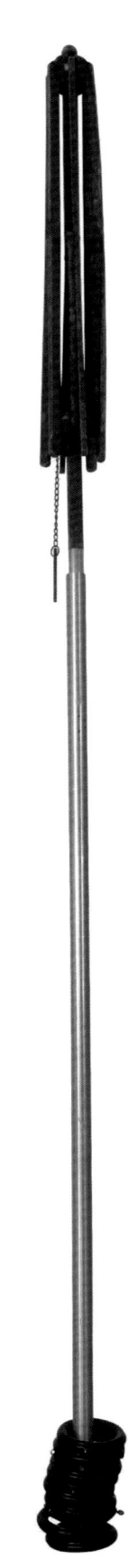

Banner
10ft x 58 inches
Wood and Metal
2013

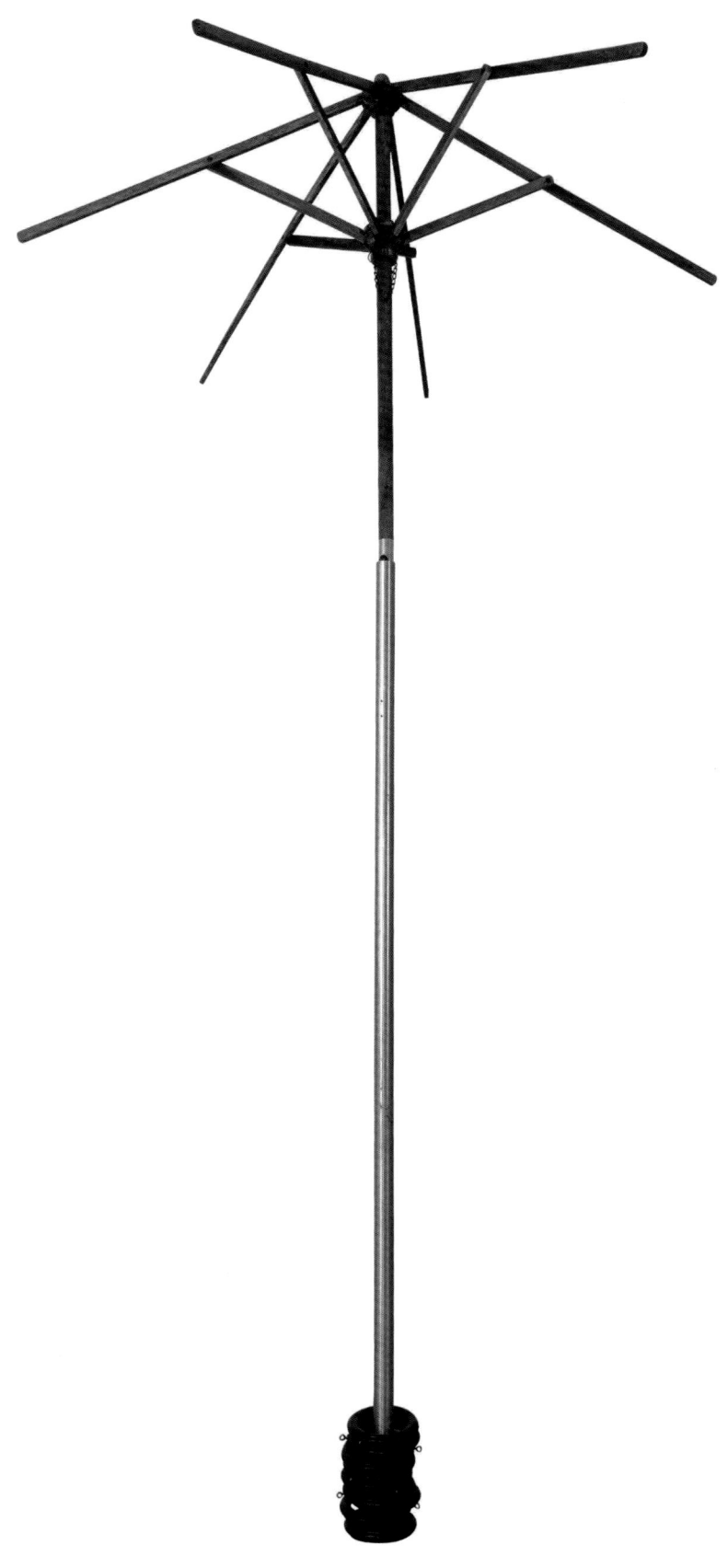

Banner (Alternate View)

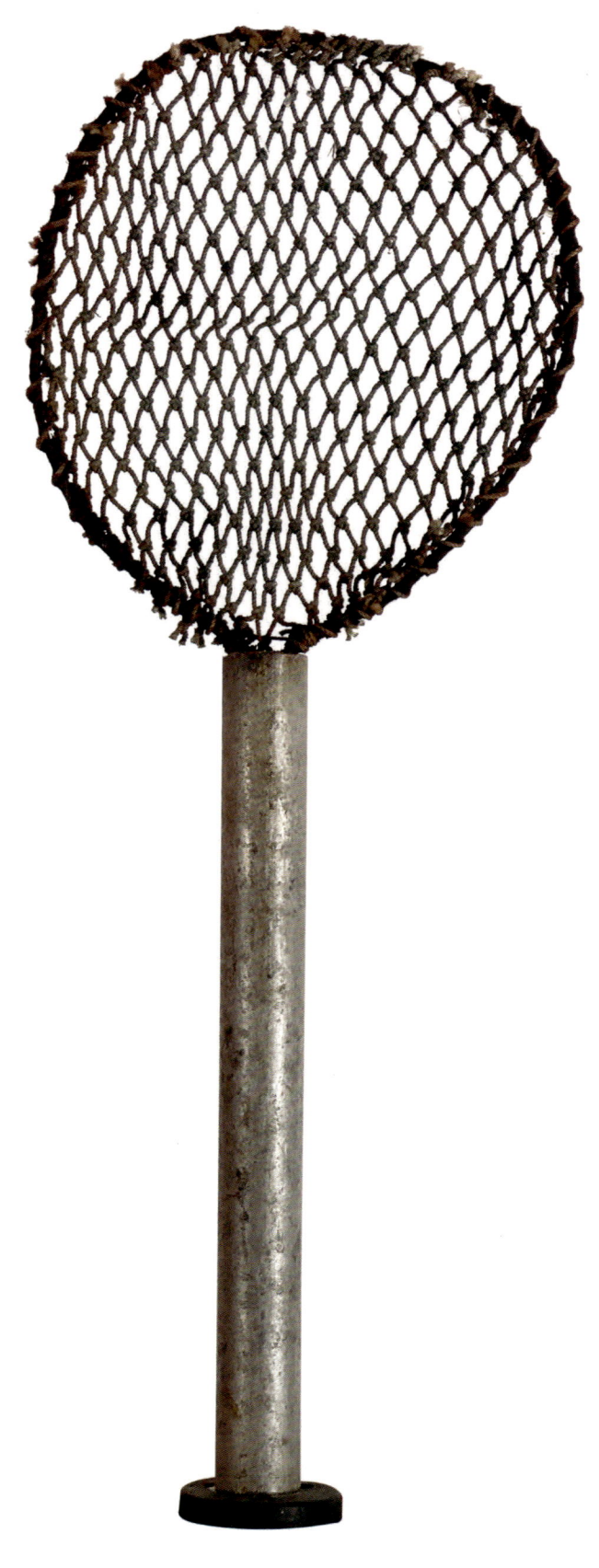

Dipper
22 x 9 x 3 inches
Steel and Nylon Netting
2024

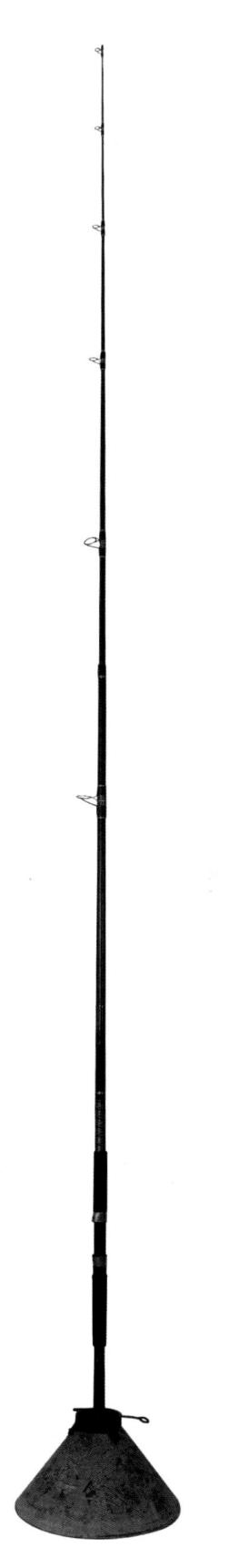

Transmitter
133 x 14 inches
Metal and Fiberglass
2013

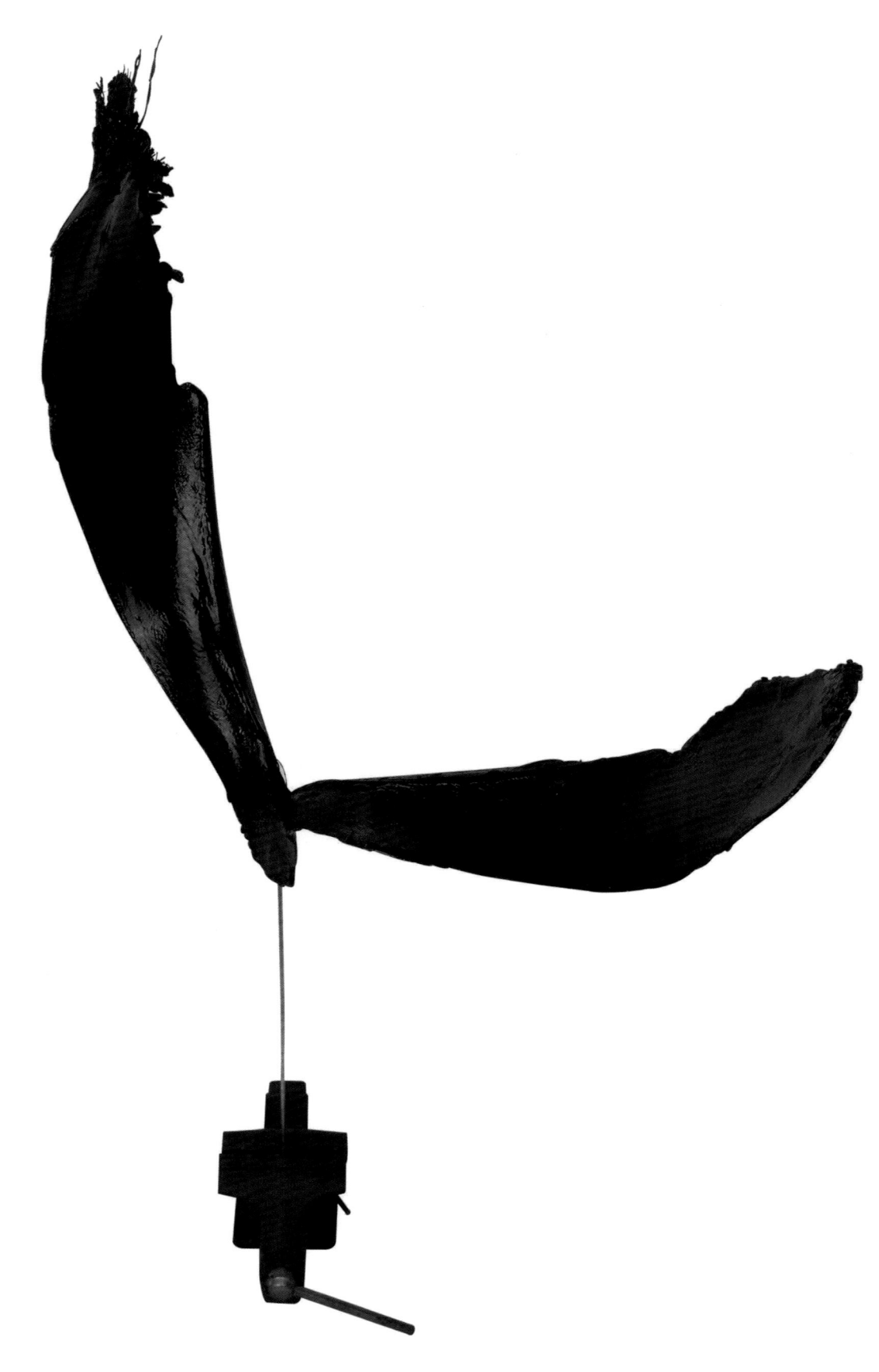

Caduceus
46 x 22 x 16 inches
Wood w/ Vise
2013

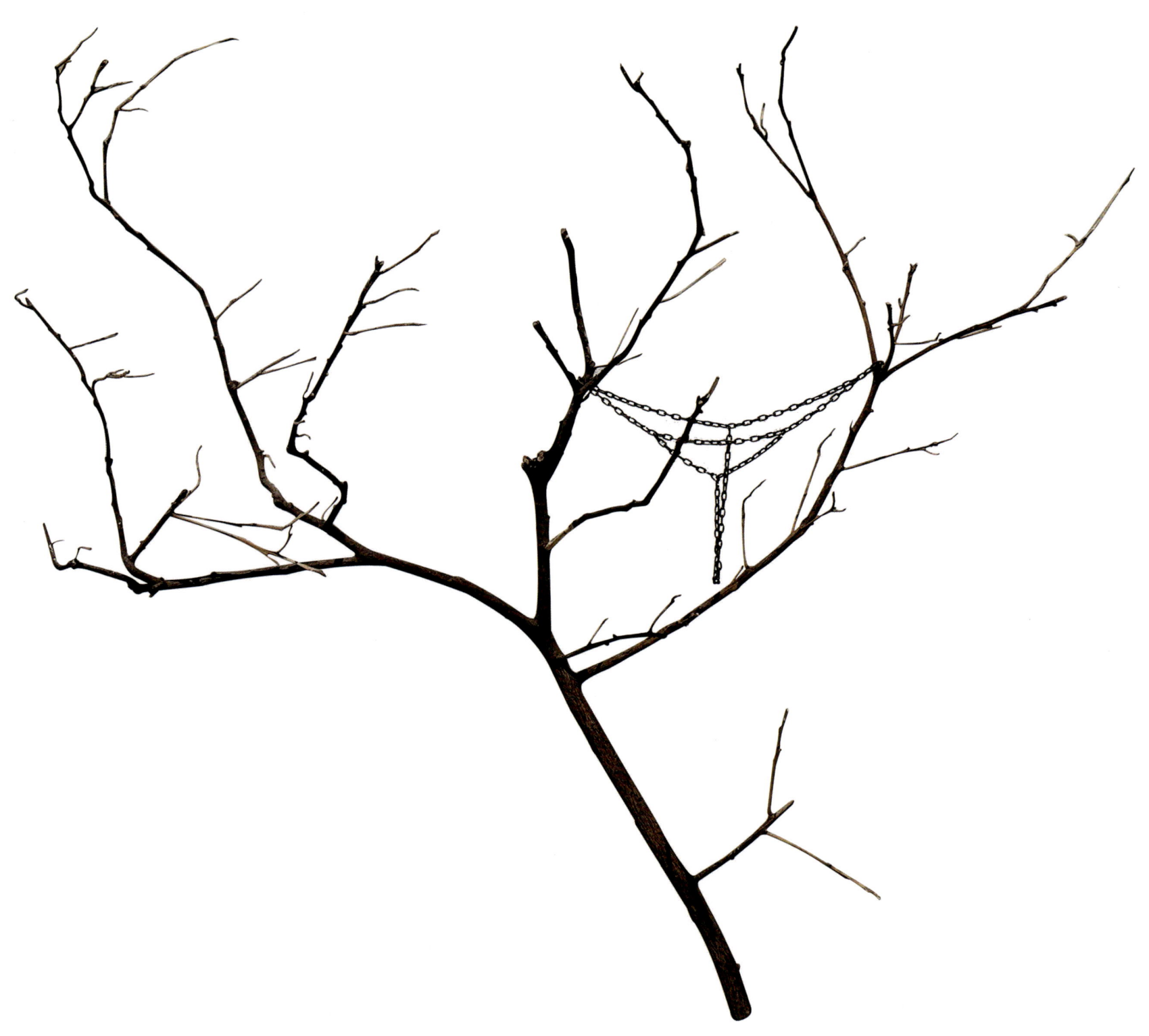

Throw
36 x 36 inches
Tree Branch w/ Chain
2013

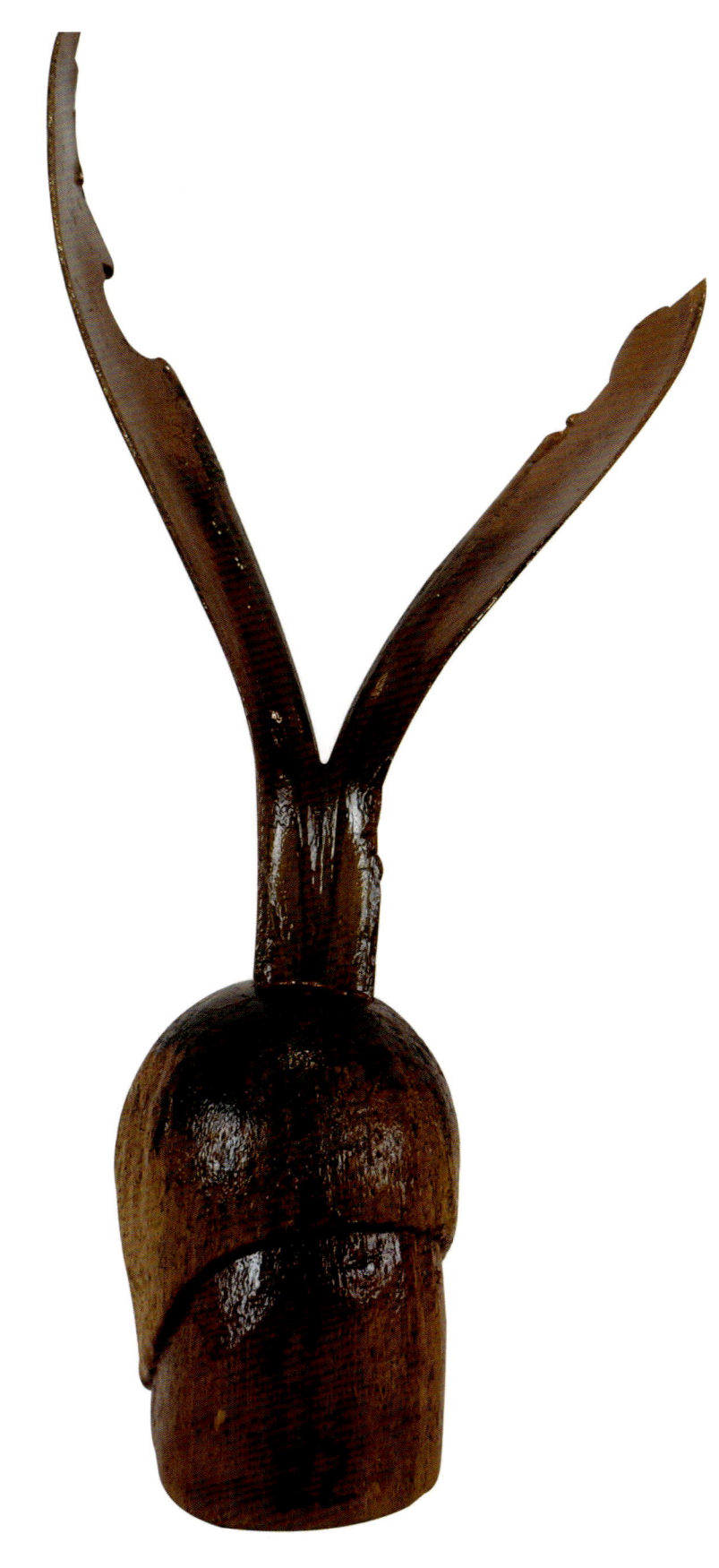

Sentinel 1
27 x 6 inches
Wood w/ Stain
2016

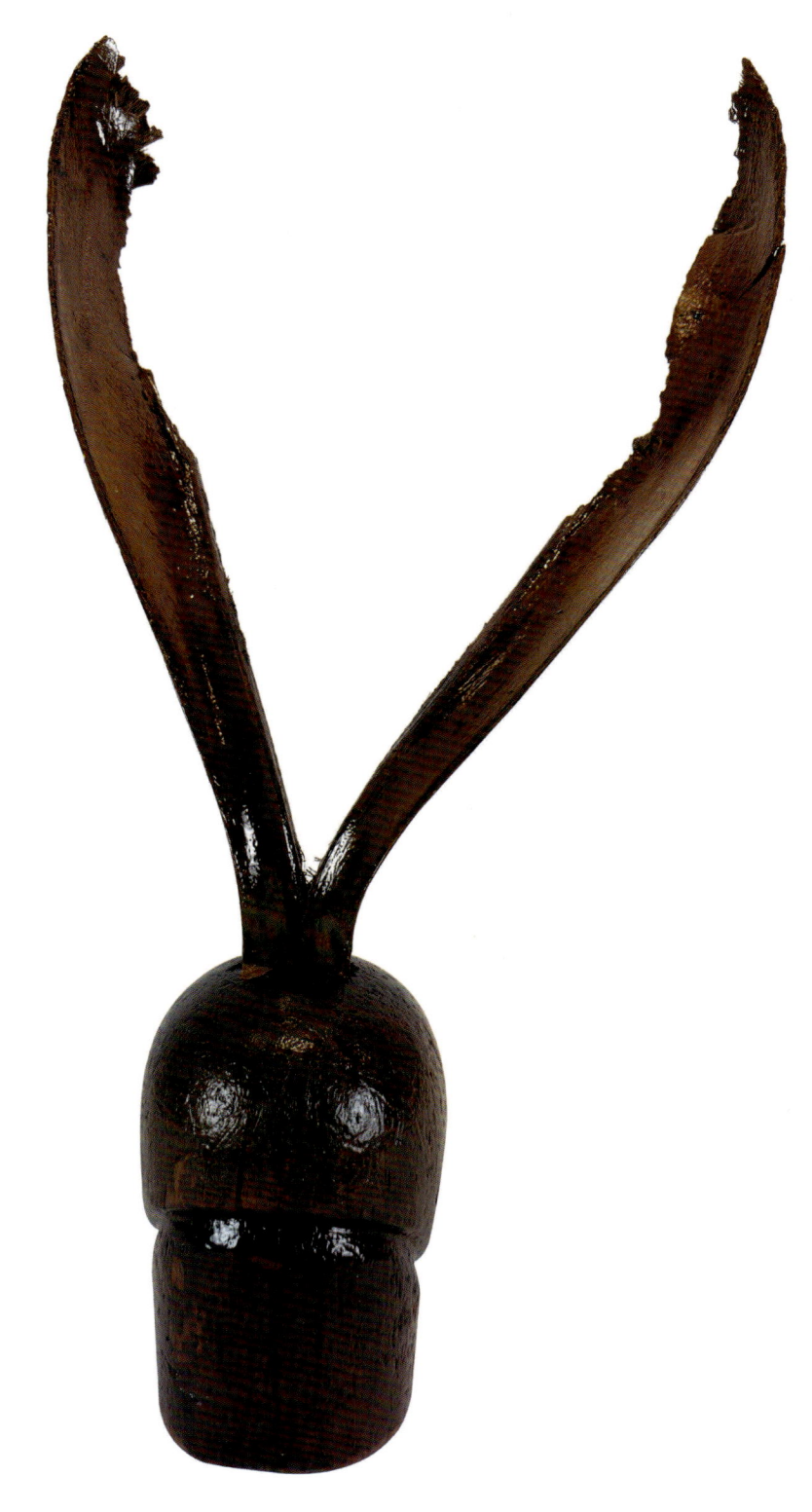

Sentinel 2
27 x 6 inches
Wood w/ Stain
2016

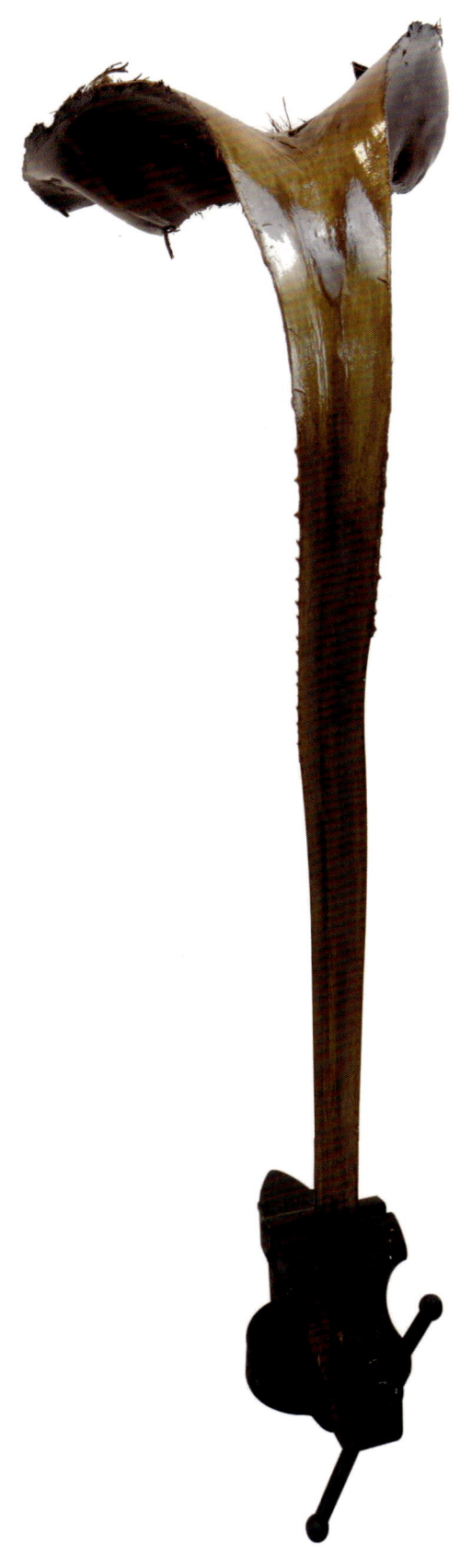

Herald
46 x 16 x 14 inches
Wood w/ Vise
2016

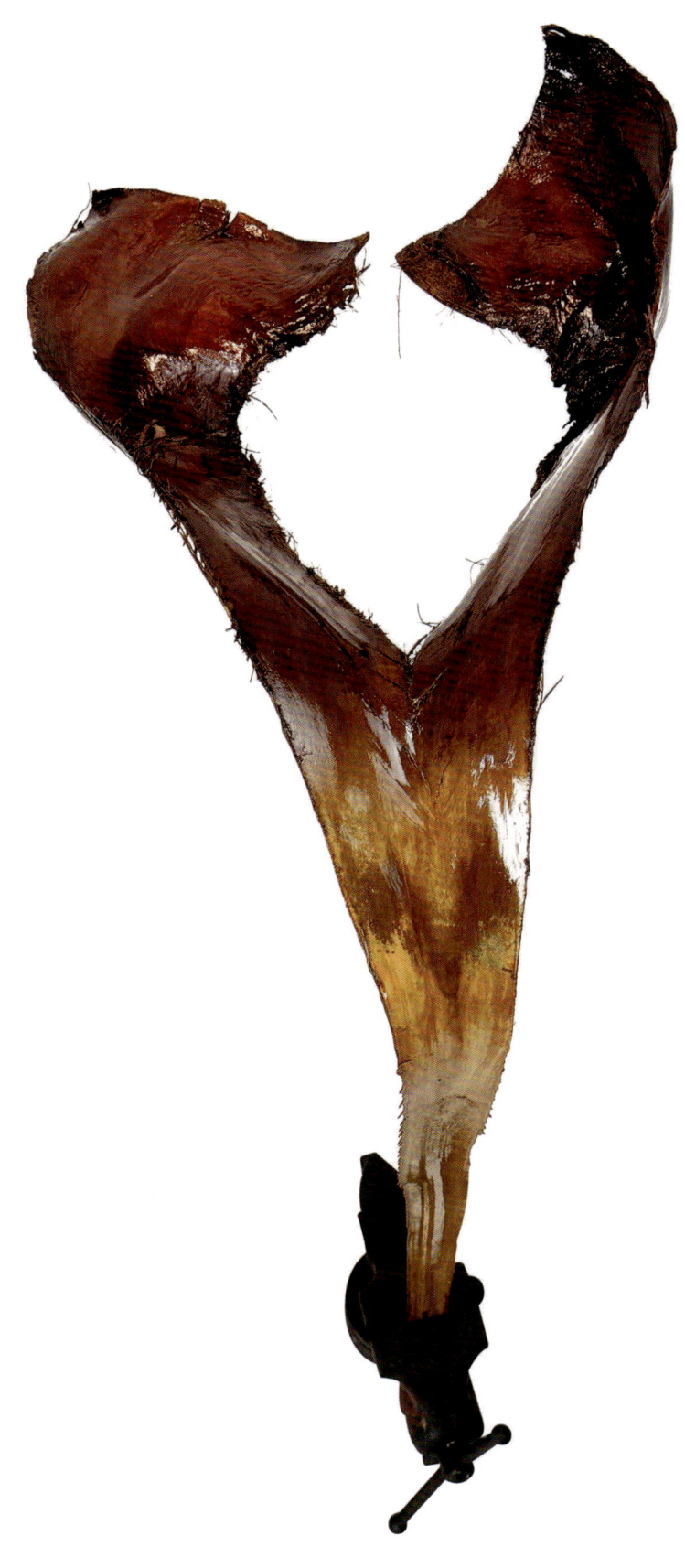

Herald (Detail)

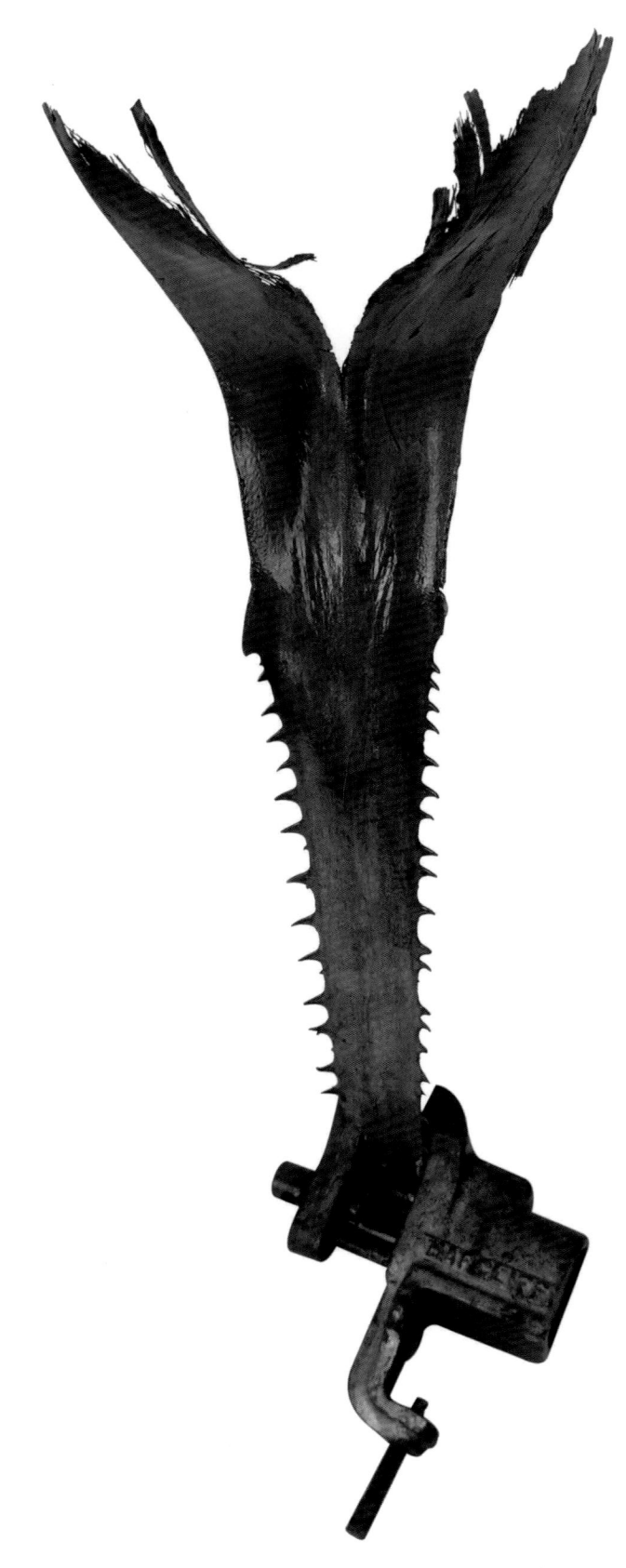

Siren
22 x 11 x 9 inches
Wood w/ Vise
2014

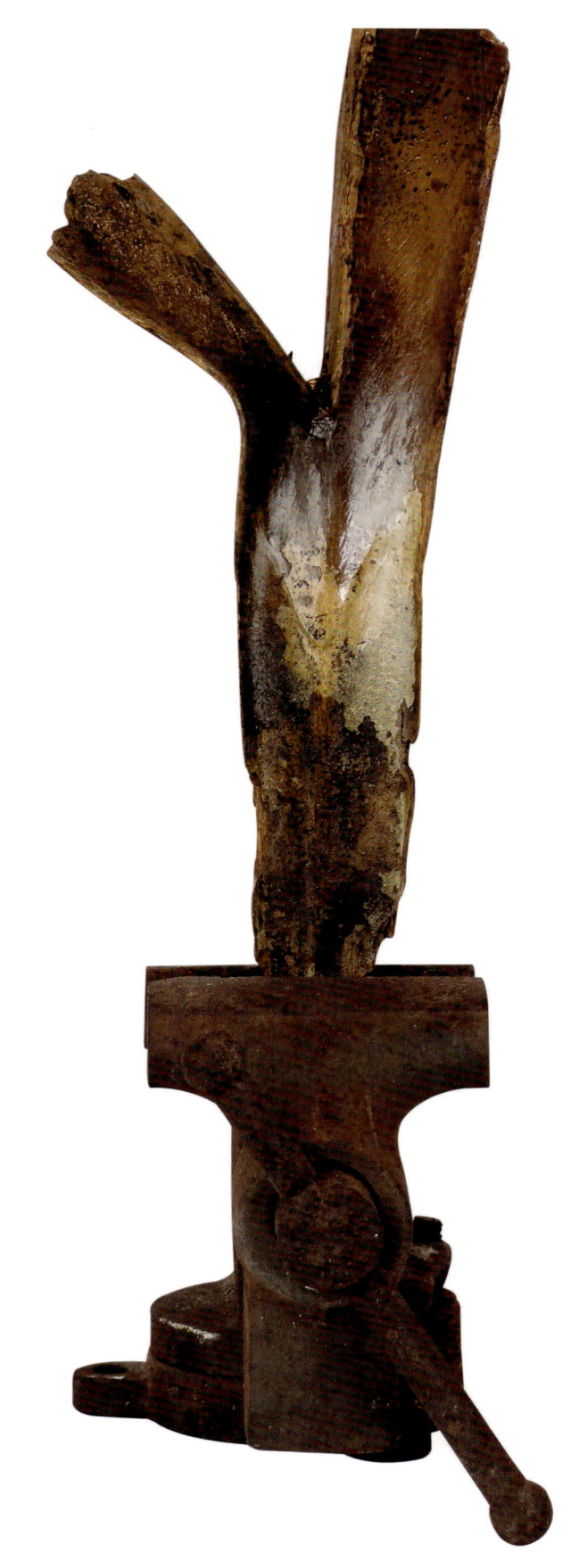

The Sign of the Poet
15 ½ x 9 x 4 inches
Wood w/ Vise
2016

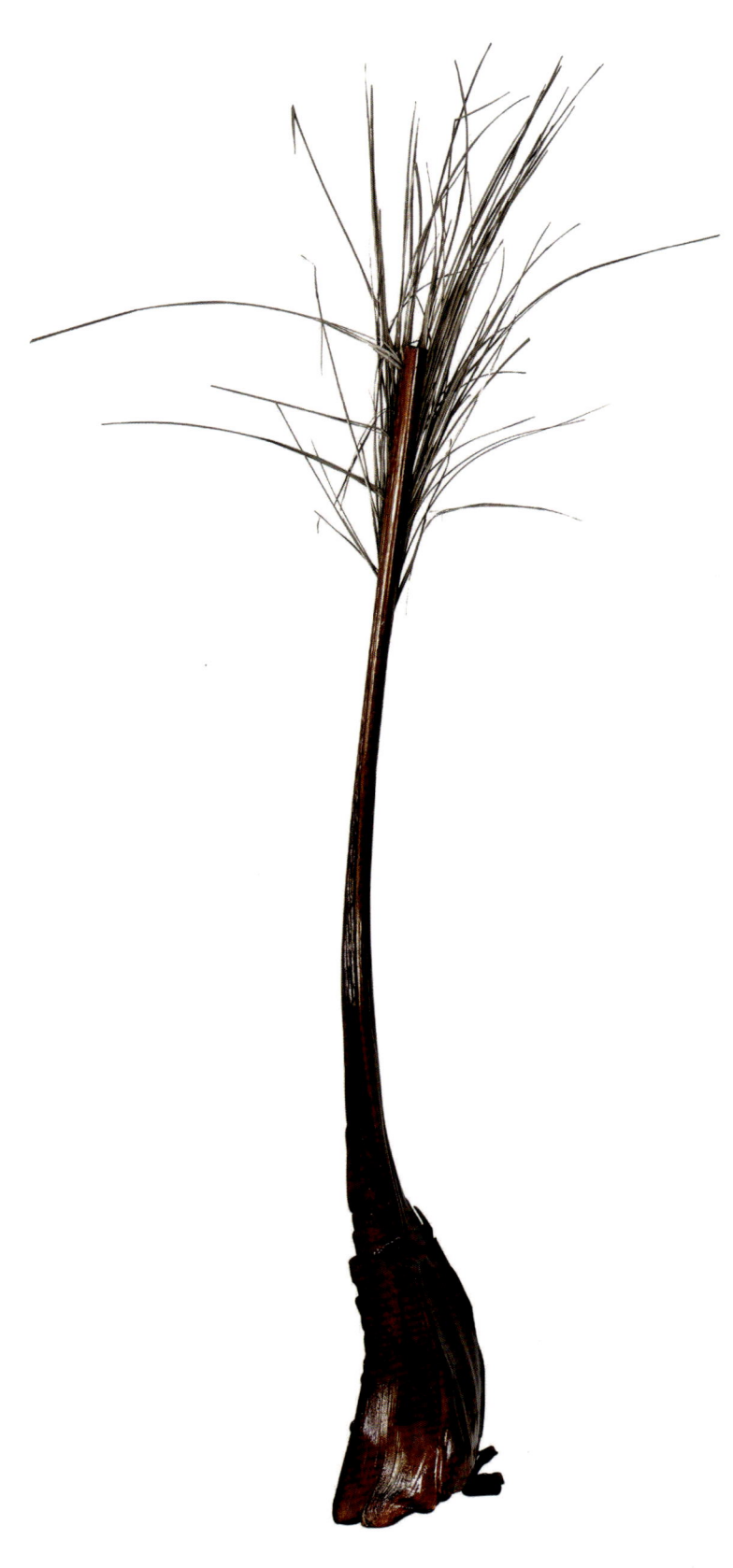

The Upright
114 x 17 inches
Wood
2011

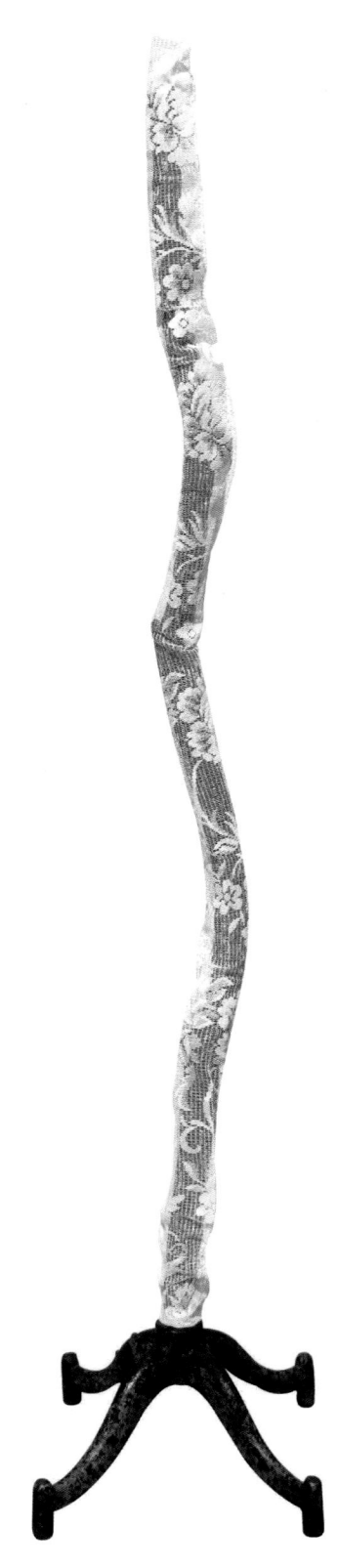

Sleeve
58 x 12 x 12 inches
Fabric, Wood and Metal
2013

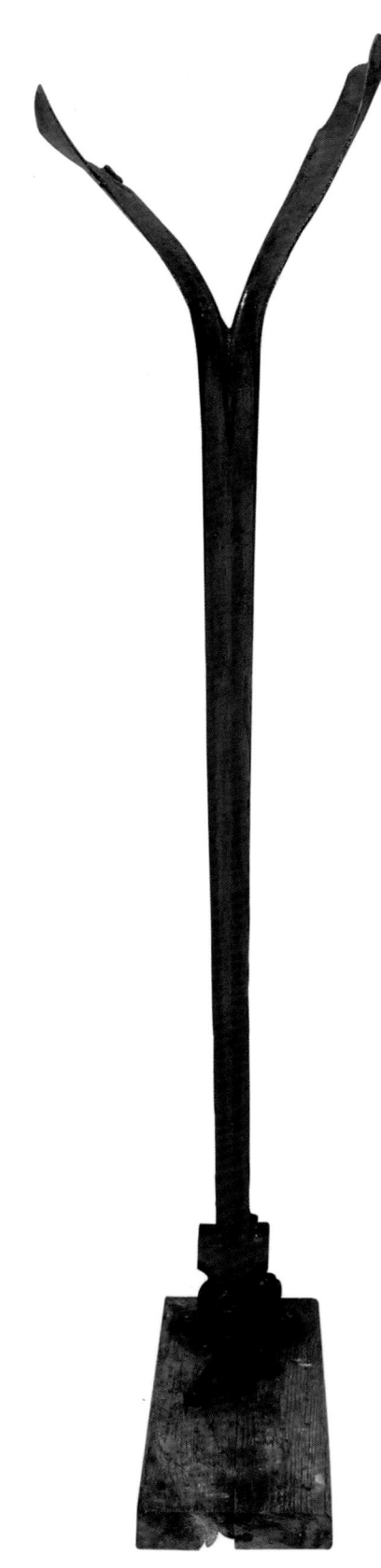

Monument I
57 x 14 x 16 inches
Wood w/ Vise Mounted on Wood
2014

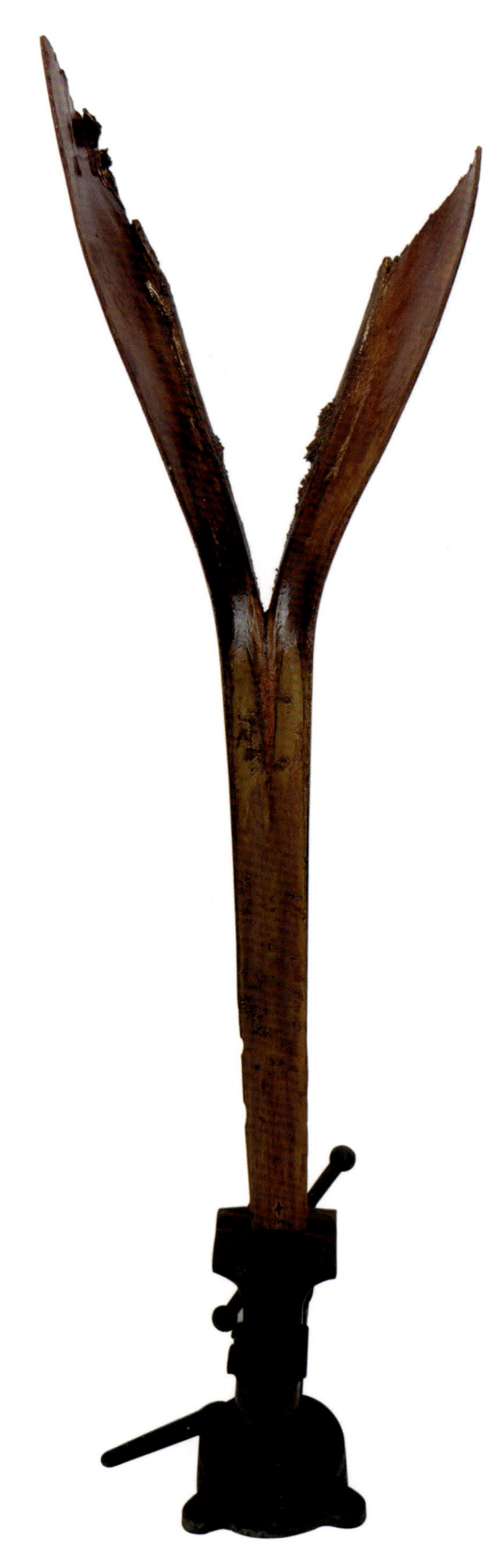

Envoy
39 x 11 x 10 inches
Wood w/ Vise
2015

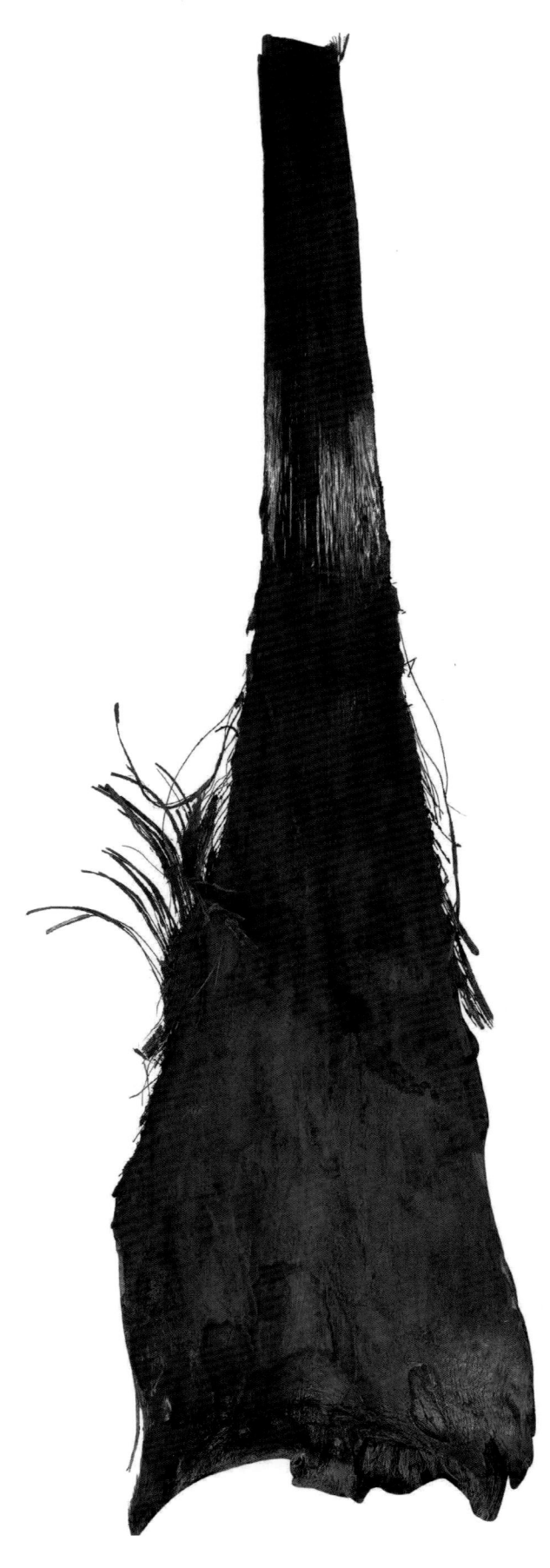

Bass
50 x 20 ½ x 14 inches
Wood
2008

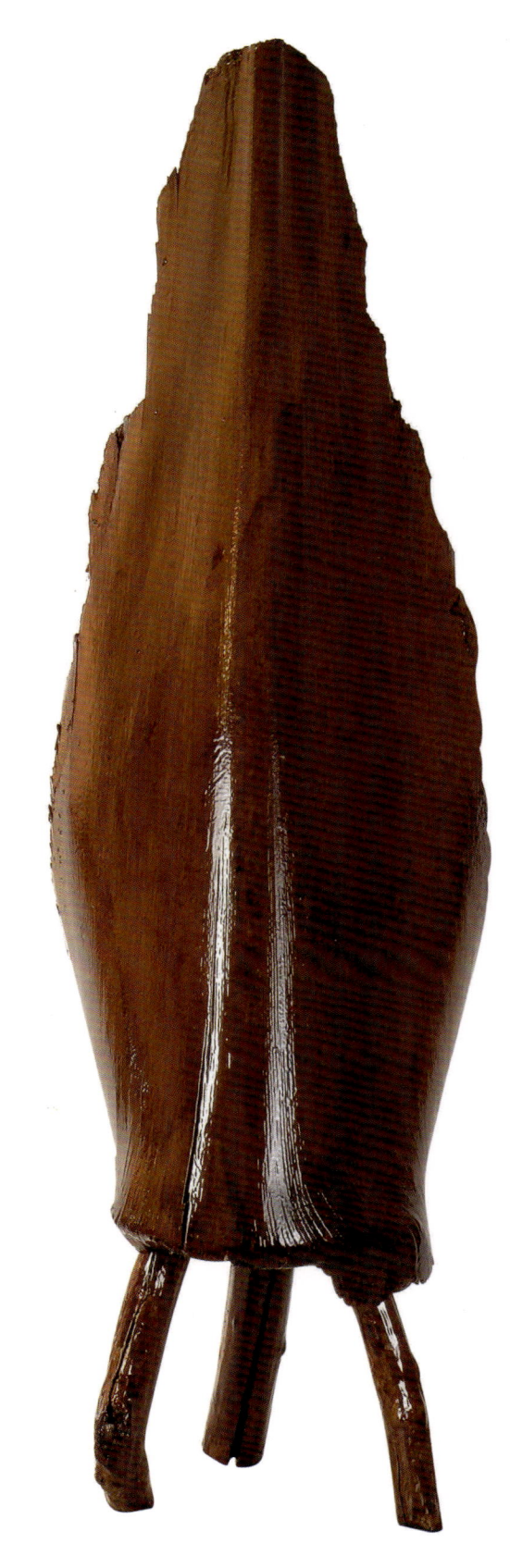

Midor
32 x 10 x 5 inches
Wood
2017

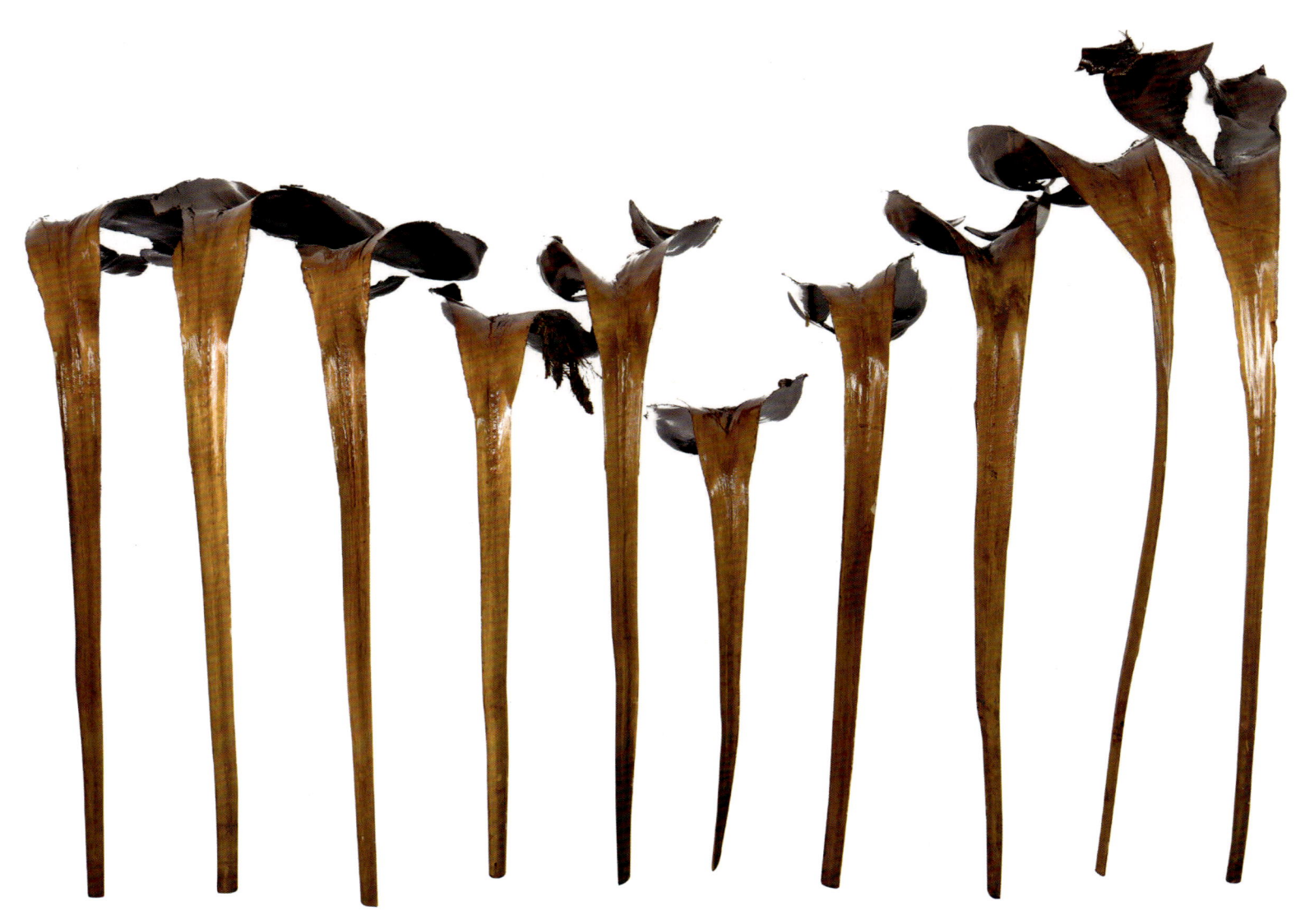

The Ensemble
63 x 144 x 24 inches
Wood
2014

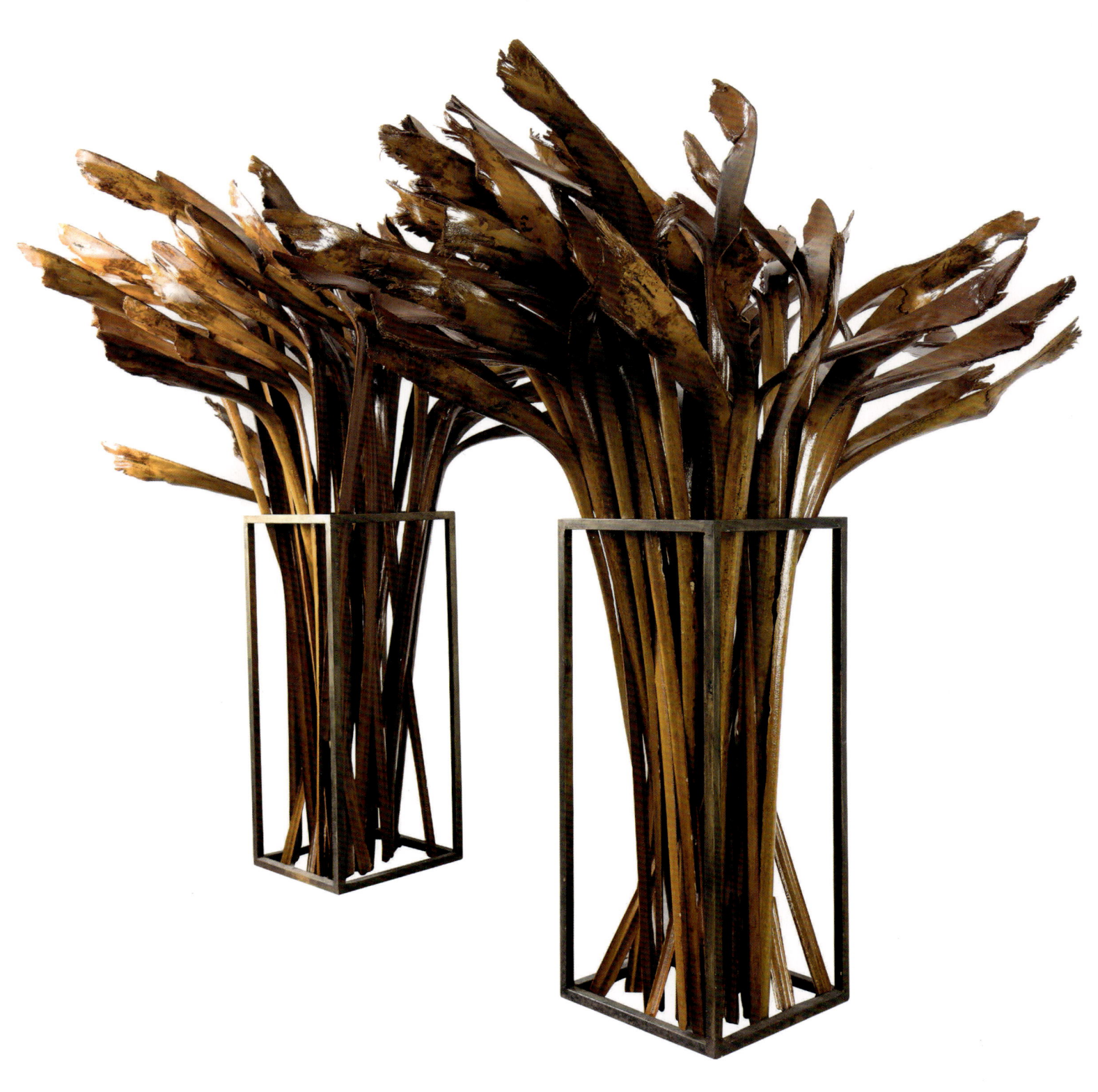

Vanguard of the Wands
65 x 60 inches
Wood in Metal Stands
2010-2024

"Successful work has a question why you're doing pick this object over that I don't spend a lot of time

sense of urgency. You don't something or why did I object on any given day. judging my work. **"**

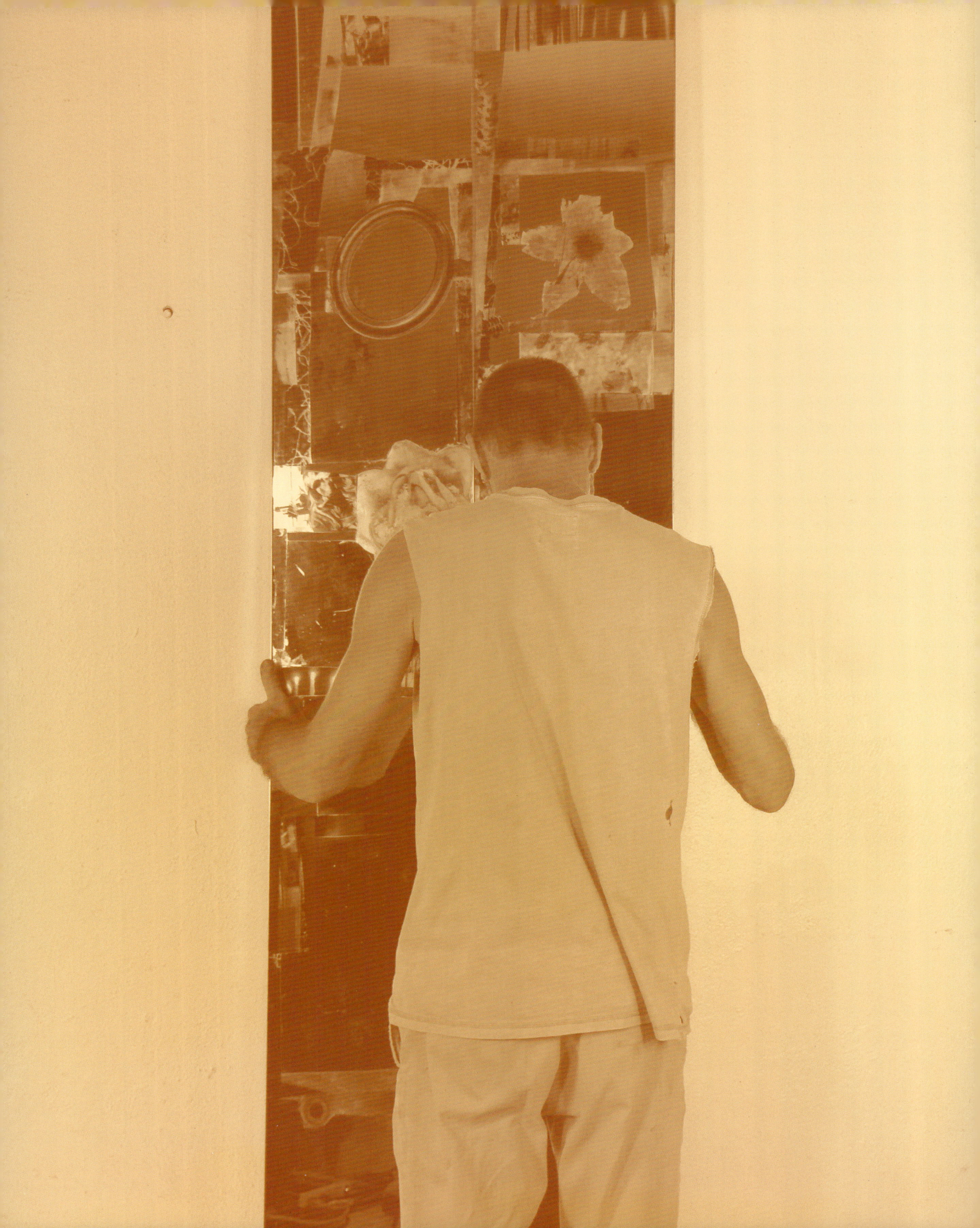

MIRROR, ALUMINUM & STEEL

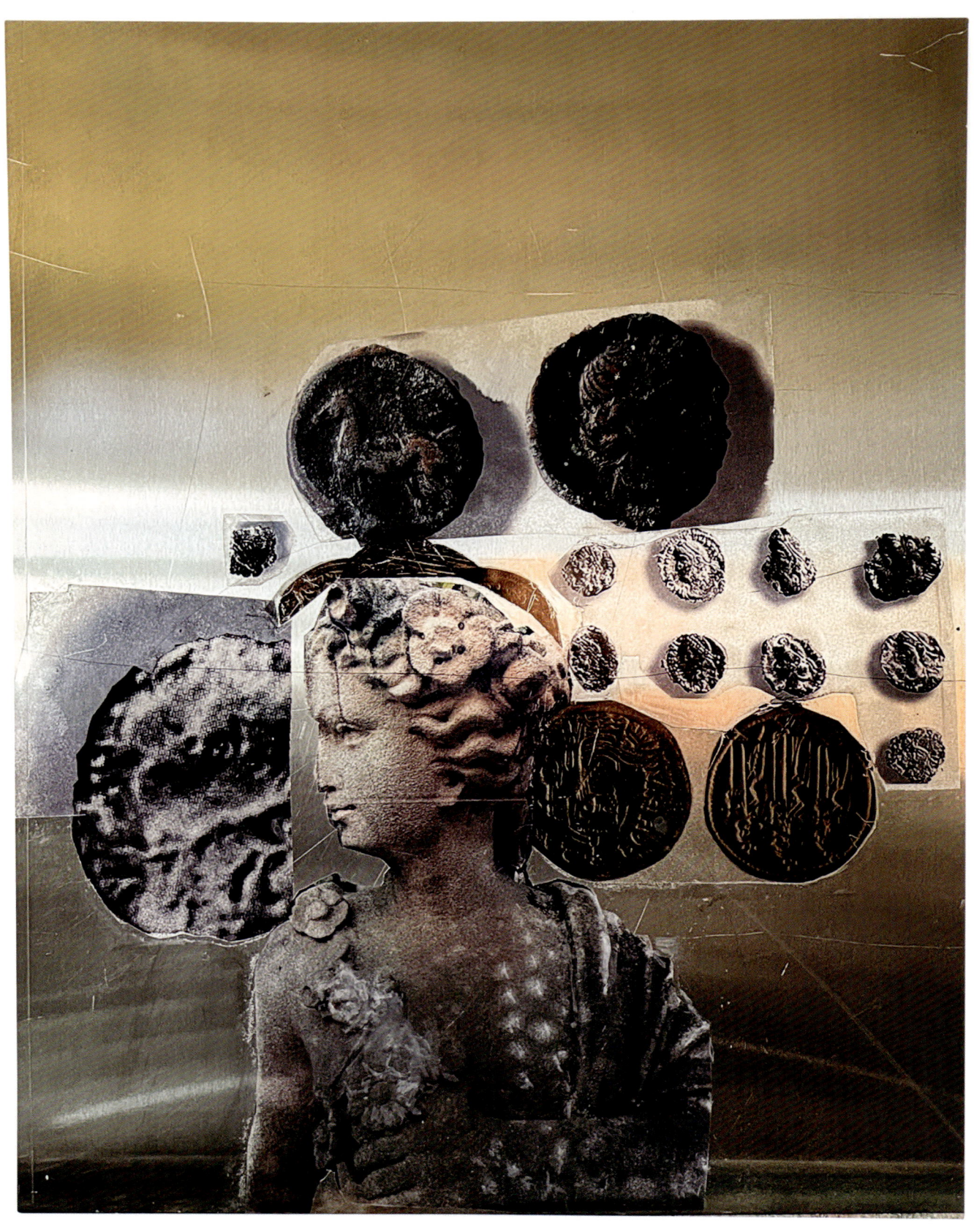

Parable III
20 x 16 inches
Print on Paper
2022

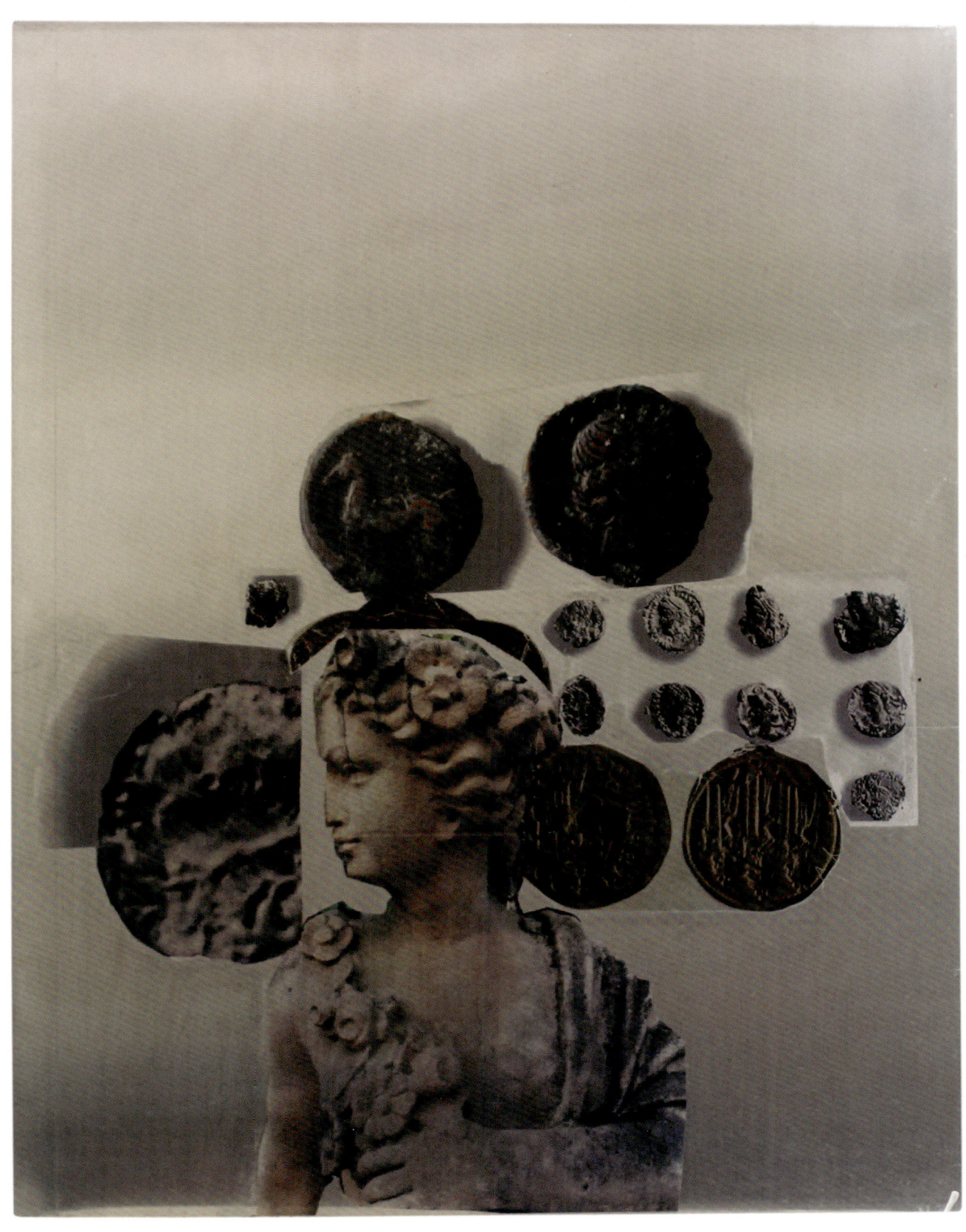

Parable III
20 x 16 inches
Mixed Media on Steel
2022

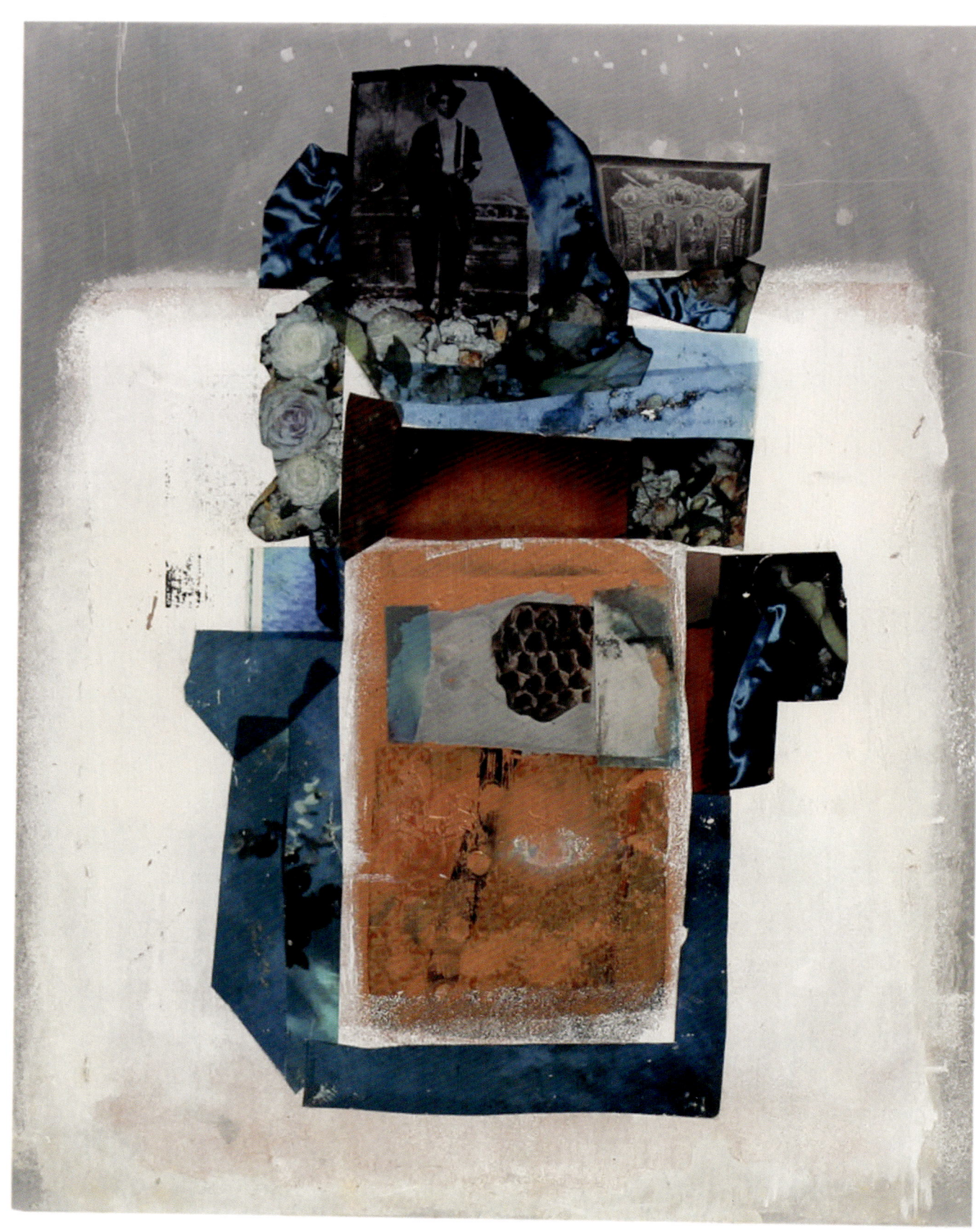

Blue Amédé I
20 x 16 inches
Mixed Media on Aluminum
2014

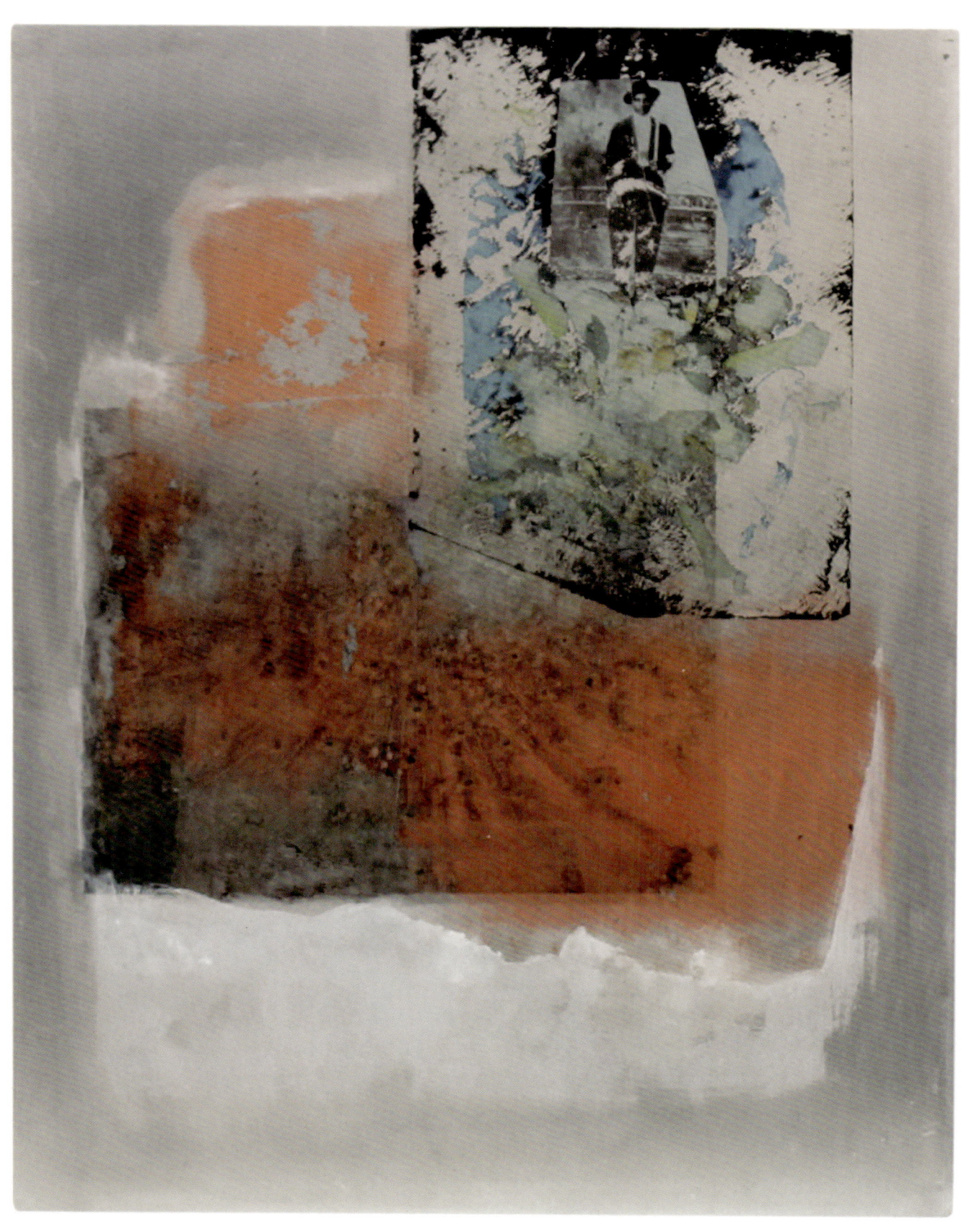

Blue Amédé 2
20 x 16 inches
Mixed Media on Aluminum
2014

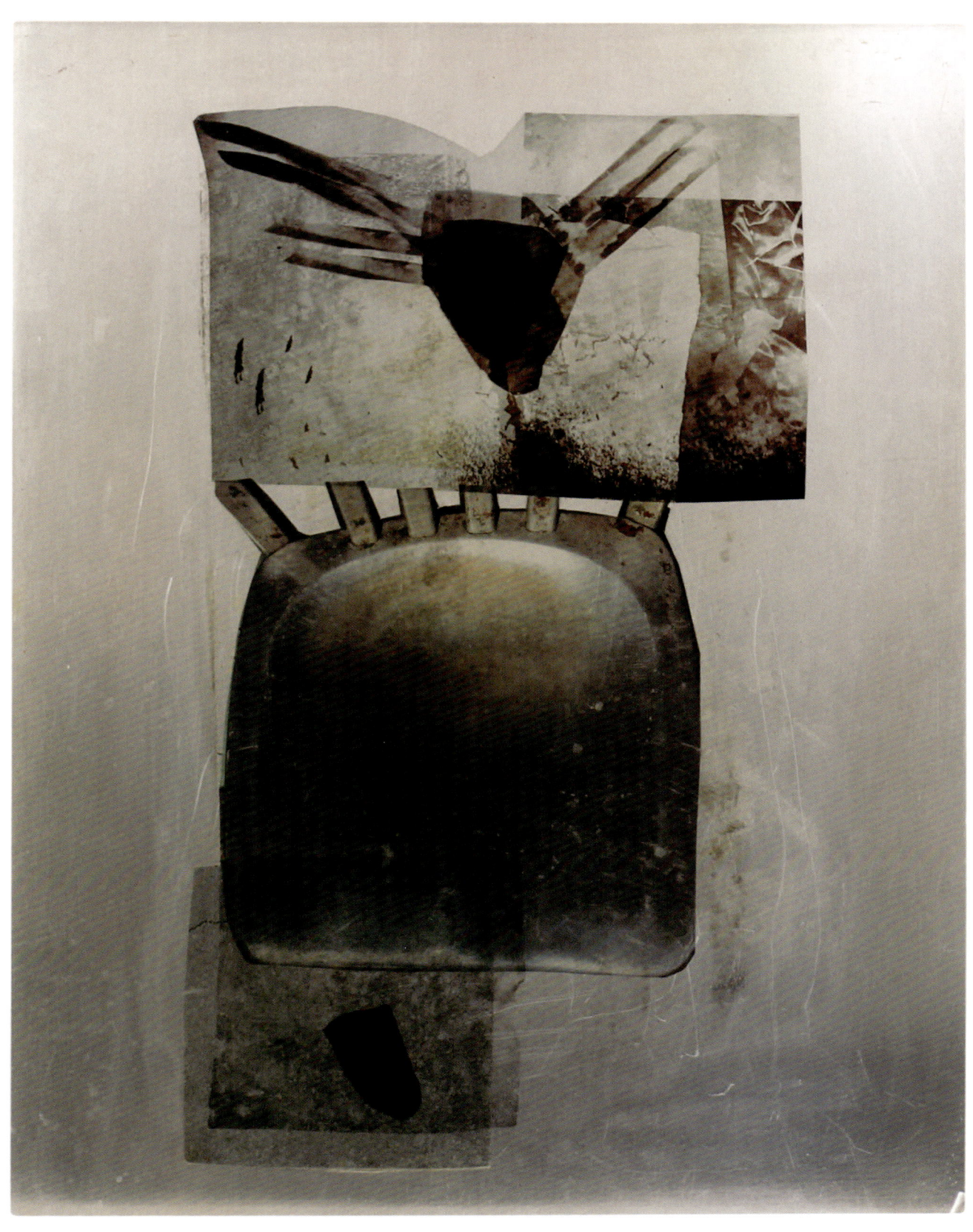

Untitled Series 1 of 11
20 x 16 inches
Mixed Media on Aluminum
2016

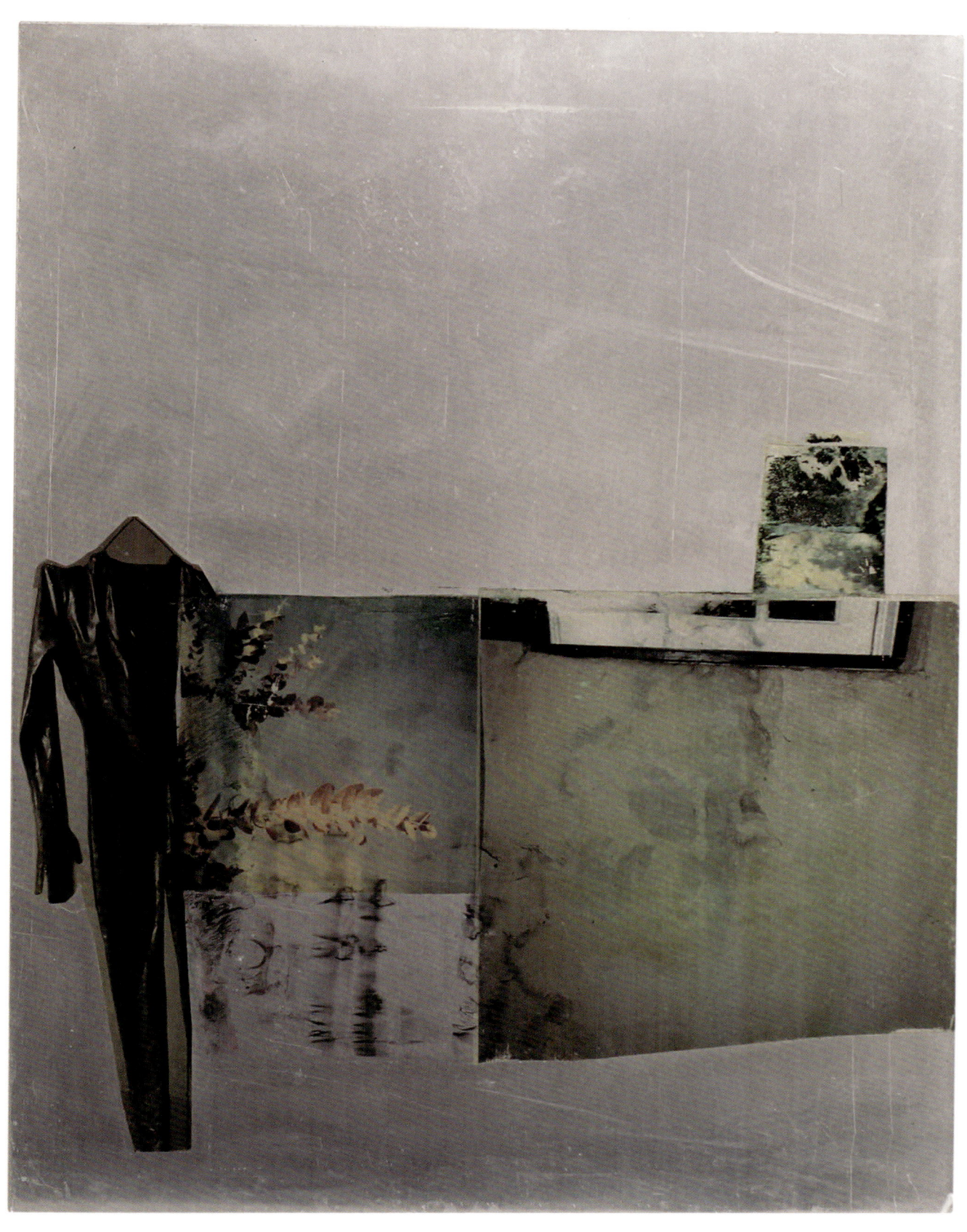

Untitled Series 2 of 11
20 x 16 inches
Mixed Media on Aluminum
2016

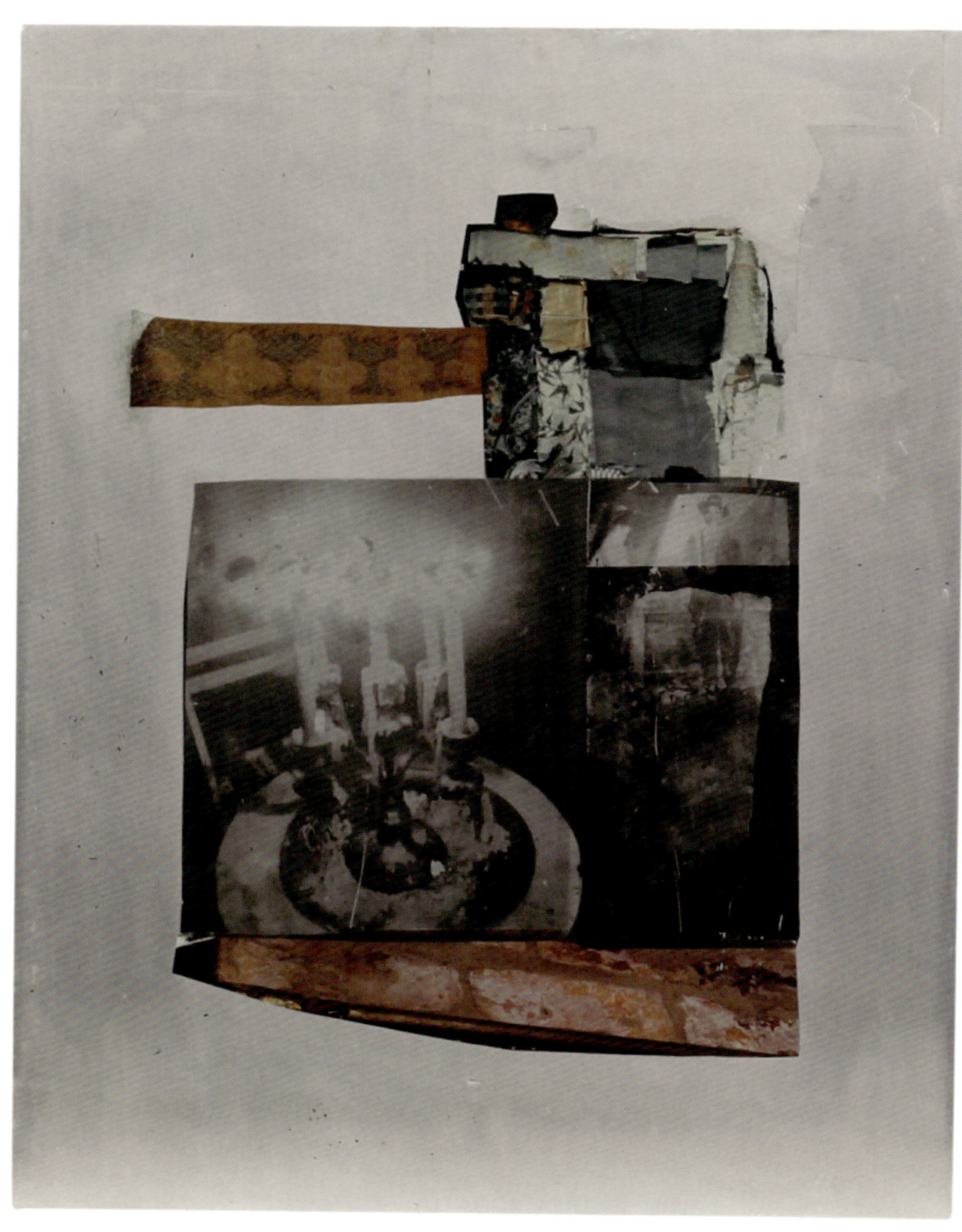

Untitled Series 3 of 11
20 x 16 inches
Mixed Media on Aluminum
2016

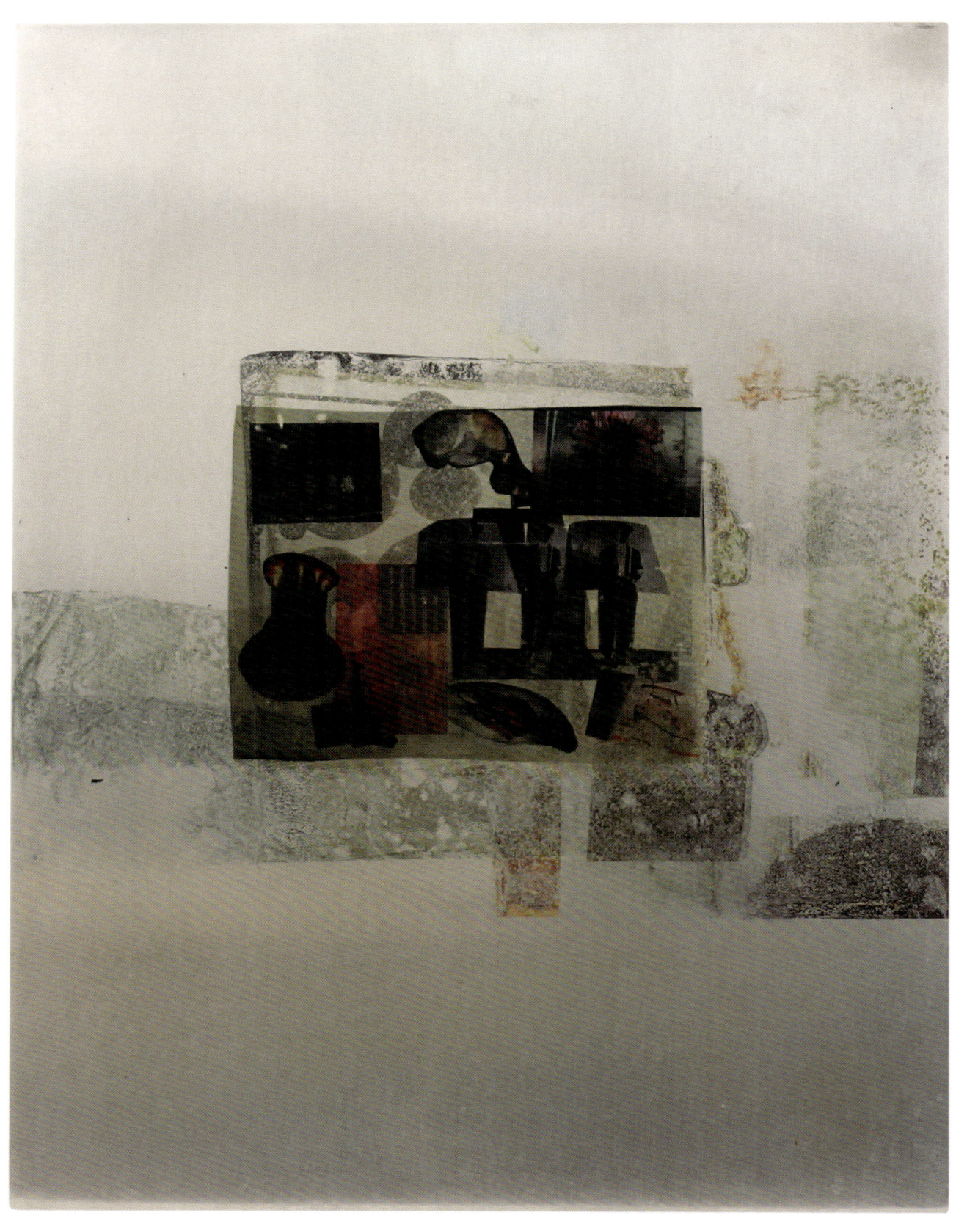

Untitled Series 4 of 11
20 x 16 inches
Mixed Media on Aluminum
2016

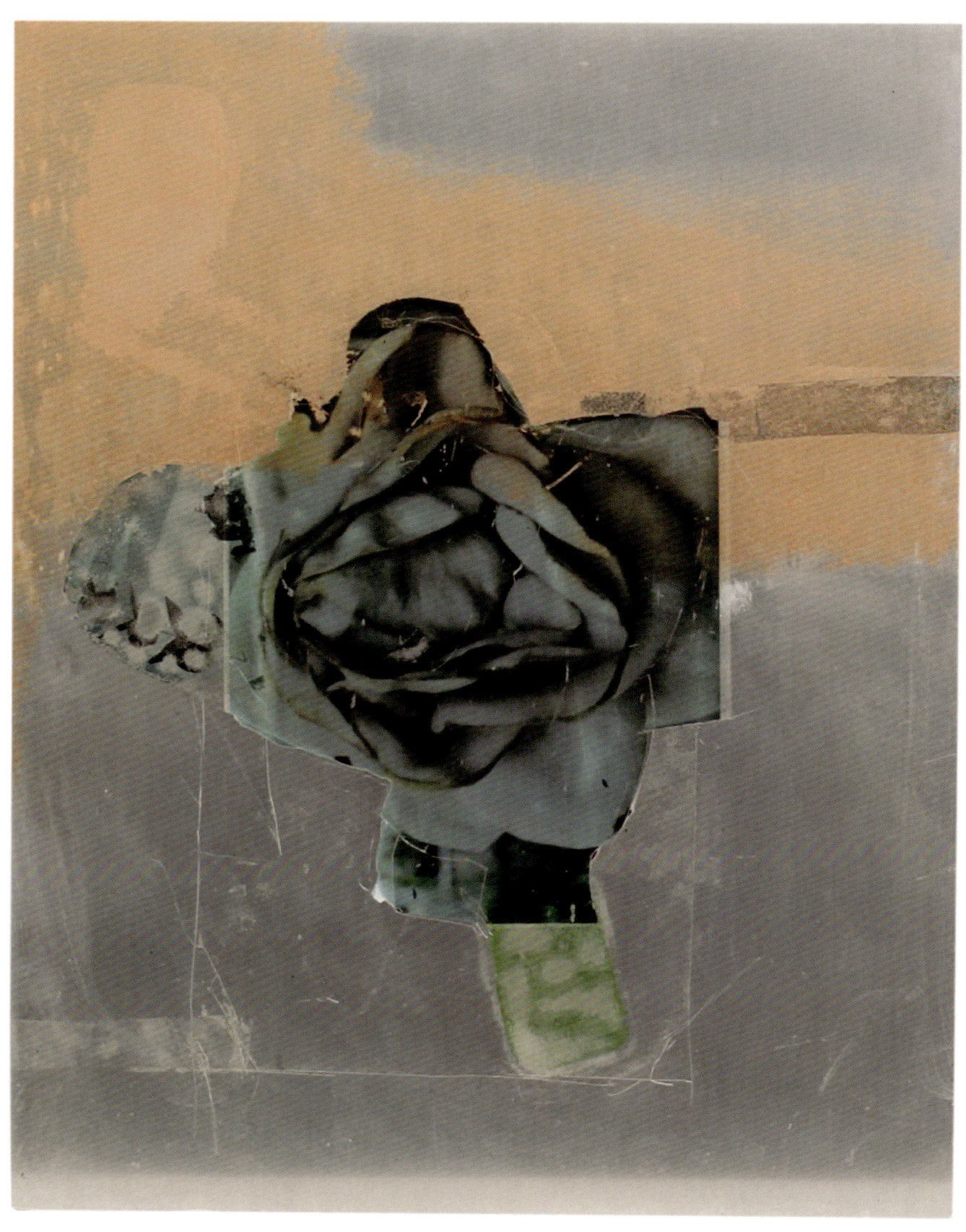

Untitled Series 5 of 11
20 x 16 inches
Mixed Media on Aluminum
2016

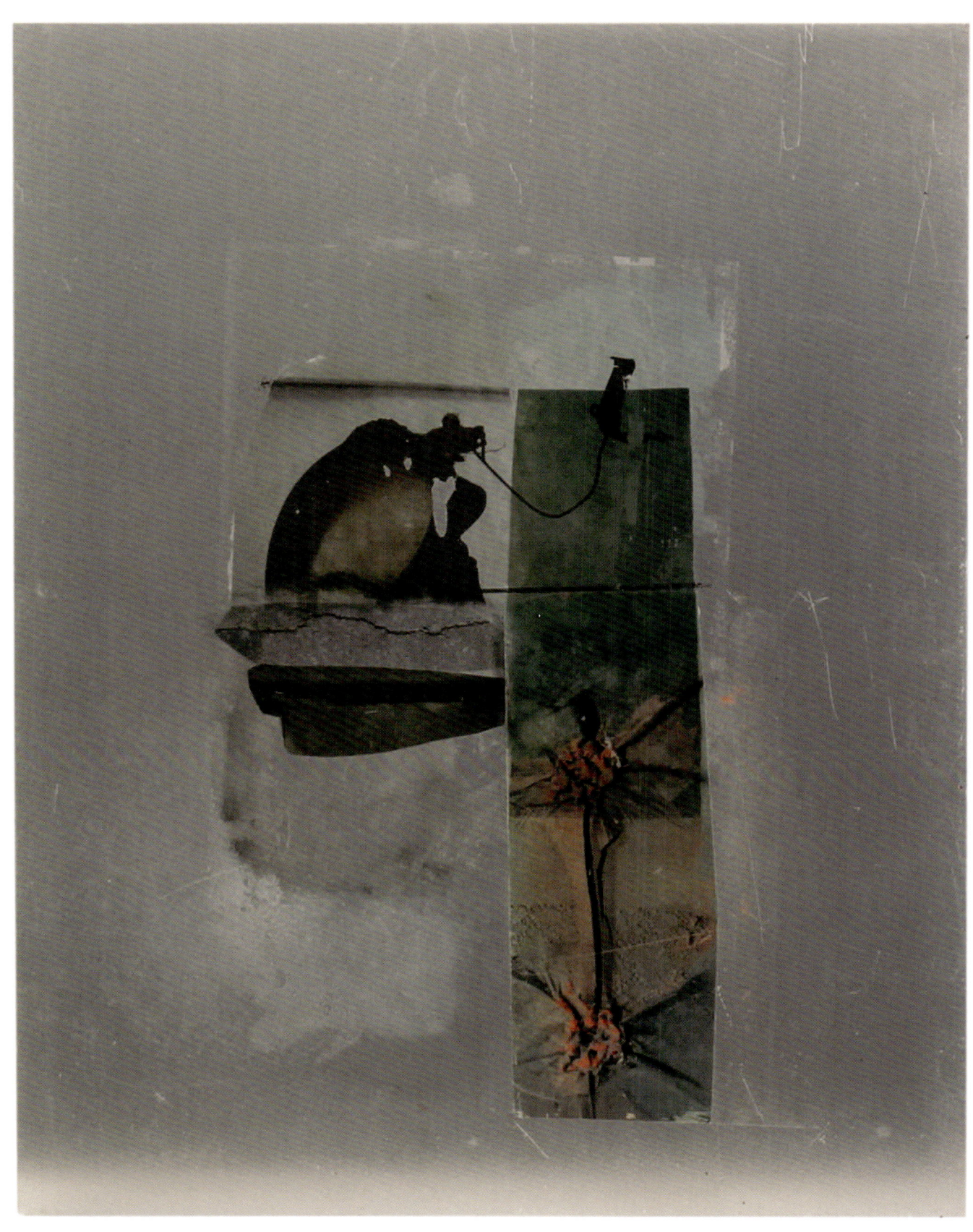

Untitled Series 6 of 11
20 x 16 inches
Mixed Media on Aluminum
2016

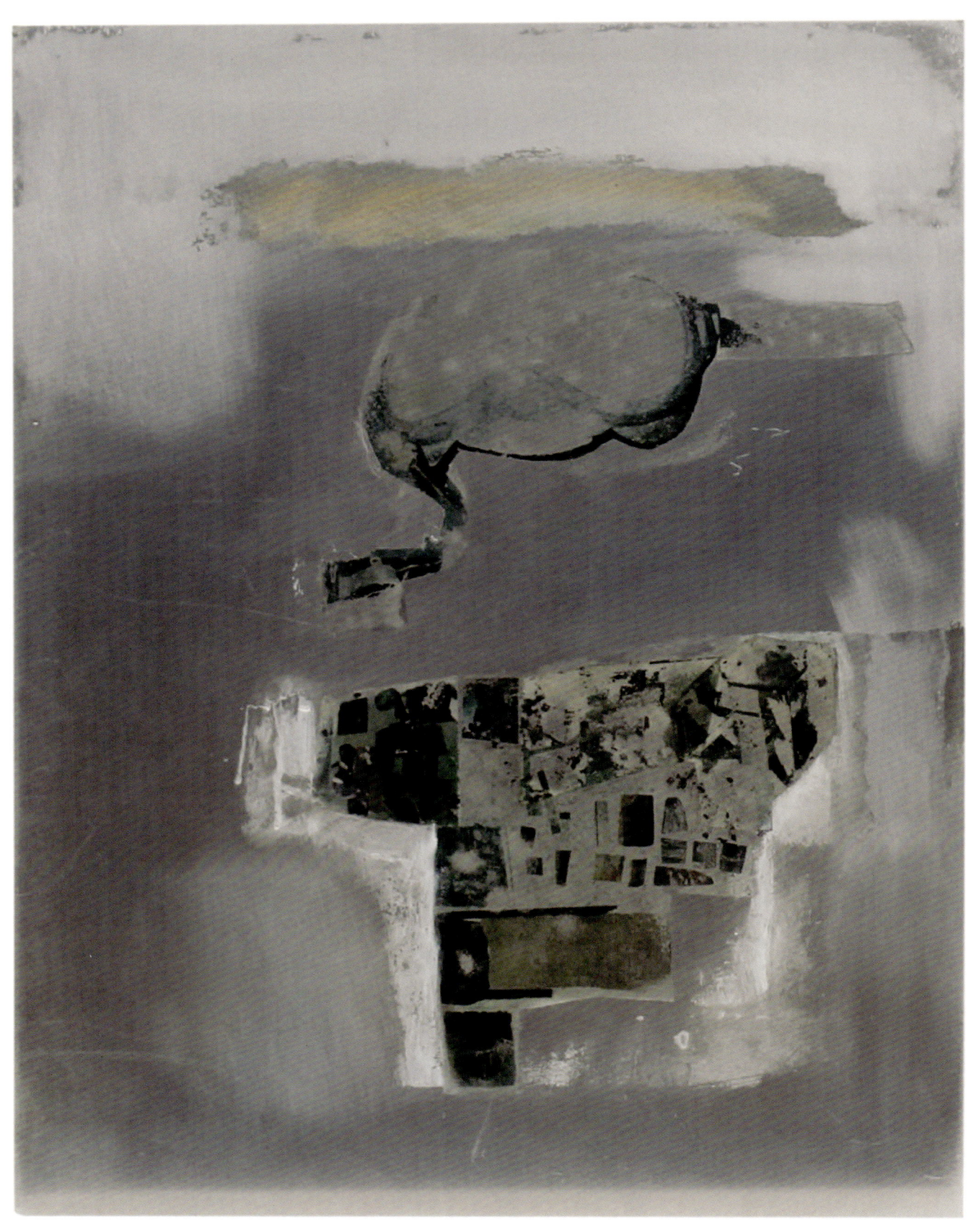

Untitled Series 7 of 11
20 x 16 inches
Mixed Media on Aluminum
2016

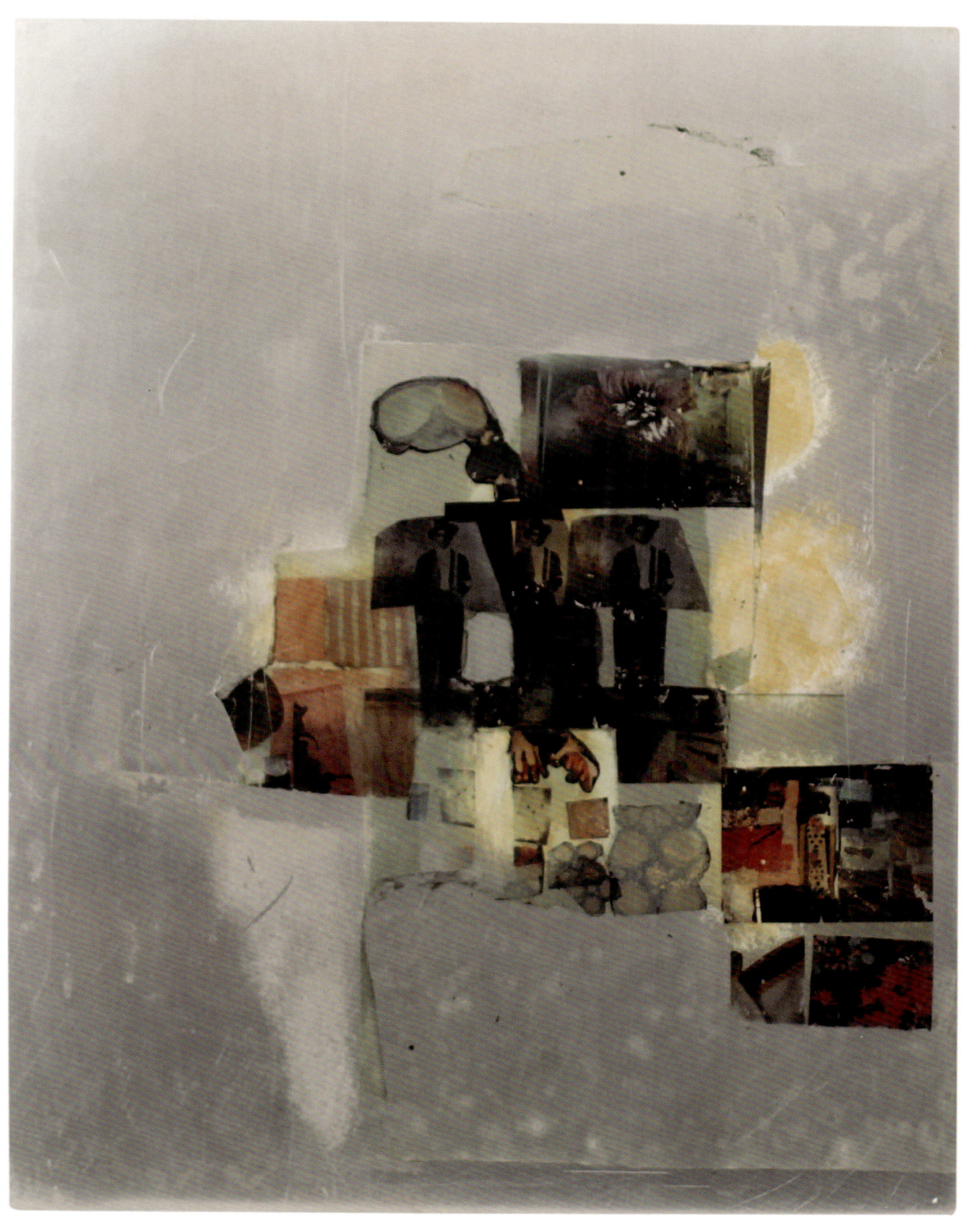

Untitled Series 8 of 11
20 x 16 inches
Mixed Media on Aluminum
2016

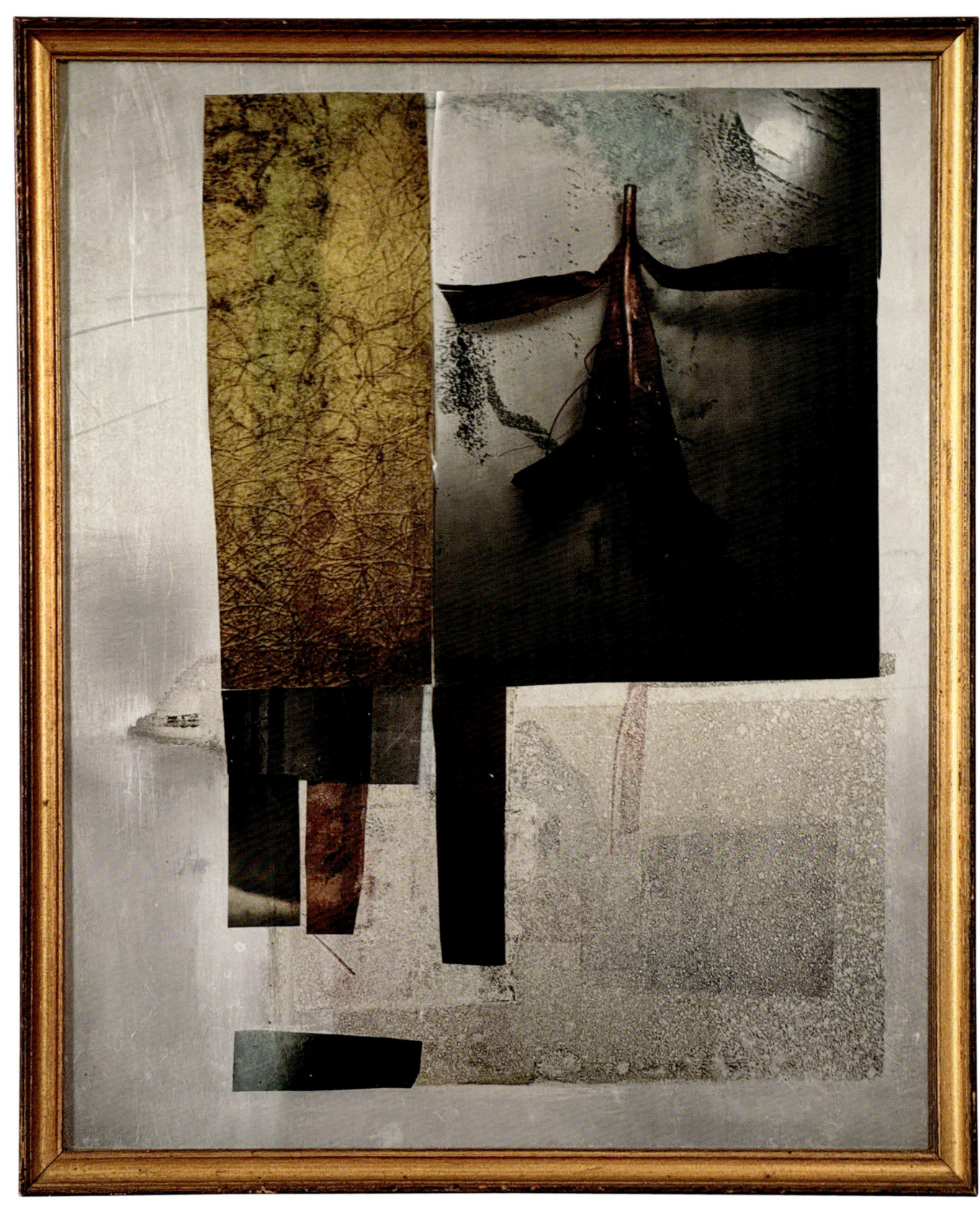

Untitled Series 9 of 11
21 x 16 inches
Mixed Media on Aluminum
2016

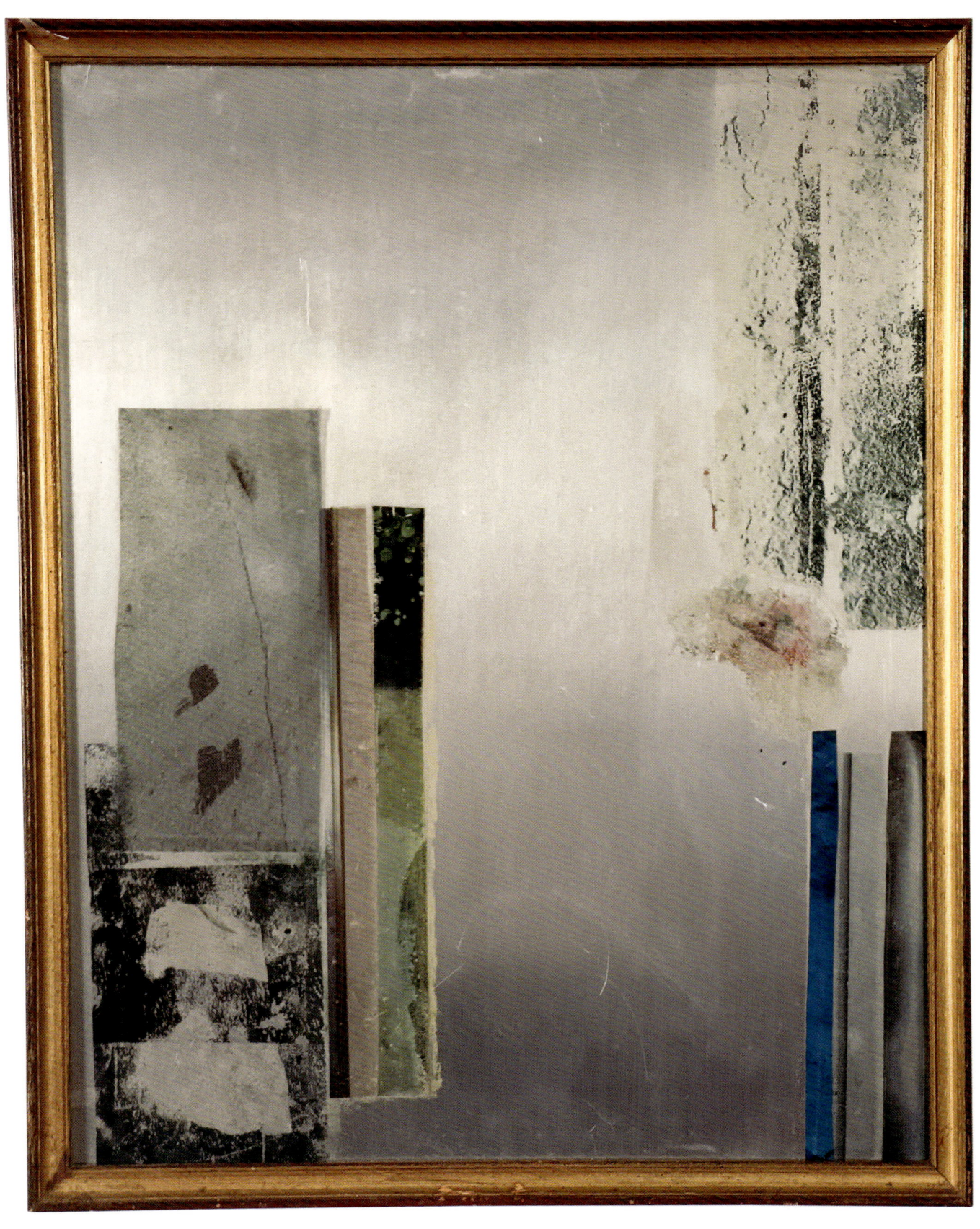

Untitled Series 10 of 11
21 x 16 inches
Mixed Media on Aluminum
2016

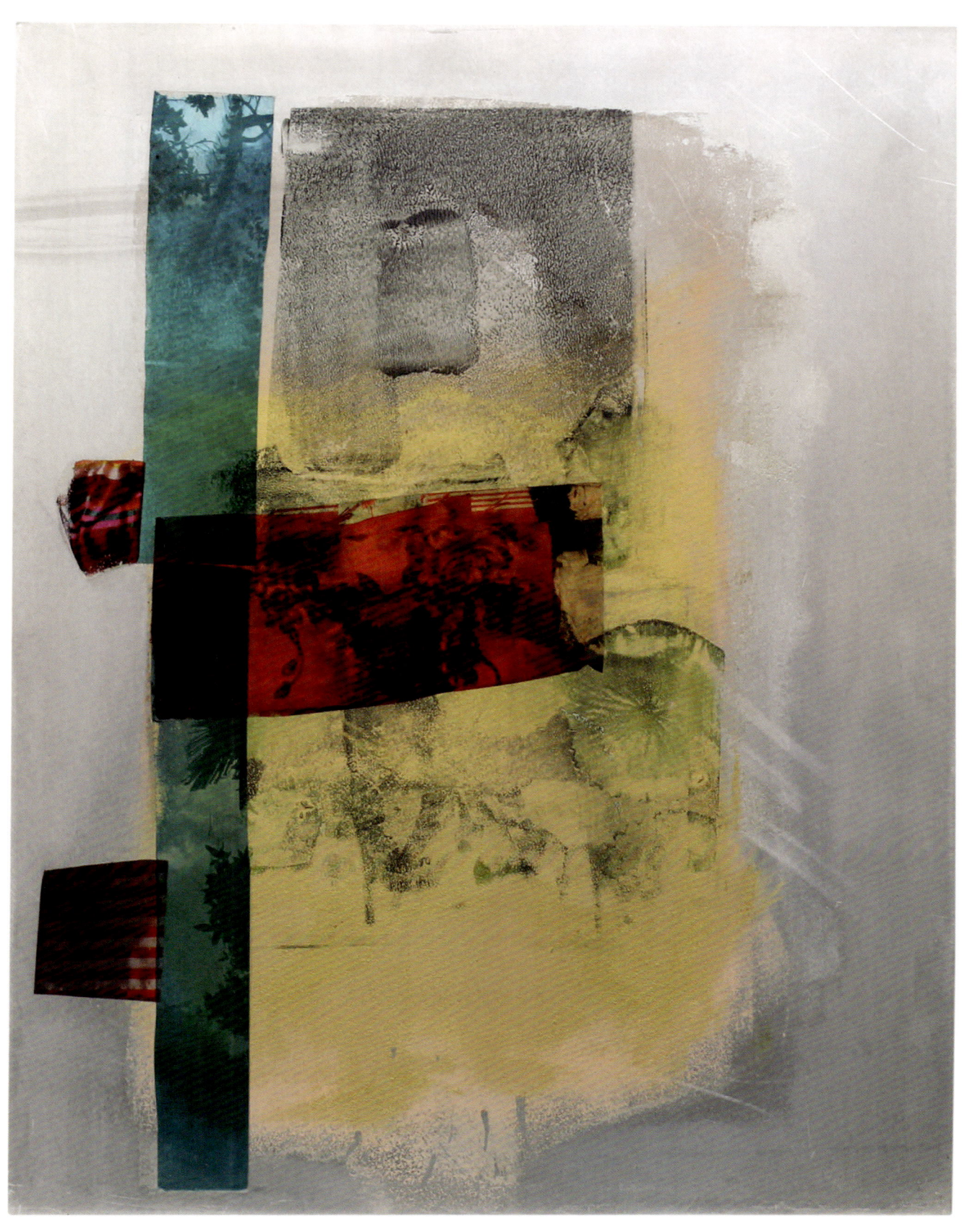

Untitled Series 11 of 11
20 x 16 inches
Mixed Media on Aluminum
2016

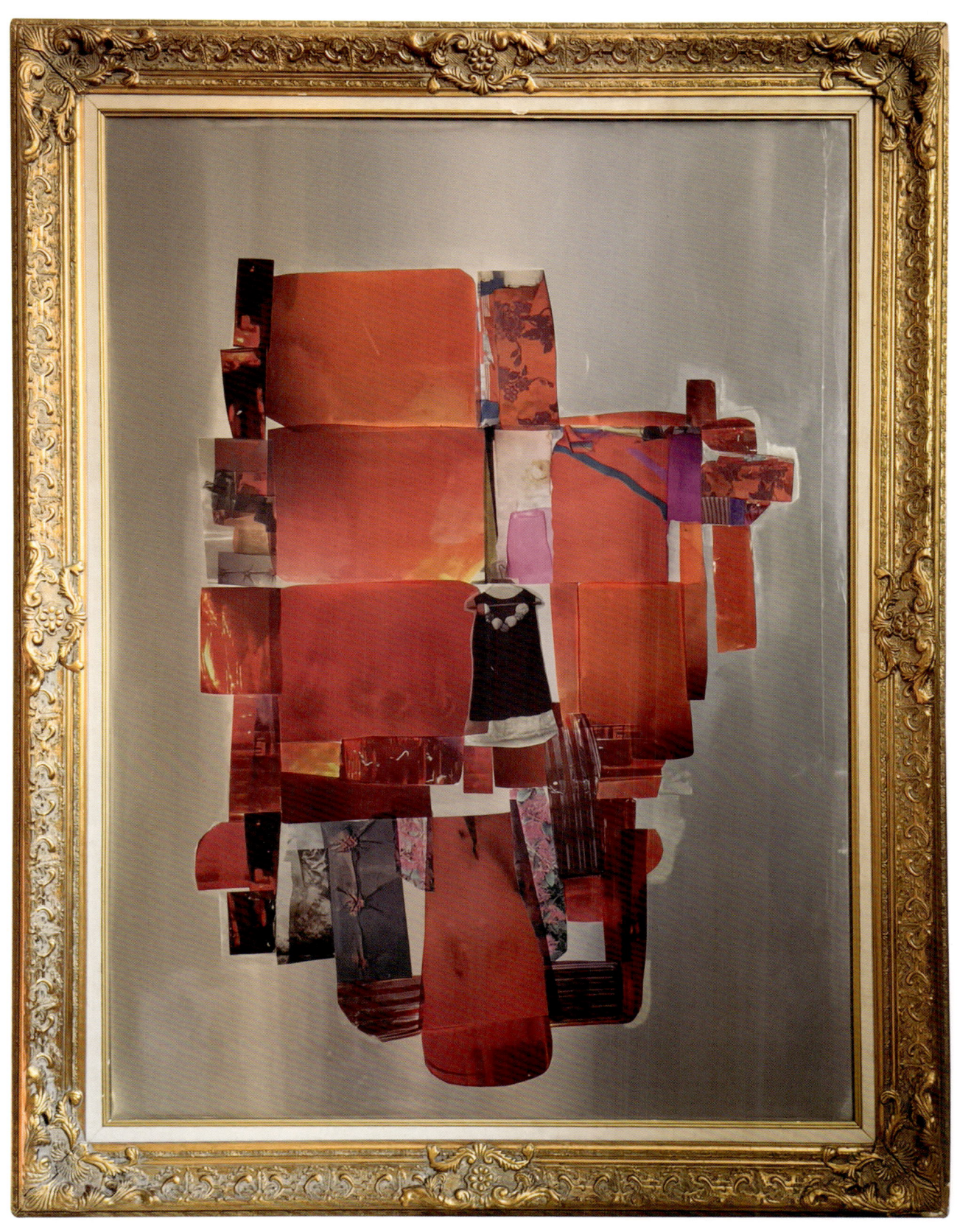

Float
57 x 45 inches
Mixed Media on Aluminum
2011

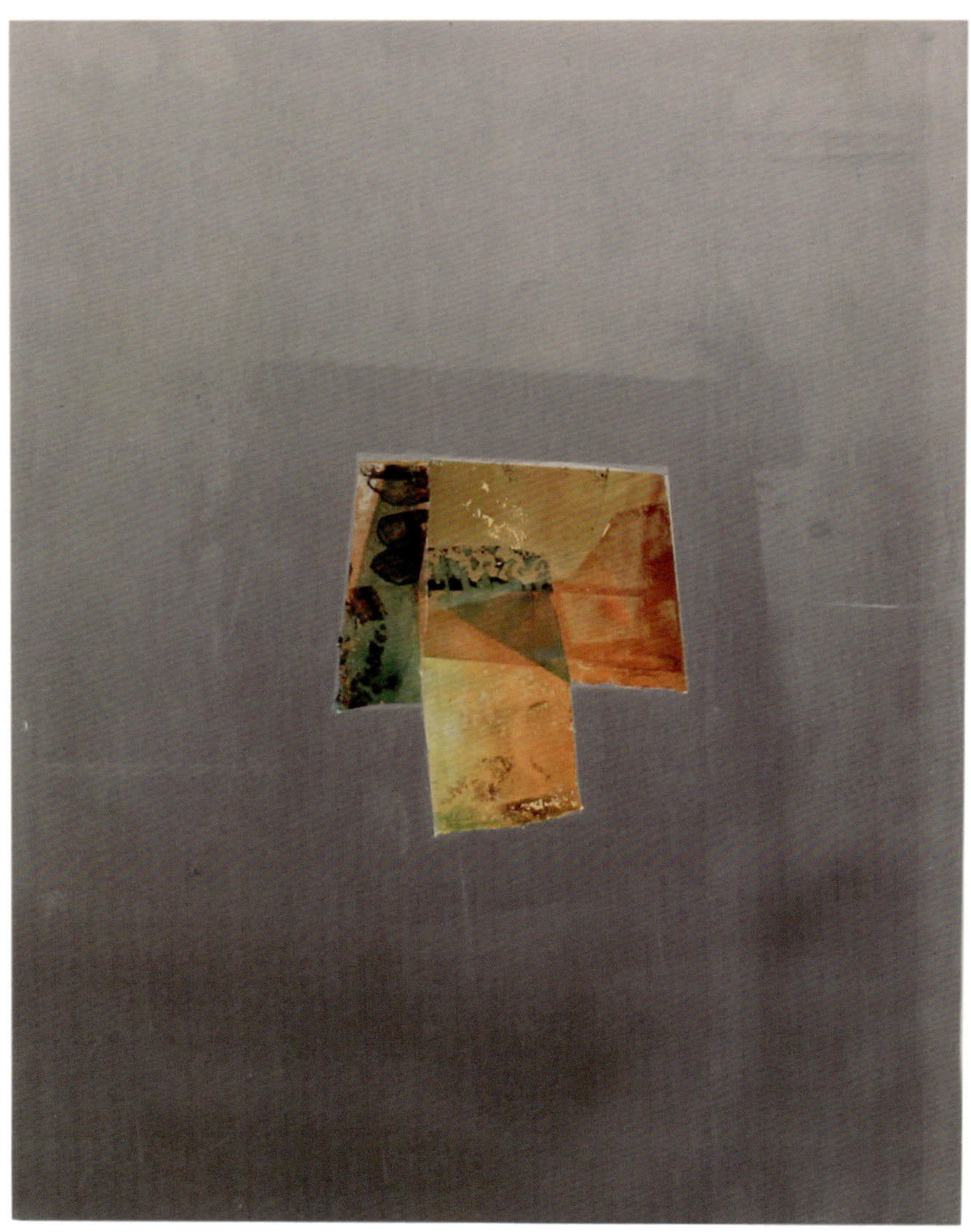

Ramp
20 x 16 inches
Mixed Media on Steel
2021

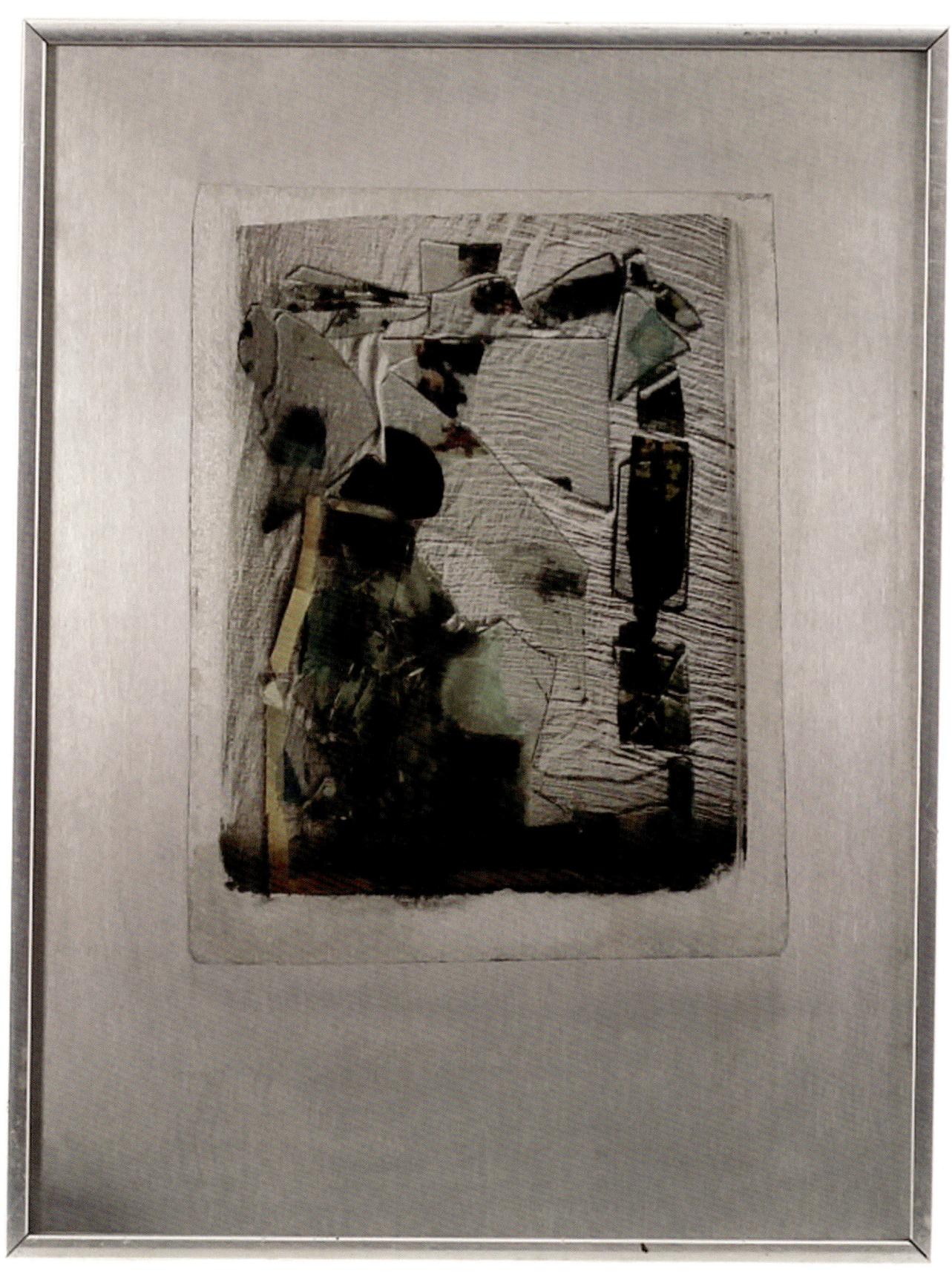

Reassembled Torso
12 ½ x 16 ¾ inches
Transparency on Aluminum
2017

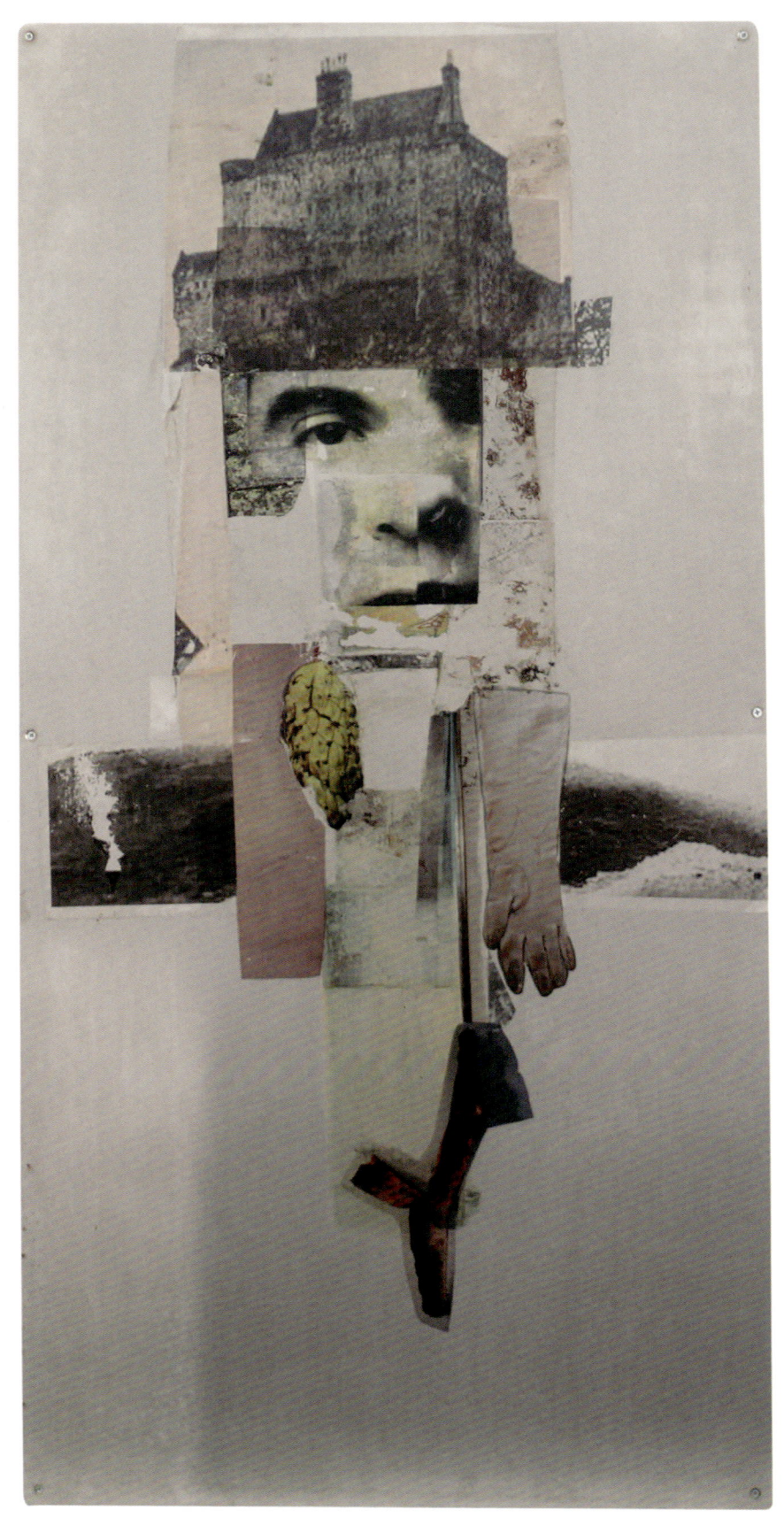

Highlands
48 x 24 inches
Mixed Media on Steel
2018

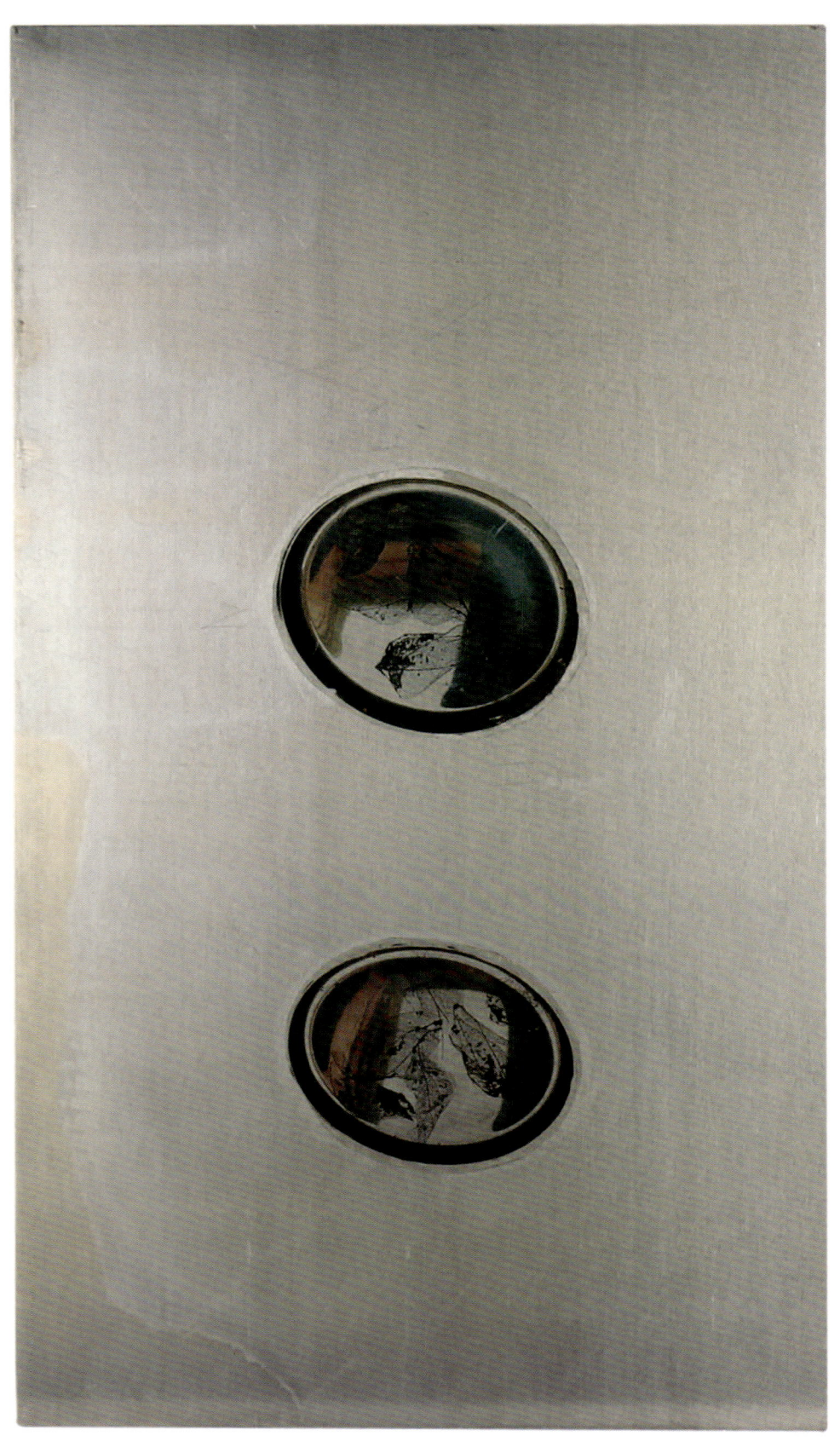

The Spooky Action of Leaves
24 x 14 inches
Mixed Media on Aluminum
2024

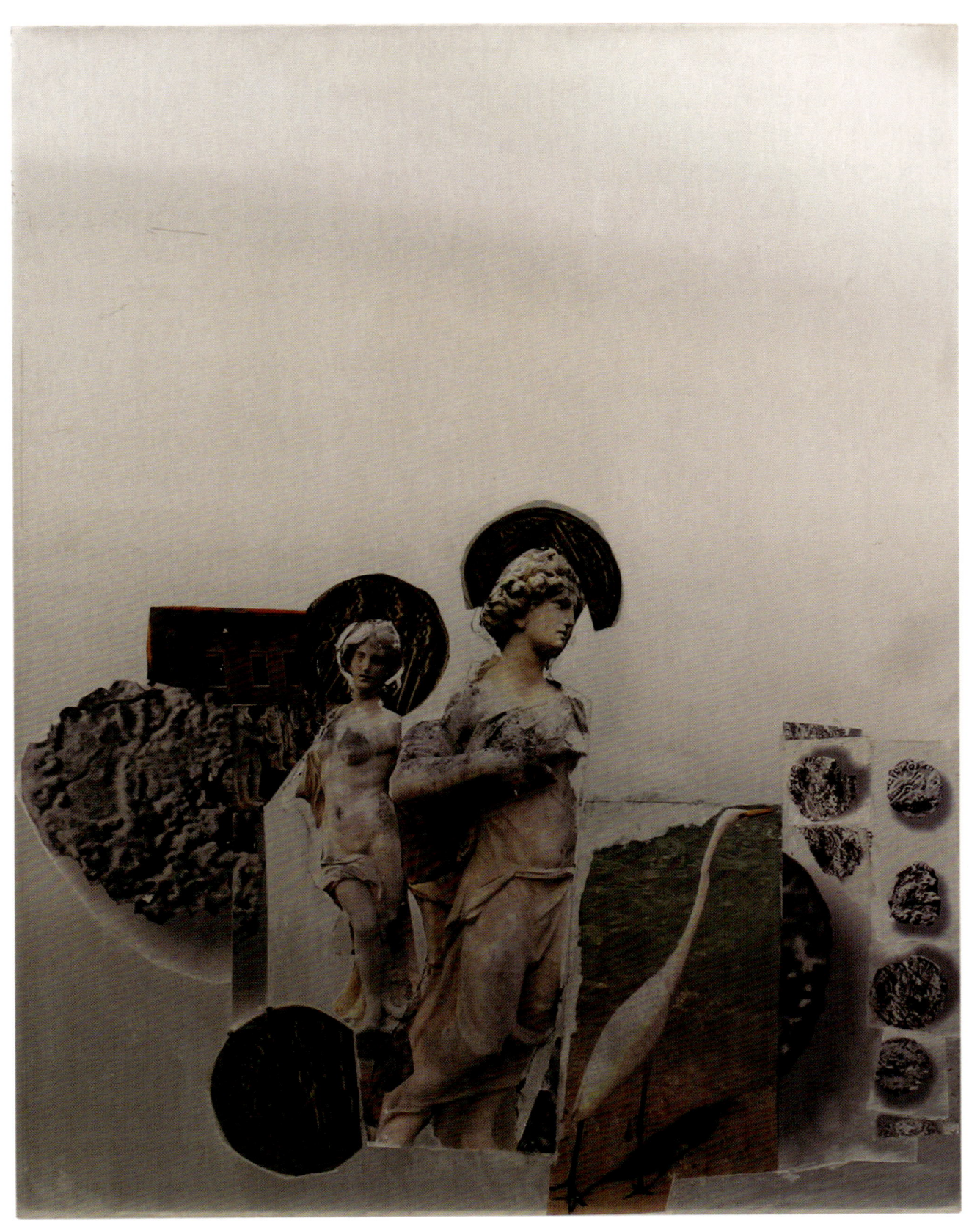

Parable I
20 x 16 inches
Mixed Media on Steel
2022

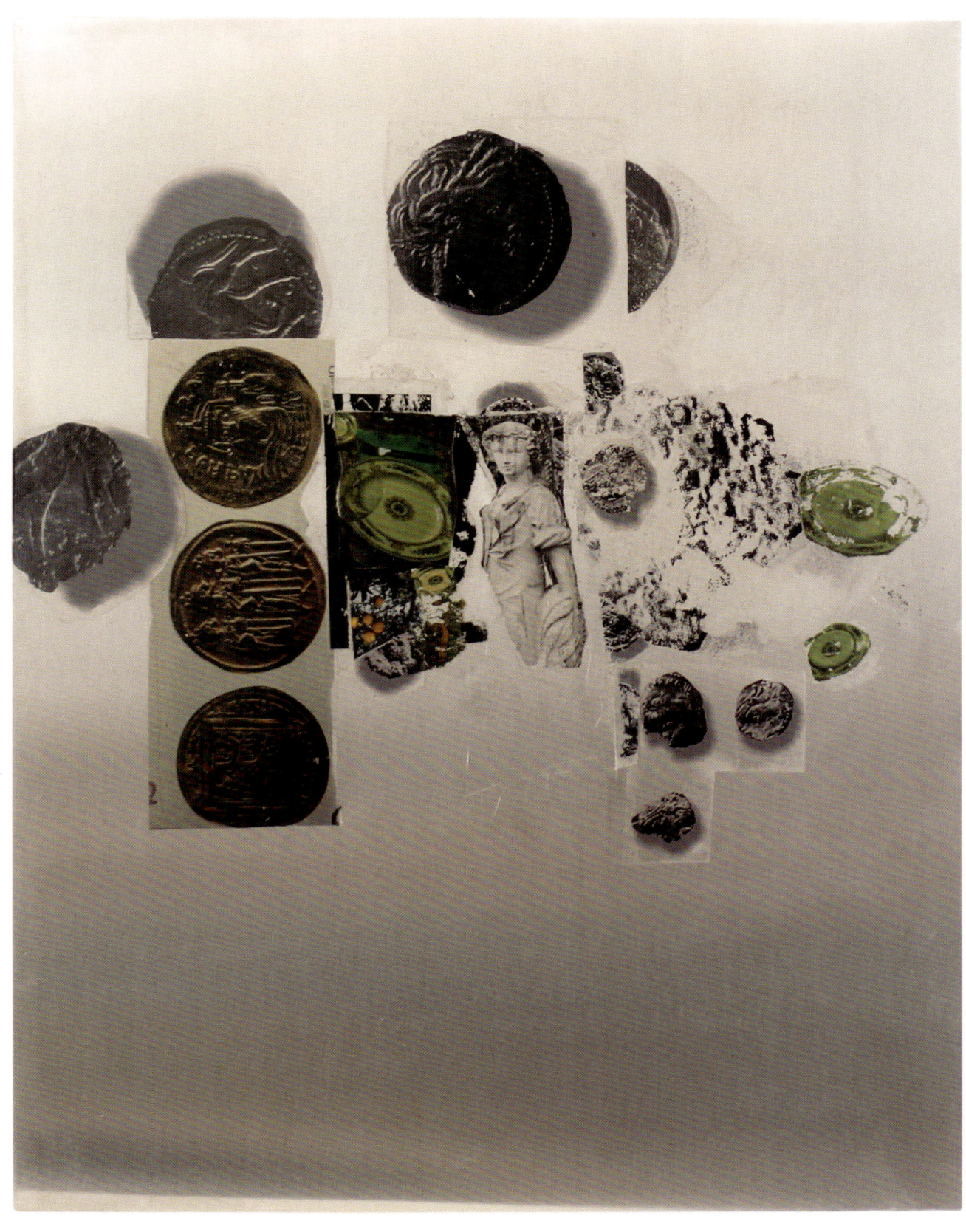

Parable II
20 x 16 inches
Mixed Media on Steel
2022

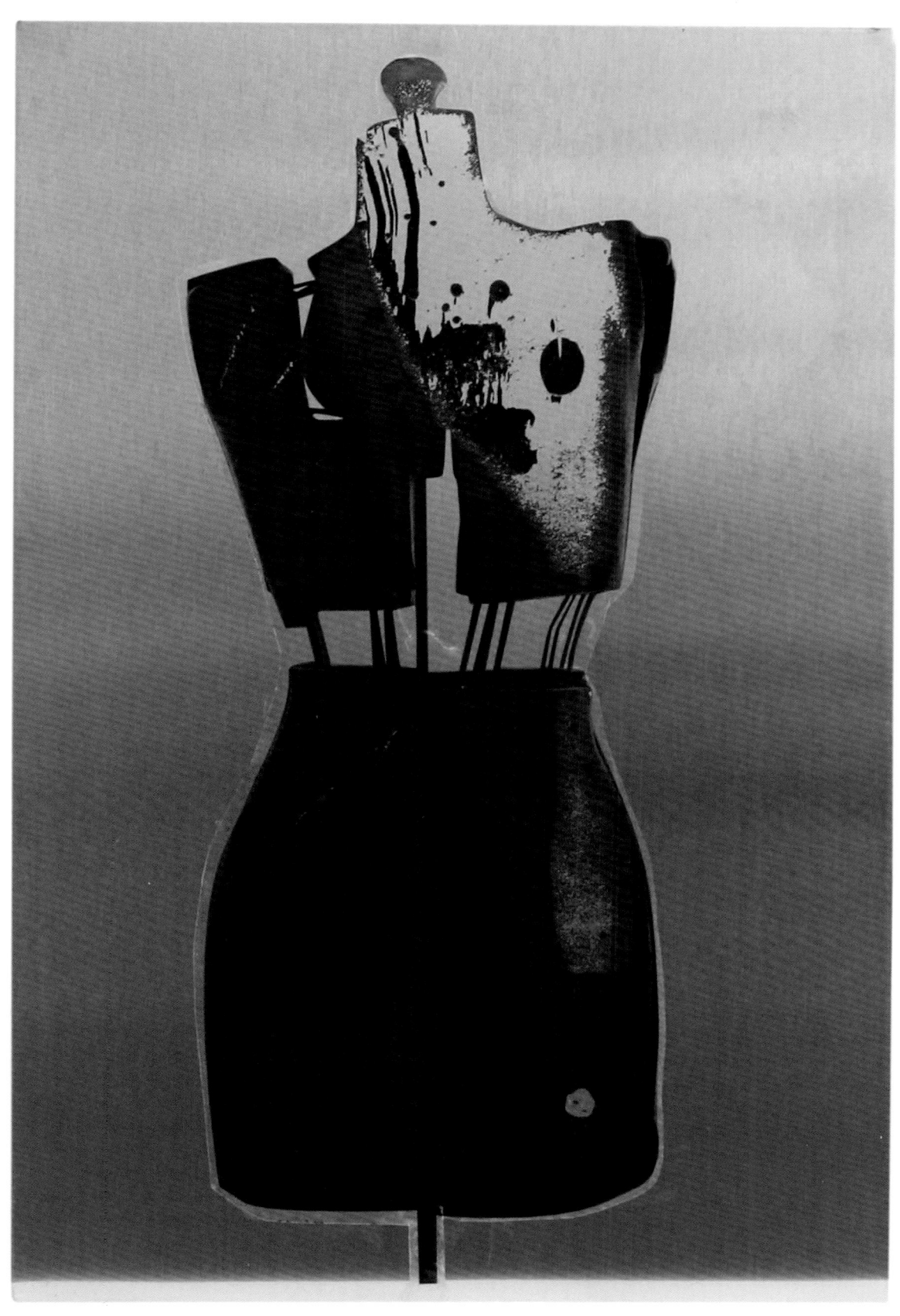

Relief 4 (Steel Test)
24 x 18 inches
Print on Water Soluble Film, Steel Substrate
2022

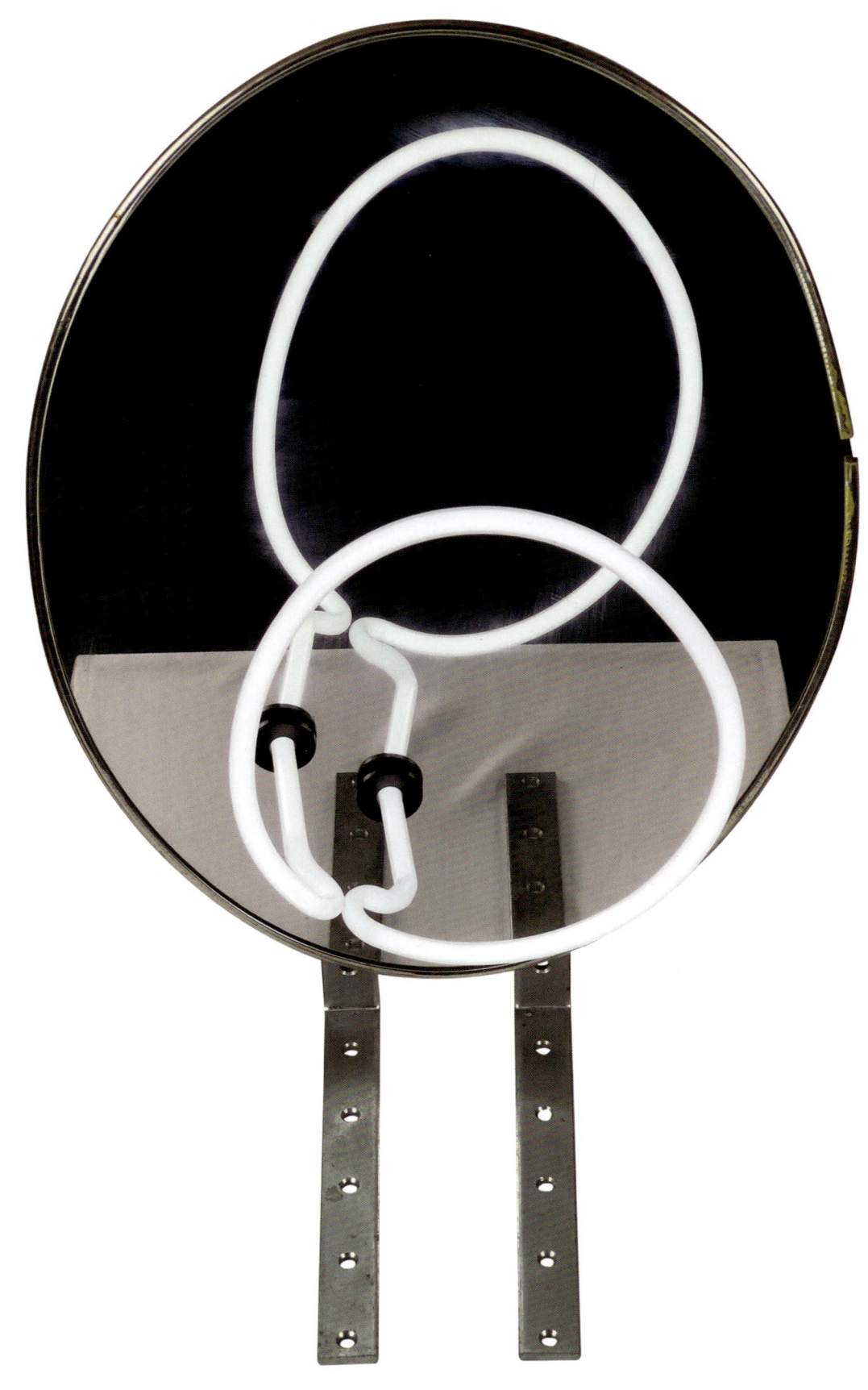

Smoke Ring
25 x 16 ½ x 15 inches
Mirror with Neon Lamp
2011

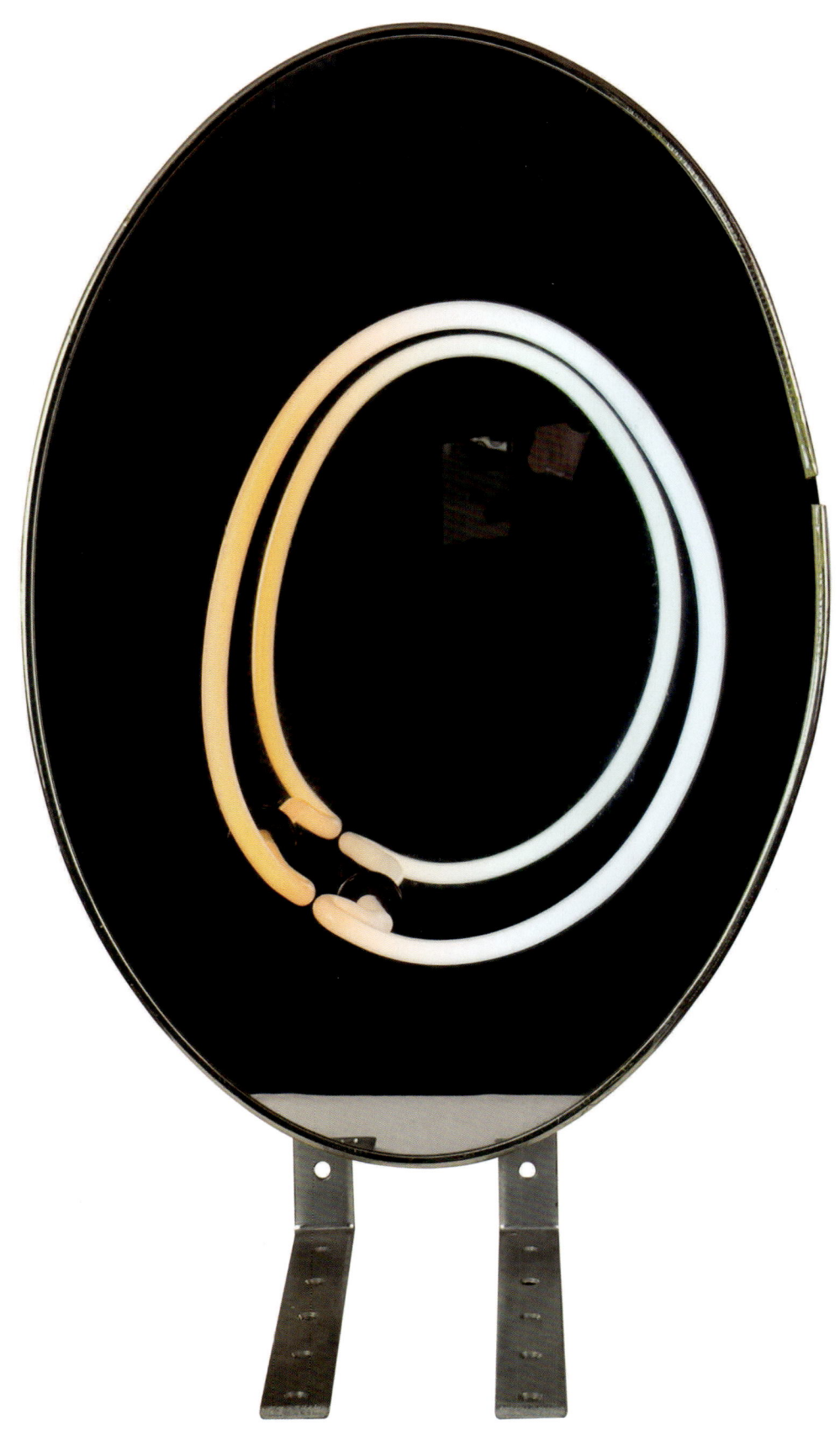

Smoke Ring (Detail)

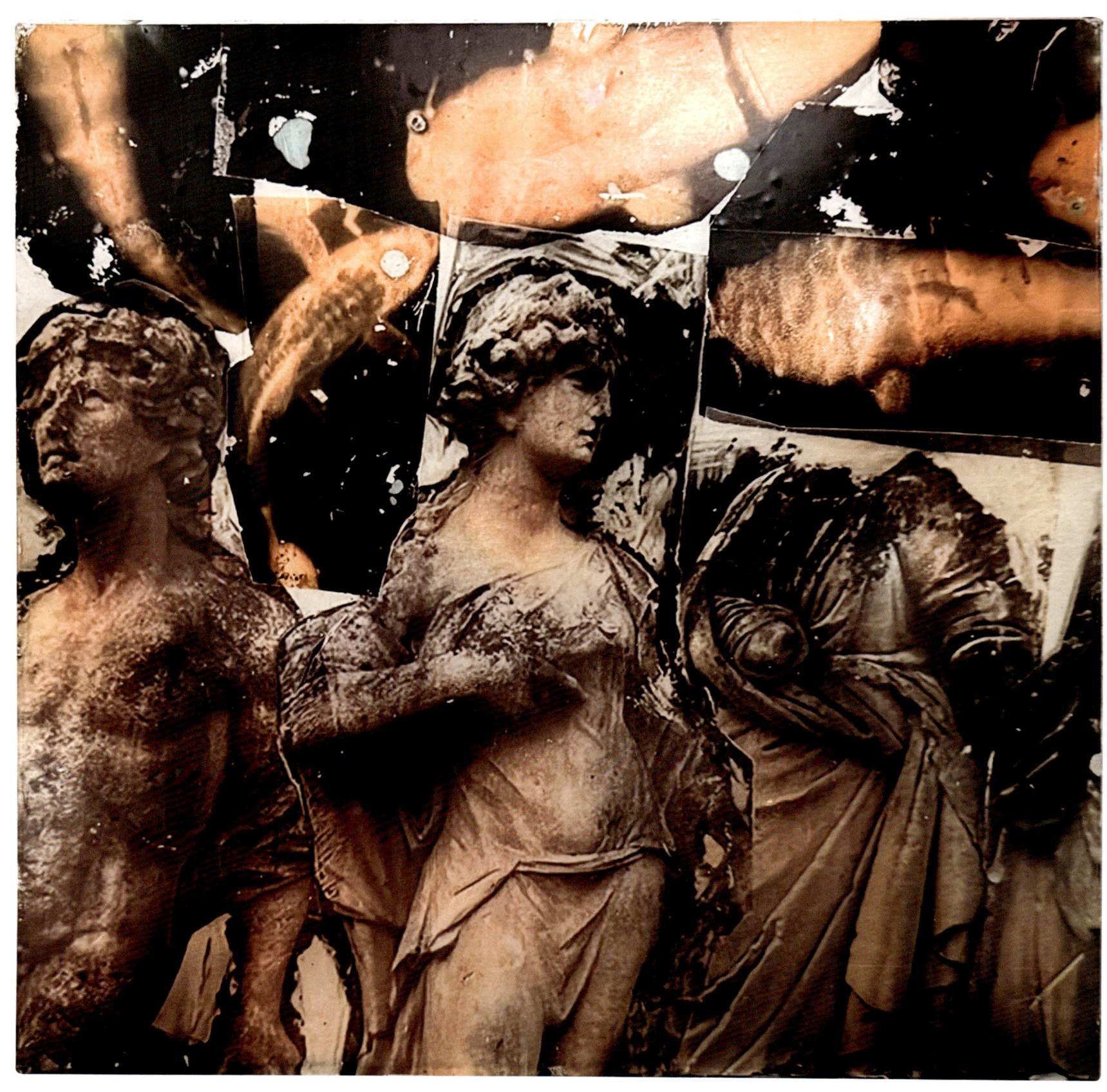

Square Tile No. 1
15 x 15 inches
Photo Collage w/ Aluminum Substrate
2023

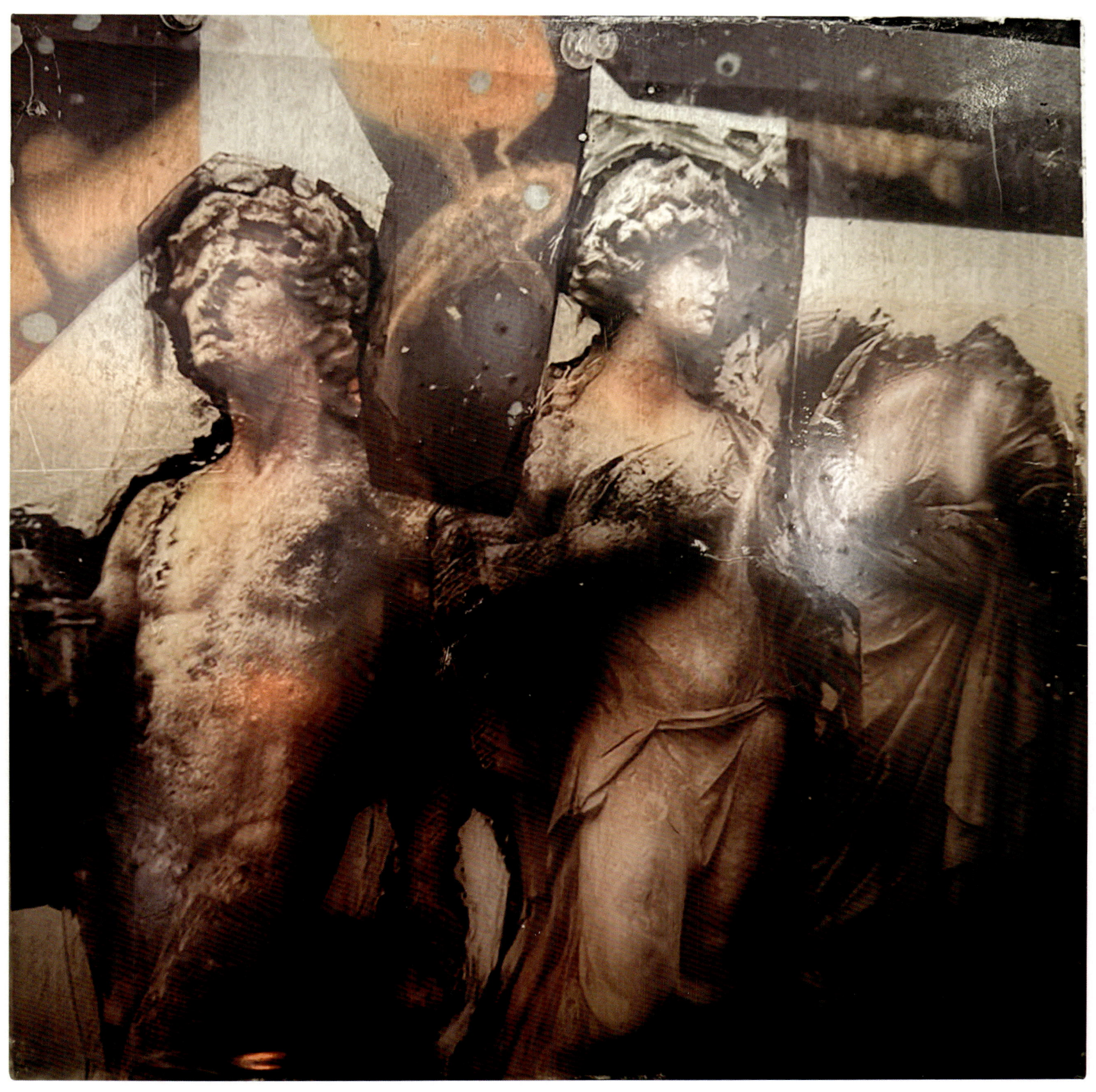

Square Tile No. 2
15 x 15 inches
Photo Collage w/ Aluminum Substrate
2023

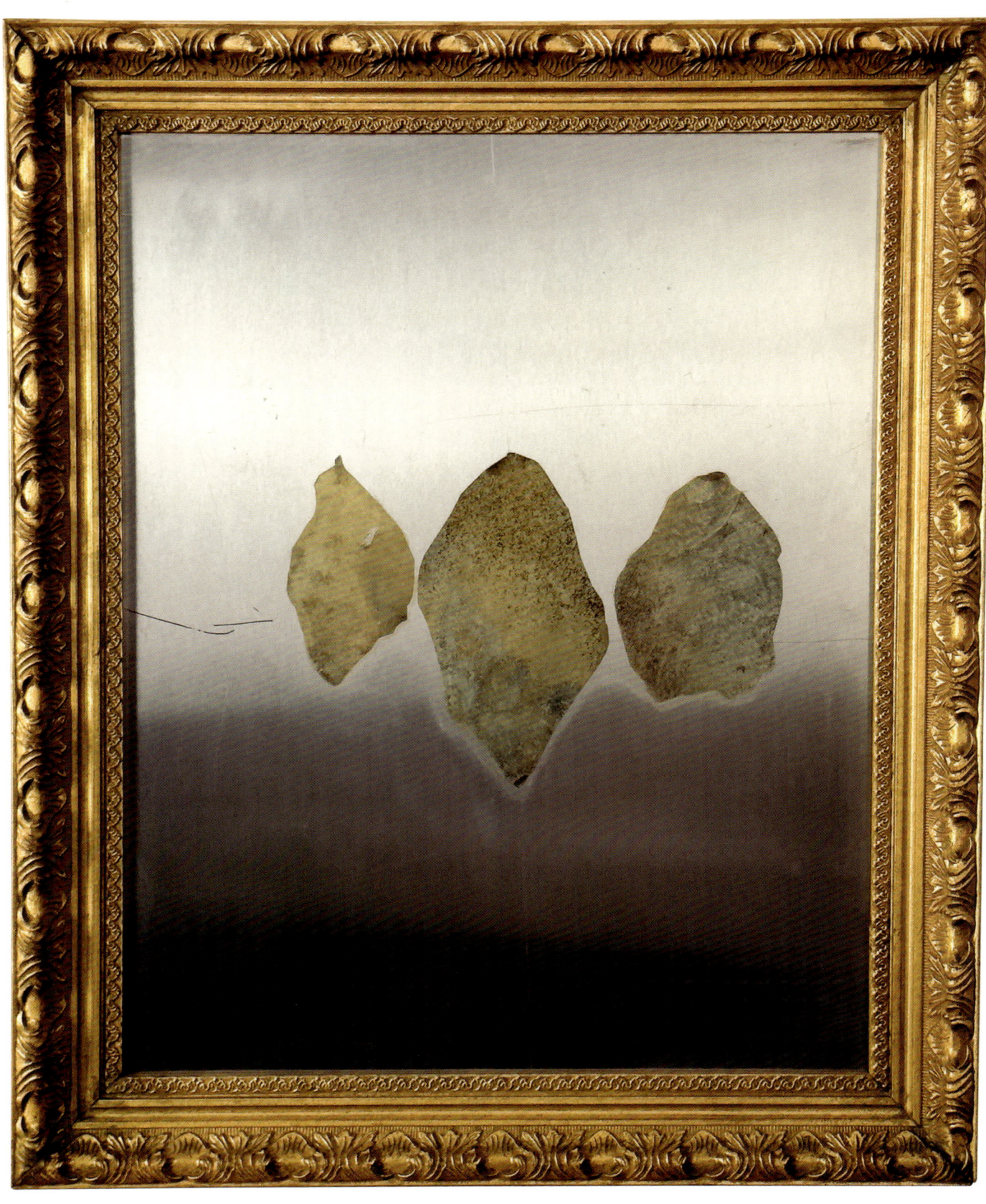

The Treasure
24 x 20 ½ inches
Mixed Media on Steel
2014

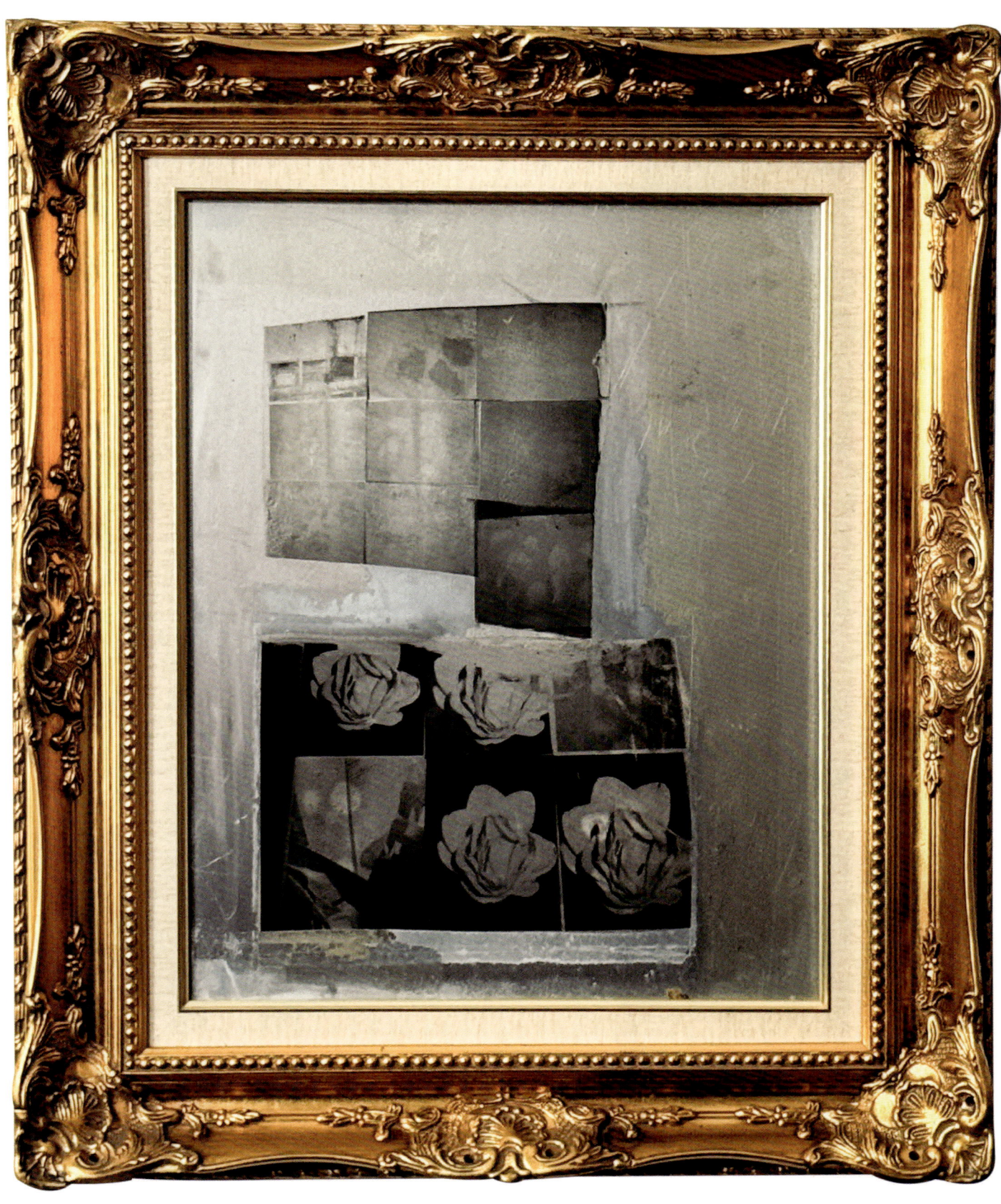

The Chateau
29 x 24 inches
Mixed Media on Aluminum
2014

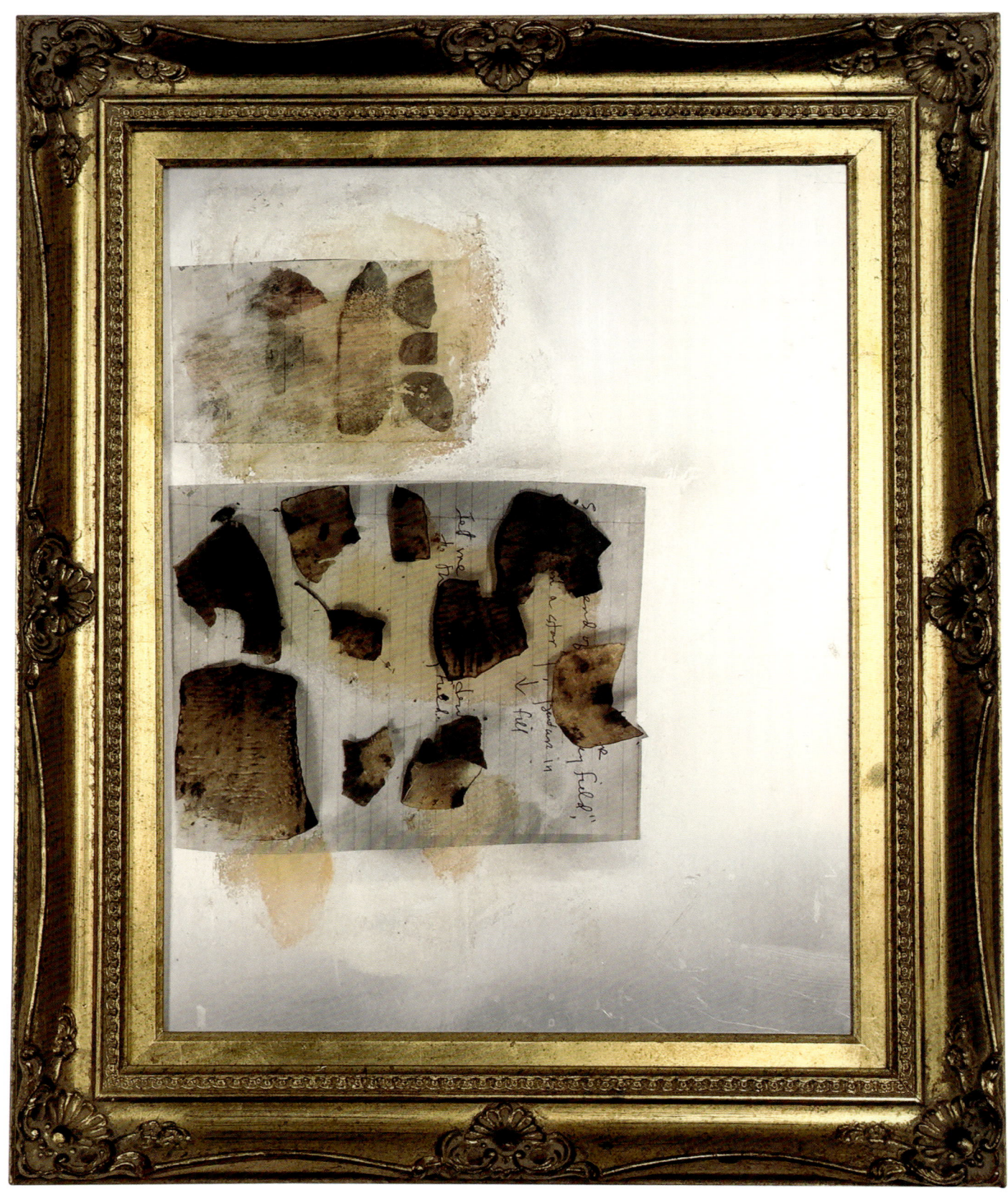

Relic
24 x 21 inches
Mixed Media on Aluminum
2017

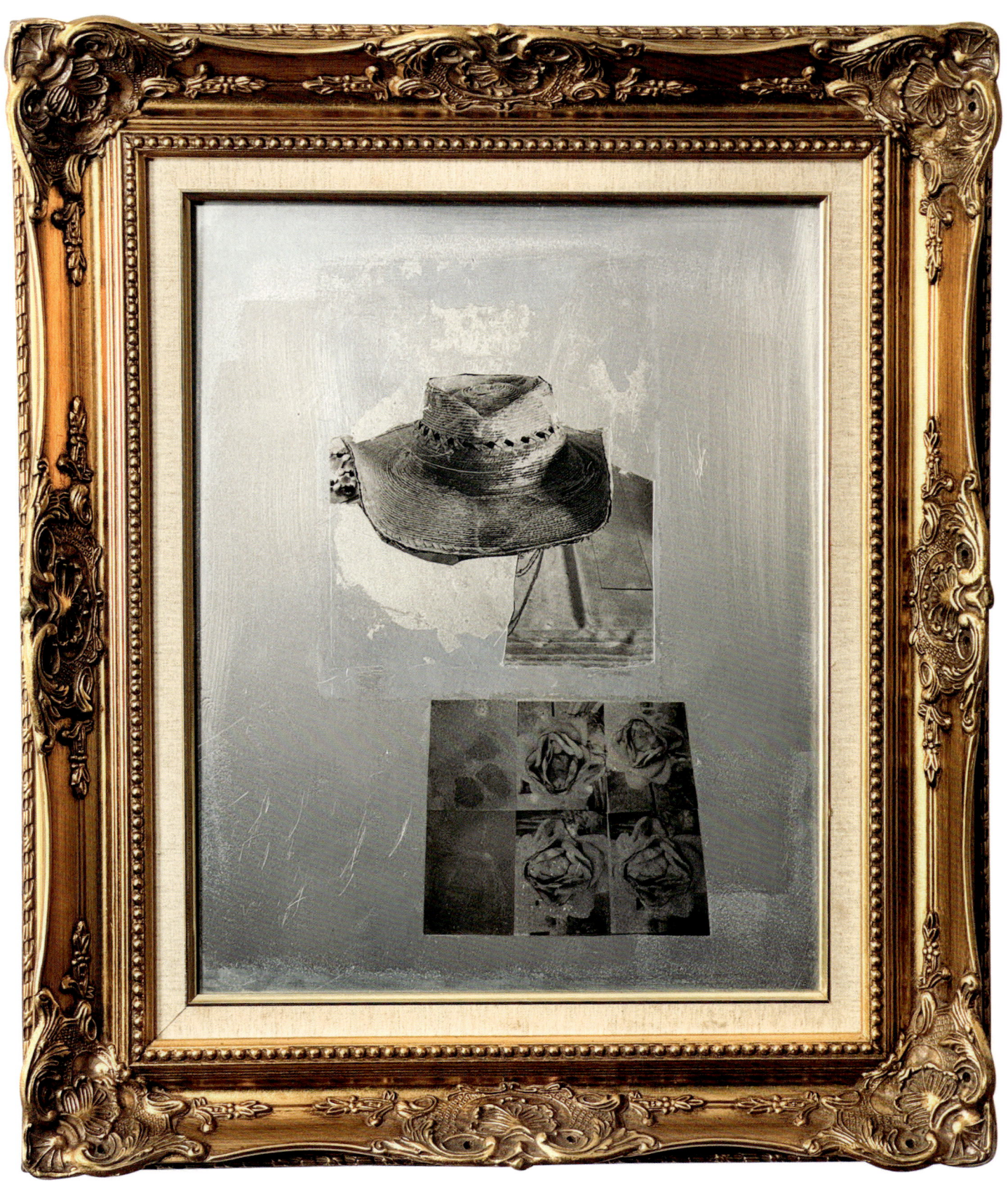

A Pilgrimage to The Pyramid of the Sun (08/08/08)
29 x 24 inches
Mixed Media on Aluminum
2014

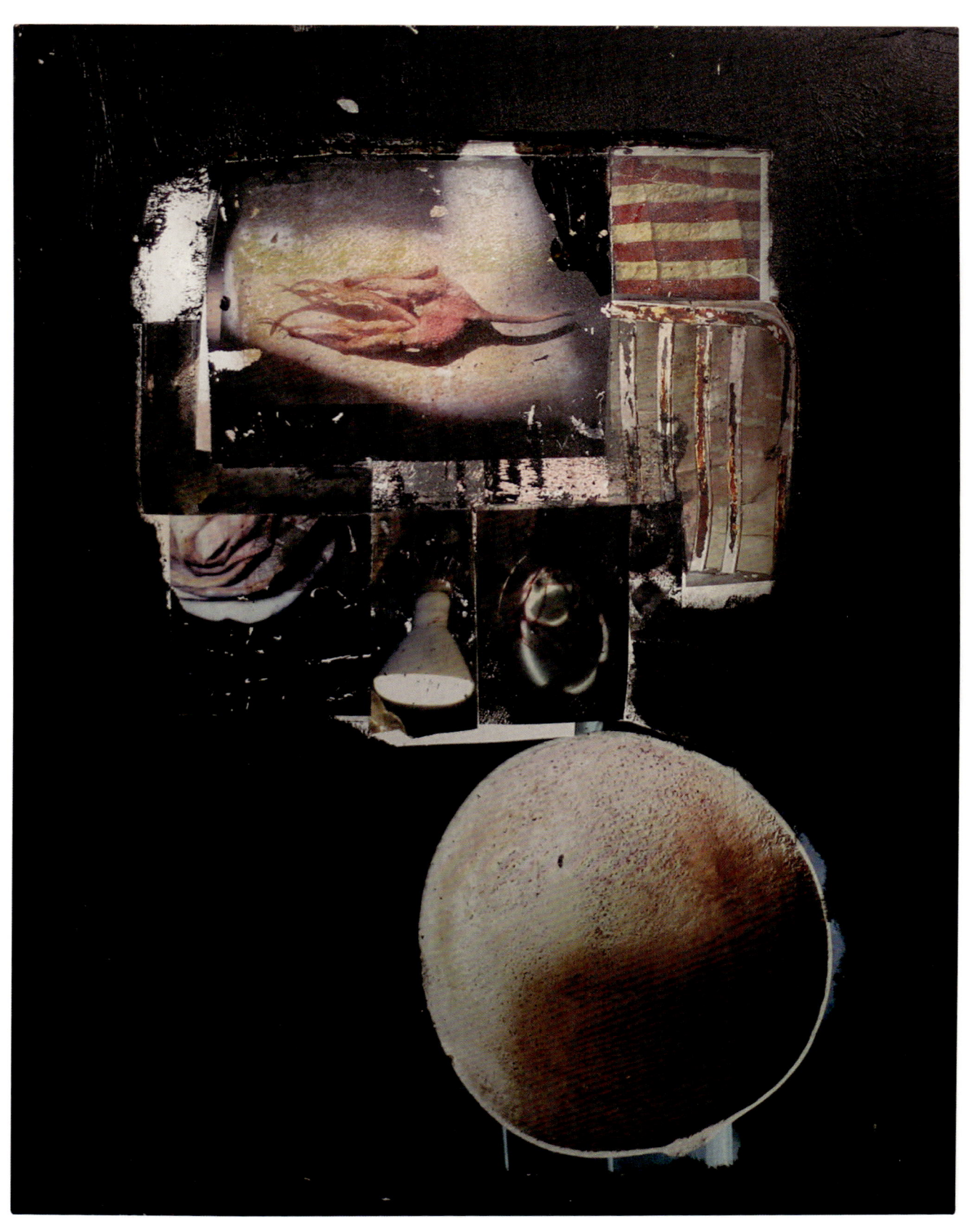

A Night in The Laboratory
20 x 16 inches
Mixed Media on Aluminum
2019

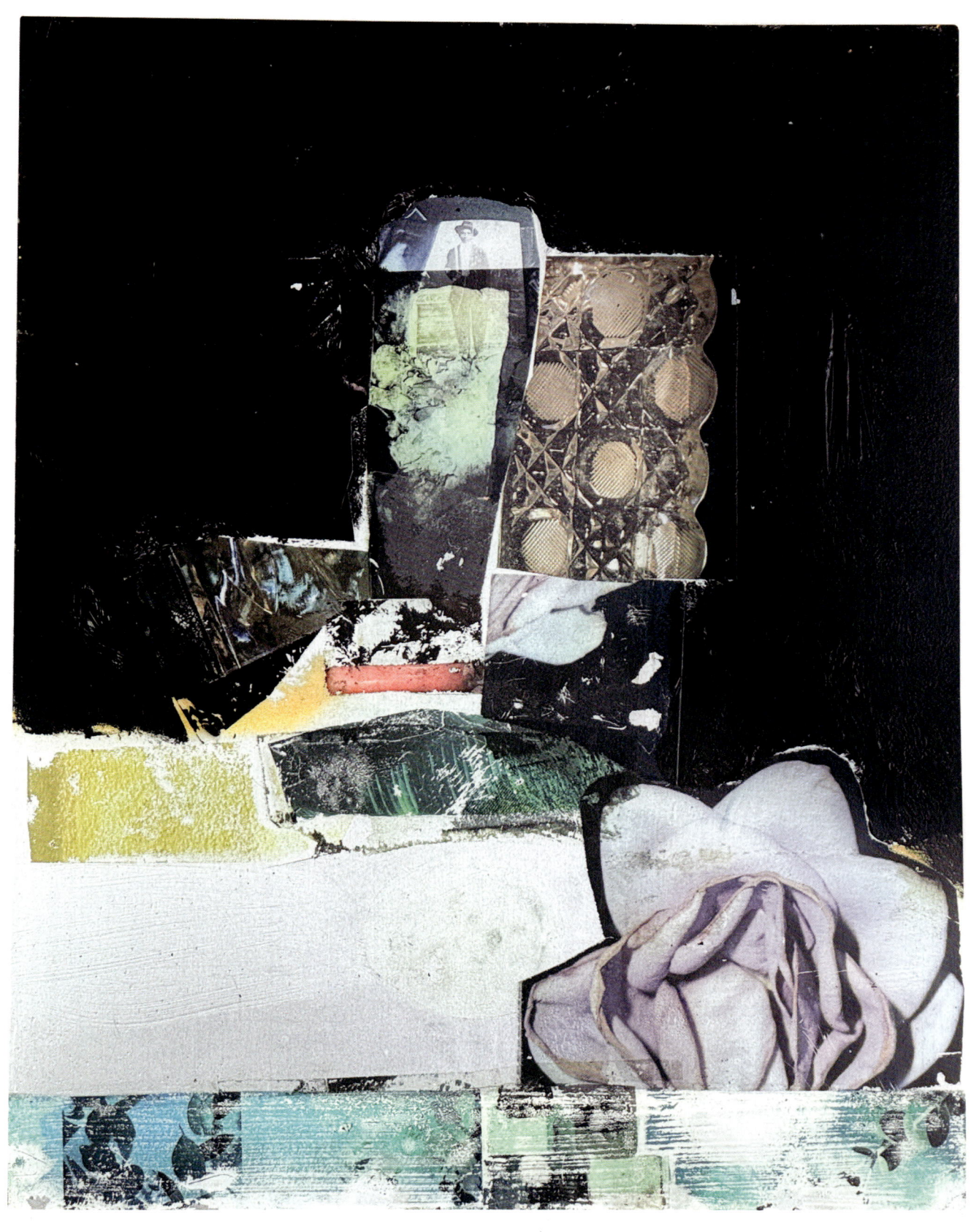

A Night in the Greenhouse
20 x 16 inches
Mixed Media on Aluminum
2017

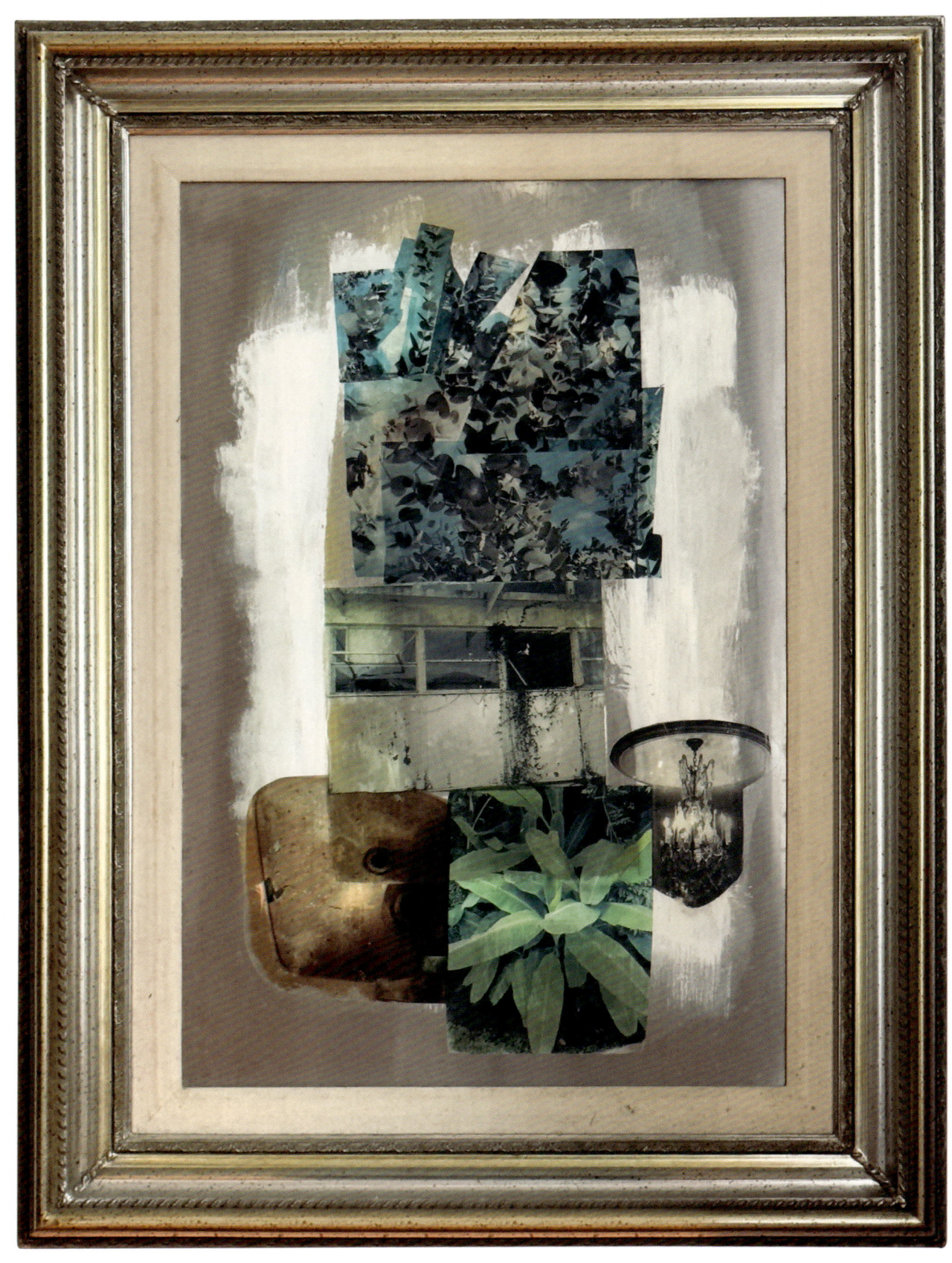

Campus
48 x 36 inches
Mixed Media Mounted on Aluminum
2016

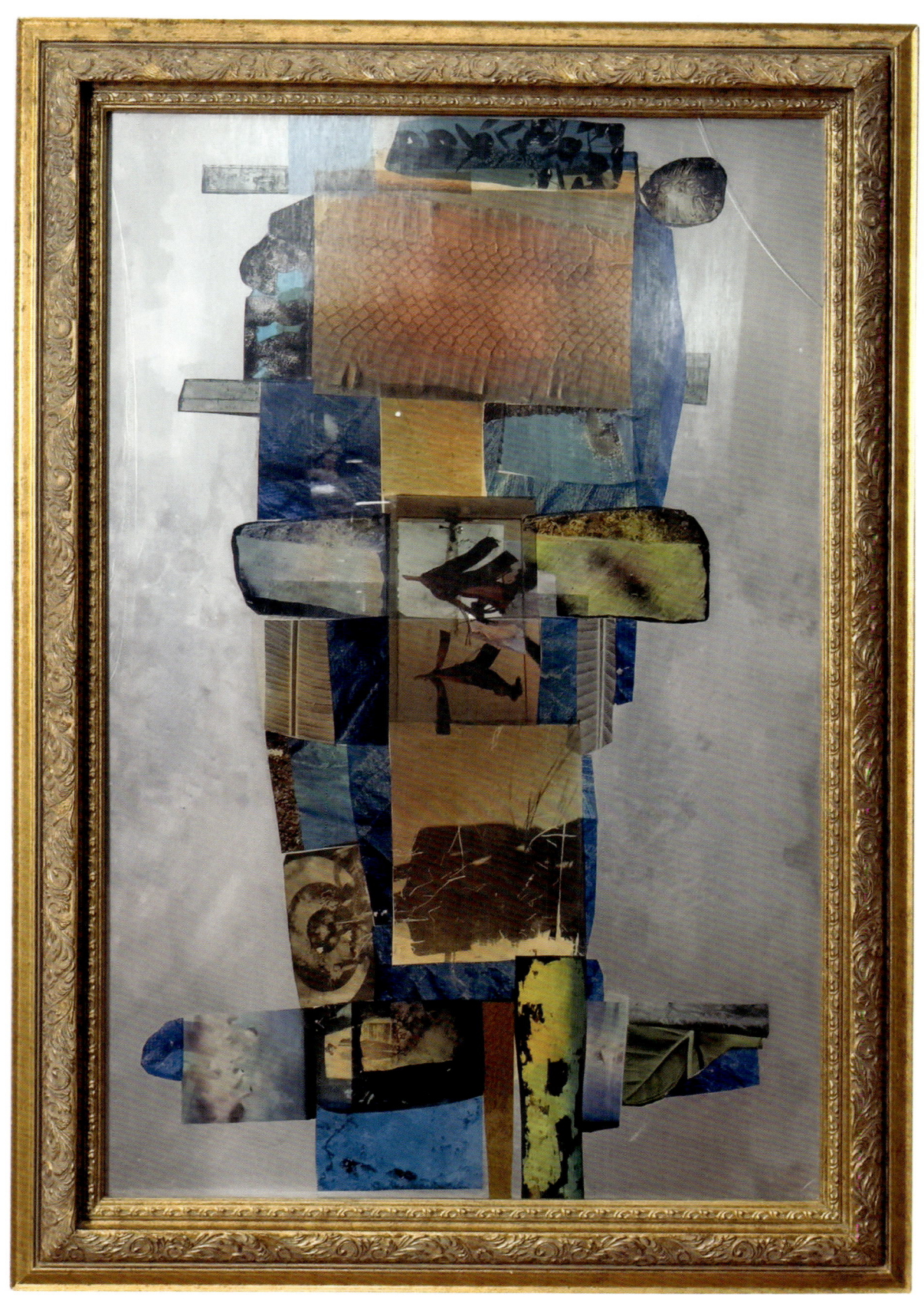

Totem
42 x 29 ½ inches
Mixed Media on Aluminum
2018

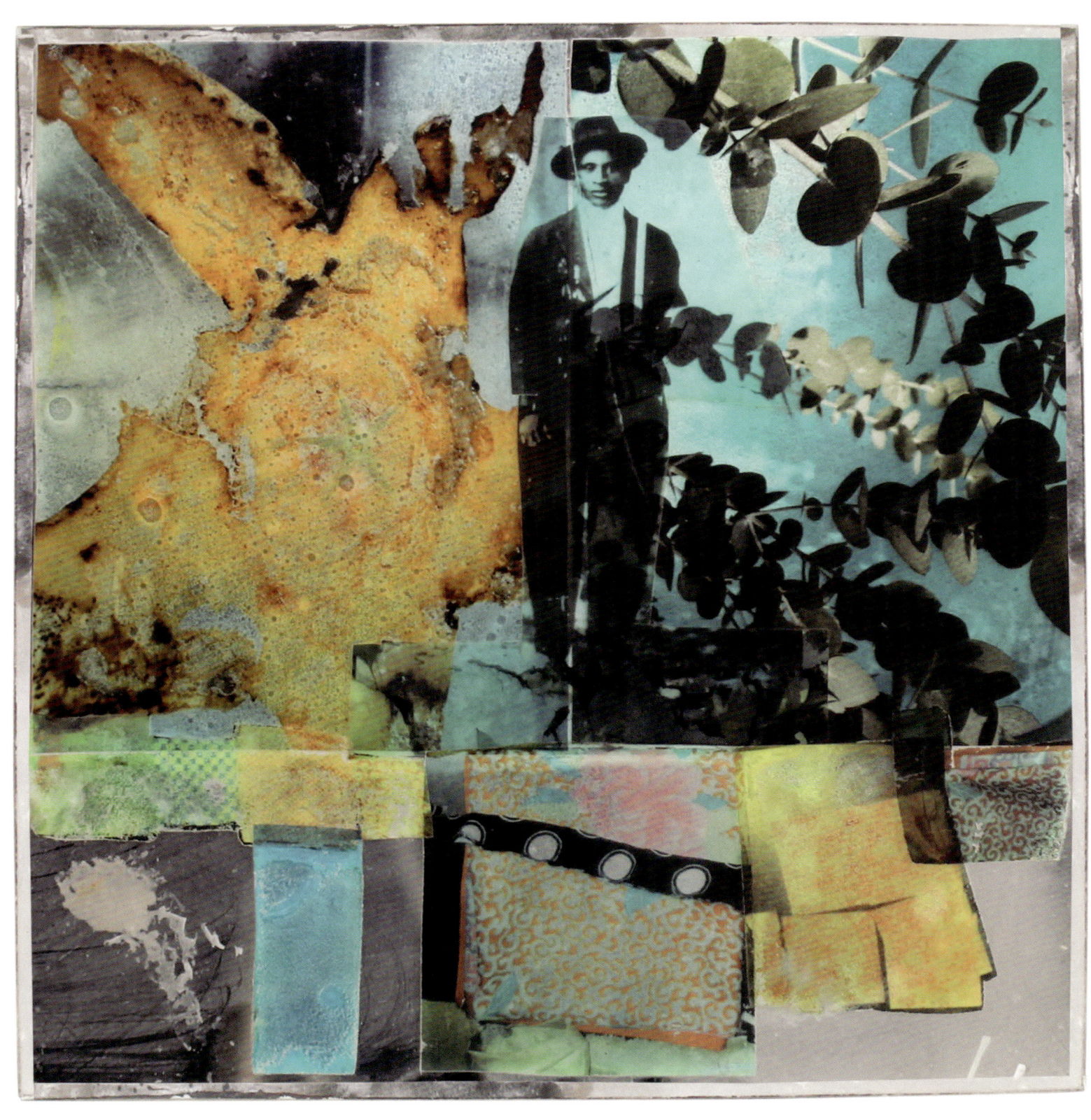

Blue Amédé (Mirrored Tile #1)
16 x 16 inches
Photo Collage Mounted on Mirror
2013

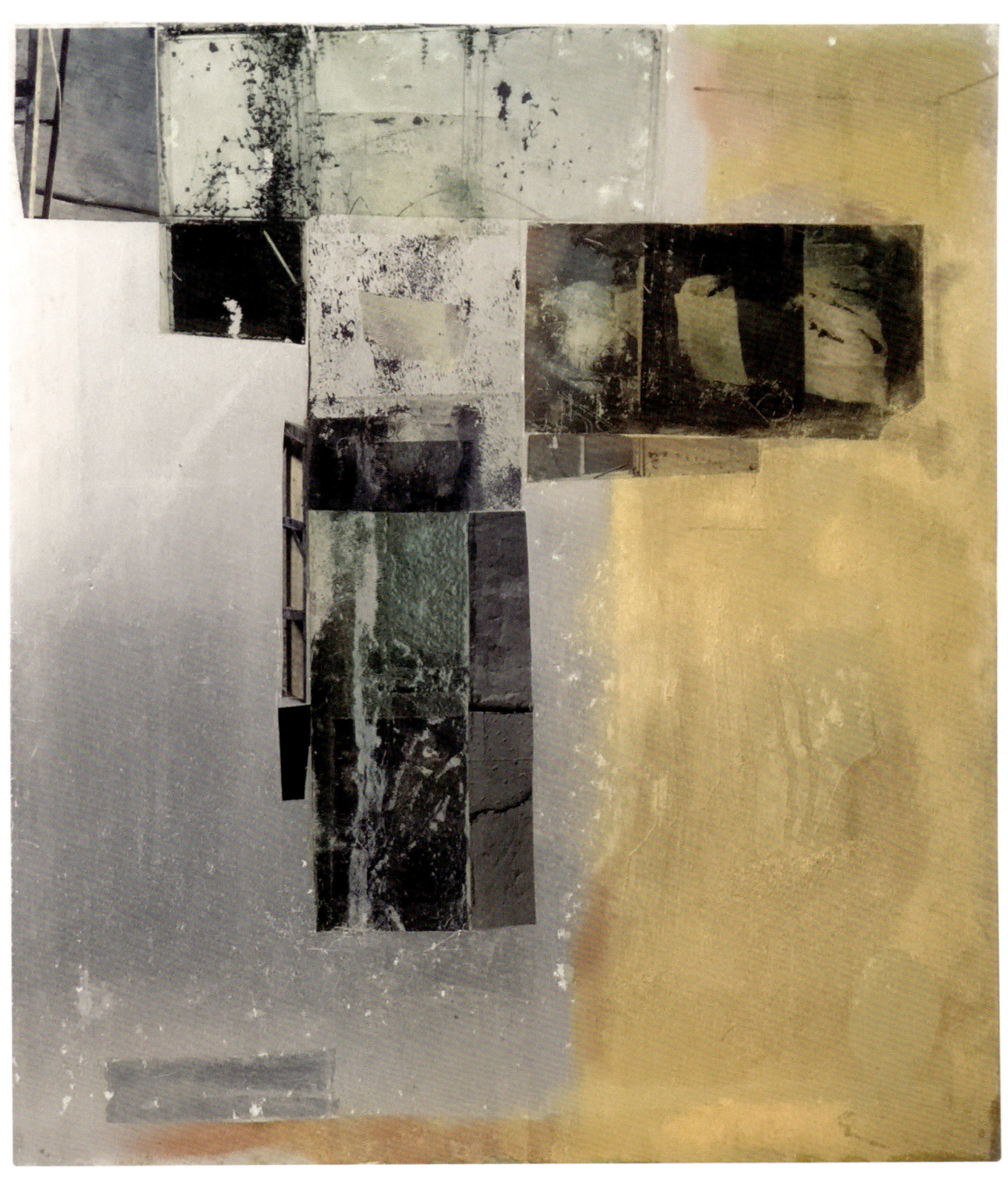

The Doorway to the Pathway
22 ¾ x 19 ½ inches
Mixed Media on Aluminum
2015

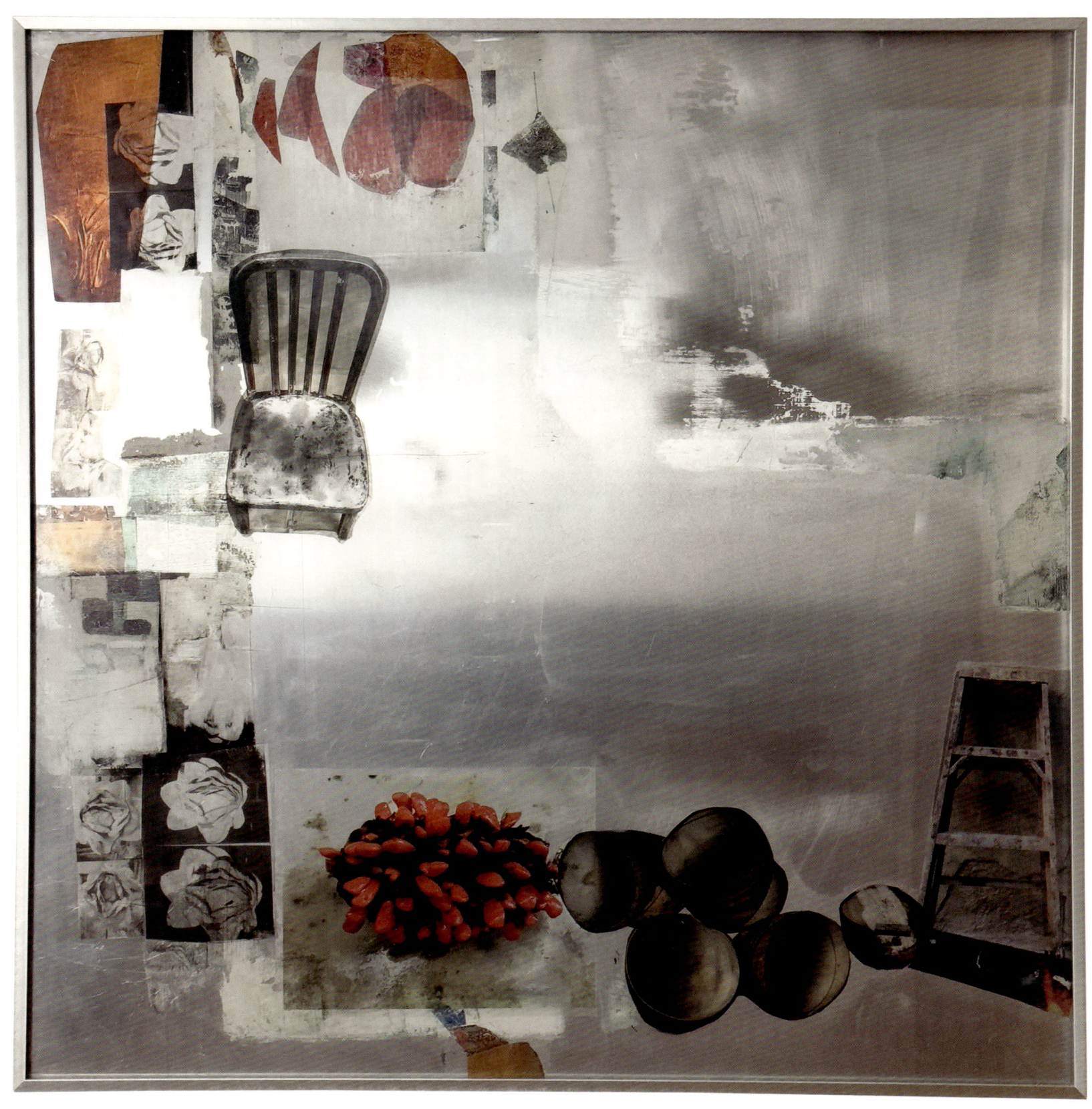

Chapo's Room
36 x 36 inches
Mixed Media on Aluminum
2015

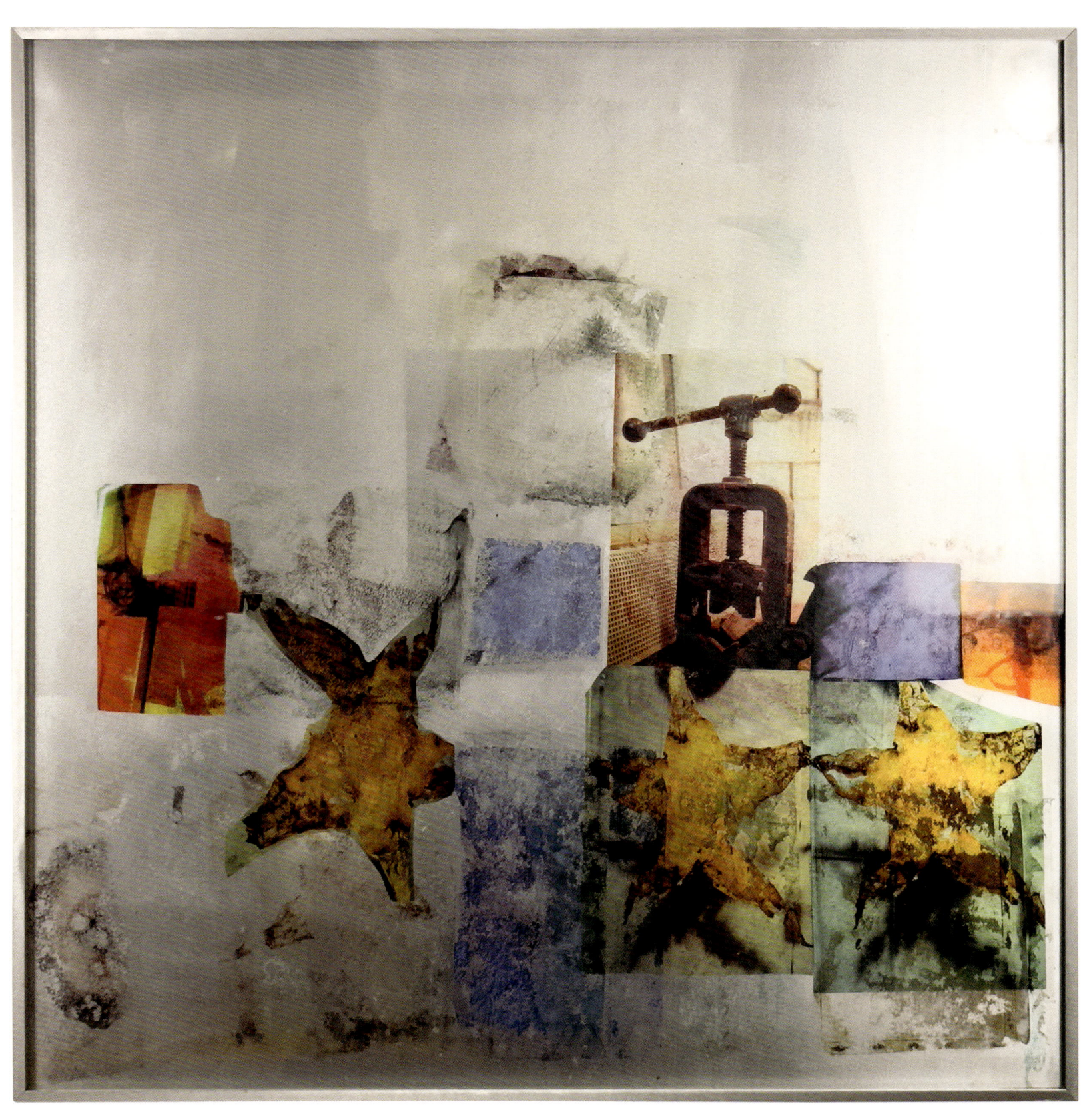

Amédé Triptych (Left Panel)
36 x 36 inches
Mixed Media on Aluminum
2015

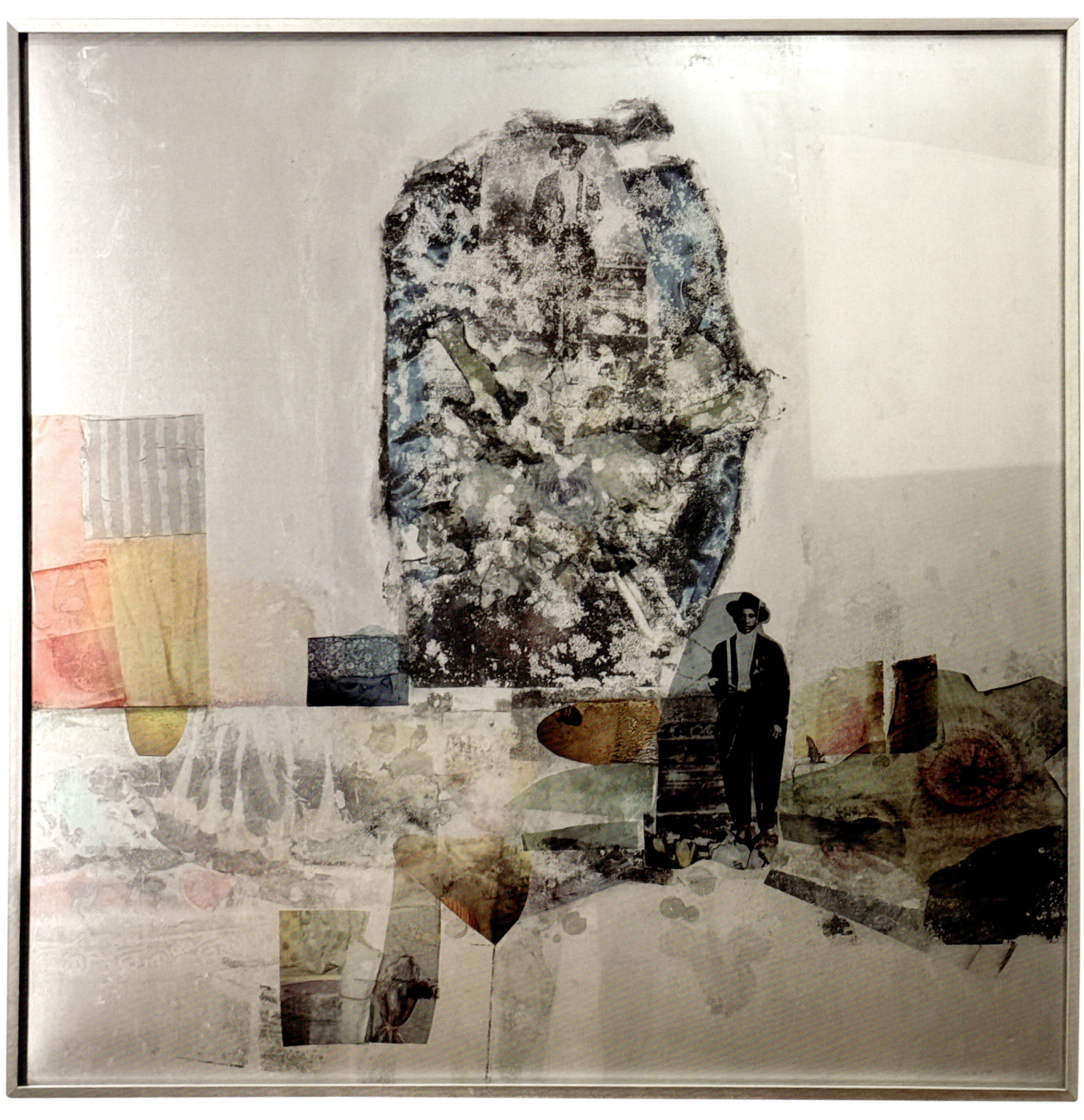

Amédé Triptych (Center Panel)
36 x 36 inches
Mixed Media on Aluminum
2015

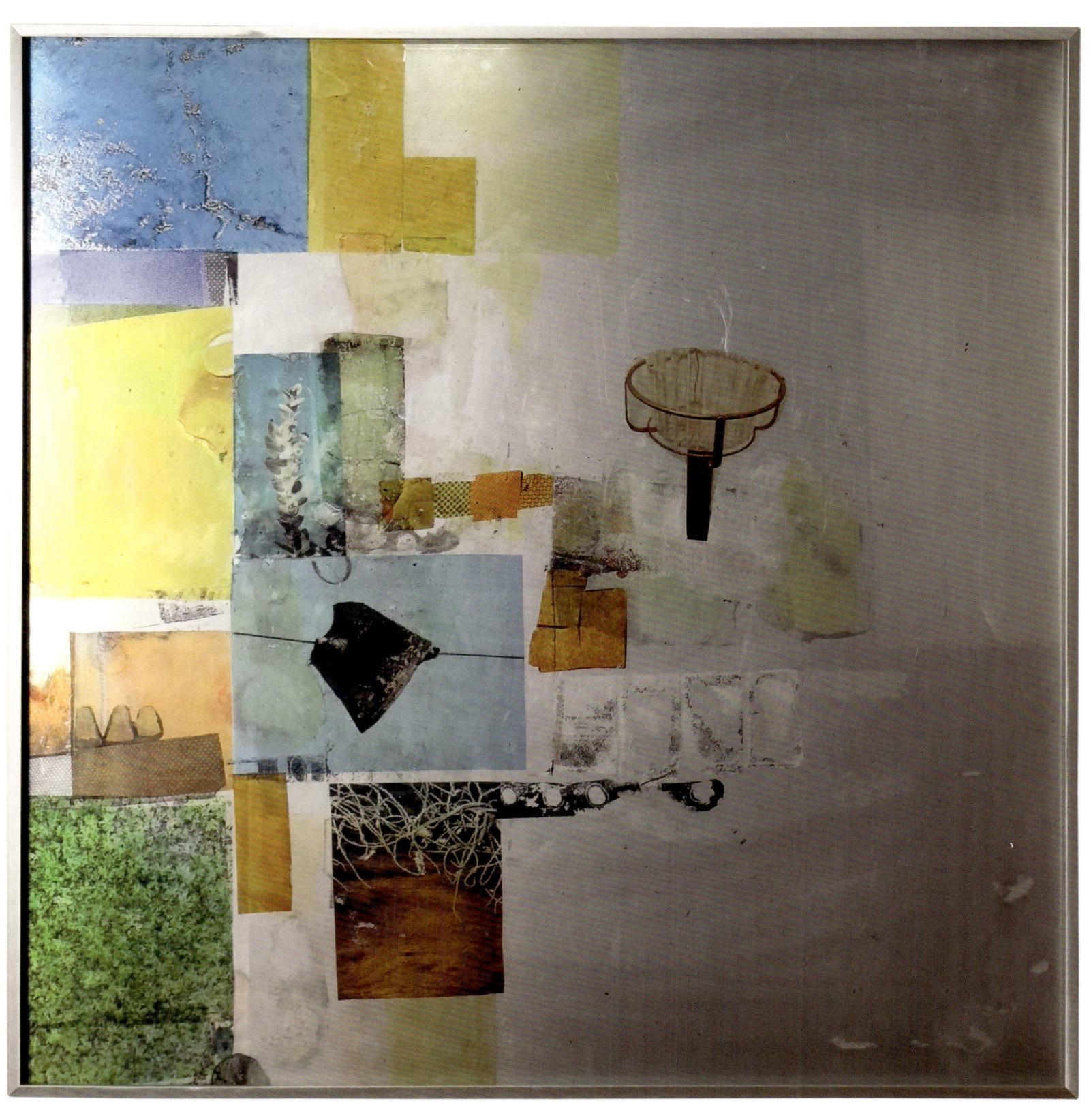

Amédé Triptych (Right Panel)
36 x 36 inches
Mixed Media on Aluminum
2015

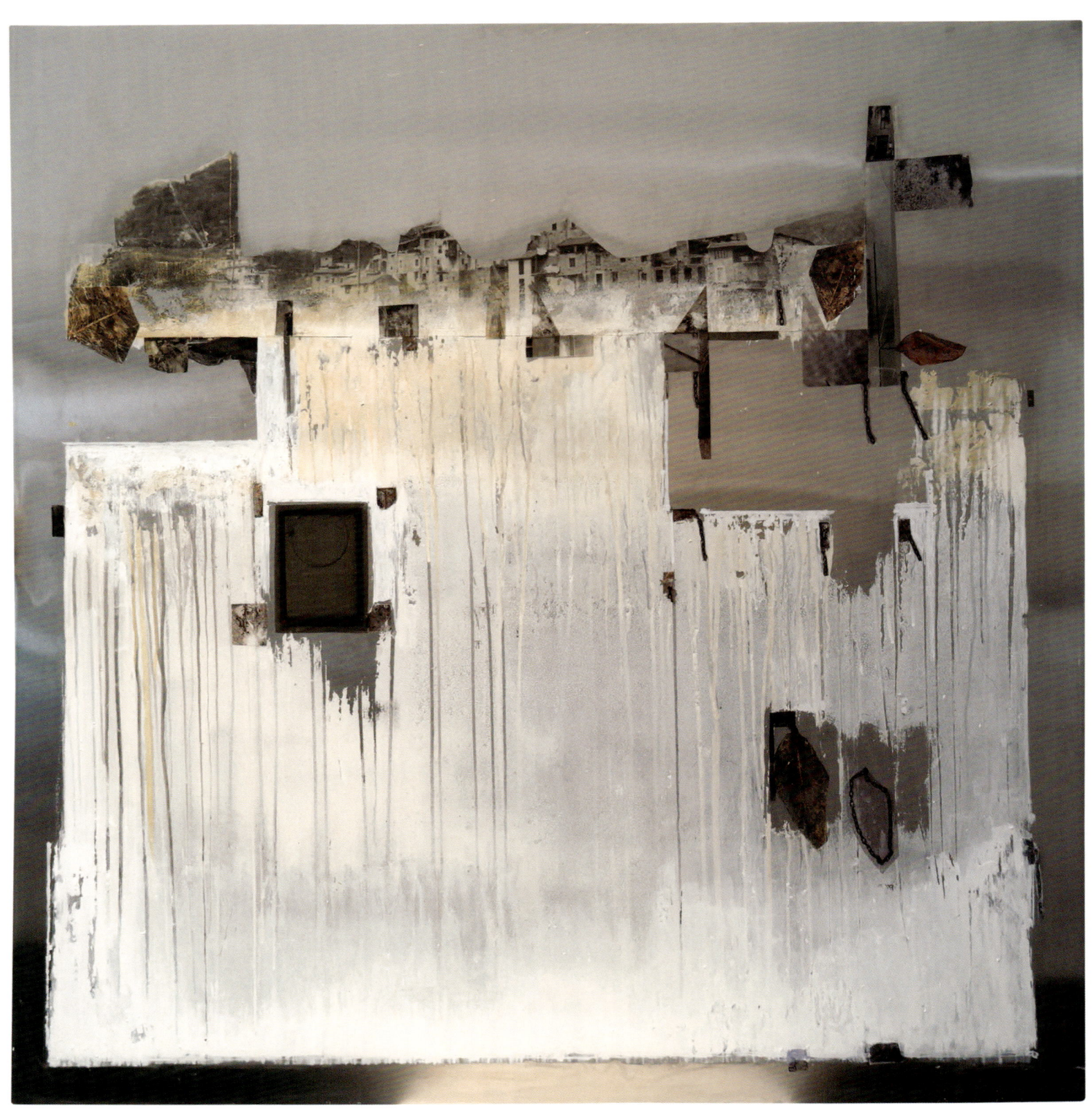

The Event in The Village
48 x 48 inches
Mixed Media on Steel
2024

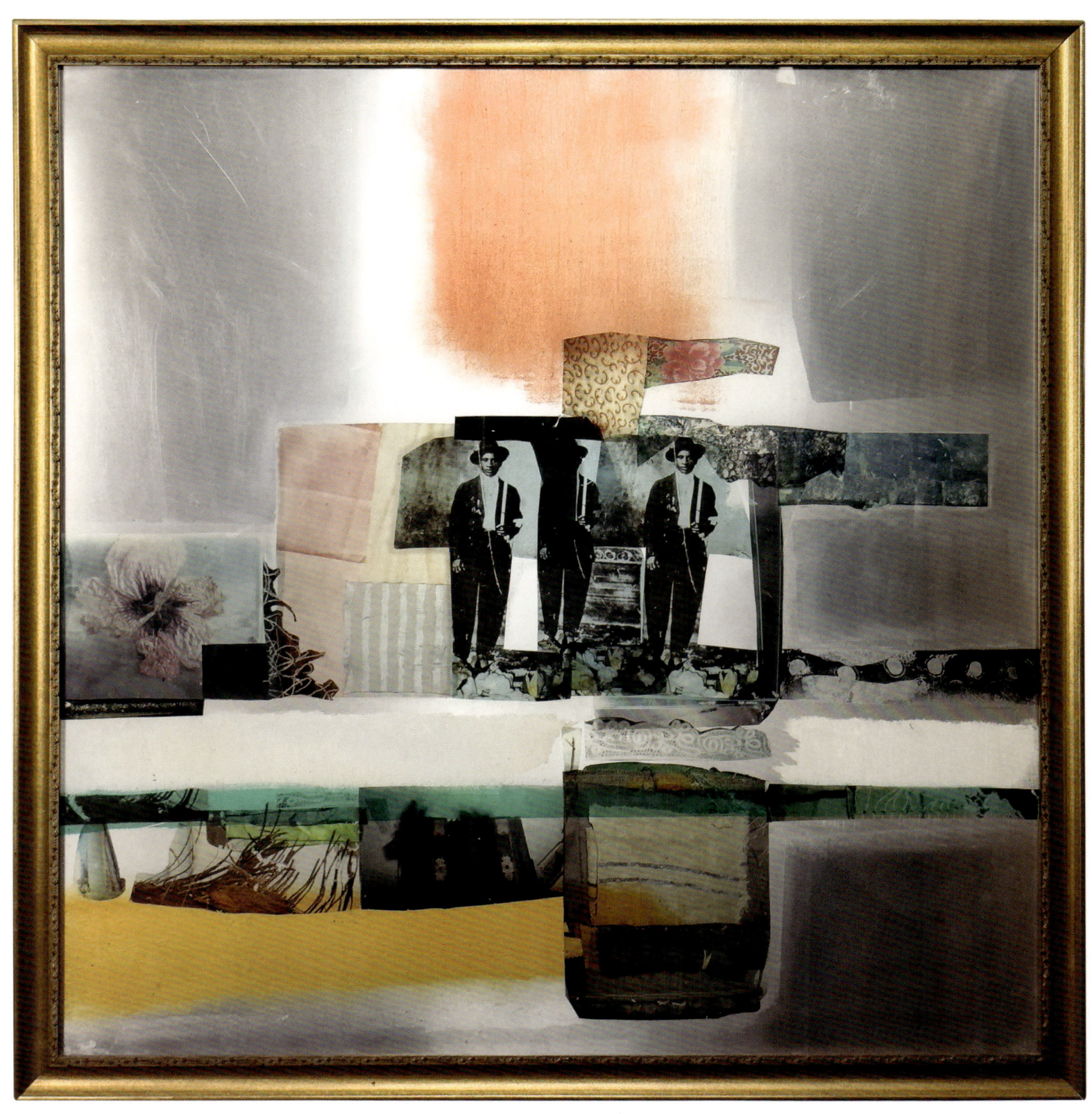

La Vie de Musicien
36 x 36 inches
Mixed Media on Aluminum
2015

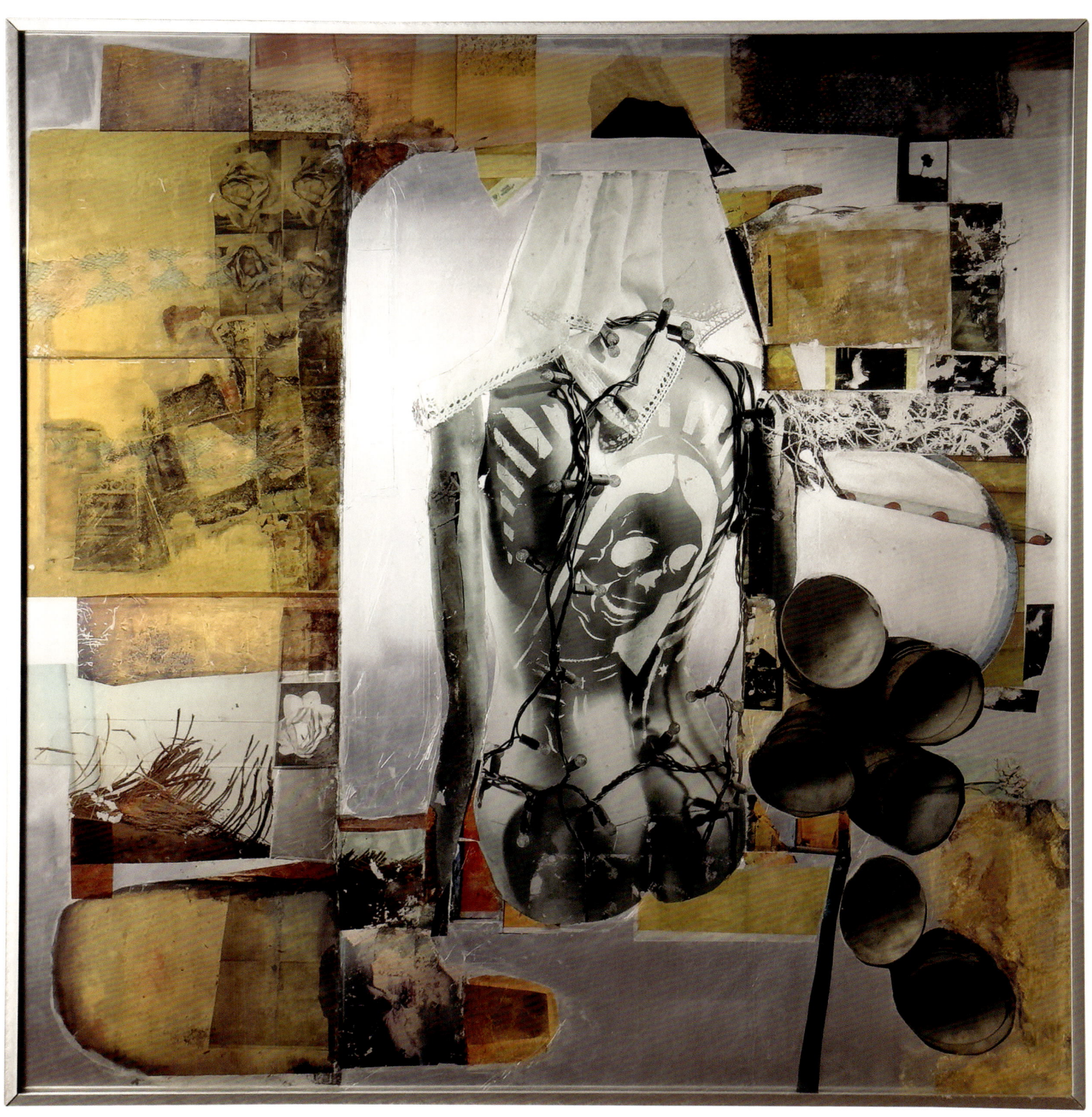

Santissima
36 x 36 inches
Mixed Media on Aluminum
2016

154

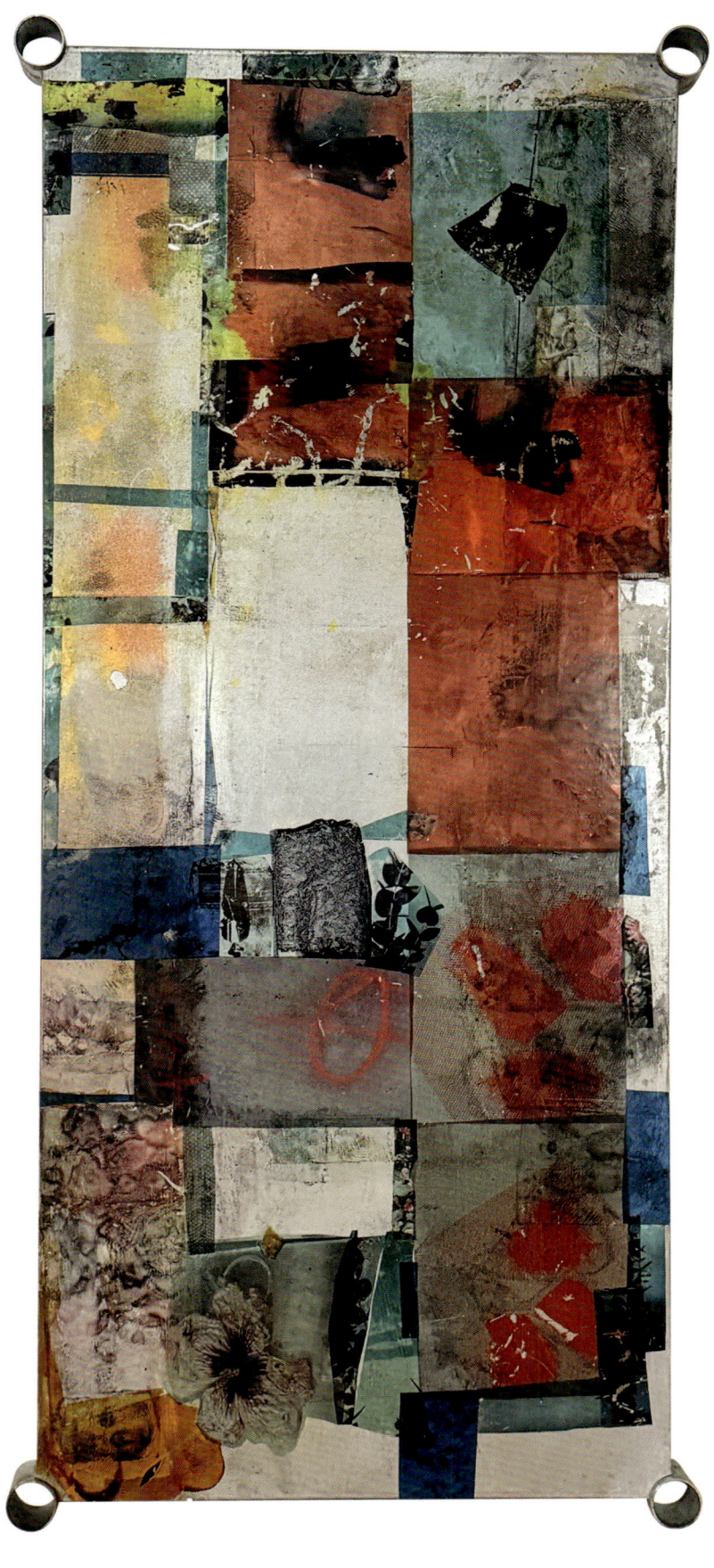

Prayer Runner
56 x 26 x 2 ½ inches
Mixed Media on Steel
2015

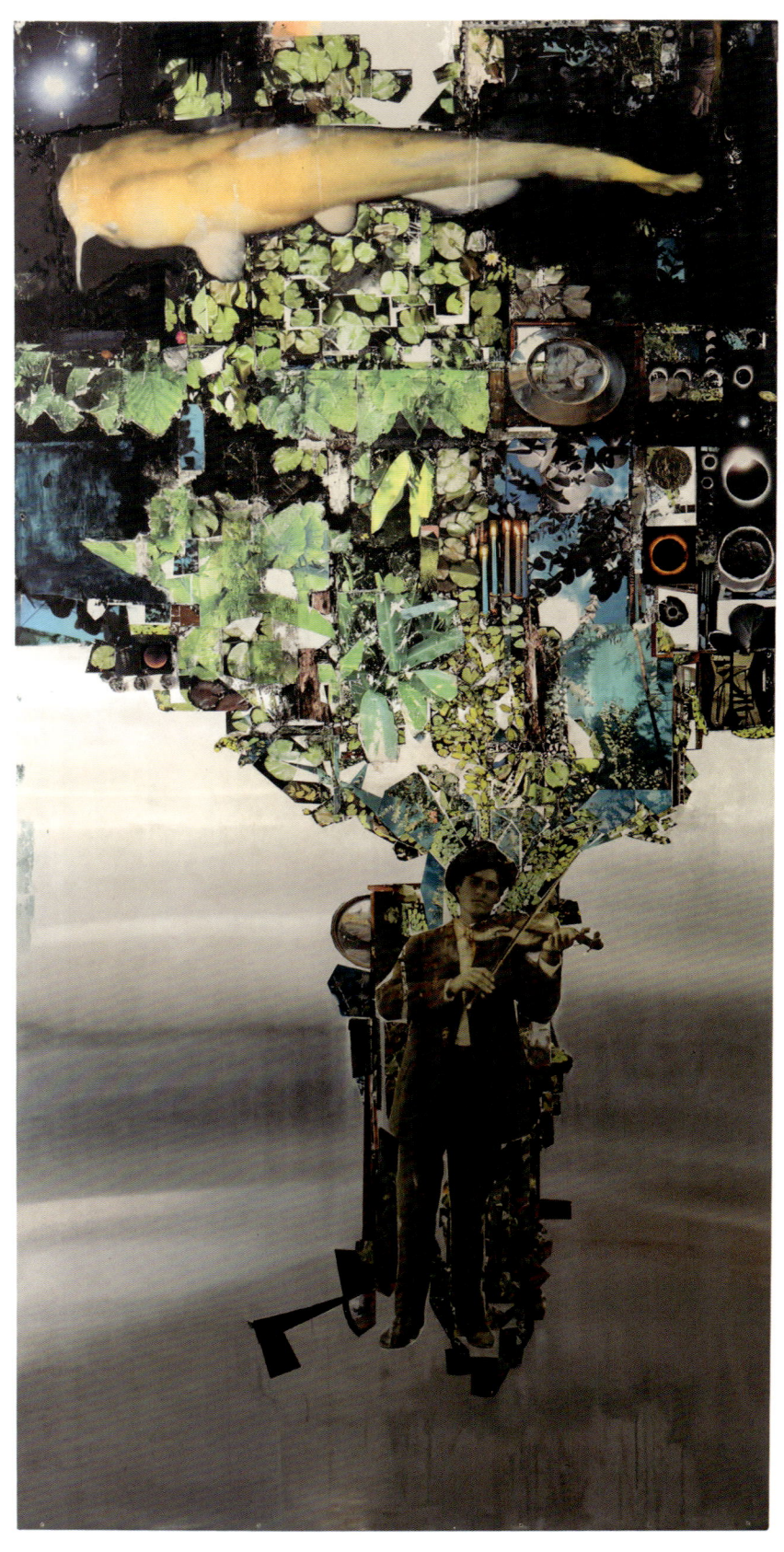

Till's Reel
8ft x 4ft
Mixed Media on Steel
2022

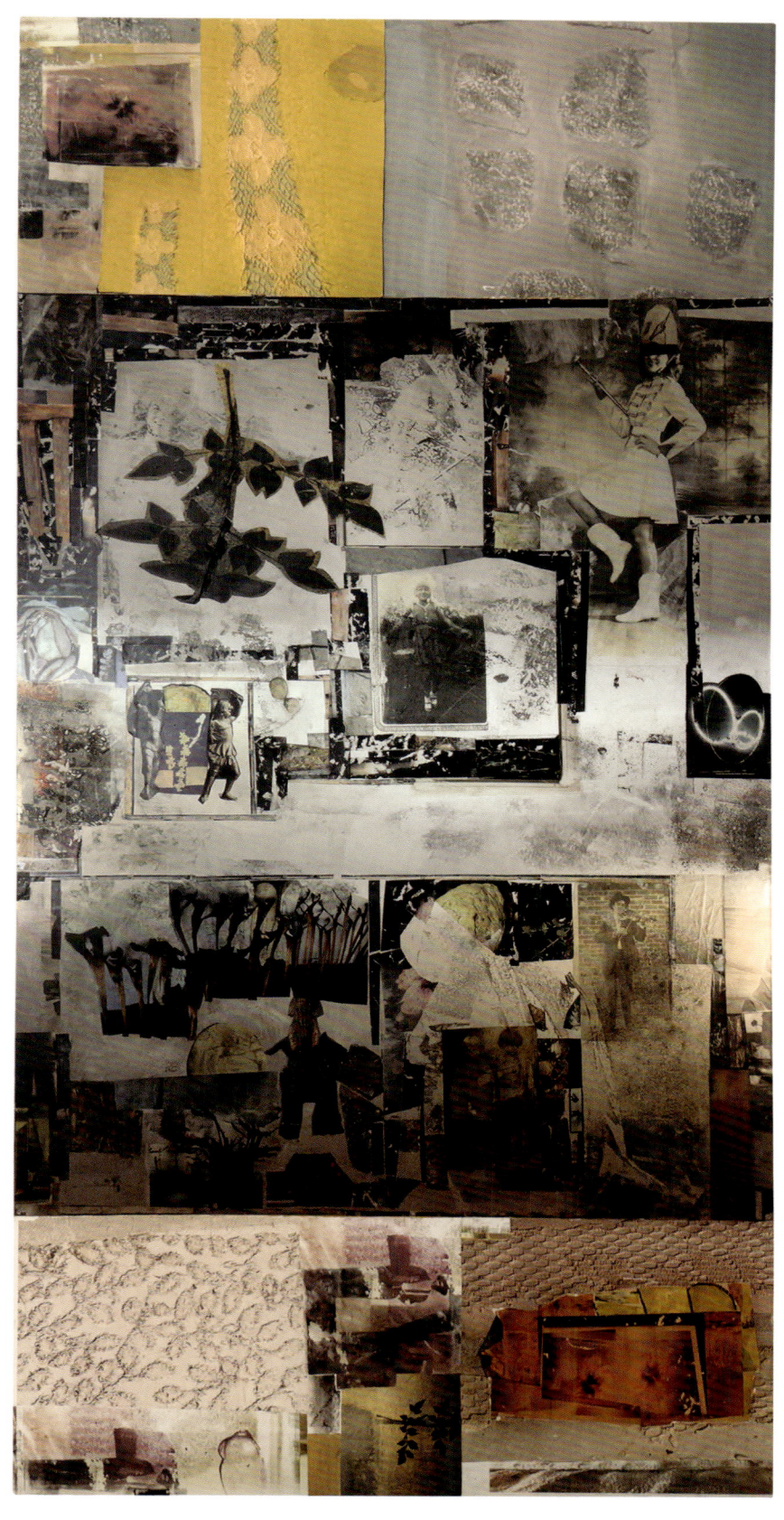

The Homestead
8ft x 4ft
Mixed Media on Steel
2020

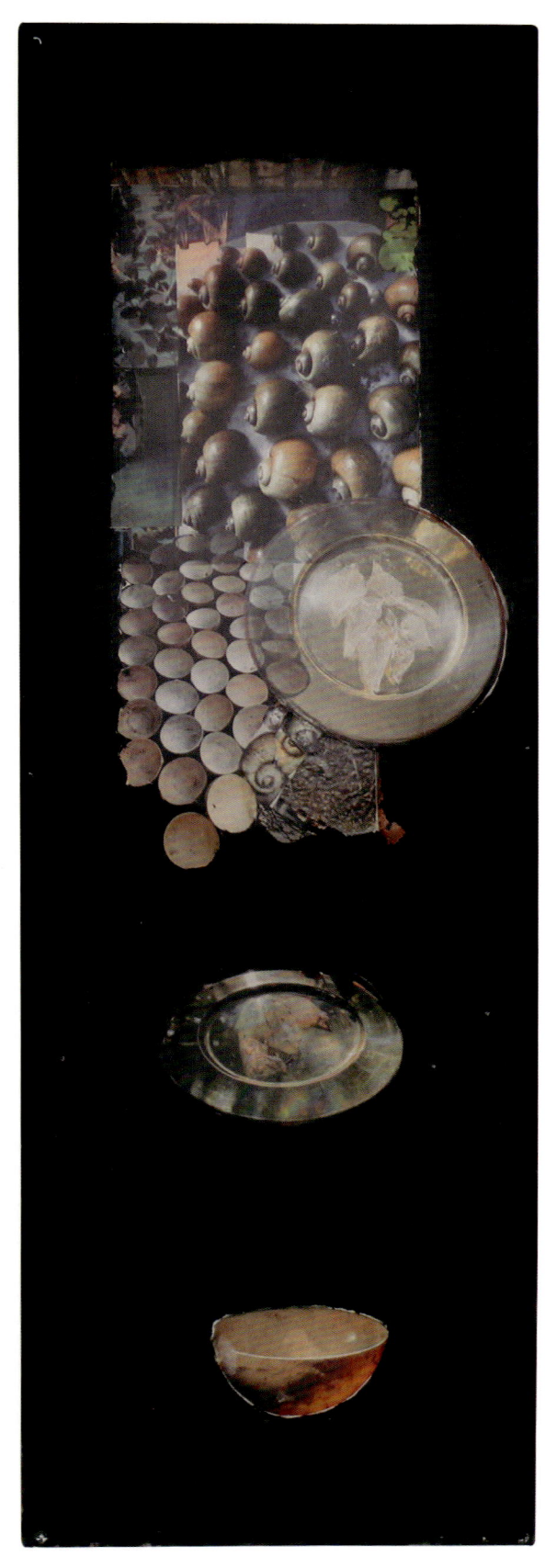

Black Board
48 x 16 inches
Mixed Medium on Steel
2016

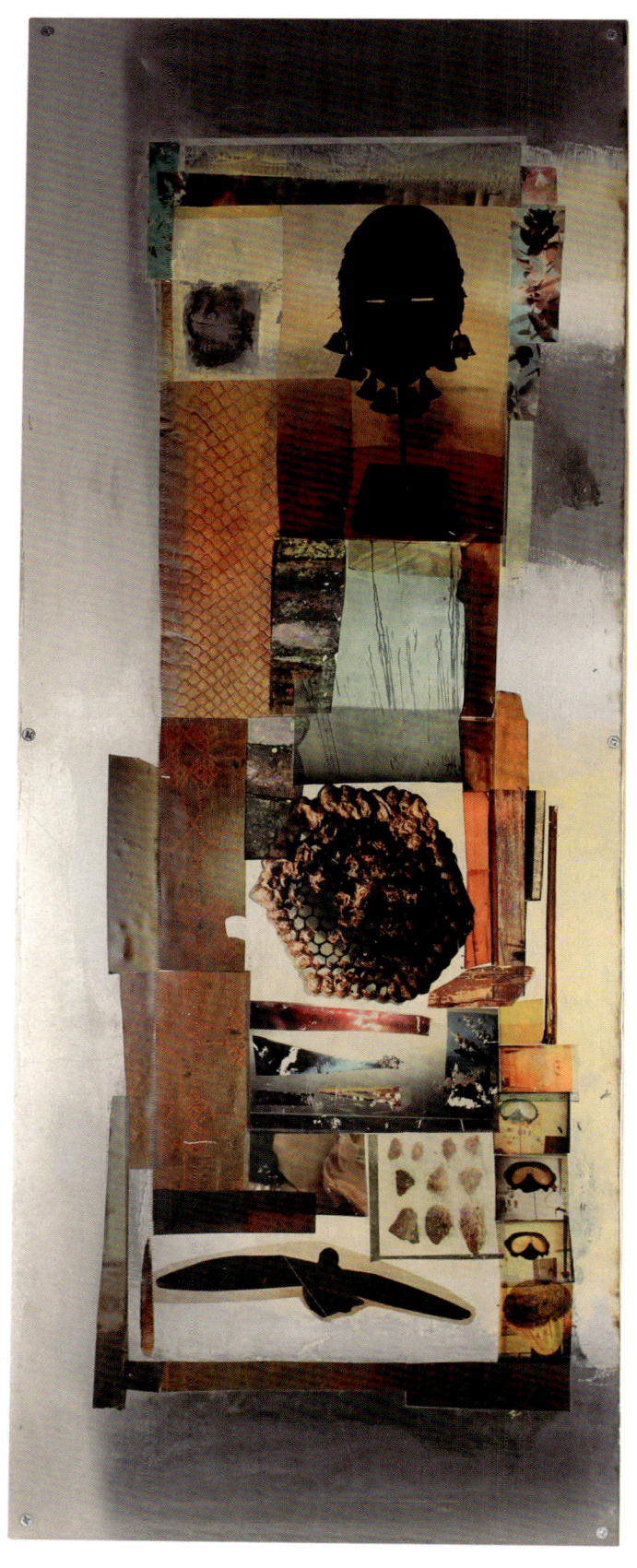

Recliner
48 x 19 inches
Mixed Media on Steel
2016

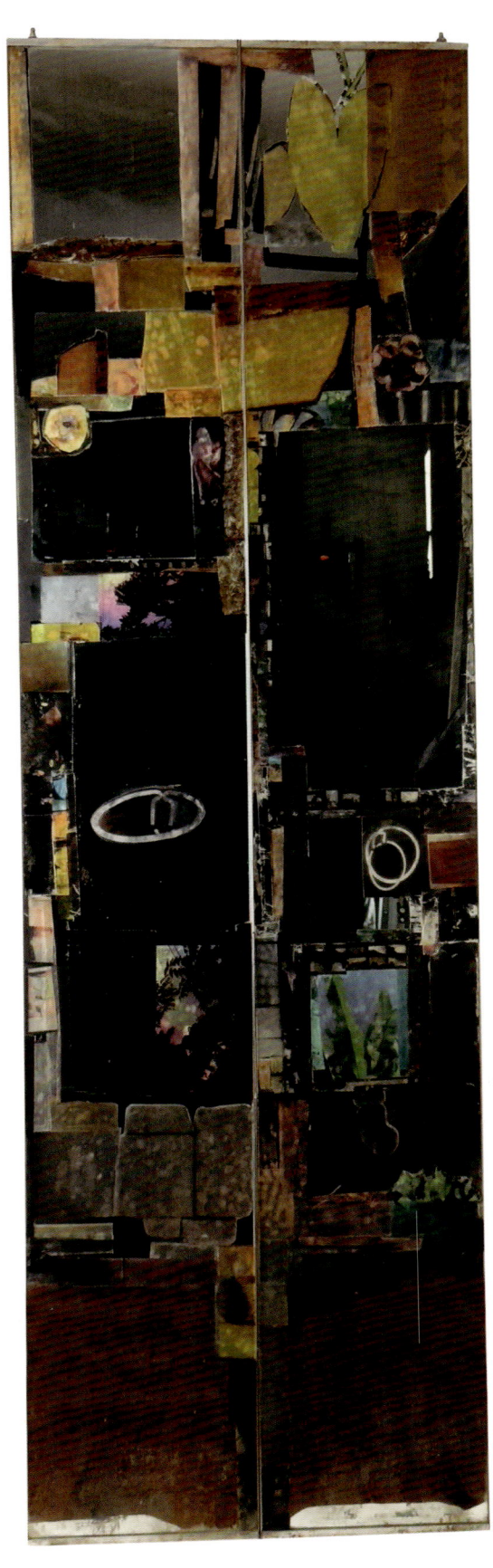

Folding Mirror (Left Panel)
78 x 23 ½ inches
Transparencies on Mirrored Glass
2015

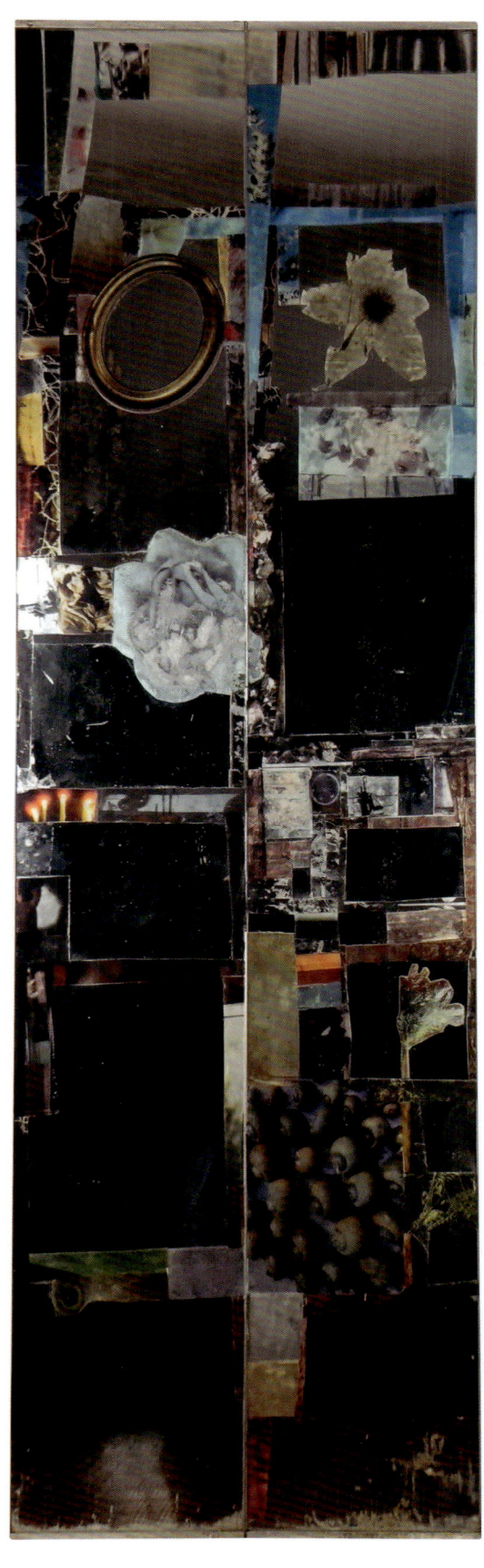

Folding Mirror (Right Panel)
78 x 23 ½ inches
Transparencies on Mirrored Glass
2015

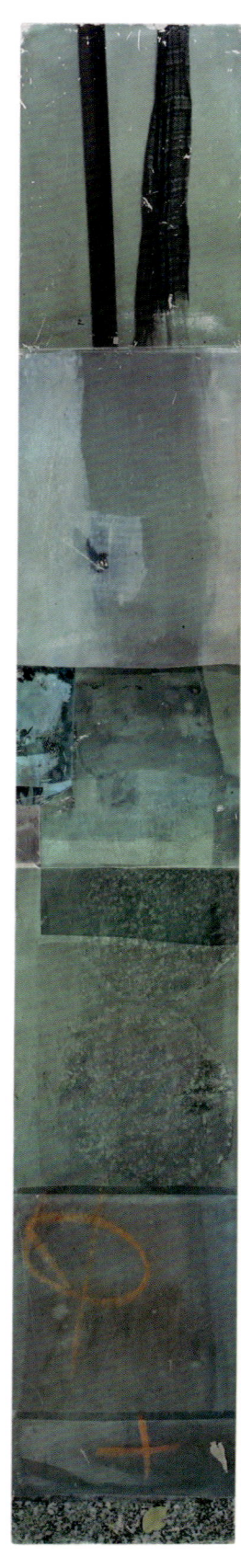

Tower 1
50 x 7 ½ inches
Mixed Media on Steel
2009

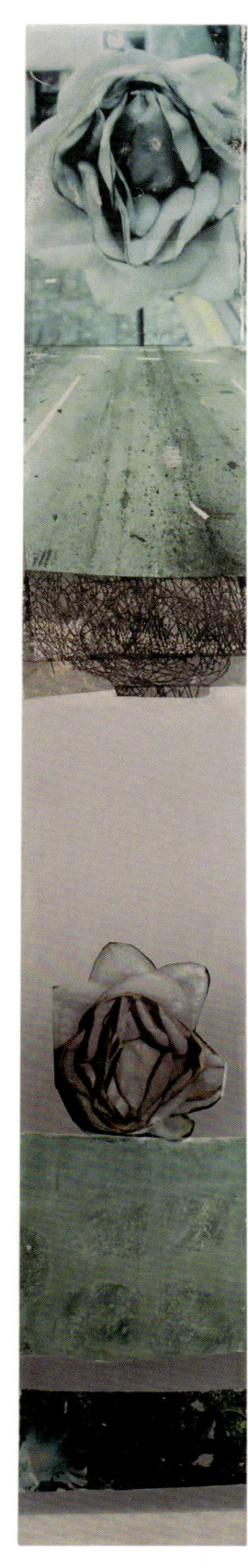

Tower 2
50 x 7 ½ inches
Mixed Media on Steel
2009

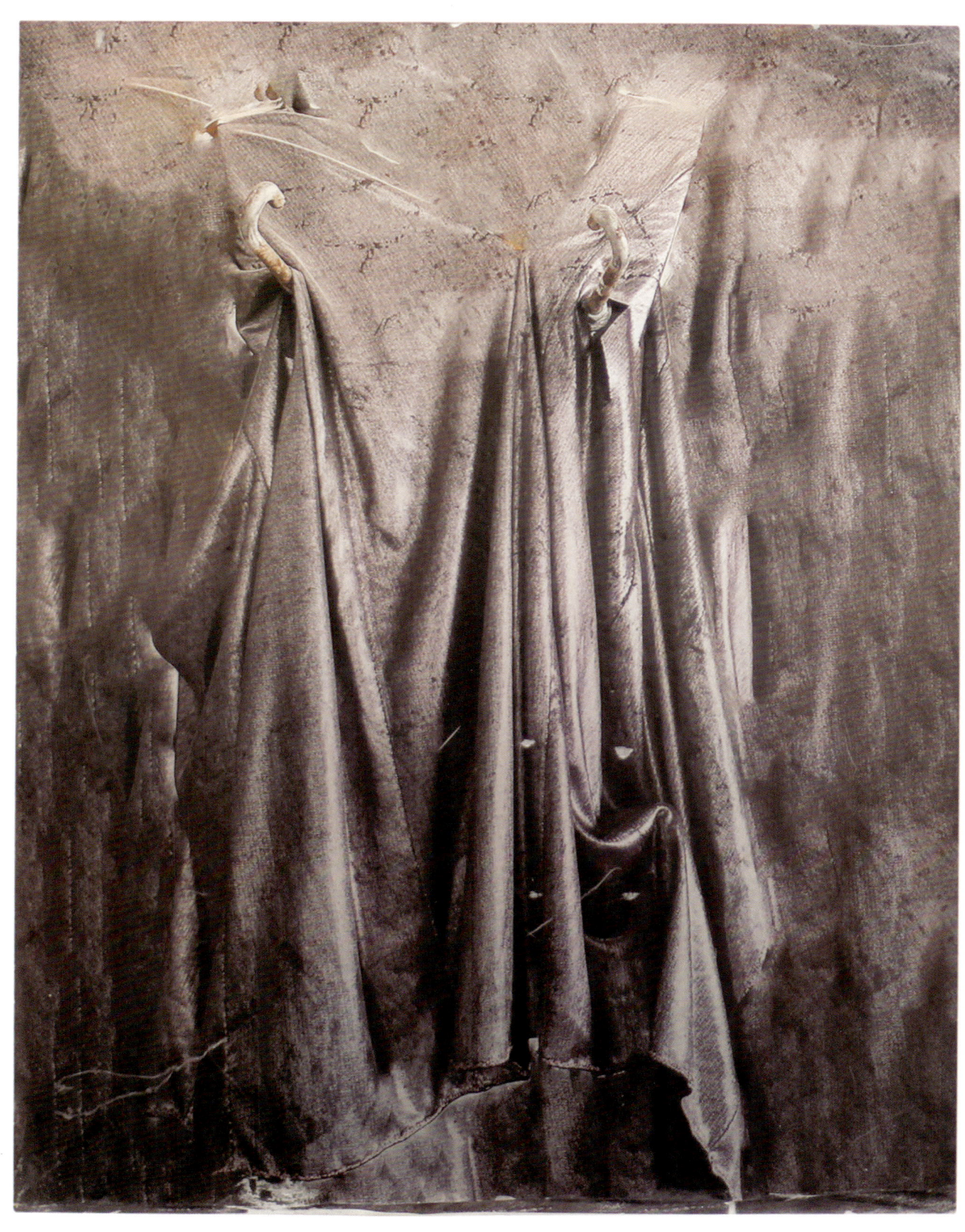

Drum Harness
27 x 22 inches
Archival Color Print
2020

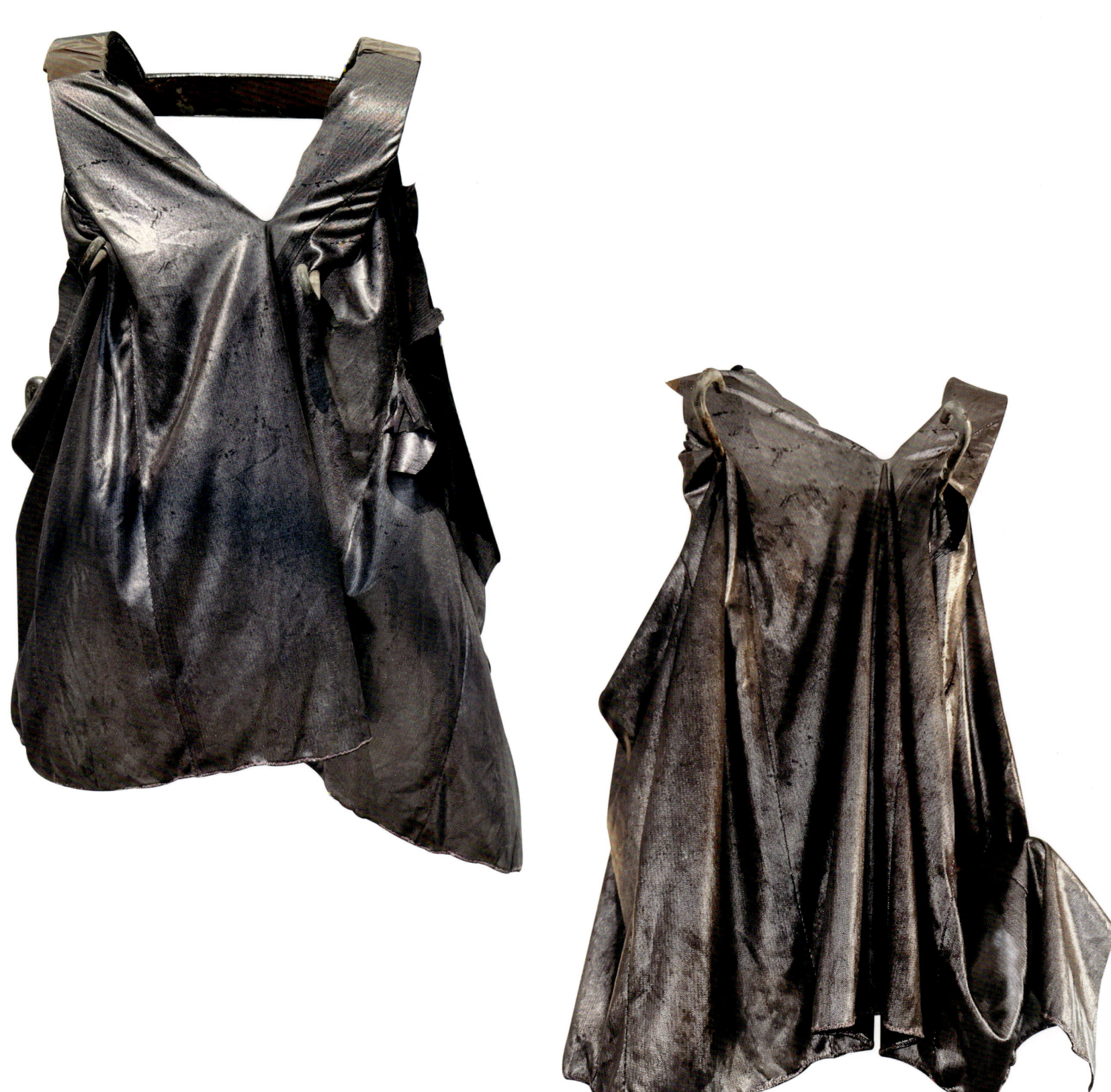

Drum Harness
10 x 17 x 12 inches
Fabric, Metal and Fiberglass
2020

" Somebody told me artist in the 3rd grade... If you tell someone will ask you: Oh, can

once everyone is an
So what happens?
you're an artist, they
you draw a horsey?

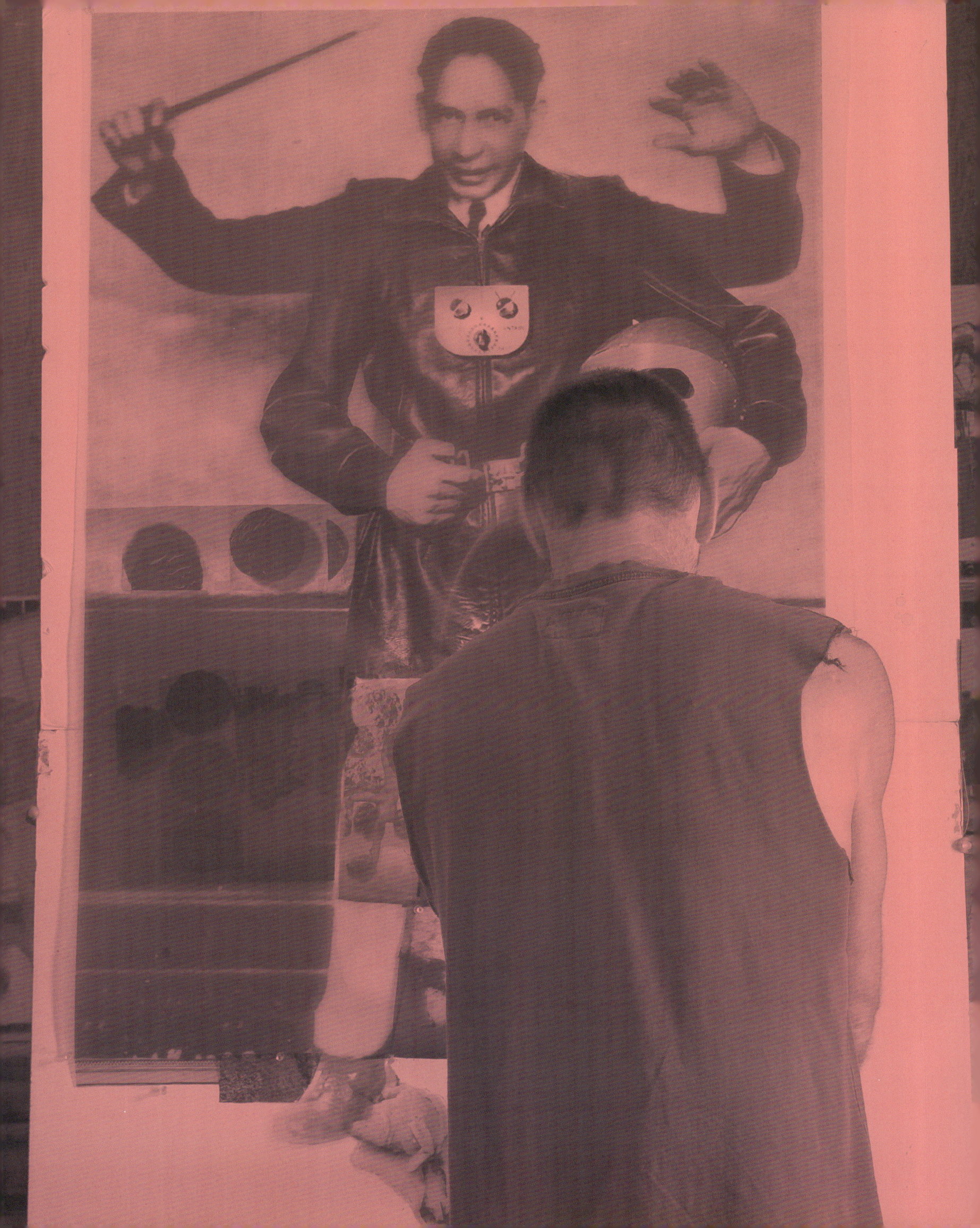

COLLAGE,
GLASS TILE, GLASS,
PLEXIGLASS &
LIGHTBOX

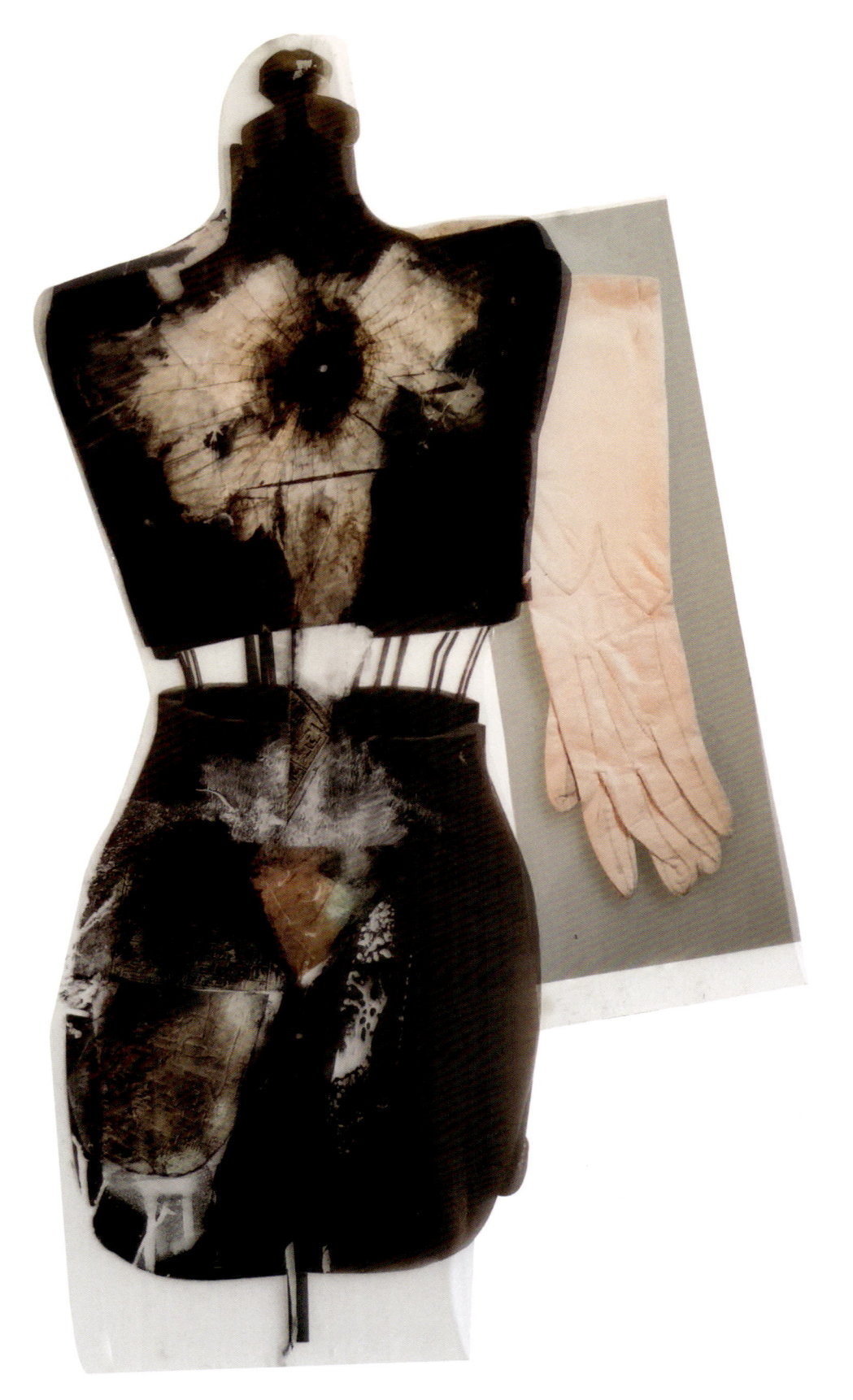

Relief 6
30 x 20 inches
Photo Transparency
2024

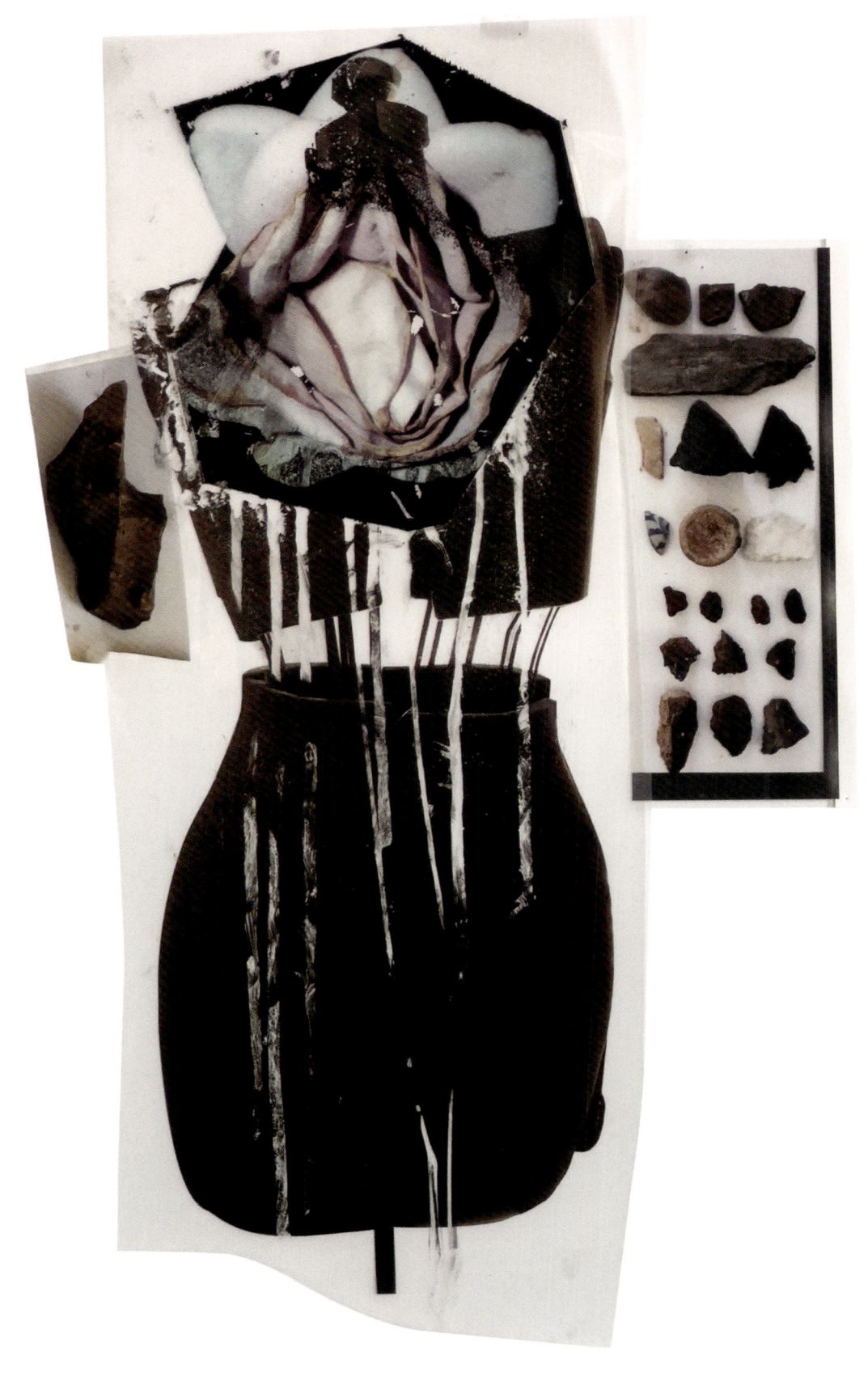

Relief 7
30 x 20 inches
Photo Transparency
2024

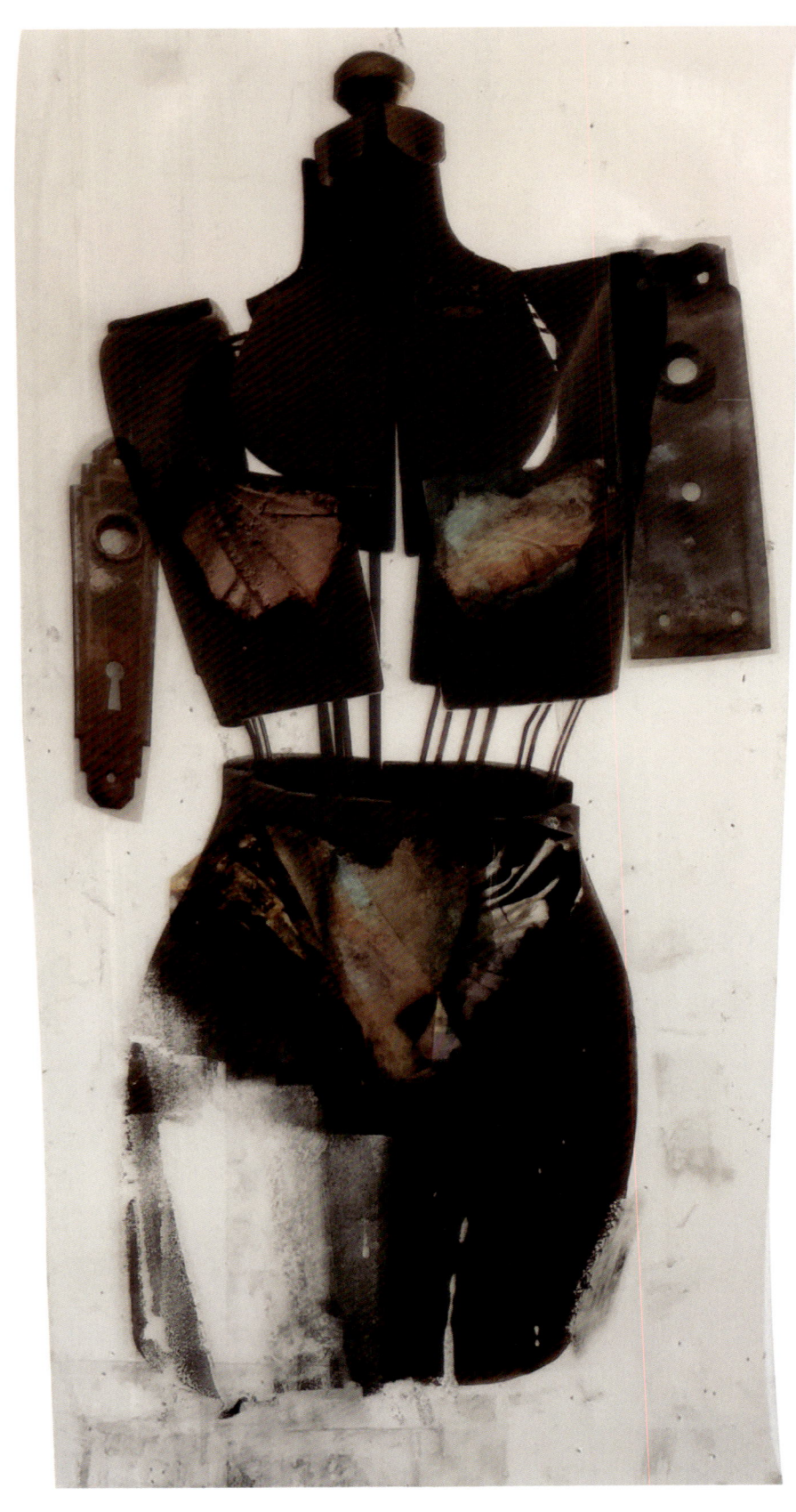

Relief 8
30 x 20 inches
Photo Transparency
2024

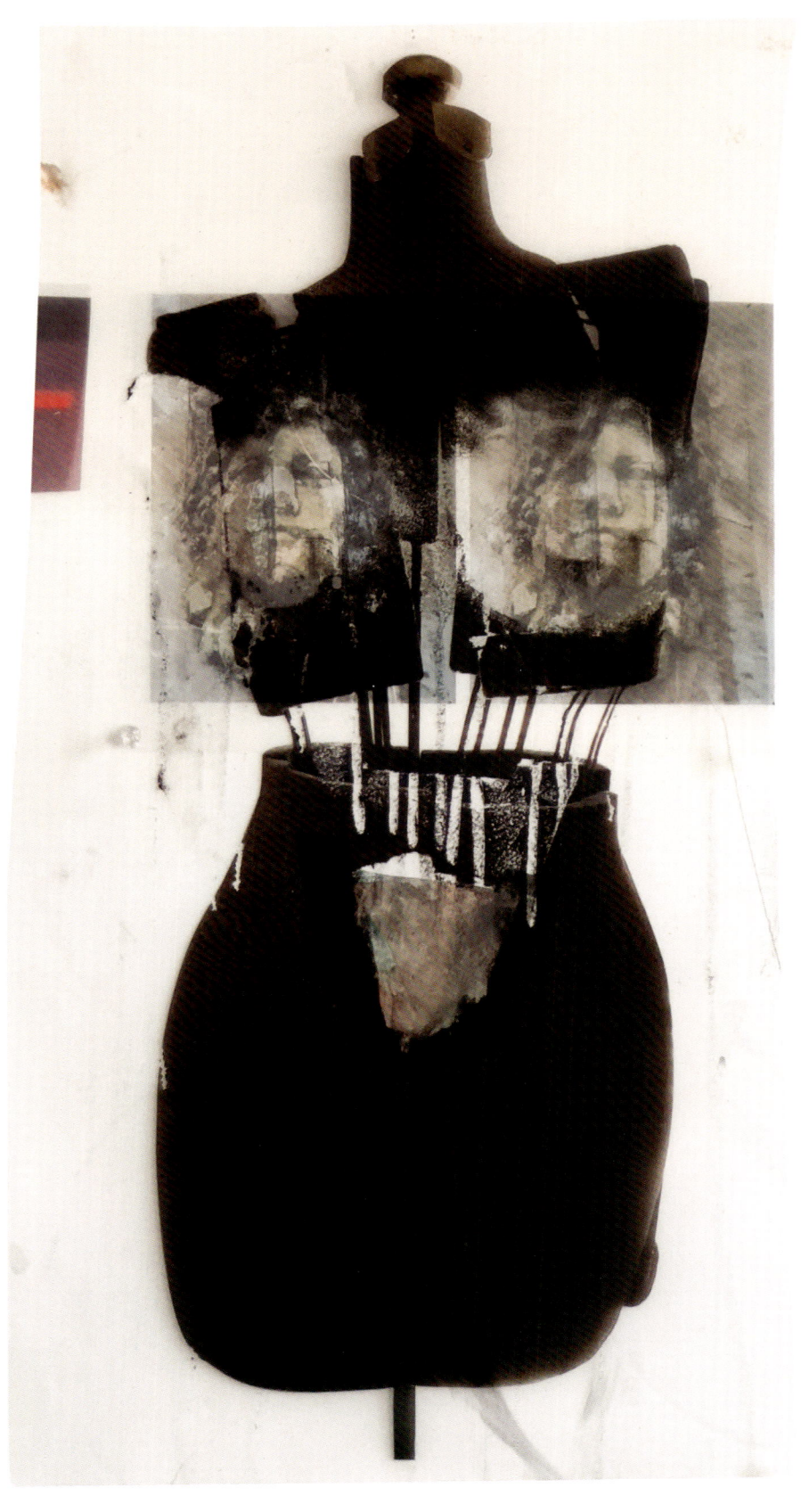

Relief 9
30 x 20 inches
Photo Transparency
2024

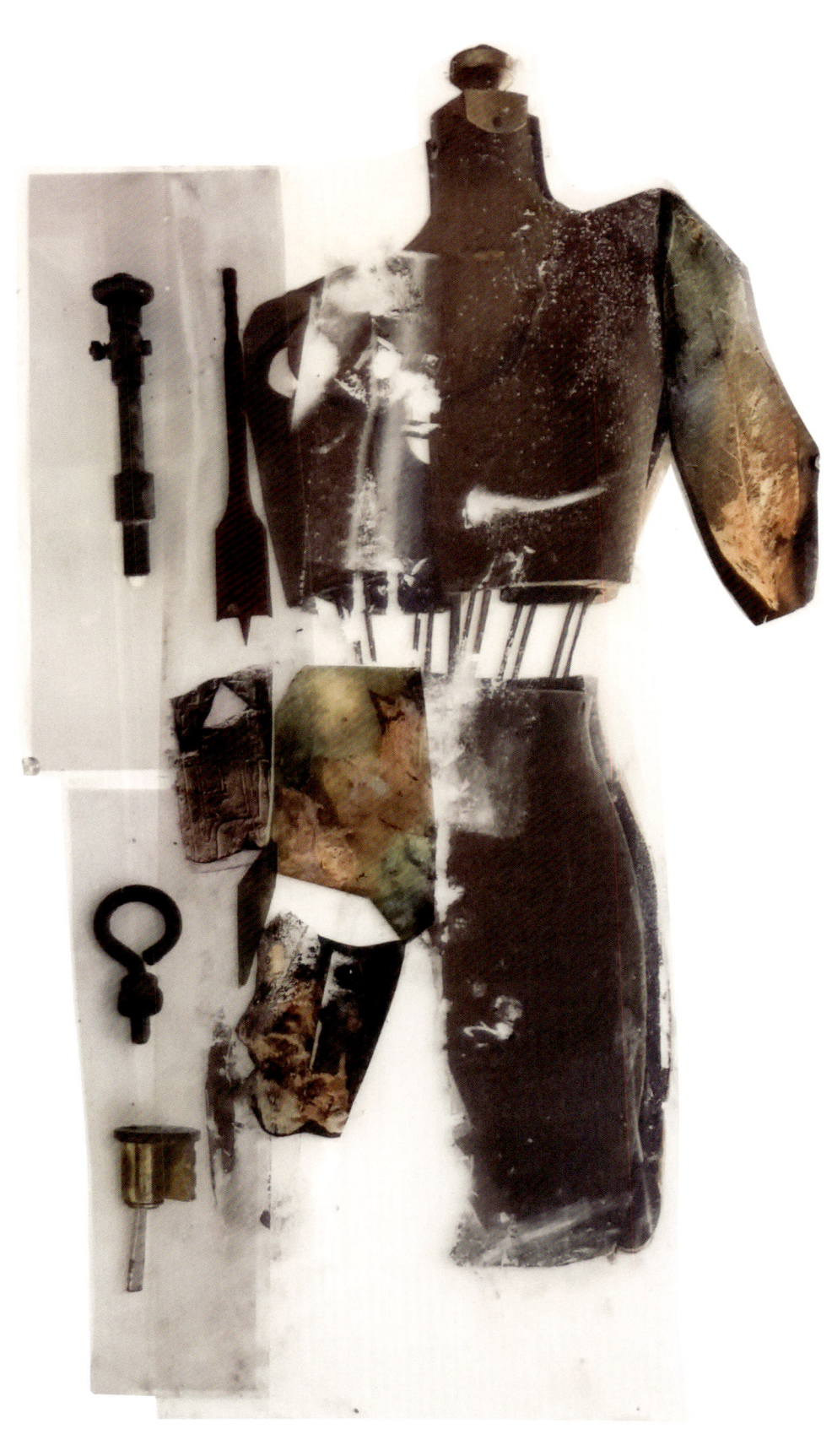

Relief 10
30 x 20 inches
Photo Transparency
2024

174

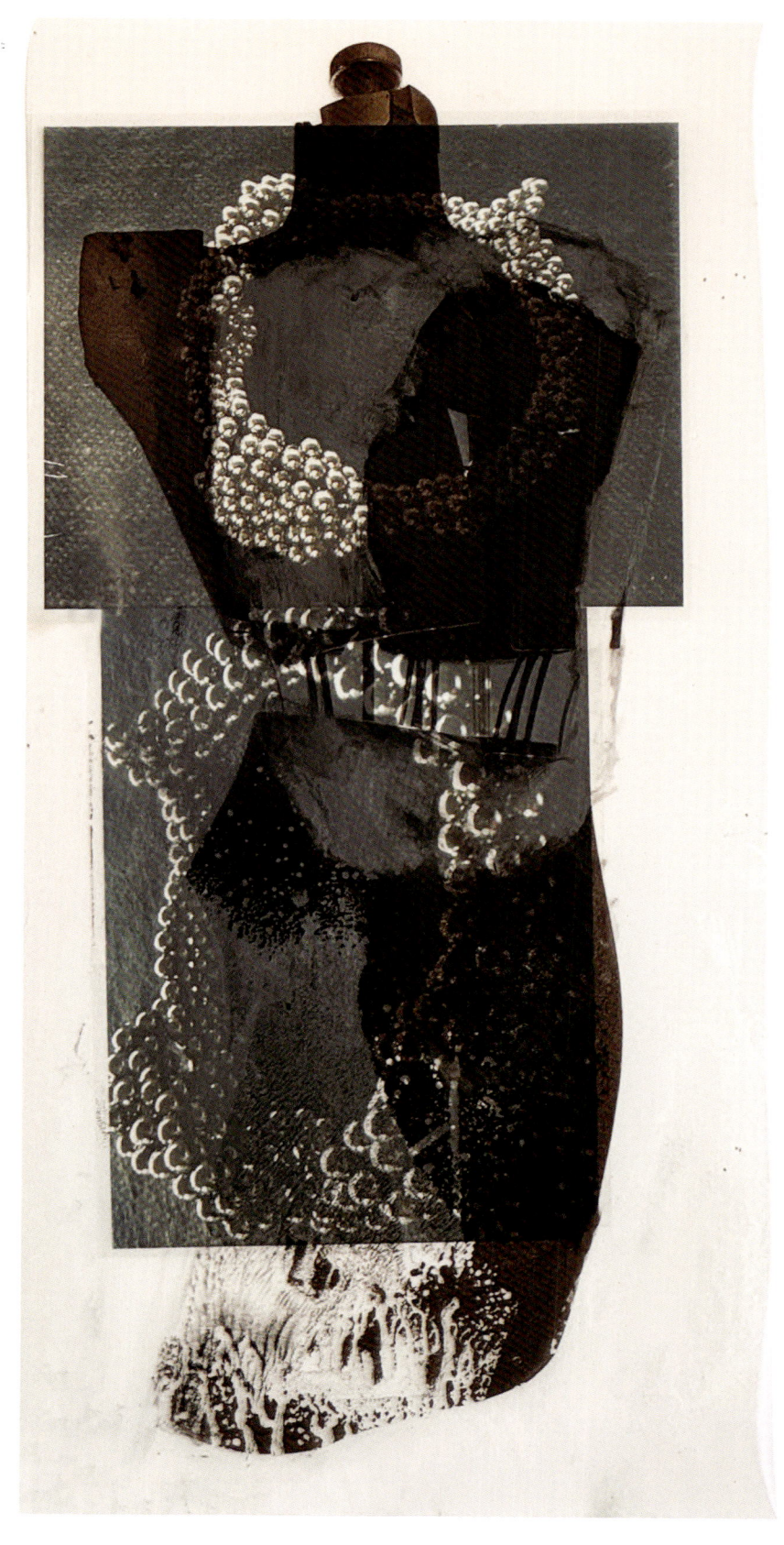

Relief 11
30 x 20 inches
Photo Transparency
2024

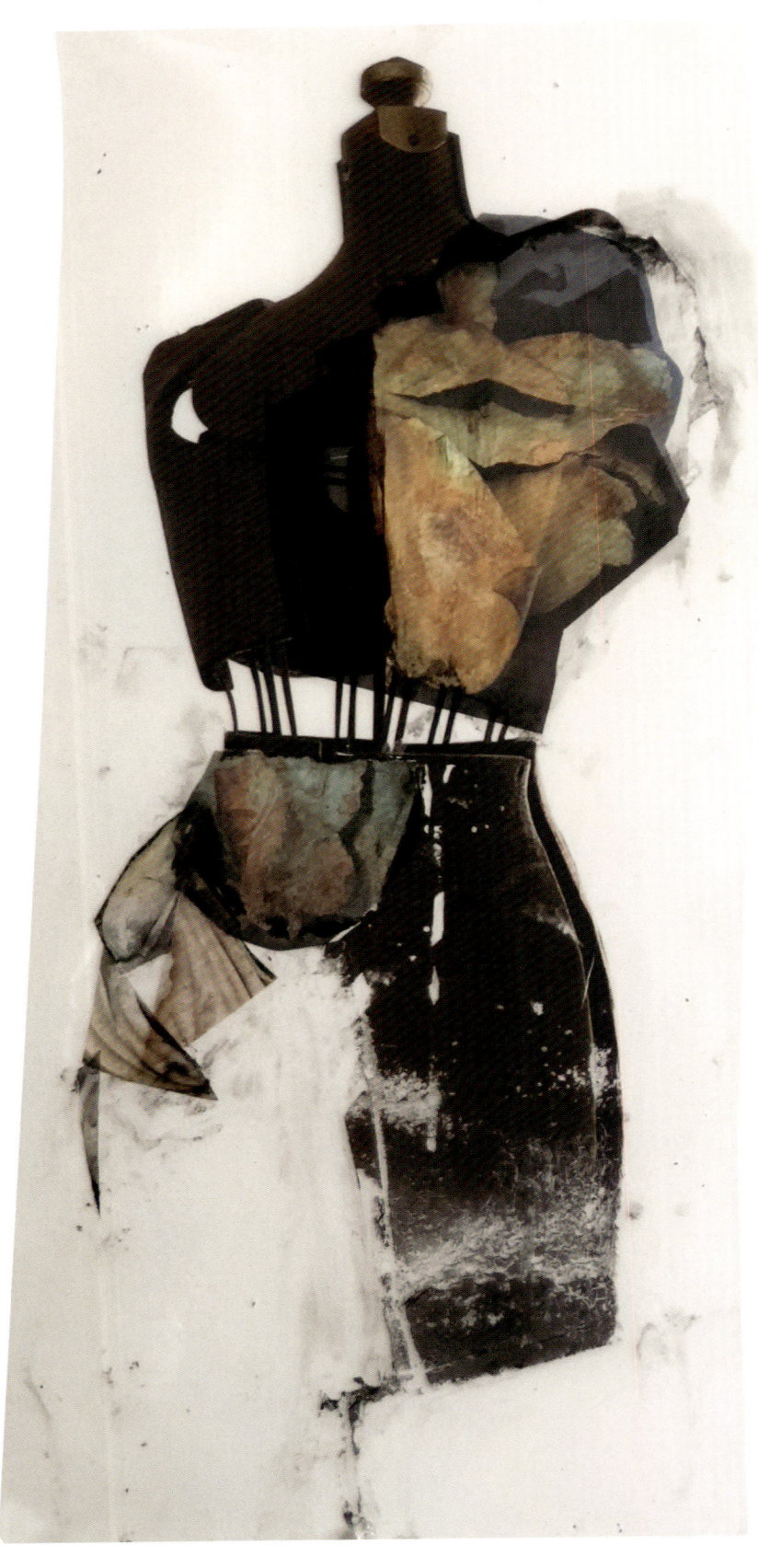

Relief 12
30 x 20 inches
Photo Transparency
2024

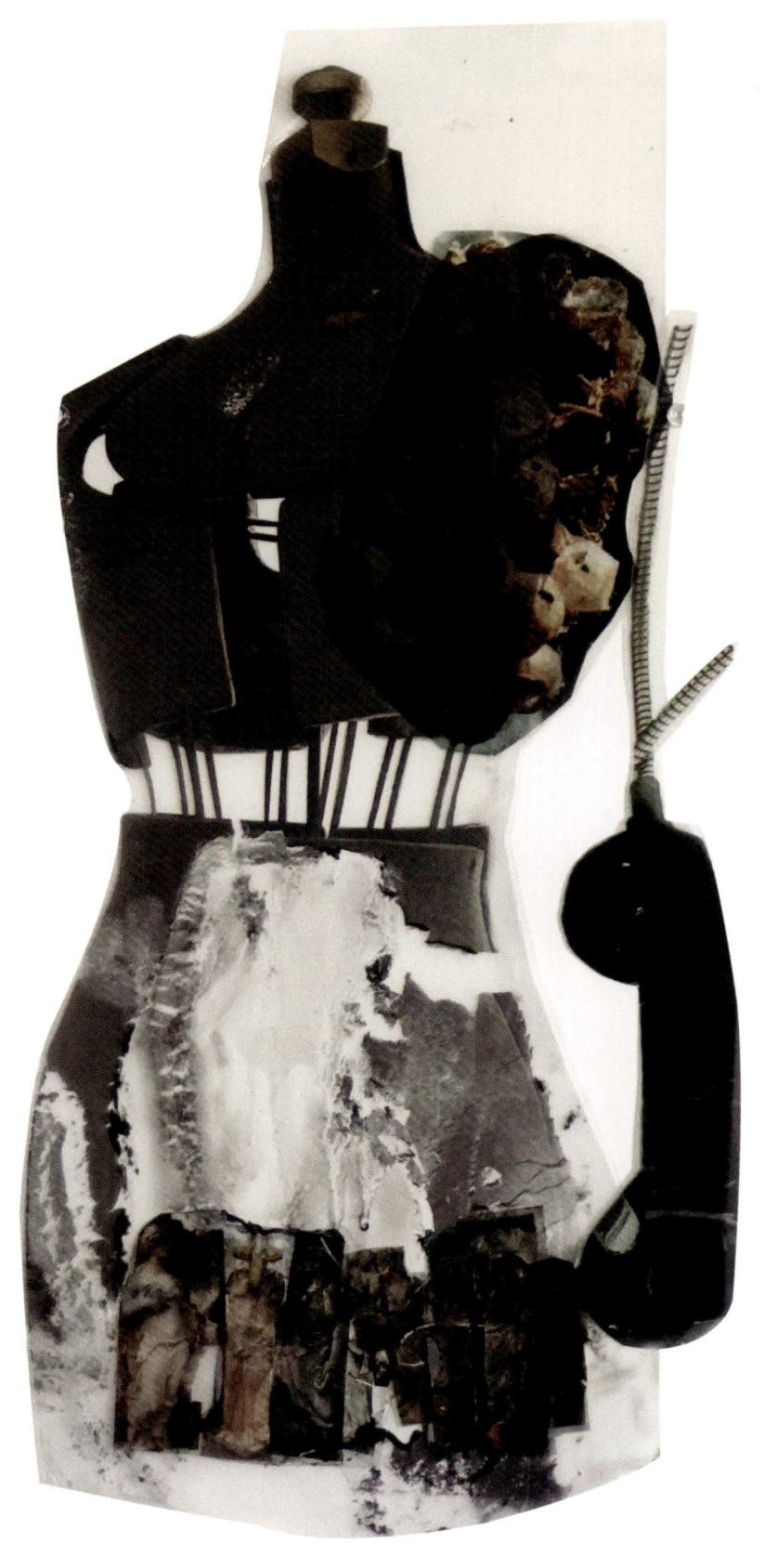

Relief 13
30 x 20 inches
Photo Transparency
2024

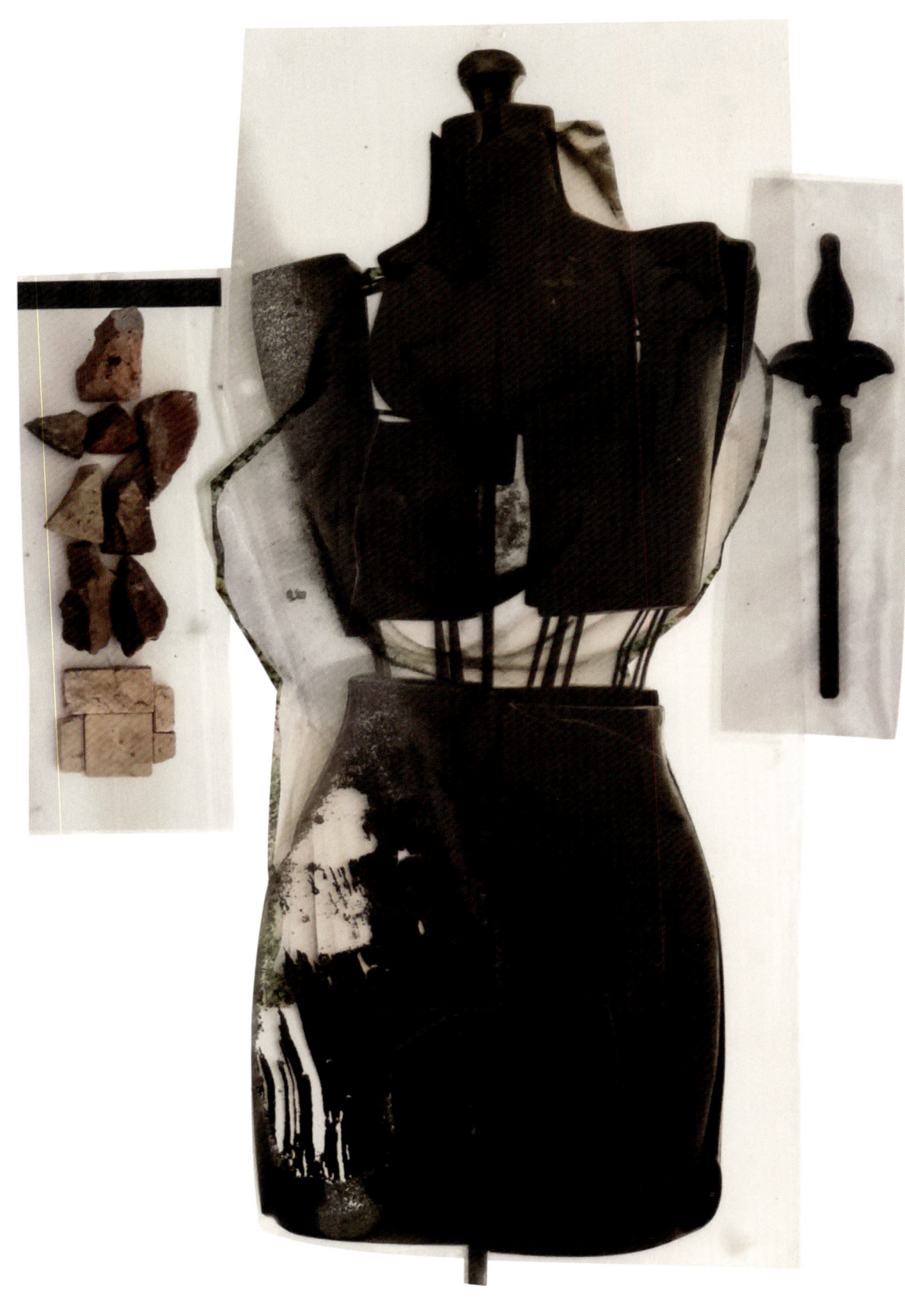

Relief 14
30 x 20 inches
Photo Transparency
2024

178

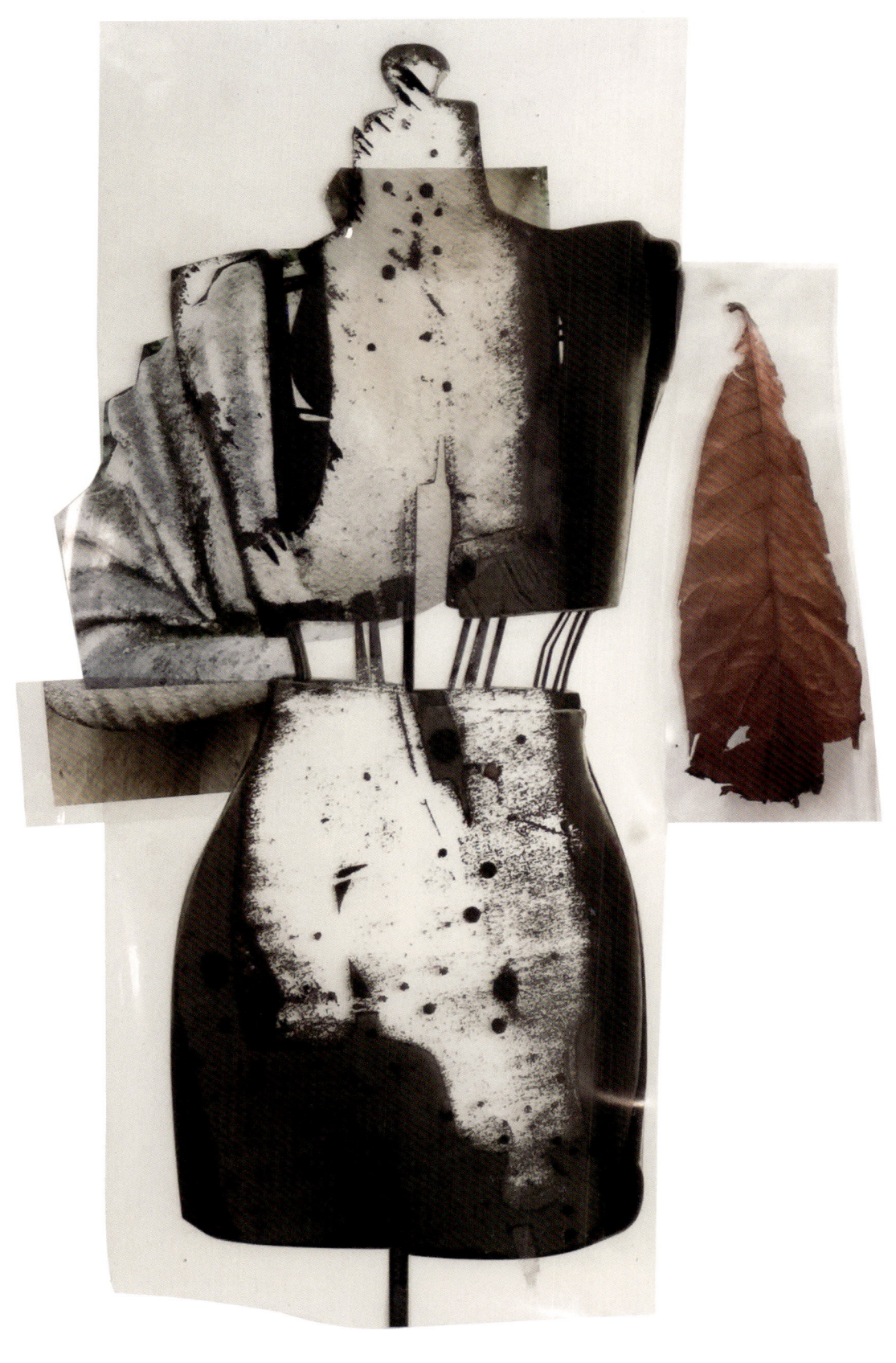

Relief 15
30 x 20 inches
Photo Transparency
2024

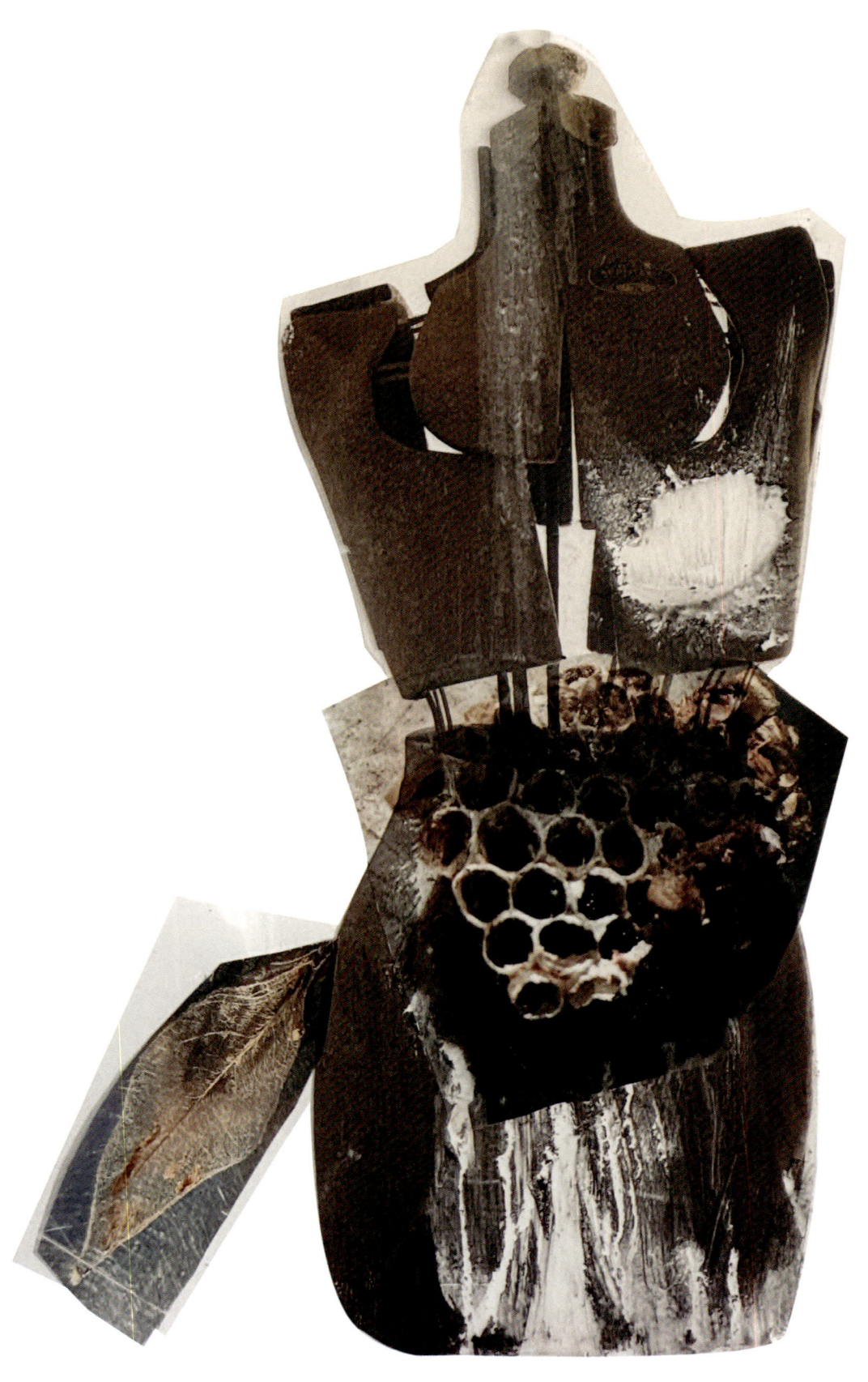

Relief 16
30 x 20 inches
Photo Transparency
2024

180

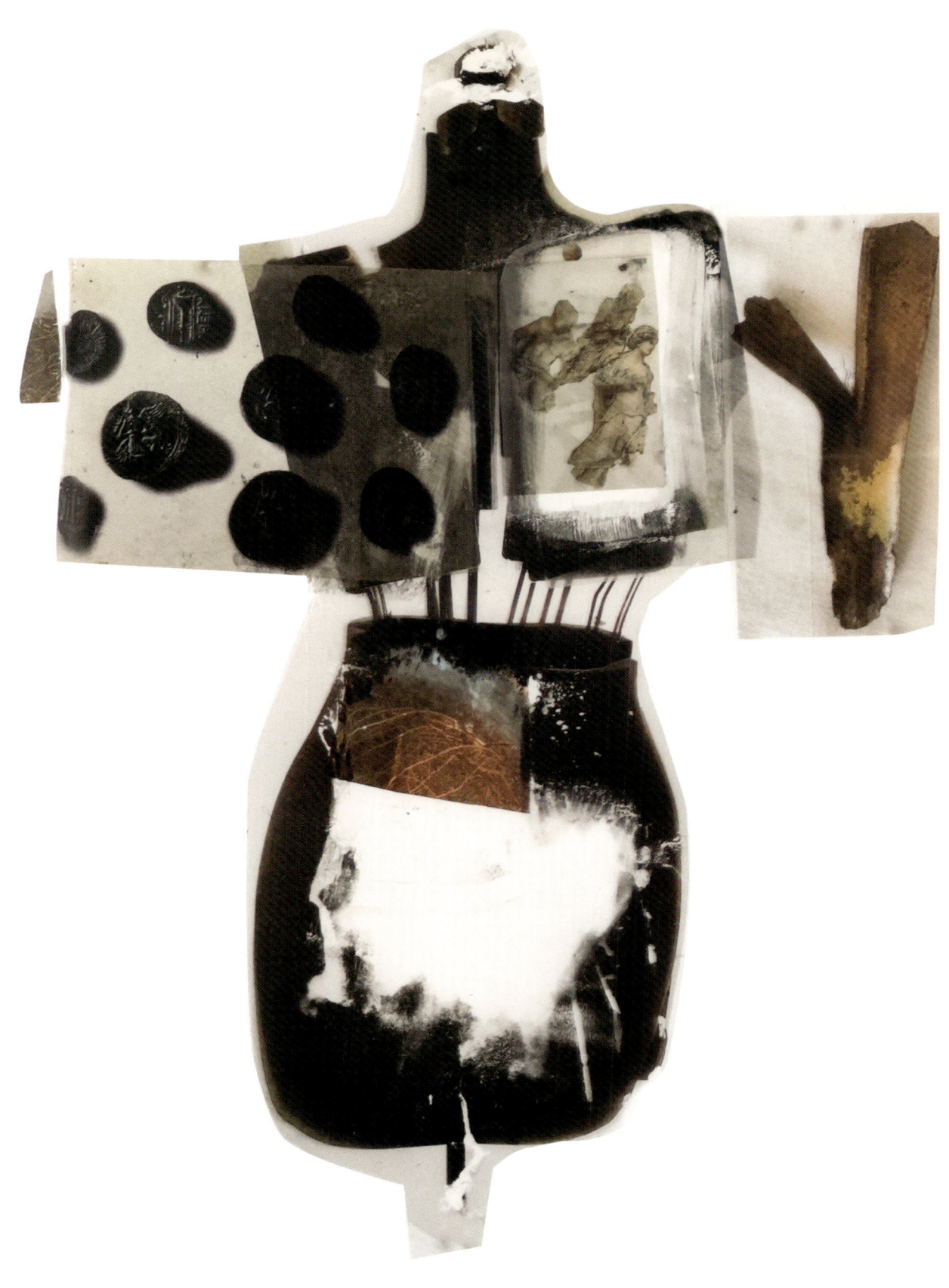

Relief 17
30 x 20 inches
Photo Transparency
2024

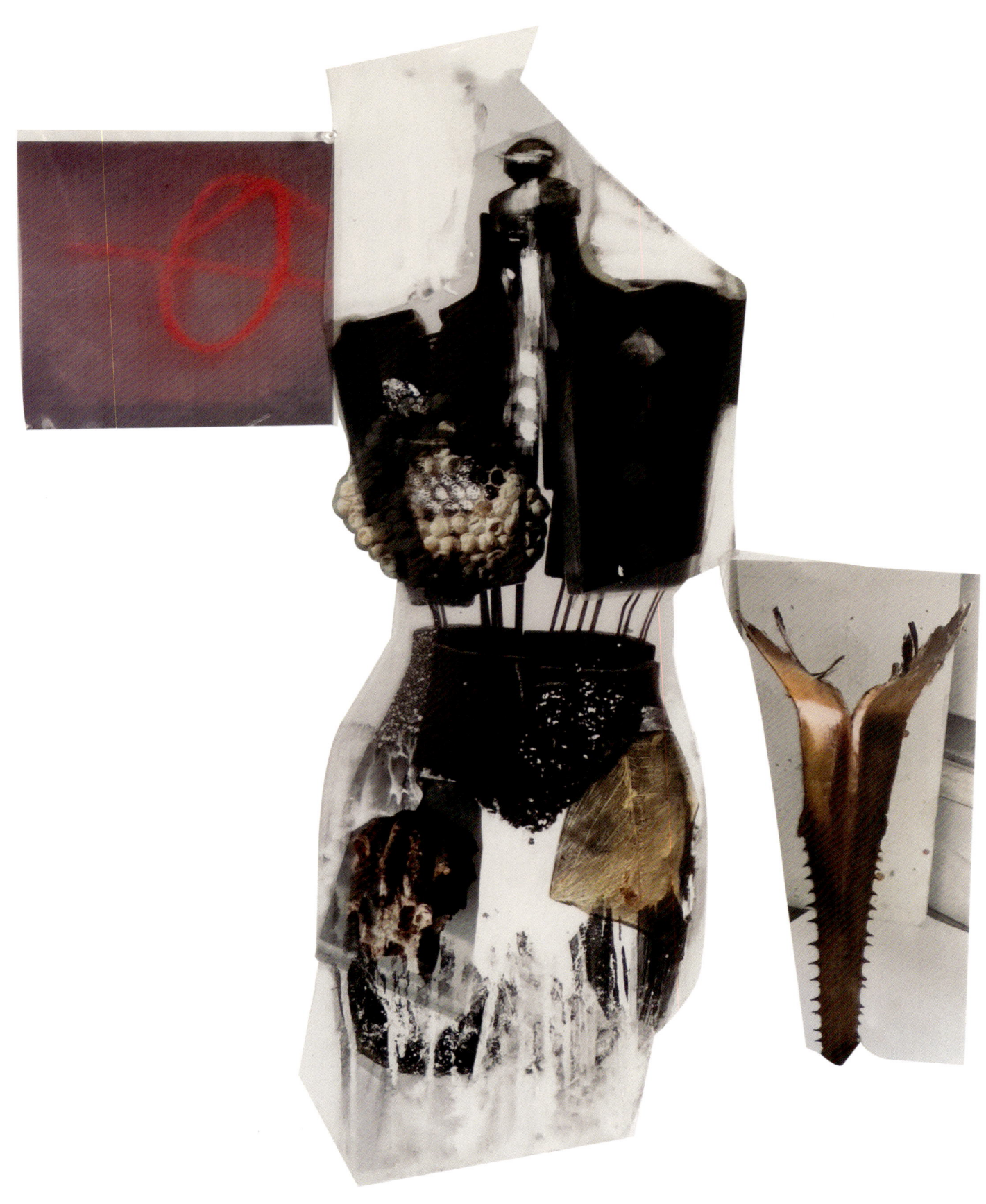

Relief 18
30 x 20 inches
Photo Transparency
2024

182

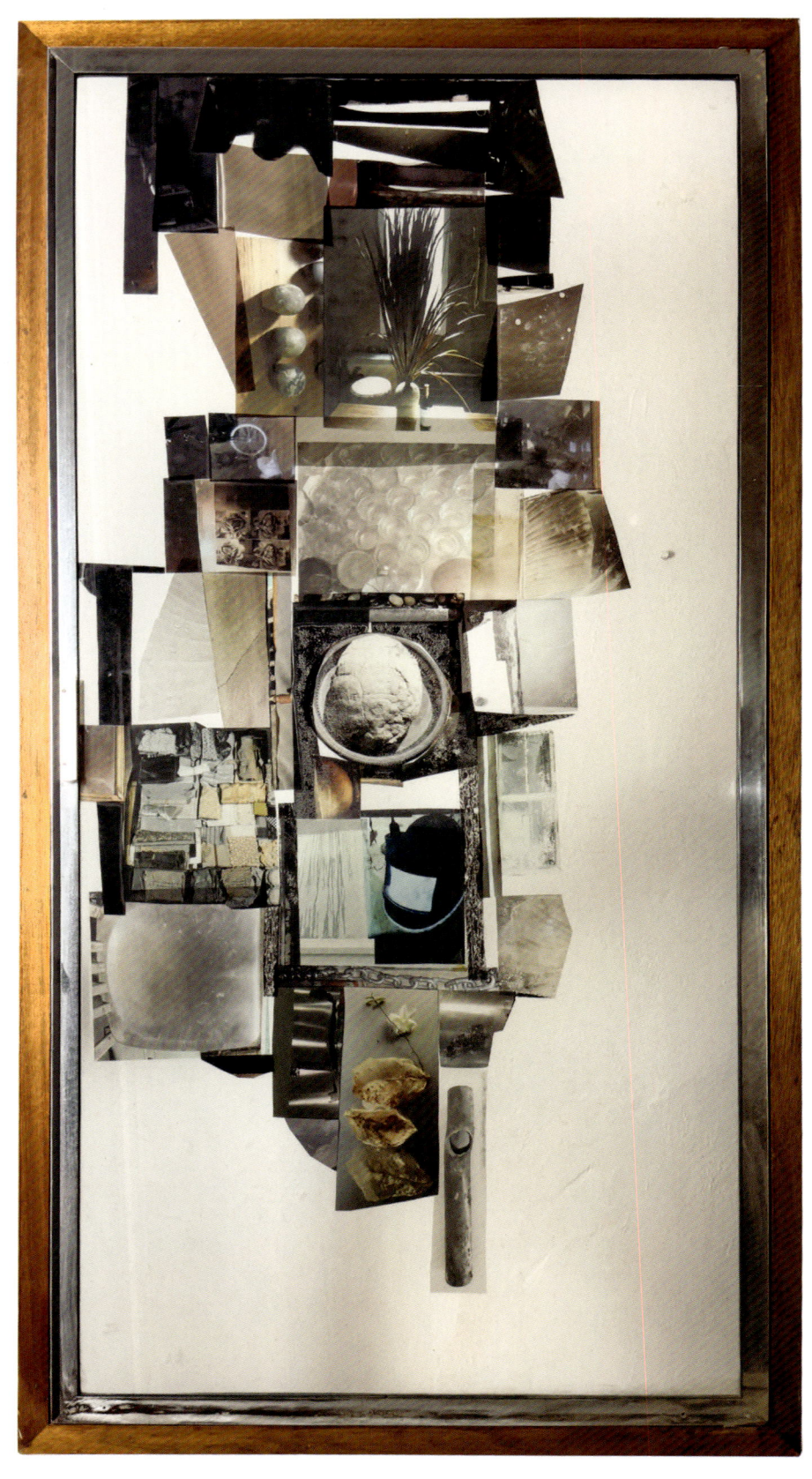

Interior
68 x 36 inches
Photo Collage on Glass Door
2017

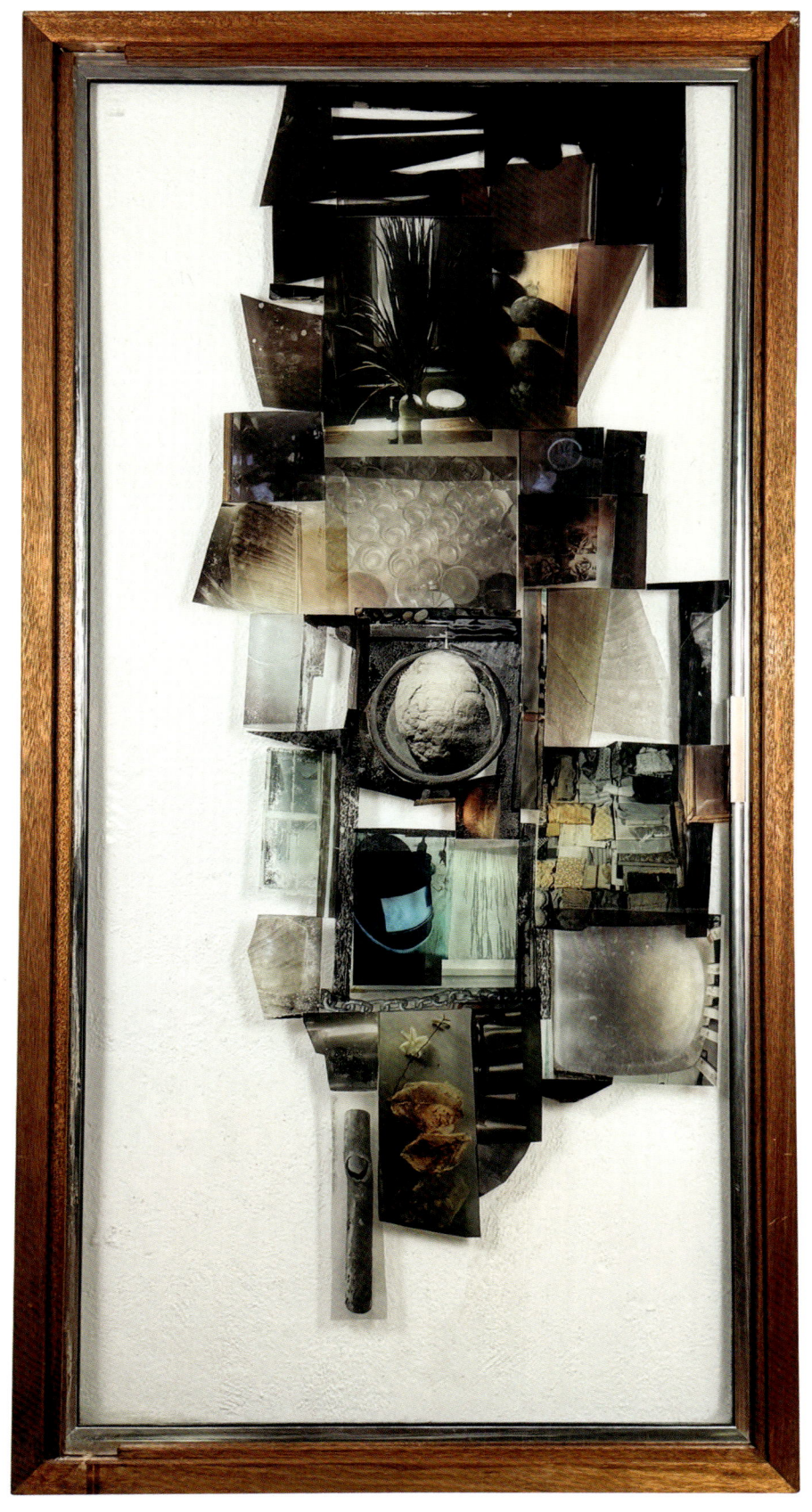

Interior (Back View)

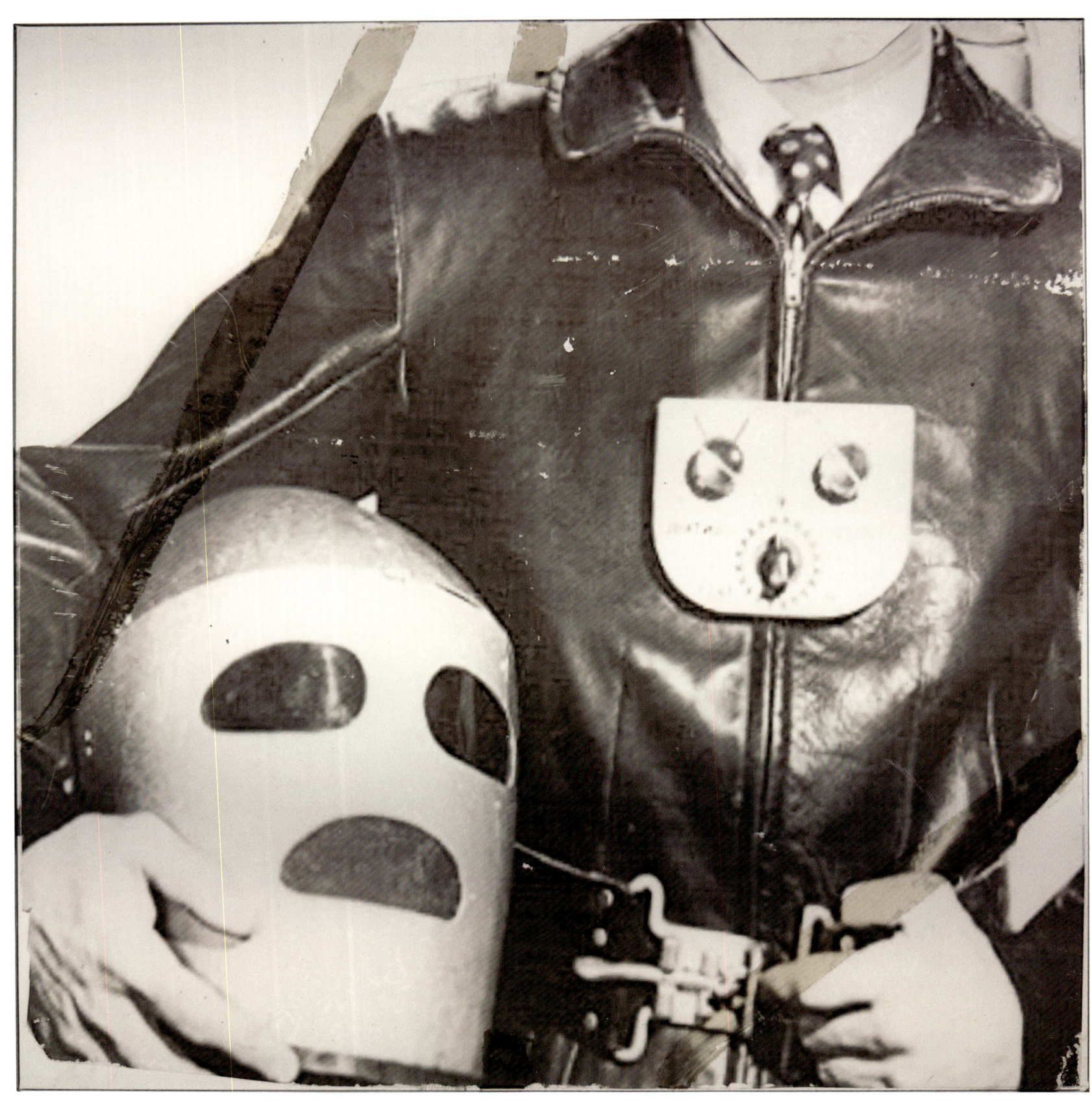

Square Tile 5
15 x 15 inches
Print on Glass w/ Aluminum Substrate
2024

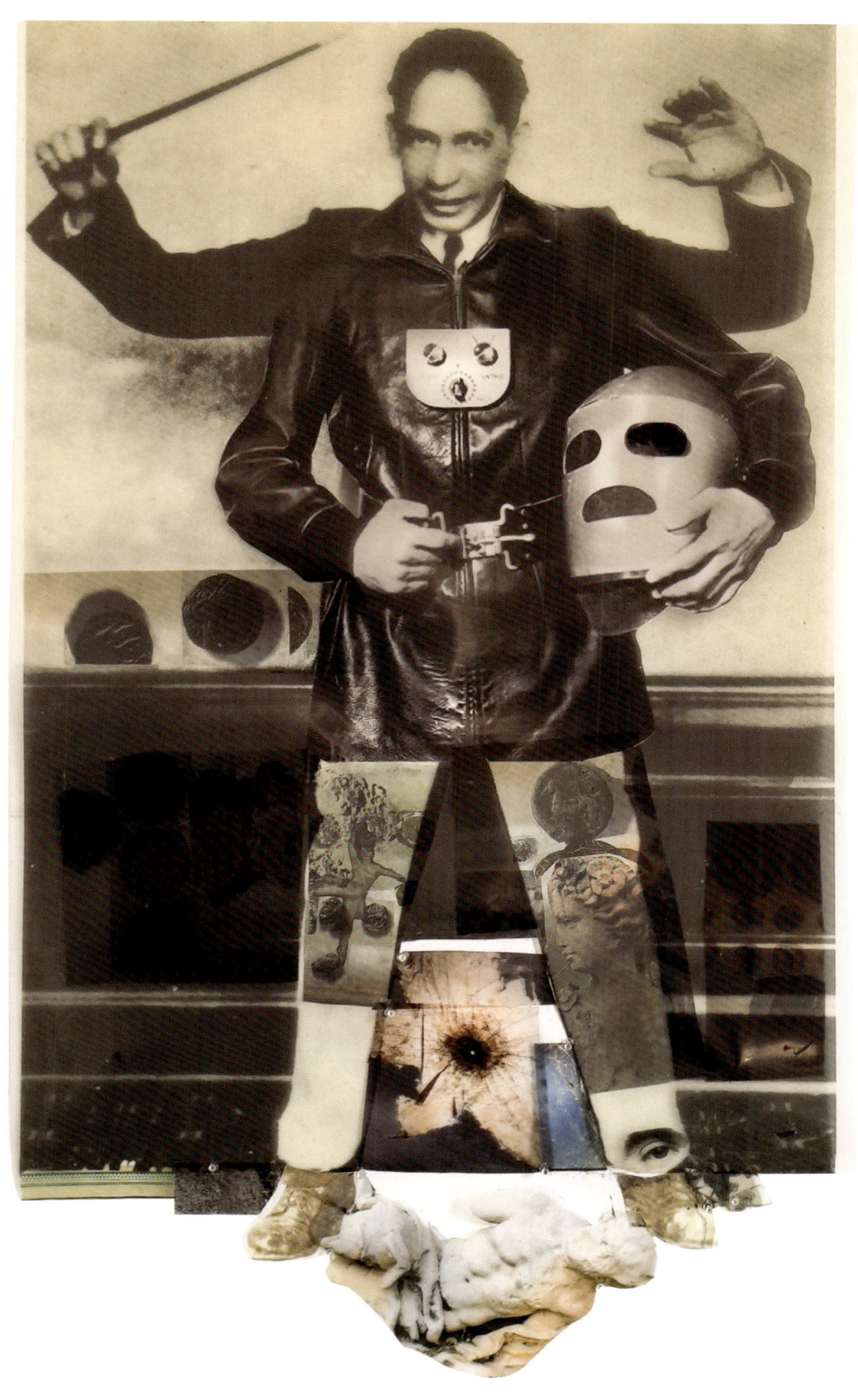

Nataraja
64 X 40 inches
Mixed Media
2024

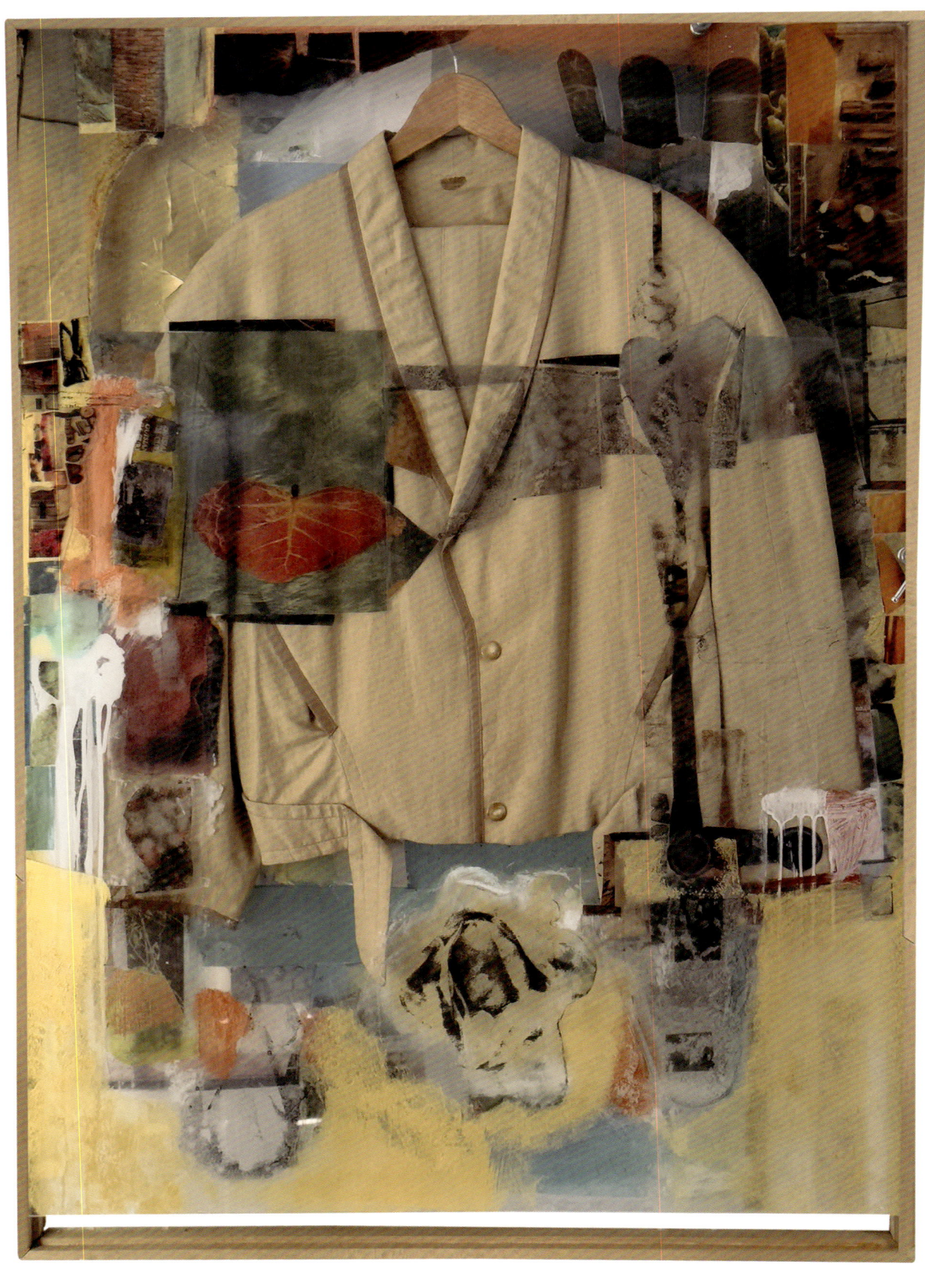

Suit
46 ¼ x 34 x 2 inches
Mixed Media
2020

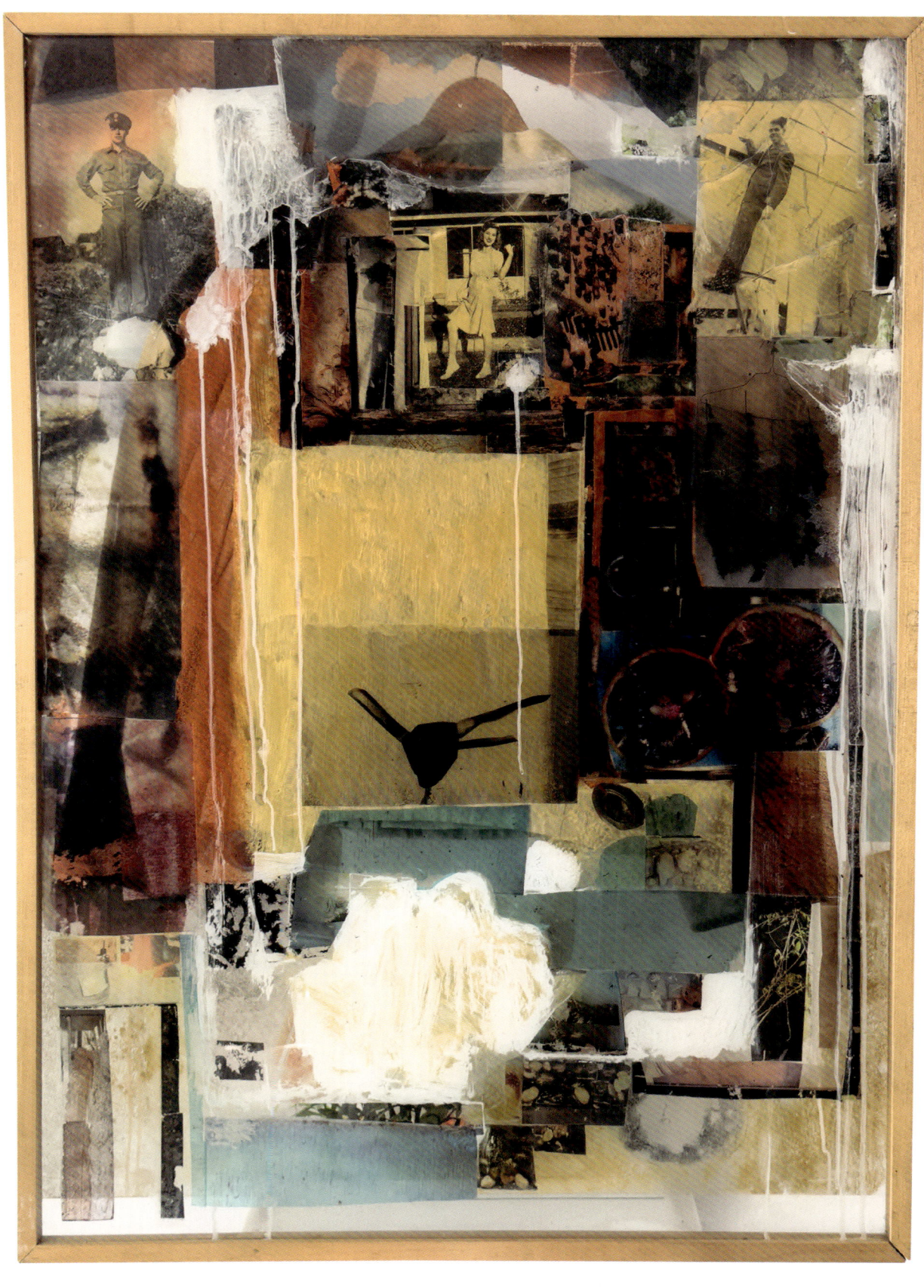

Suit (Back View)

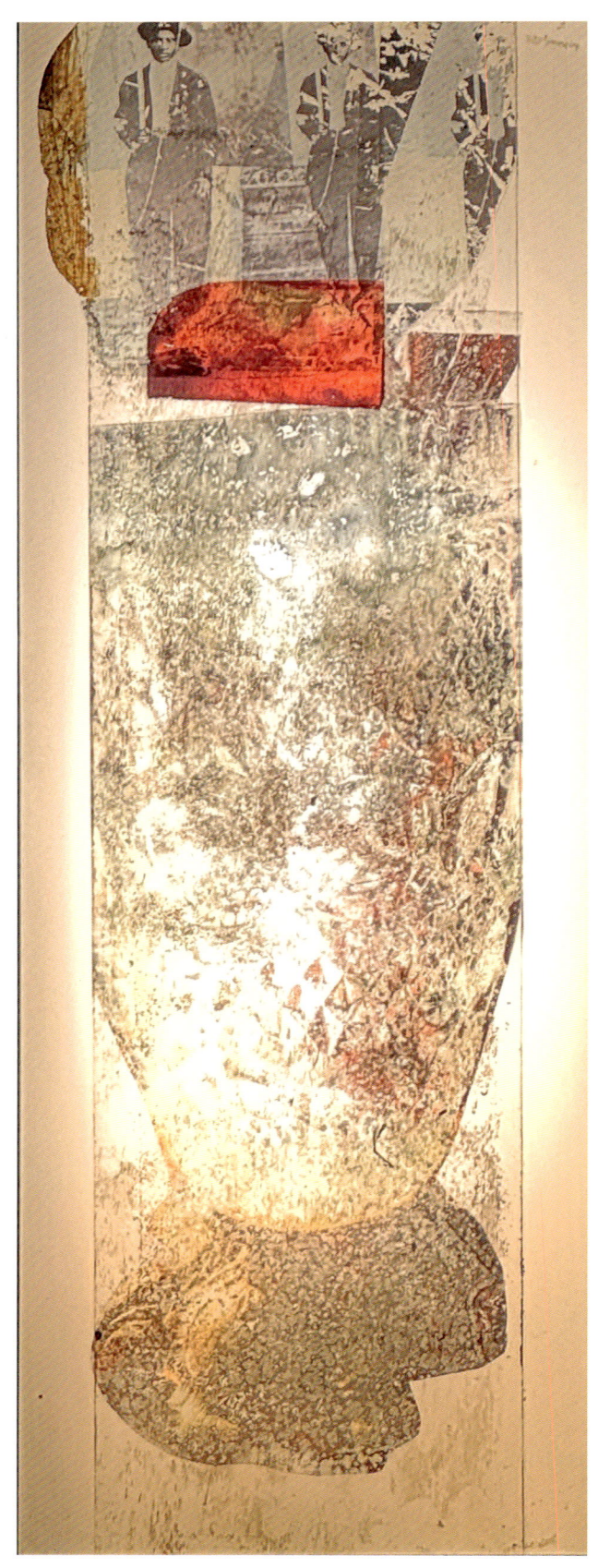

Novena
15 ½ x 6 ¾ x 2 ½ inches
Mixed Media on Plexiglass w/ Lightbox
2017

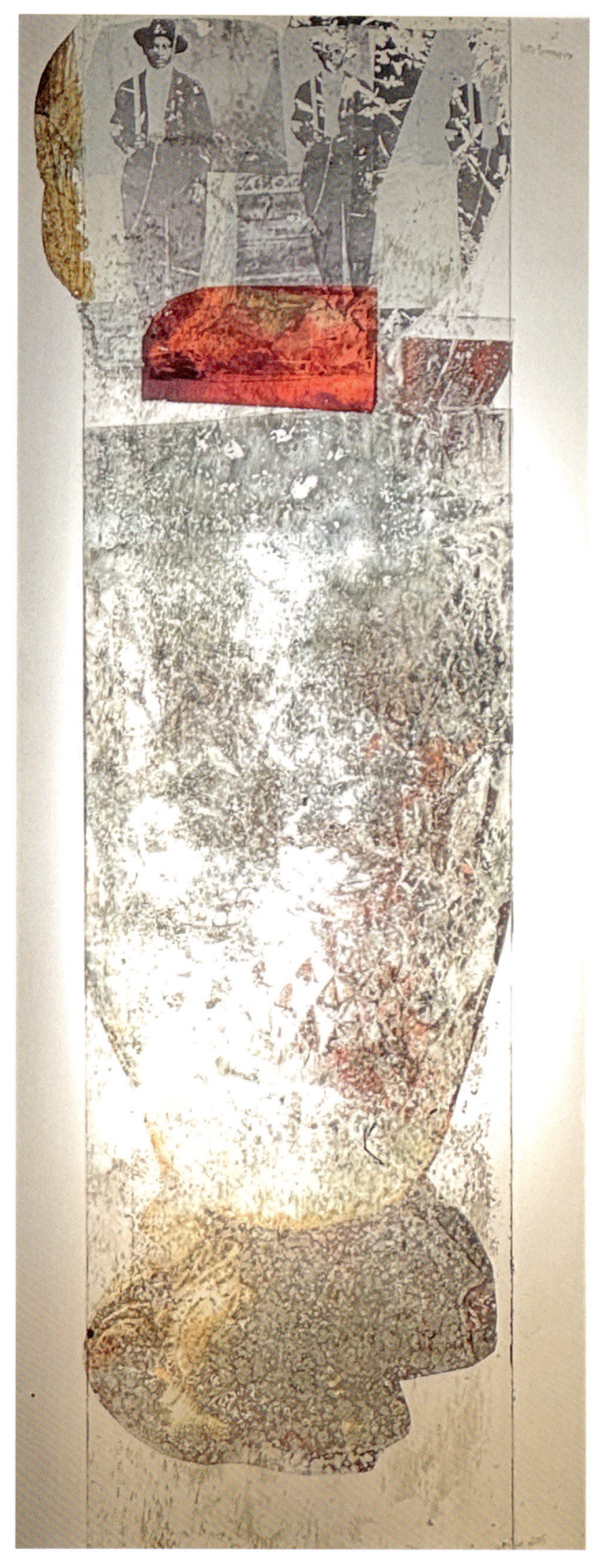

Novena (Alternate View)

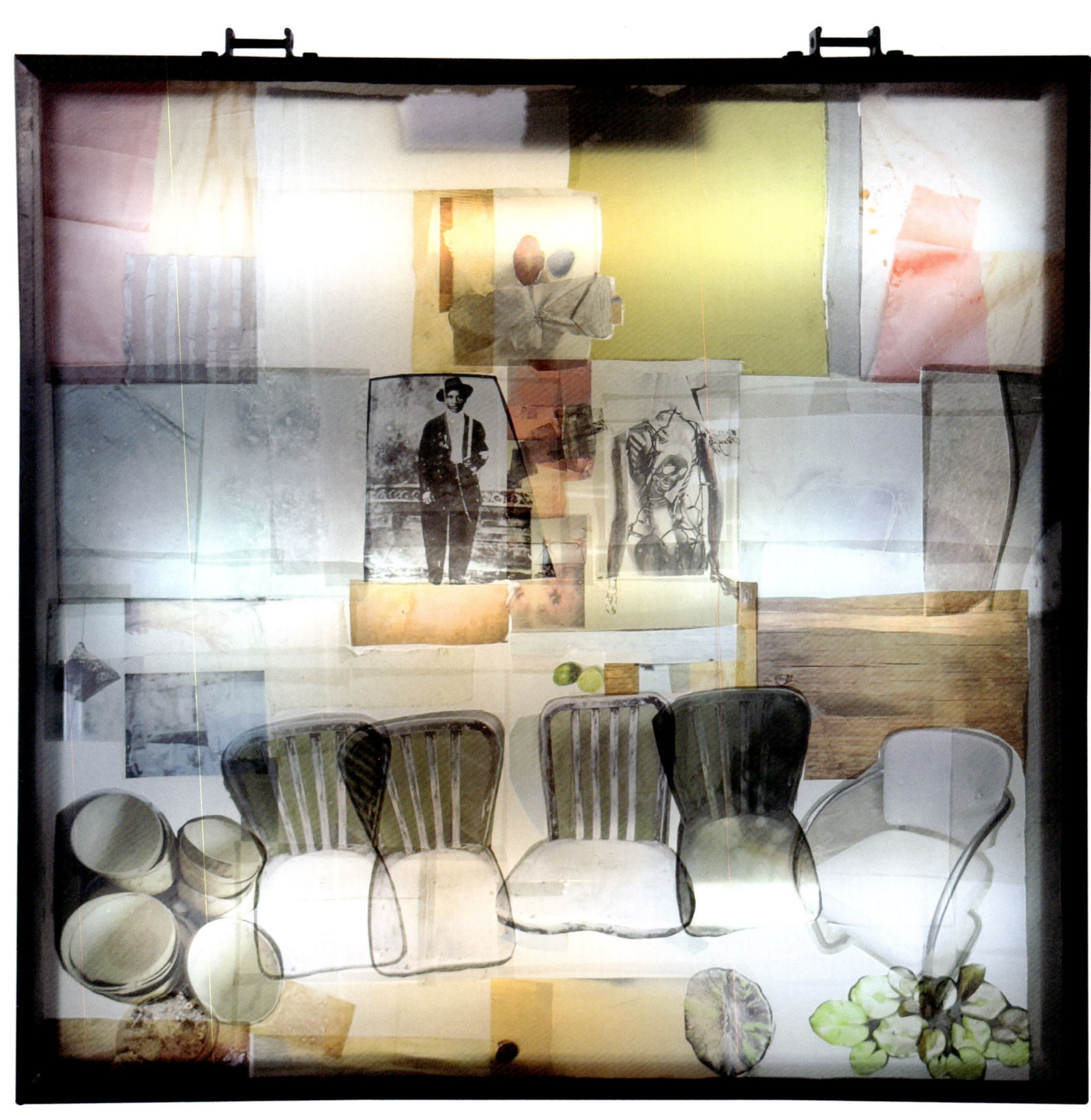

Backstage (Side A)
36 x 36 inches
Mixed Media on Lightbox
2015

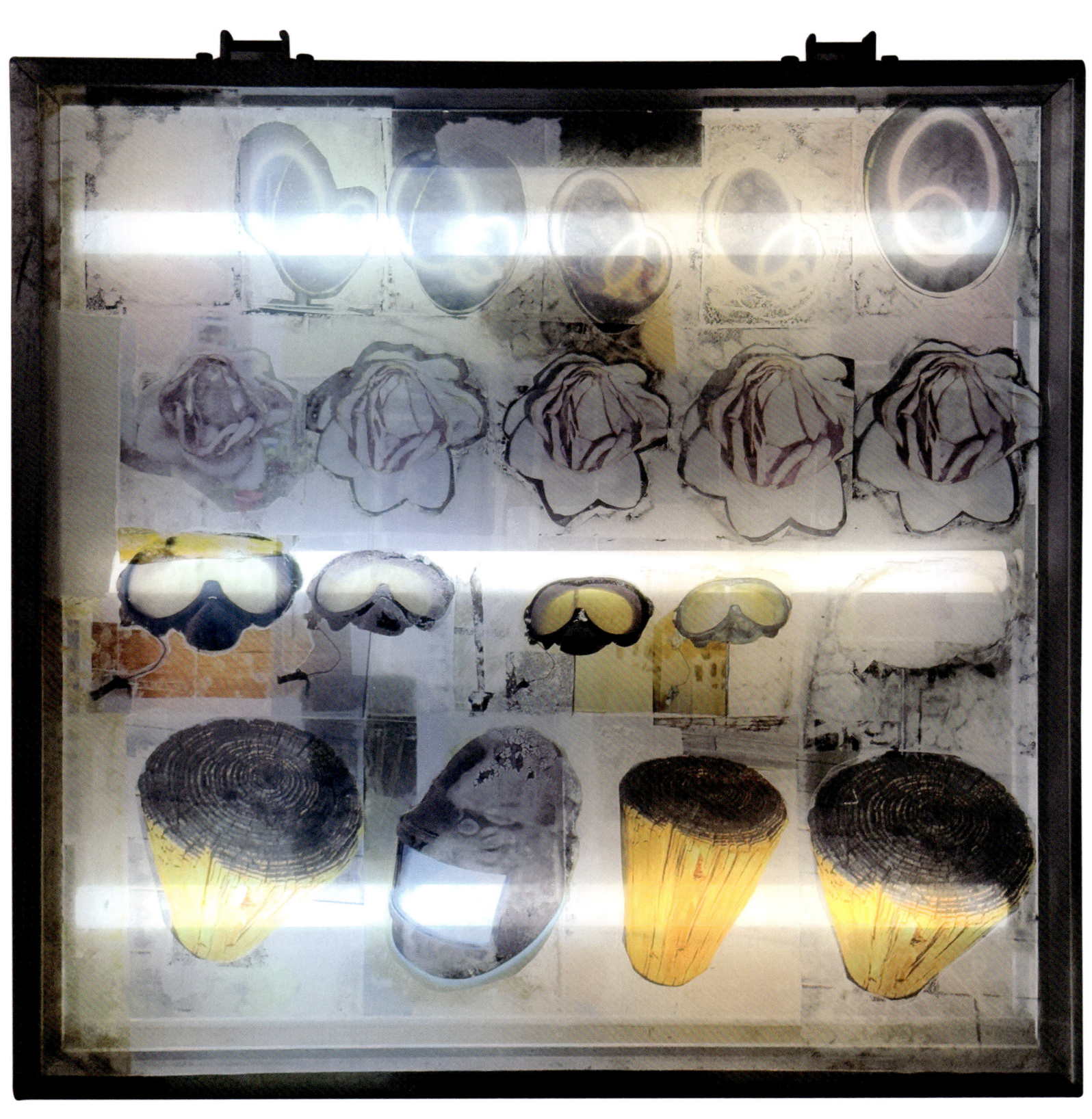

Backstage (Side B)
36 x 36 inches
Mixed Media on Lightbox
2015

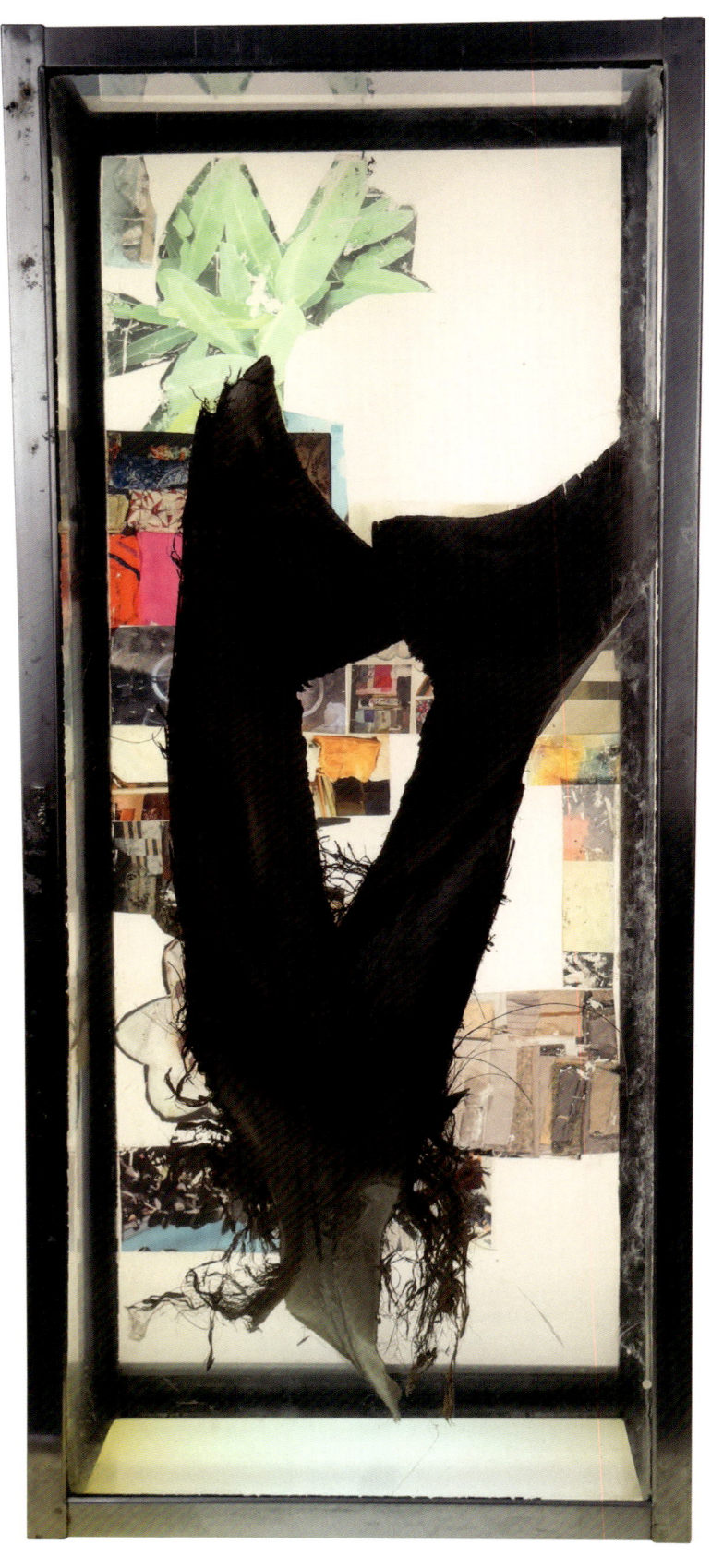

Nightstand
36 x 16 ½ x 10 inches
Mixed Media
2016

194

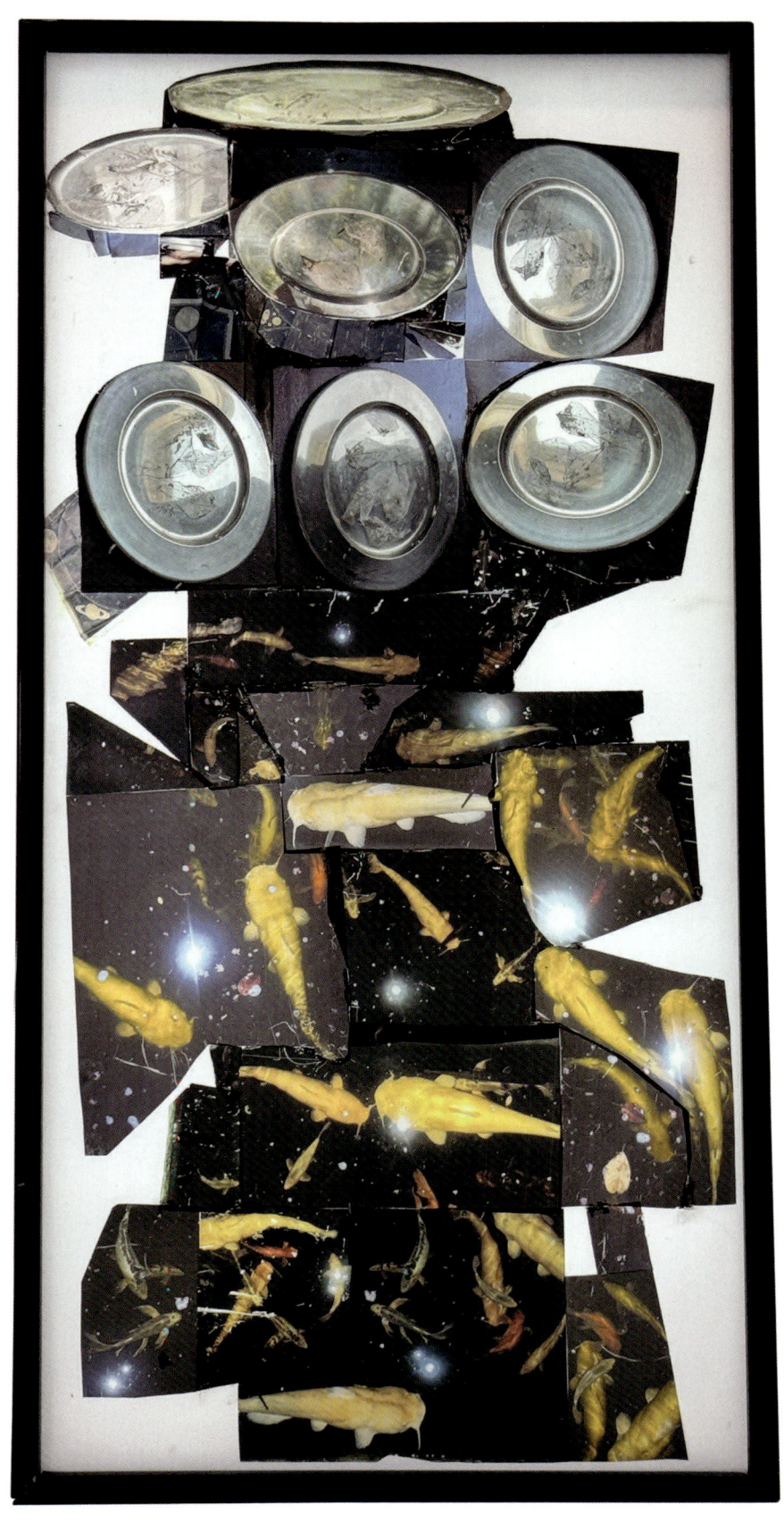

The Backyard
48 ½ x 24 ¼ x 6 ½ inches
Mixed Media Mounted on Lightbox
2020

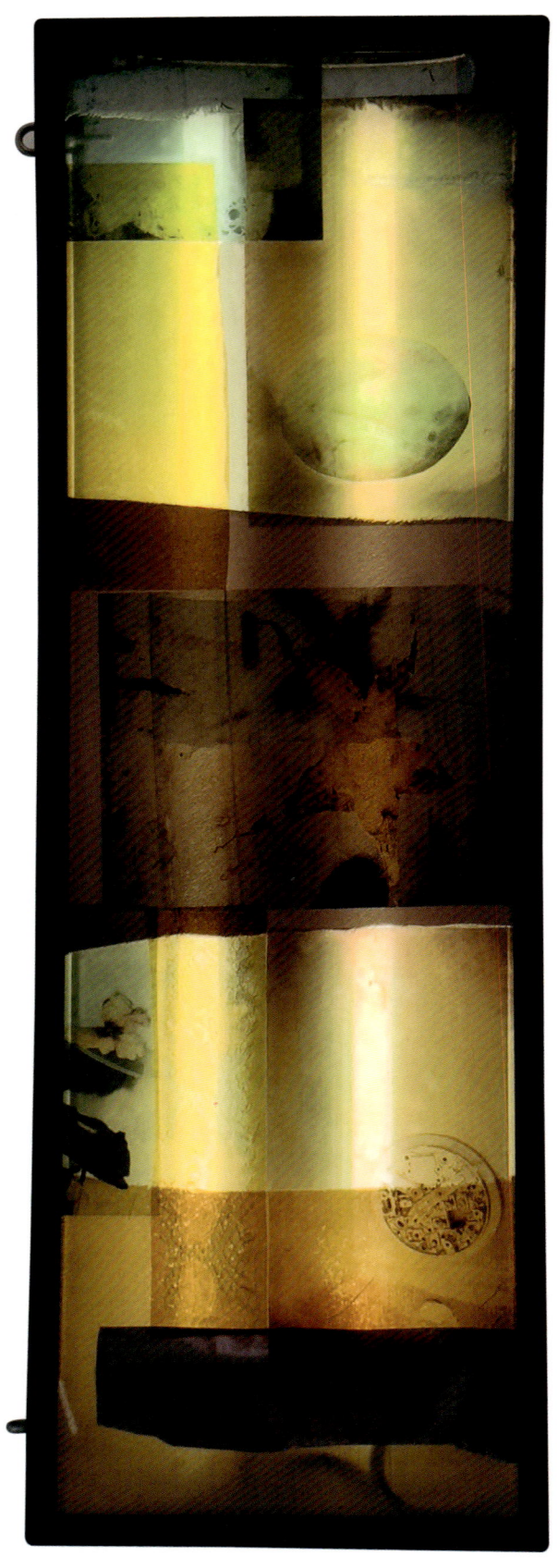

Nightlight
43 x 12 ½ x 6 ¼ inches
Photo Collage, Fabric and Transparencies Mounted on Lightbox
2010

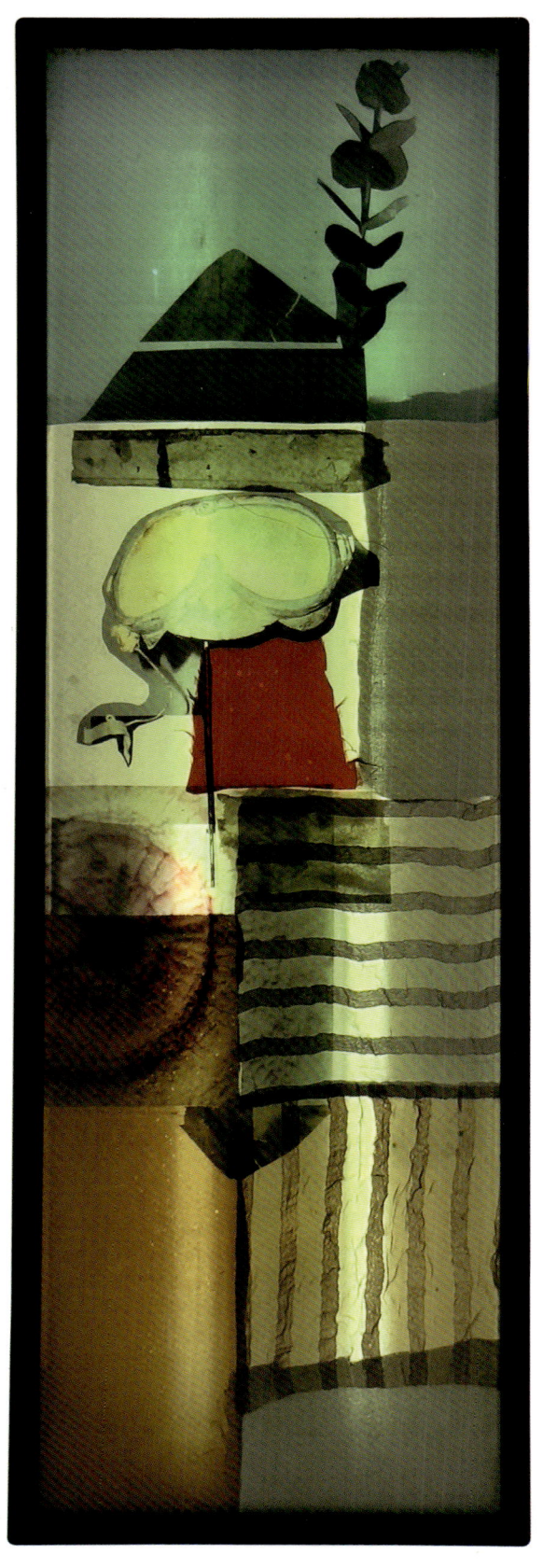

Nightlight (Back View)

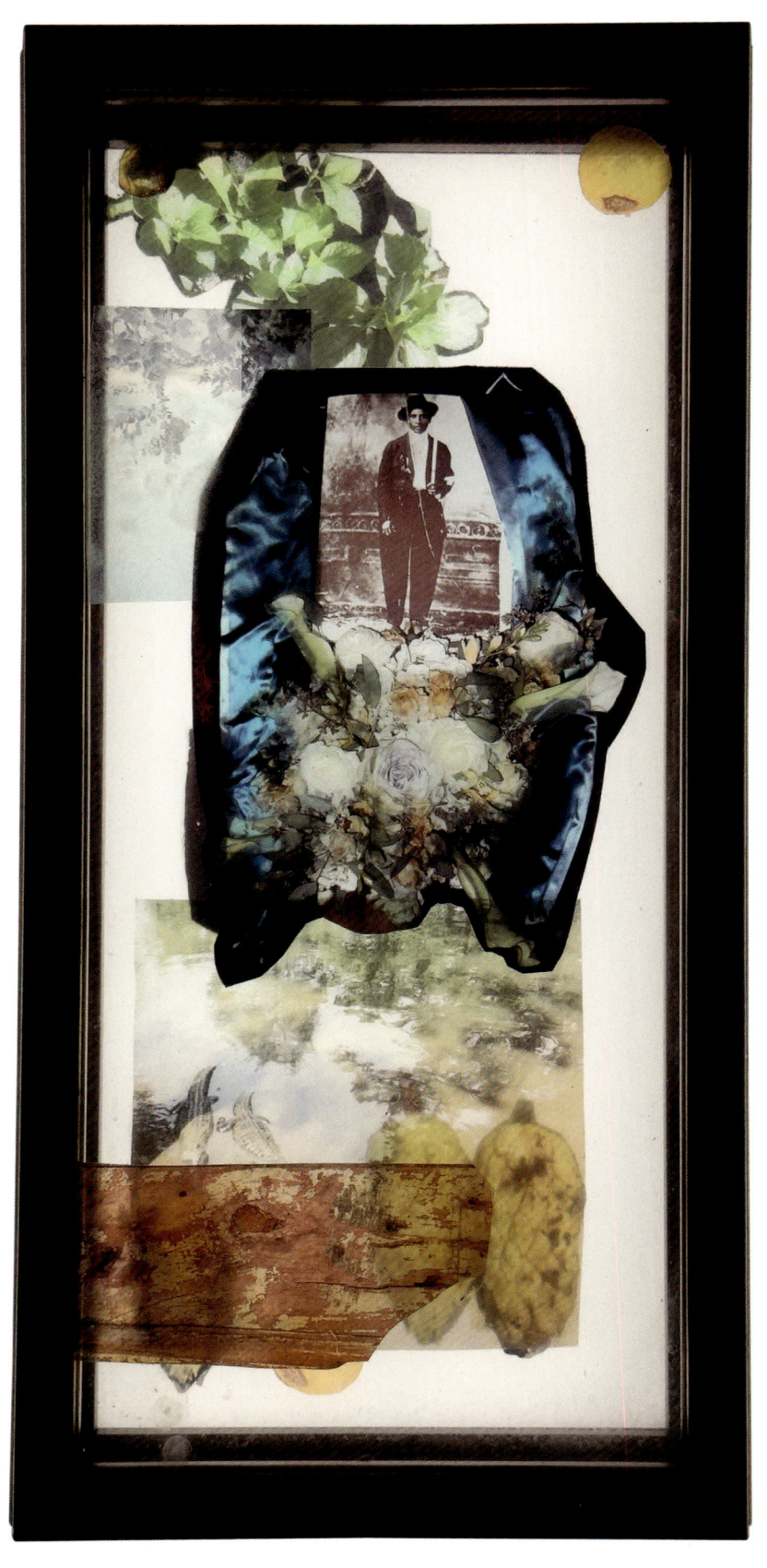

Blue Amédé Shadow Box
24 x 12 x 4 inches
Mixed Media, Layered Glass, Wood Frame
2016

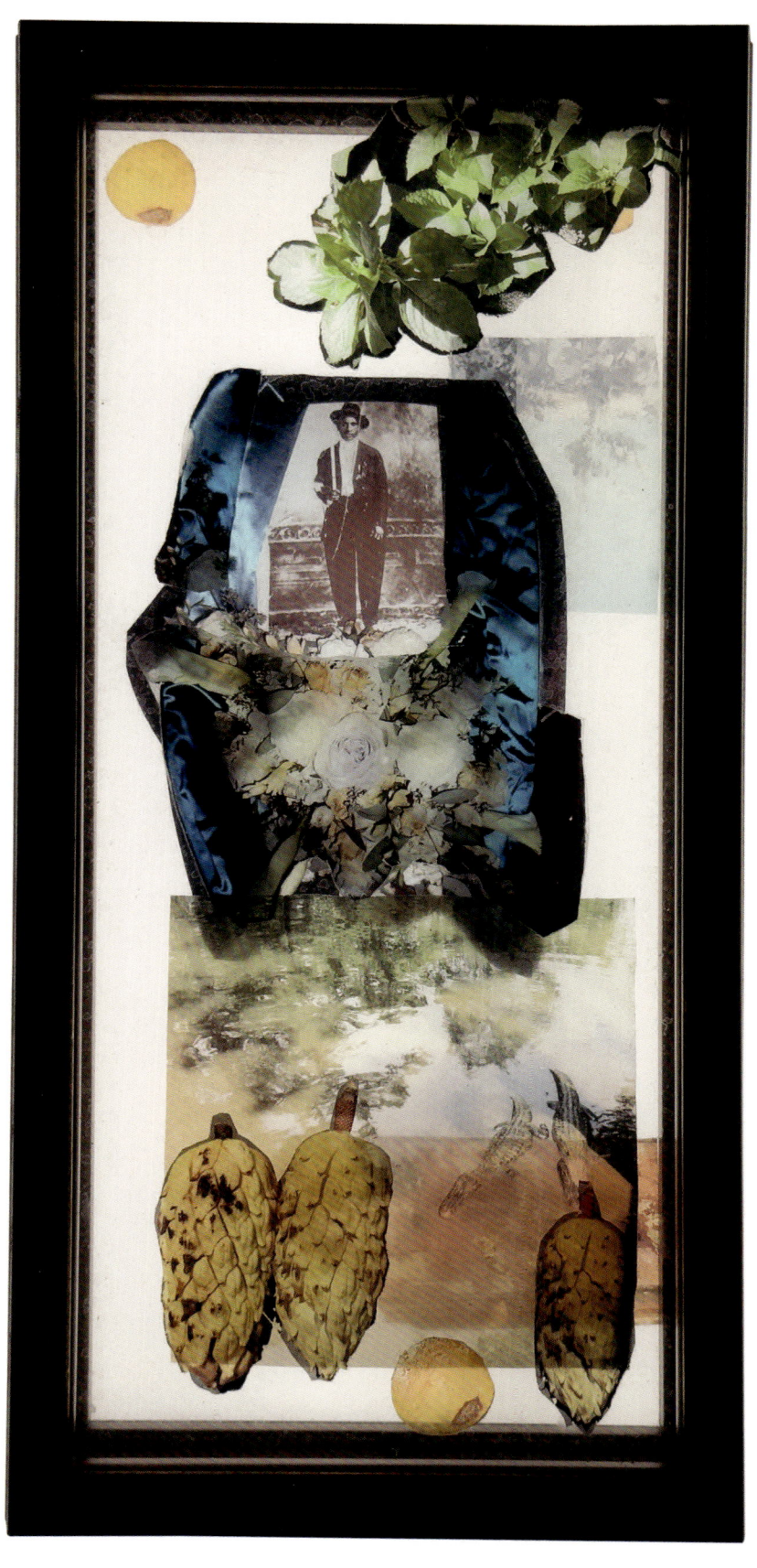

Blue Amédé Shadow Box (Back View)

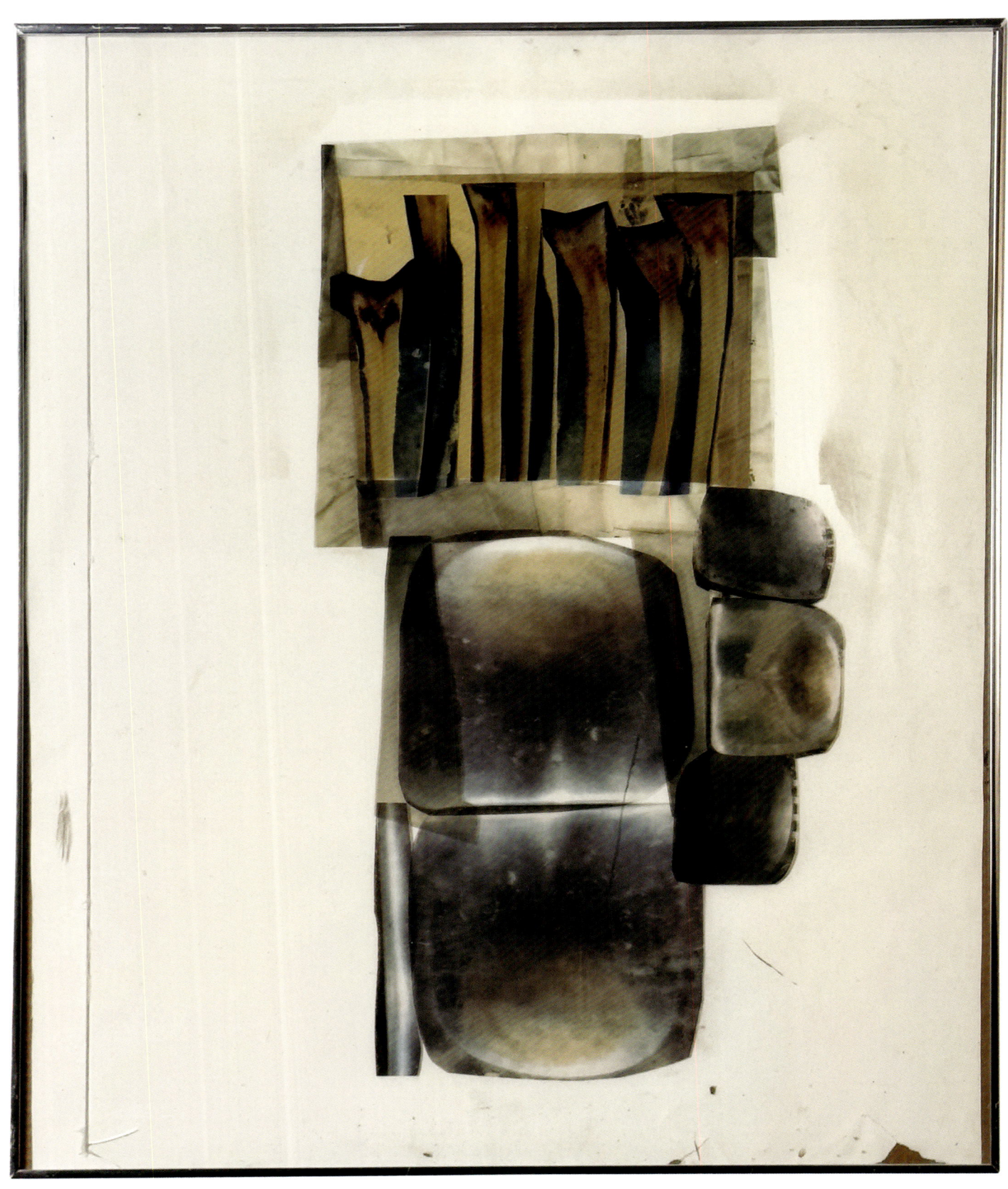

Early Chair 1
30 x 26 ¼ inches
Mixed Media Collage on Plexiglass
2018

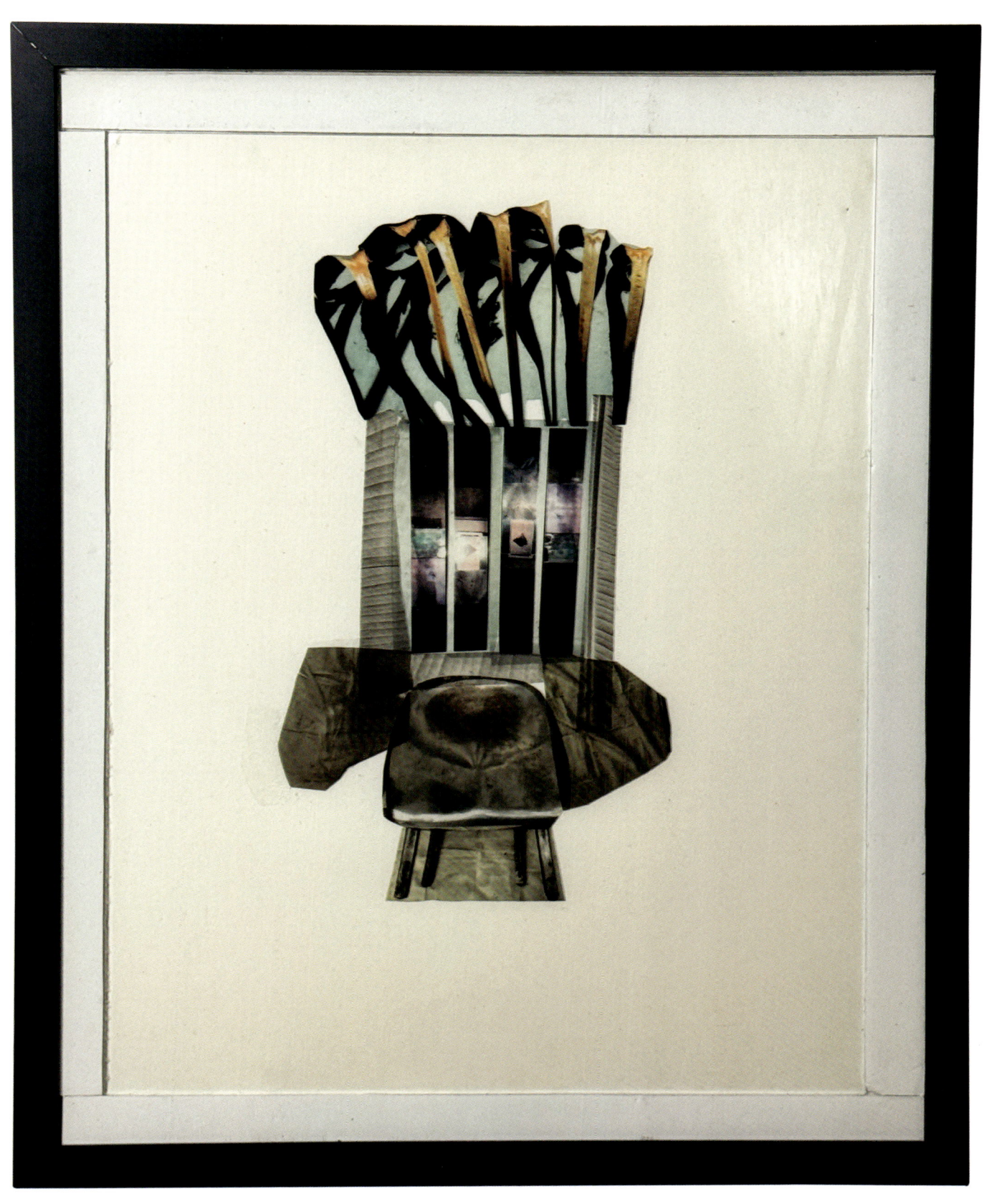

Early Chair 2
36 x 30 inches
Mixed Media Collage on Plexiglass
2018

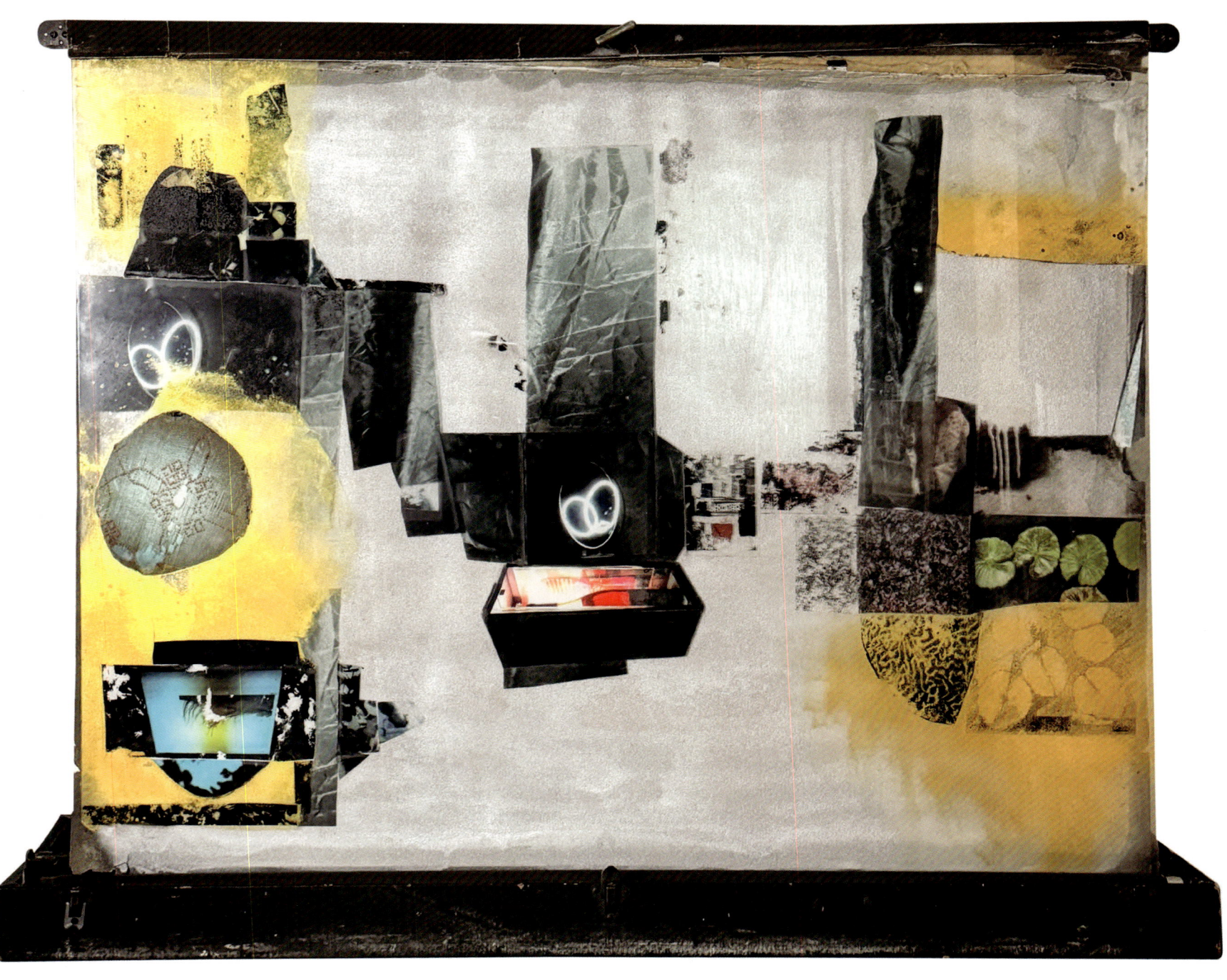

Map
35 x 44 inches
Mixed Media on Plexiglass w/ Silver Screen Substrate
2016

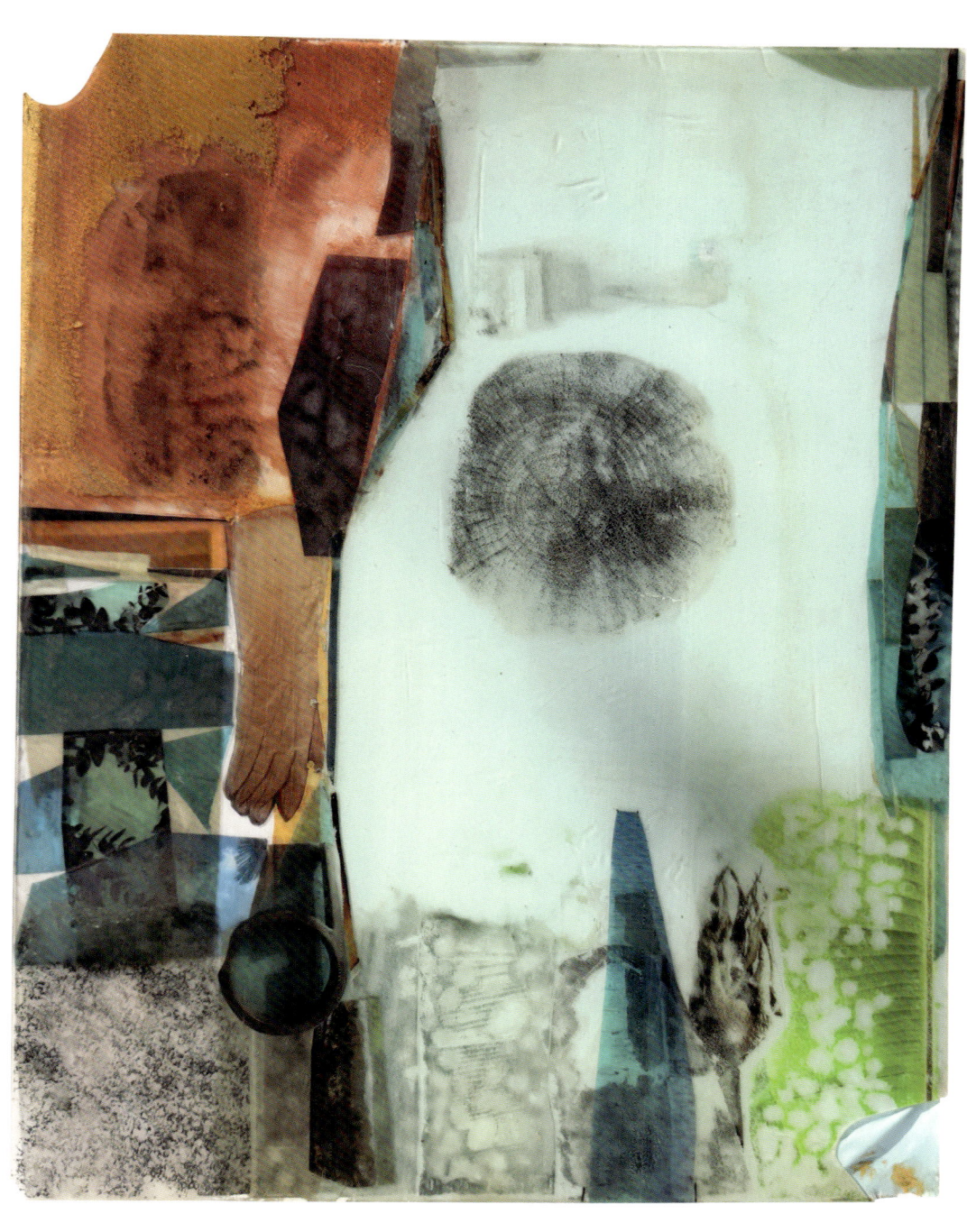

Danser II
24 x 18 inches
Mixed Media on White Plexiglass
2017

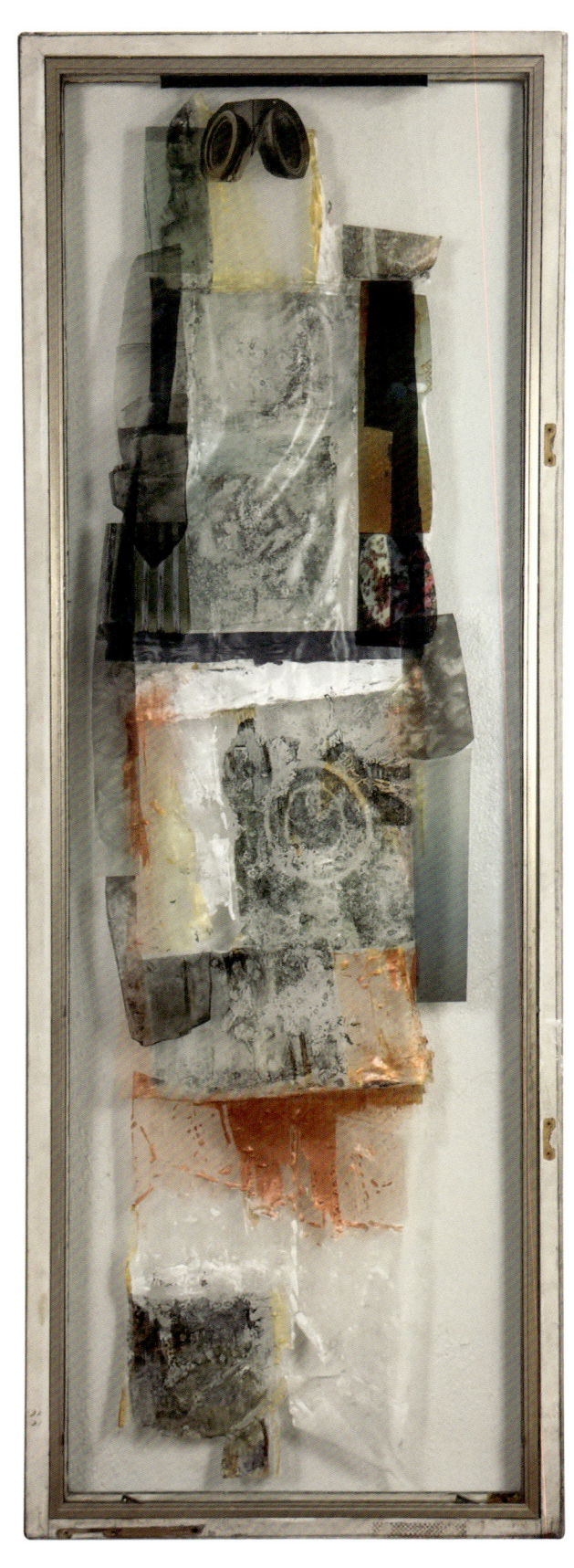

New Suit
63 x 22 ½ inches
Mixed Media between Layered Glass
2016

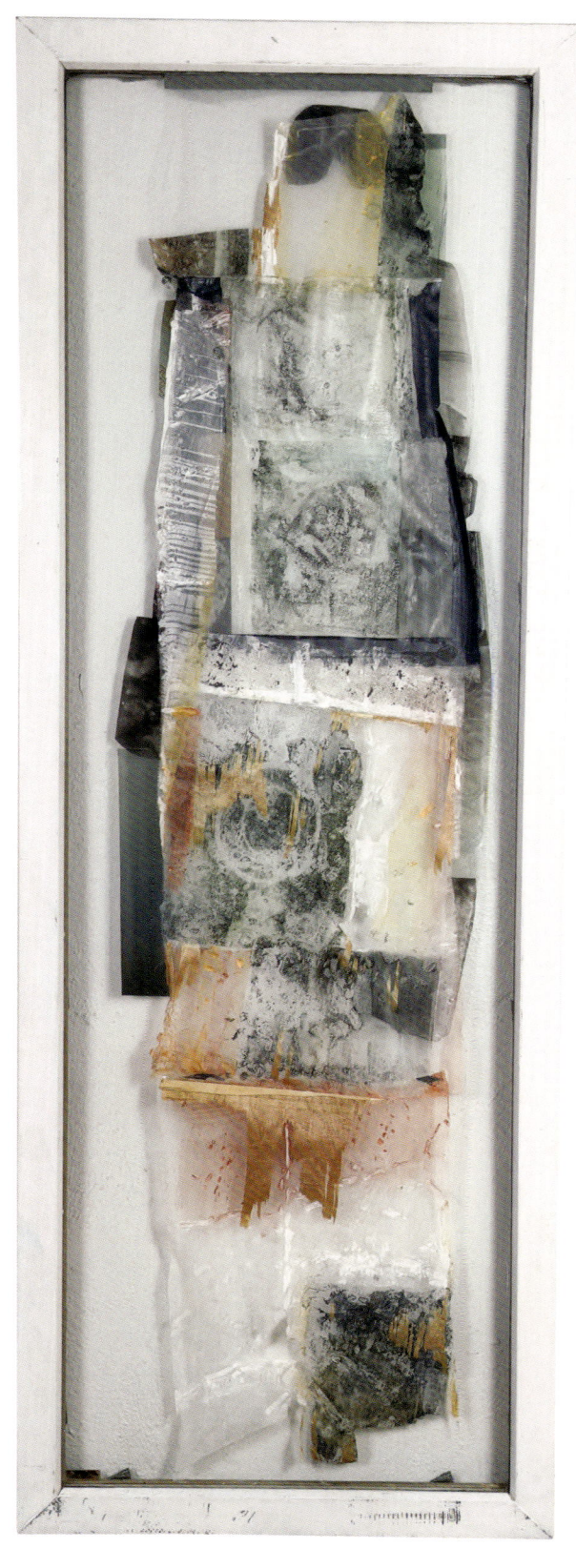

New Suit (Back View)

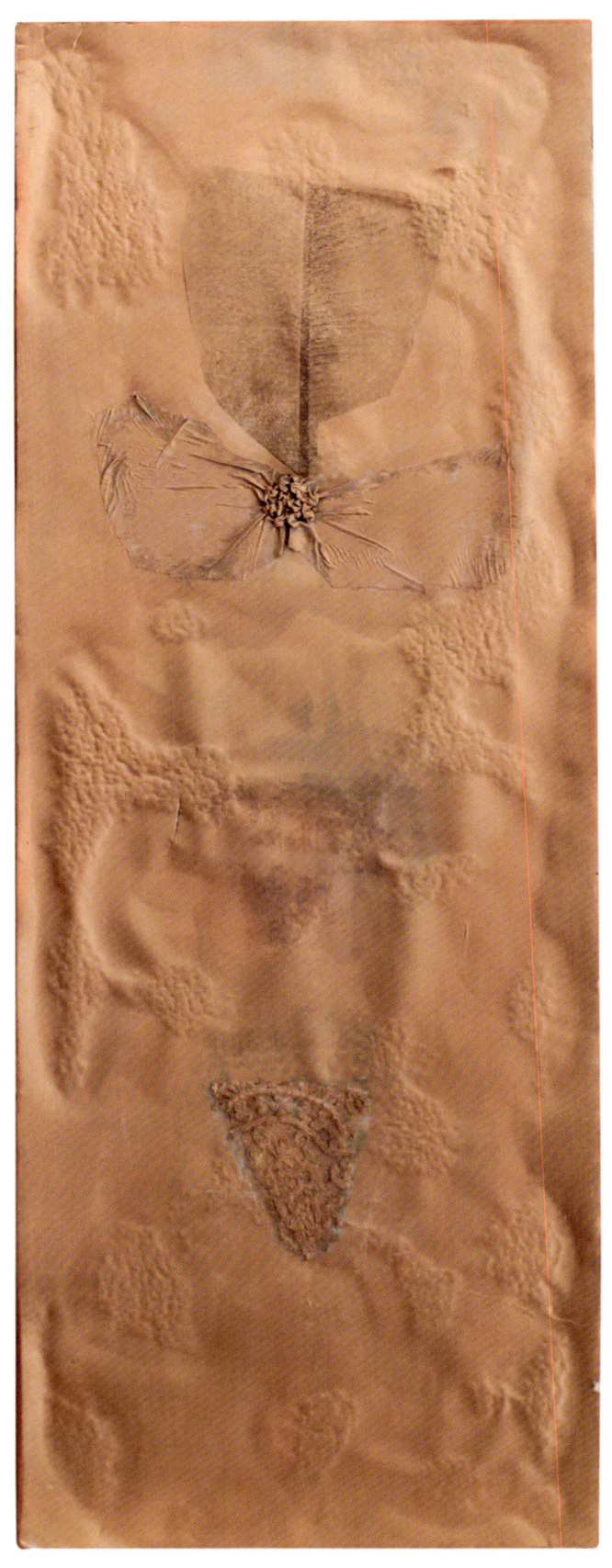

Bikini
37 x 14 inches
Paint and Fabric on Foamboard
2011

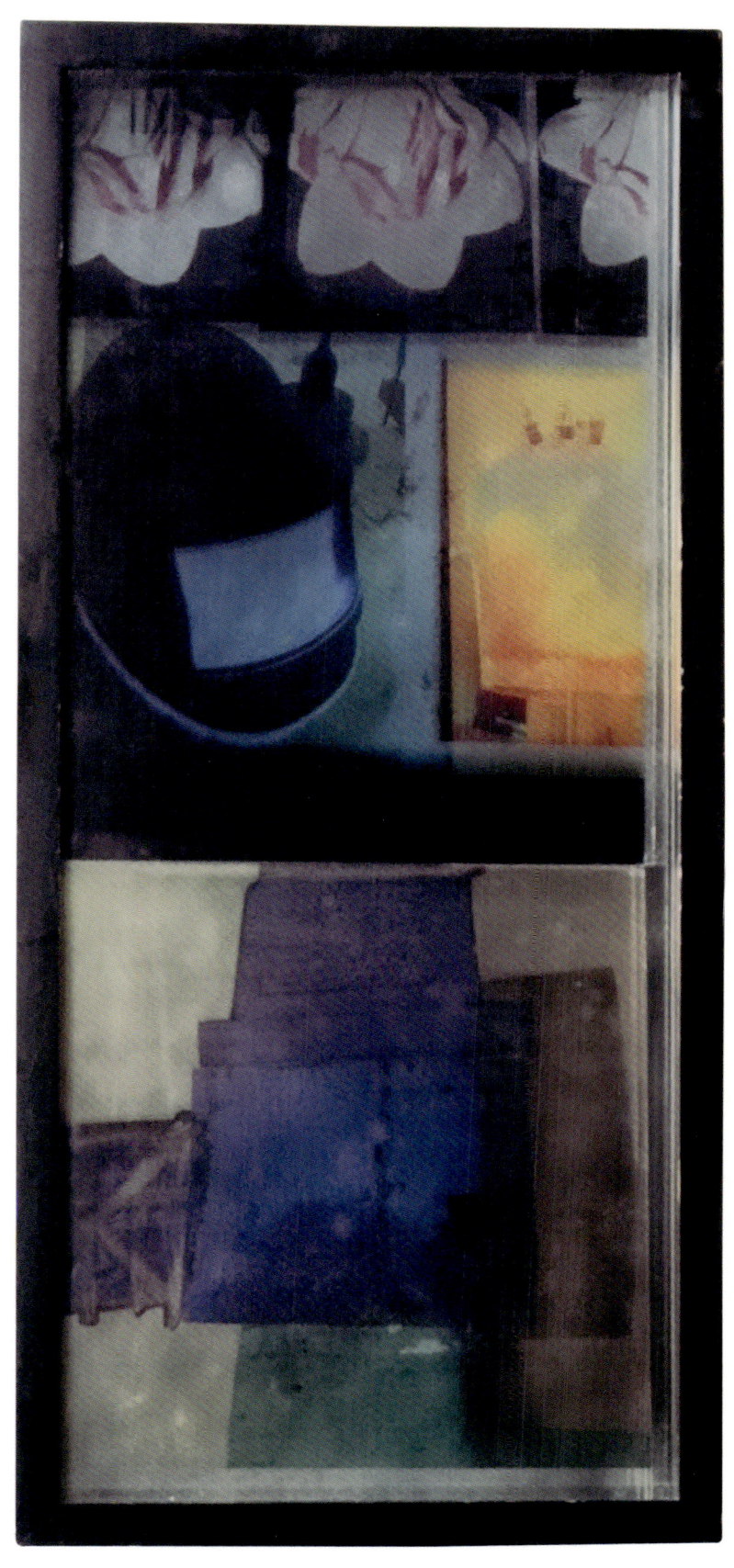

Bookend
21 x 9 ¾ inches
Mixed Media, Mirror, Layered Glass
2017

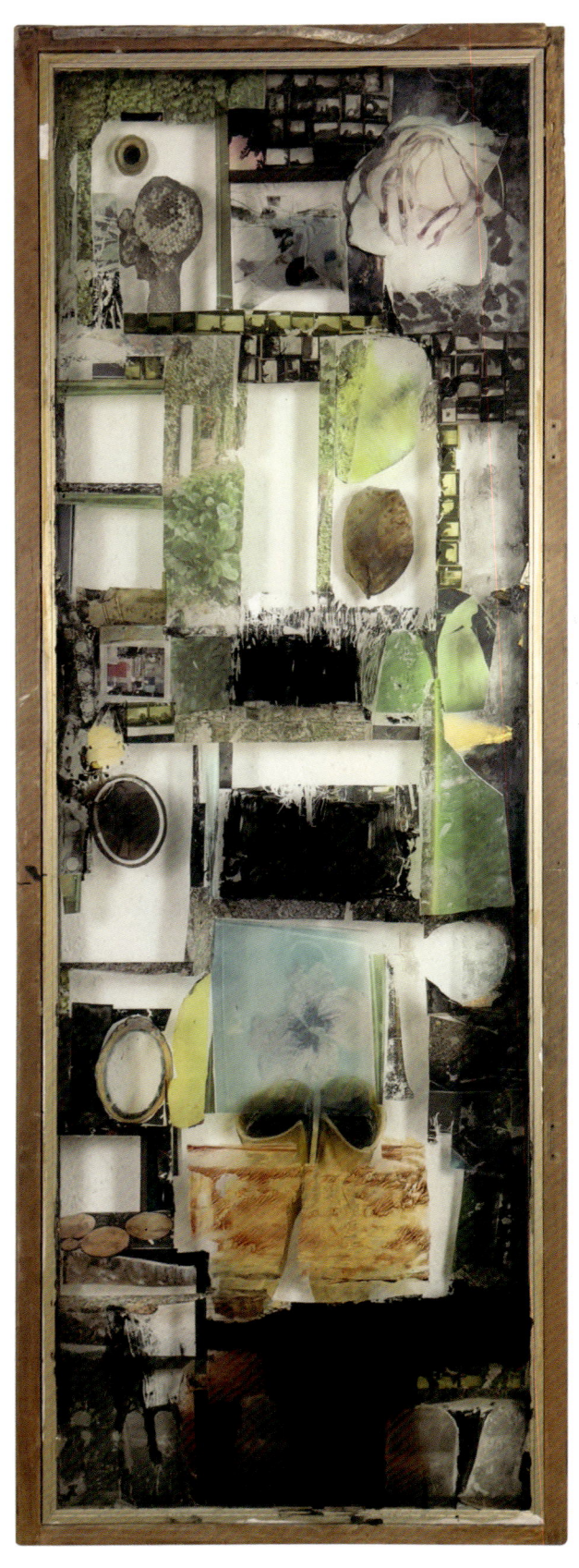

Idyll
63 x 23 inches
Mixed Media on Layered Glass
2016

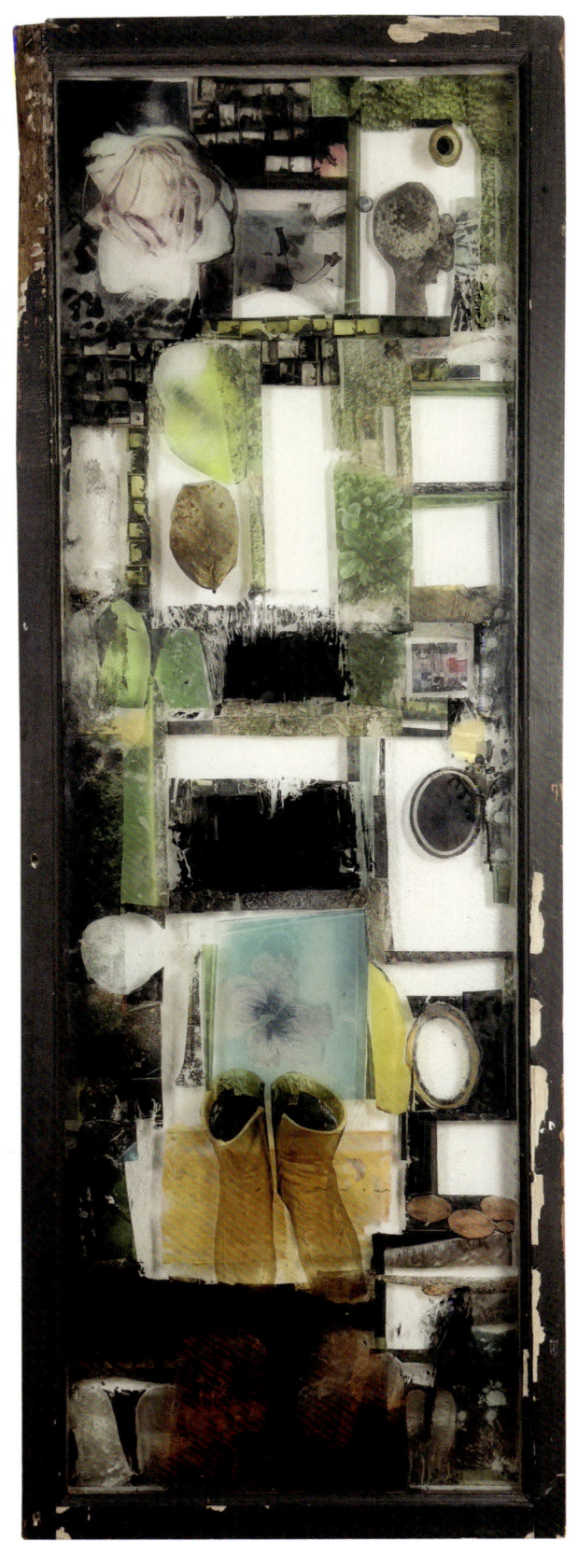

Idyll (Back View)

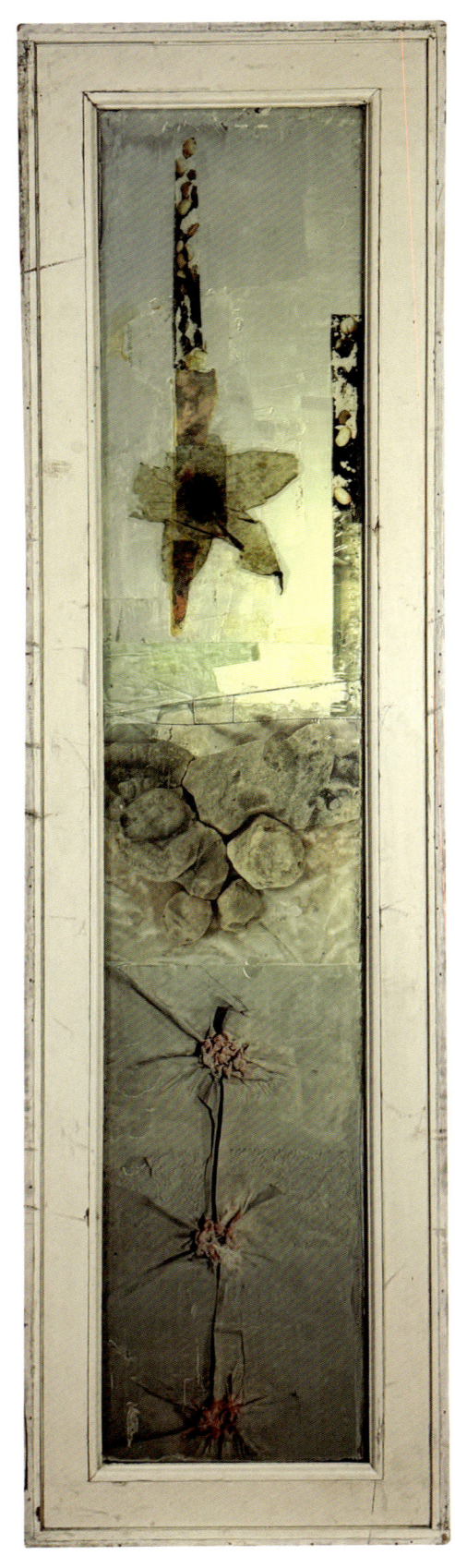

Window Box
62 x 17 inches
Mixed Media on Glass
2016

210

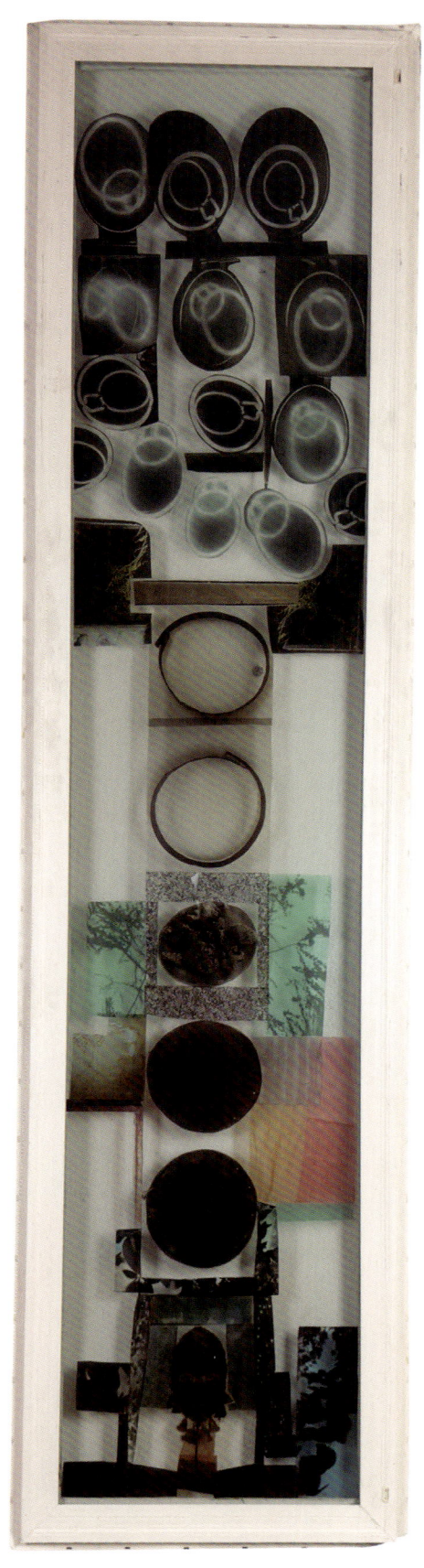

Mantra
97 x 25 ½ inches
Mixed Media on Glass
2017

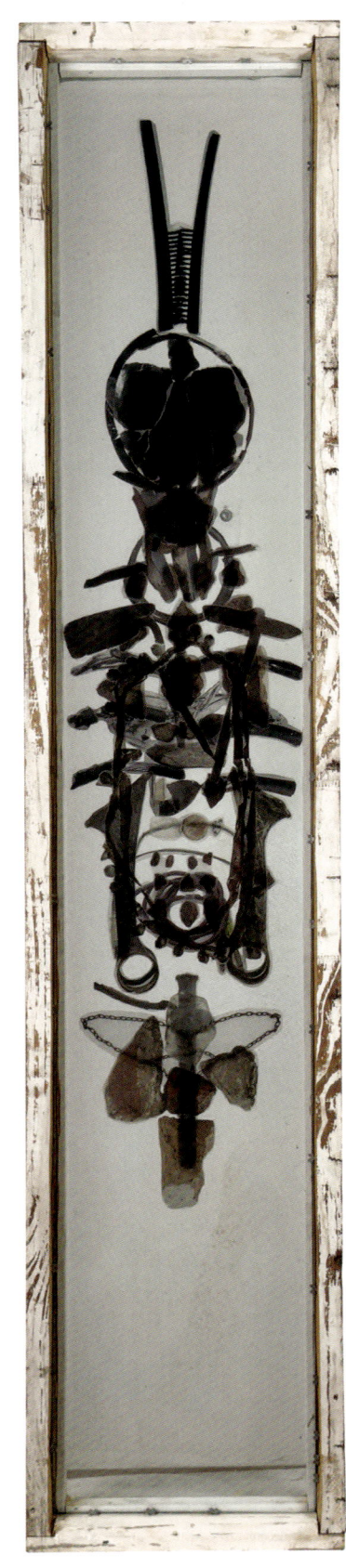

Mummy
65 x 14 inches
Mixed Media on Layered Glass
2017

212

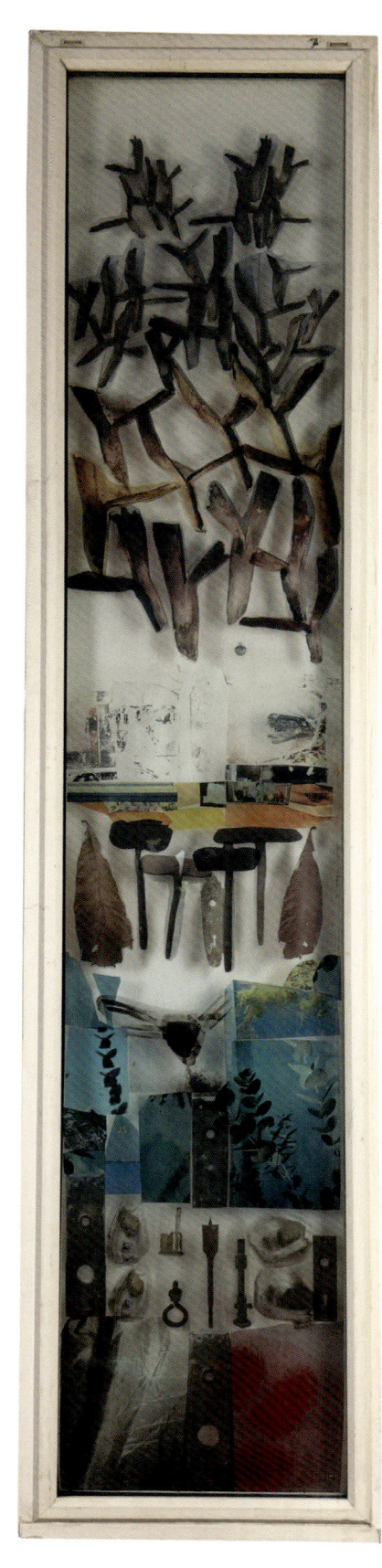

Allegory
97 x 25 ½ inches
Mixed Media on Glass
2017

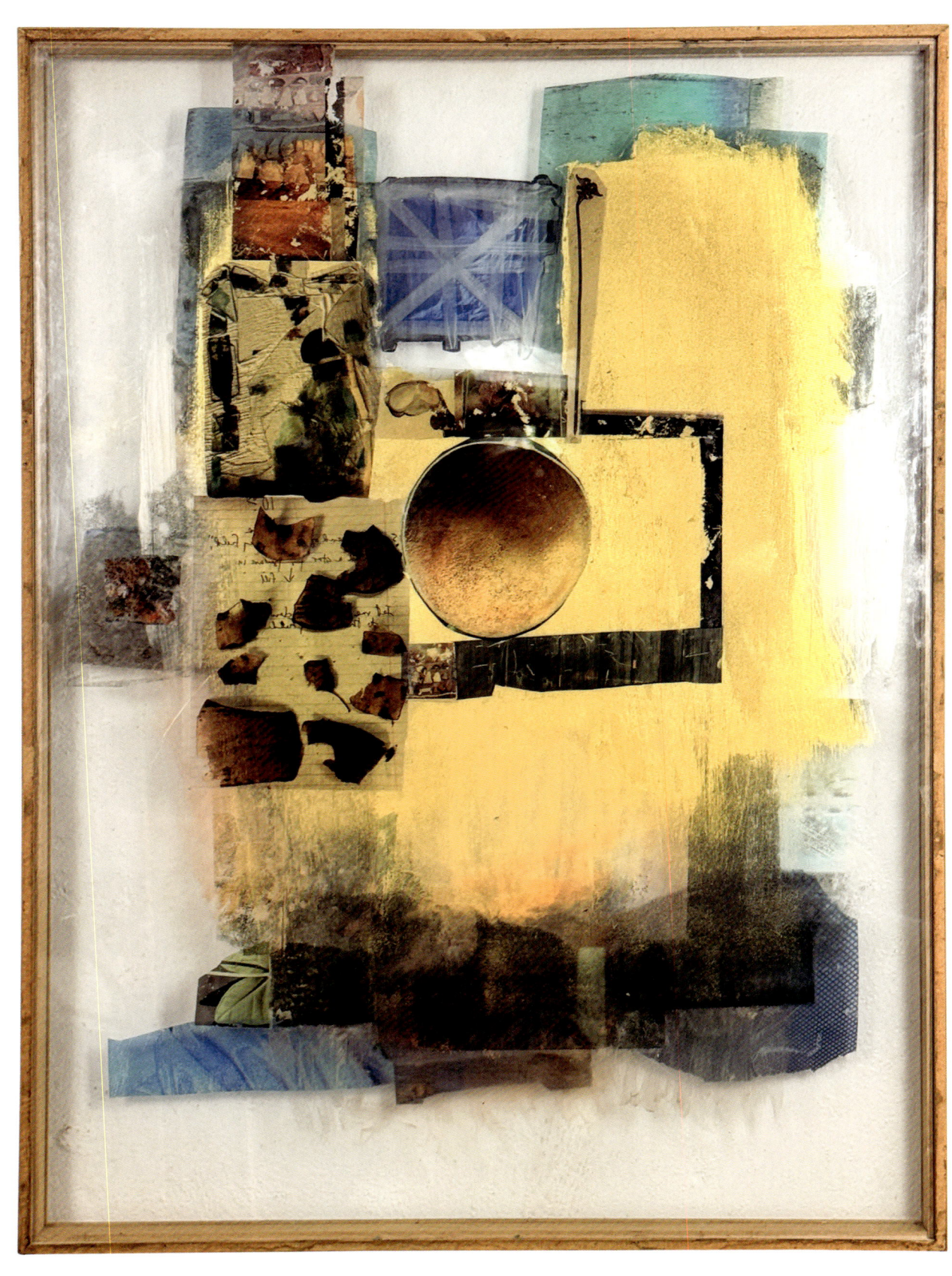

Tarp (Front)
44 x 32 inches
Mixed Media on Layered Plexiglass
2018

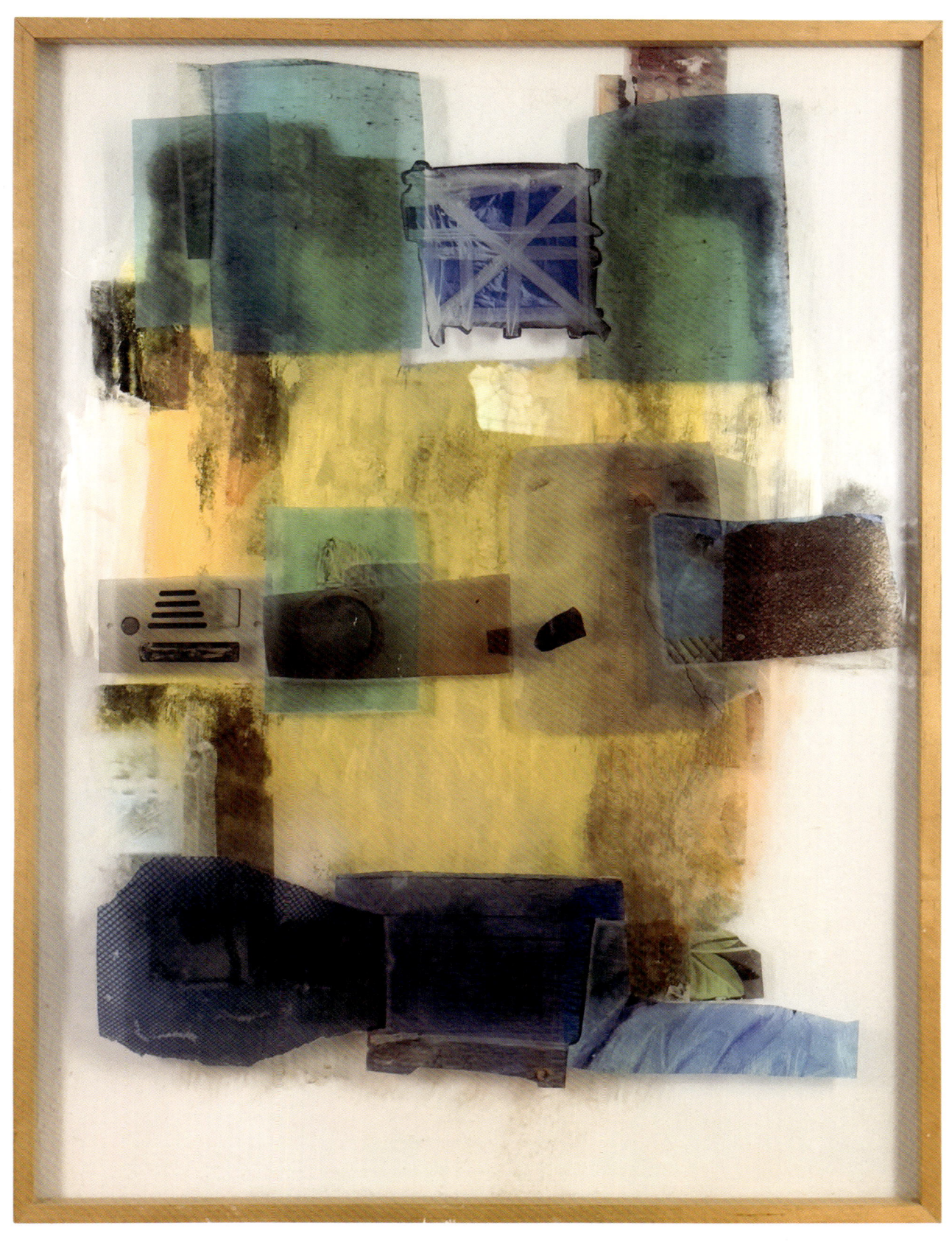

Tarp (Back View)

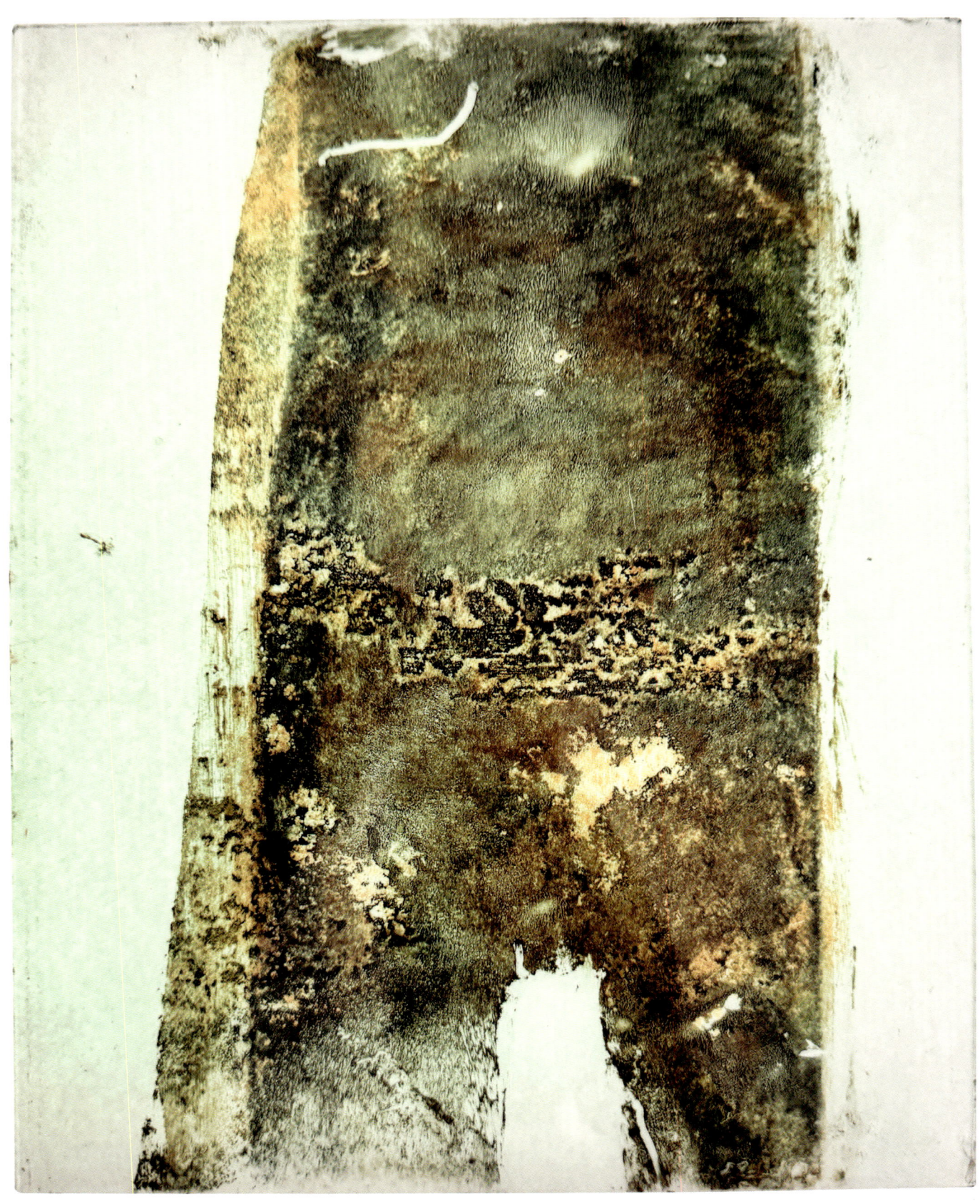

Odalesque
11 x 7 inches
Mixed Media on Glass
2018

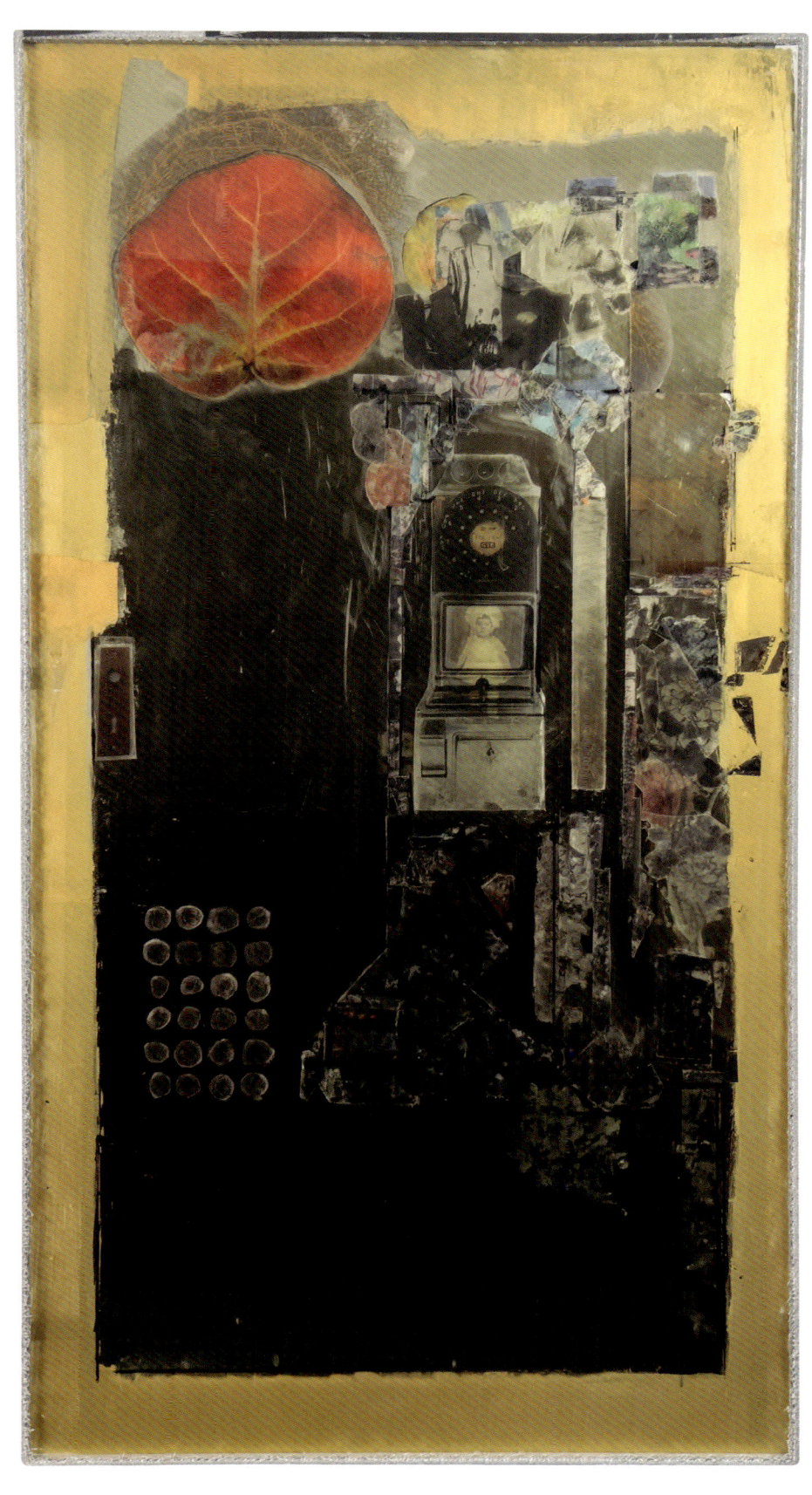

Earl King's Office
96 x 48 inches
Mixed Media on Glass
2024

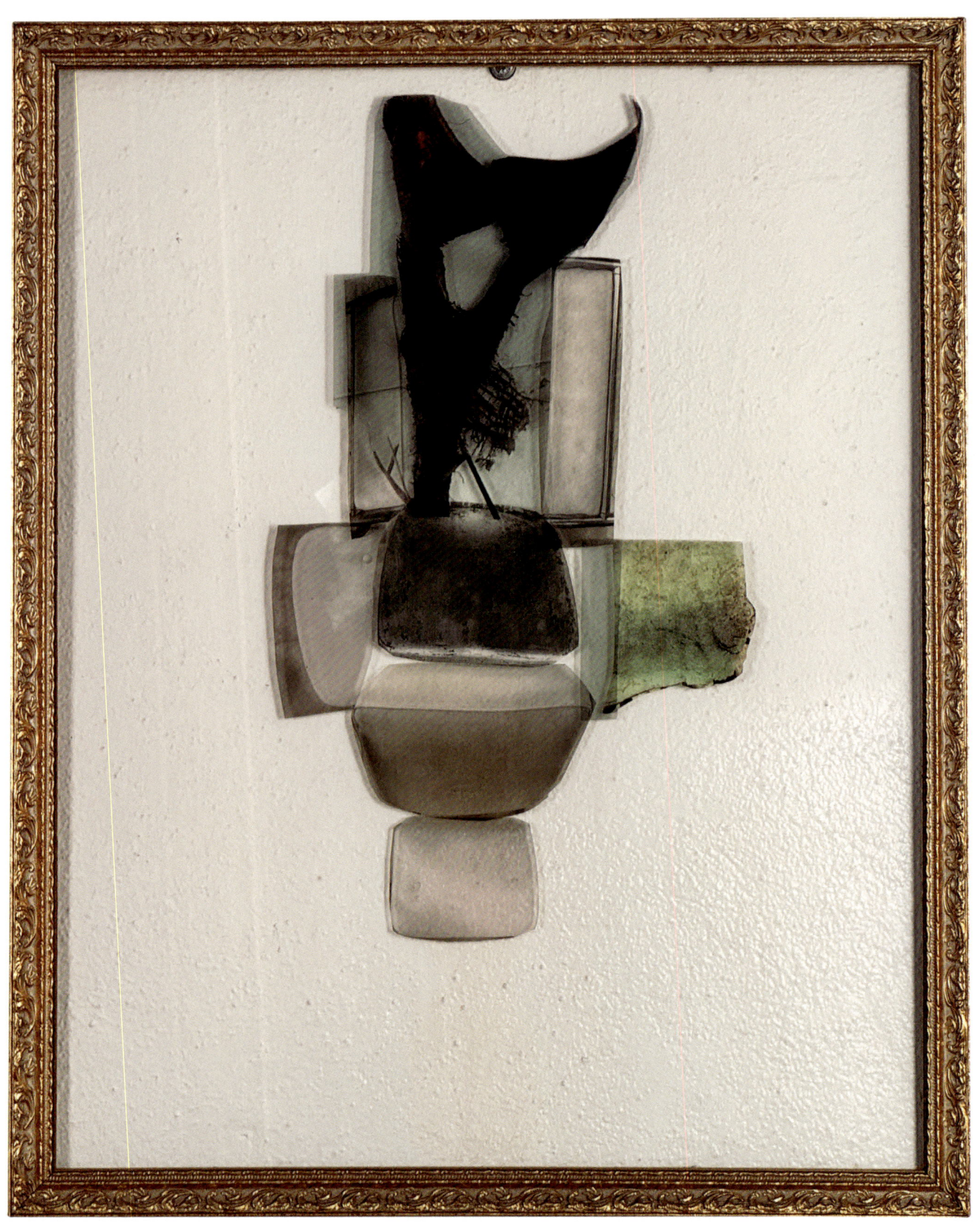

Early Chair 3
40 x 30 inches
Photo Collage on Plexiglass
2018

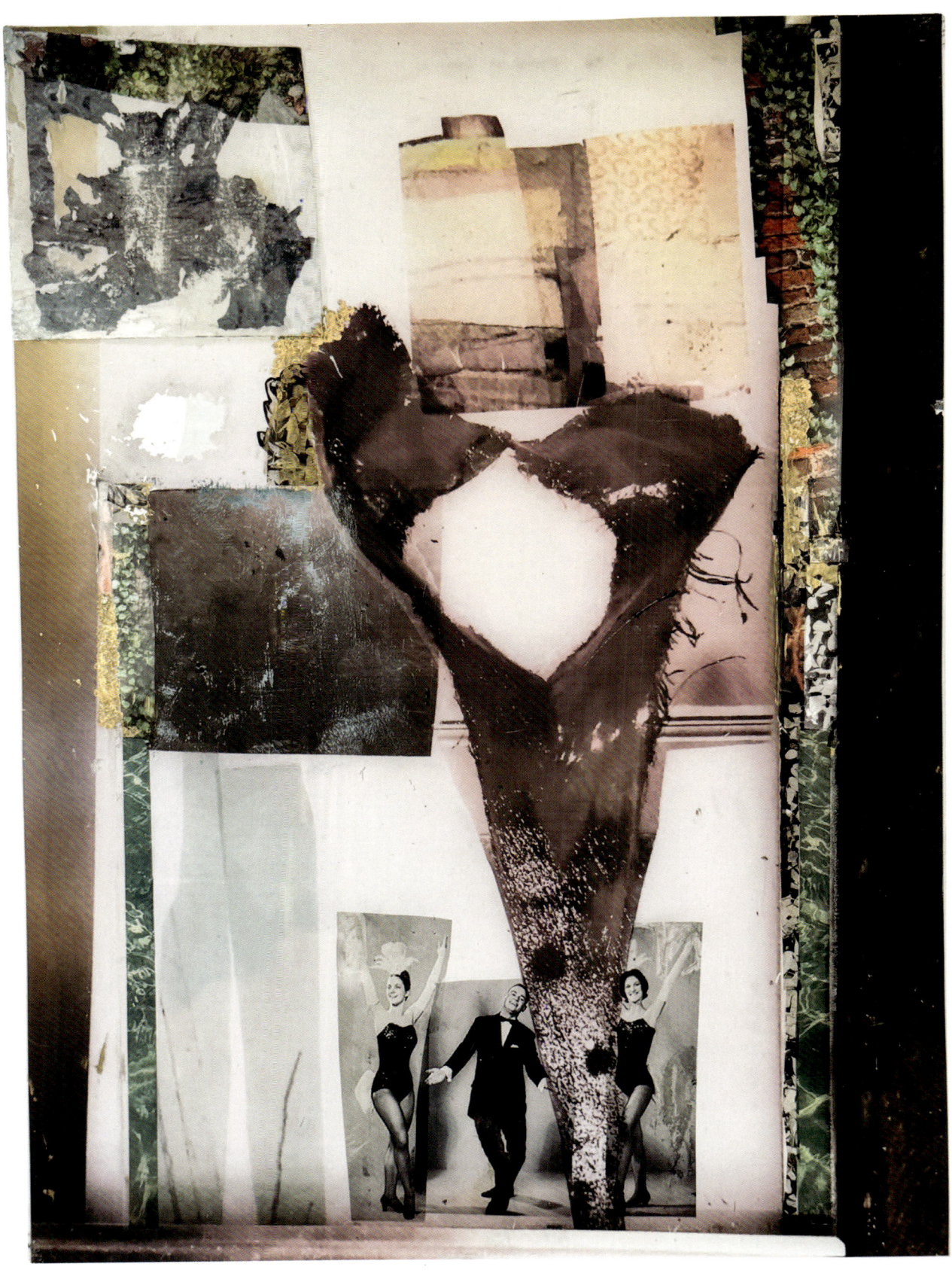

Curtain Call
40 x 30 inches
Mixed Media on Foam
2024

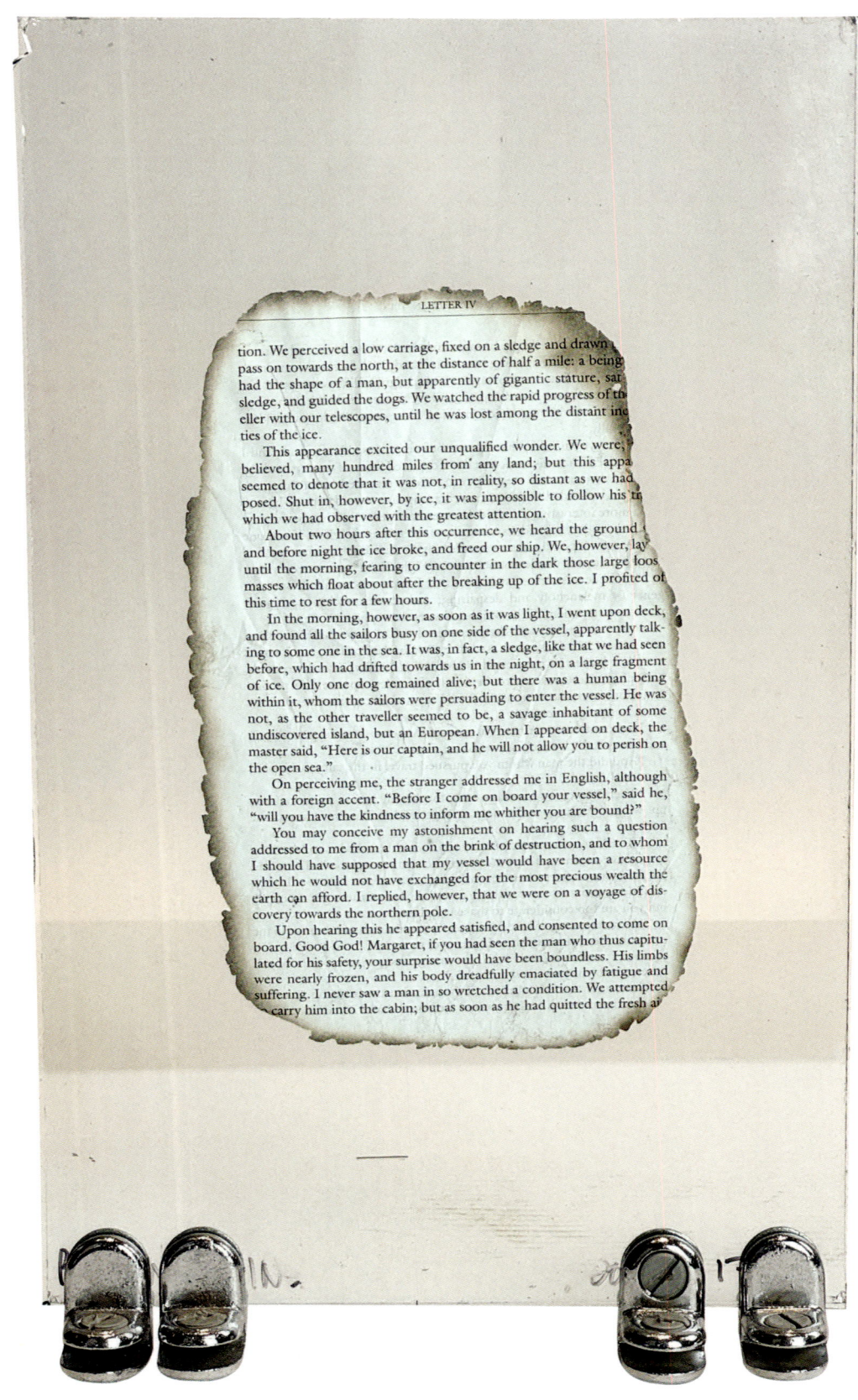

Burned Page from Frankenstein Blown Against My Studio Door
8 ½ x 6 ½ inches
Paper and Glass
2021

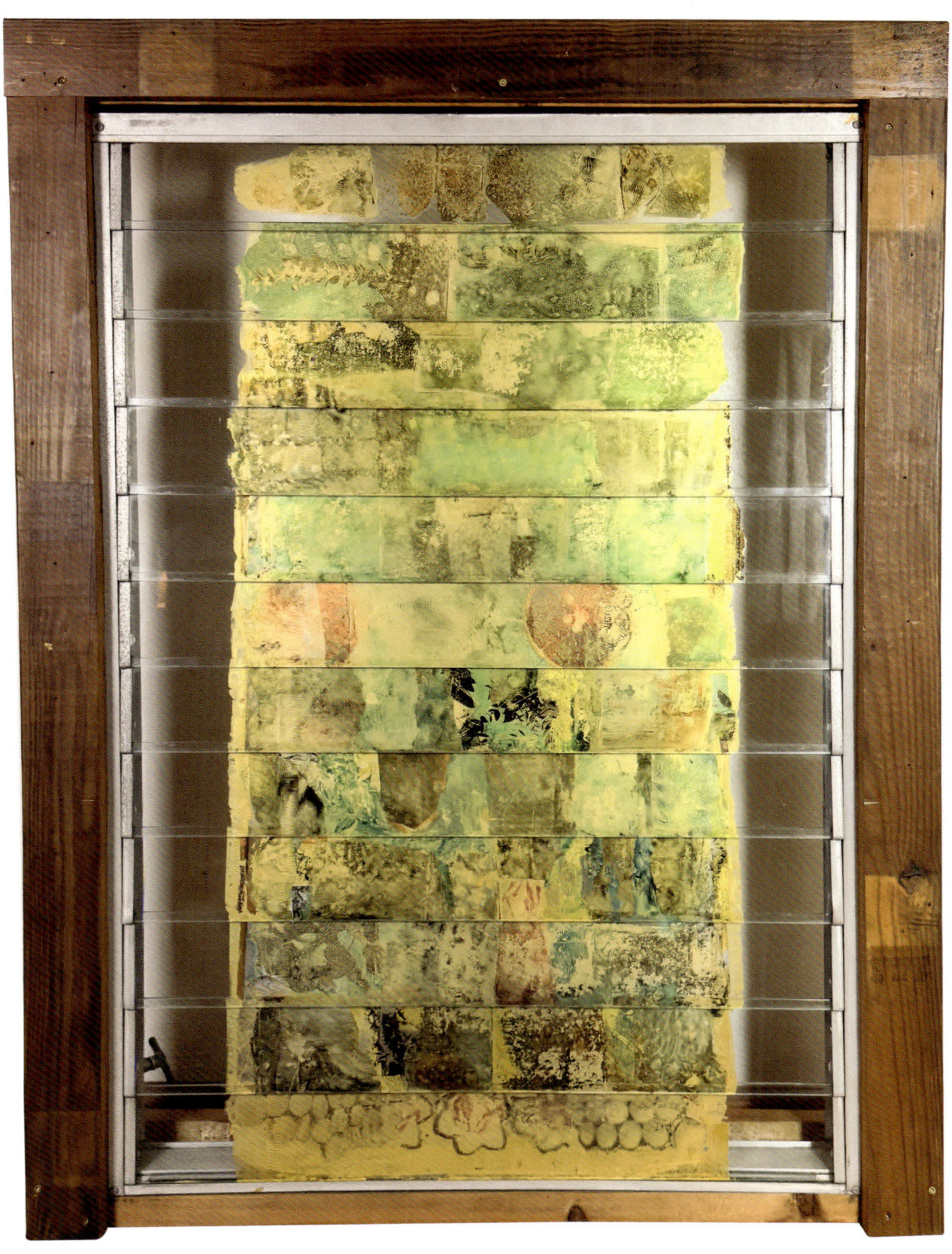

Quilt
60 ½ x 41 inches
Mixed Media, Louvered Glass
2016

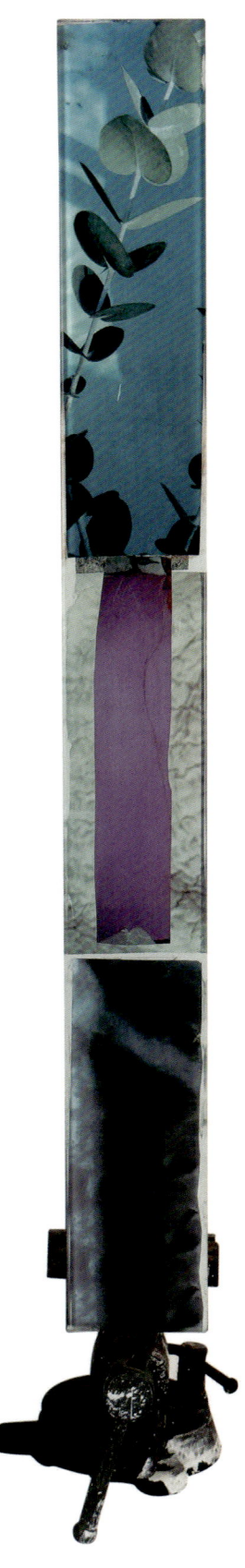

Monolith
30⅛ x 9 ½ inches
Mixed Media on Glass w/ Vise
2010

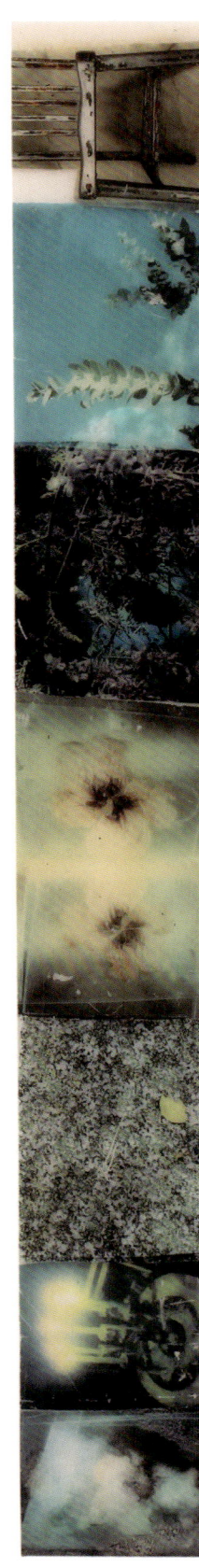

Slot
49 ½ x 6 inches
Mixed Media on White Plexiglass
2008

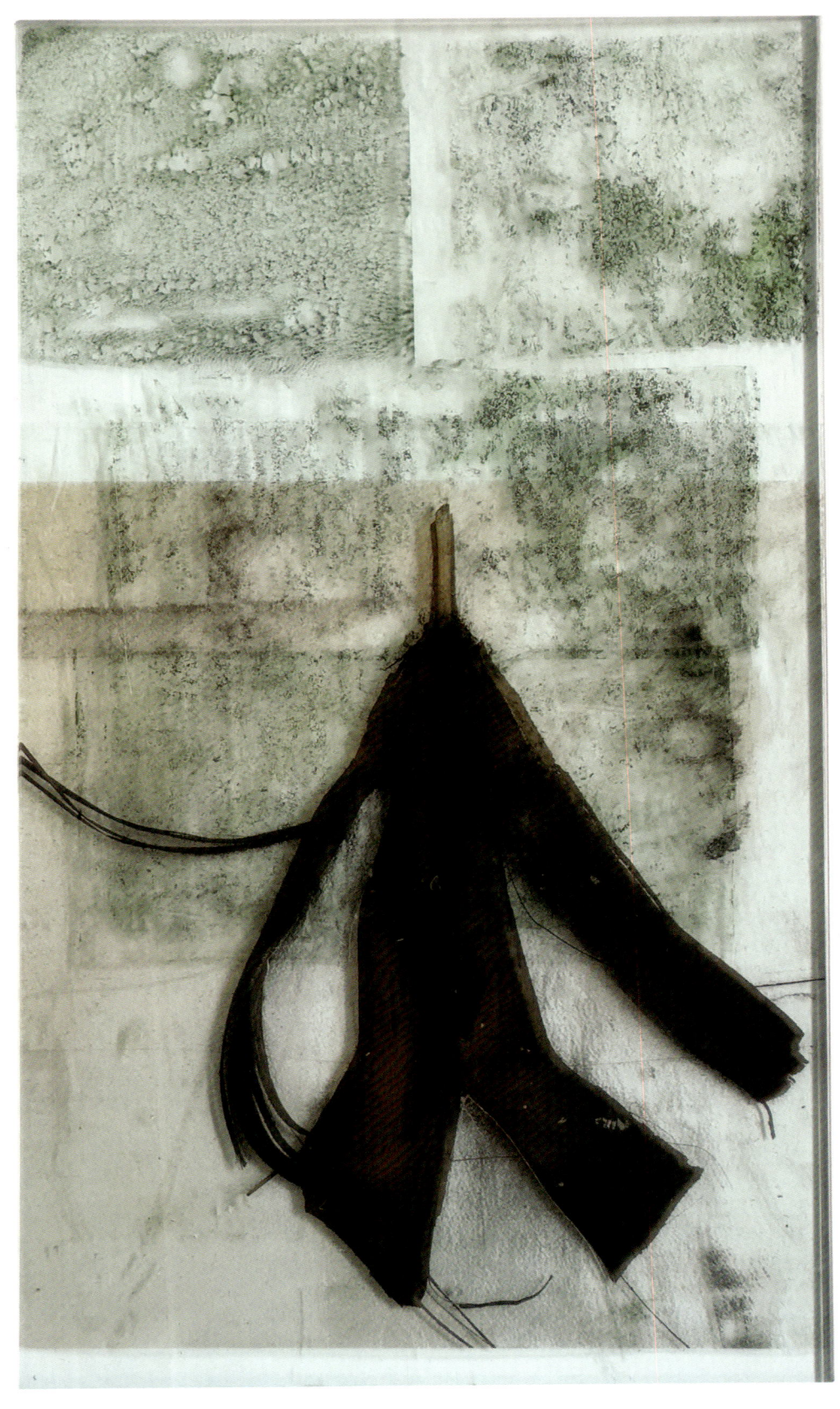

Glass Relief 2
24 x 14 inches
Mixed Media on Layered Glass
2024

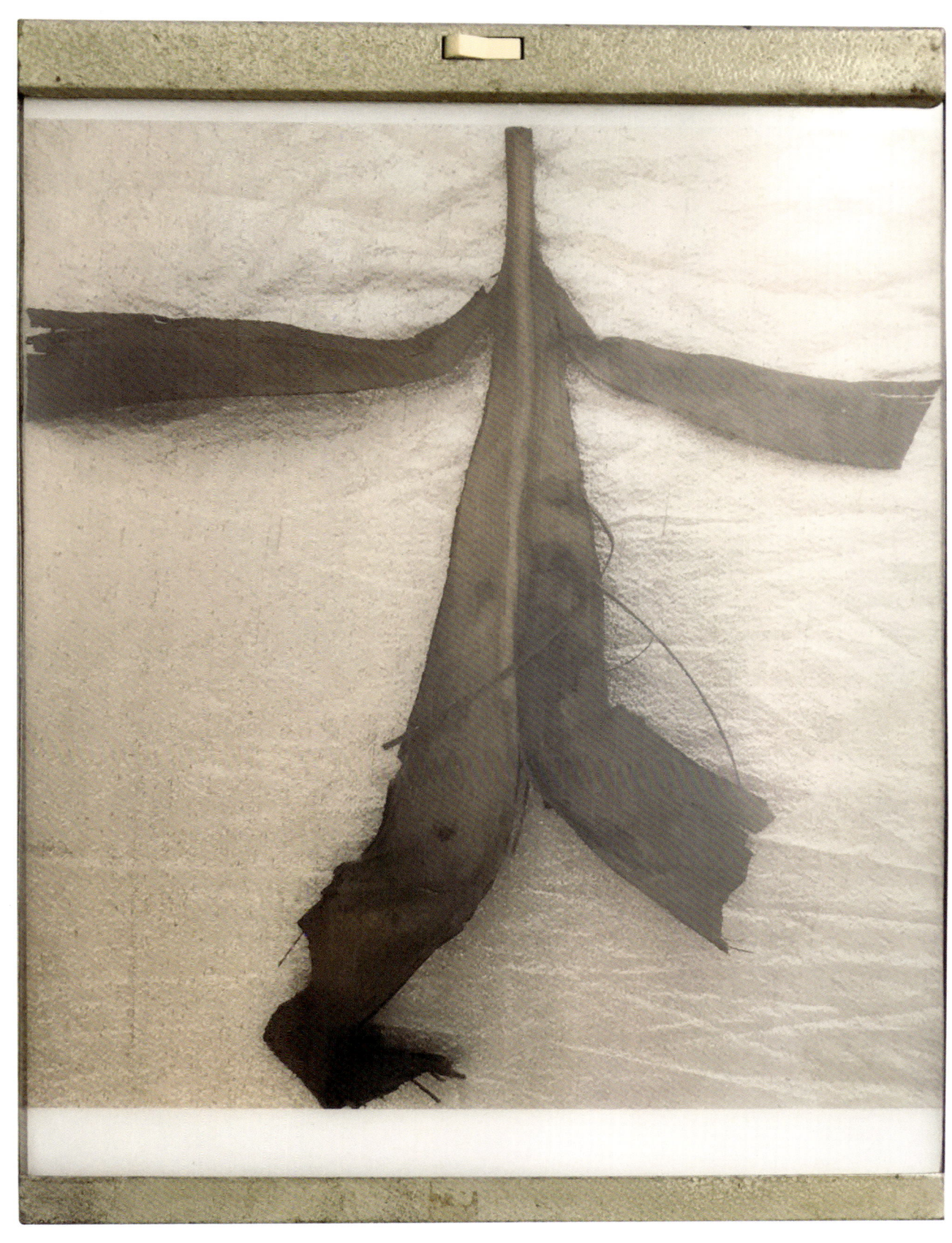

Untitled
18 x 14 inches
Color Print on Lightbox
2022

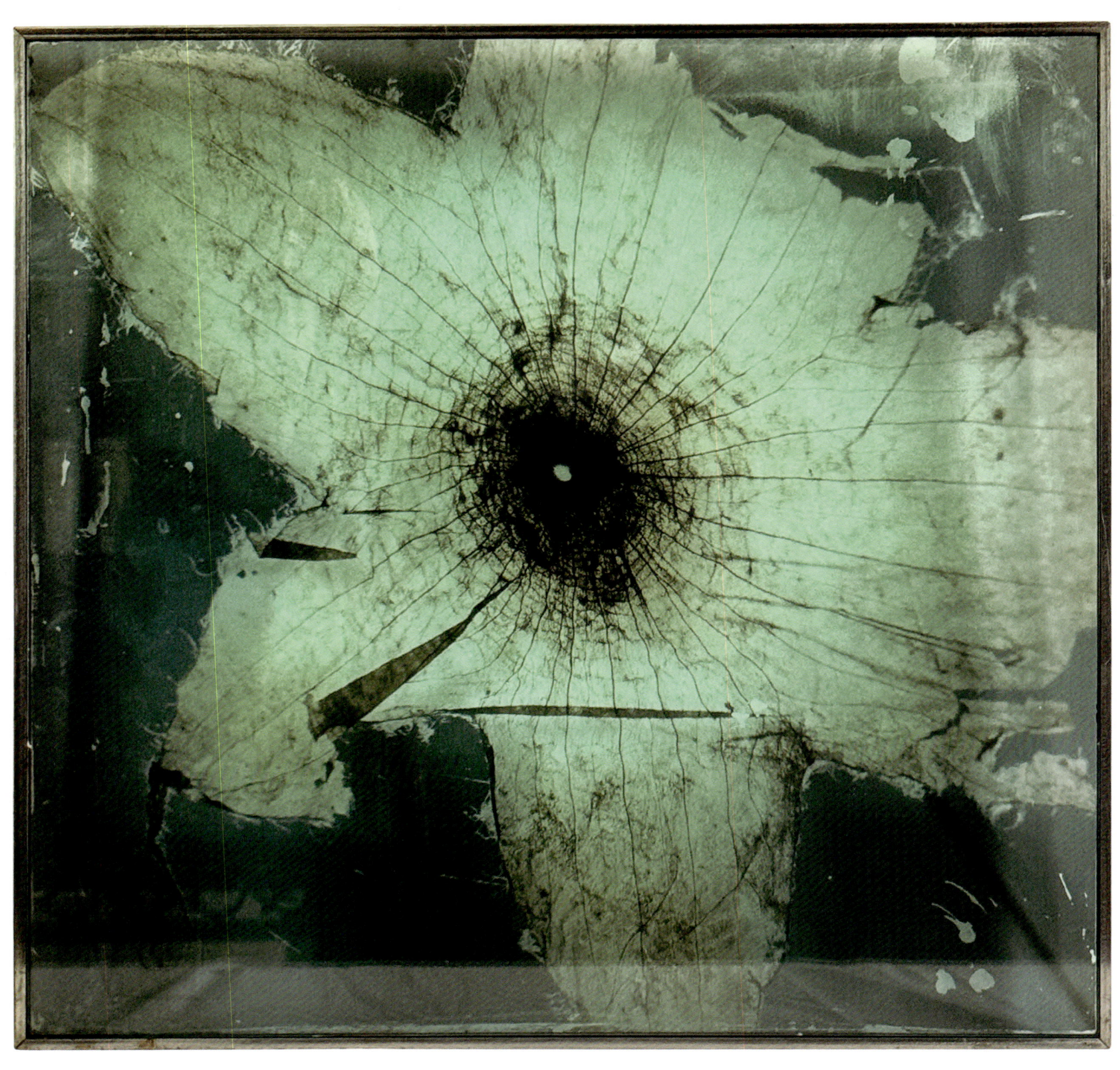

White Hole
33 ¼ x 35 ½ inches
Print on Glass
2017

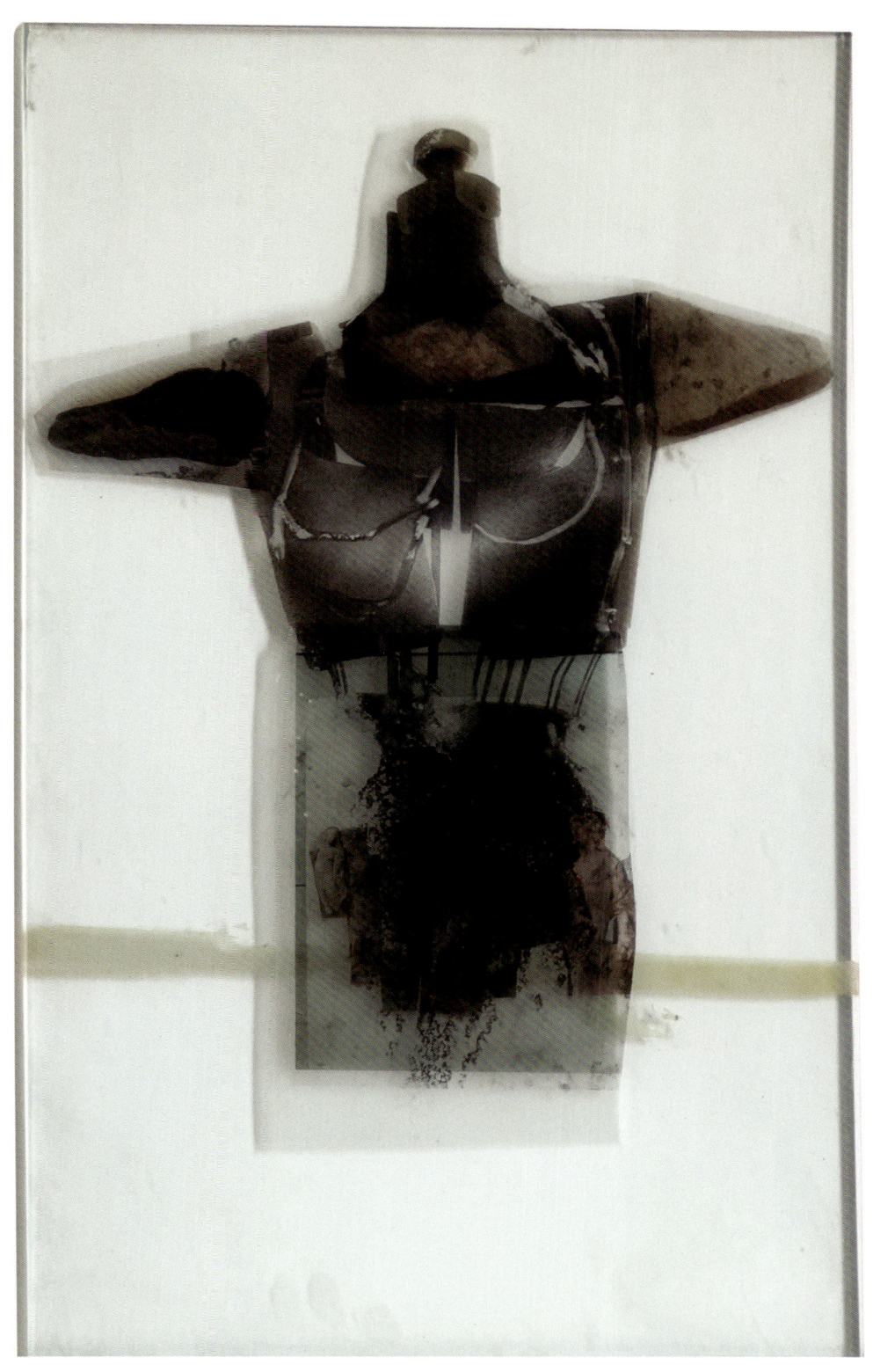

Glass Relief 1
24 x 15 inches
Mixed Media, Print on Layered Glass
2024

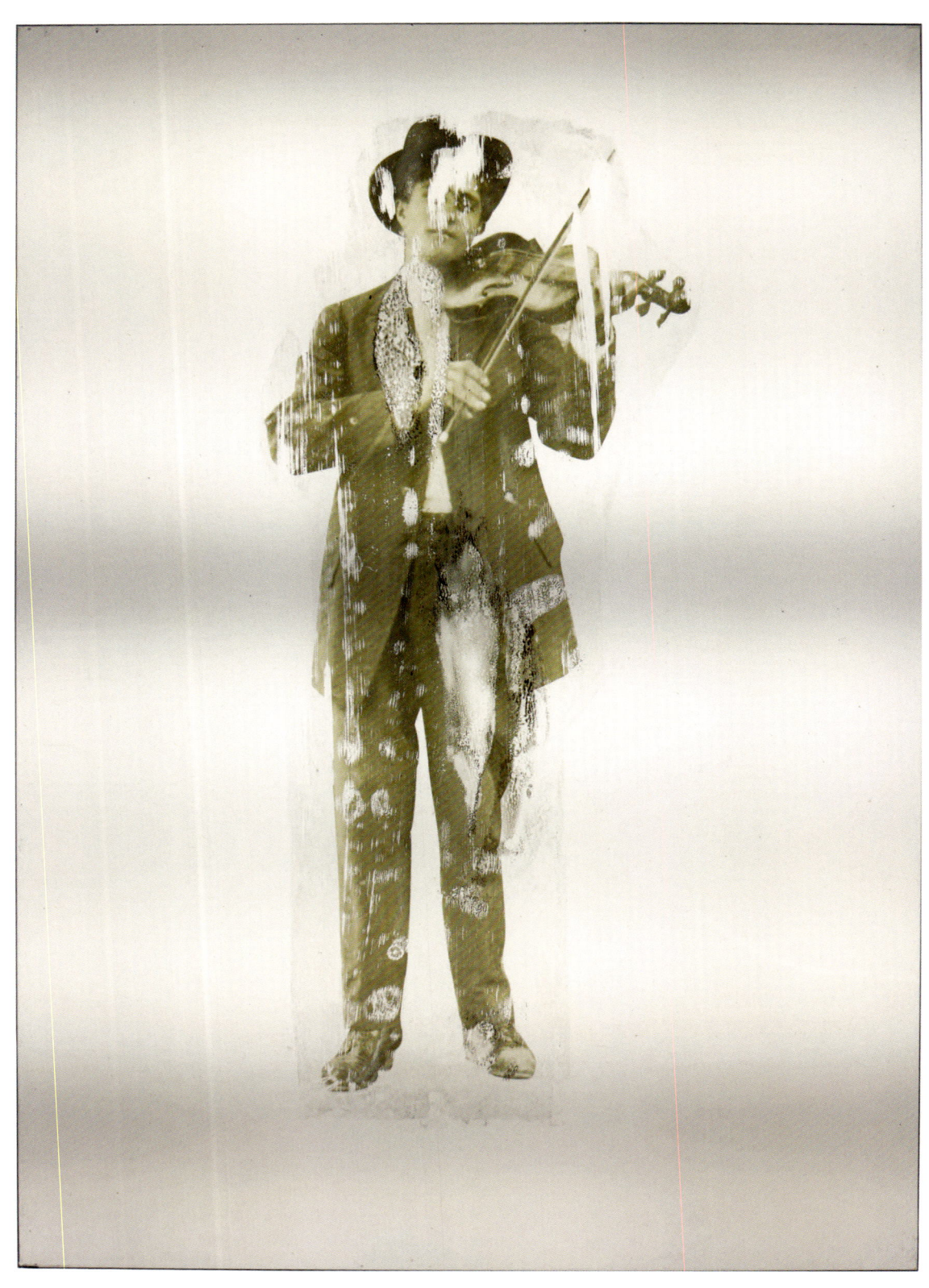

Sky Song
18 ¾ x 25 ½ inches
Illustrated Water-Soluble Print on Glass
2018

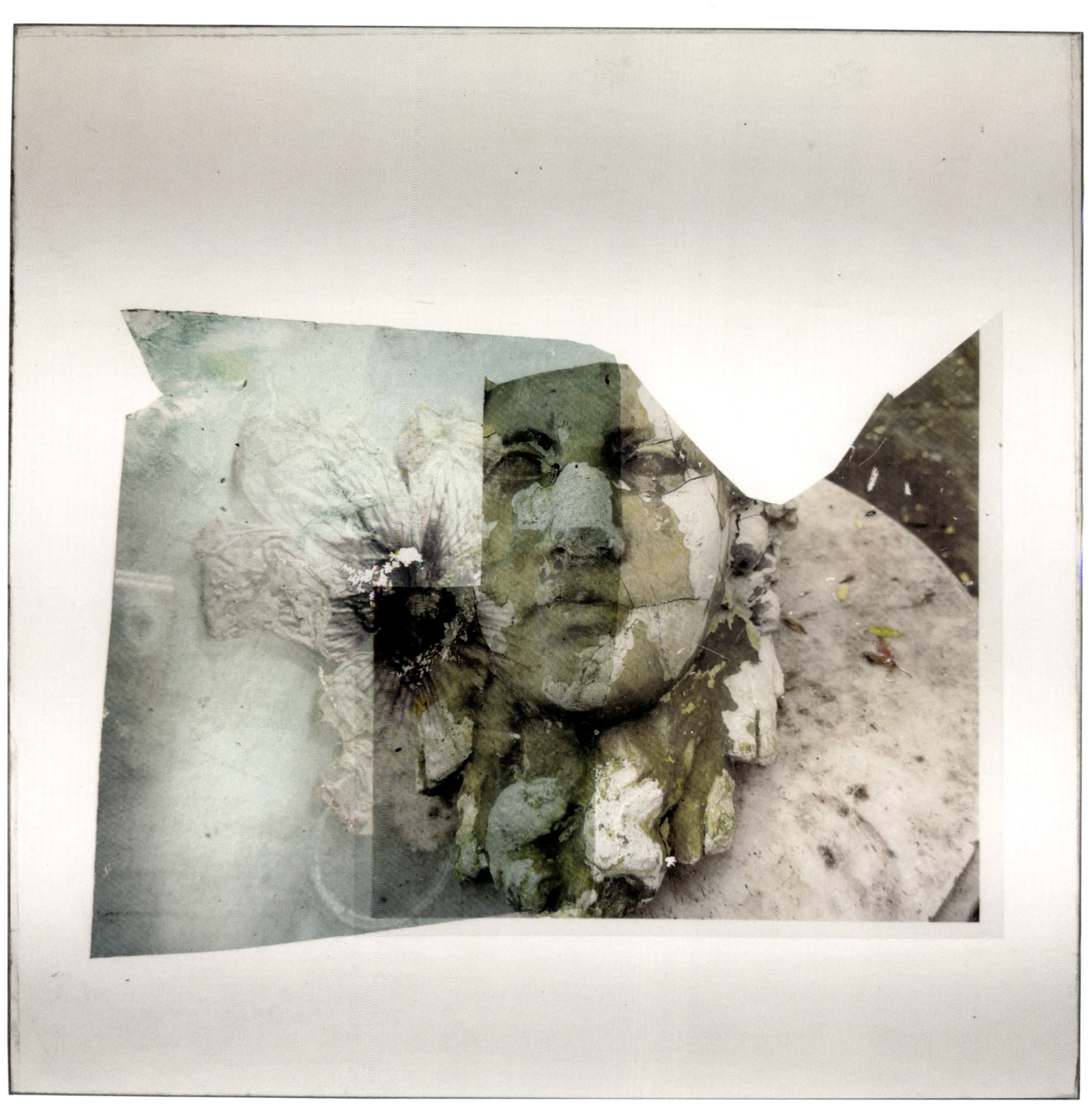

Square Tile 2
14 x 14 inches
Print on Glass w/ Aluminum Substrate
2024

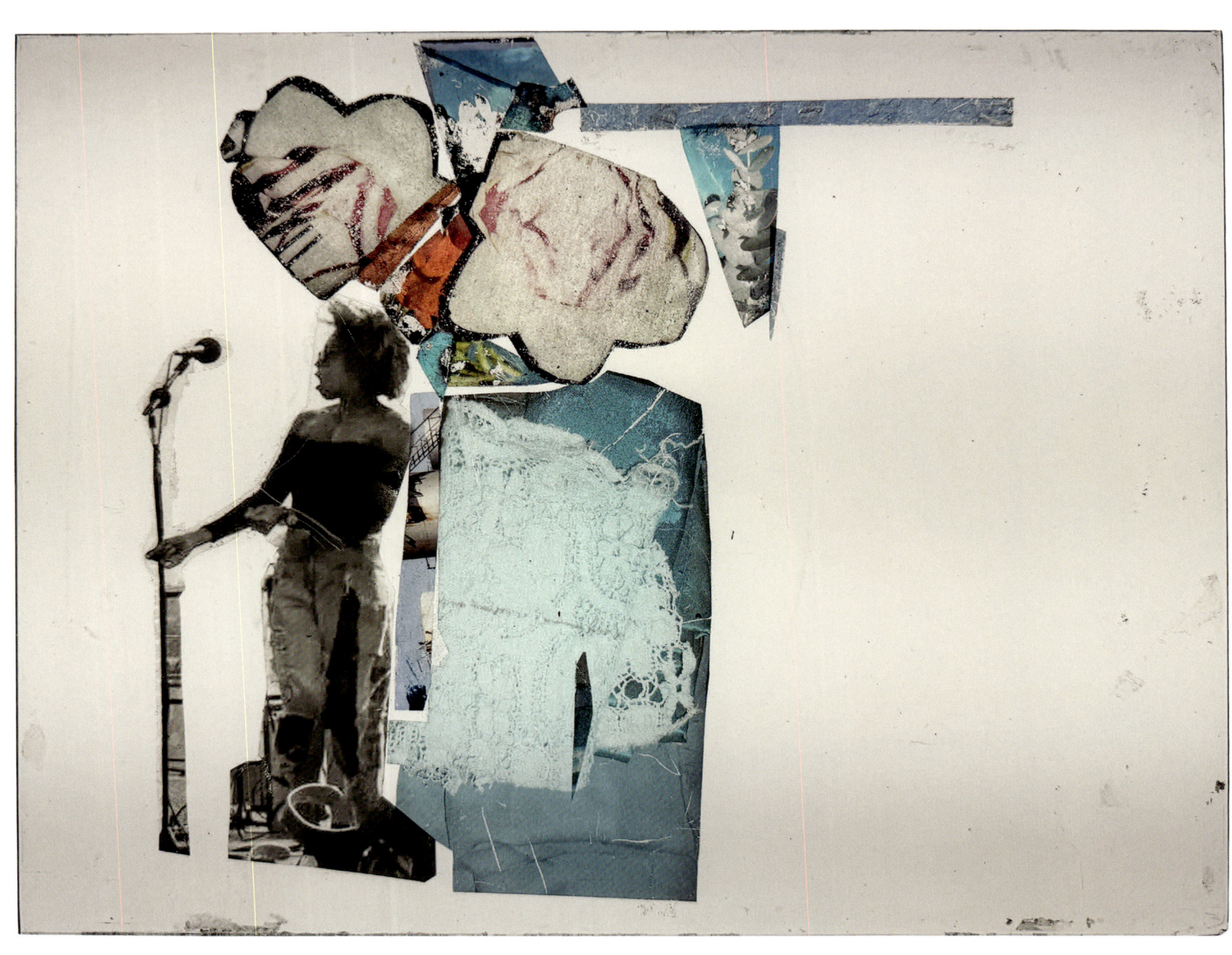

Blue Ronin I
16 x 12 inches
Mixed Media on Glass
2023

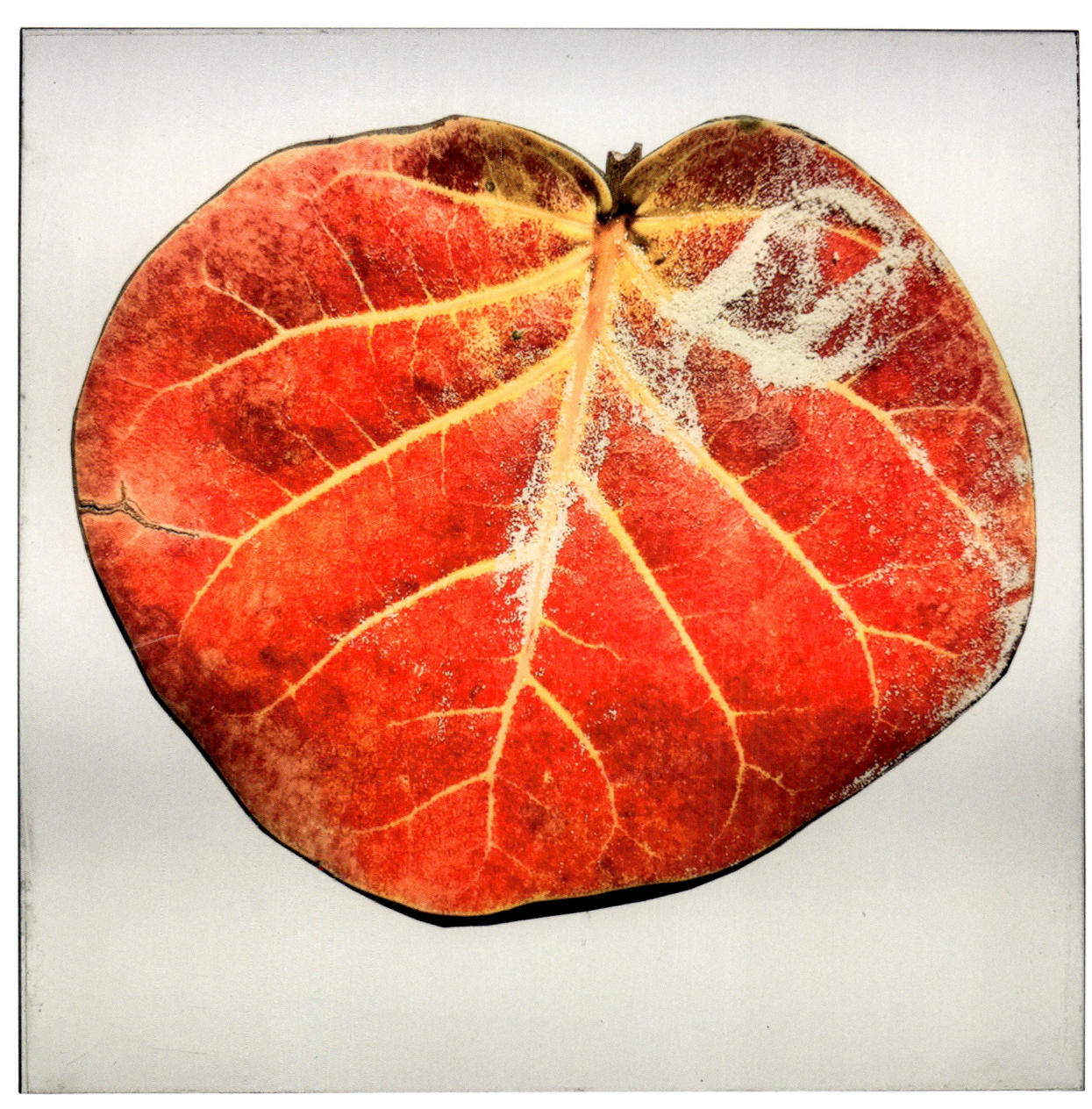

Square Tile 4
15 x 15 inches
Print on Glass w/ Aluminum Substrate
2024

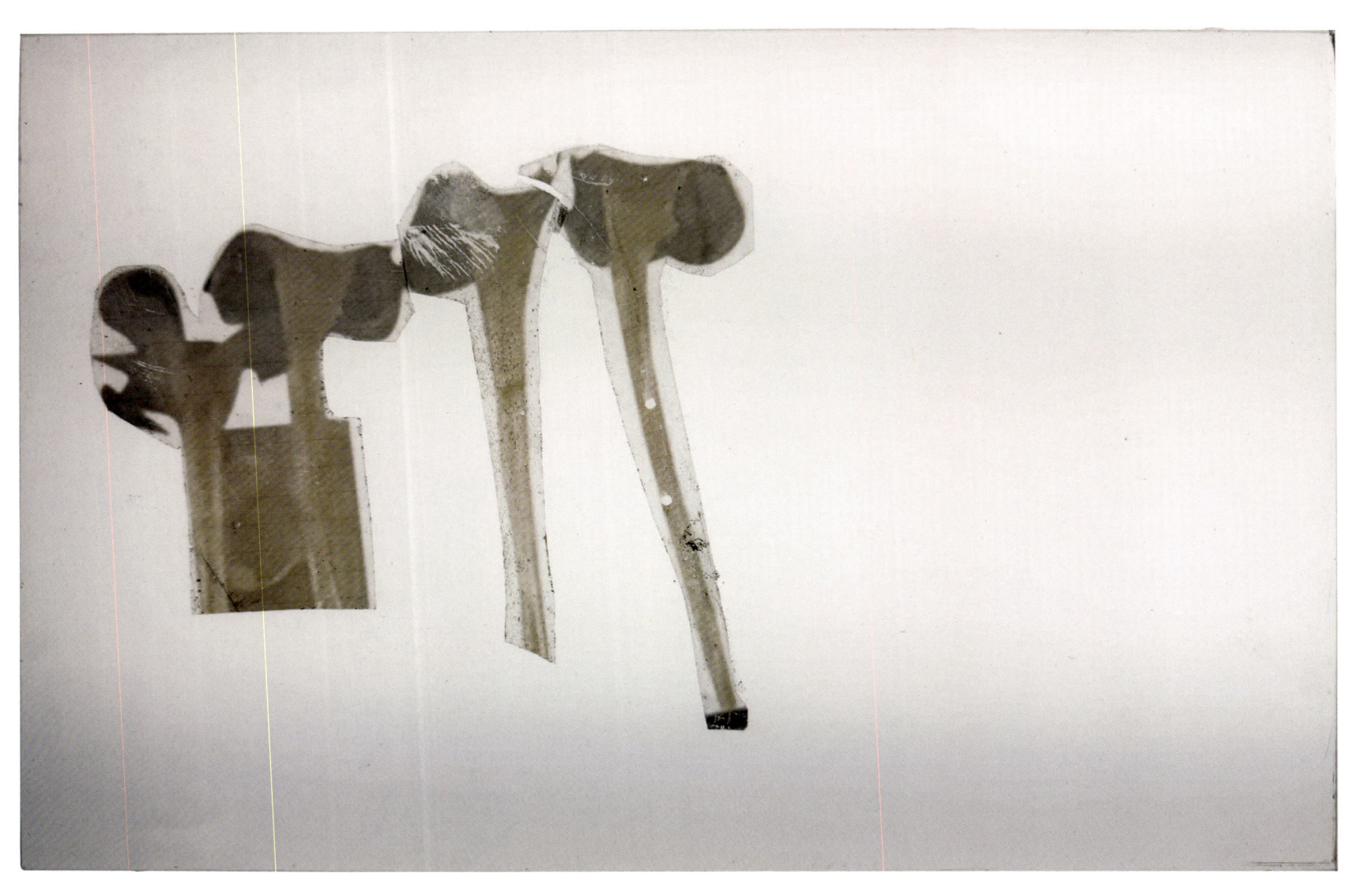

Glass Tile 4
10 x 16 inches
Mixed media on Glass w/ Aluminum Substrate
2024

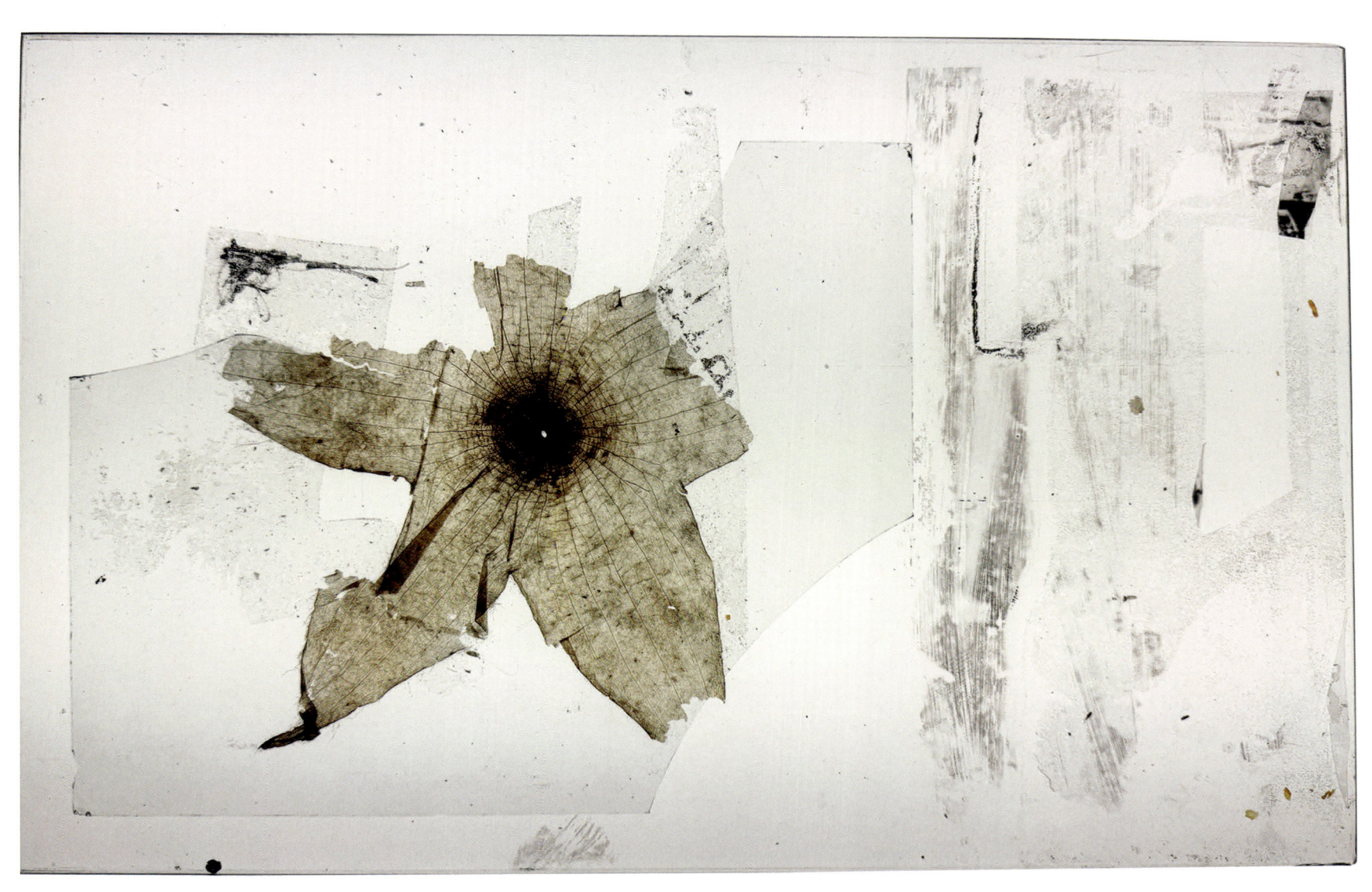

Glass Tile 3
10 x 16 inches
Mixed Media on Glass w/ Aluminum Substrate
2024

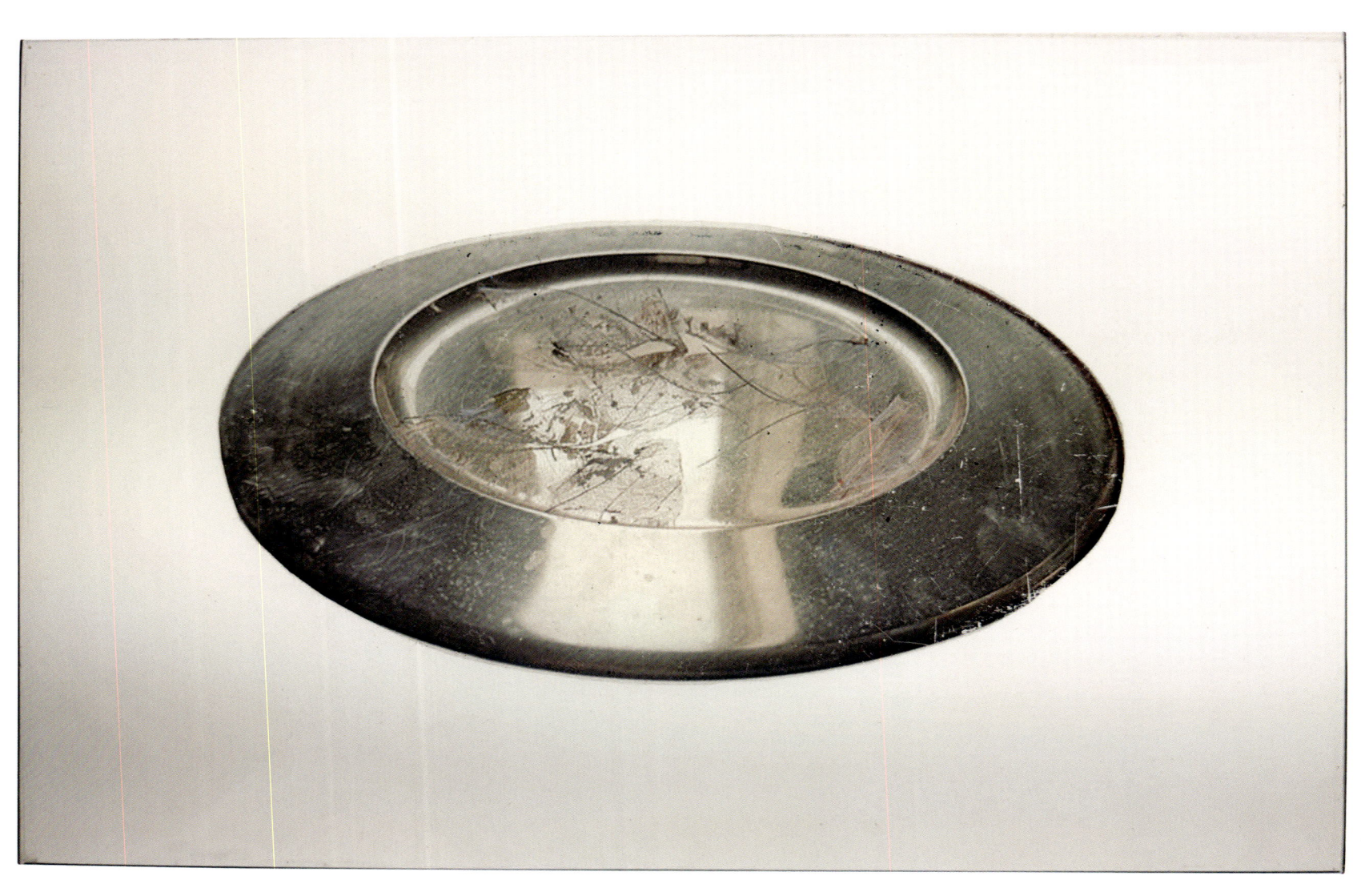

Glass Tile 1
10 x 16 inches
Print on Glass w/ Aluminum Substrate
2024

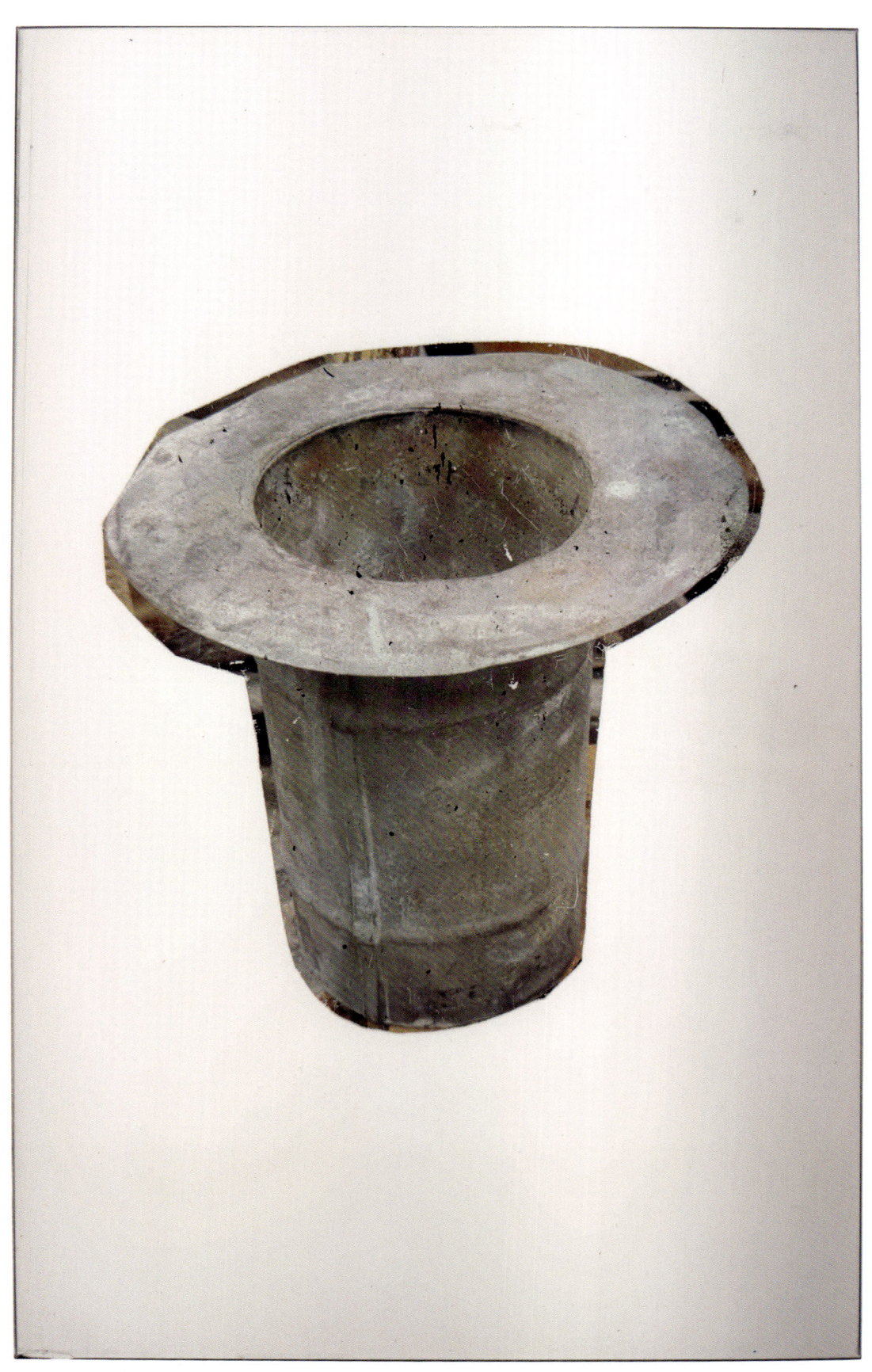

Glass Tile 2
10 x 16 inches
Print on Glass w/ Aluminum Substrate
2024

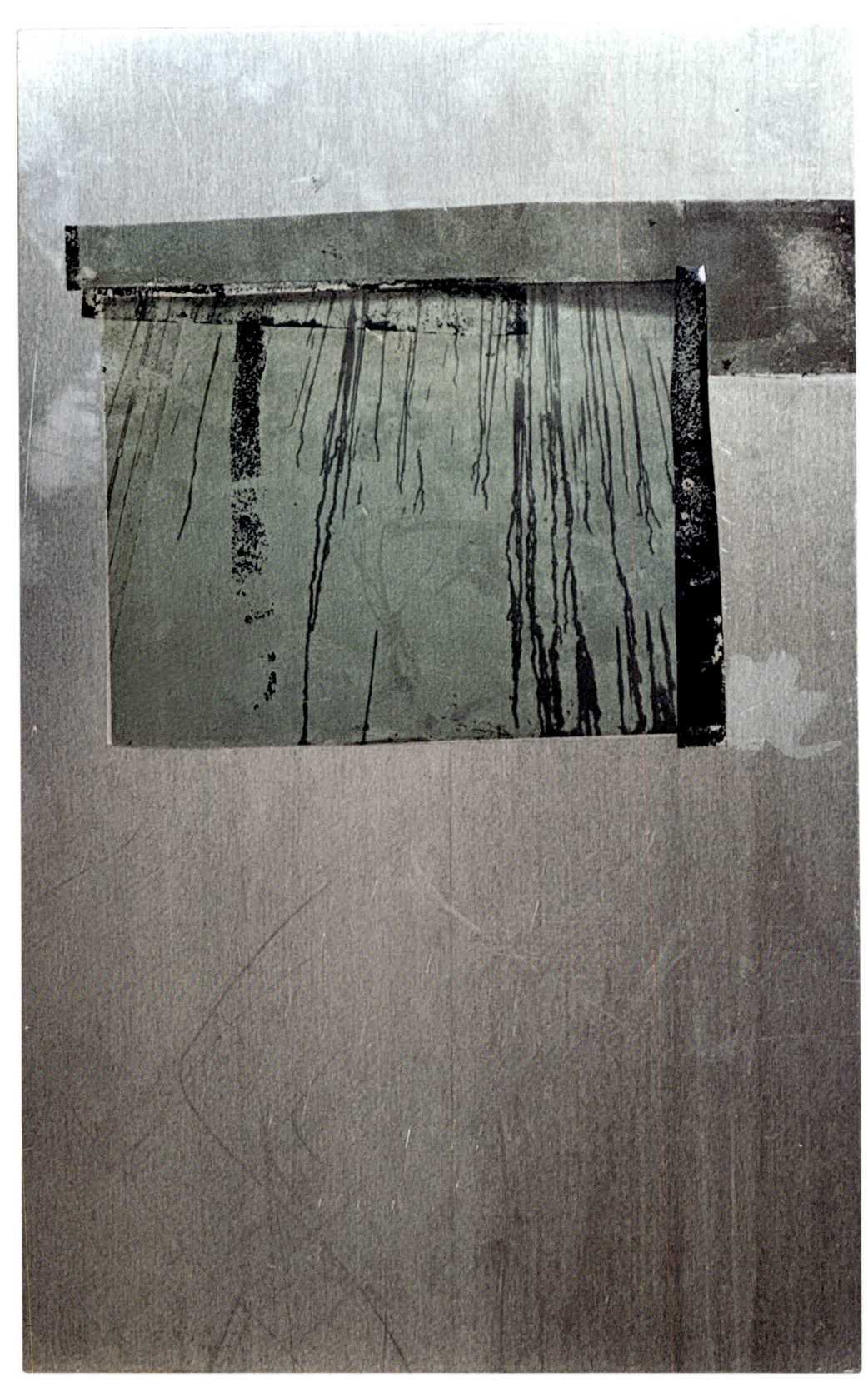

Glass Tile 8
10 x 16 inches
Mixed Media on Aluminum
2024

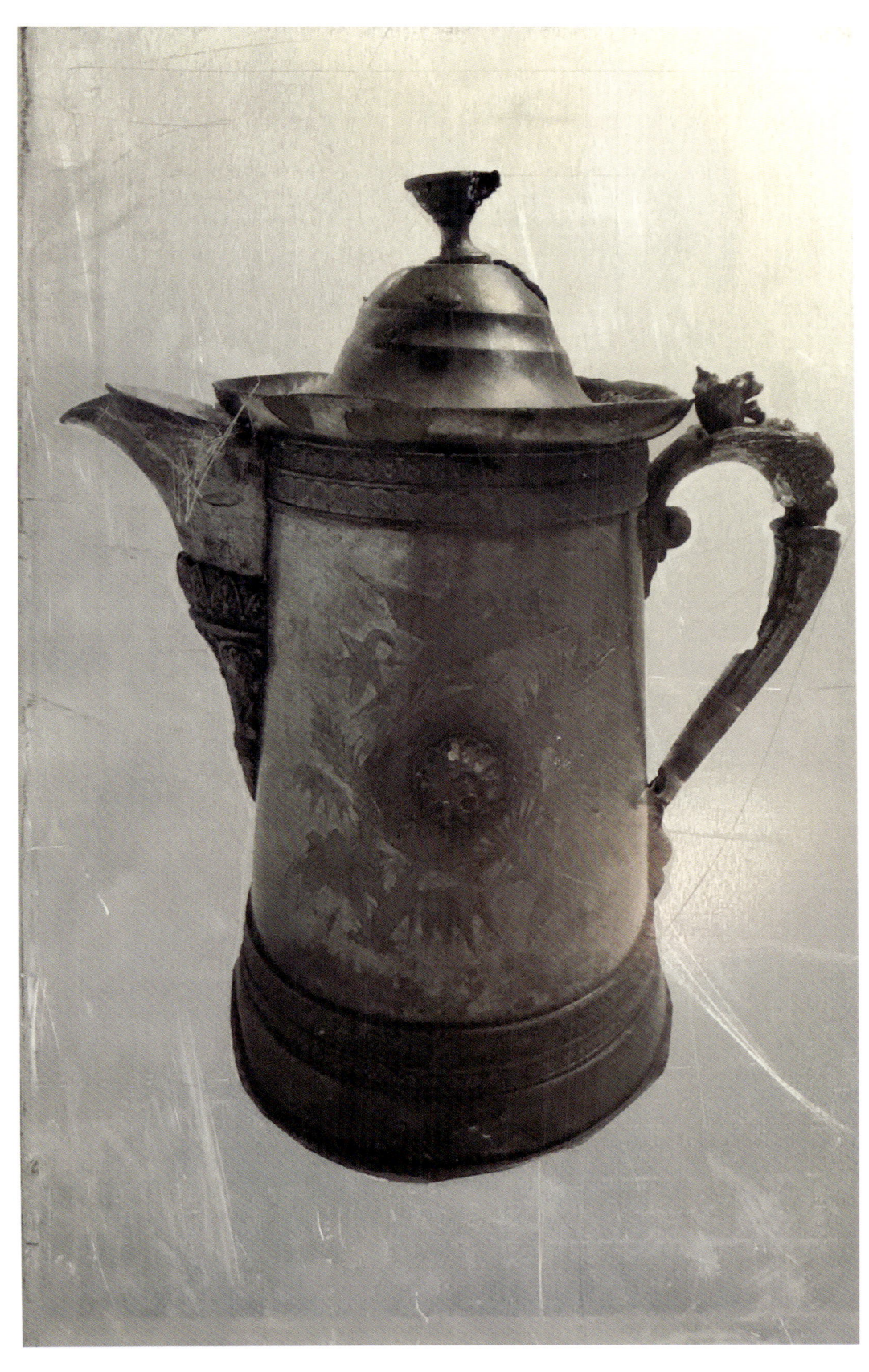

Glass Tile 9
16 x 10 inches
Print on Aluminum Substrate
2024

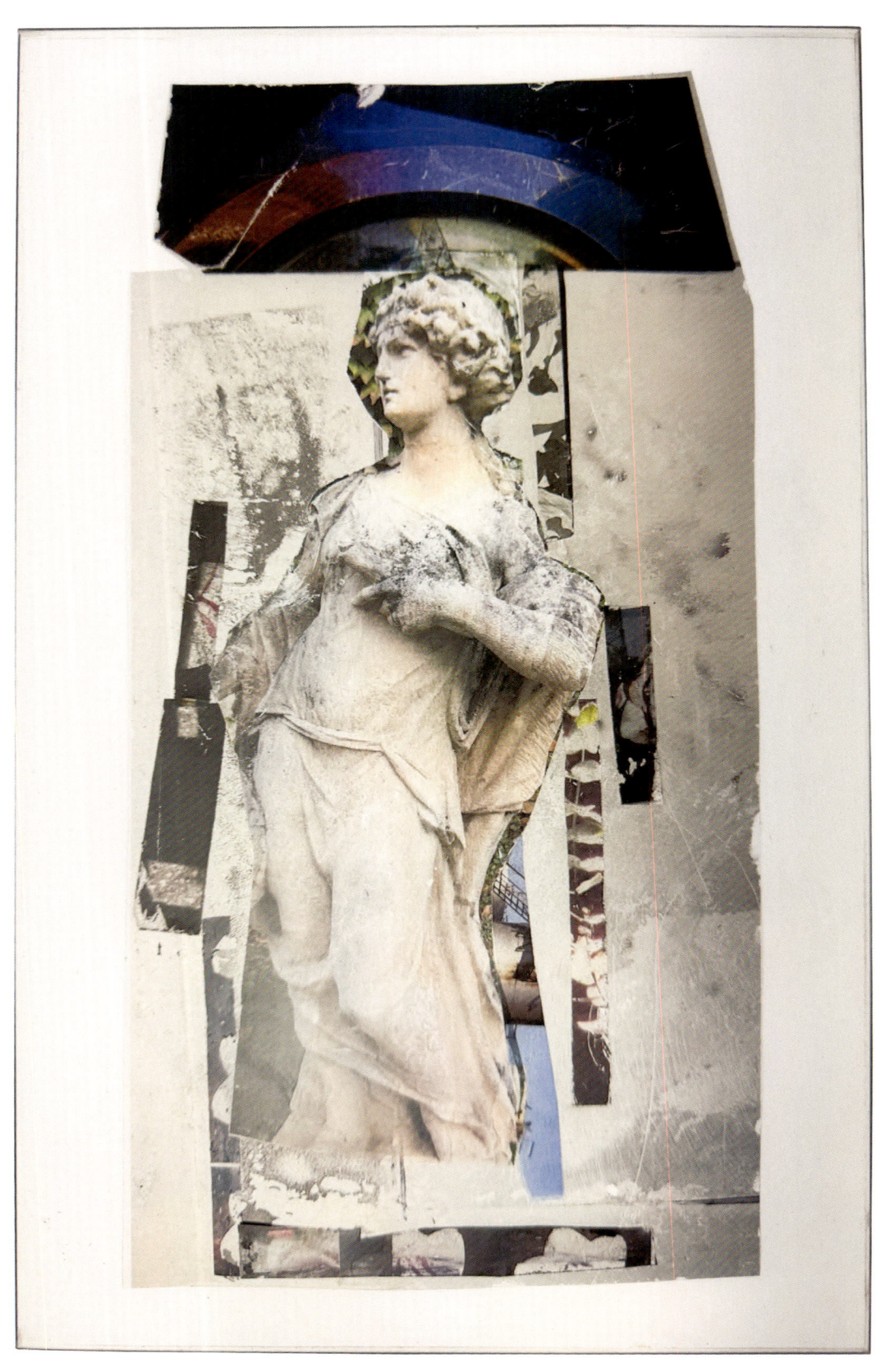

Glass Tile 5
16 x 10 inches
Mixed Media on Glass
2024

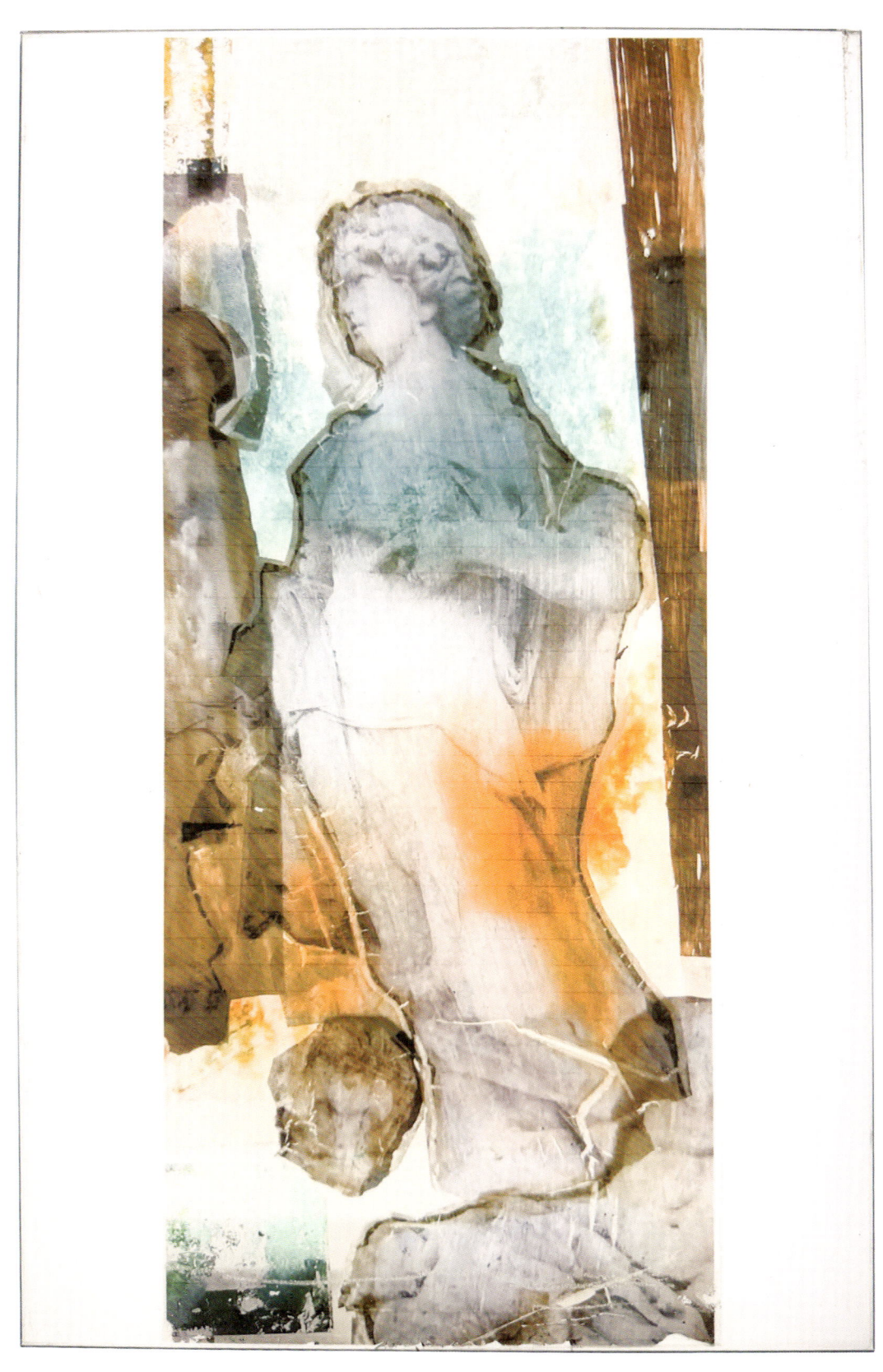

Glass Tile 6
16 x 10 inches
Mixed Media on Glass
2024

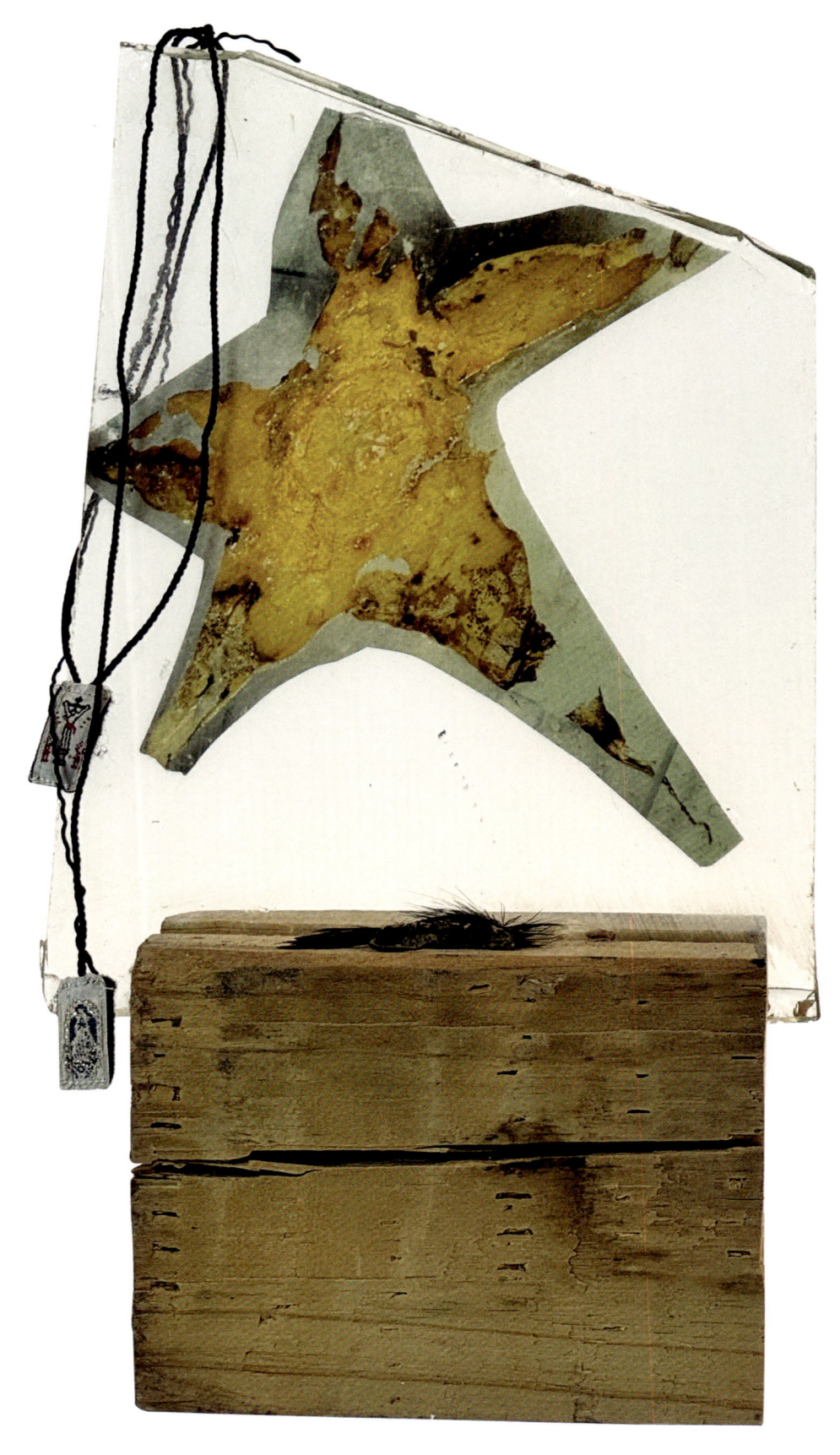

Cactus Marker
11 x 6 inches
Mixed Media
2015

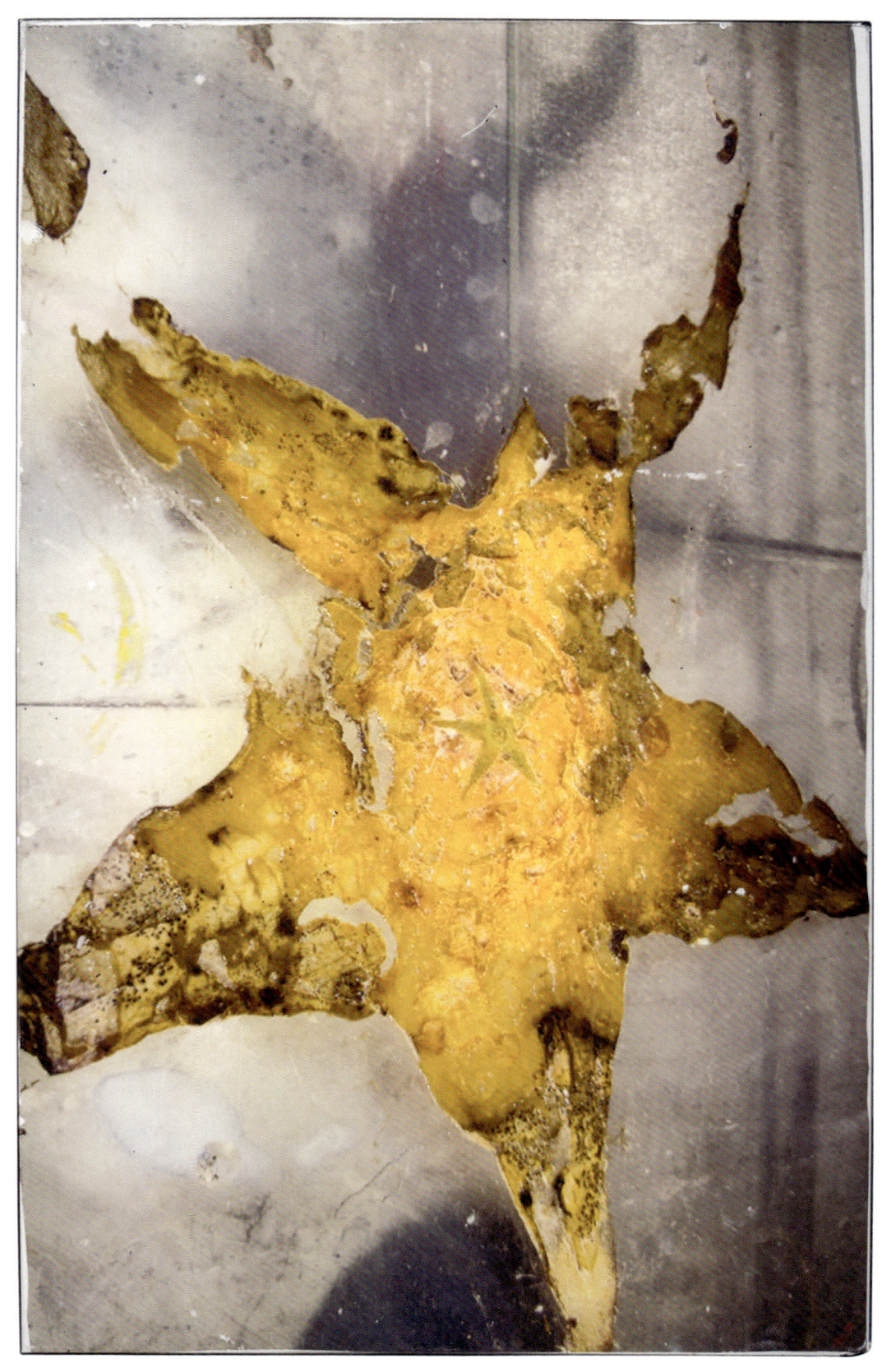

Glass Tile 7
16 x 10 inches
Print on Glass w/ Aluminum Substrate
2024

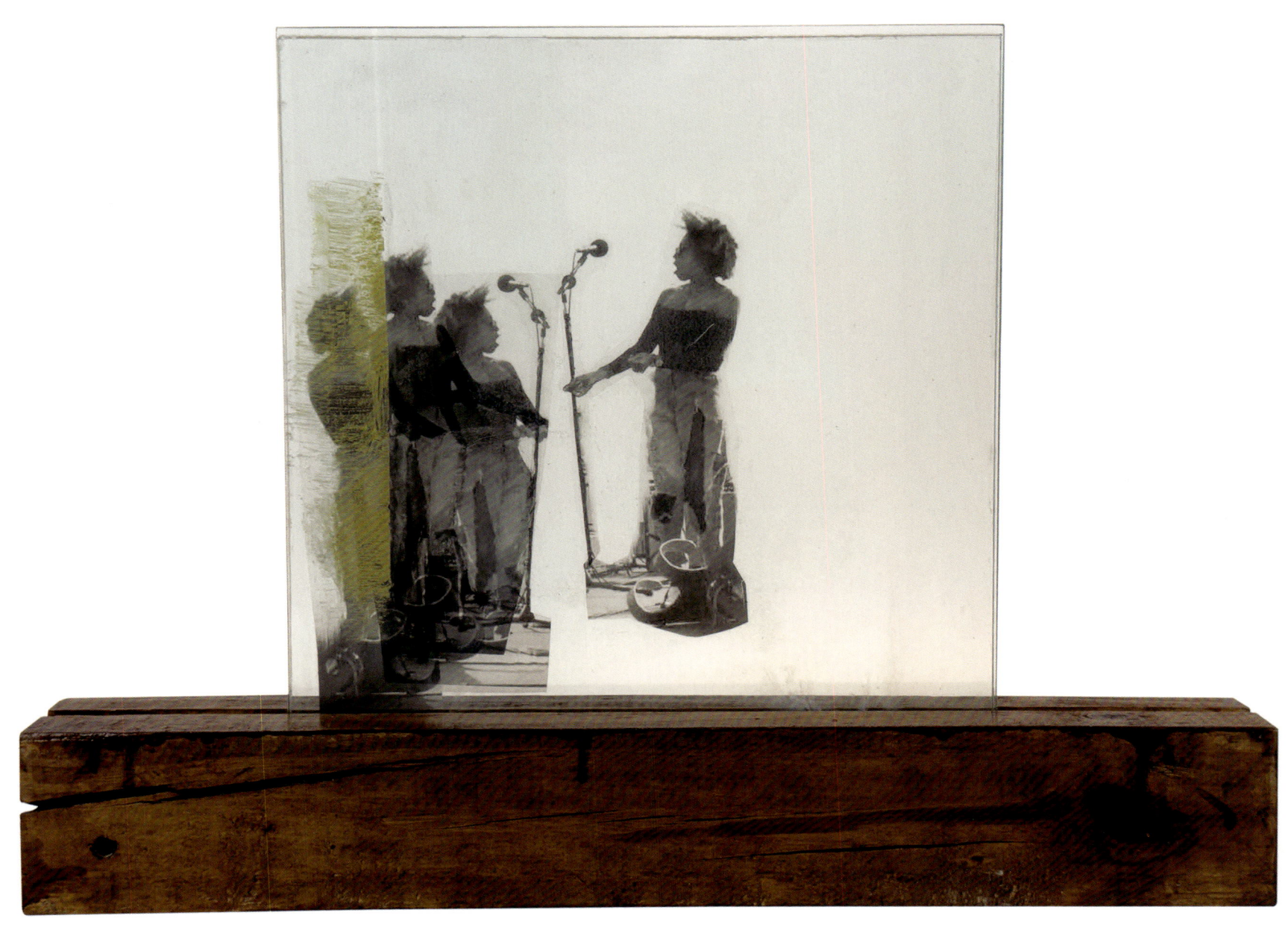

Chorus (Orbital 3)
24 x 17 ½ x 3 ½ inches
Mixed Media, Layered Glass w/ Wood Block
2022

242

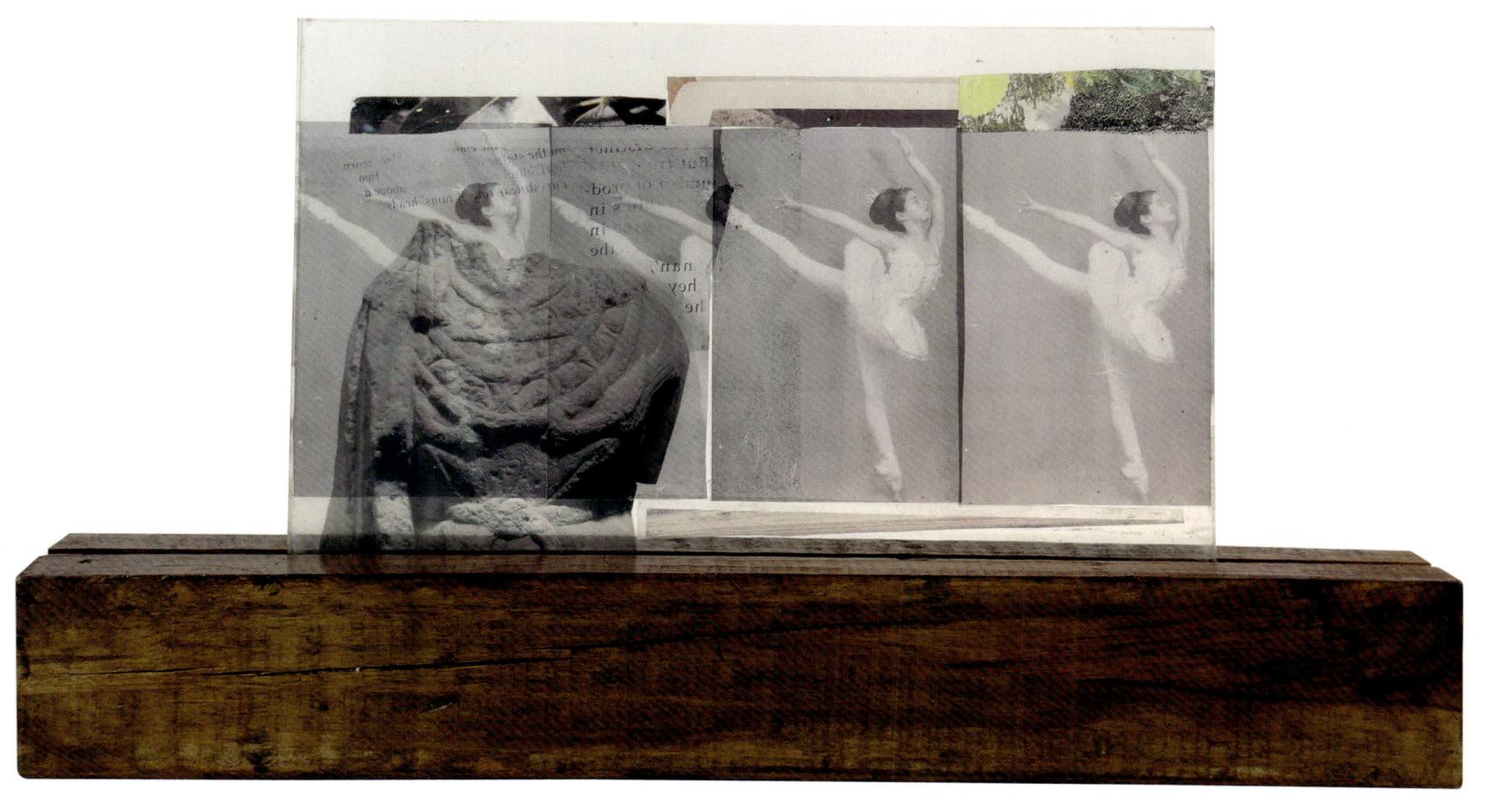

Postcard (Orbital 4)
24 x 13 x 3 ½ inches
Mixed Media, Layered Glass w/ Wood Block
2022

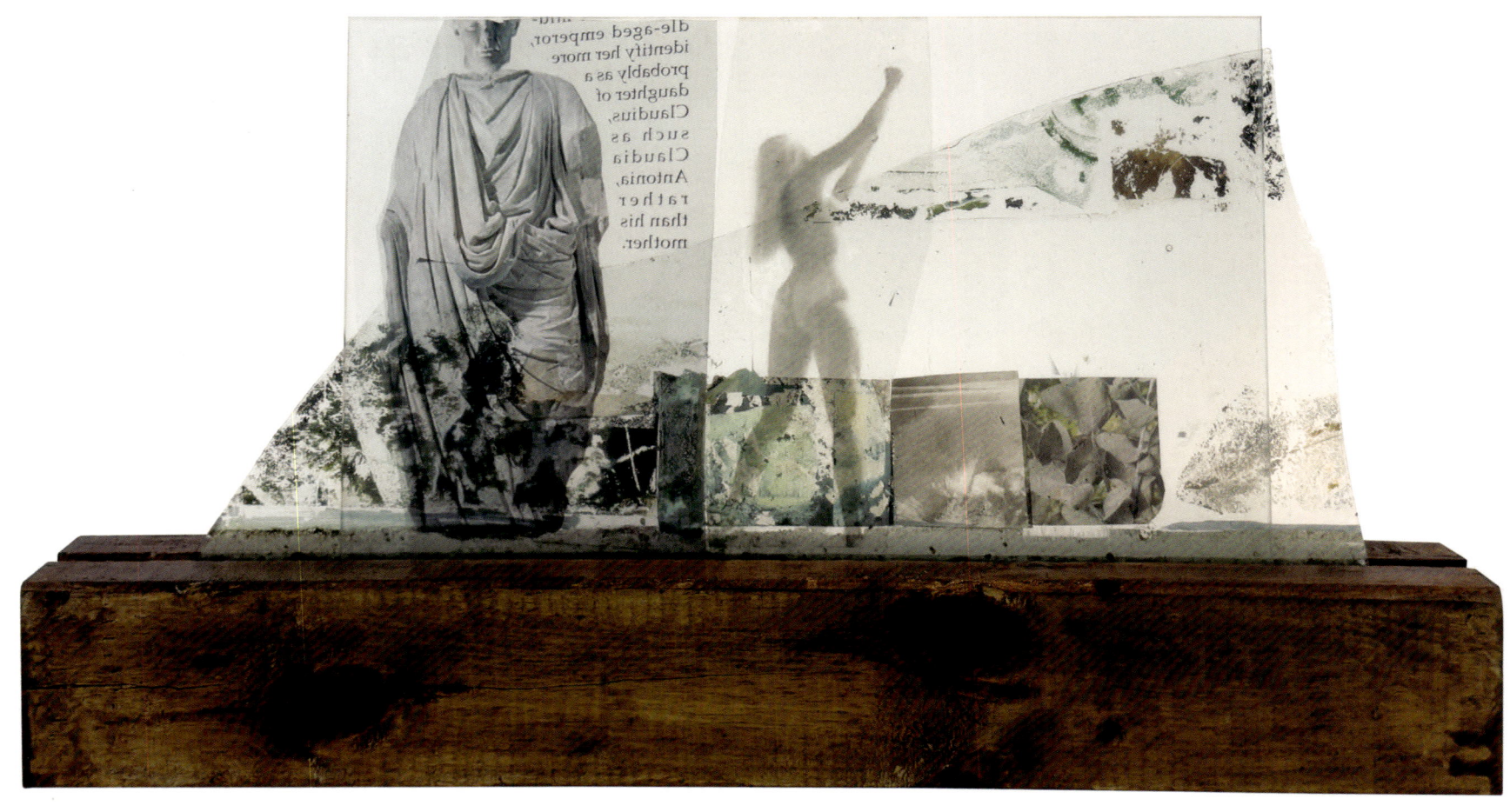

Storyboard (Orbital 1)
24 x 13 x 3 ½ inches
Mixed Media, Layered Glass w/ Wood Block
2022

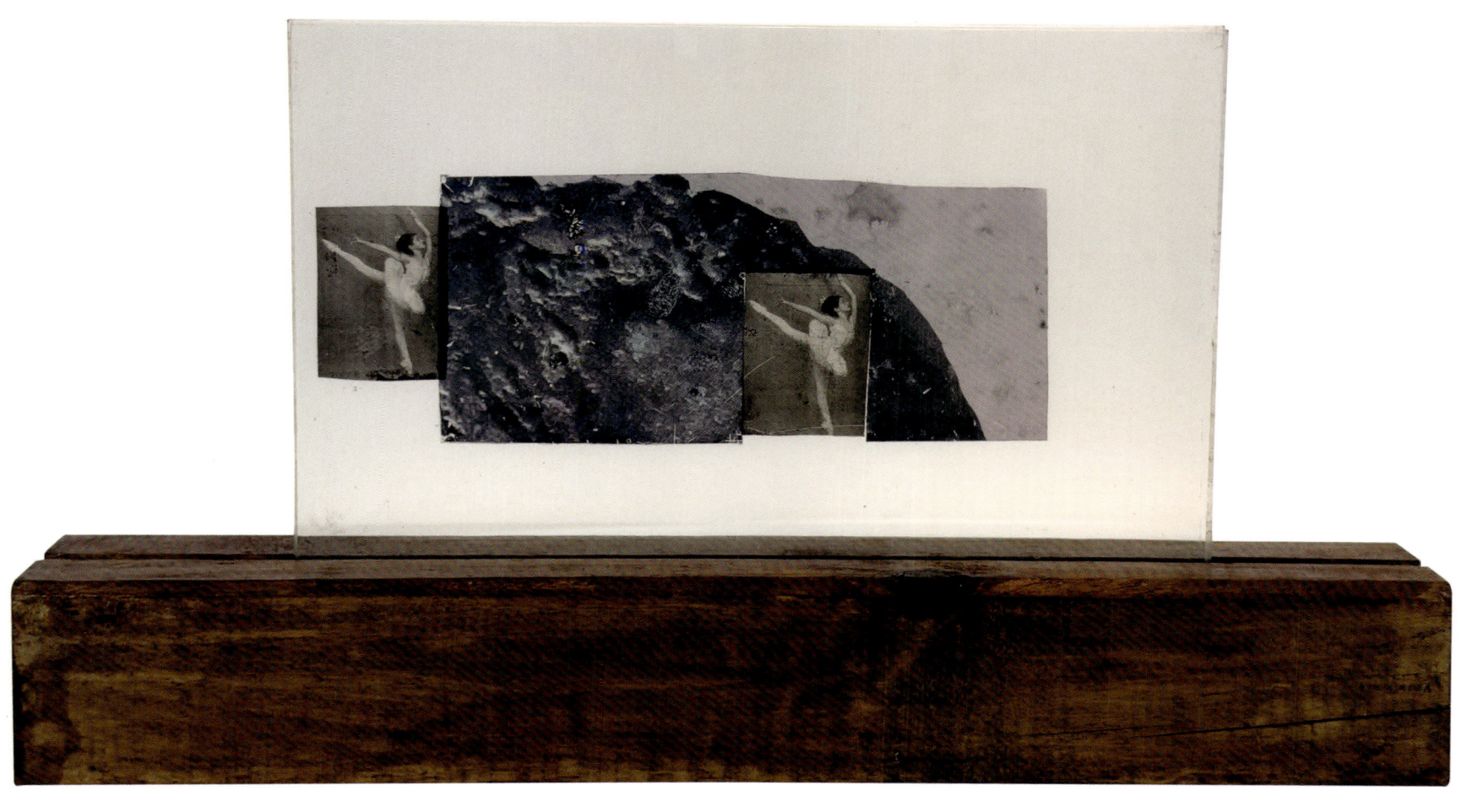

Set (Orbital 2)
24 x 13 x 3 ½ inches
Mixed Media, Layered Glass w/ Wood Block
2022

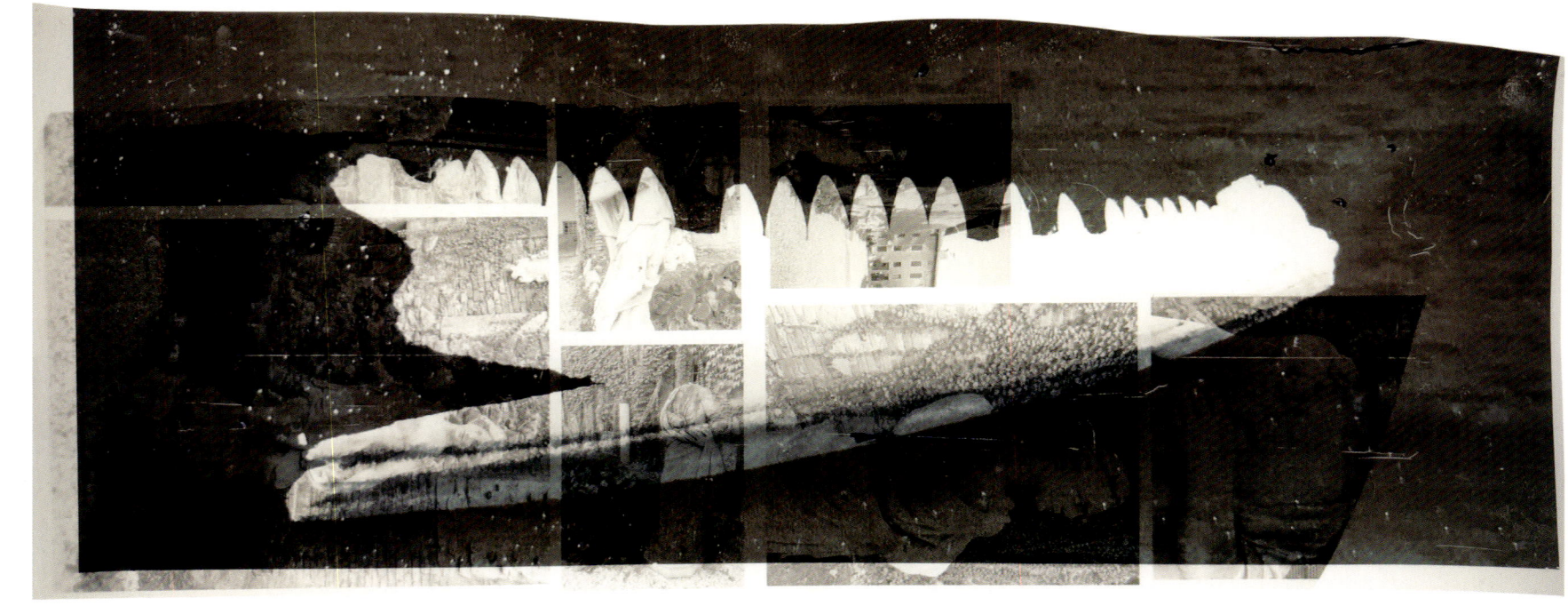

Flag
32 ½ x 13 inches
Layered Adhesive Film
2021

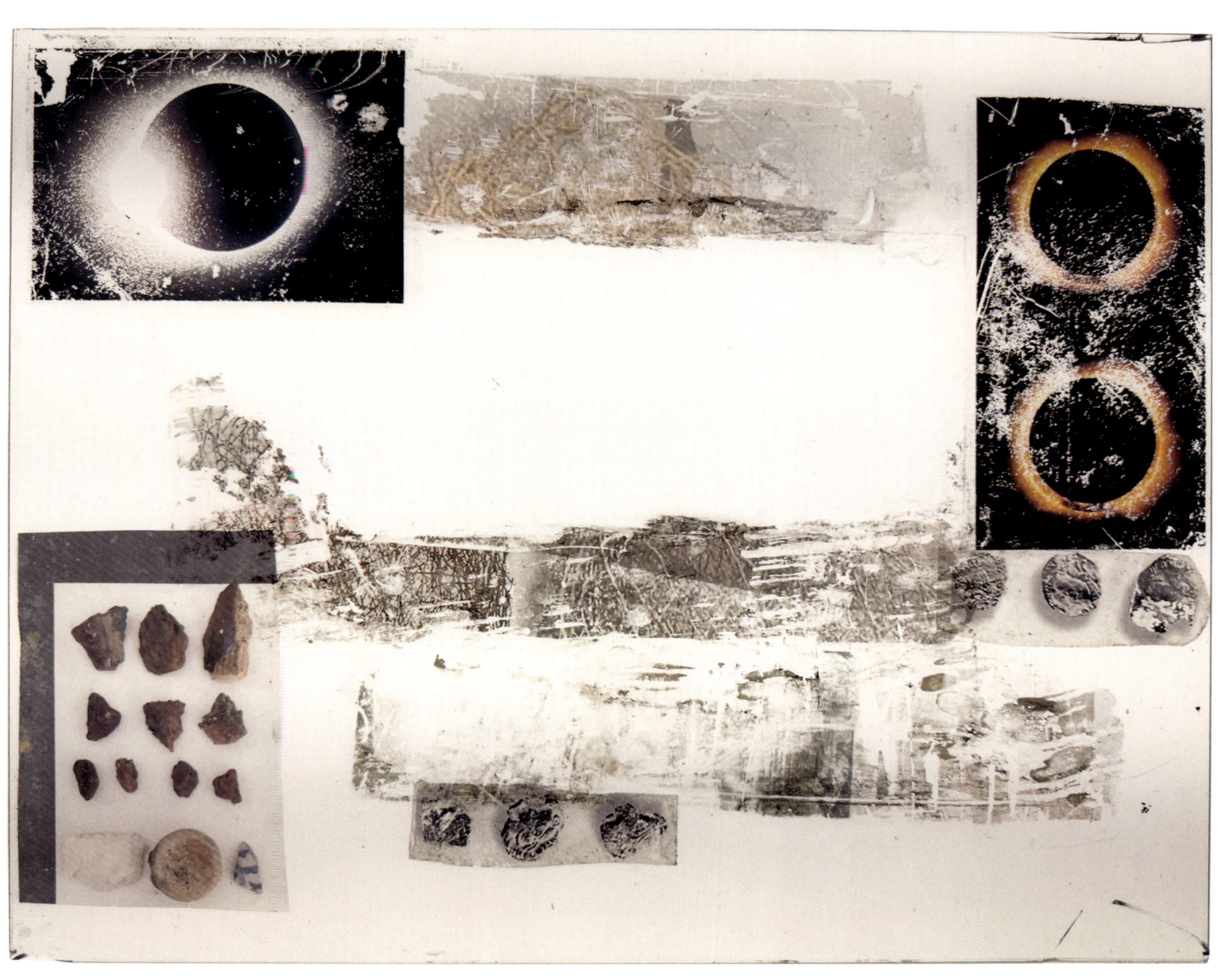

Glass Floor
15 x 19 inches
Mixed Media on Glass
2022

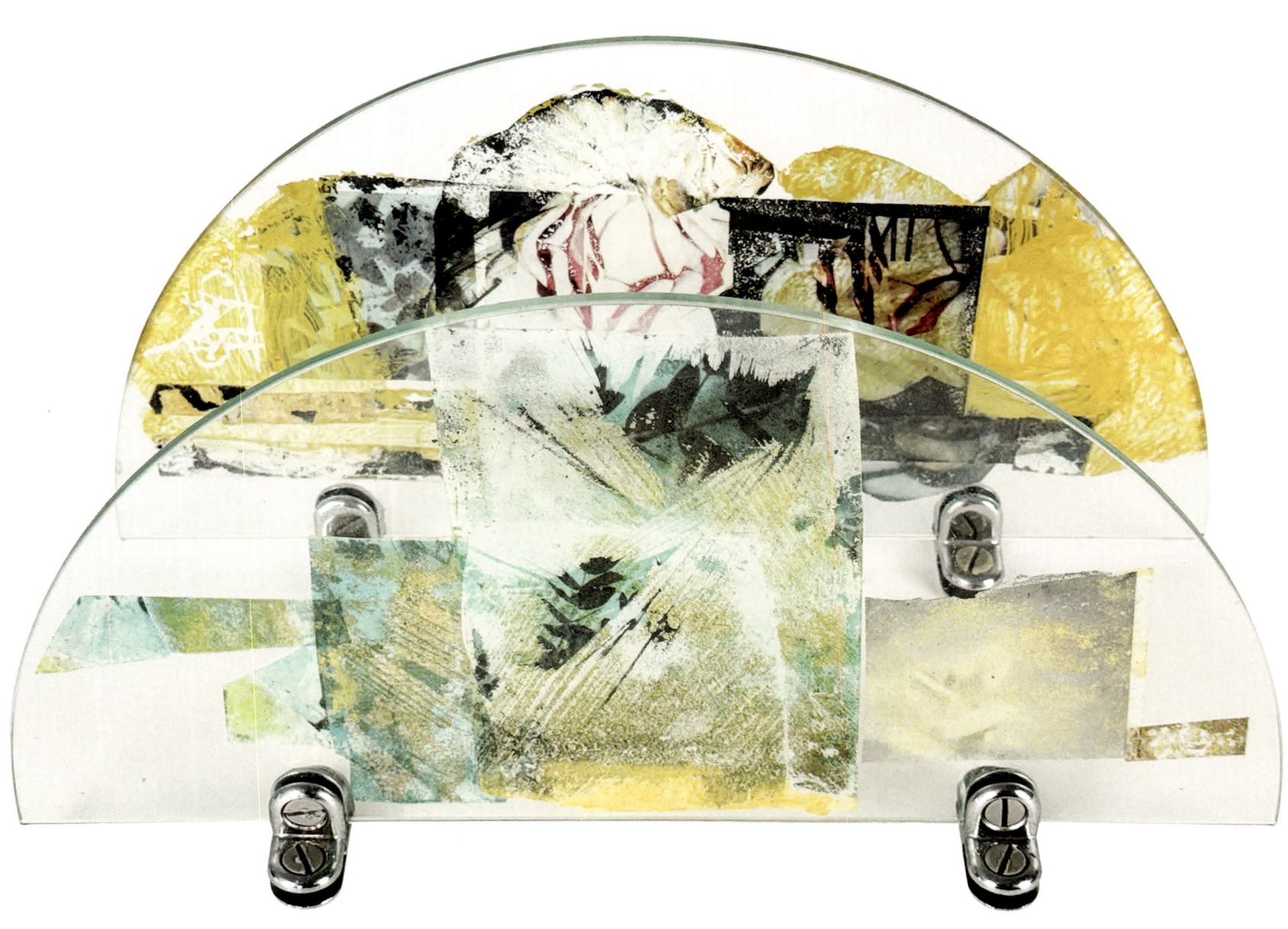

Paired Orbital
8 x 11 x 4 inches
Mixed Media on Glass
2016

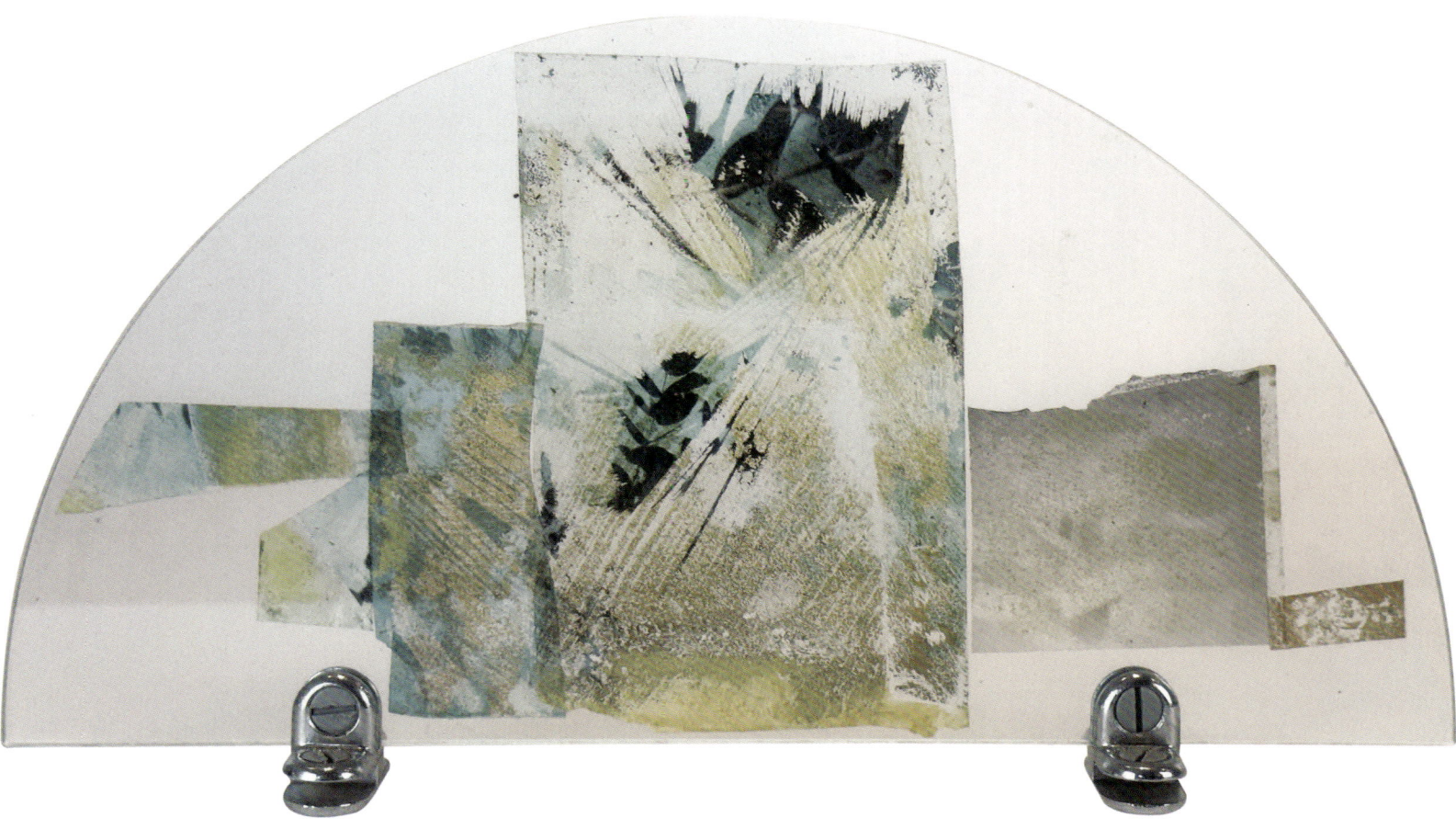

Paired Orbital: Front (Detail)

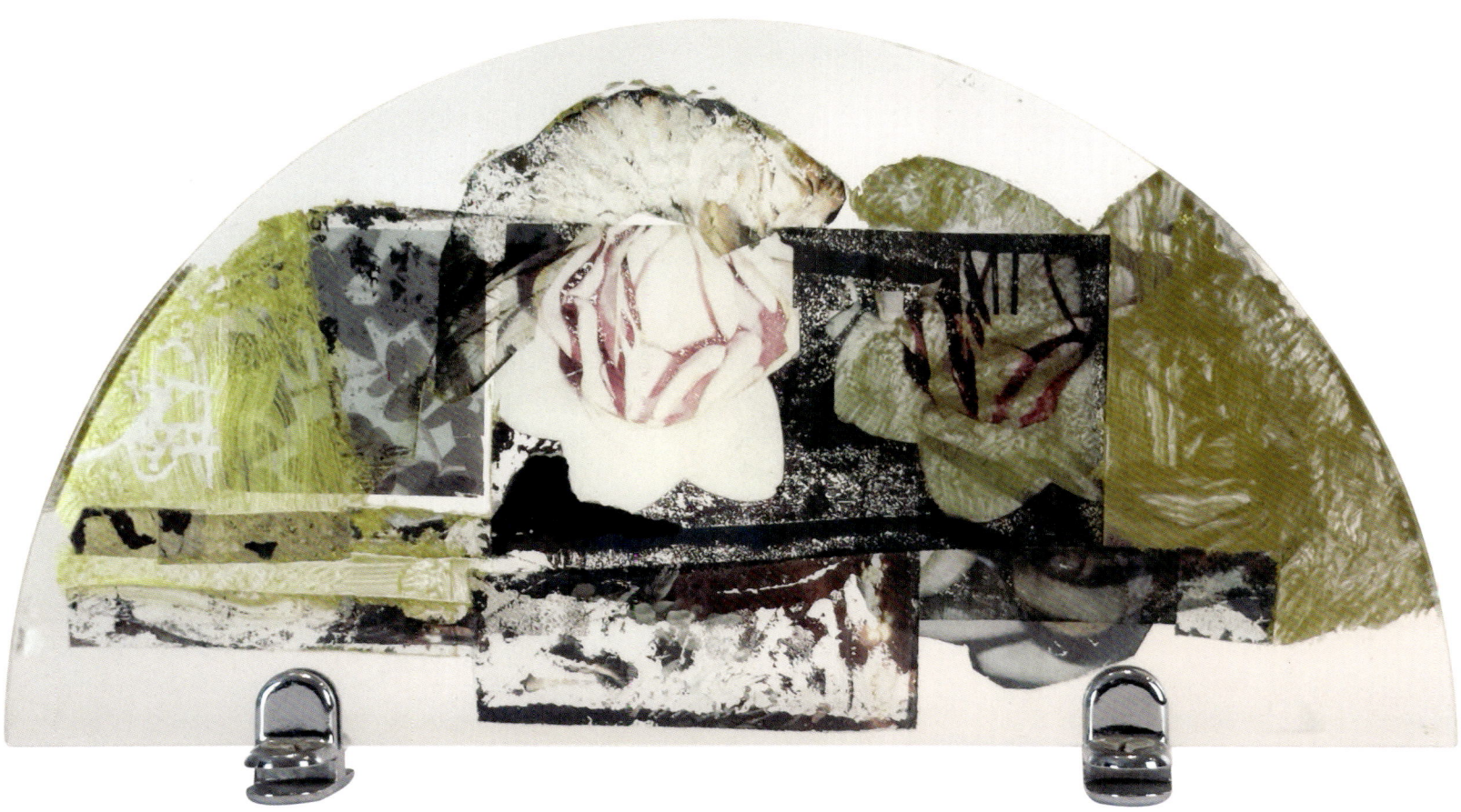

Paired Orbital: Rear (Detail)

249

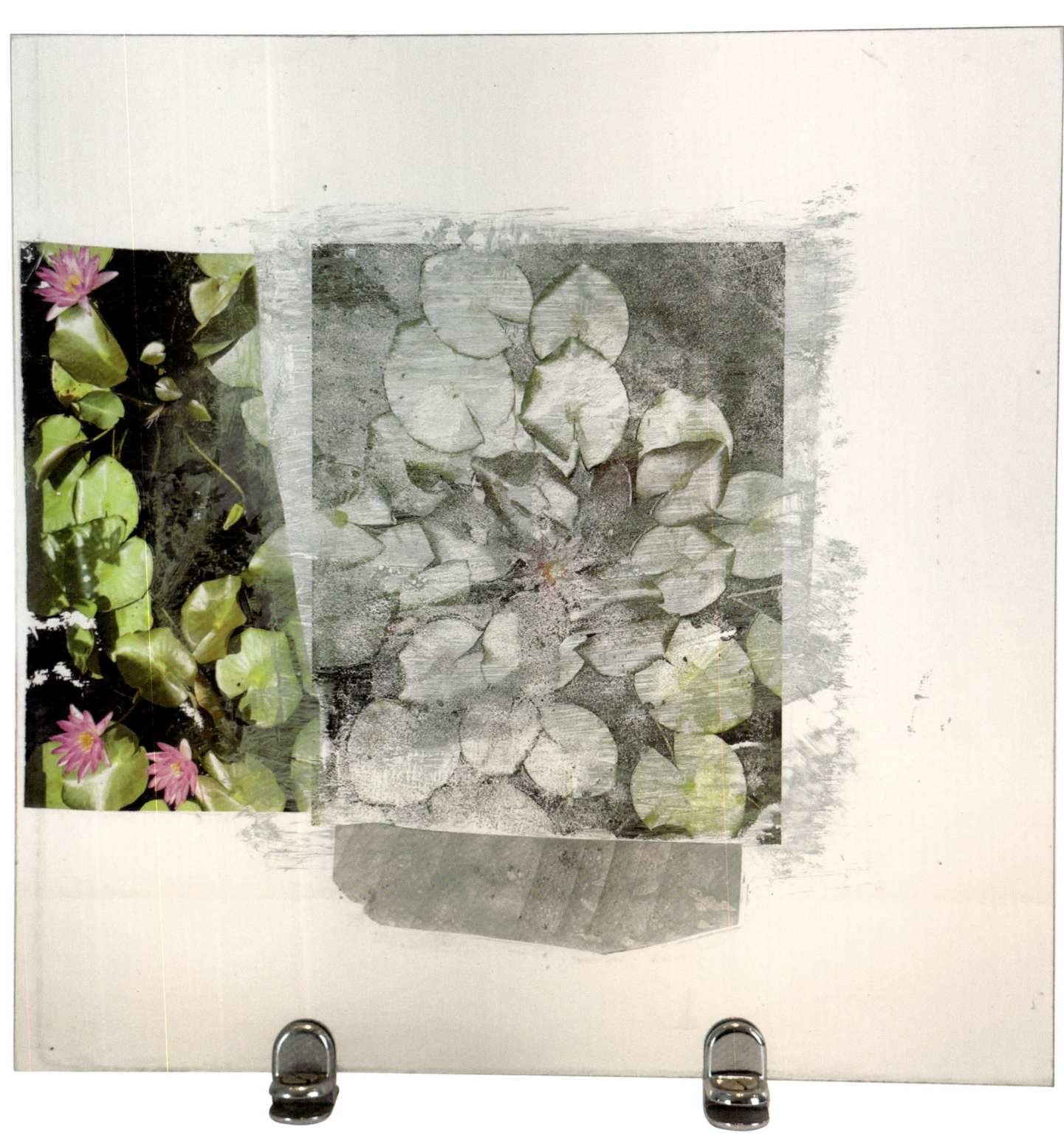

Chronicle (1 Panel)
14 x 14 inches
Mixed Media on Glass
2018

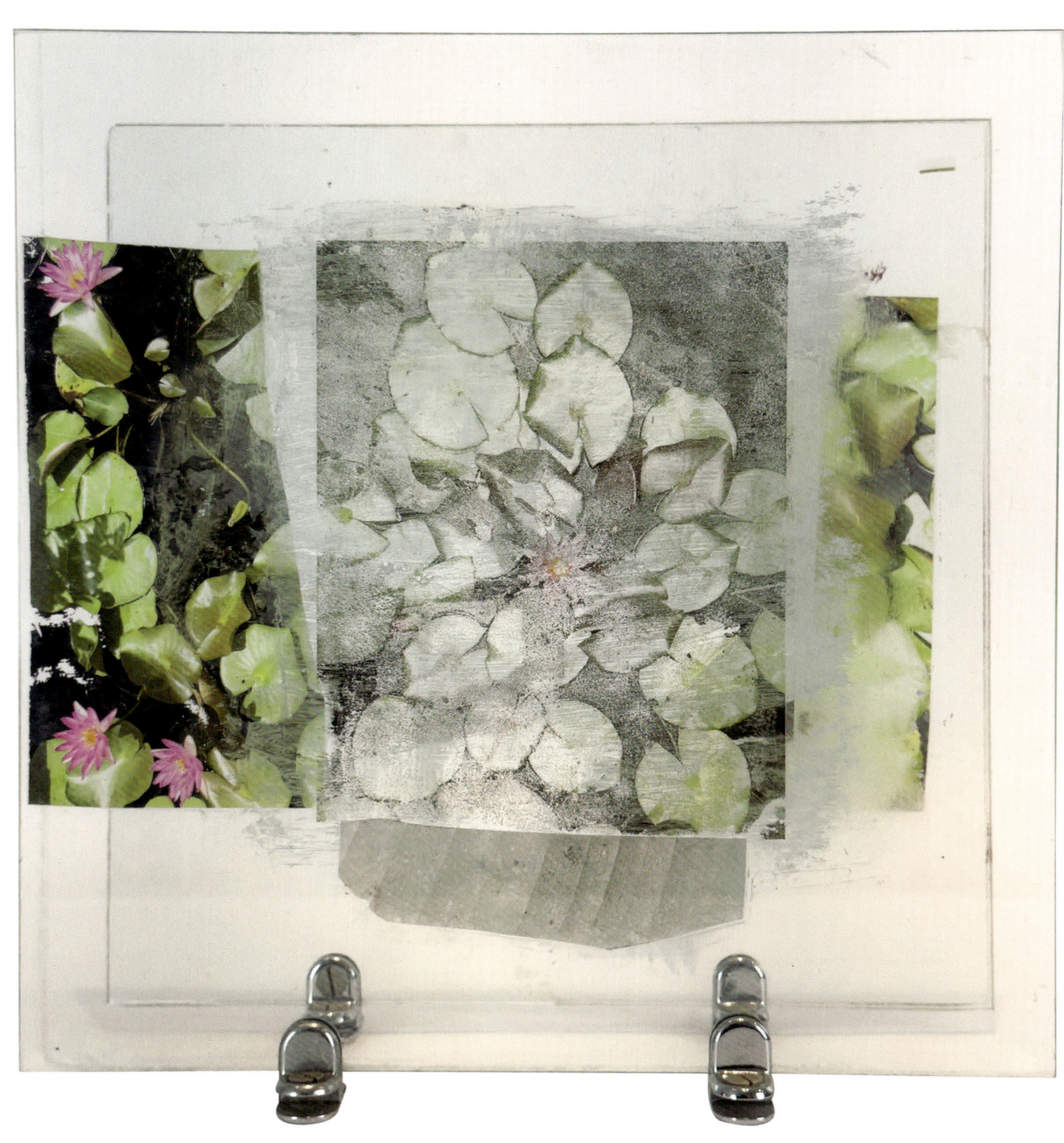

Chronicle (2 Panels)
14 x 14 x 2 inches
Mixed Media on Glass
2018

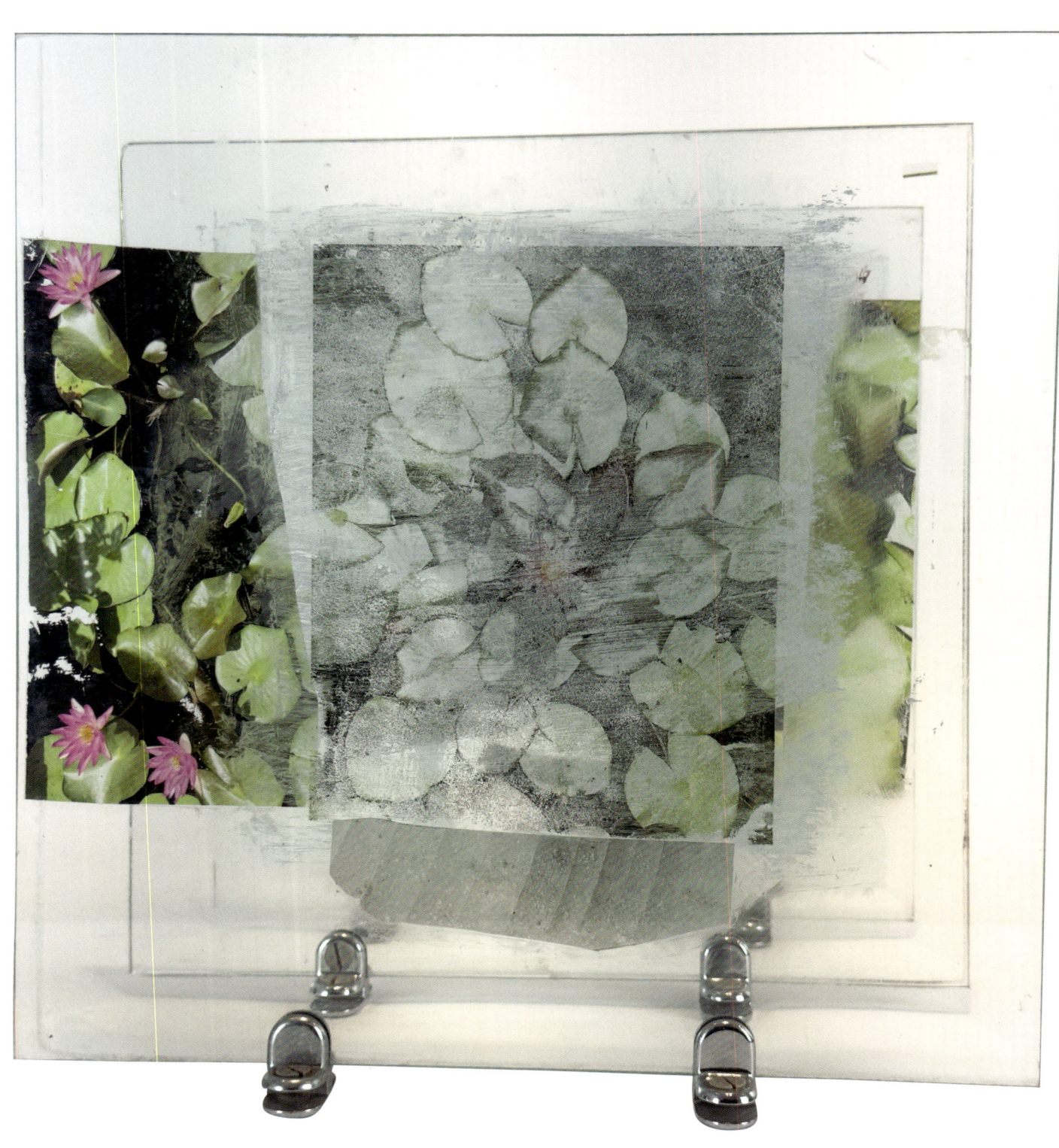

Chronicle (3 Panels)
14 x 14 x 4 inches
Mixed Media on Glass
2018

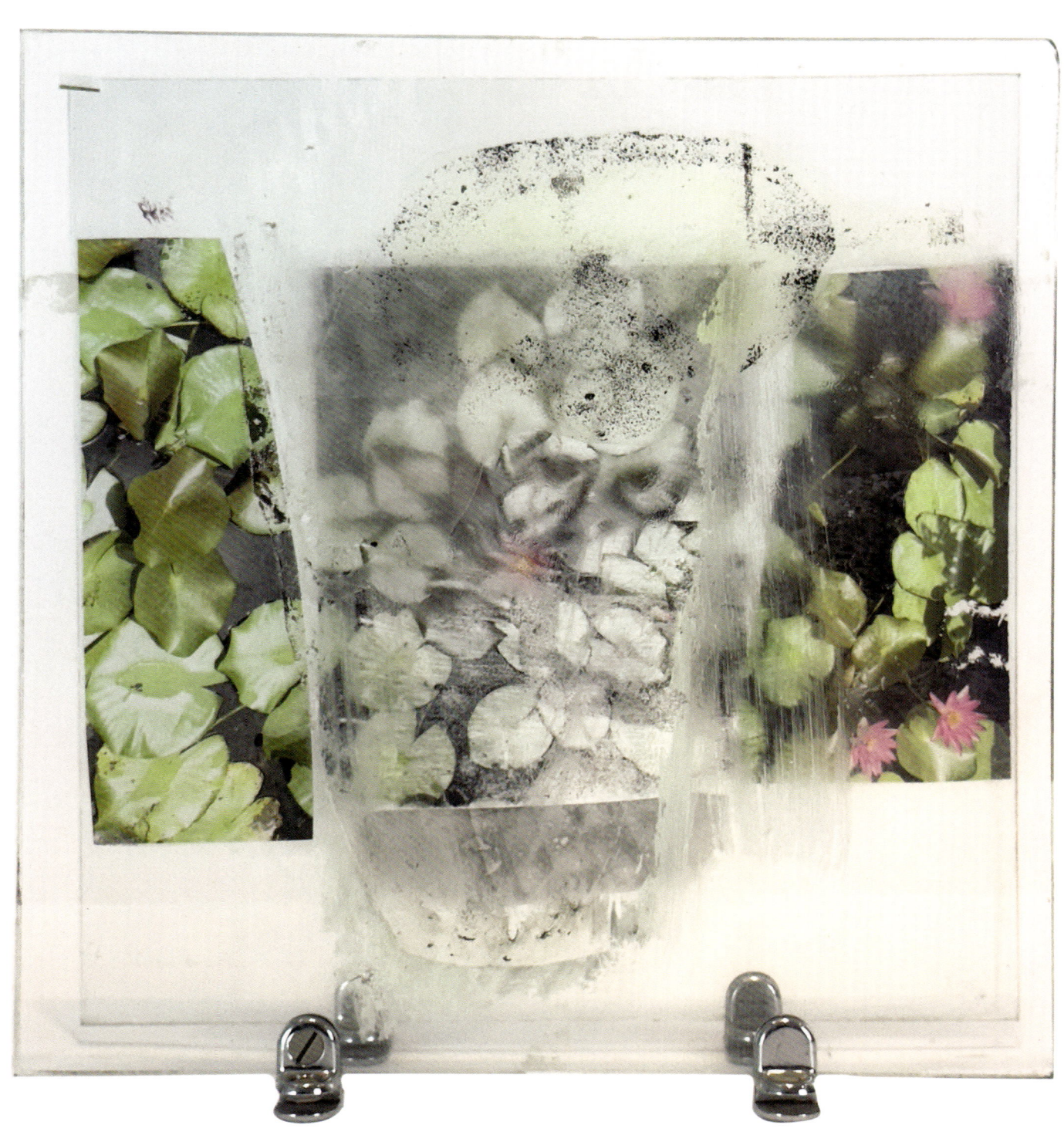

Chronicle (2 Panels: Back View)
14 x 14 x 2 inches
Mixed Media on Glass
2018

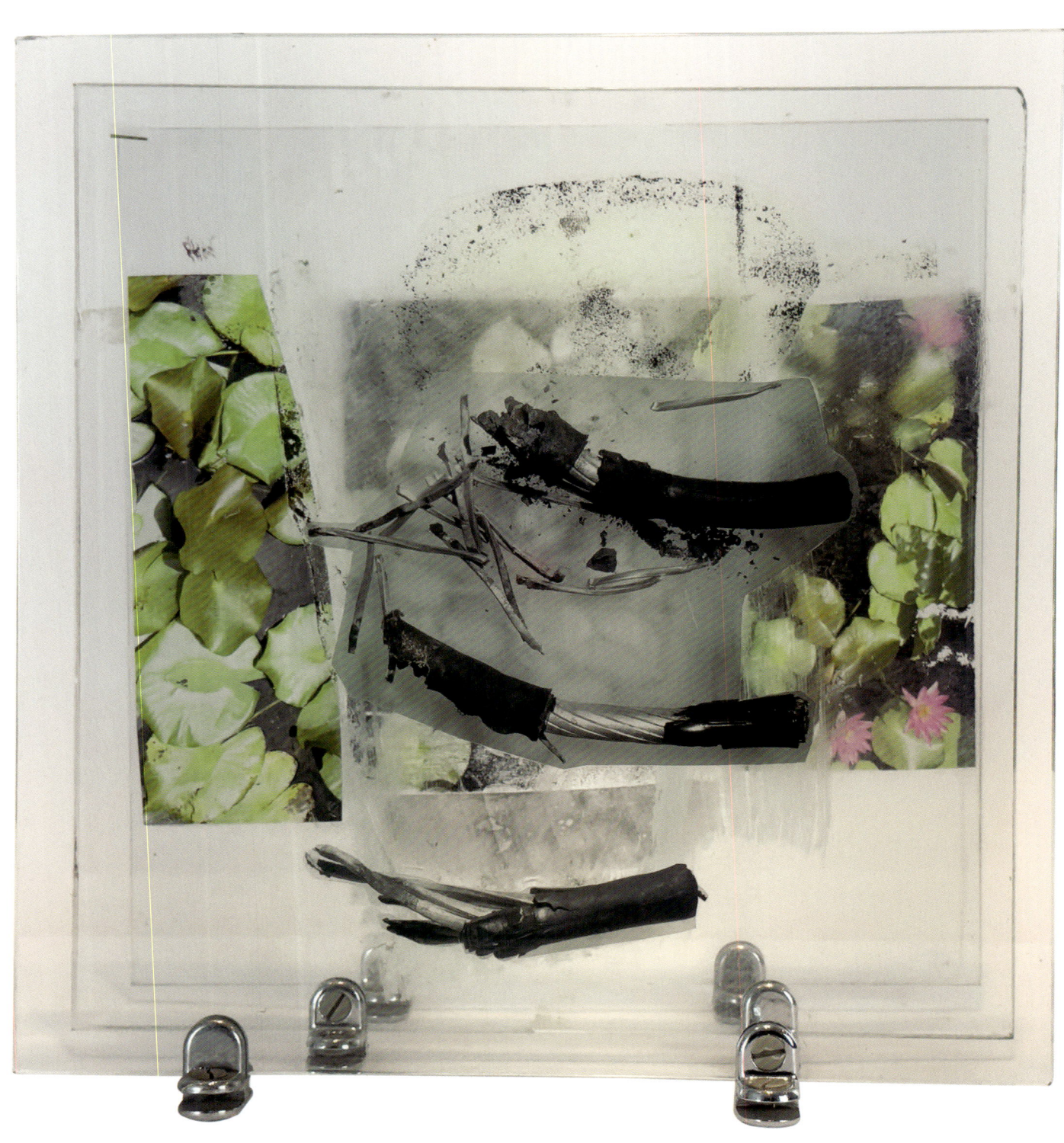

Chronicle (3 Panels: Back View)
14 x 14 x 4 inches
Mixed Media on Glass
2018

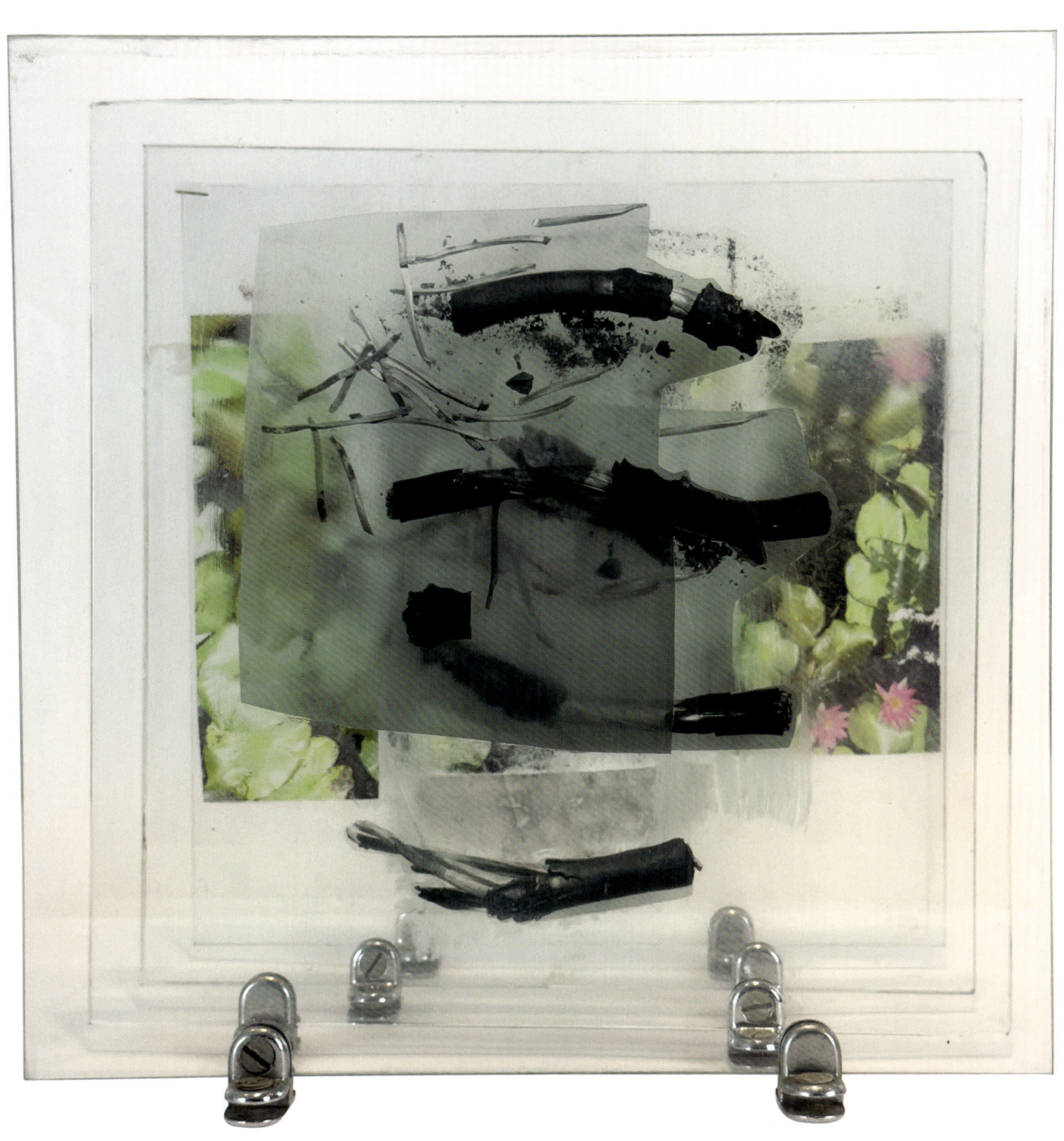

Chronicle (4 Panels: Back View)
14 x 14 x 6 inches
Mixed Media on Glass
2018

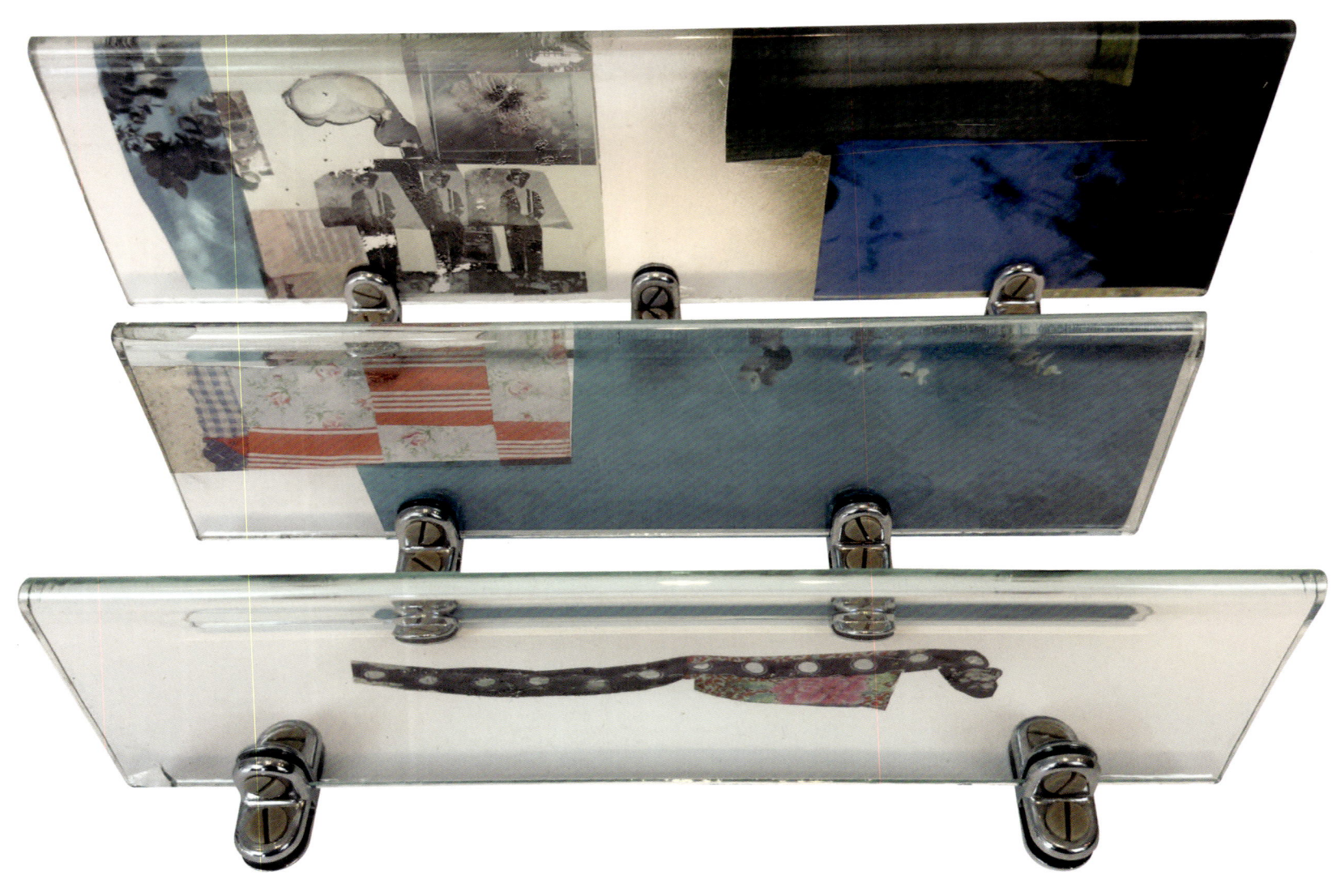

Wave (Triptych)
18 x 8 inches
Mixed Media on Glass
2017

256

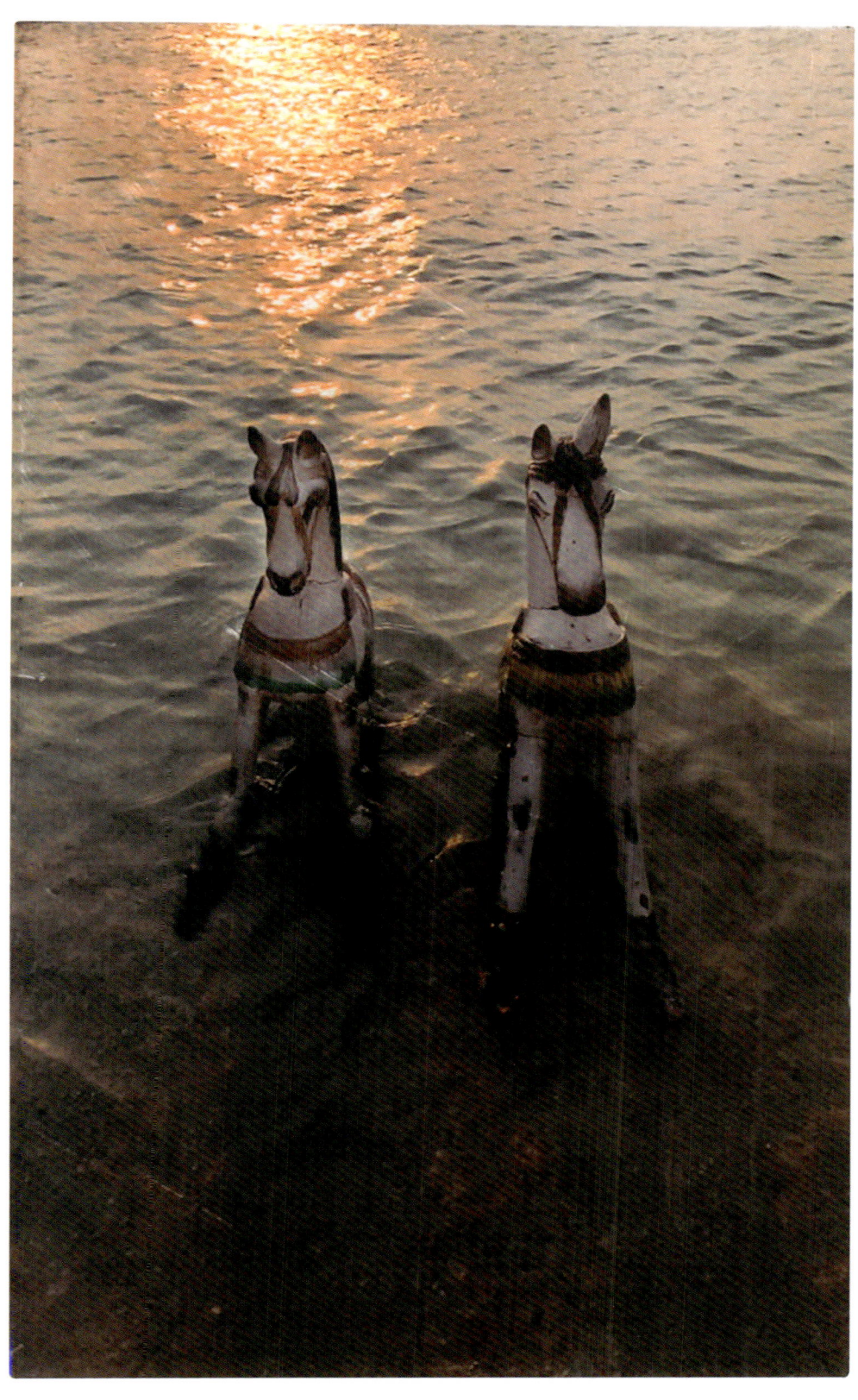

Glass Tile #1
16 x 10 inches
Print on Glass w/ Aluminum Substrate
2023

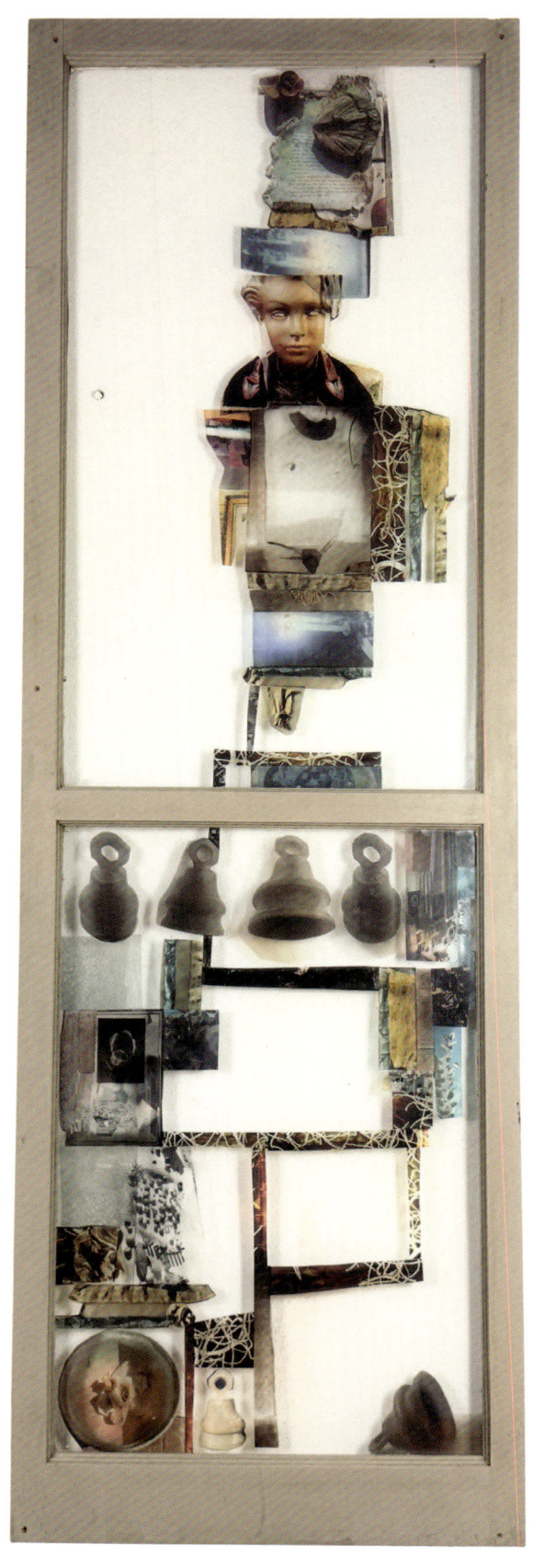

Balloon
89 x 29 ½ inches
Mixed Media on Glass
2017

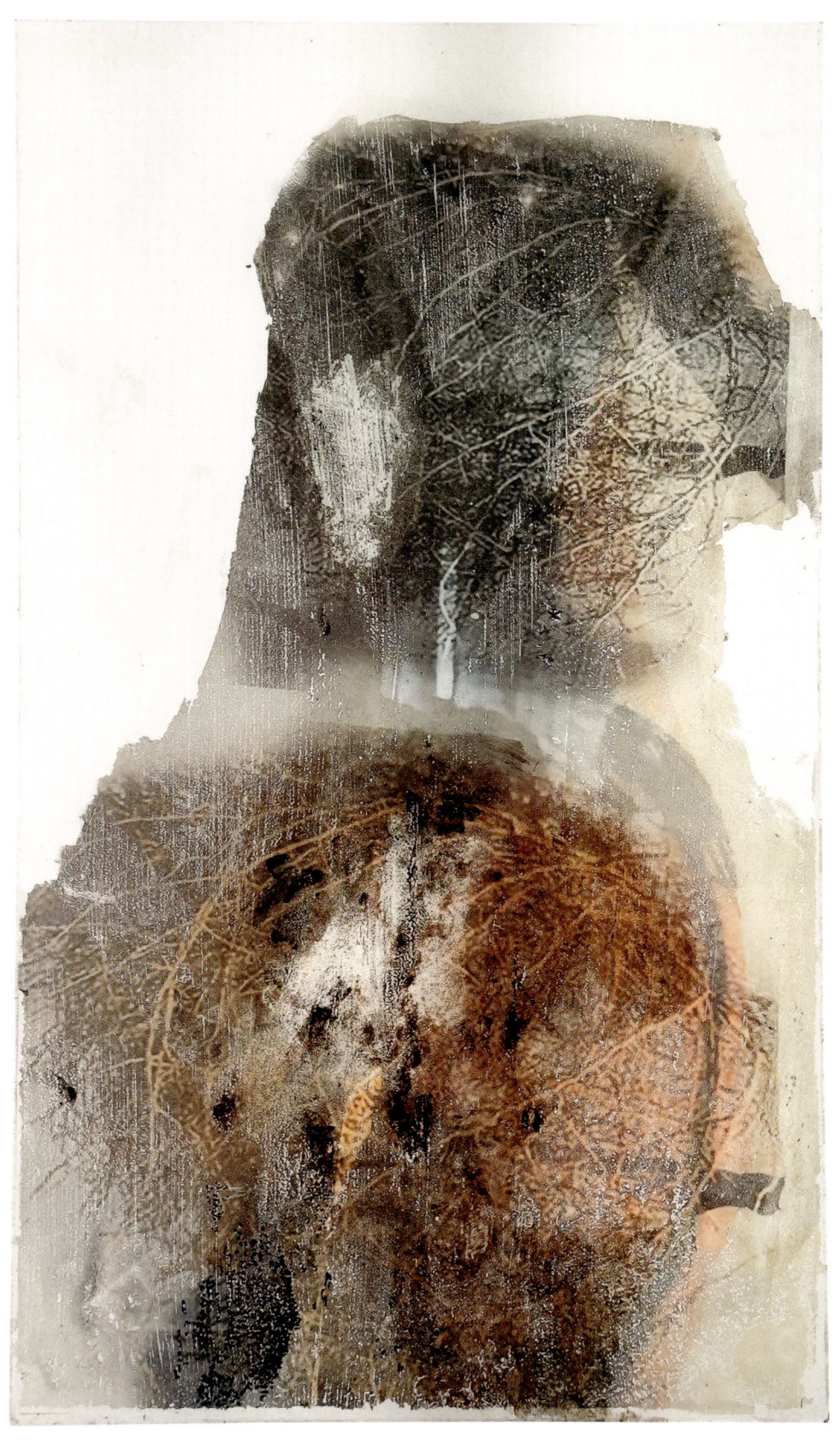

Centauride
24 x 14 inches
Mixed Media w/ Film Transfer on Glass
2021

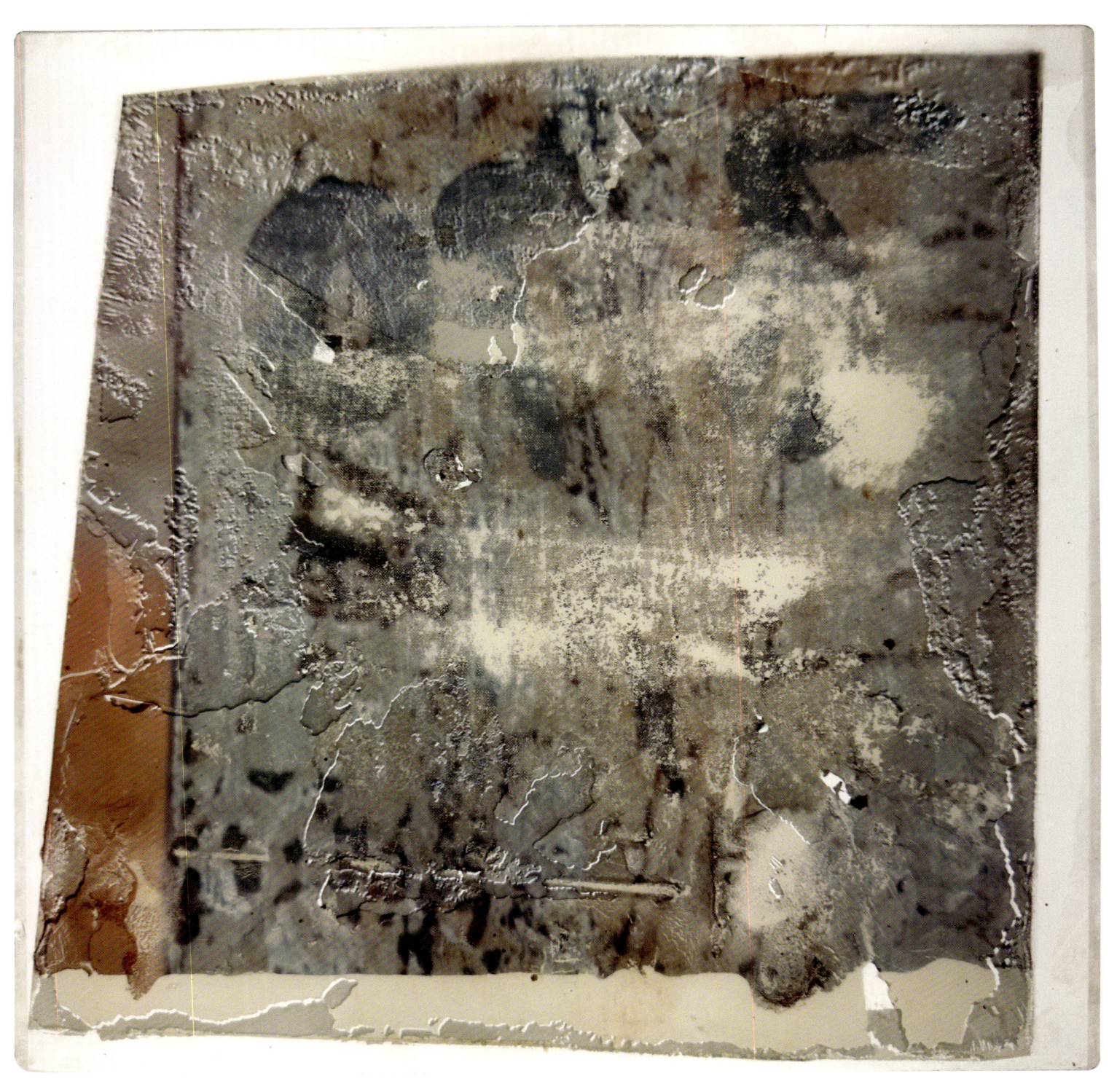

Ghost
14 x 14 inches
Mixed Media on Glass
2013

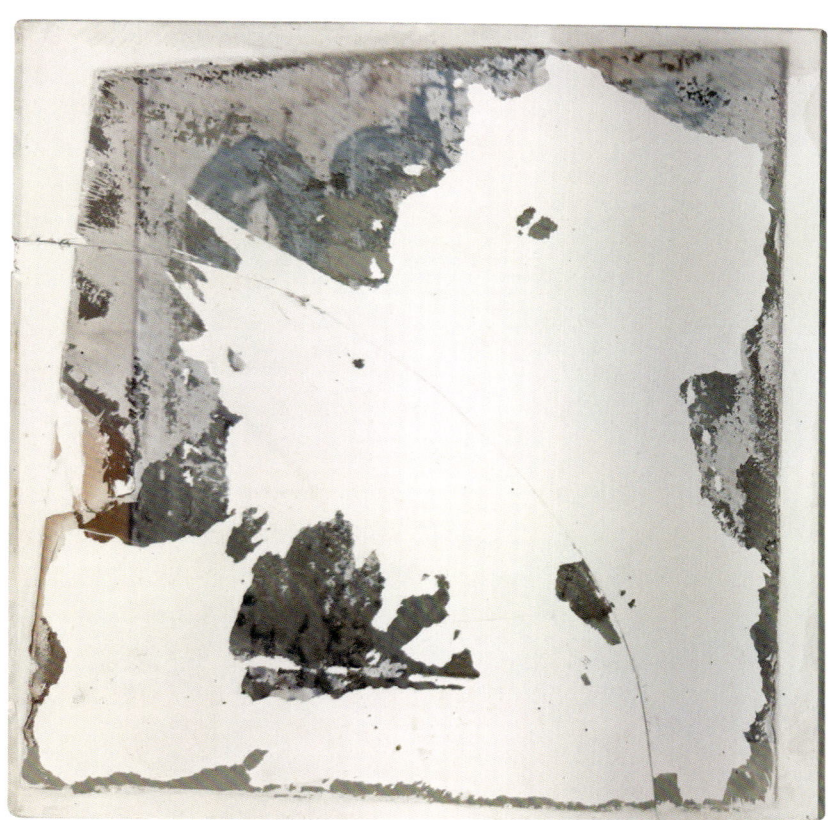

Ghost (Details)

" **The most fundamental all my endeavors is still camera**

root that spreads through photography. To me a is magic. "

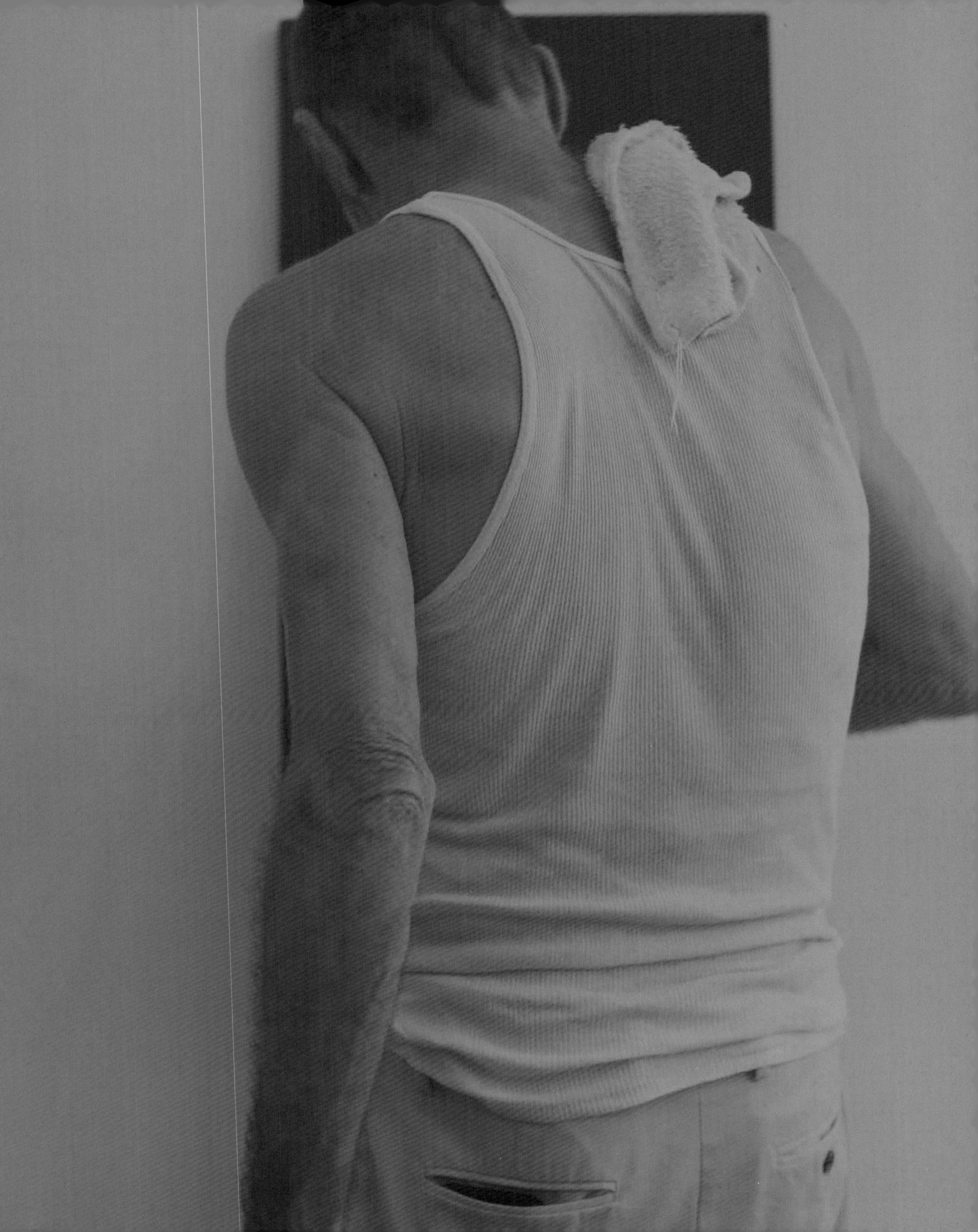

PRINTS, PAPER
& PAINTINGS

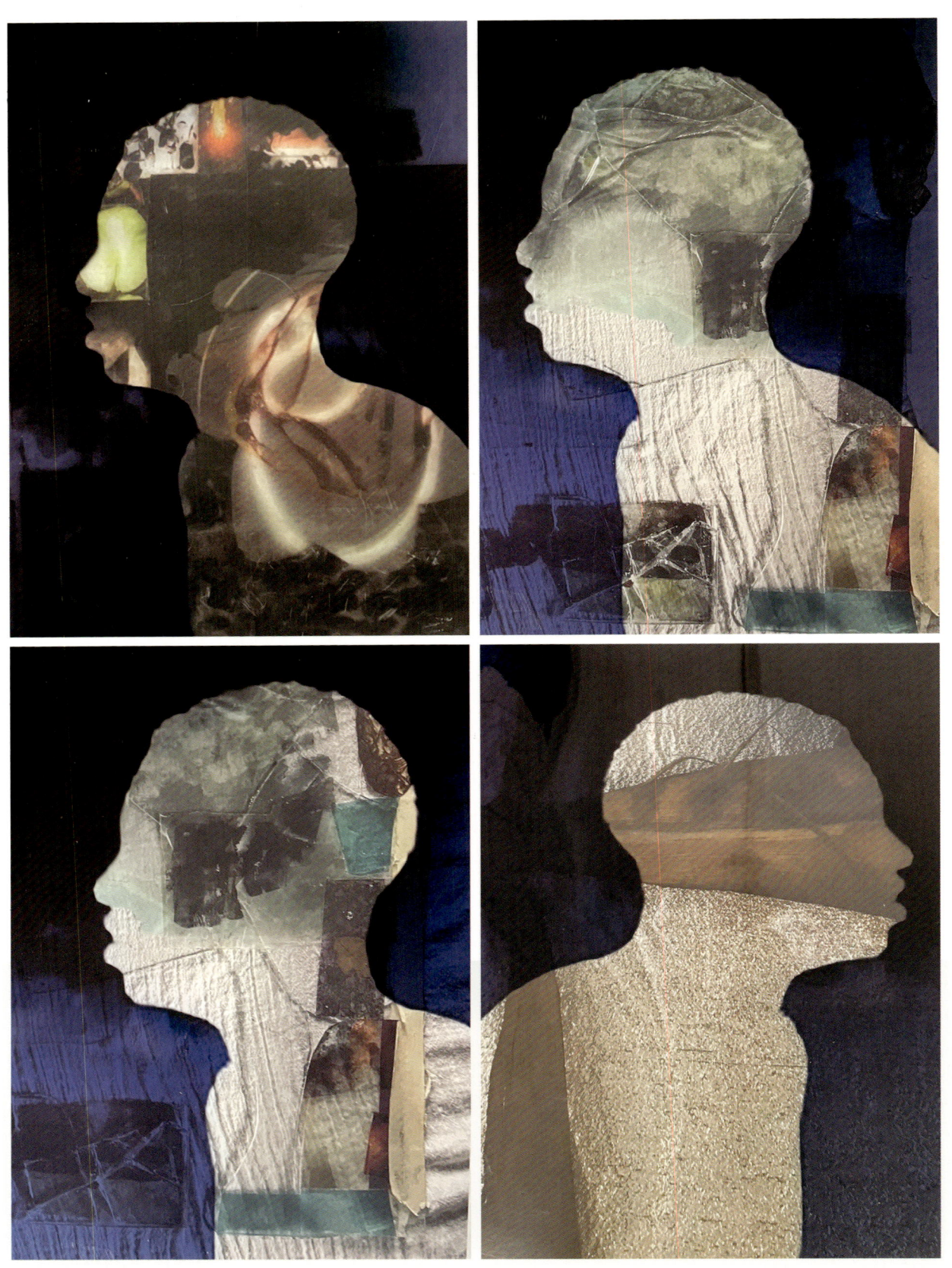

Garifuna
60 x 44 inches
Archival Color Print on Paper
2020

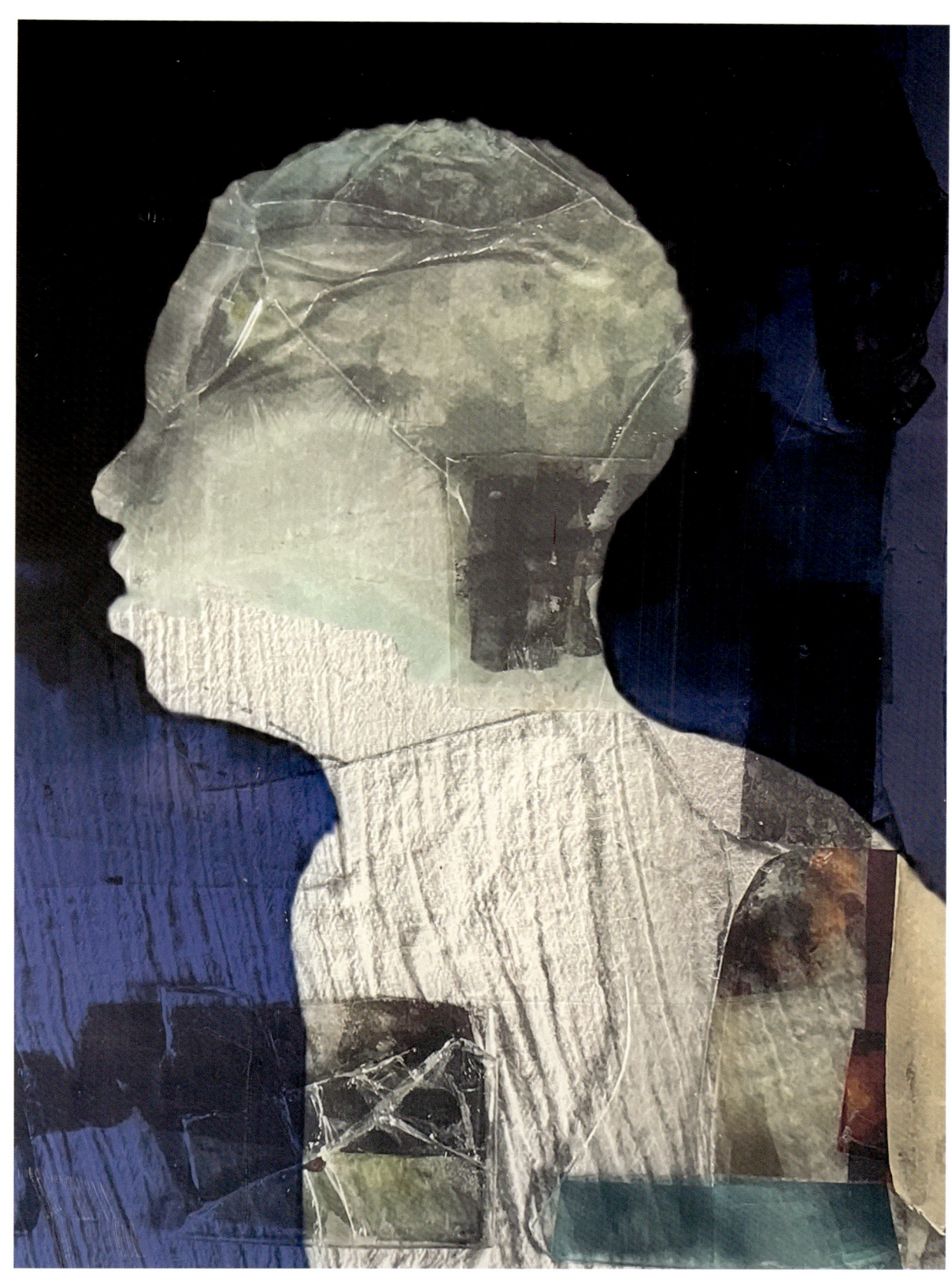

Garifuna 1
30 x 22 inches
Archival Color Print on Paper
2020

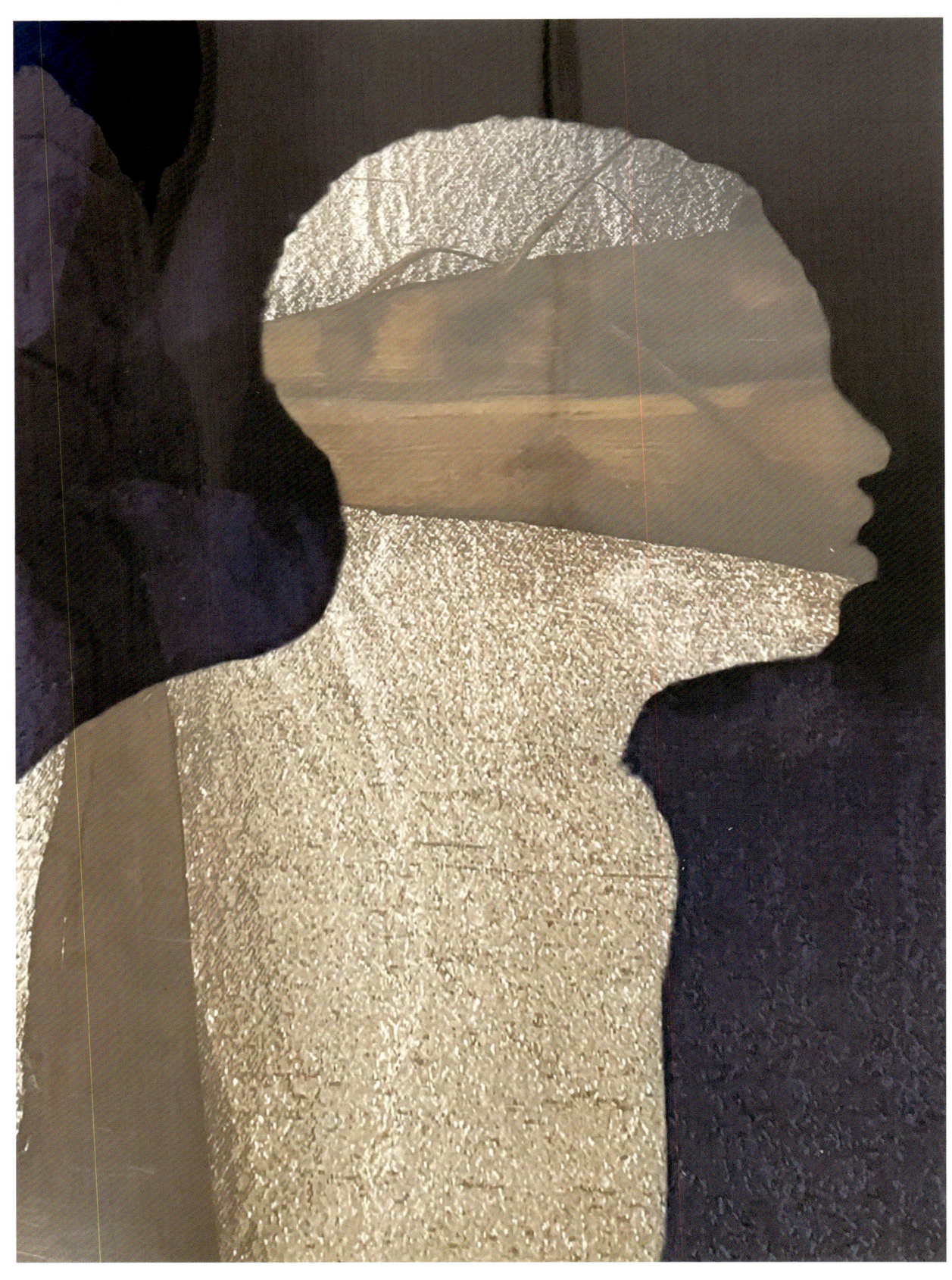

Garifuna 2
30 x 22 inches
Archival Color Print on Paper
2020

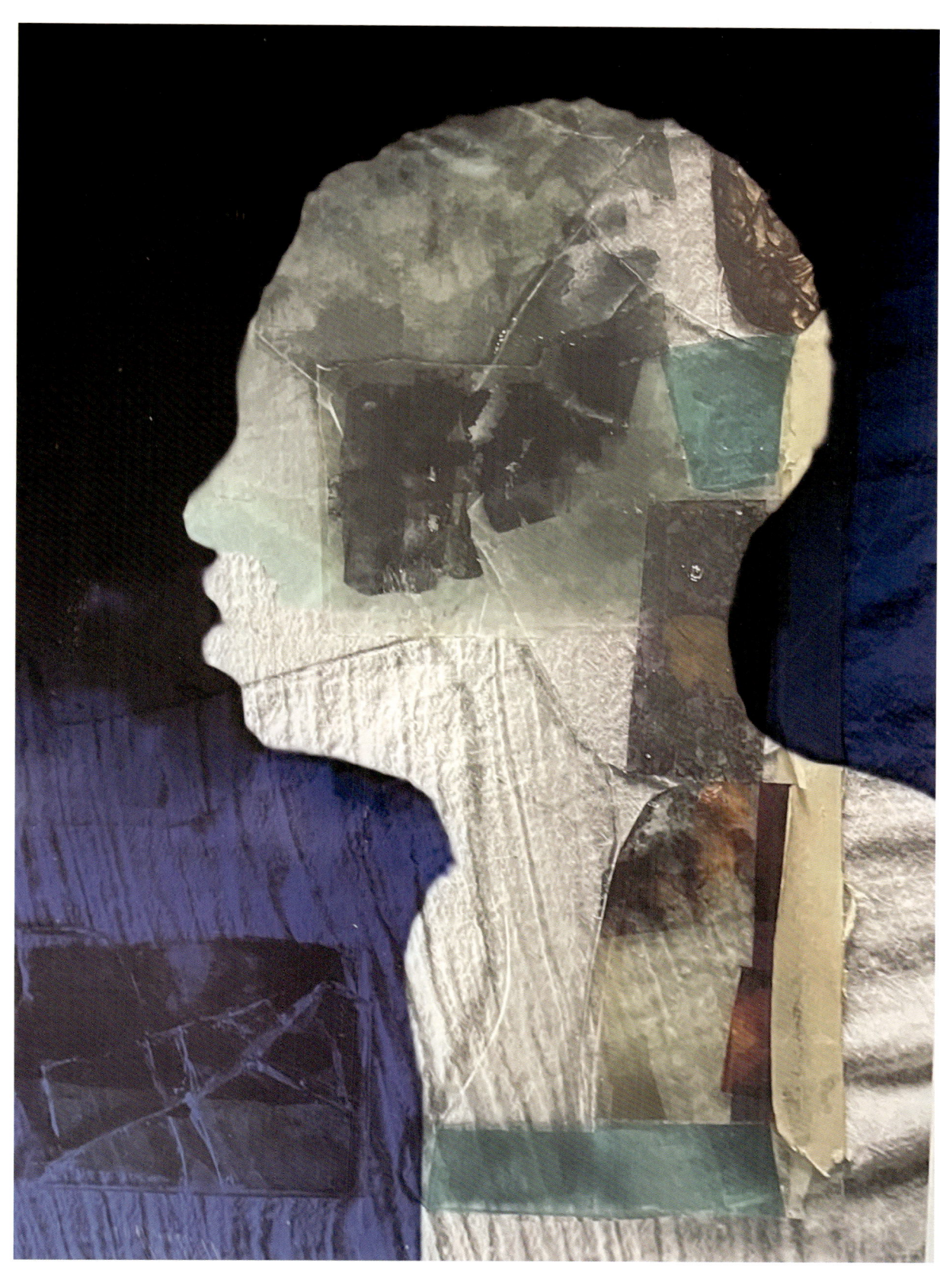

Garifuna 3
30 x 22 inches
Archival Color Print on Paper
2020

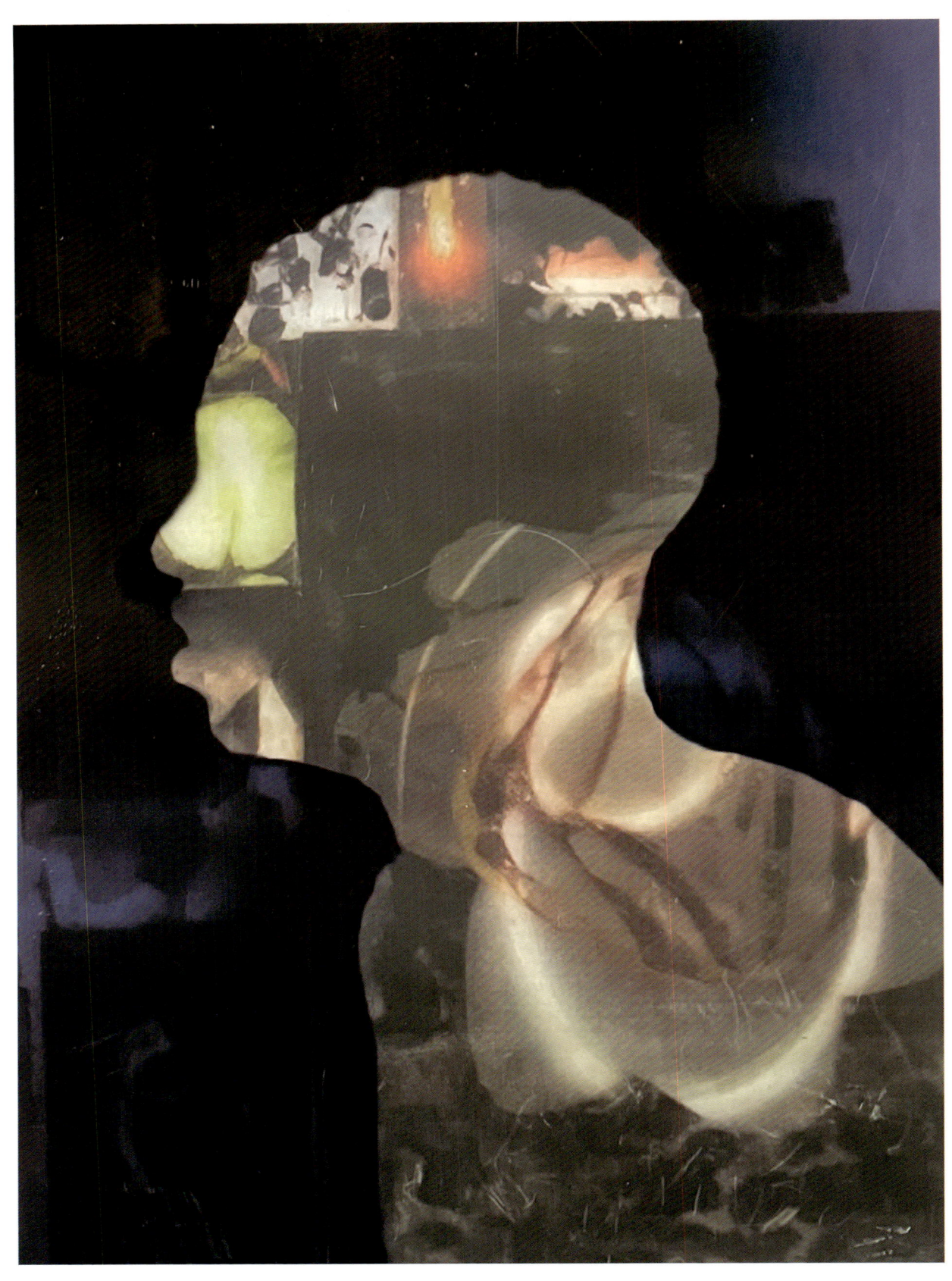

Garifuna 4
30 x 22 inches
Archival Color Print on Paper
2020

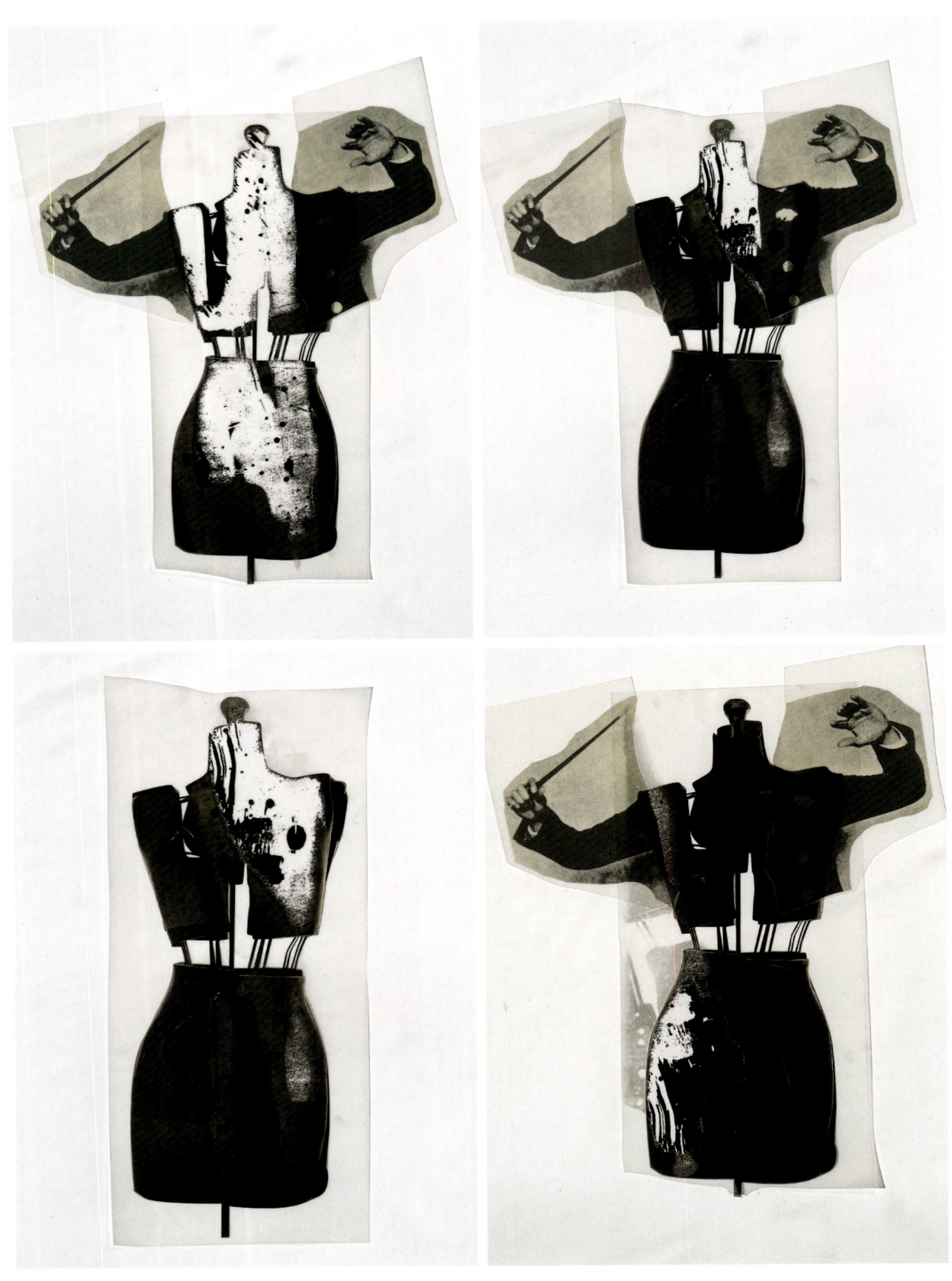

Relief 1
56 x 42 ½ inches
Mixed Media
2020

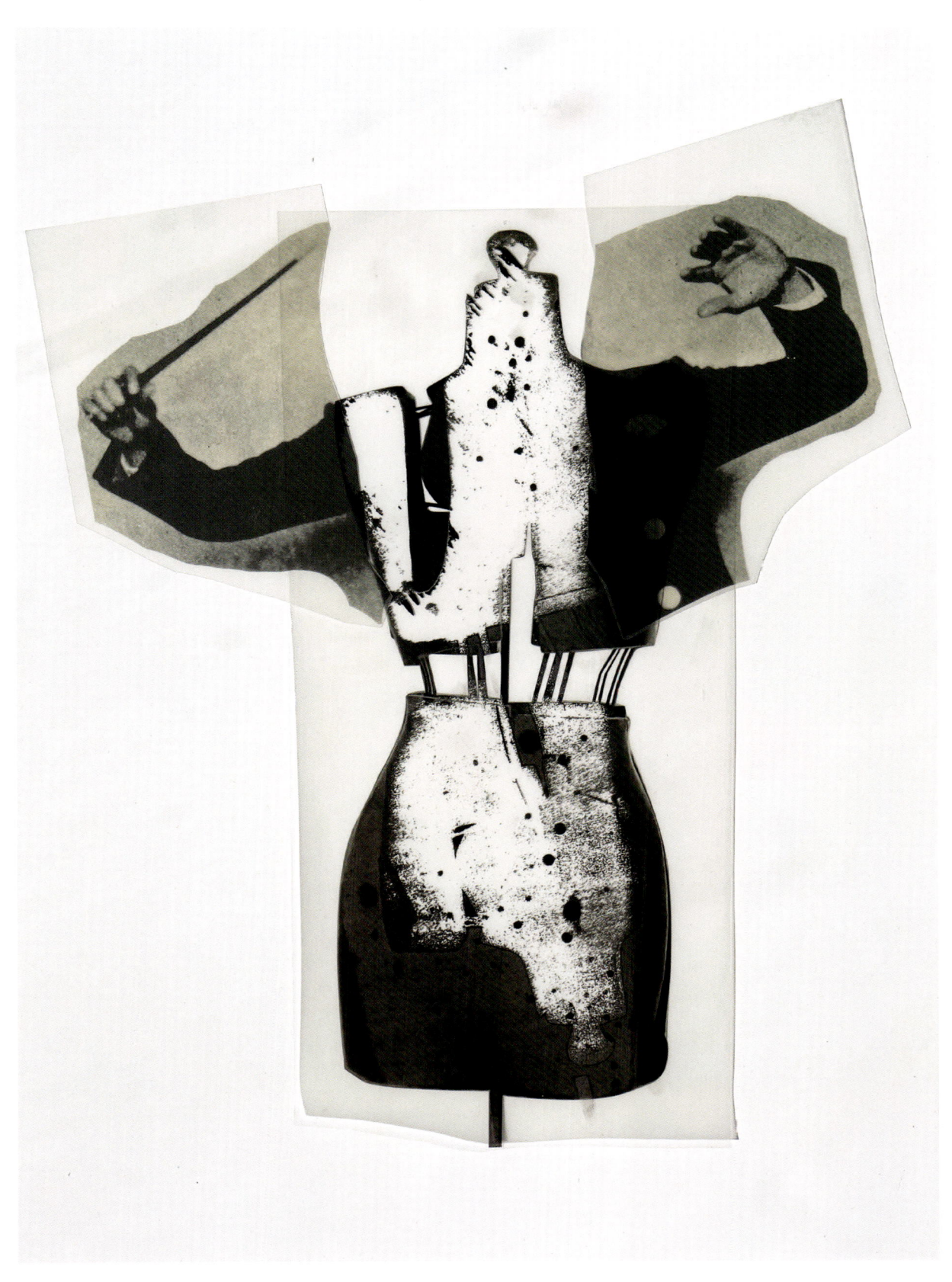

Relief 2
28 x 21 inches
Mixed Media
2020

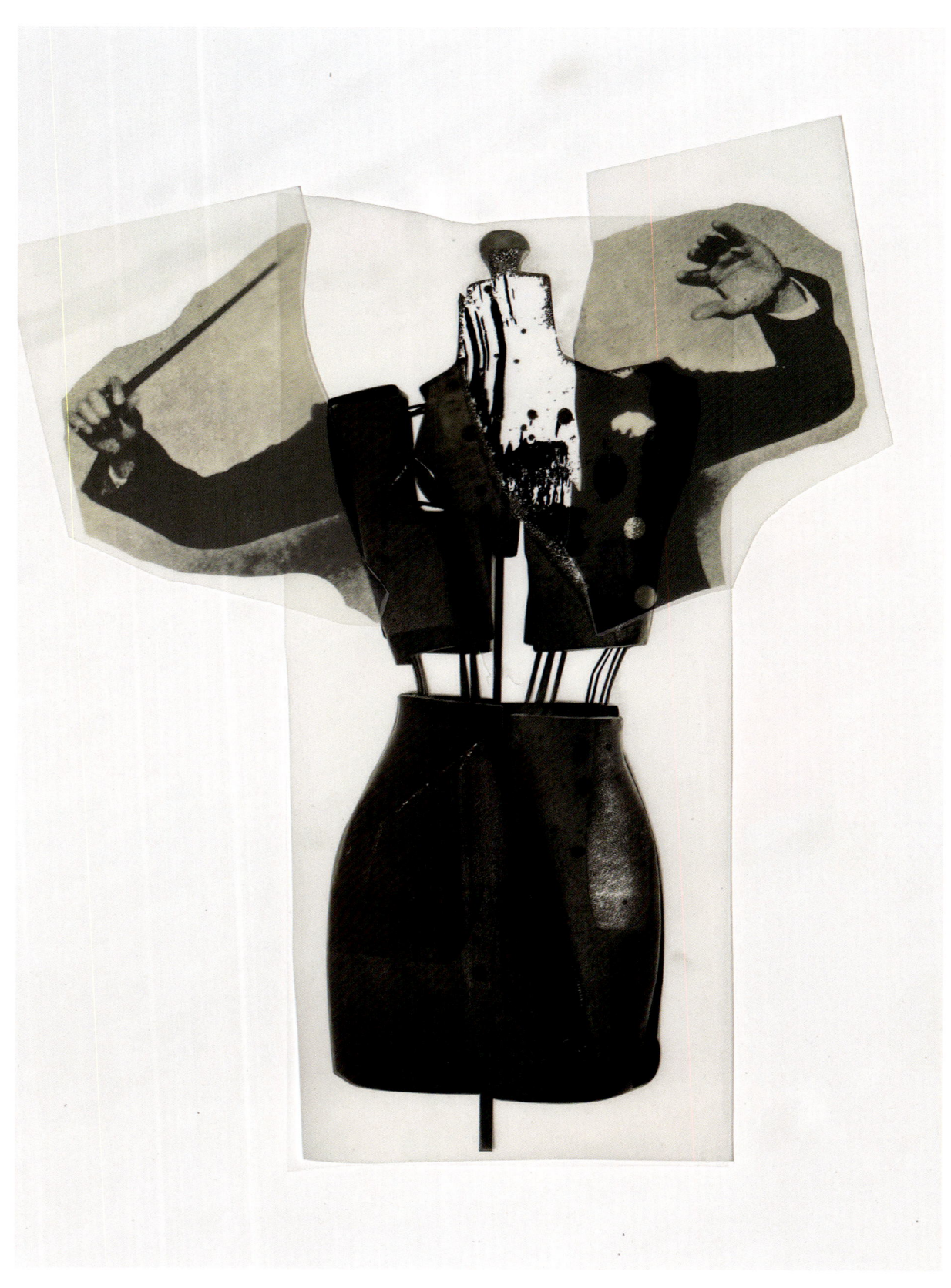

Relief 3
28 x 21 inches
Mixed Media
2020

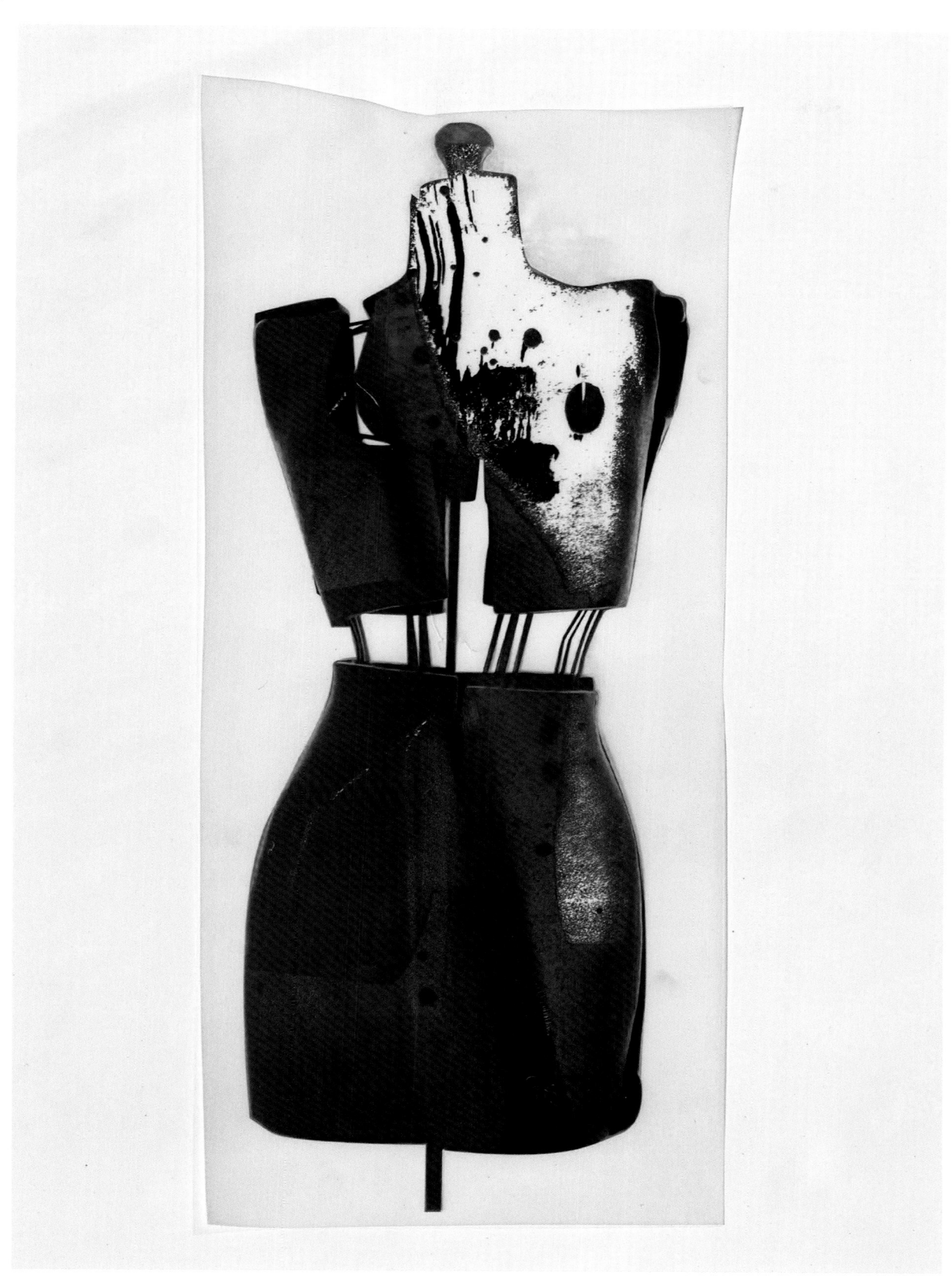

Relief 4
28 x 21 inches
Mixed Media
2020

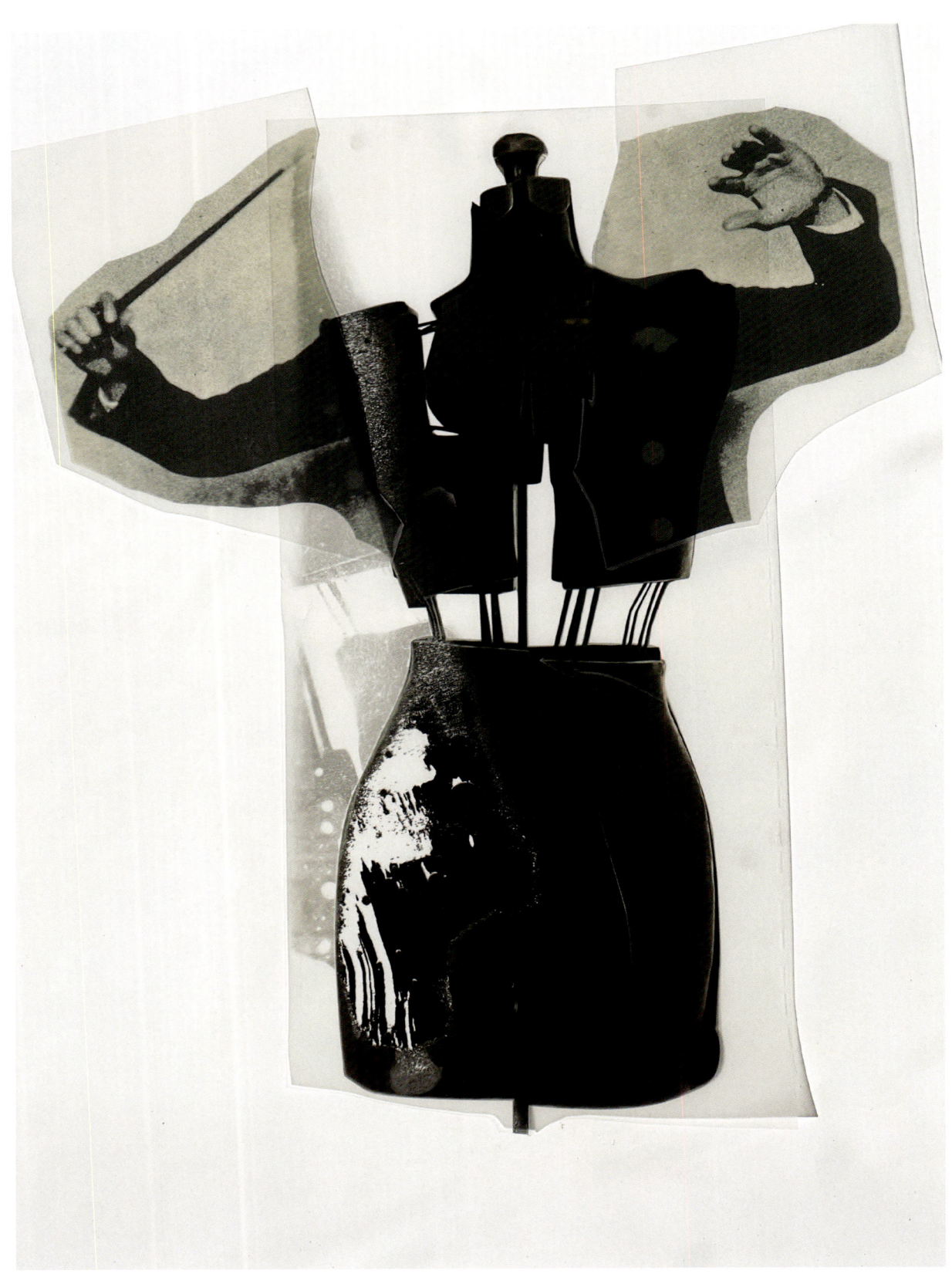

Relief 5
28 x 21 inches
Mixed Media
2020

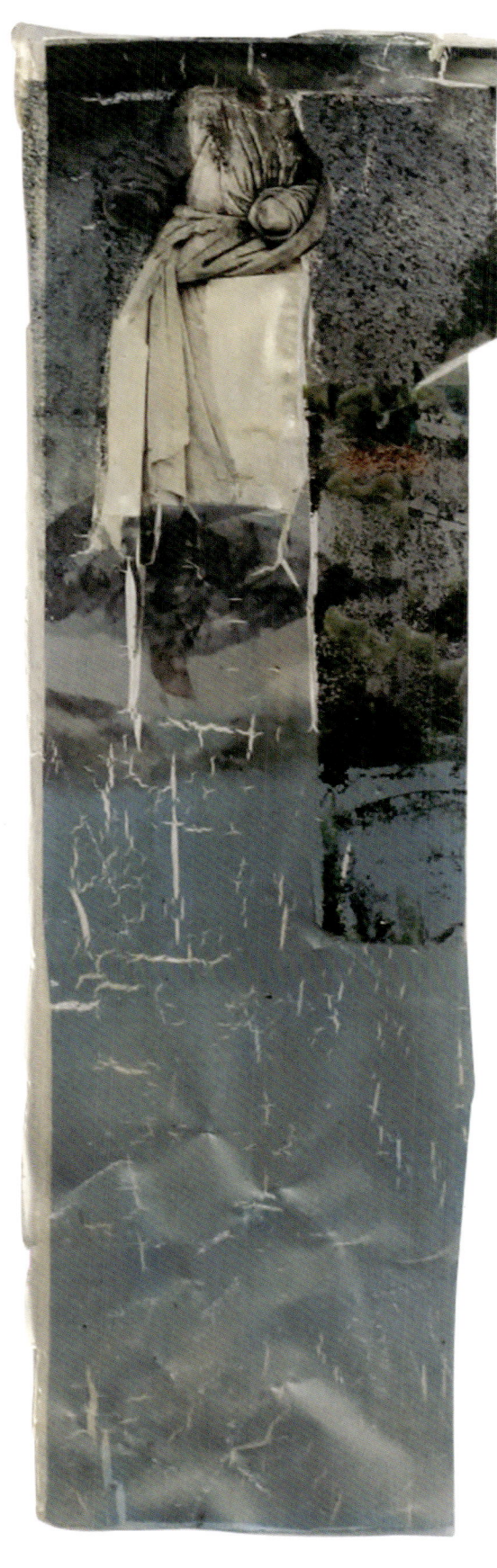

Remnant
22 x 7 inches
Mixed Media on Film
2017

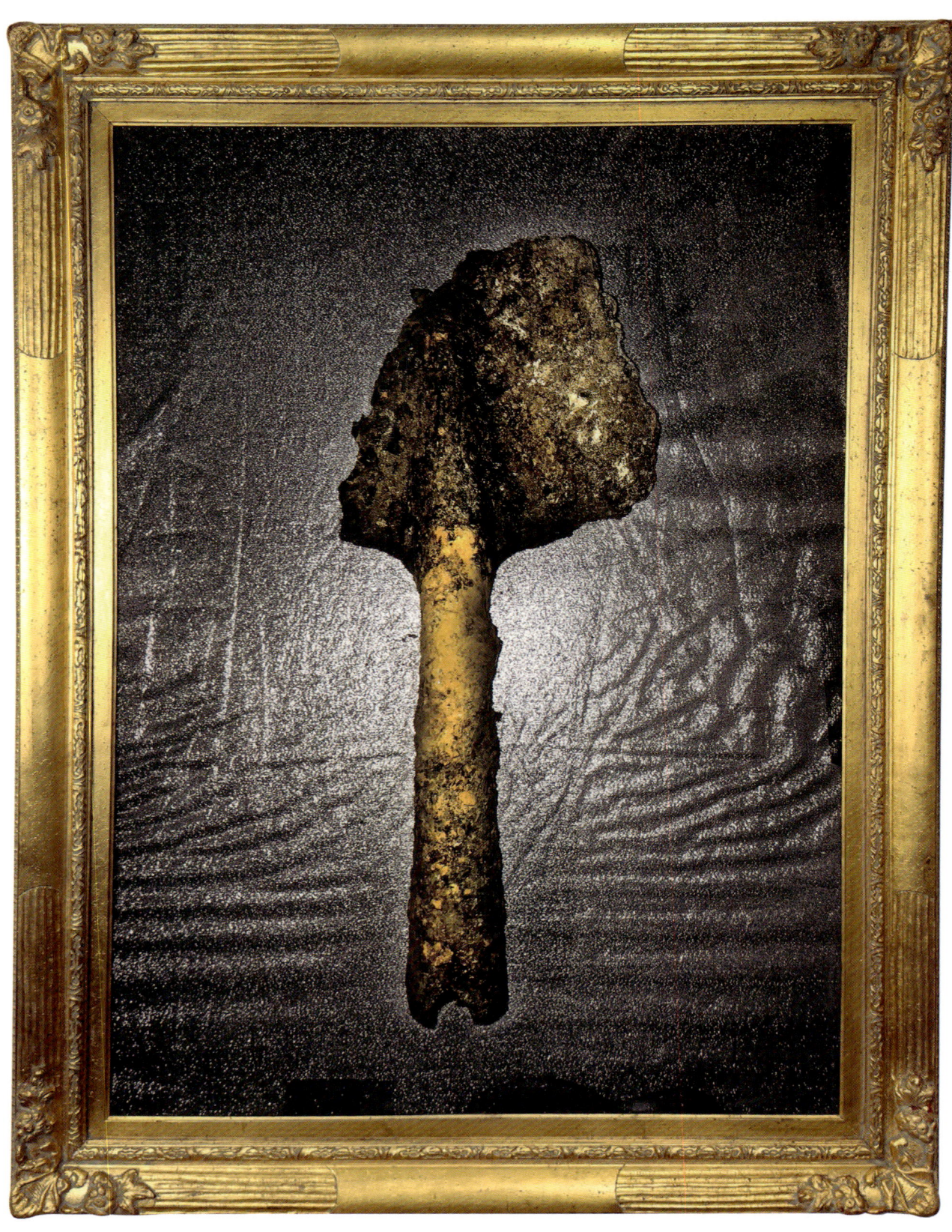

The Manifestation
56 x 45 inches
Archival Color Print on Paper
2016

278

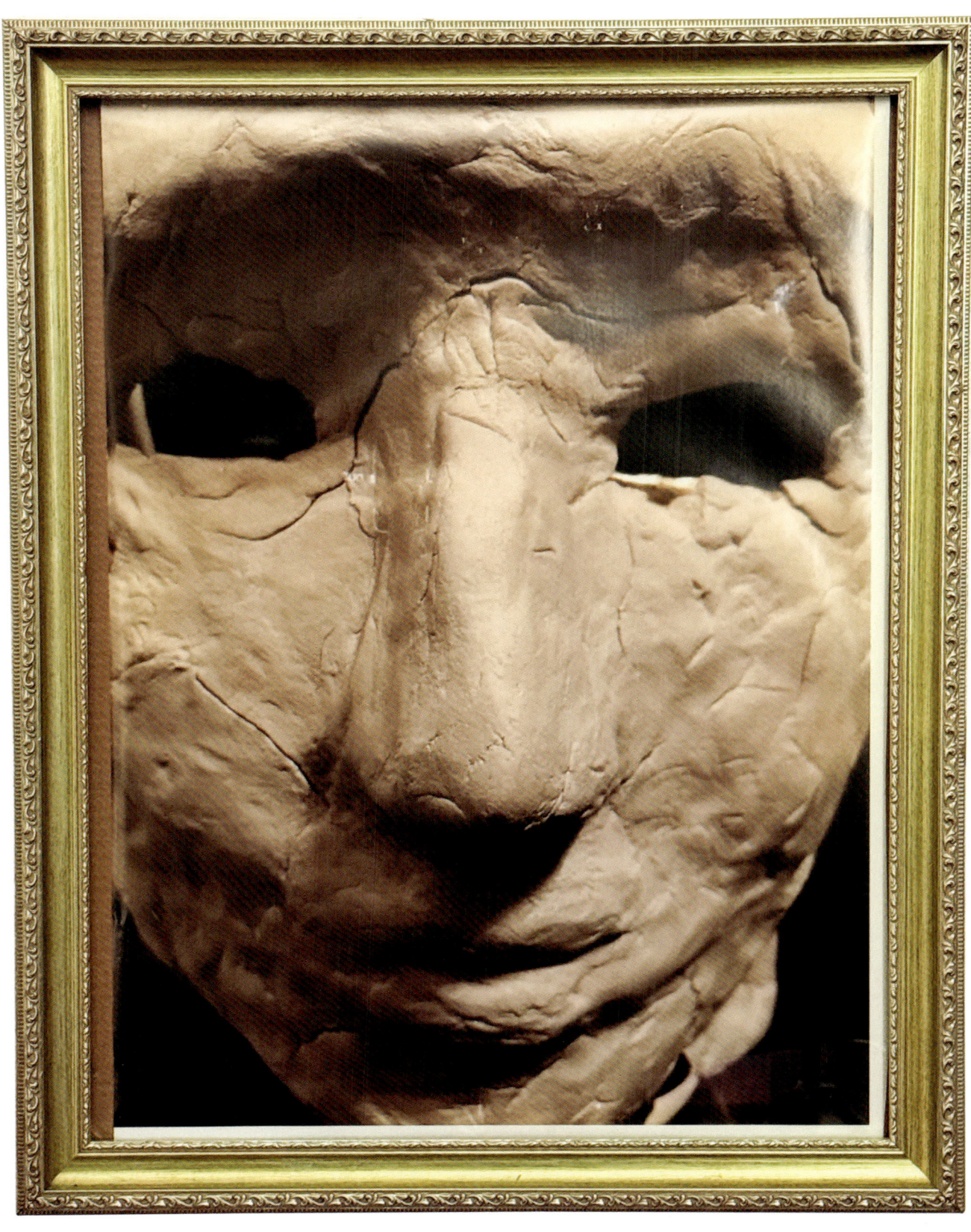

Portrait
31 ½ x 25 ½ inches
Archival Color Print on Paper
2016

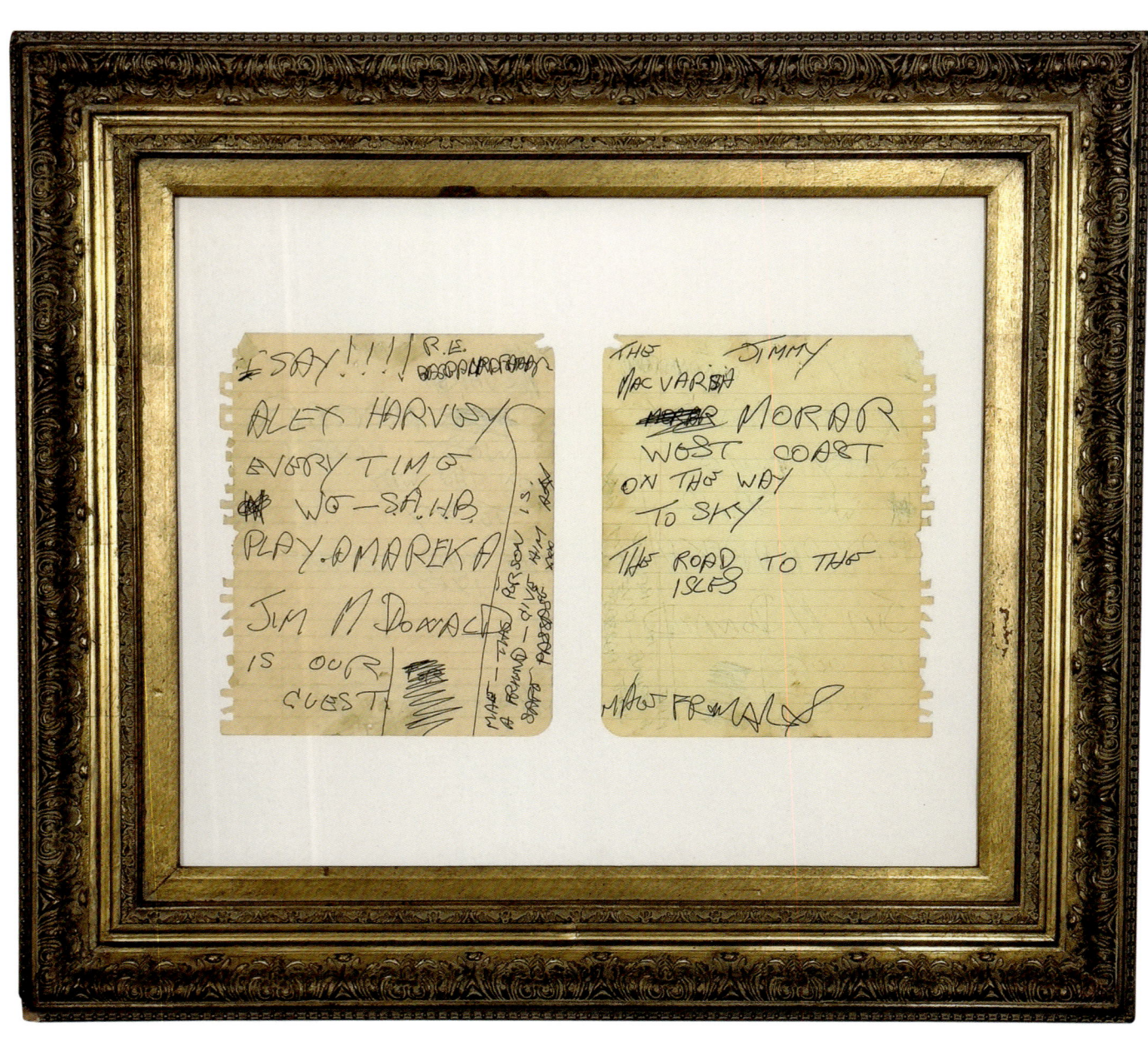

Note from Alex Harvey
28 x 32 inches
Color Print on Paper
2016

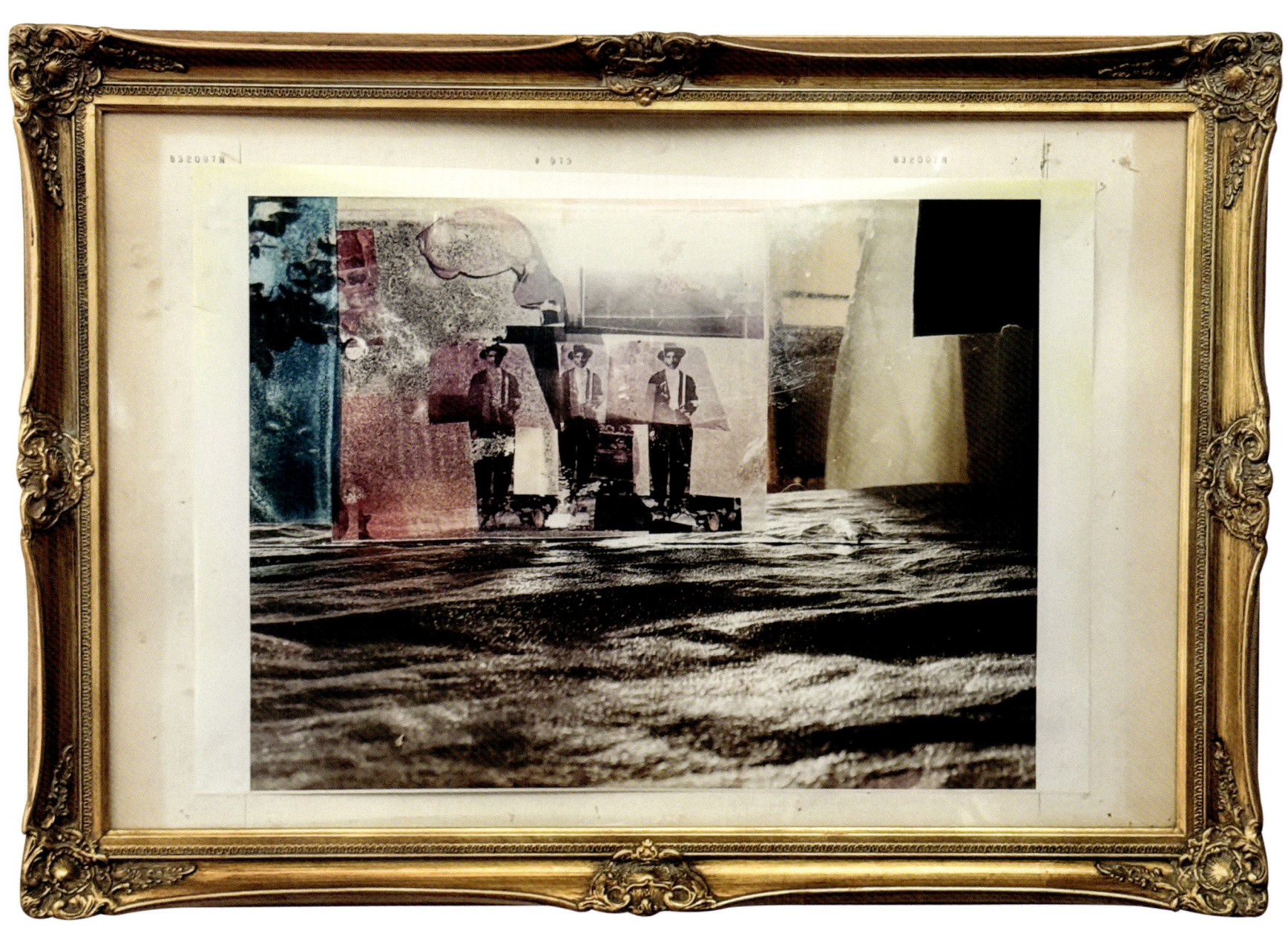

In The Club
29 ½ x 41 ½ inches
Archival Color Print on Paper
2013

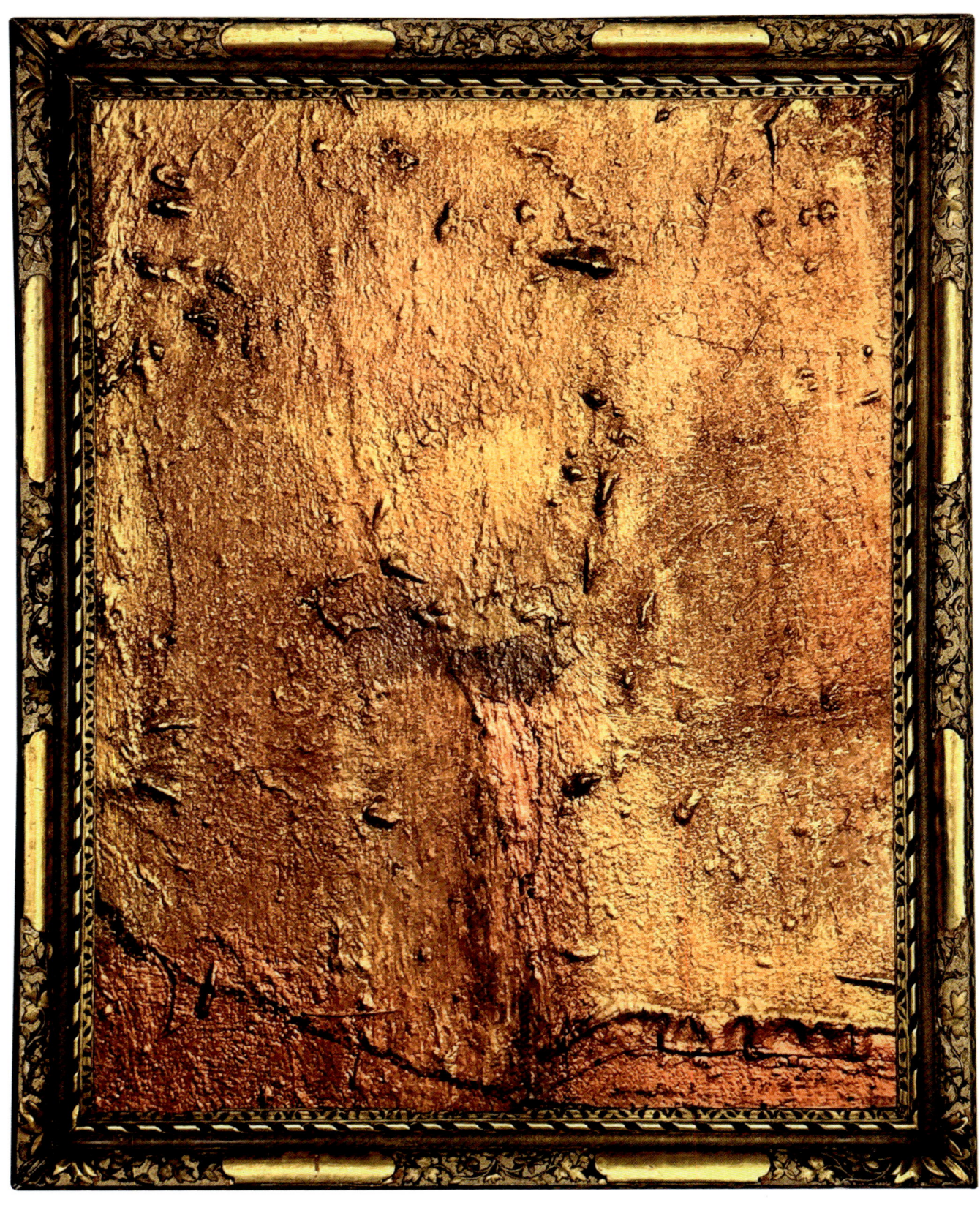

Untitled
56 ½ x 46 ¾ inches
Print on Canvas
2018

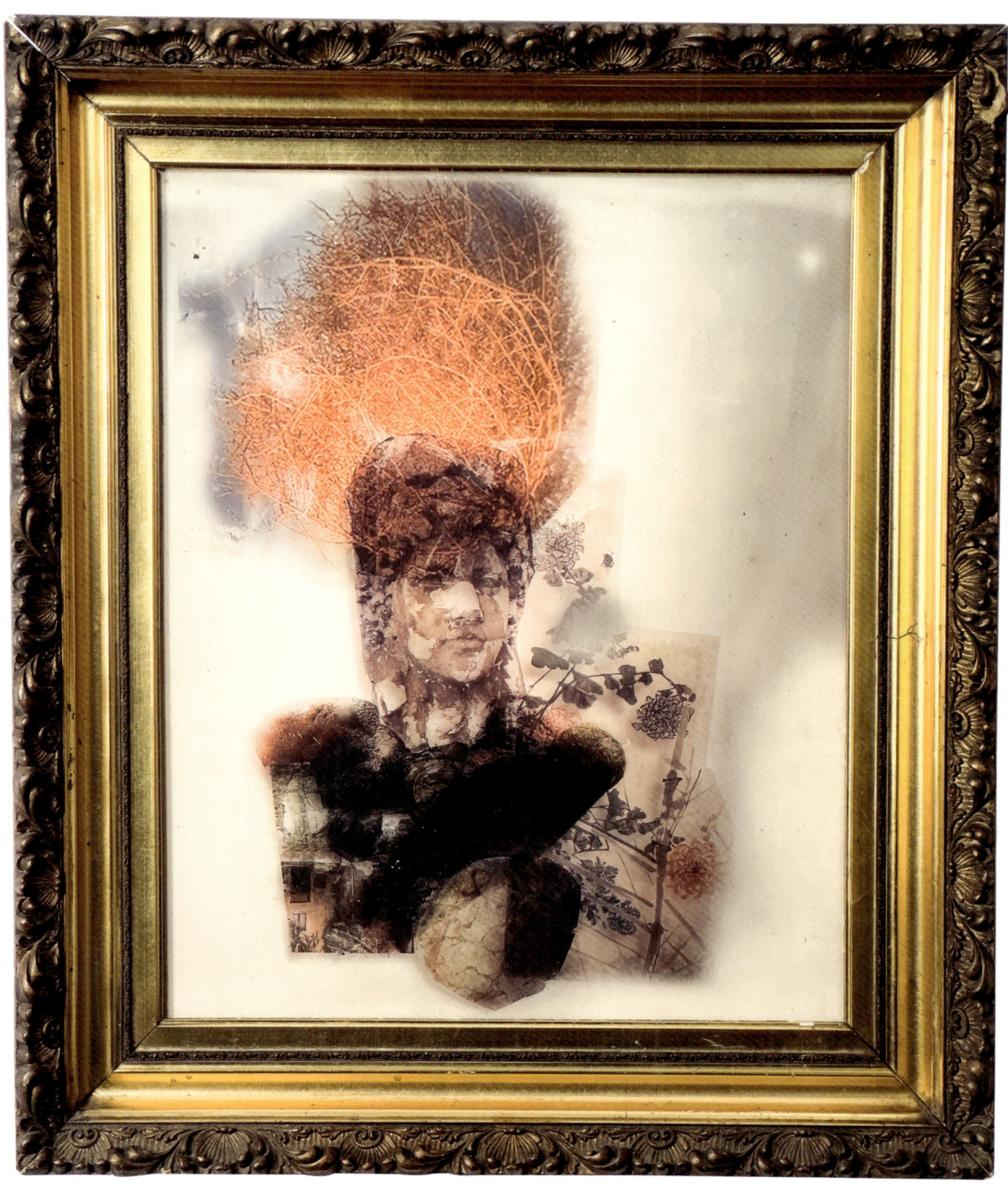

Doorstop
29 x 24 ½ inches
Archival Color Print on Paper
2018

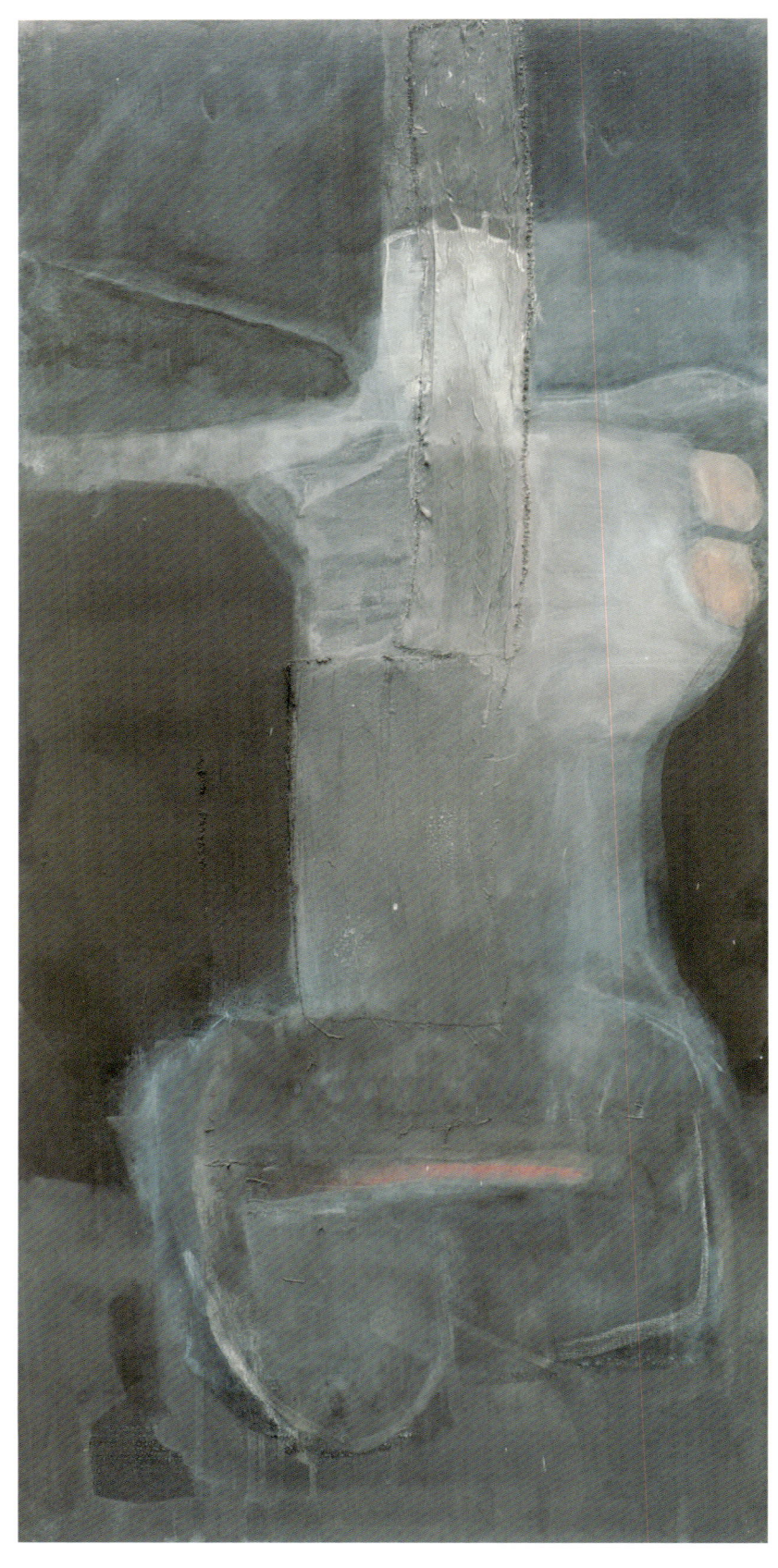

Eurytion
48 x 24 inches
Mixed Media on Canvas
2011

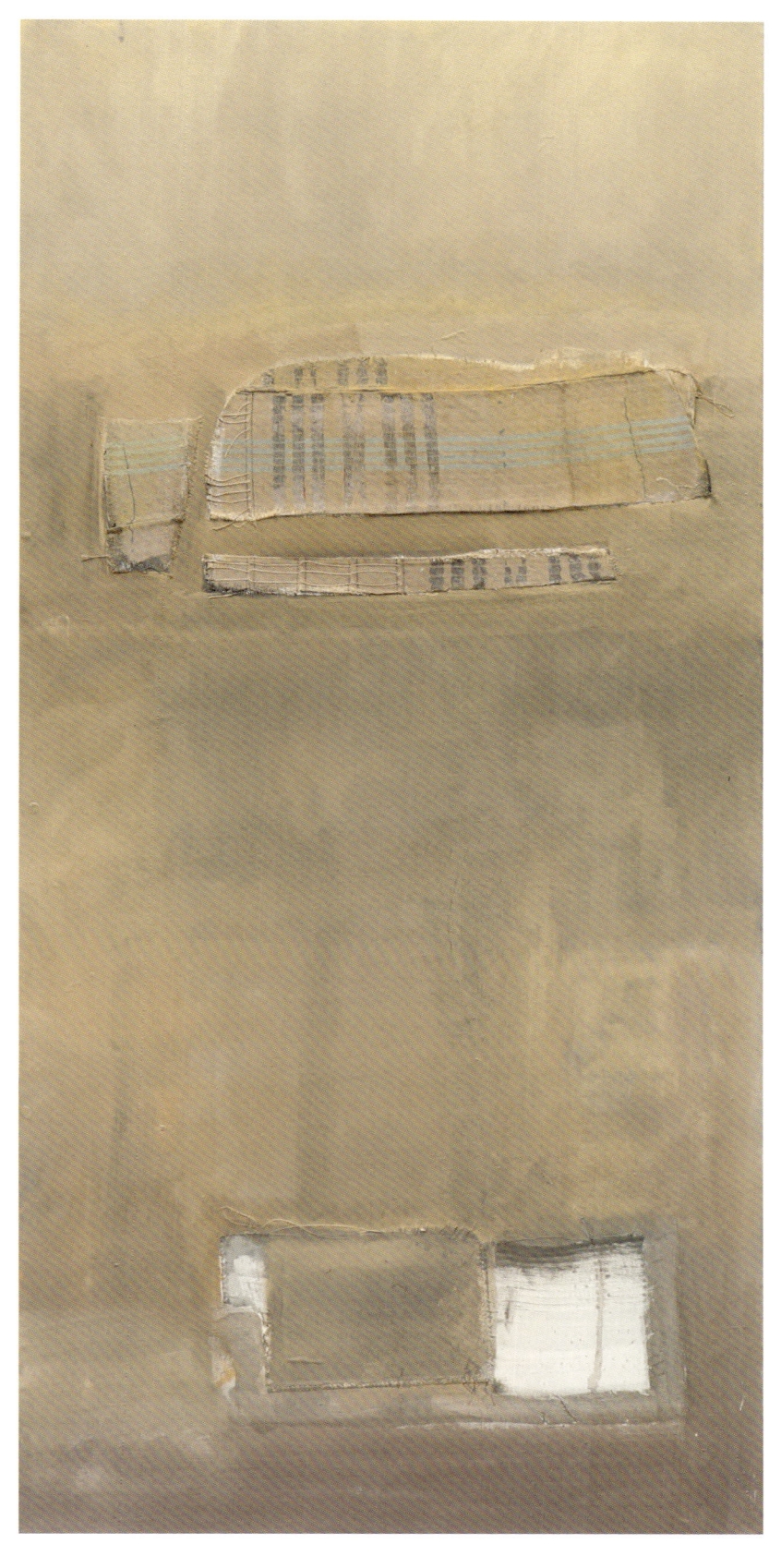

Alphonse en repose
48 x 24 inches
Mixed Media on Canvas
2010

Reflector
48 x 36 inches
Mixed Media on Canvas
2013

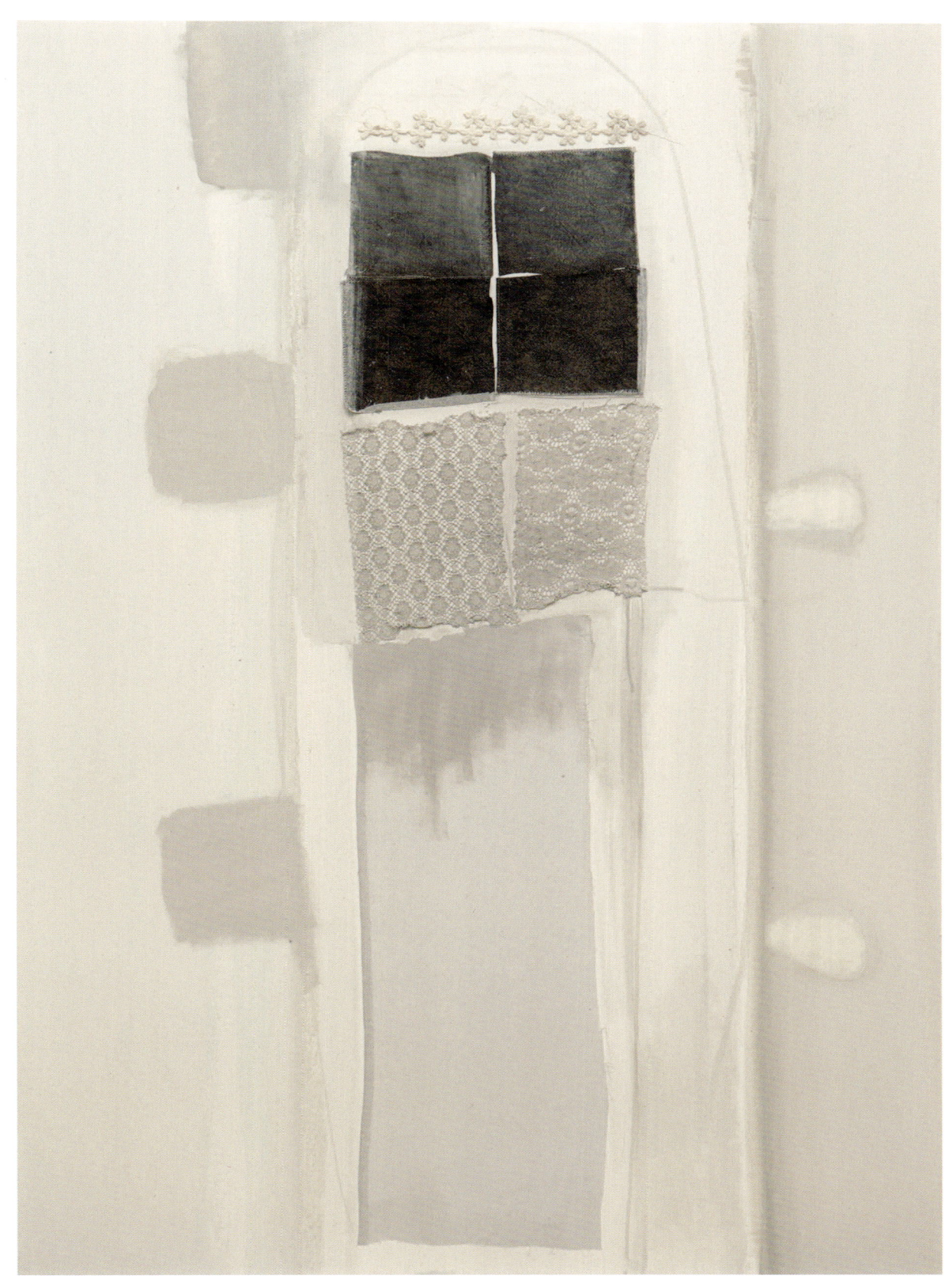

Bride of Pirithous
48 x 36 inches
Mixed Media on Canvas
2011

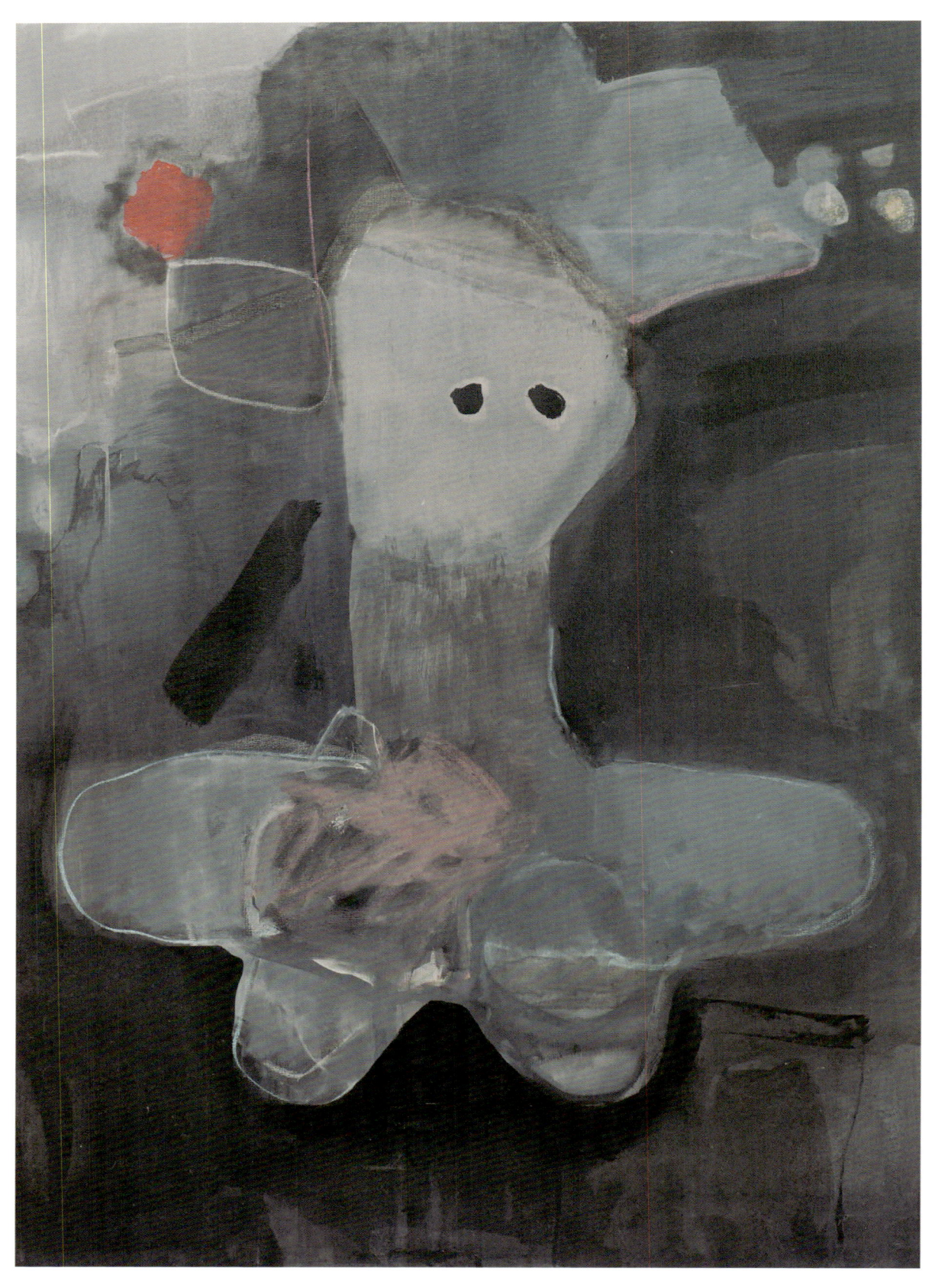

In The Vineyard of Pholus
48 x 36 inches
Mixed Media on Canvas
2011

Dove Chrysalis
48 x 36 inches
Mixed Media on Canvas
2011

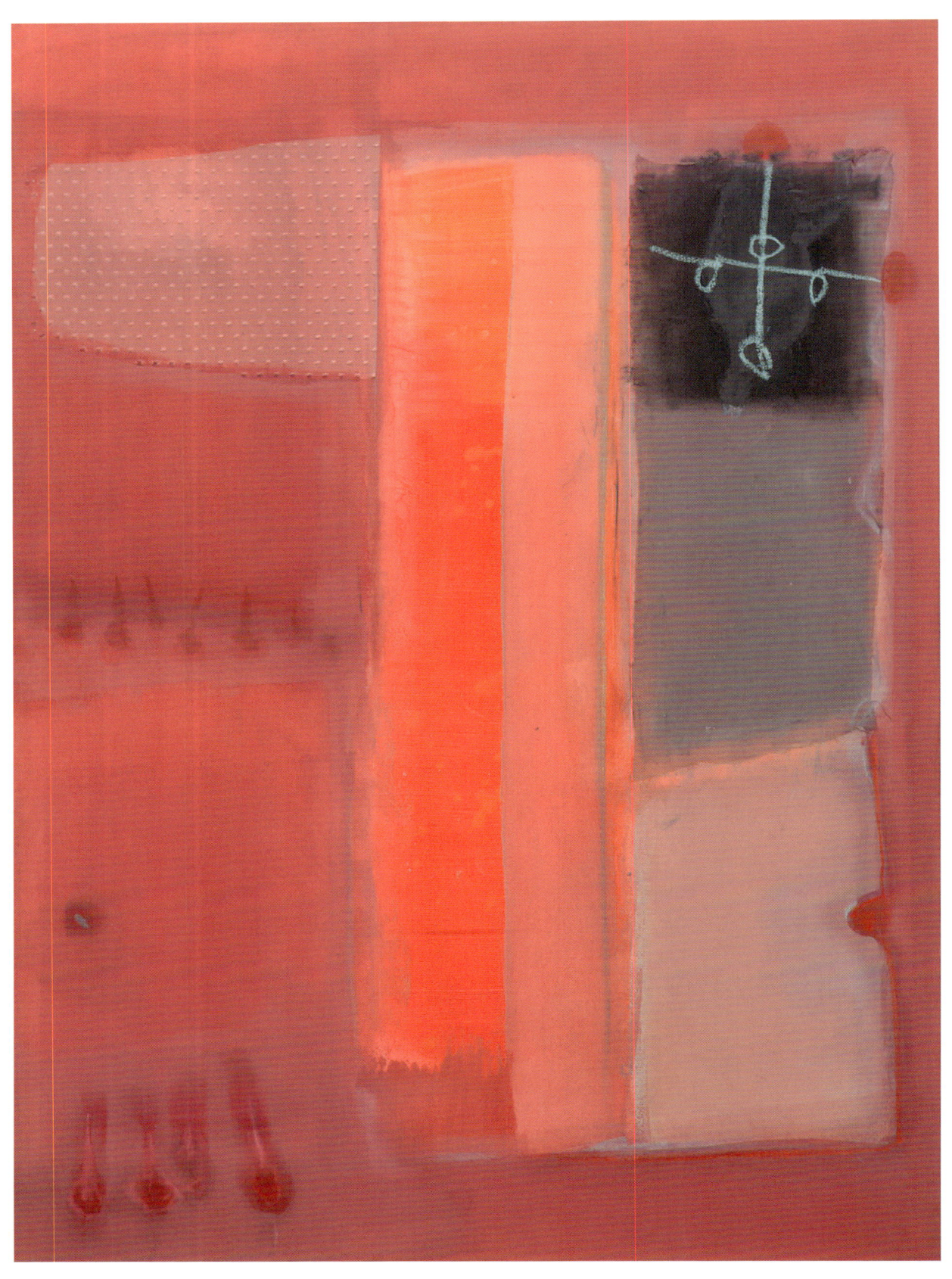

Barometrics of Spin
36 x 24 inches
Mixed Media on Canvas
2012

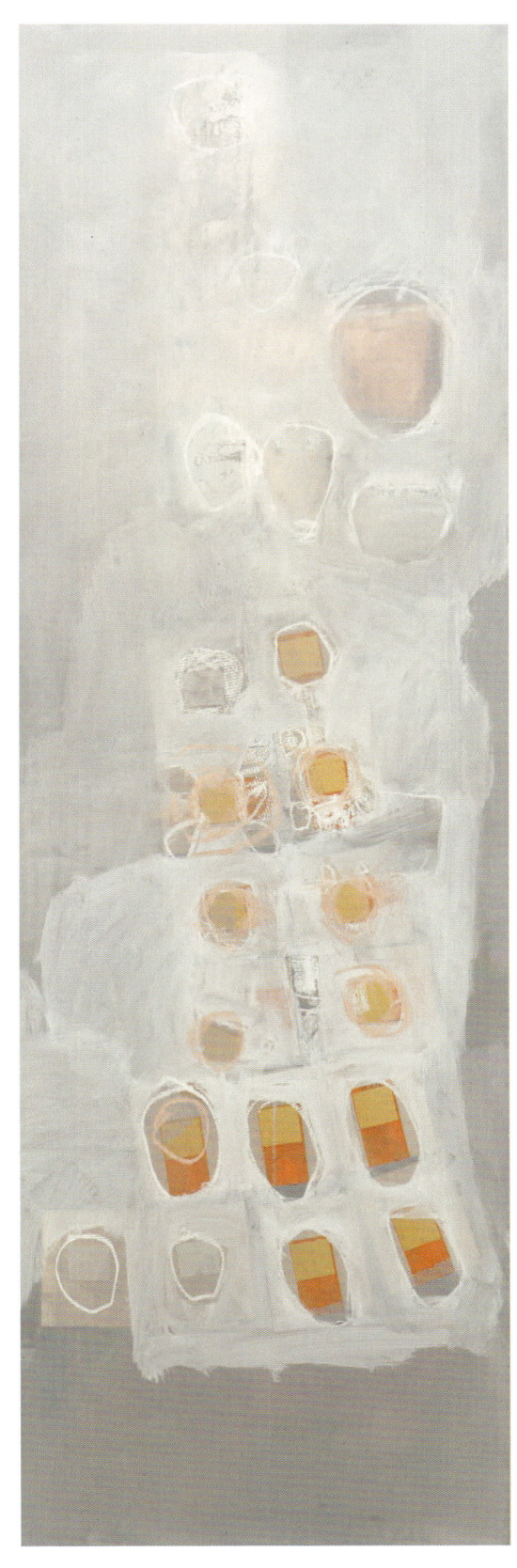

Core Sample
72 x 24 inches
Mixed Media on Canvas
2011

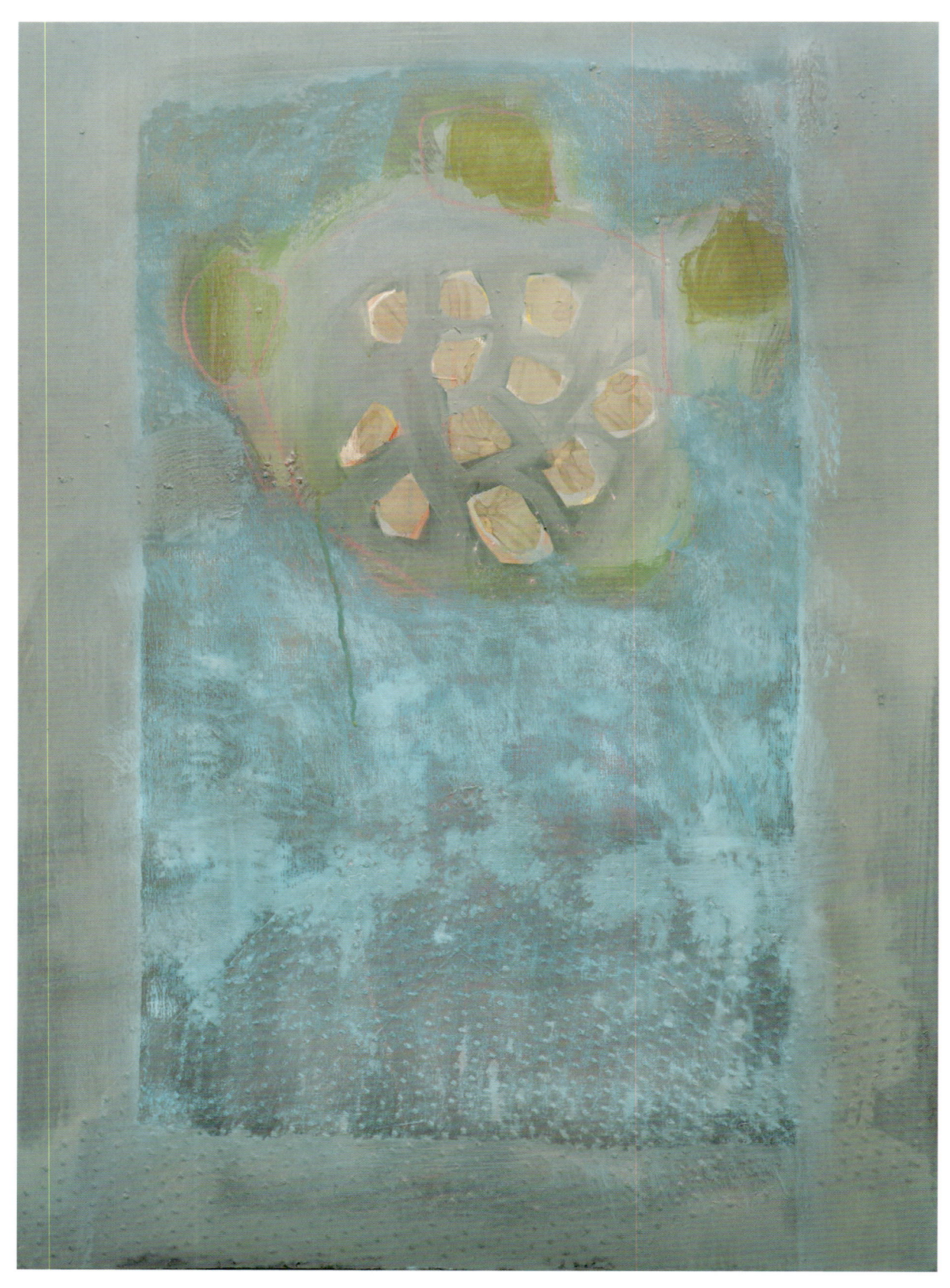

Bourré
40 x 30 inches
Mixed Media on Canvas
2011

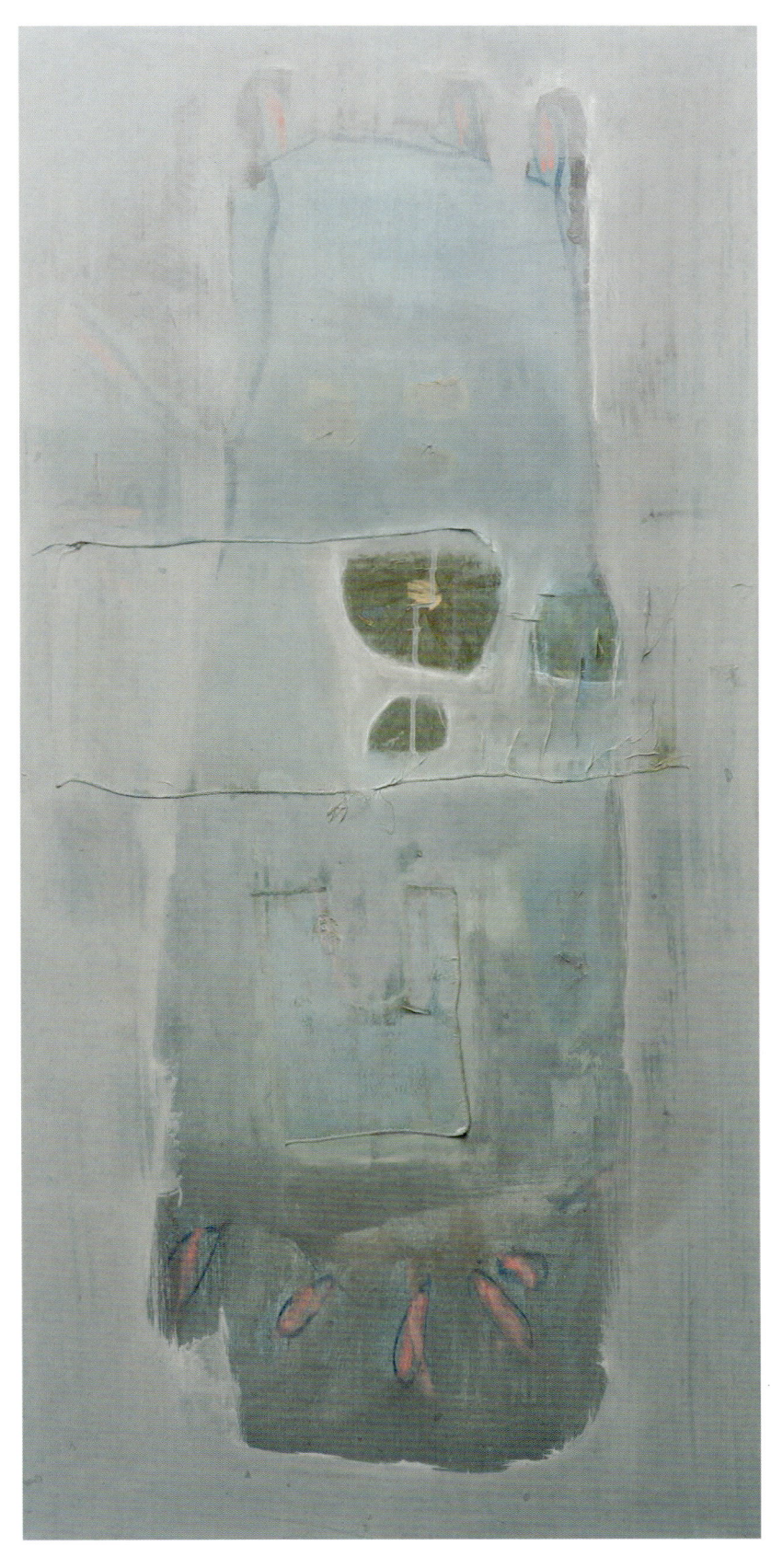

Liminal
48 x 24 inches
Mixed Media on Canvas
2012

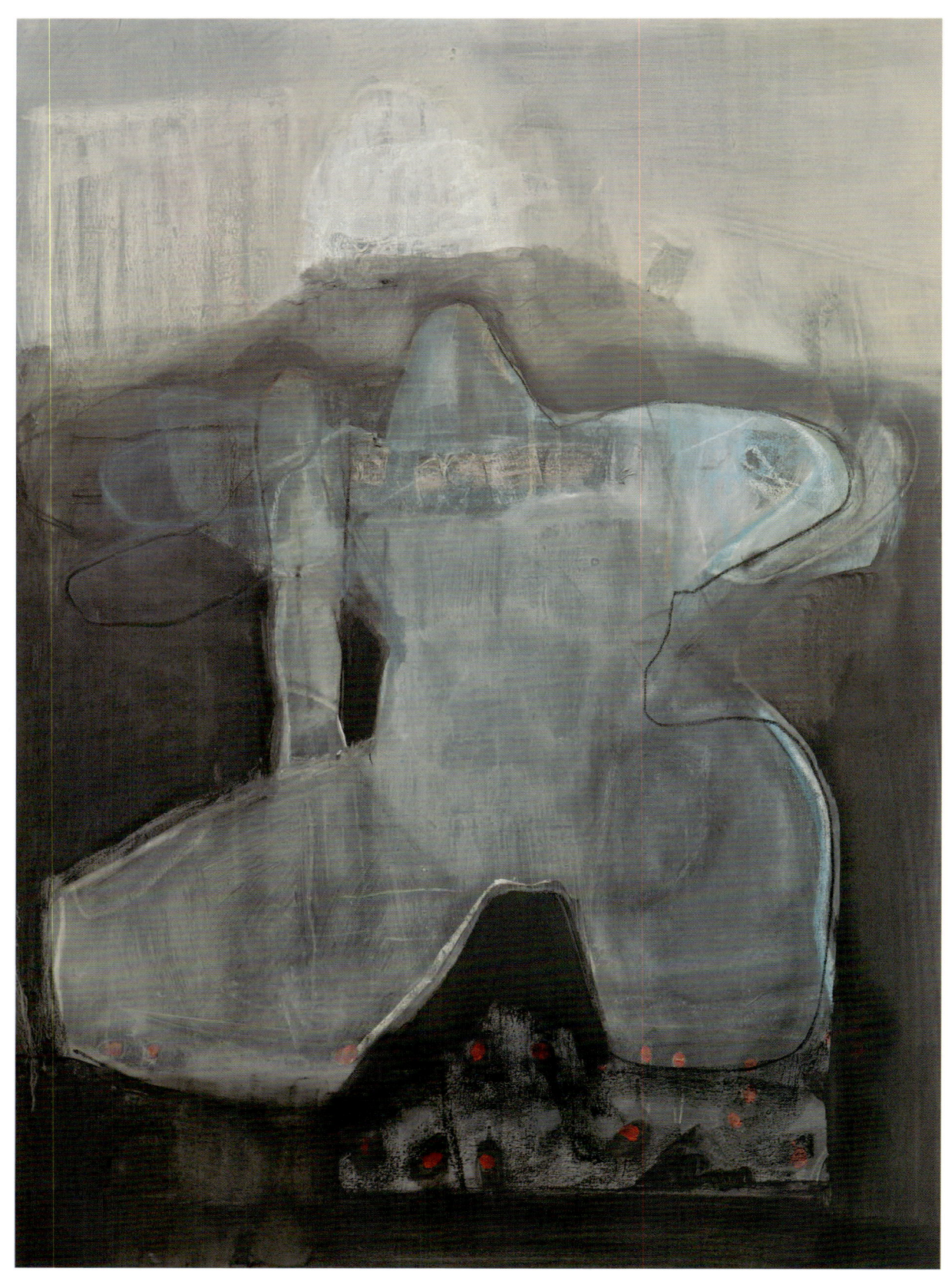

The Taking of Stilbe by Apollo
48 x 36 inches
Mixed Media on Canvas
2011

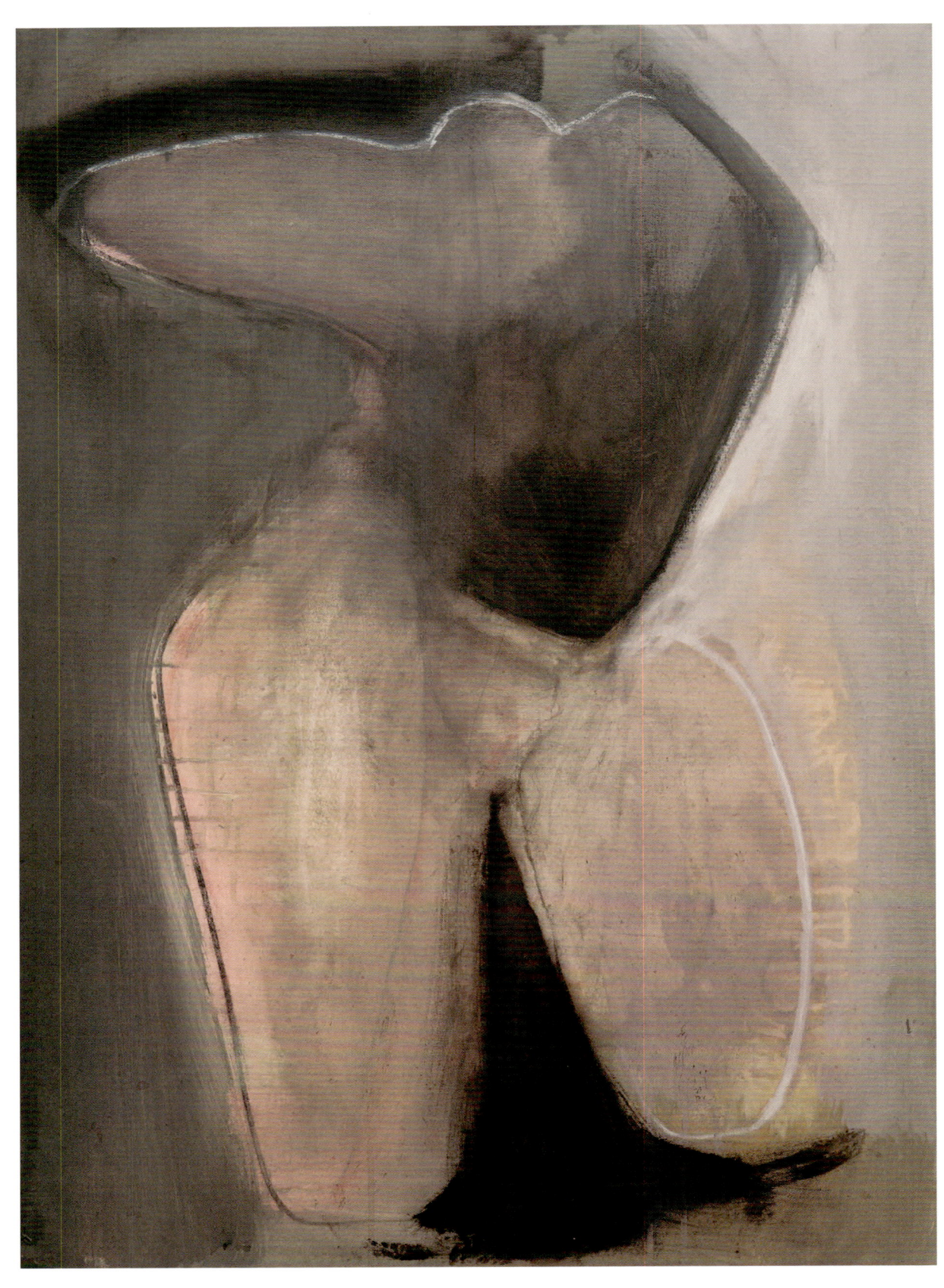

Dancer 3
40 x 30 inches
Mixed Media on Canvas
2012

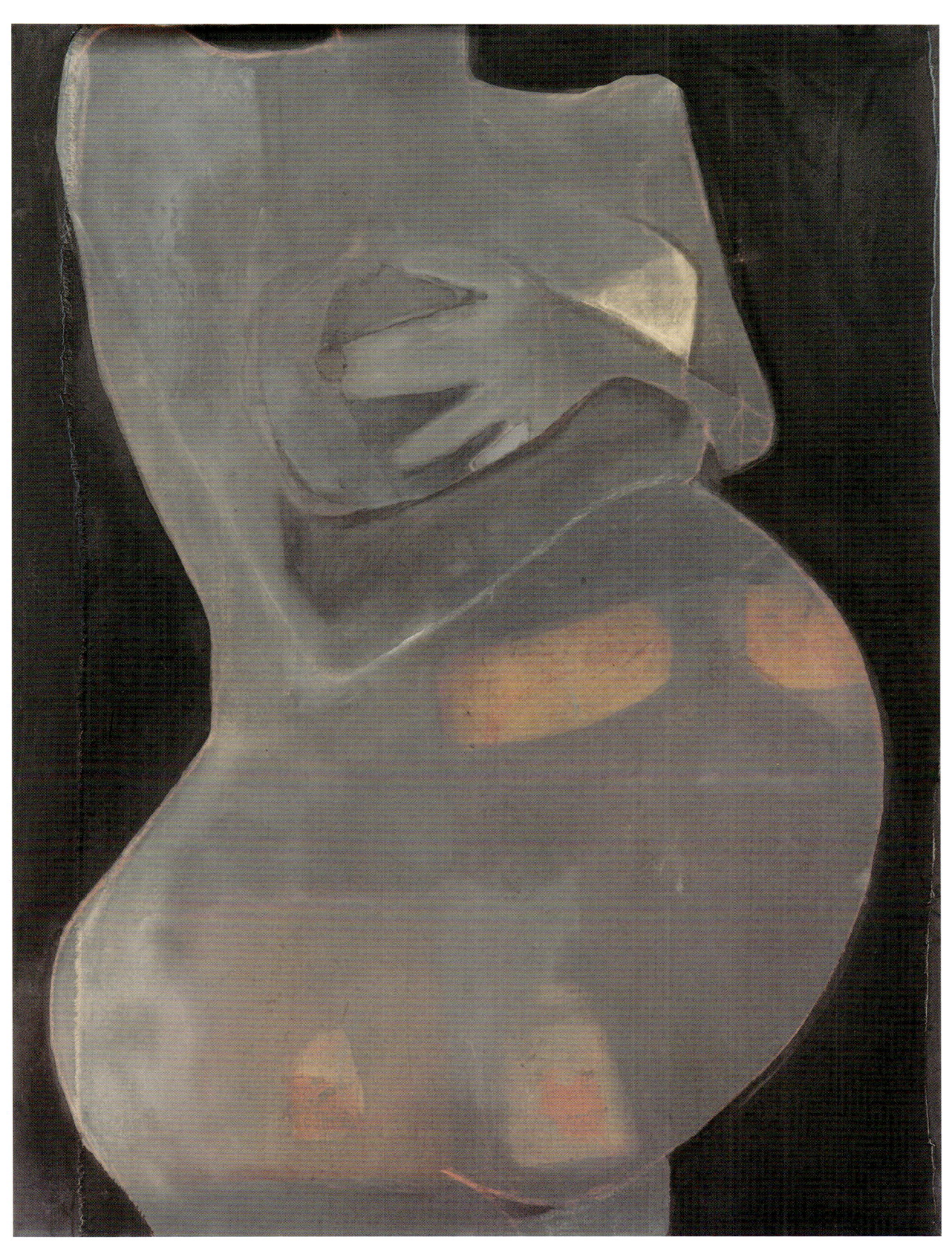

Untitled
28 X 21 ¾ inches
Mixed Media on Canvas
2011

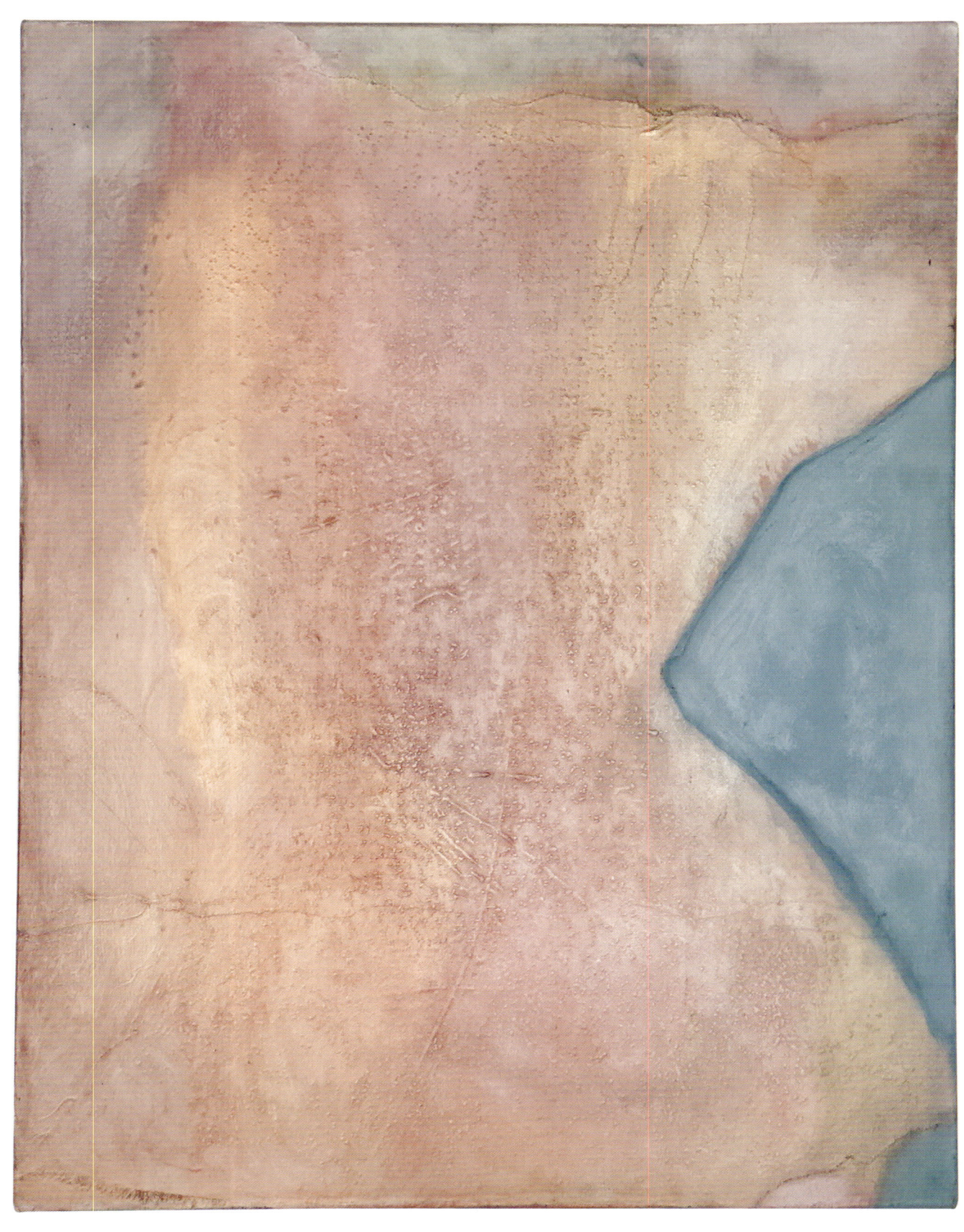

Stabby
30 X 24 inches
Mixed Media on Canvas
2014

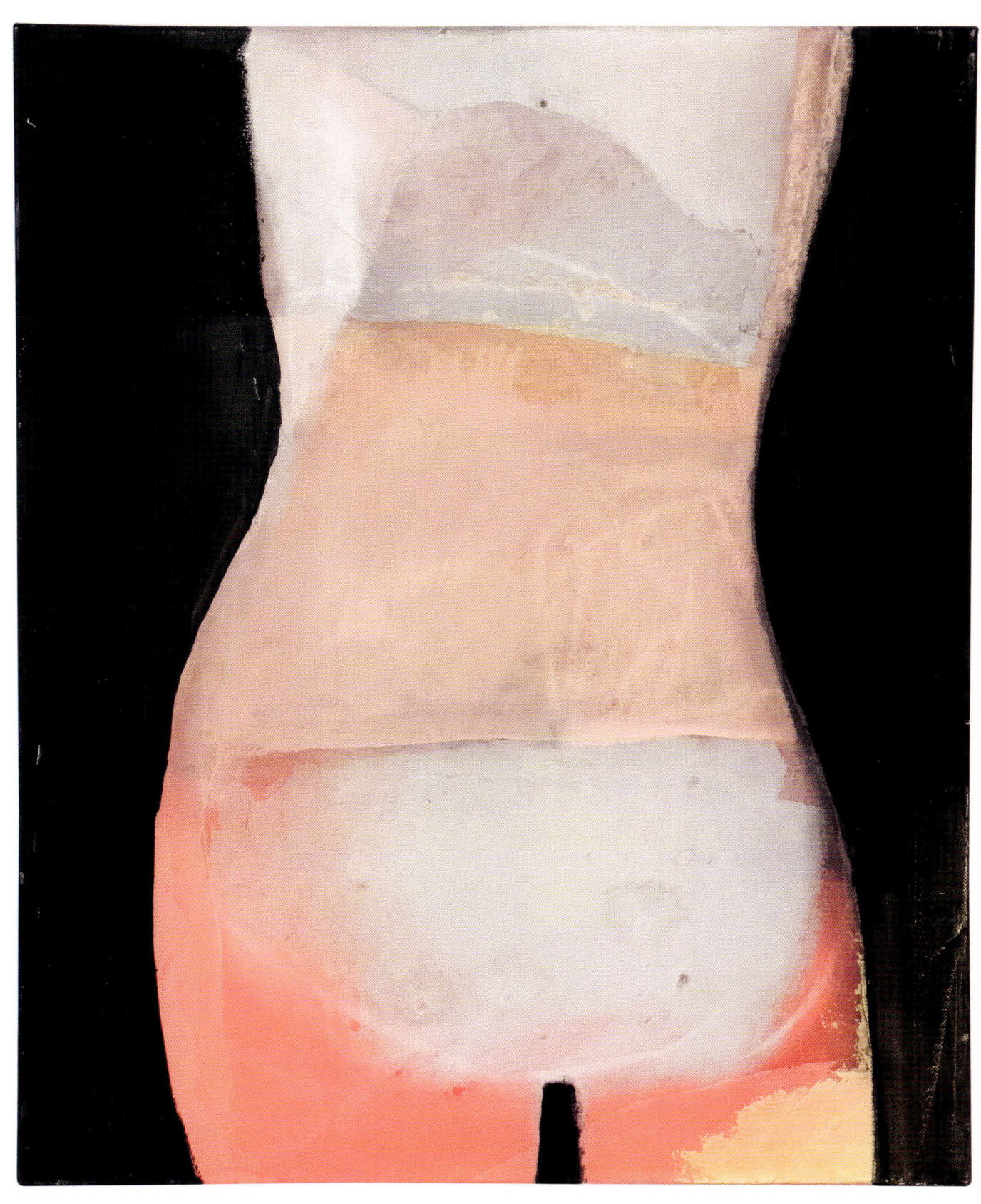

La Gringa
24 x 20 inches
Mixed Media on Canvas
2014

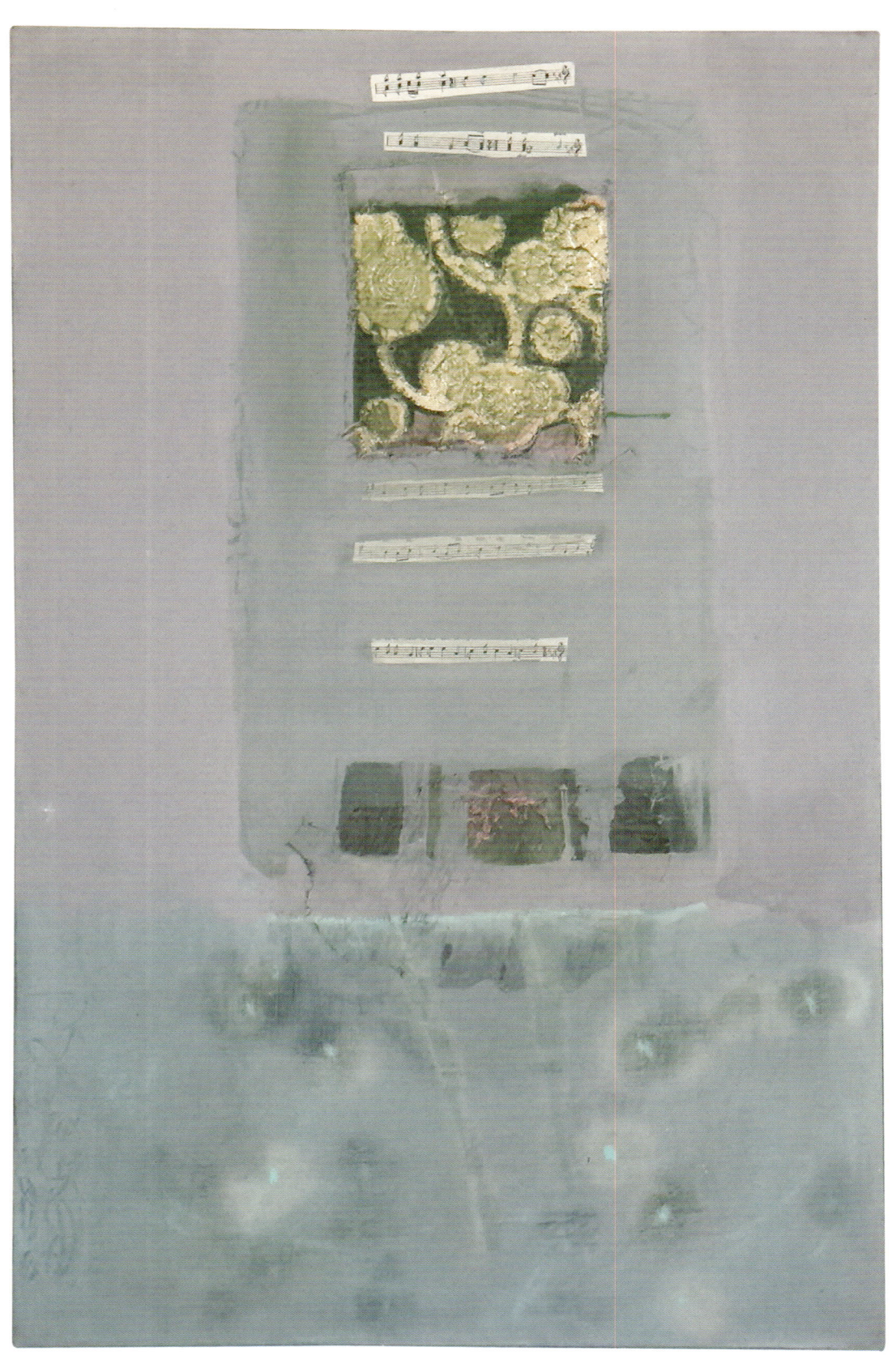

Jukebox
36 x 24 inches
Mixed Media on Canvas
2012

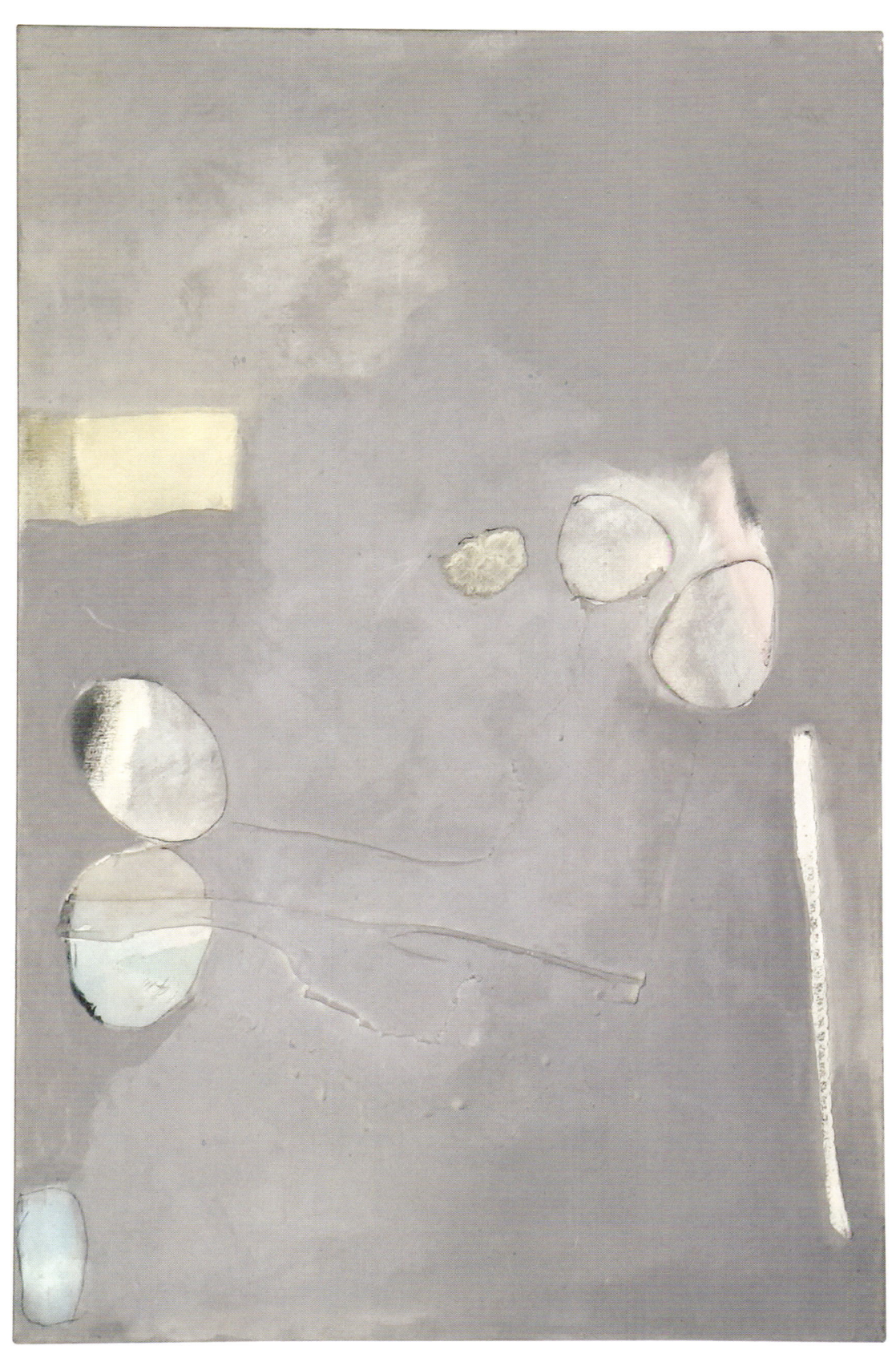

Hint
36 x 24 inches
Mixed Media on Canvas
2012

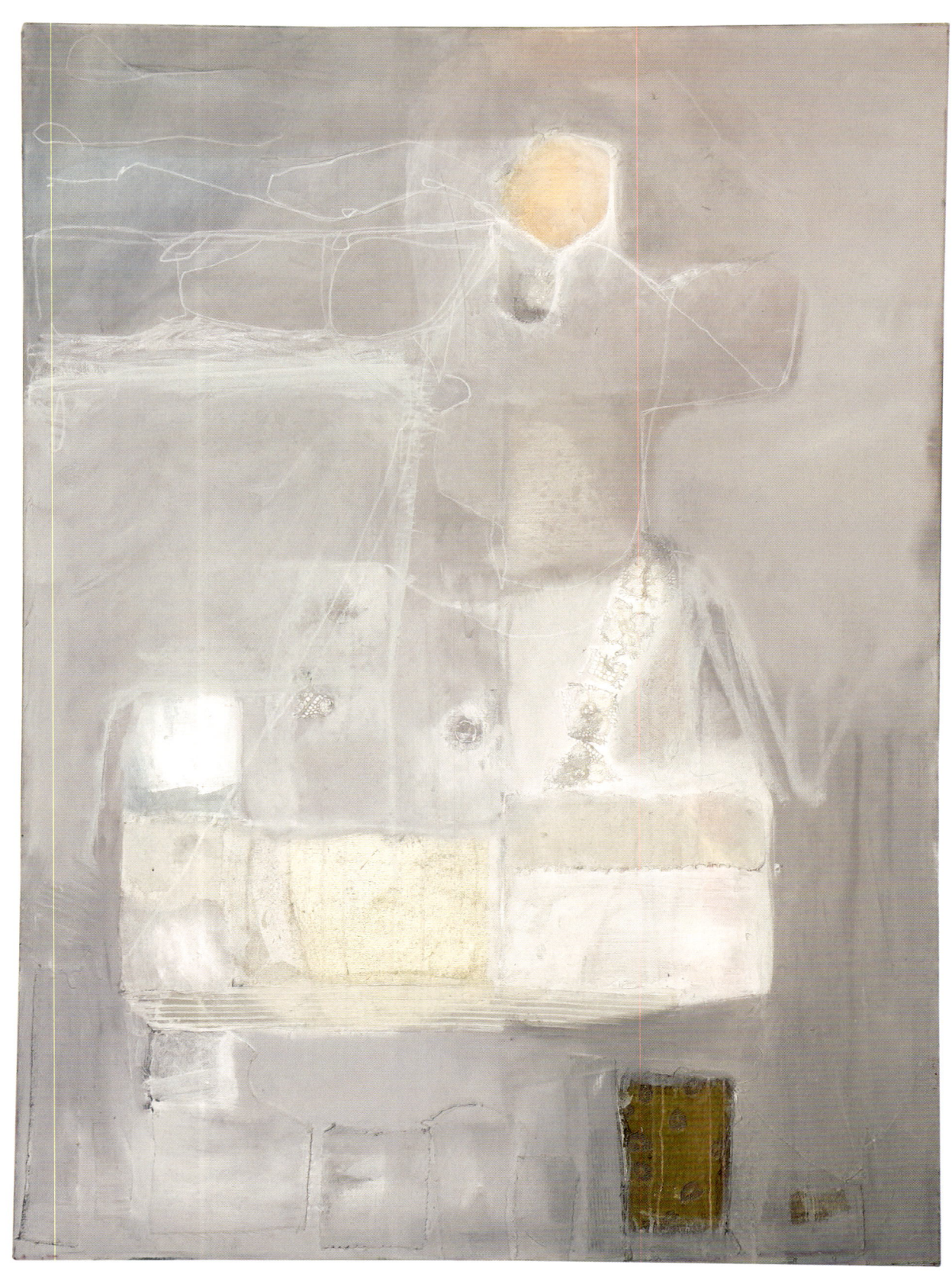

Cyllarus
48 x 36 inches
Mixed Media on Canvas
2014

302

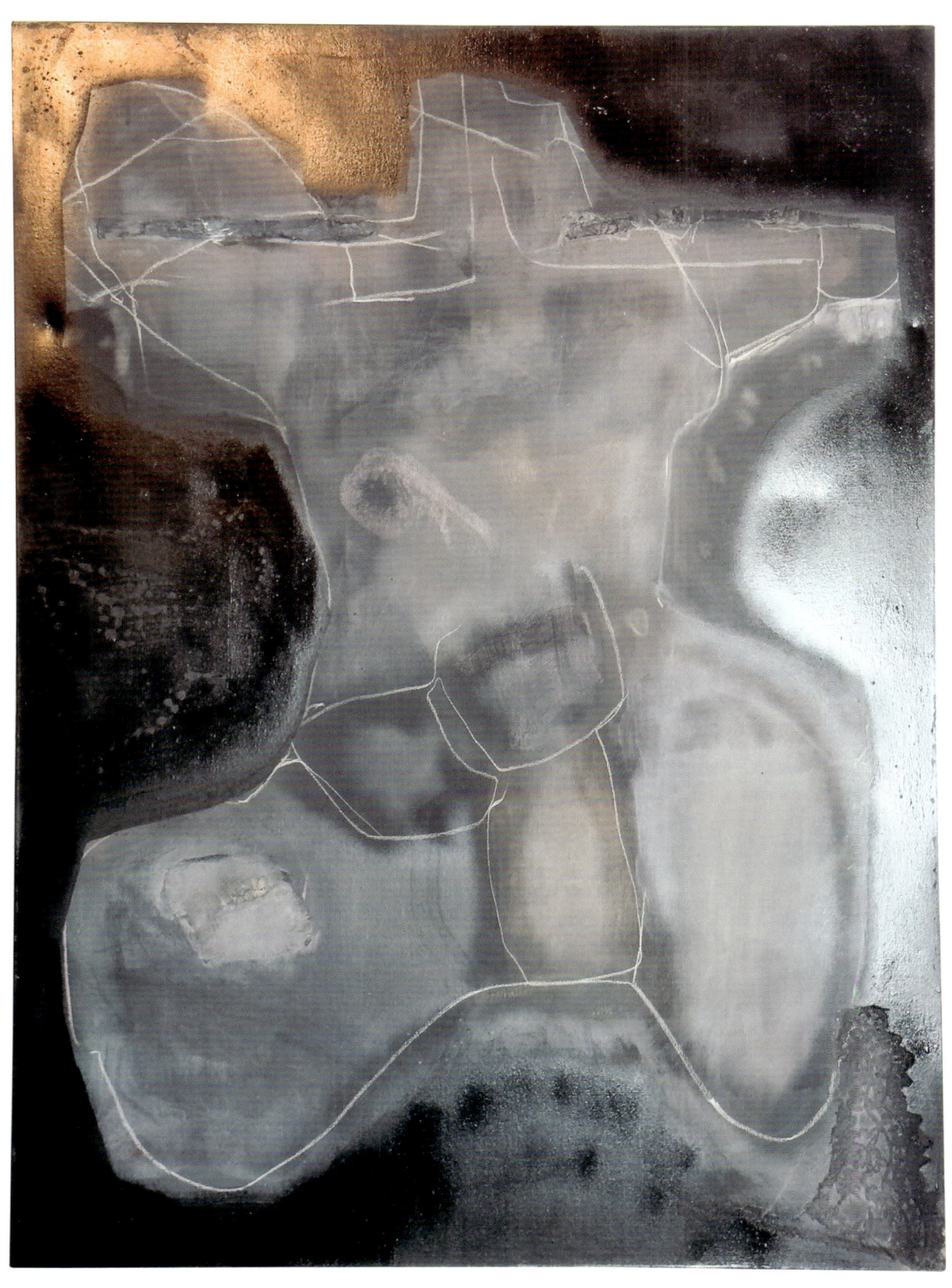

Hylonome
48 x 36 inches
Mixed Media on Canvas
2012

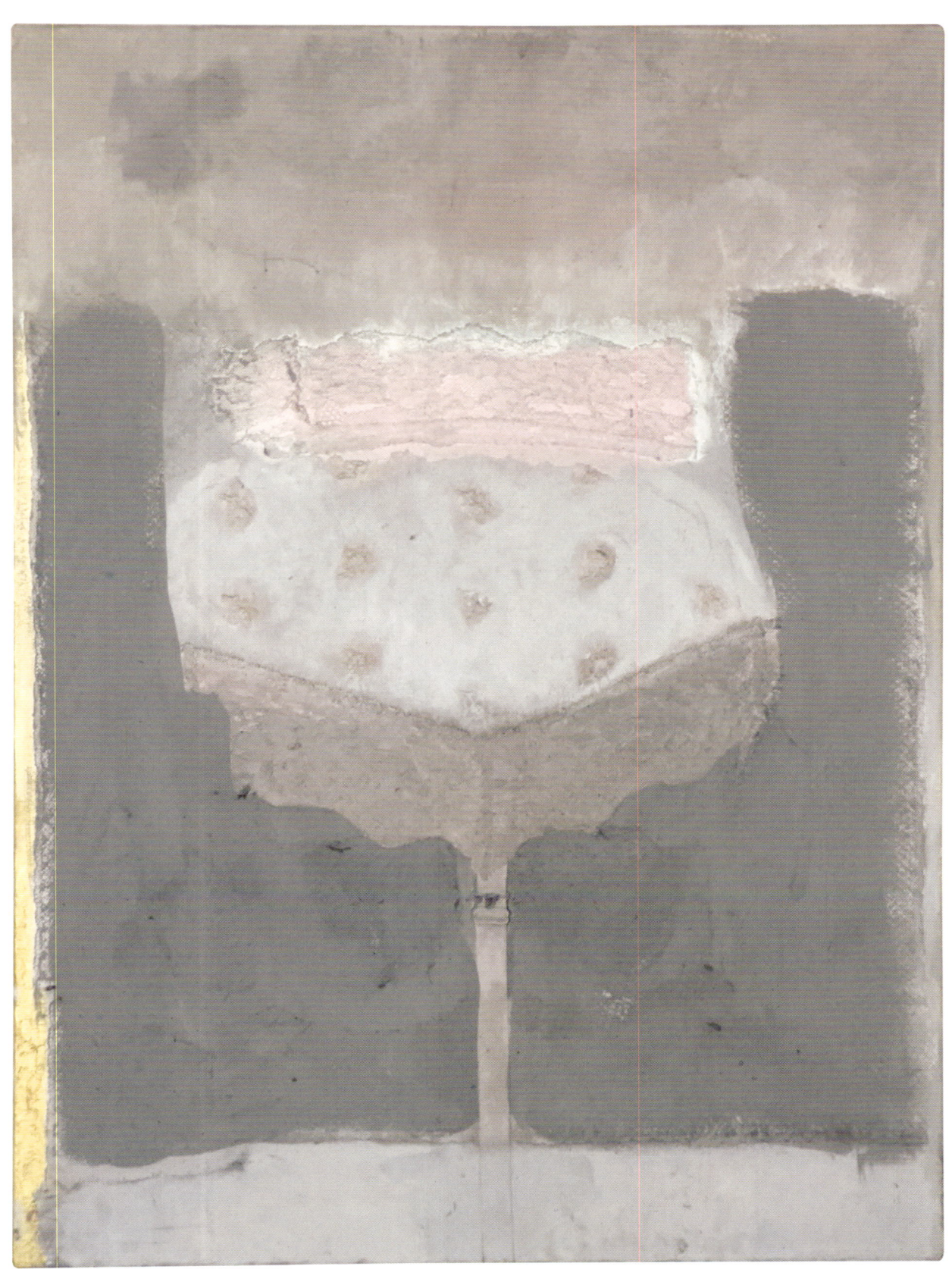

Champagne
24 x 18 inches
Mixed Media on Canvas
2008

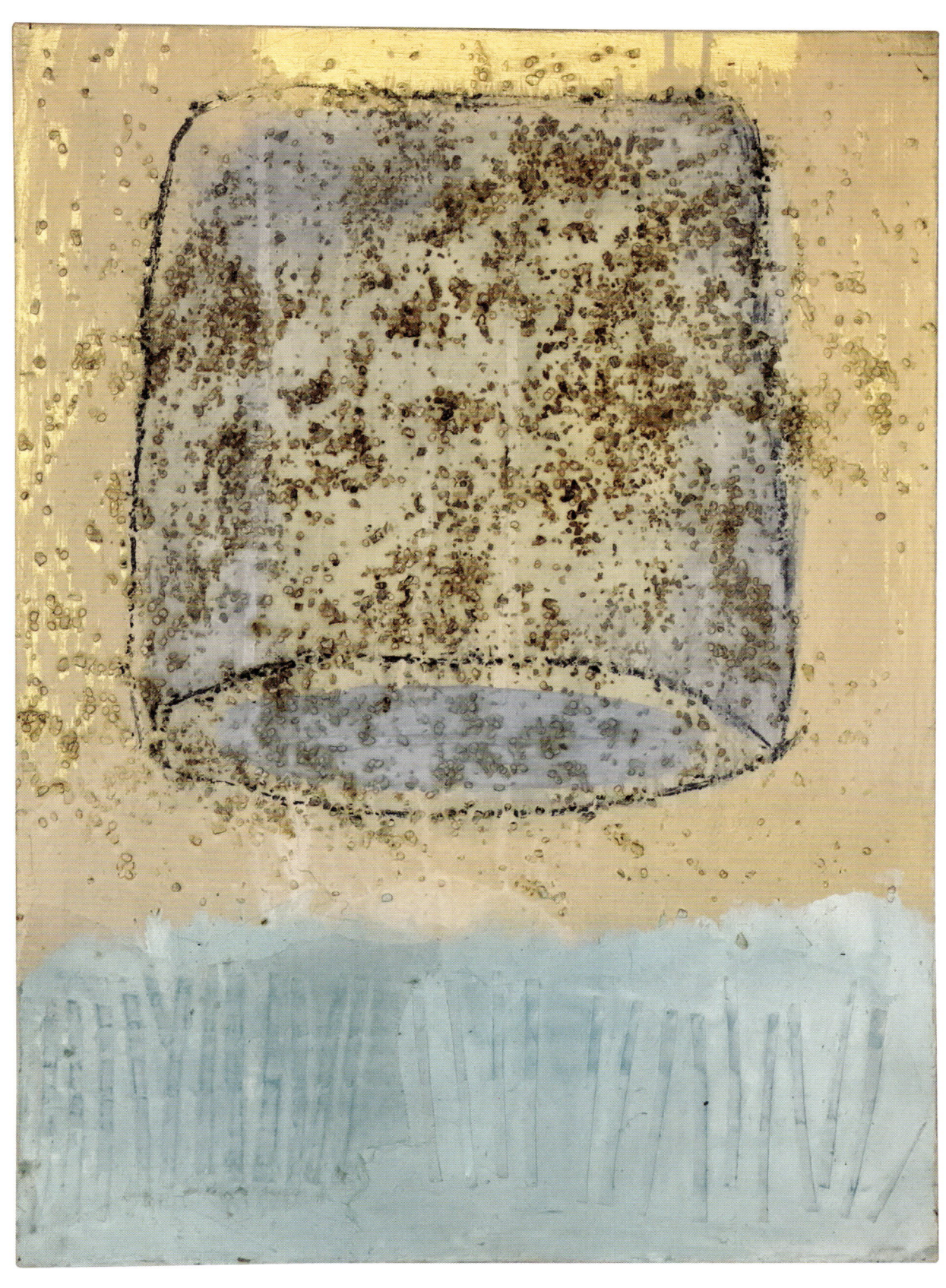

Holly Beach
24 x 18 inches
Mixed Media on Canvas
2008

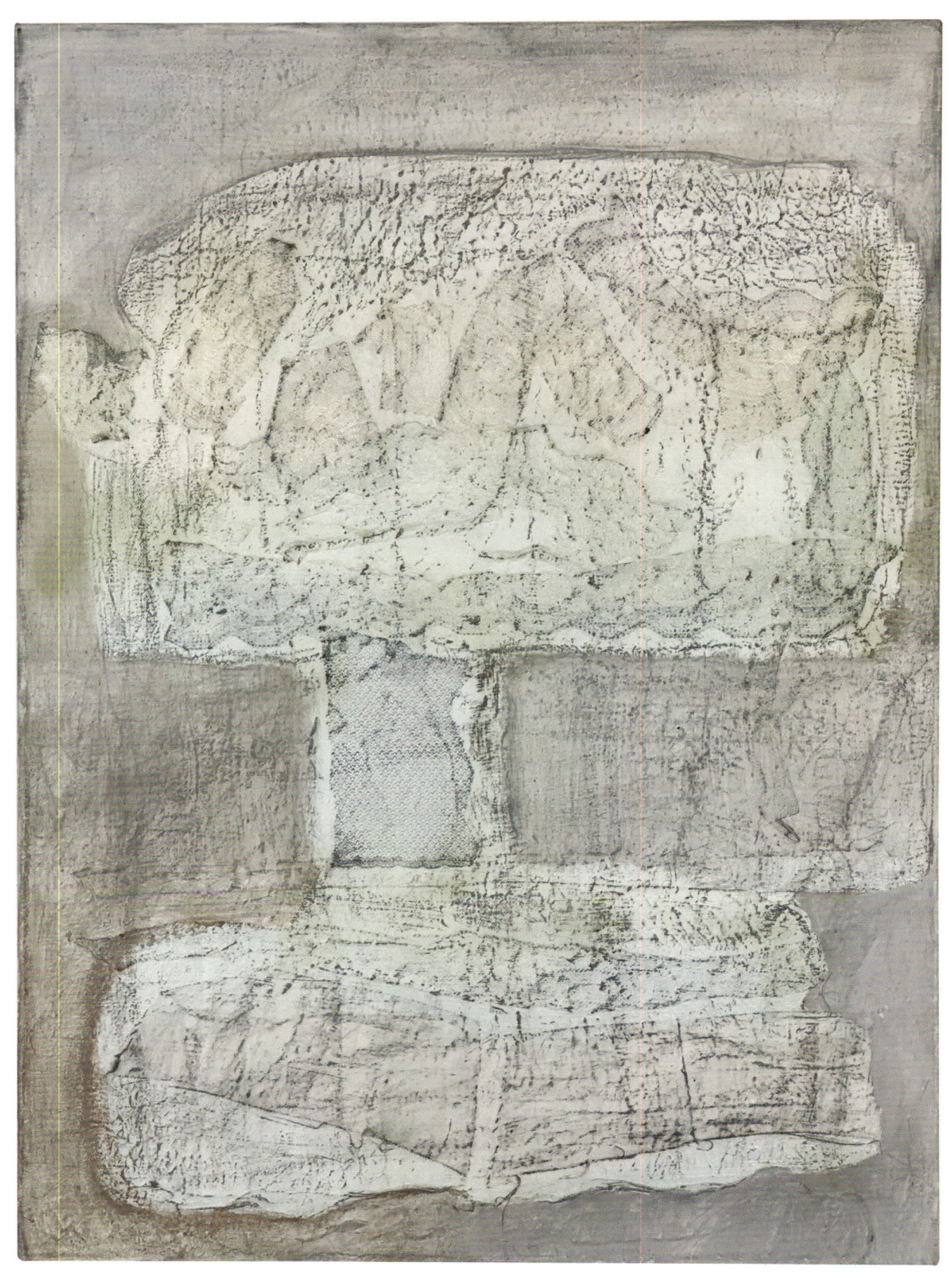

Sigh
24 x 18 inches
Mixed Media on Canvas
2008

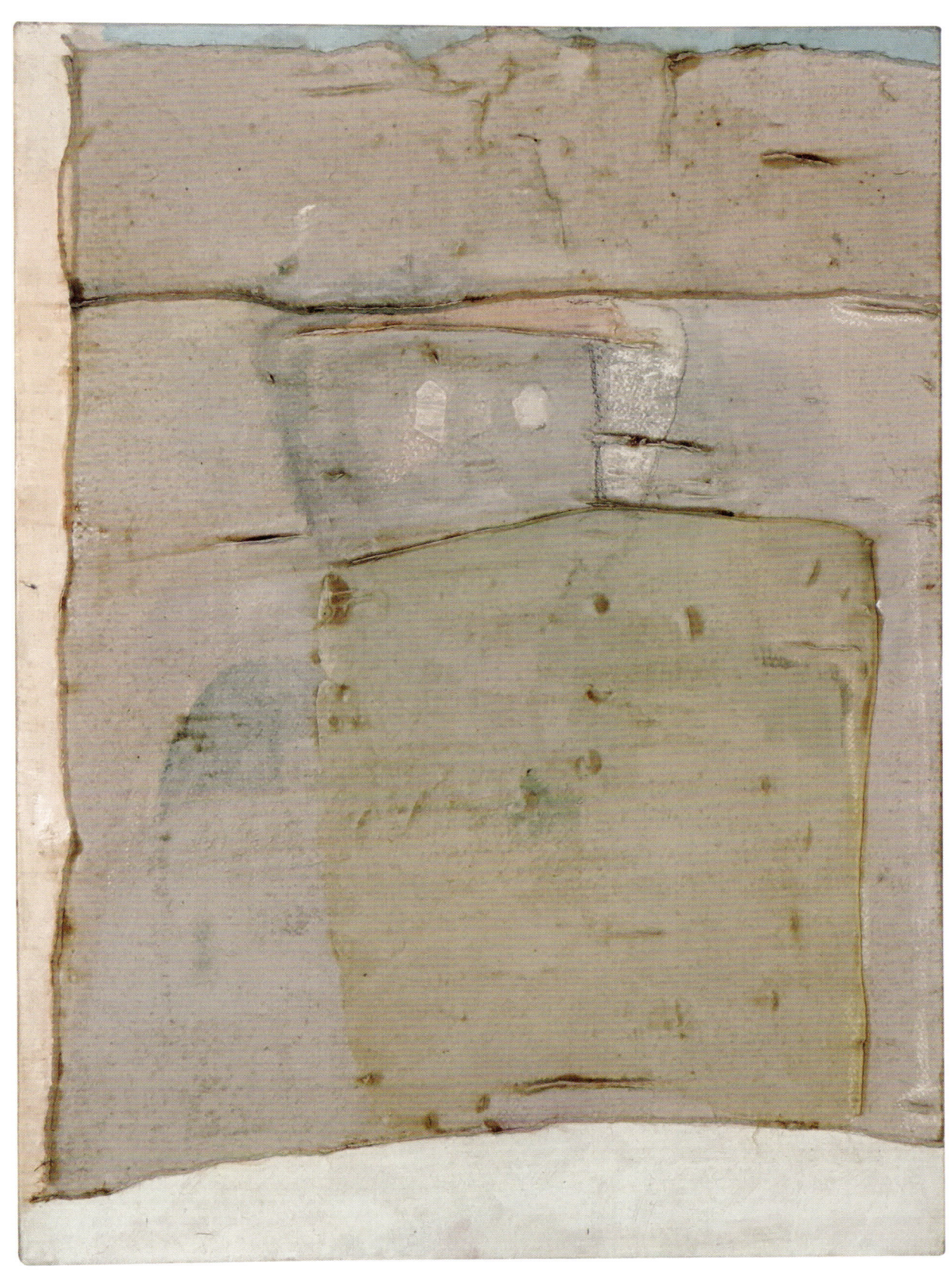

Mud Flap
24 x 18 inches
Mixed Media on Canvas
2008

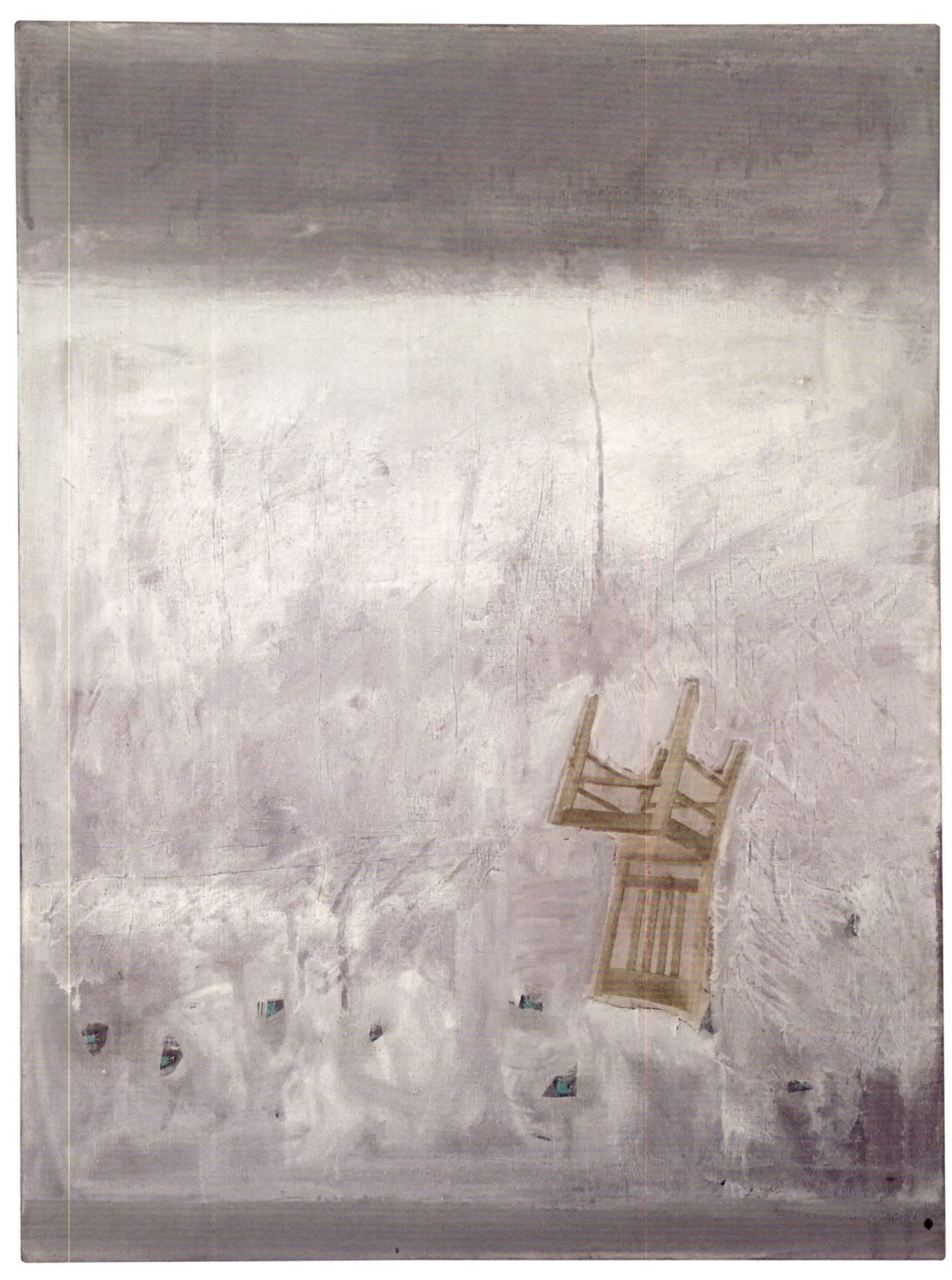

Testament
24 x 18 inches
Mixed Media on Canvas
2008

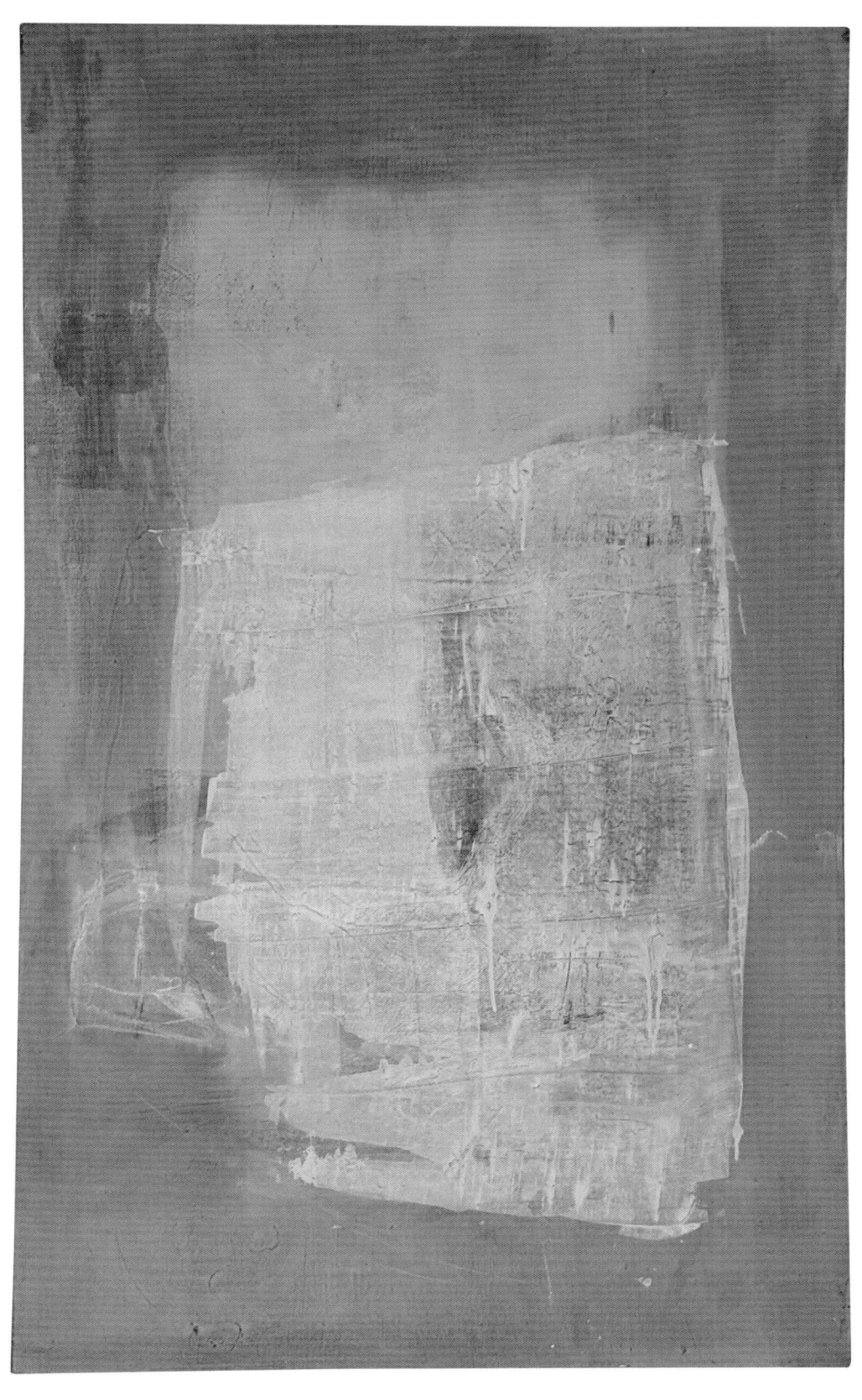

Fan
48 x 30 inches
Mixed Media on Canvas
2012

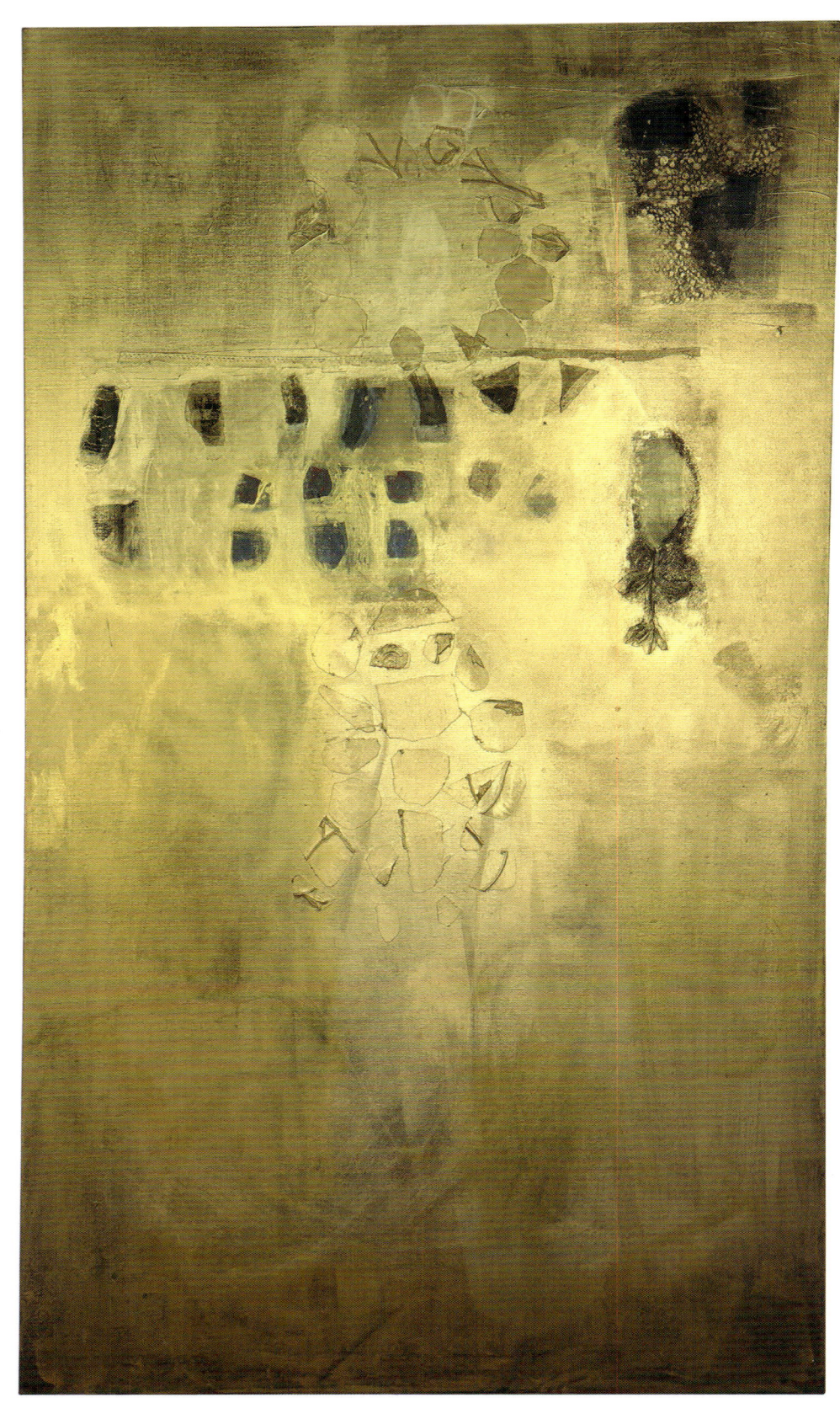

Rising Sign
60 x 36 inches
Mixed Media on Canvas
2011

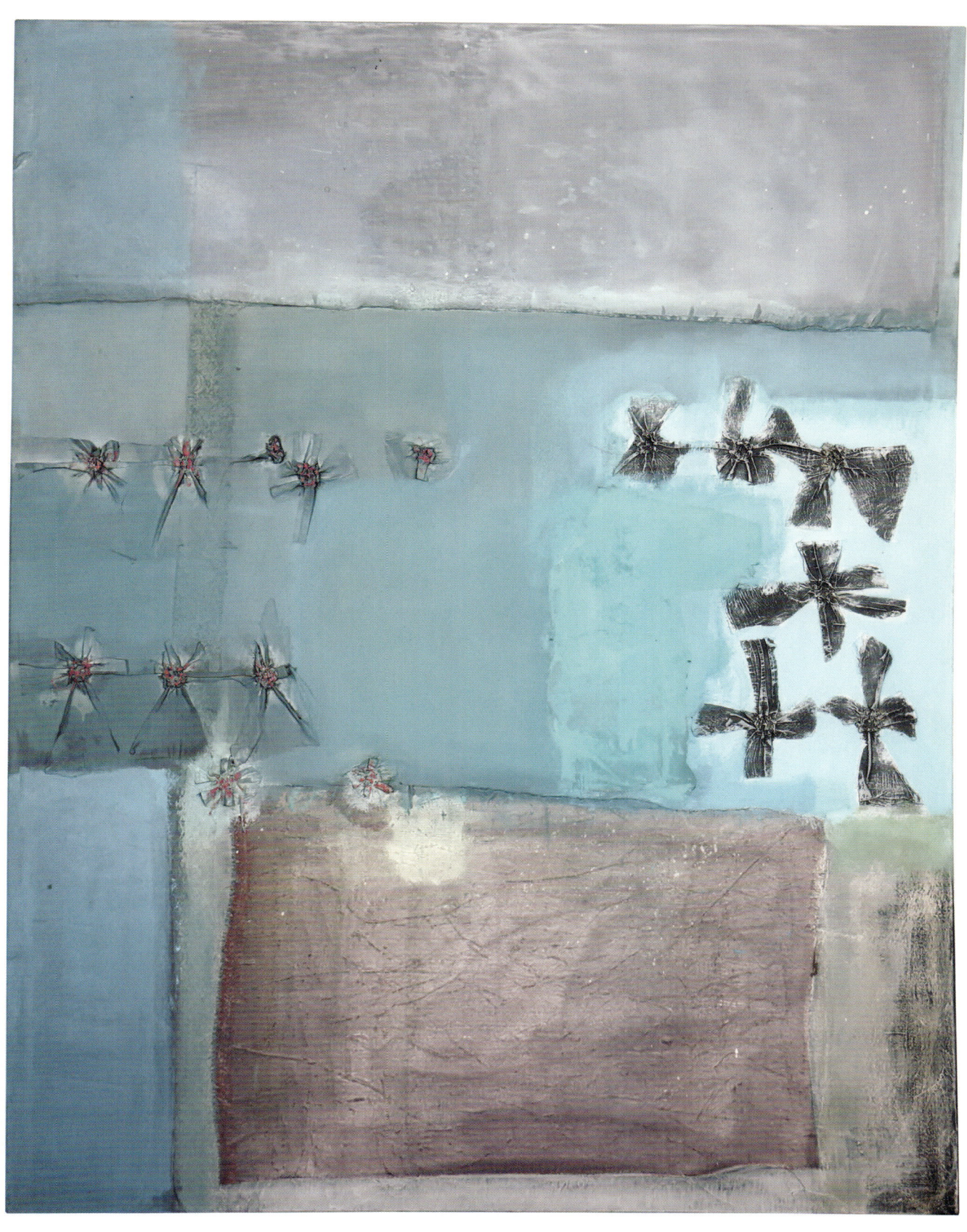

The Secrets of the Rug
60 x 48 inches
Mixed Media on Canvas
2011

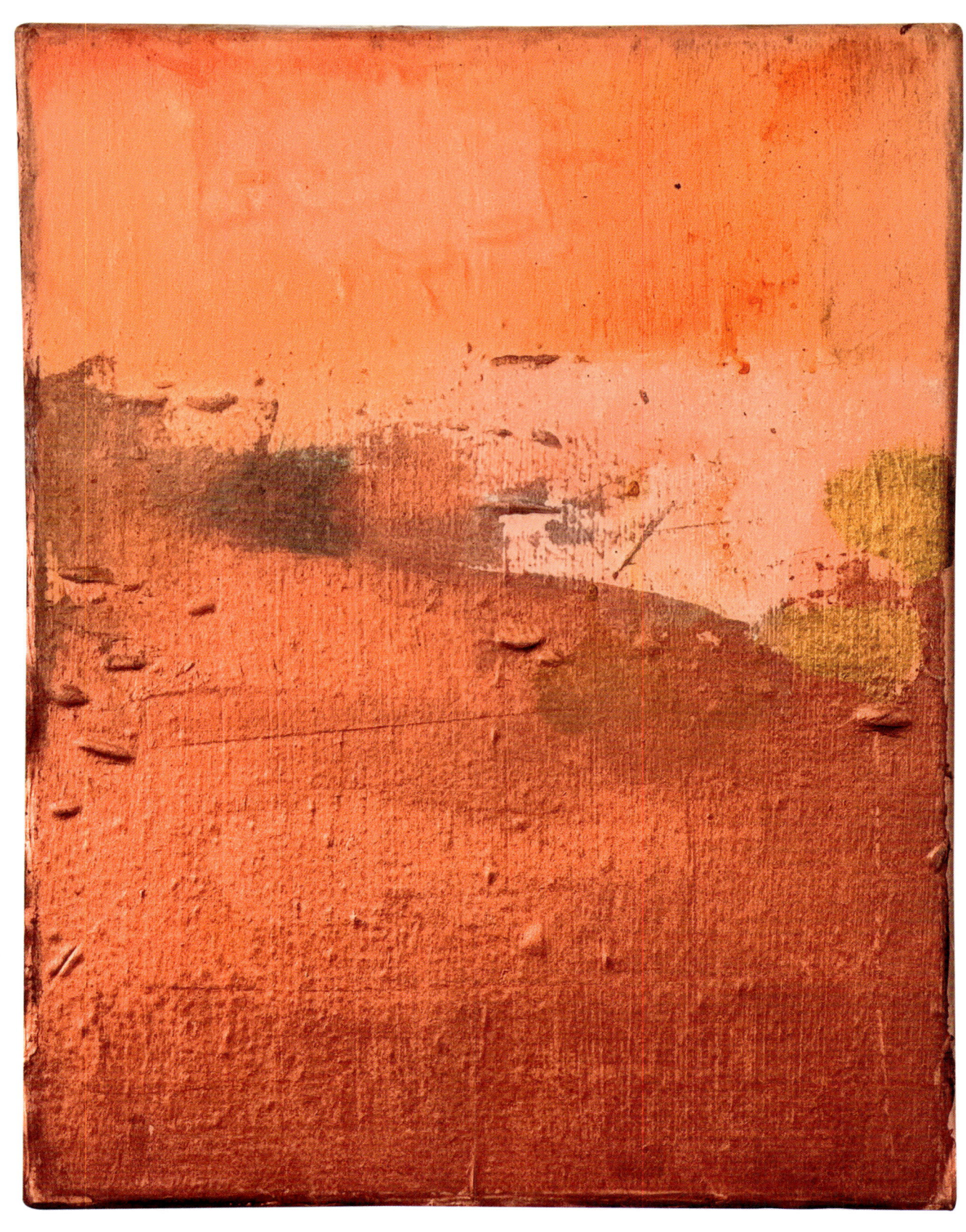

Puerto Rico (1 of 4)
14 x 11 inches
Mixed Media on Canvas
2016

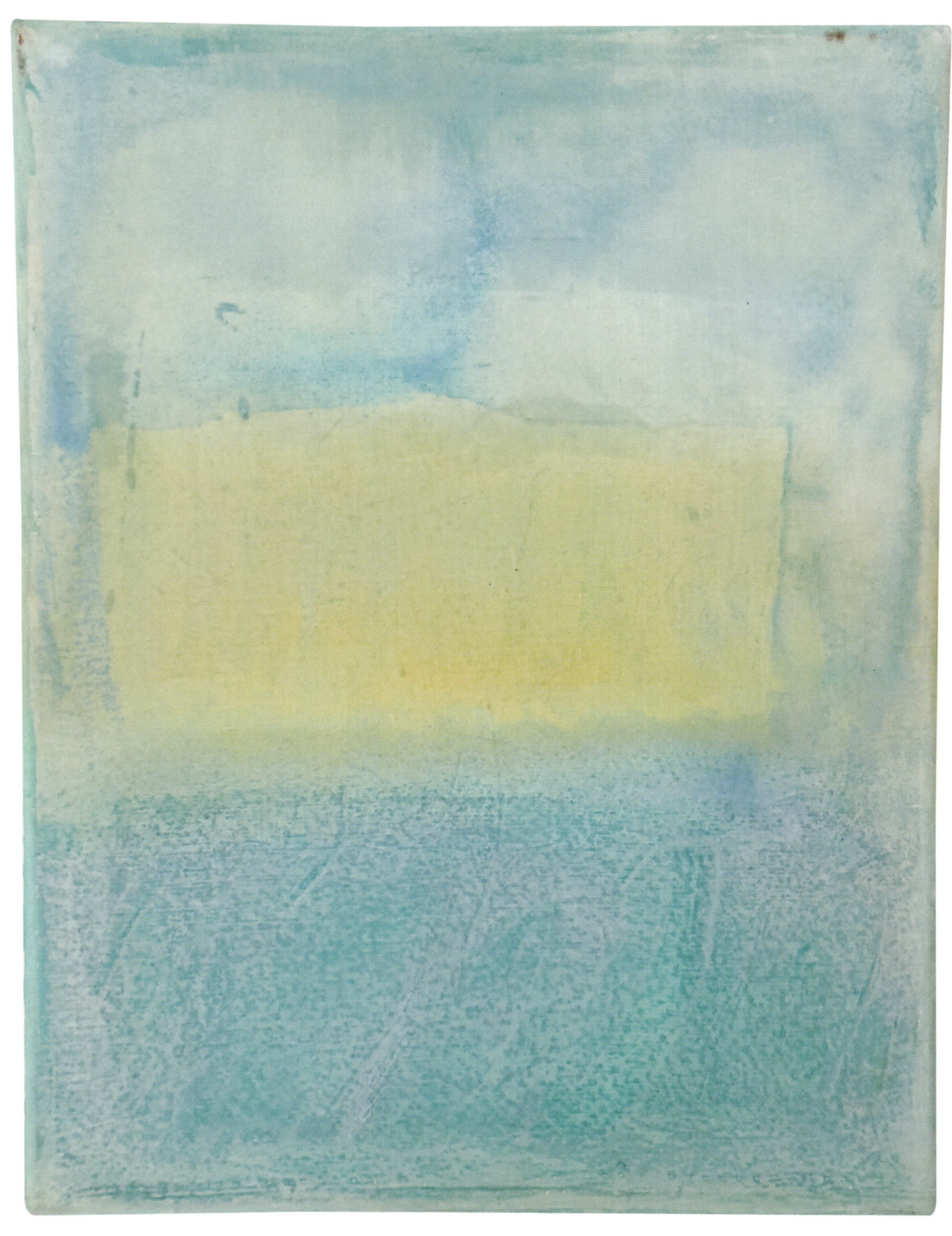

Puerto Rico (2 of 4)
14 x 11 inches
Mixed Media on Canvas
2016

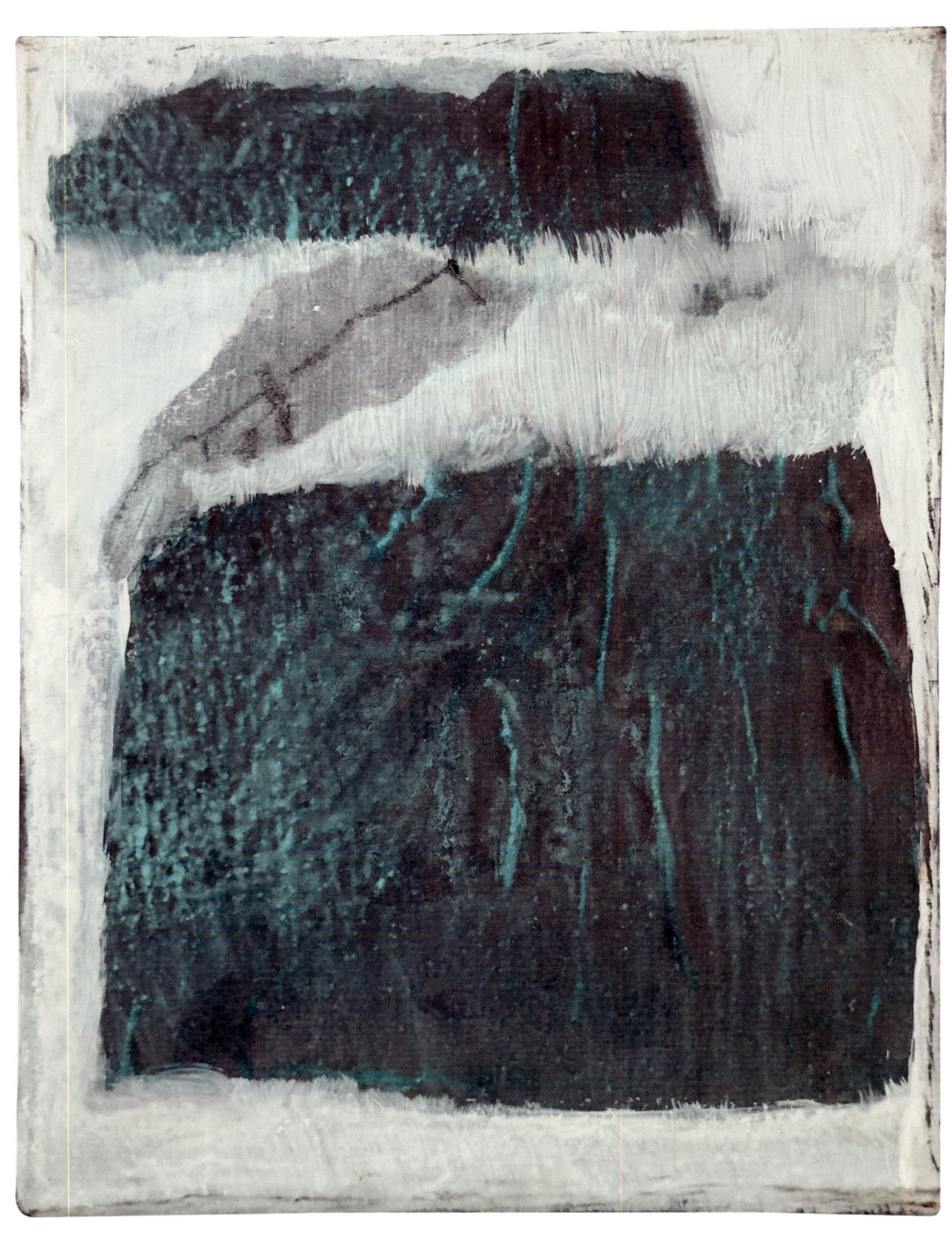

Puerto Rico (3 of 4)
14 x 11 inches
Mixed Media on Canvas
2016

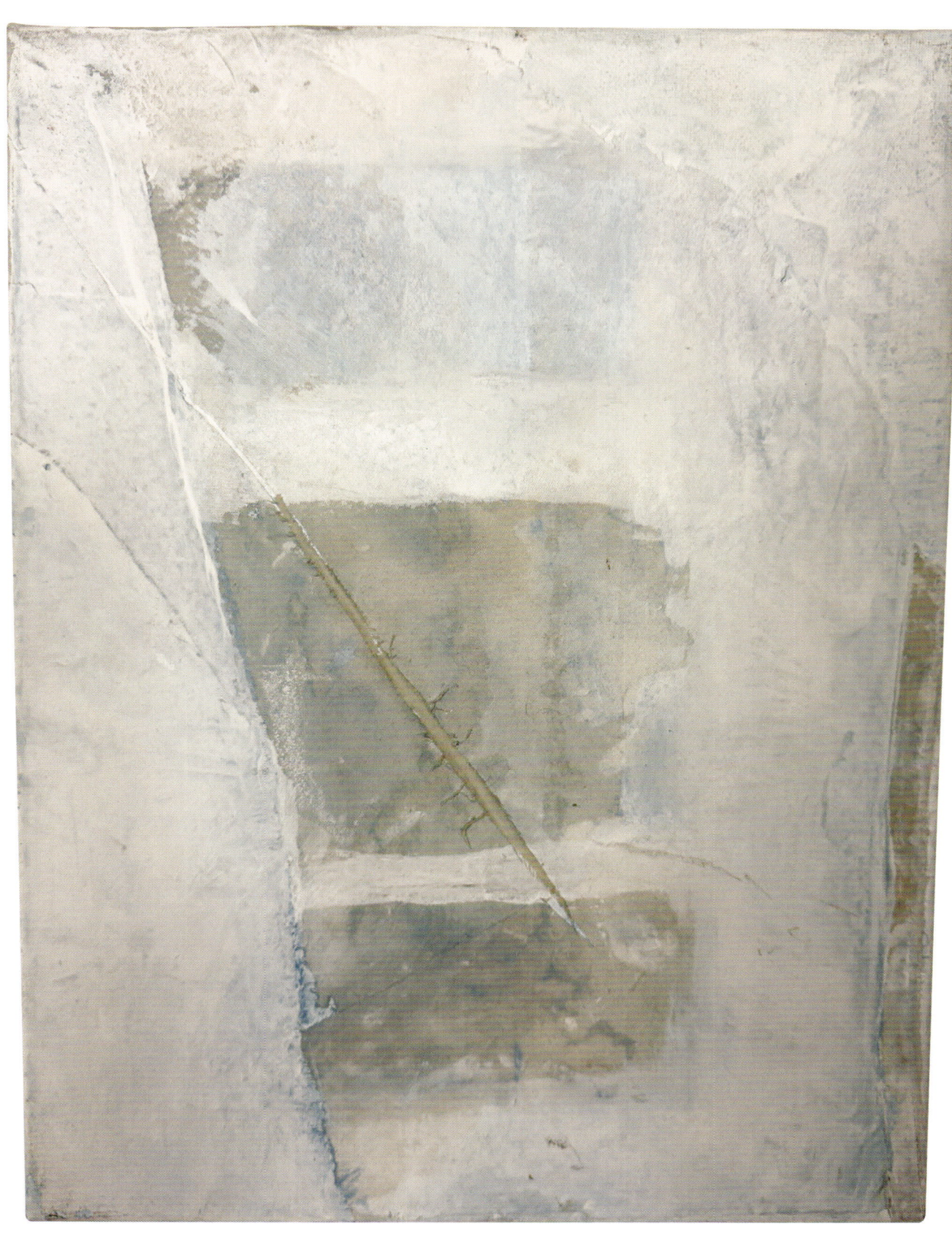

Puerto Rico (4 of 4)
14 x 11 inches
Mixed Media on Canvas
2016

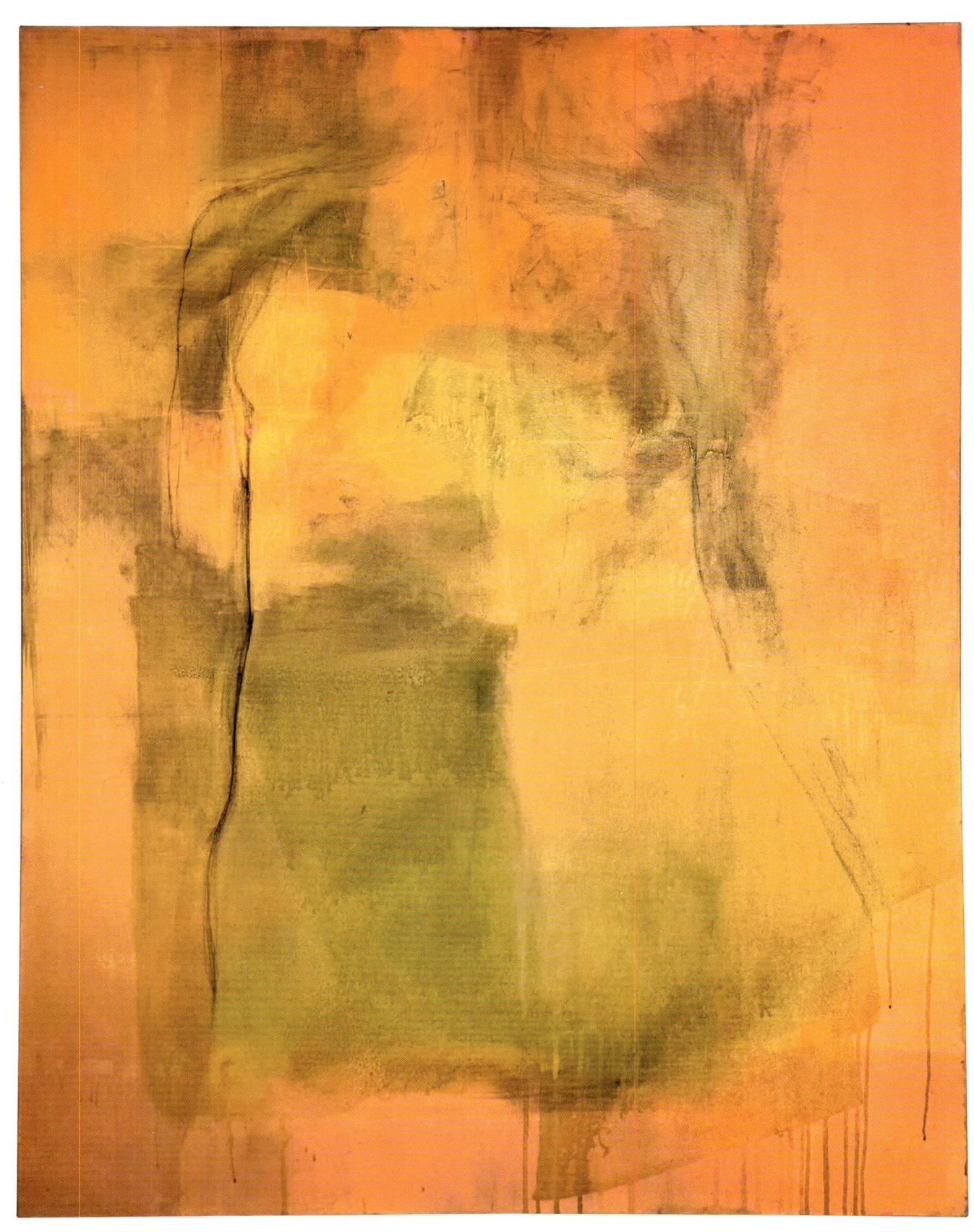

Yellow Dancer
60 x 48 inches
Mixed Media on Canvas
2010

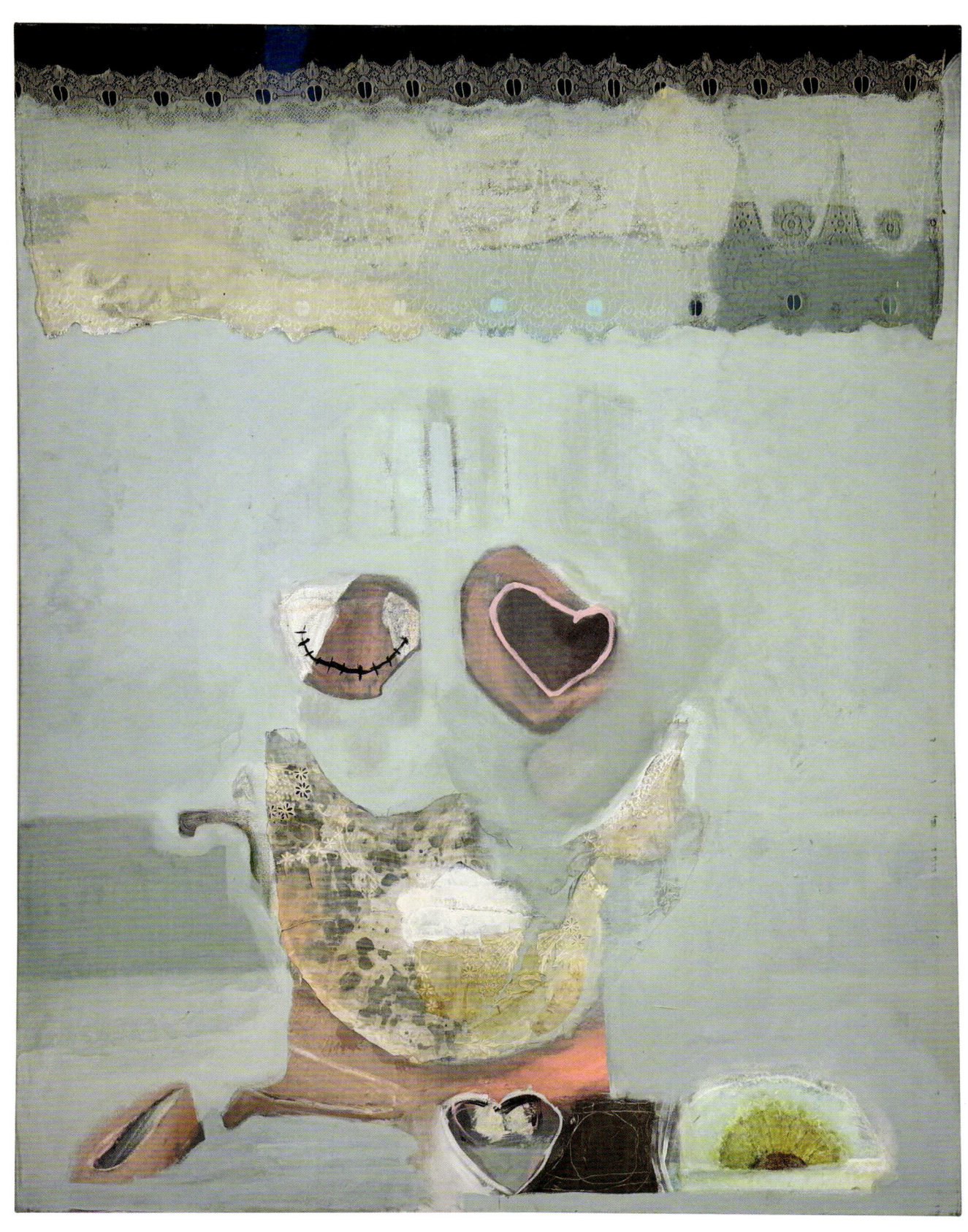

Mr. Gone
60 x 40 inches
Mixed Media
2006

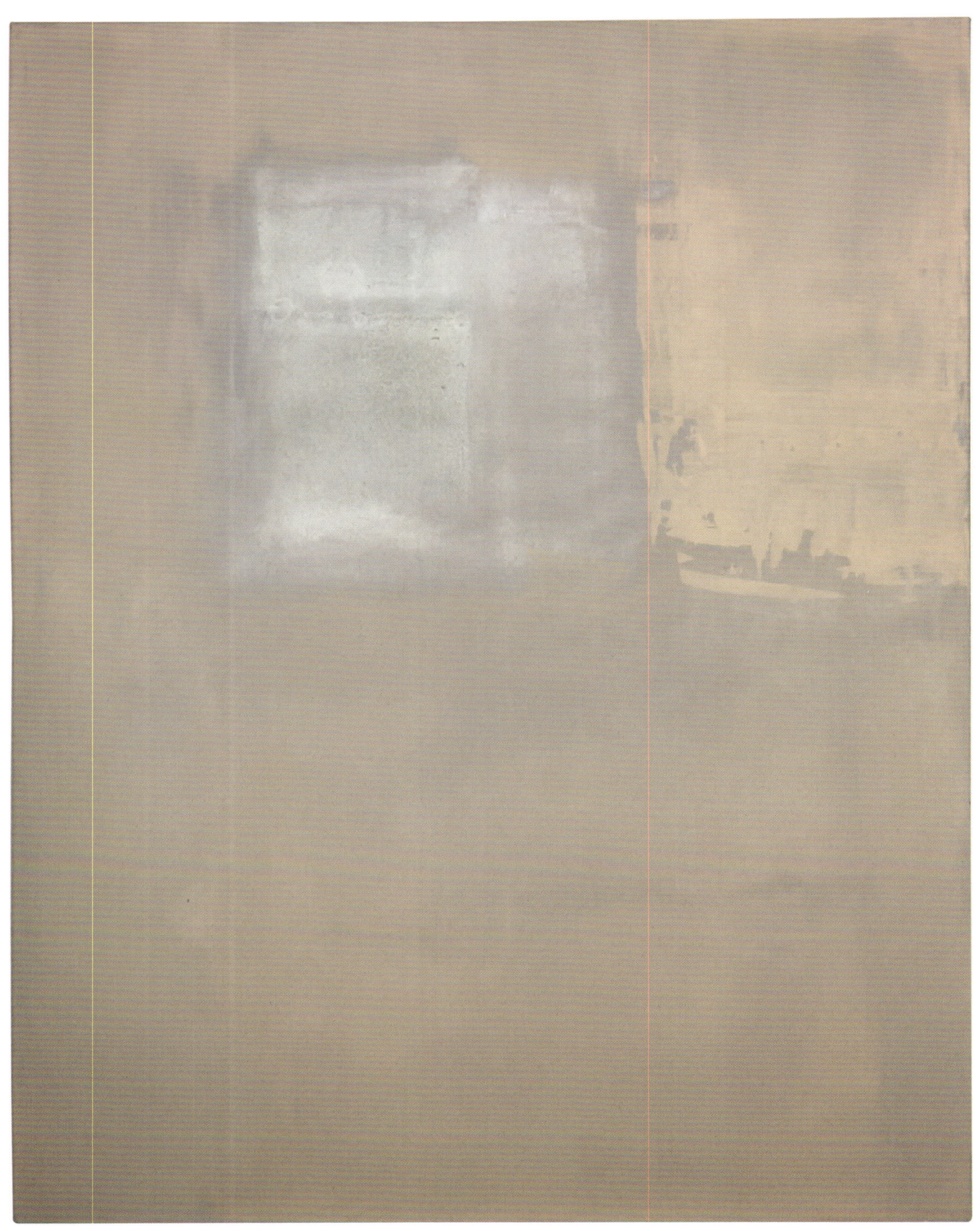

Moat
60 x 48 inches
Mixed Media on Canvas
2012

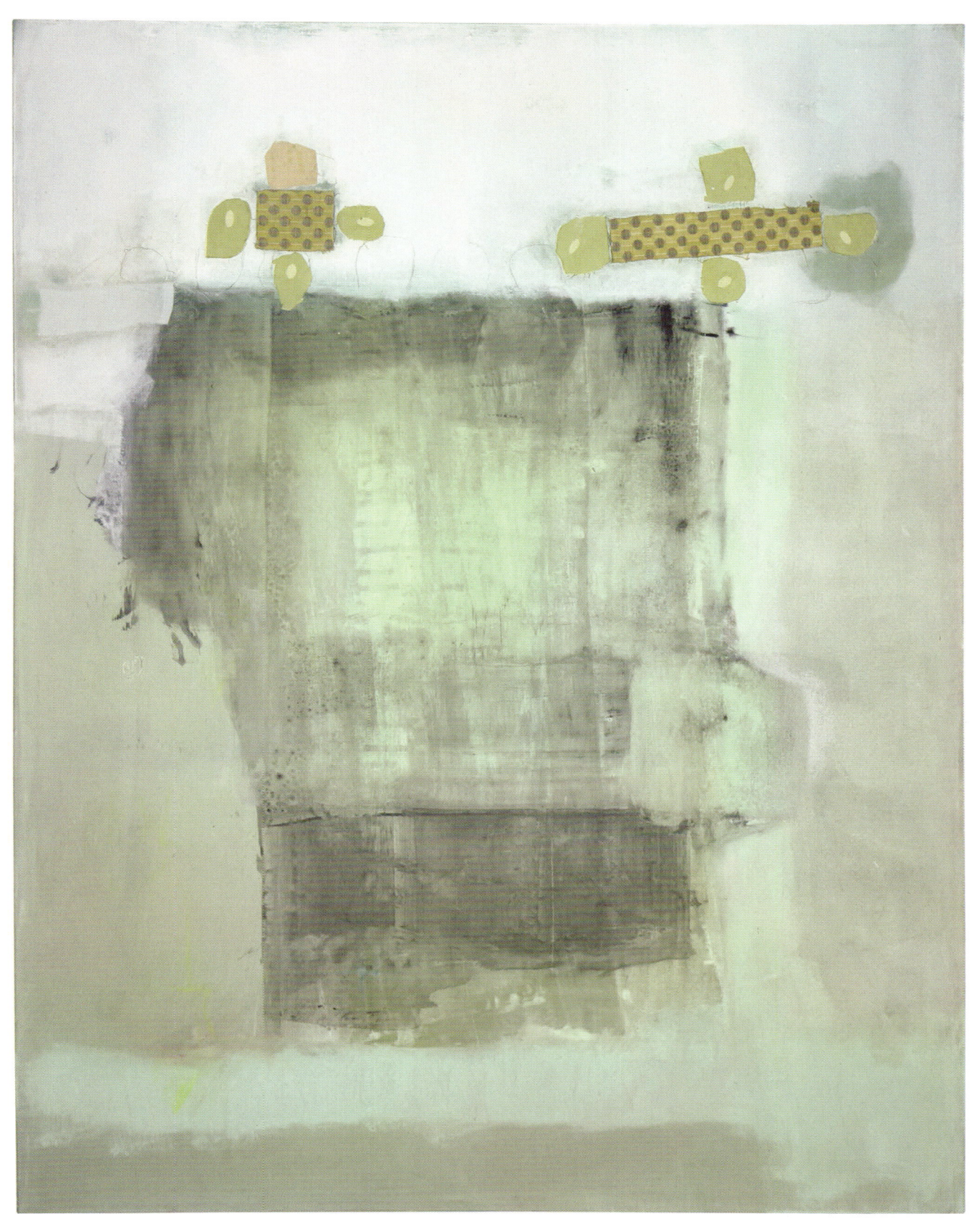

Palanquin
60 x 48 inches
Mixed Media on Canvas
2011

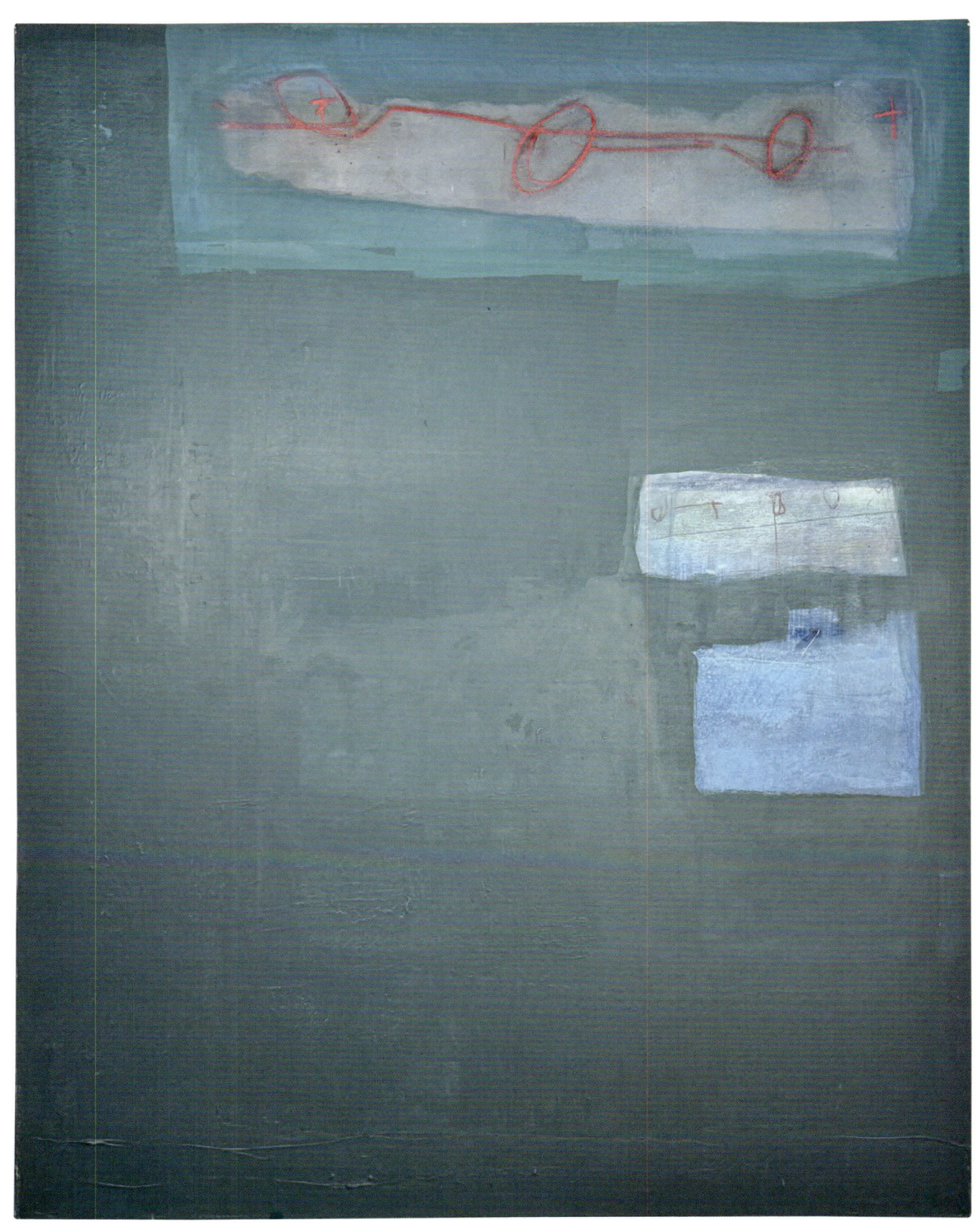

The Flying Carpet
60 x 48 inches
Mixed Media on Canvas
2012

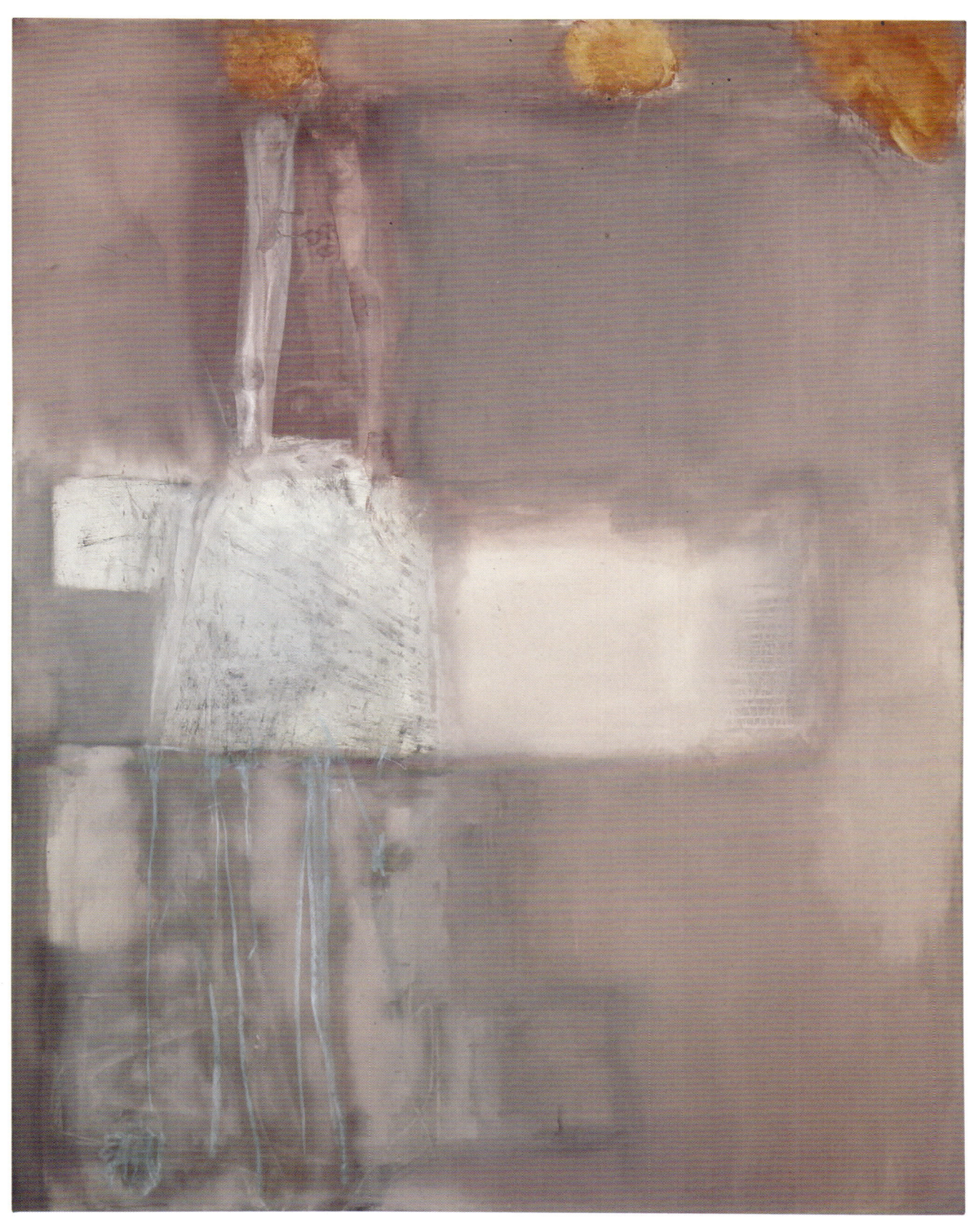

Centaurus Among the Mares
60 x 48 inches
Mixed Media on Canvas
2012

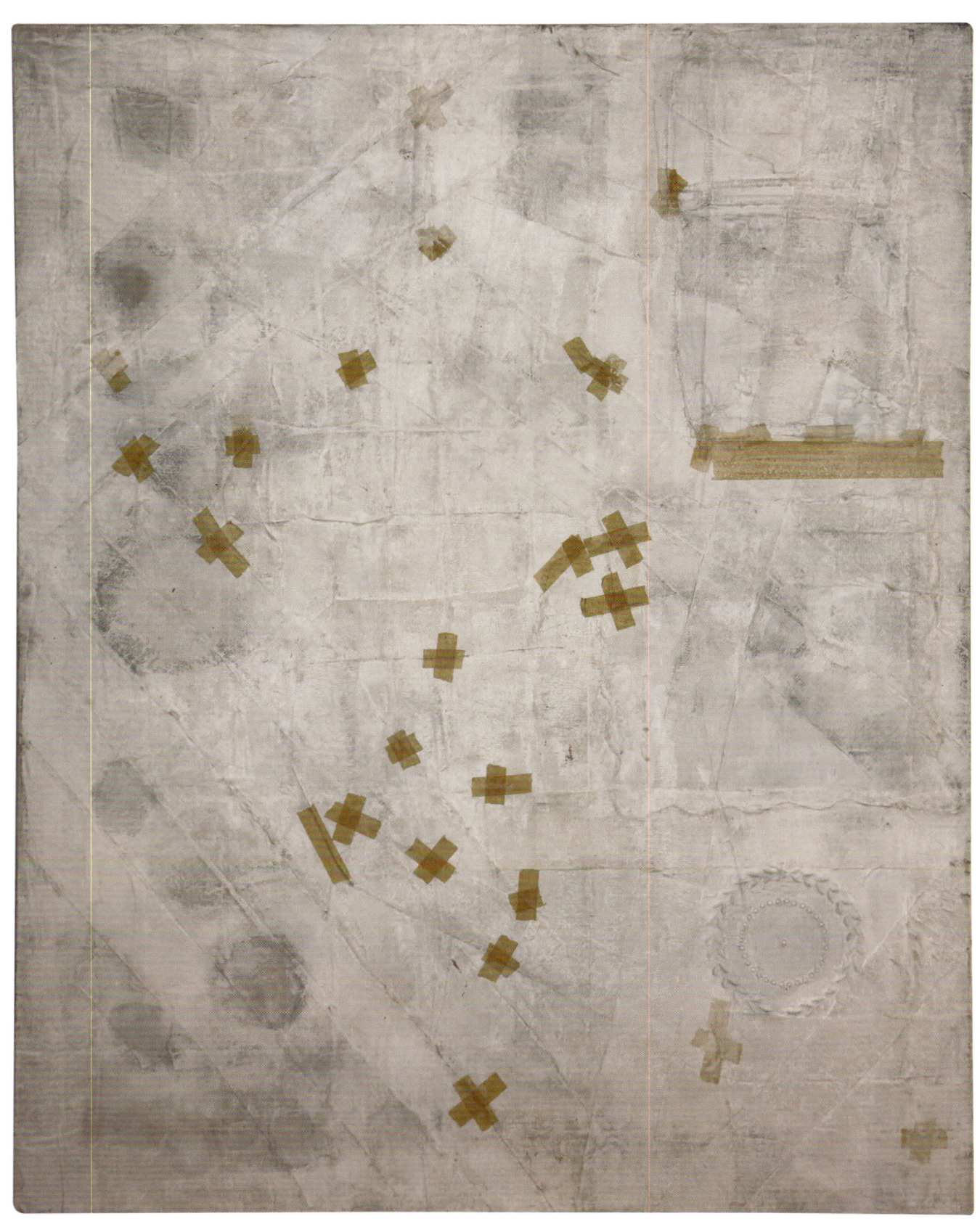

The Ceiling
60 x 48 inches
Mixed Media on Canvas
2011

Flight Path
60 x 36 inches
Mixed Media on Canvas
2013

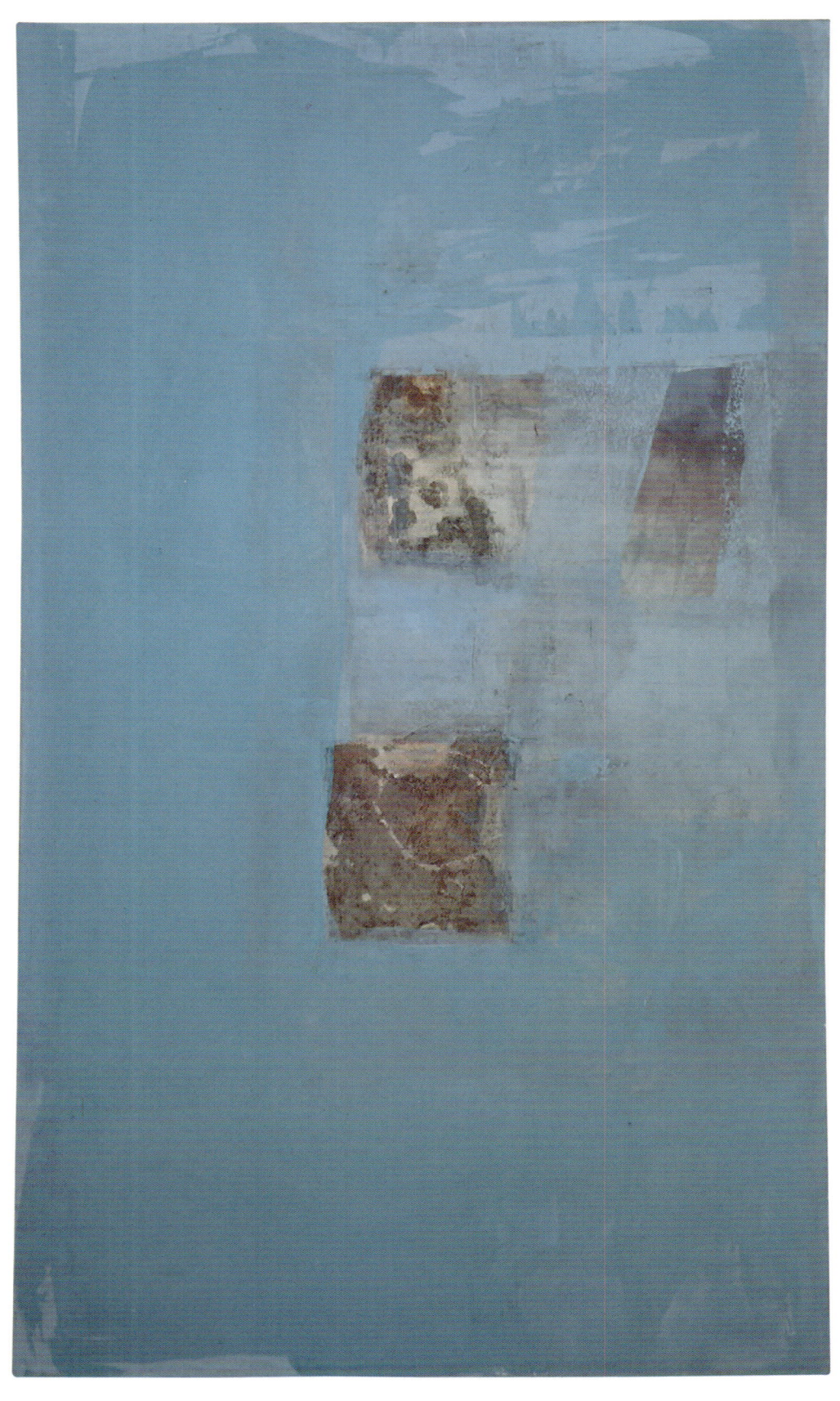

Athol
60 x 30 inches
Mixed Media on Canvas
2012

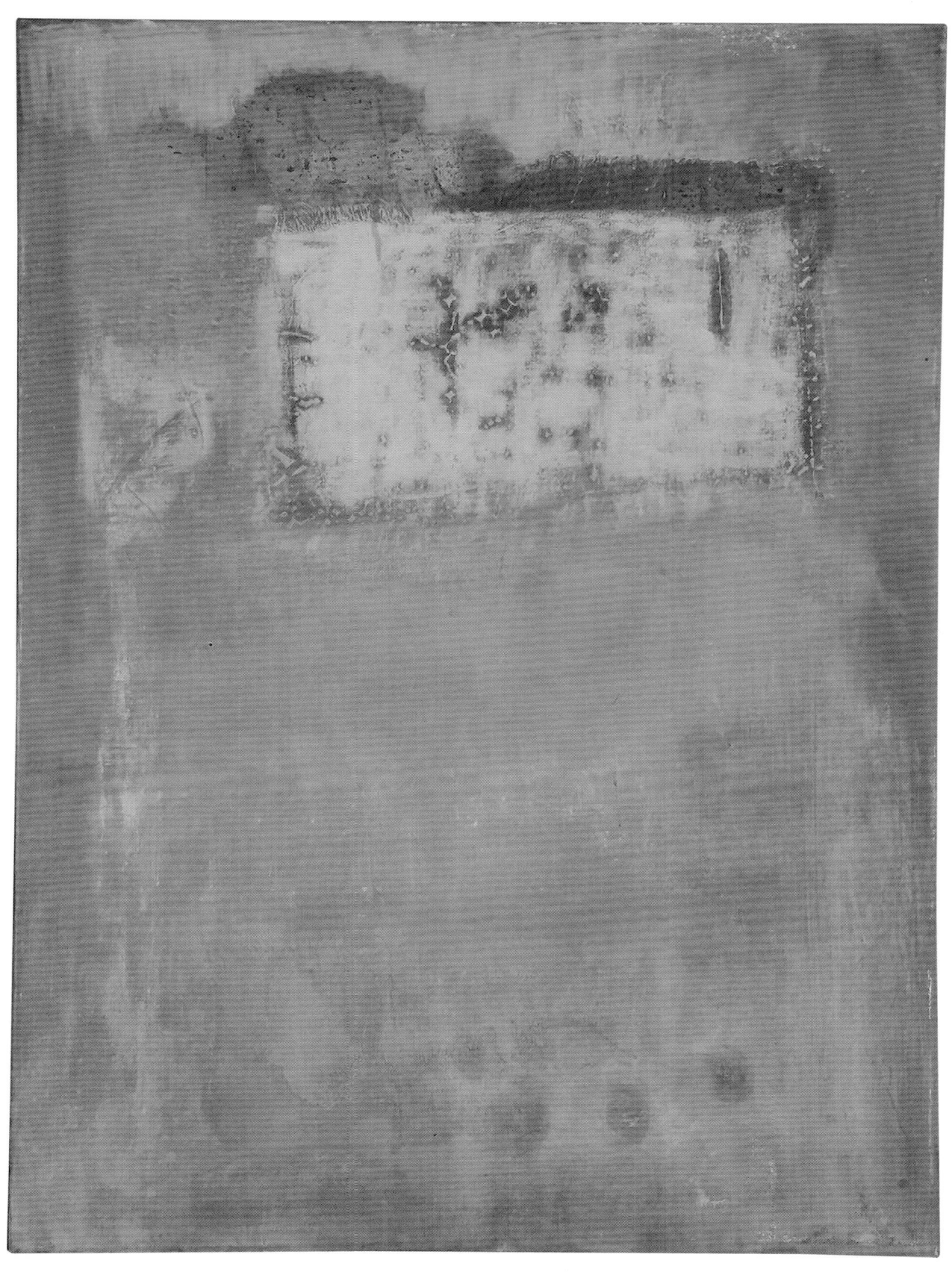

Moonlit Landscape
40 x 30 inches
Mixed Media on Canvas
2013

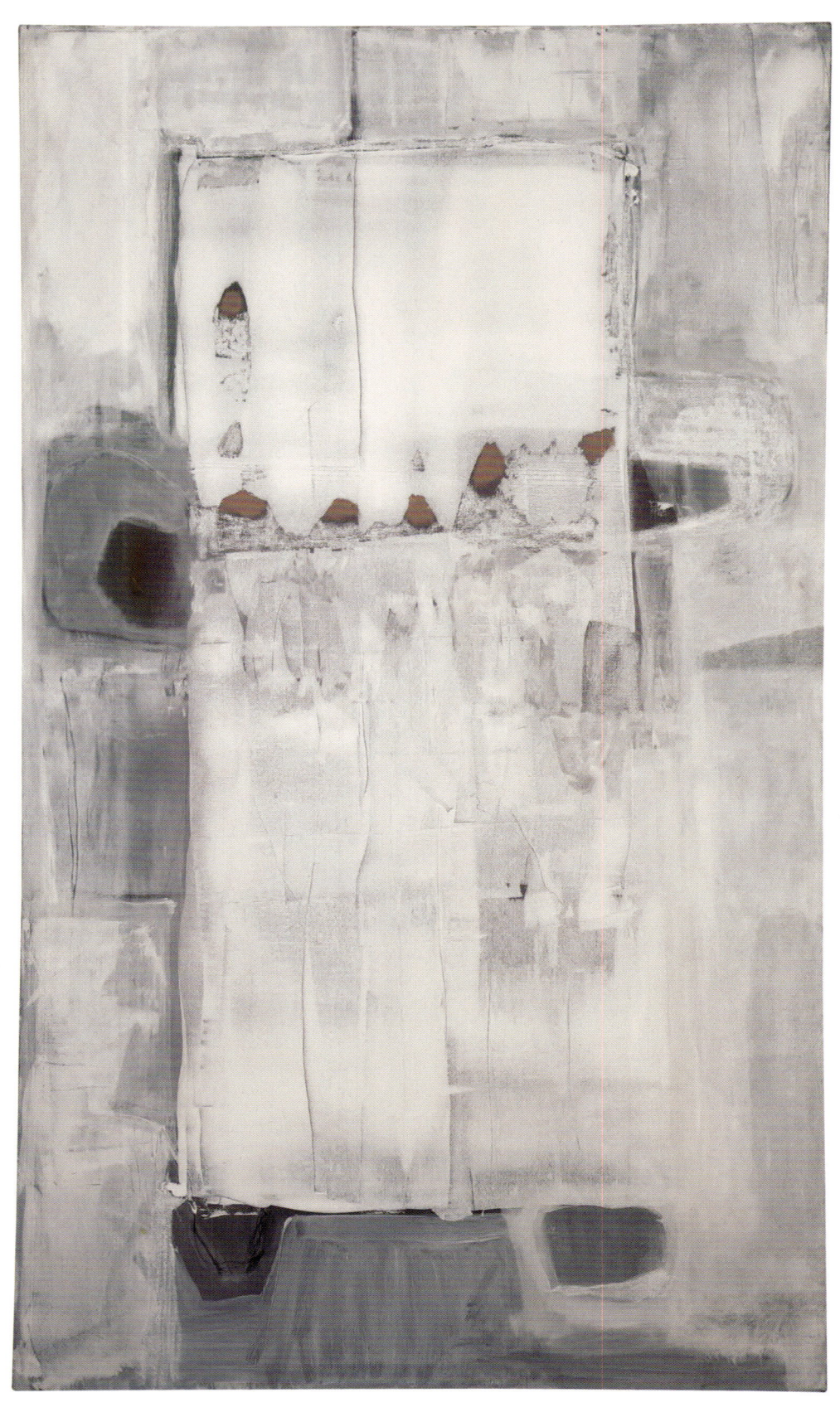

Fridge
60 x 36 inches
Mixed Media on Canvas
2012

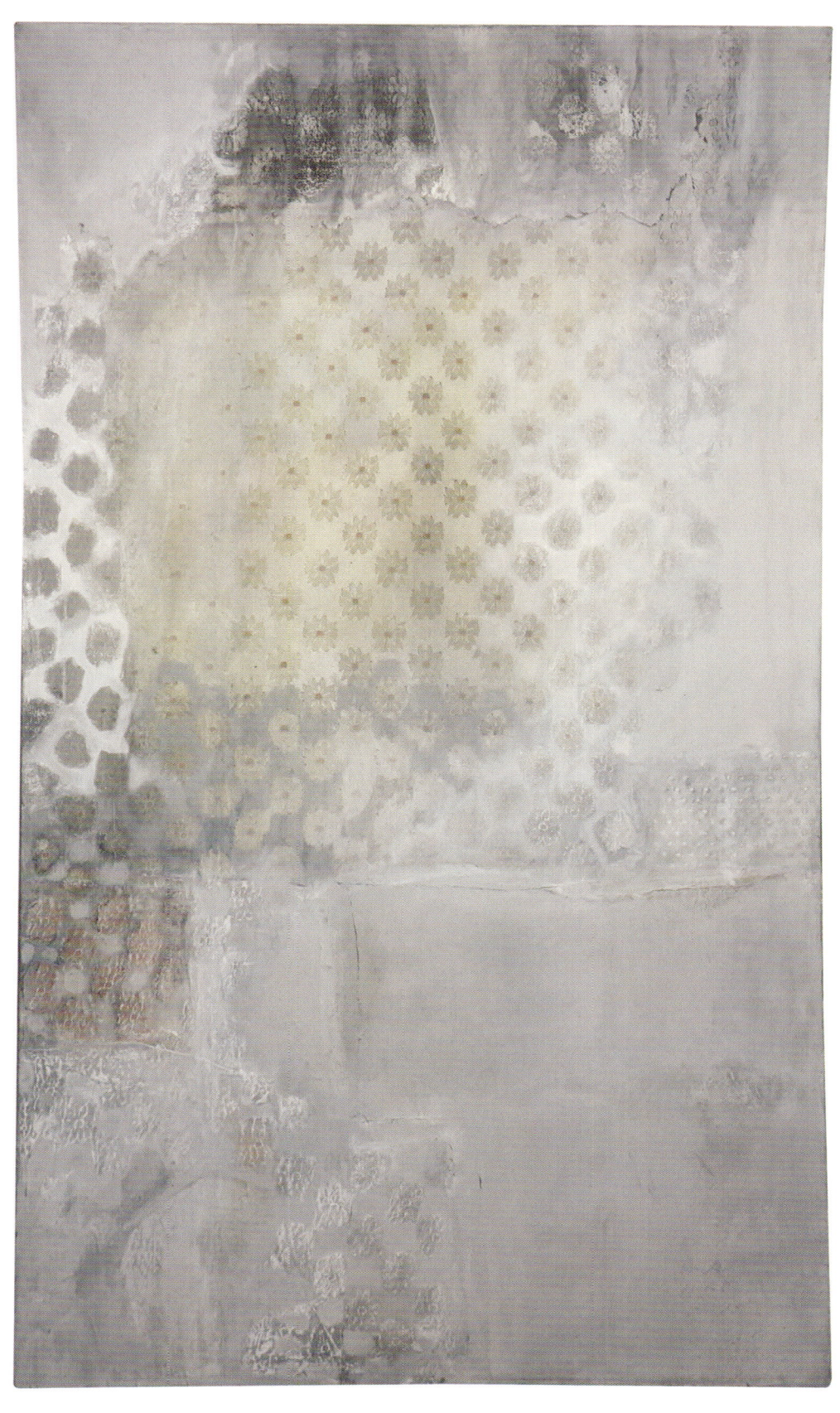

Jockey
60 x 36 inches
Mixed Media on Canvas
2013

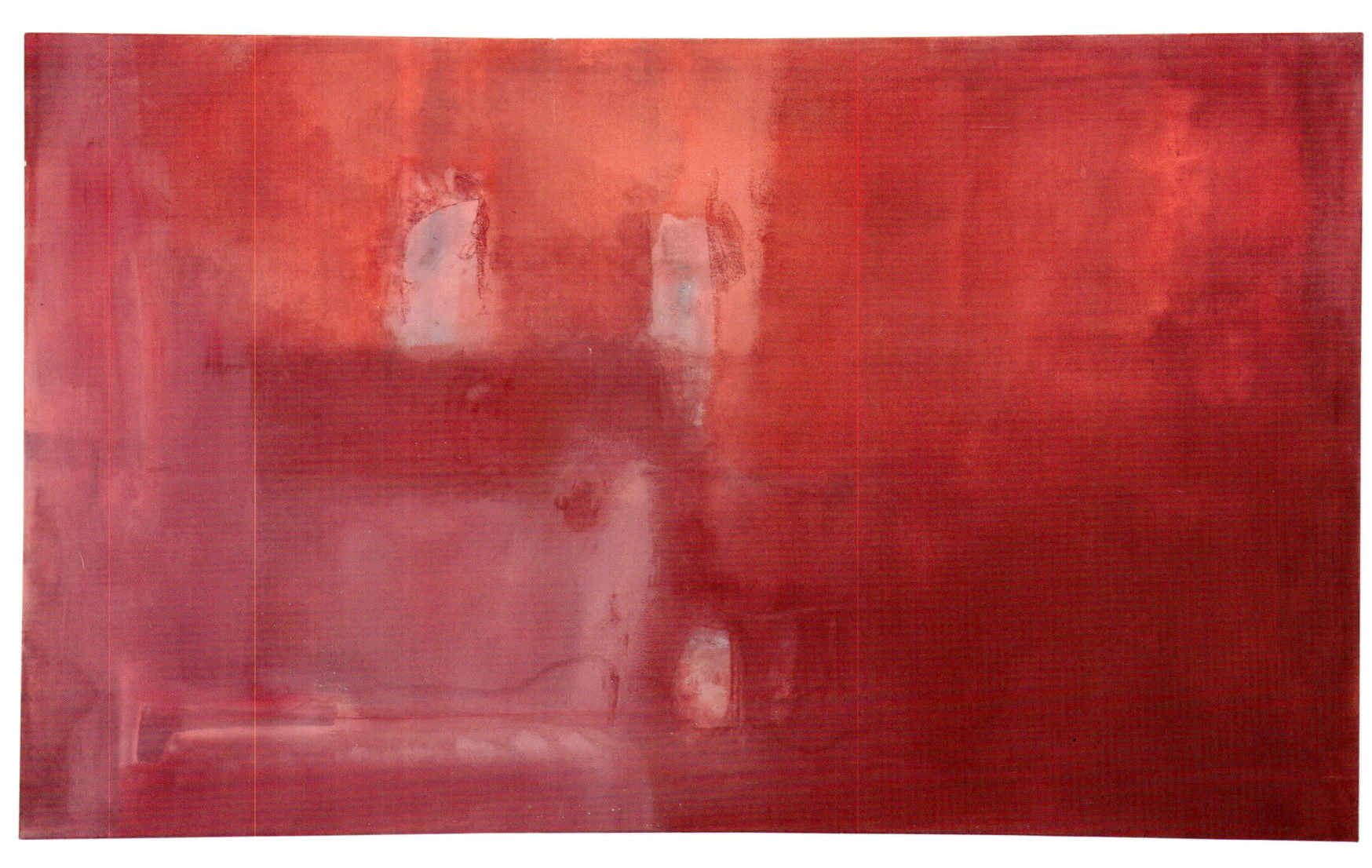

Rudy's Bunker
60 x 36 inches
Mixed Media on Canvas
2011

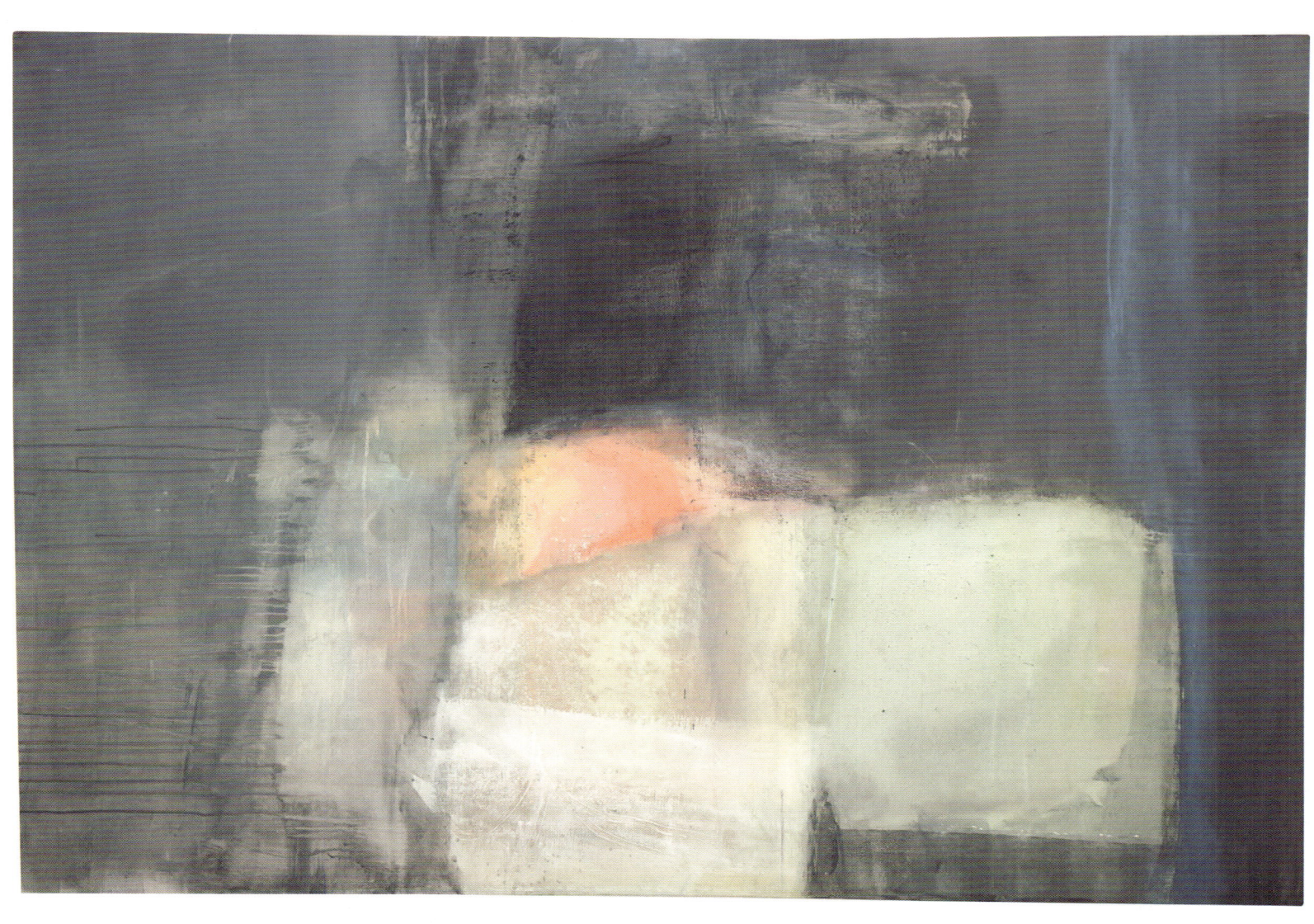

Dancer 4
48 x 72 inches
Mixed Media on Canvas
2014

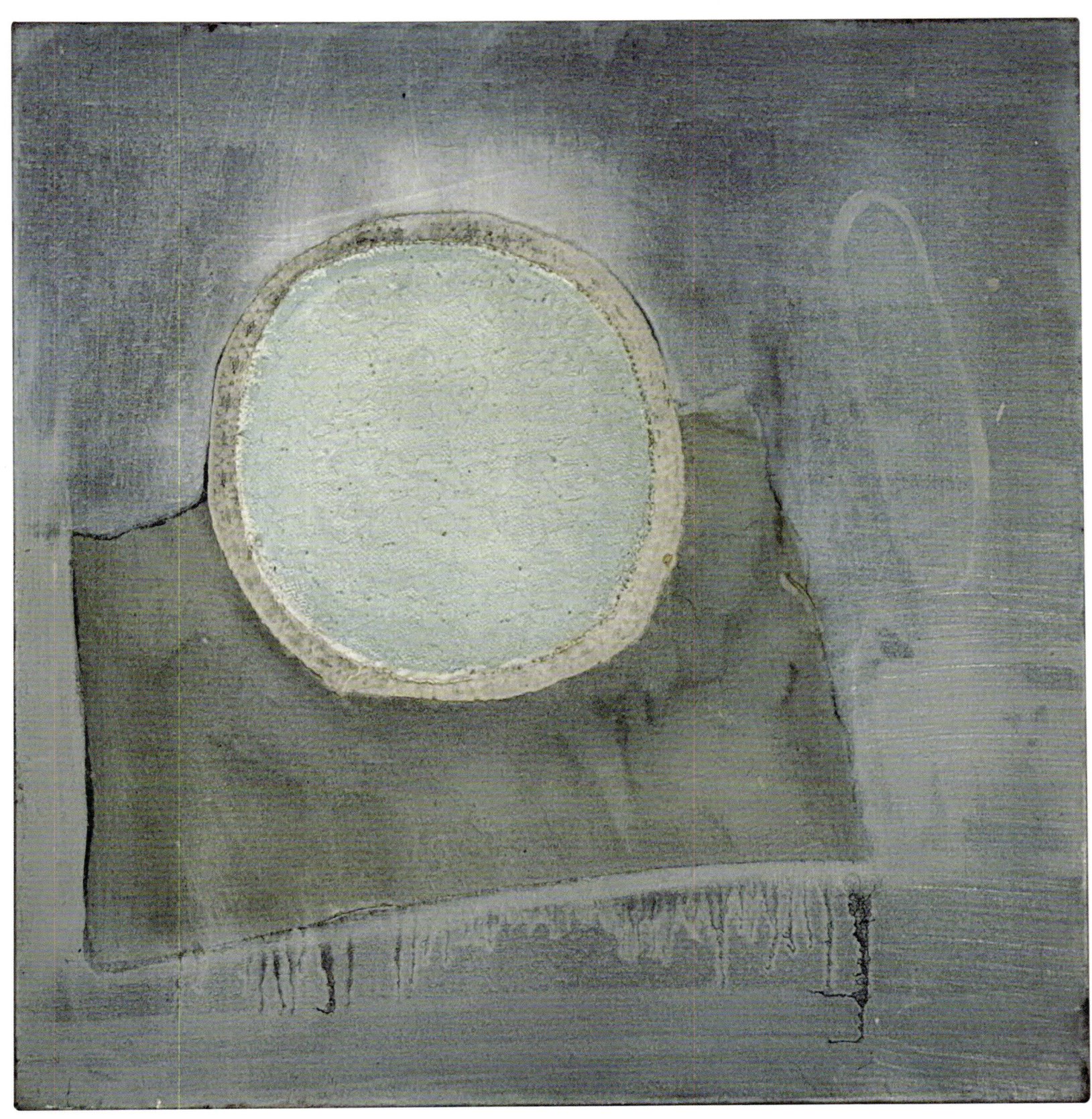

Porthole
20 x 20 inches
Mixed Media on Canvas
2012

330

The Arena
36 x 24 inches
Mixed Media on Canvas
2014

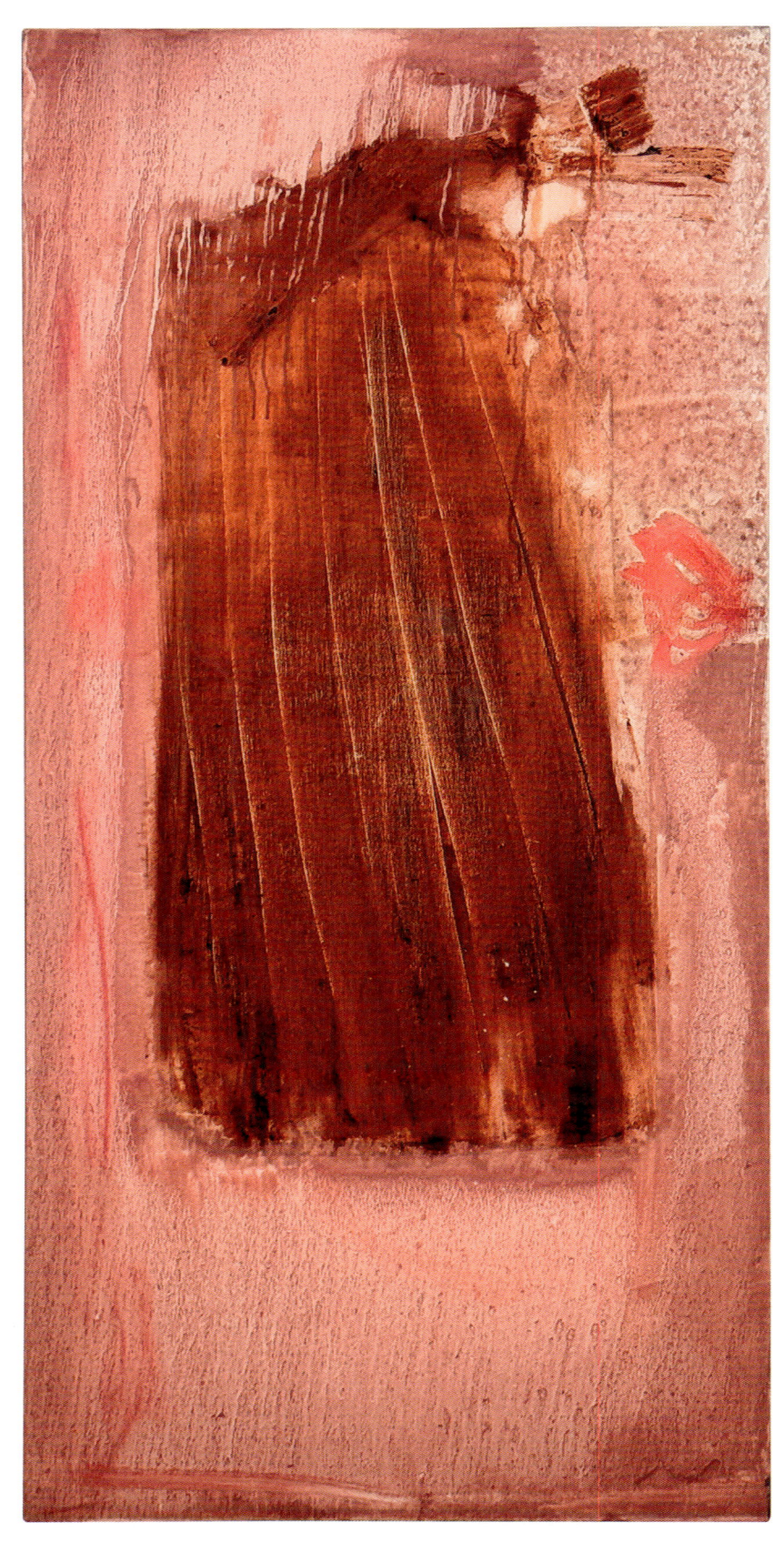

Cloak
48 x 24 inches
Mixed Media on Canvas
2013

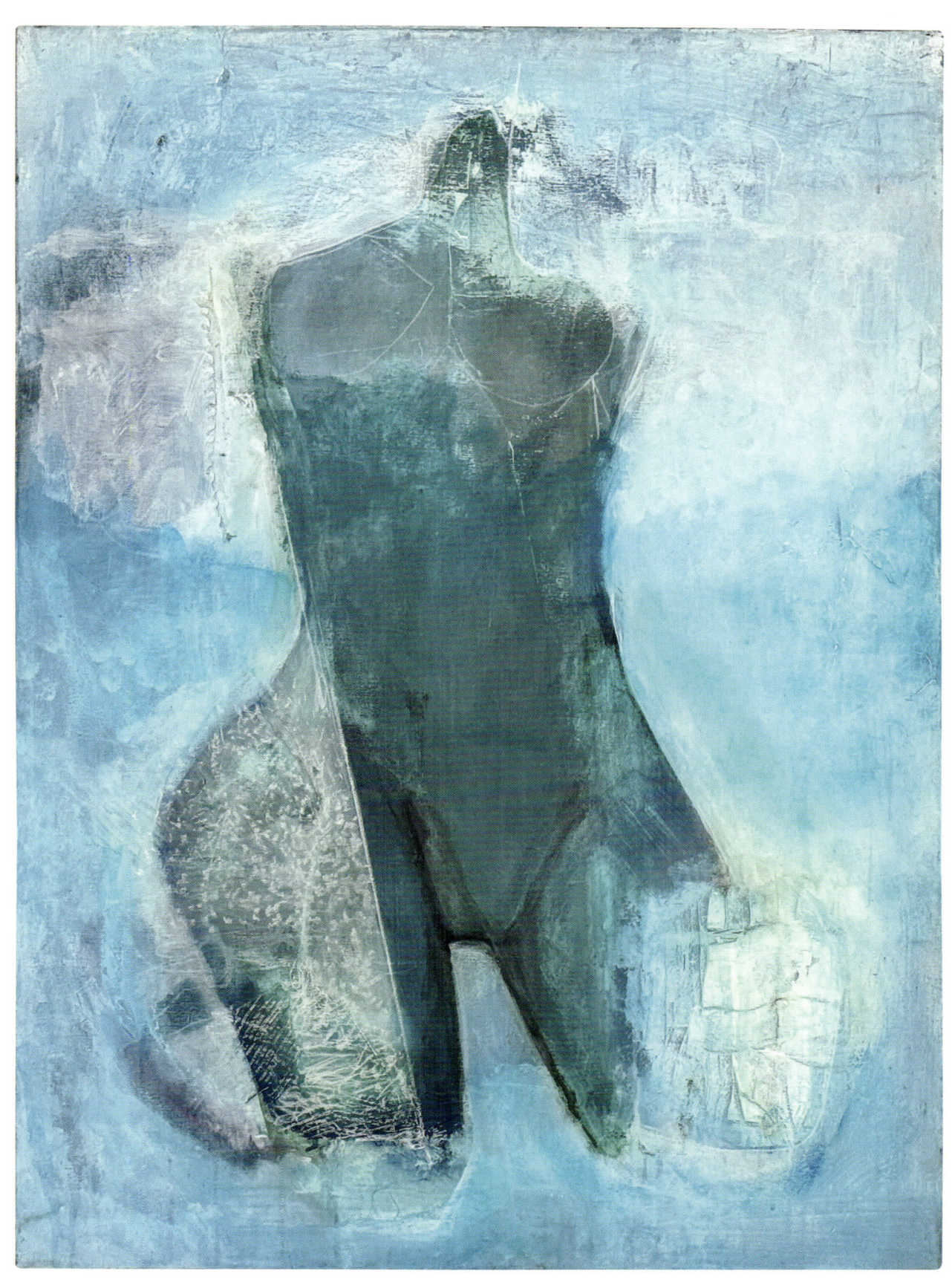

Nephele
40 x 30 inches
Mixed Media on Canvas
2011

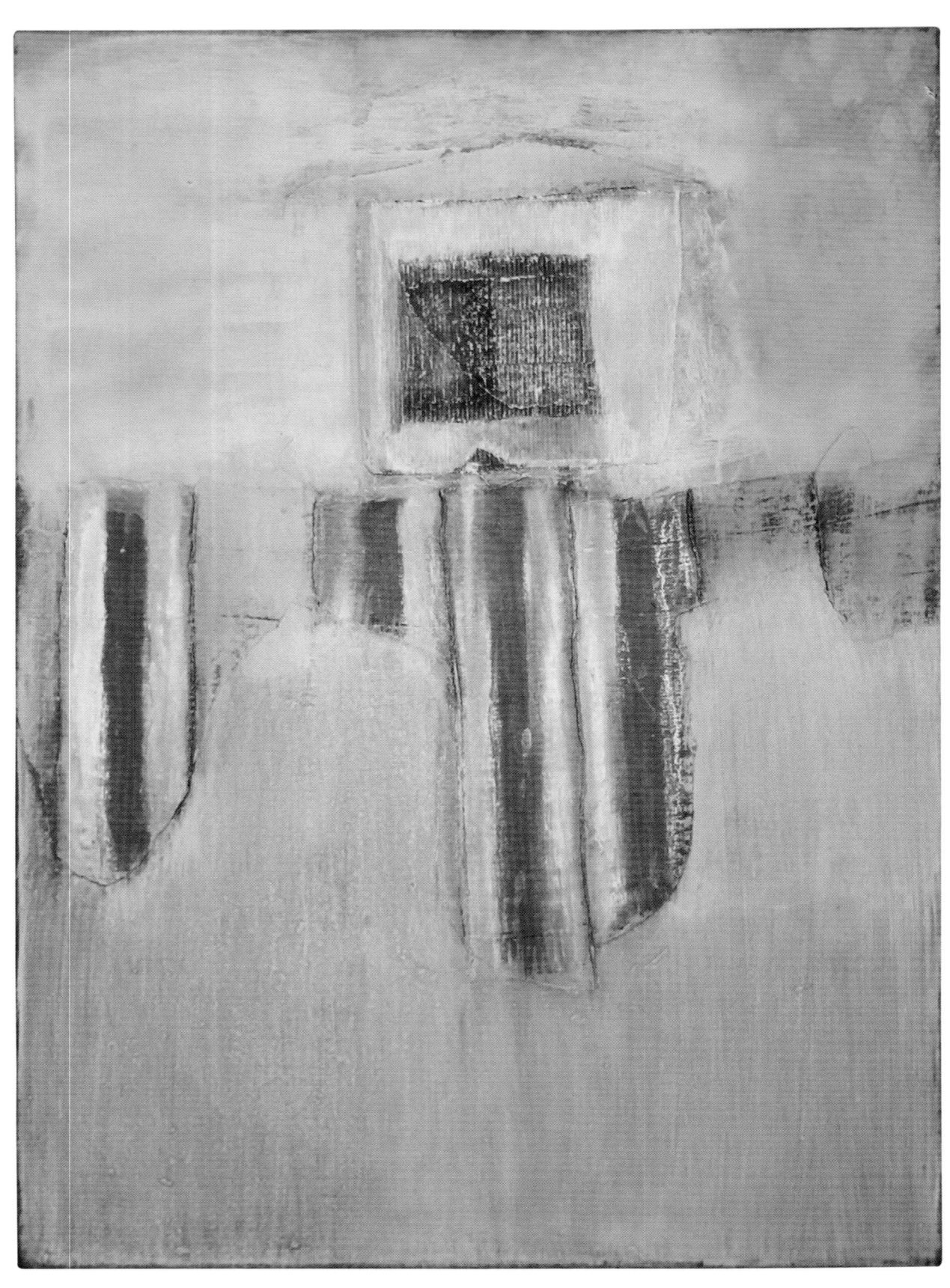

The Repairman's Hut
40 x 30 inches
Mixed Media on Canvas
2011

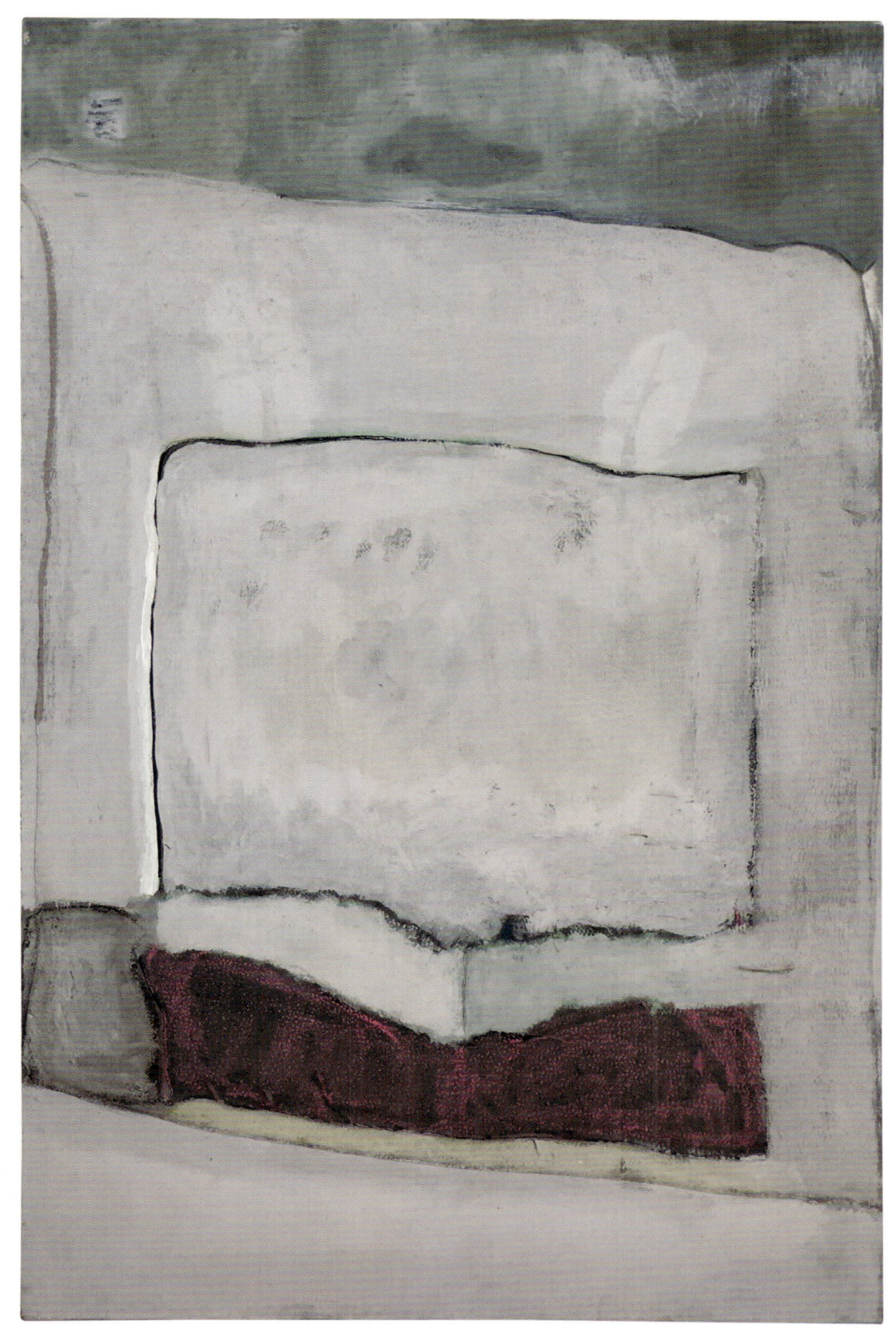

Landfall
36 x 24 inches
Mixed Media on Canvas
2012

Scarecrow
36 x 24 inches
Mixed Media on Canvas
2012

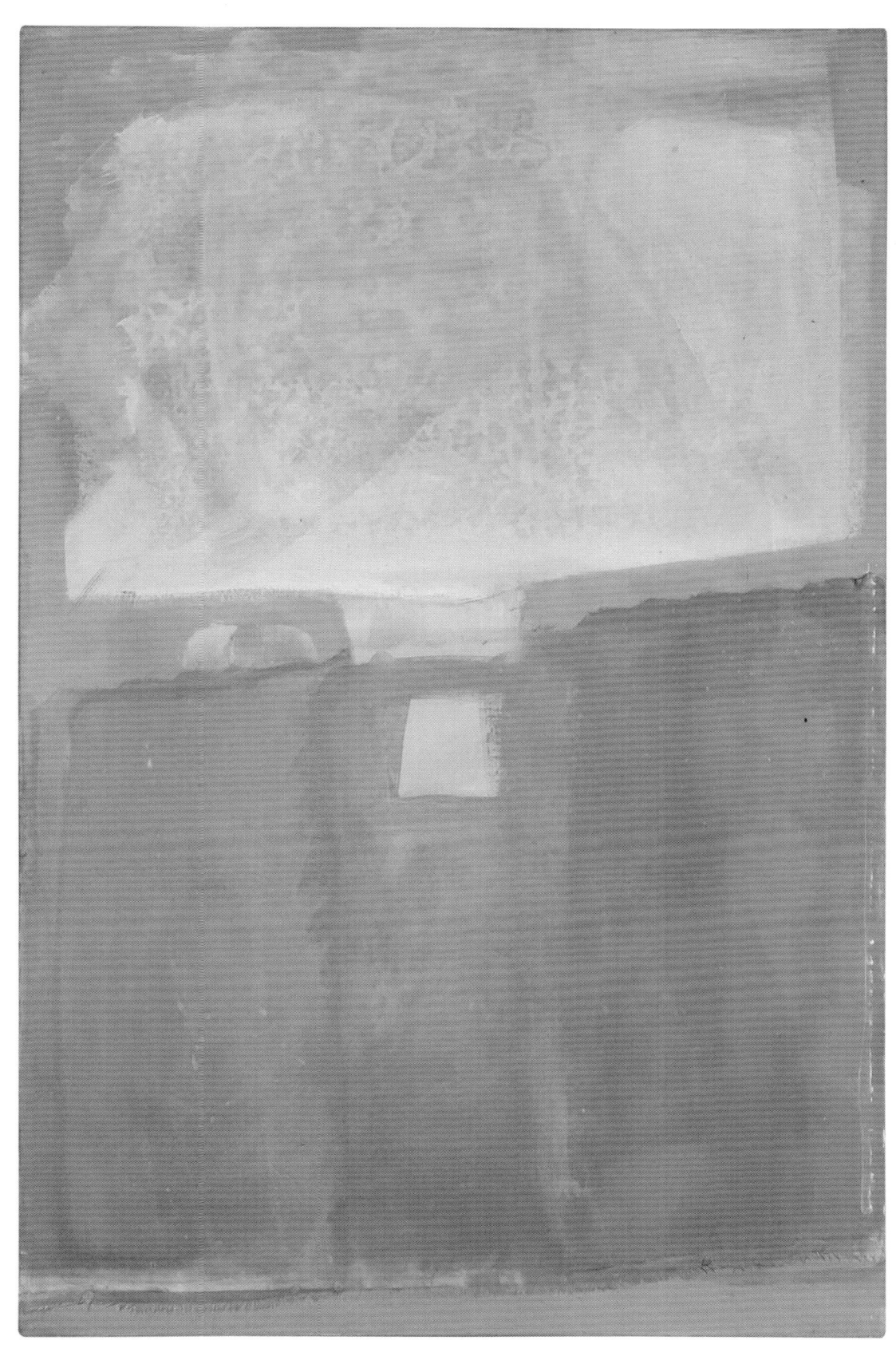

Gulf Spray
36 x 24 inches
Mixed Media on Canvas
2012

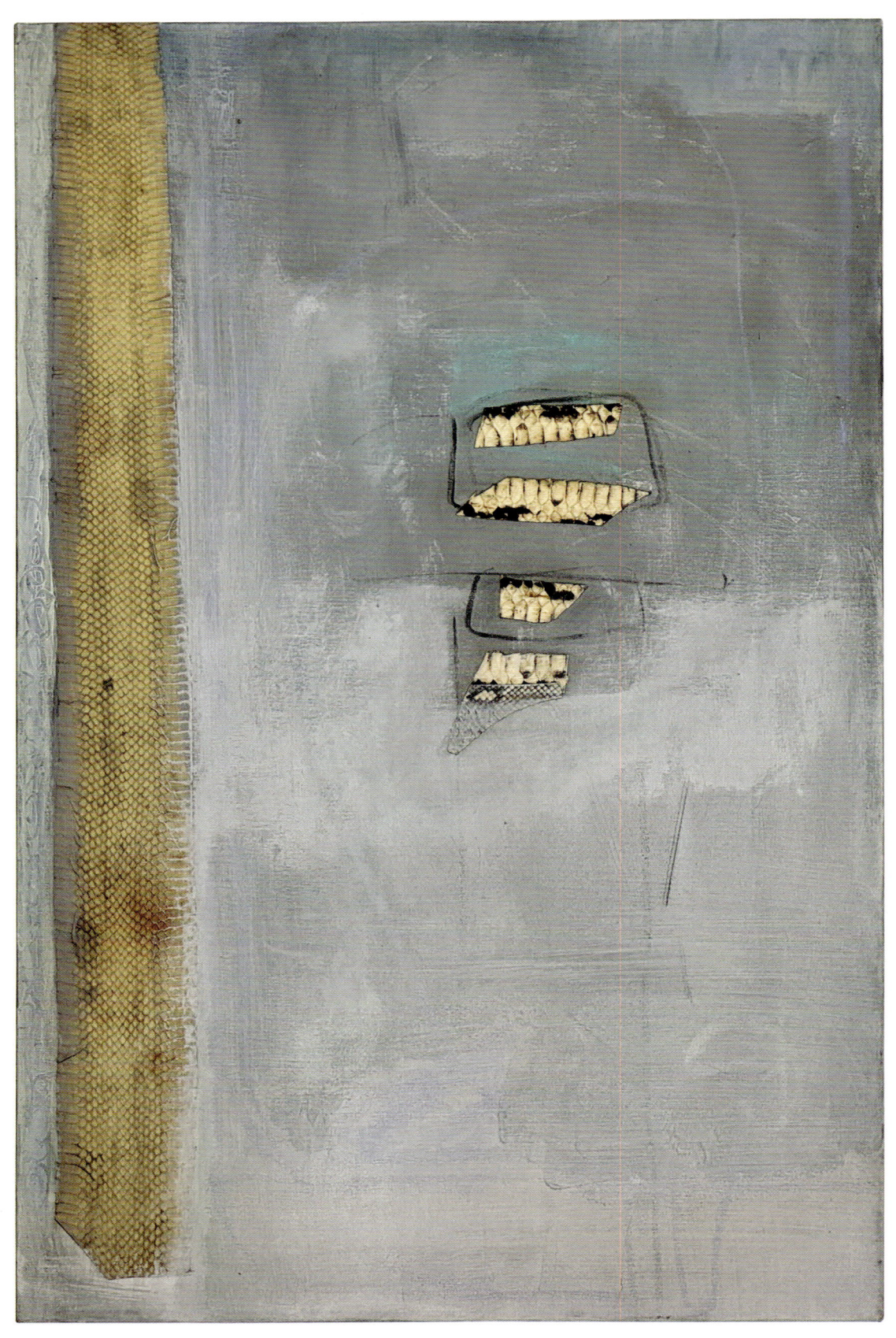

Skinner's Blues
36 x 24 inches
Mixed Media on Canvas
2011

338

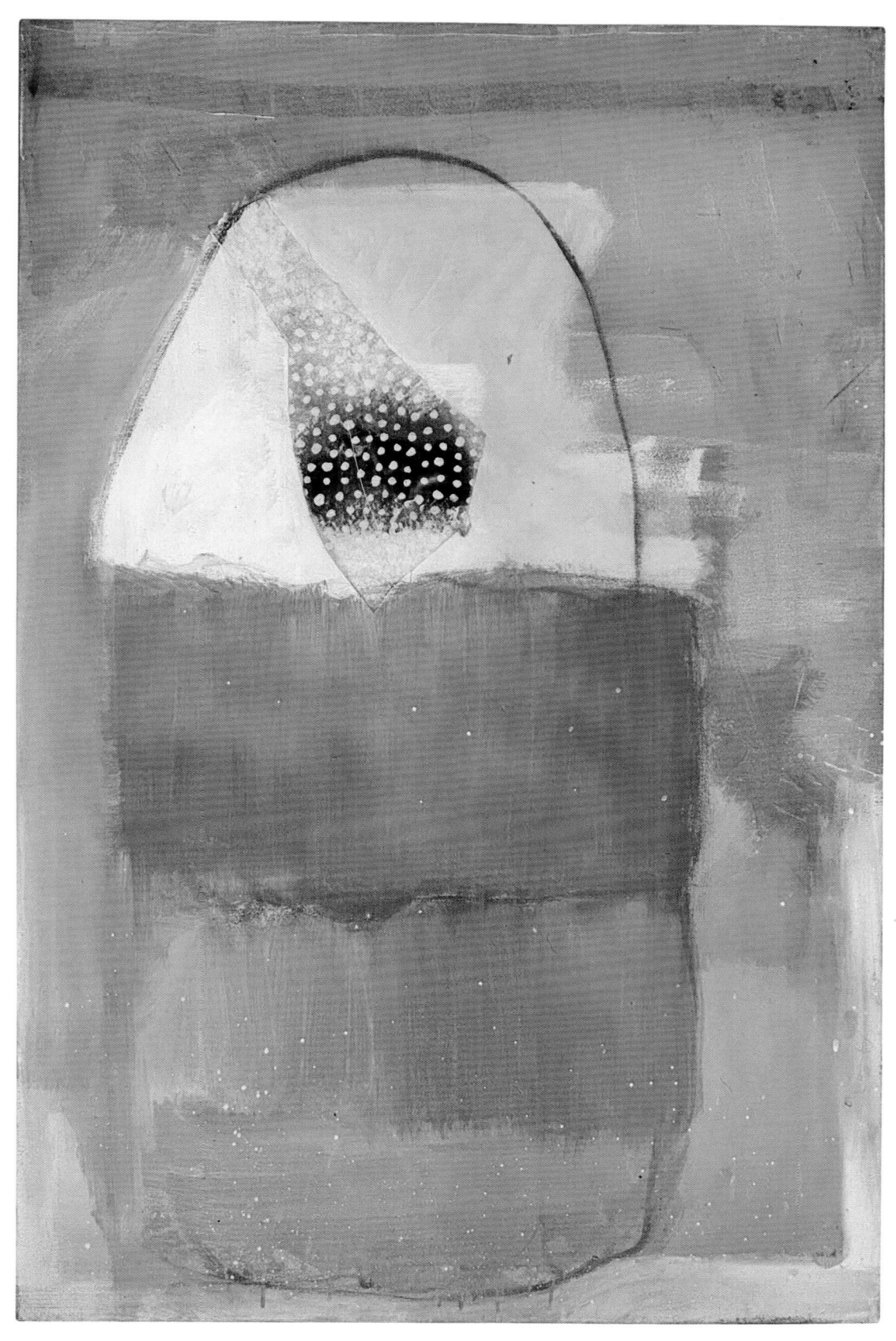

Delivery
36 x 24 inches
Mixed Media on Canvas
2012

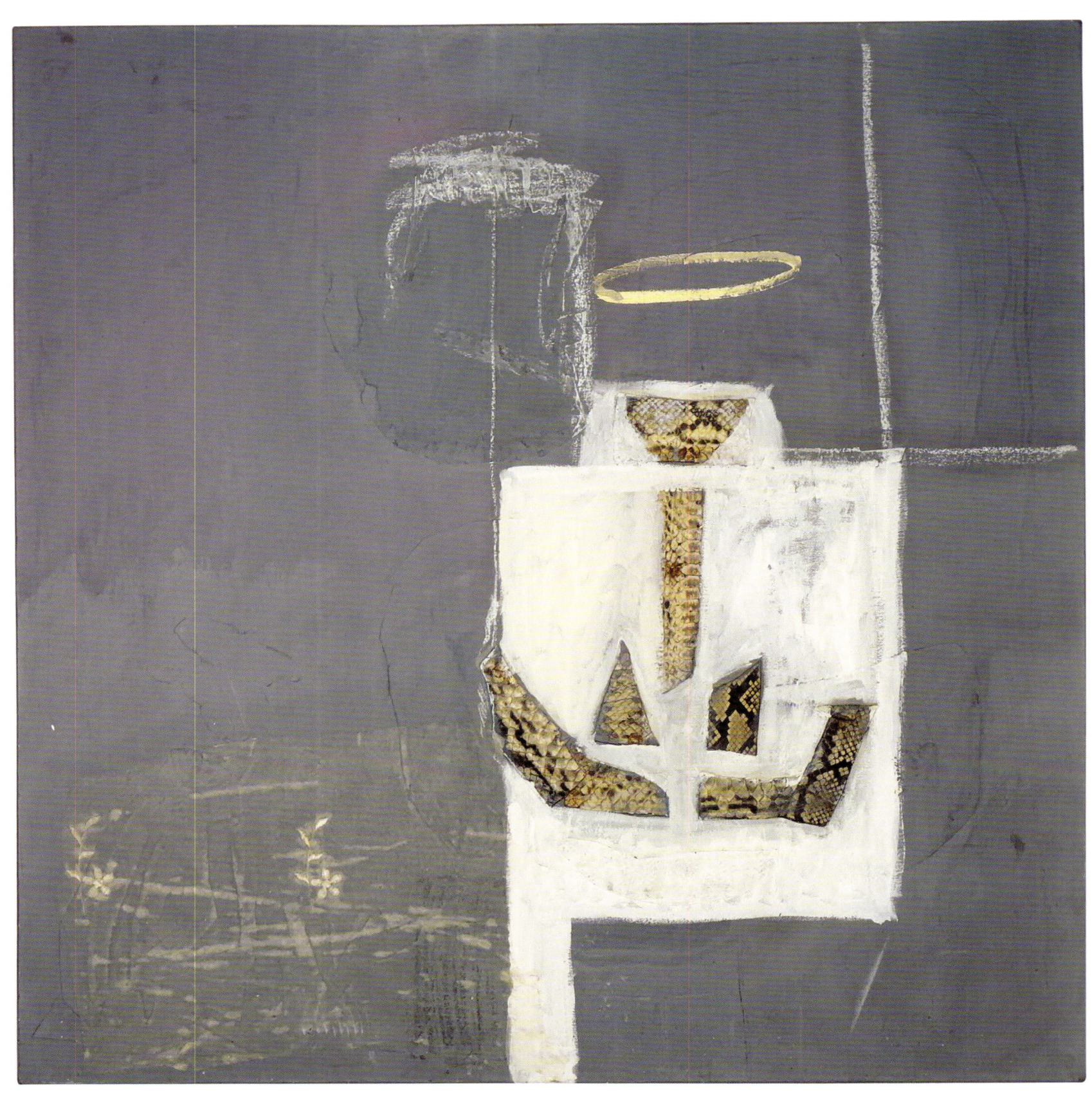

The Numbering of the Sands
30 x 30 inches
Mixed Media on Canvas
2010

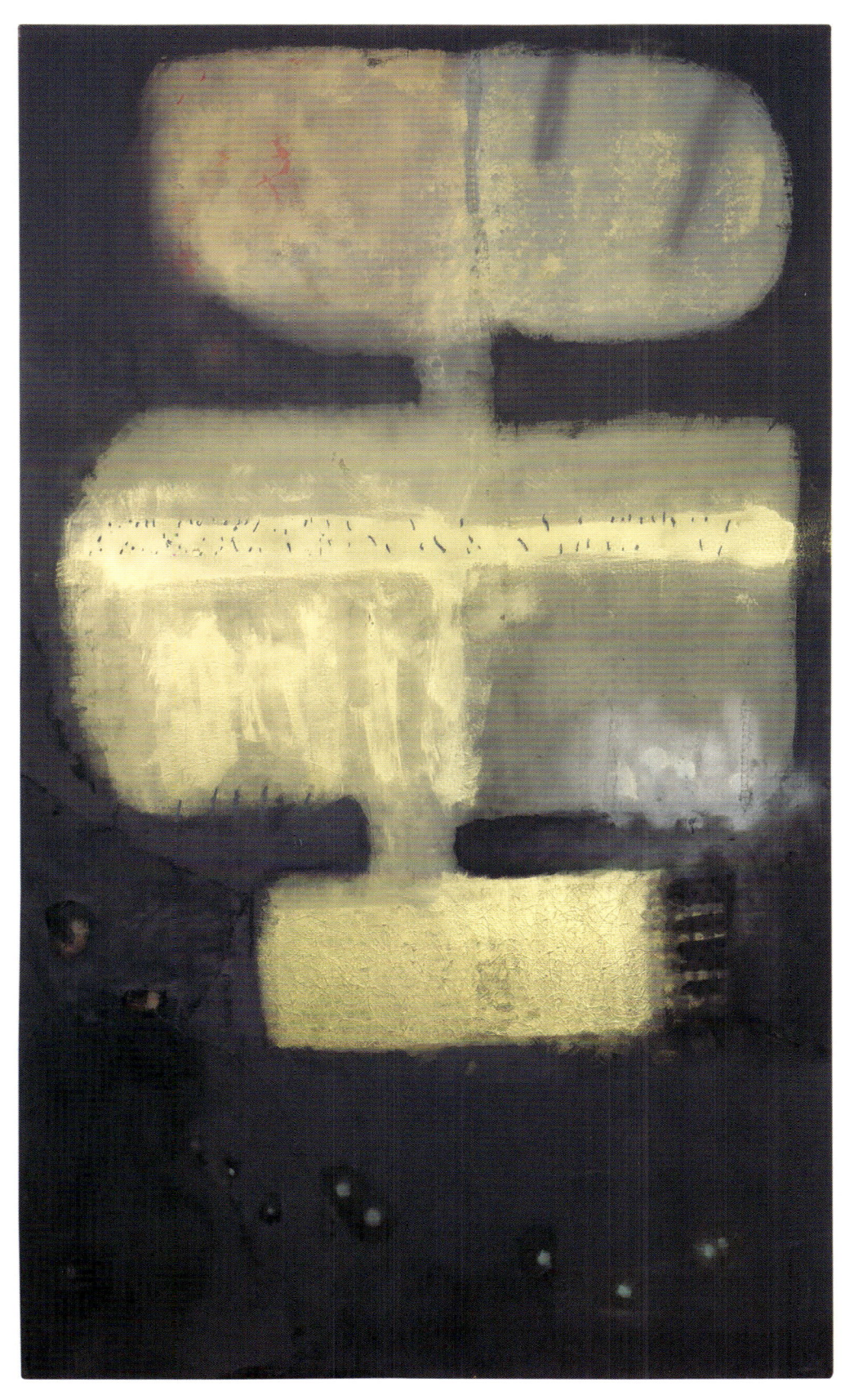

Submersible
60 x 36 inches
Mixed Media on Canvas
2009

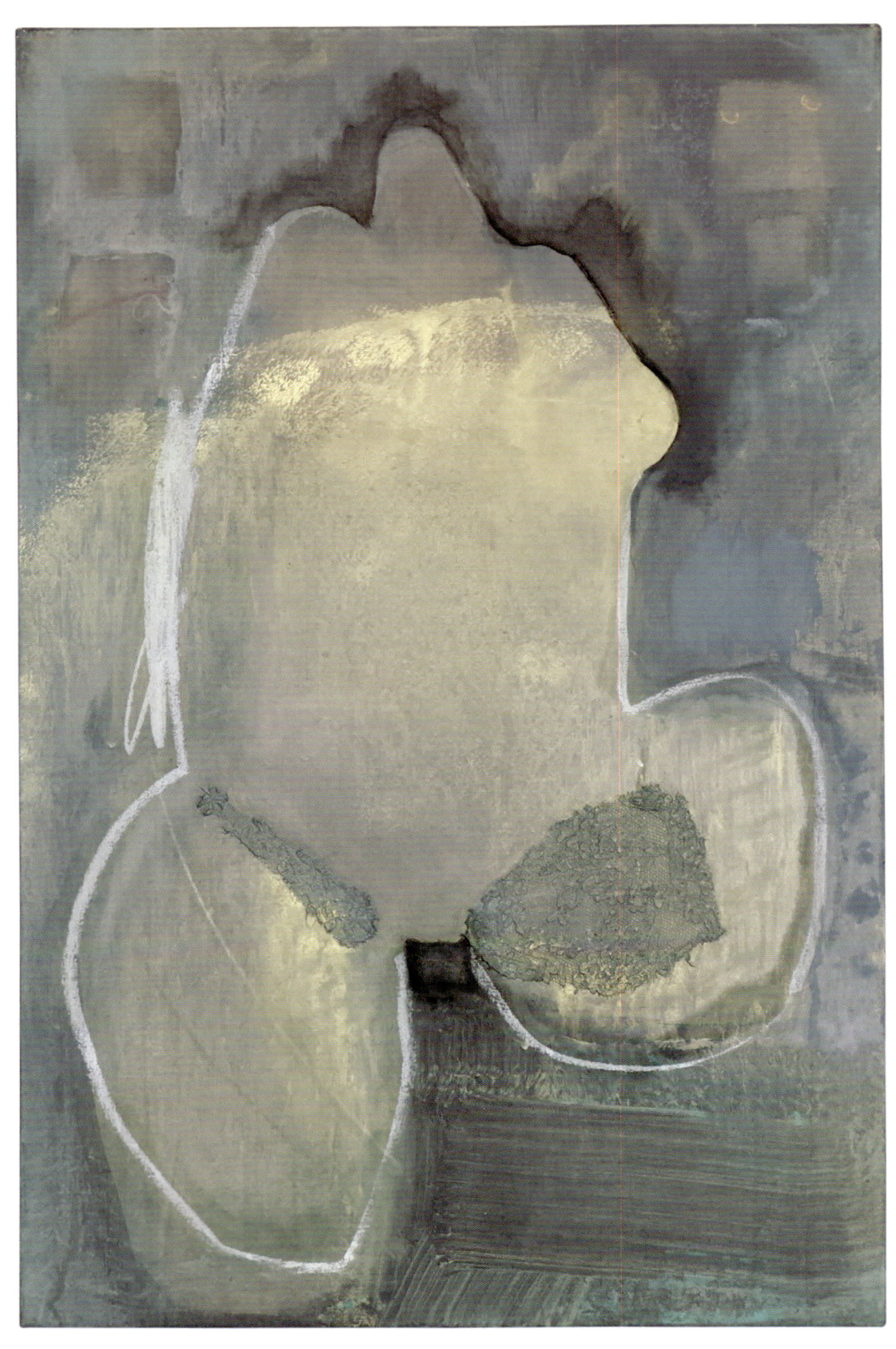

Dancer
36 x 24 inches
Mixed Media on Canvas
2011

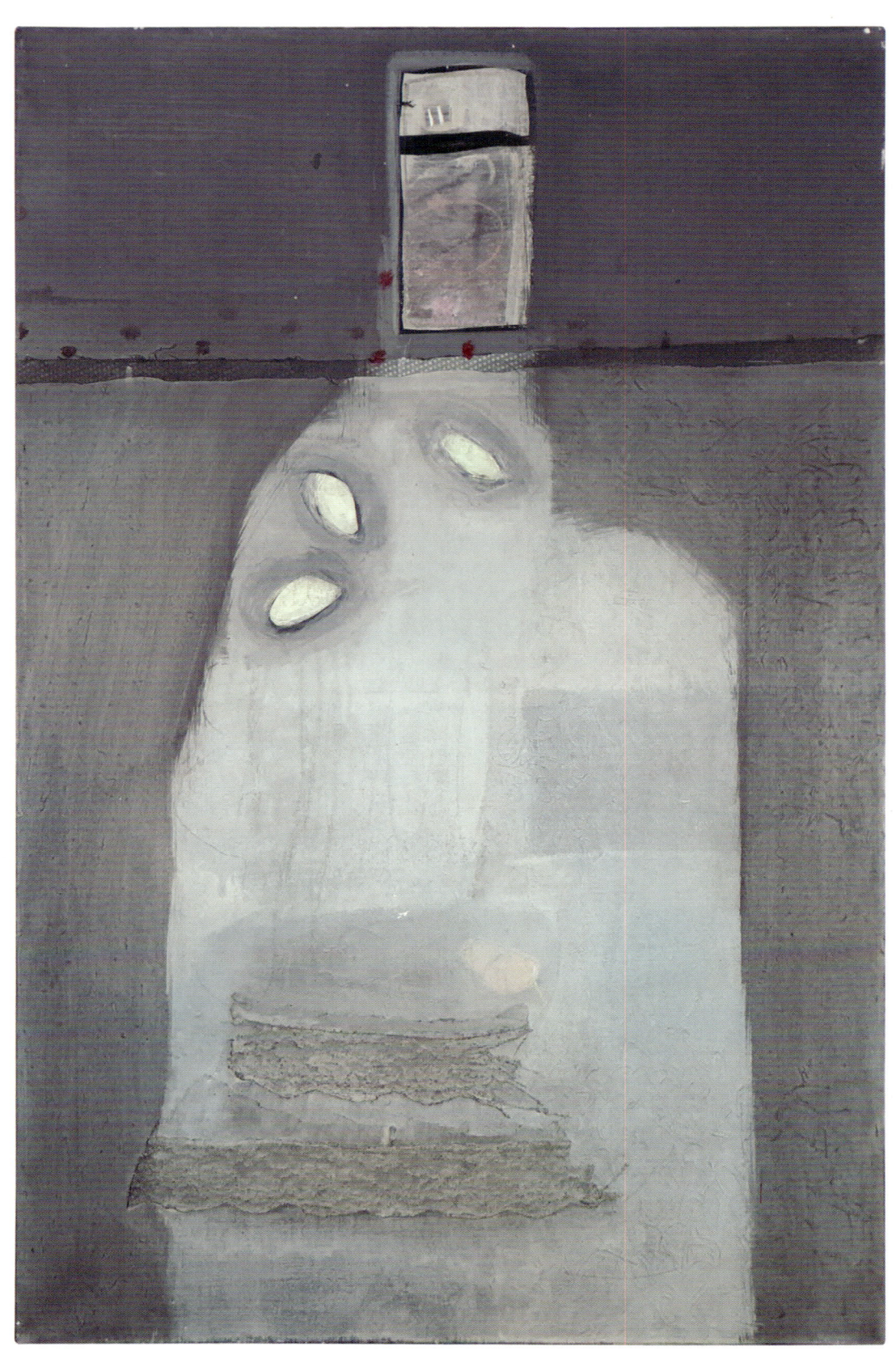

Canestack (Half Gallon)
36 x 24 inches
Mixed Media on Canvas
2012

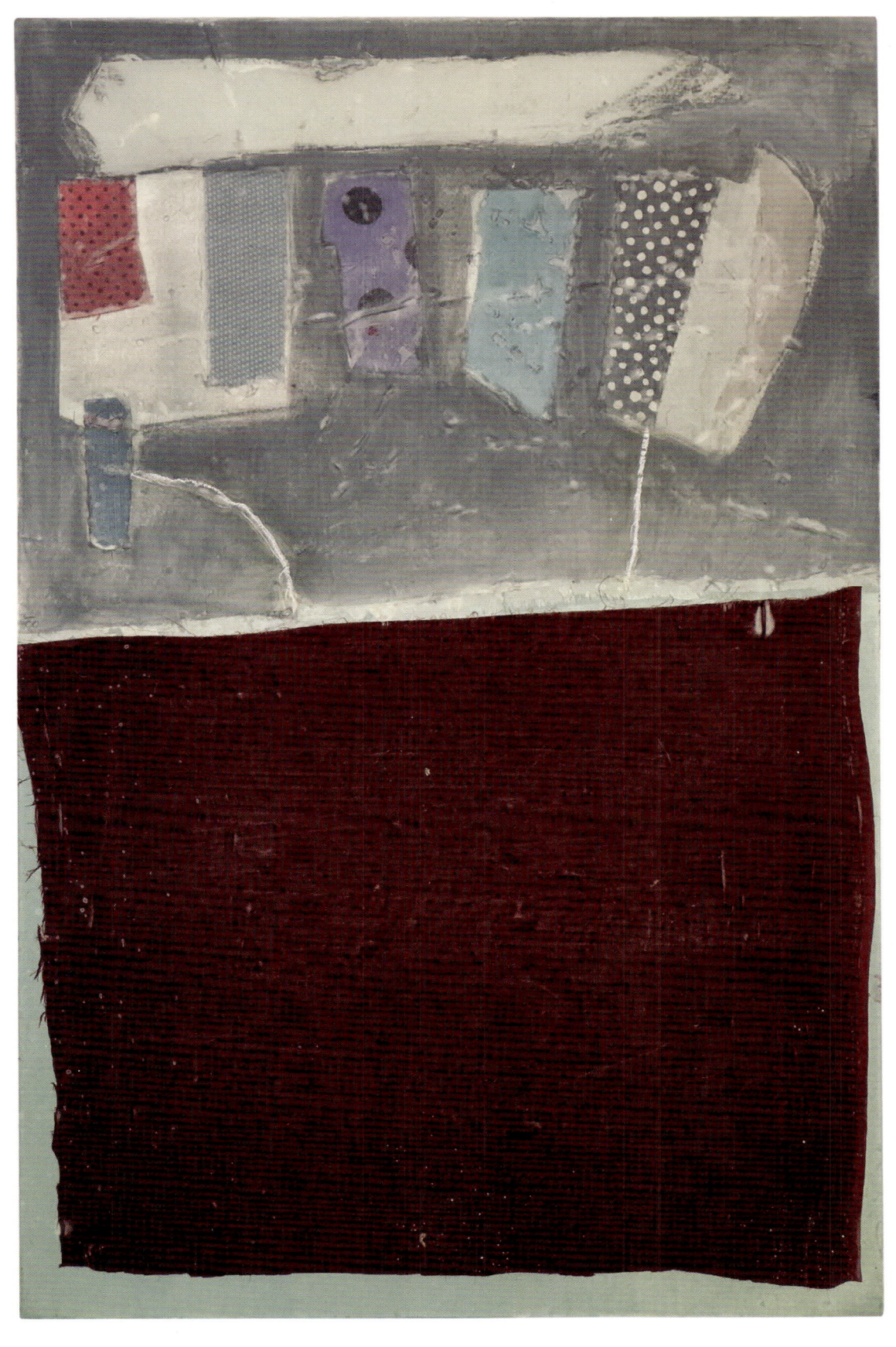

Pandora's Clothesline
36 x 24 inches
Mixed Media on Canvas
2012

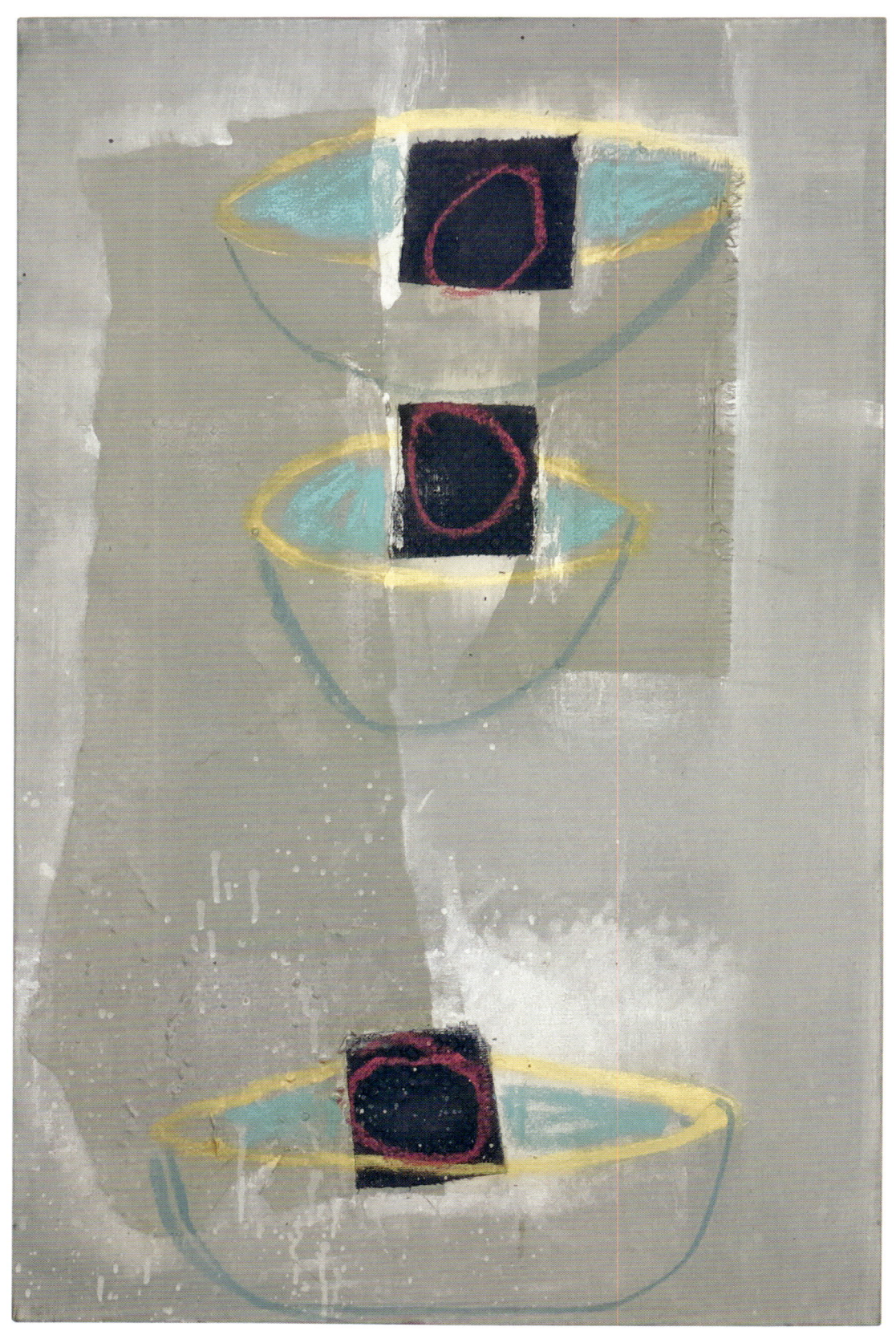

Fountain
36 x 24 inches
Mixed Media on Canvas
2012

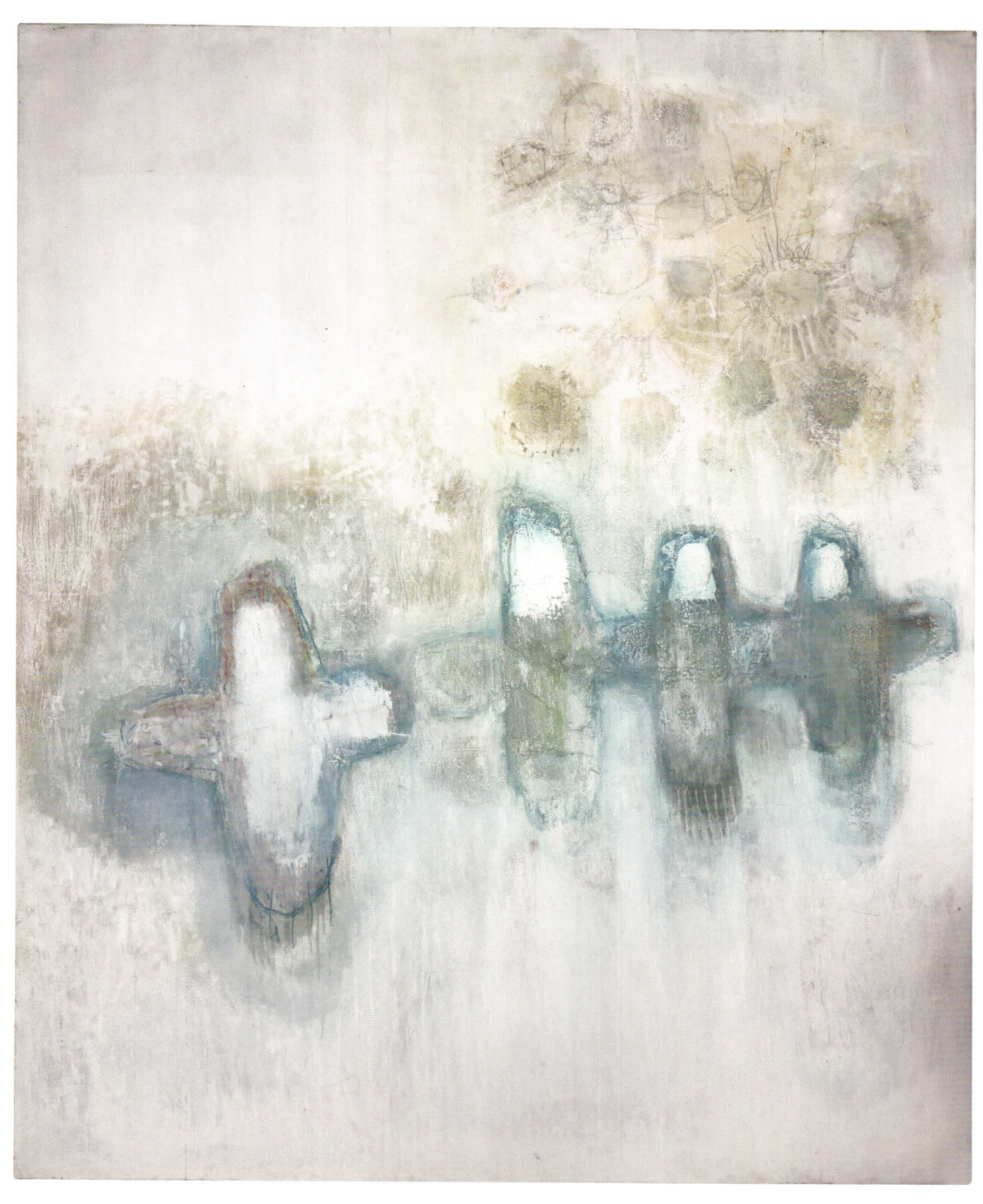

The Gnostics
72 x 60 inches
Mixed Media on Canvas
2016

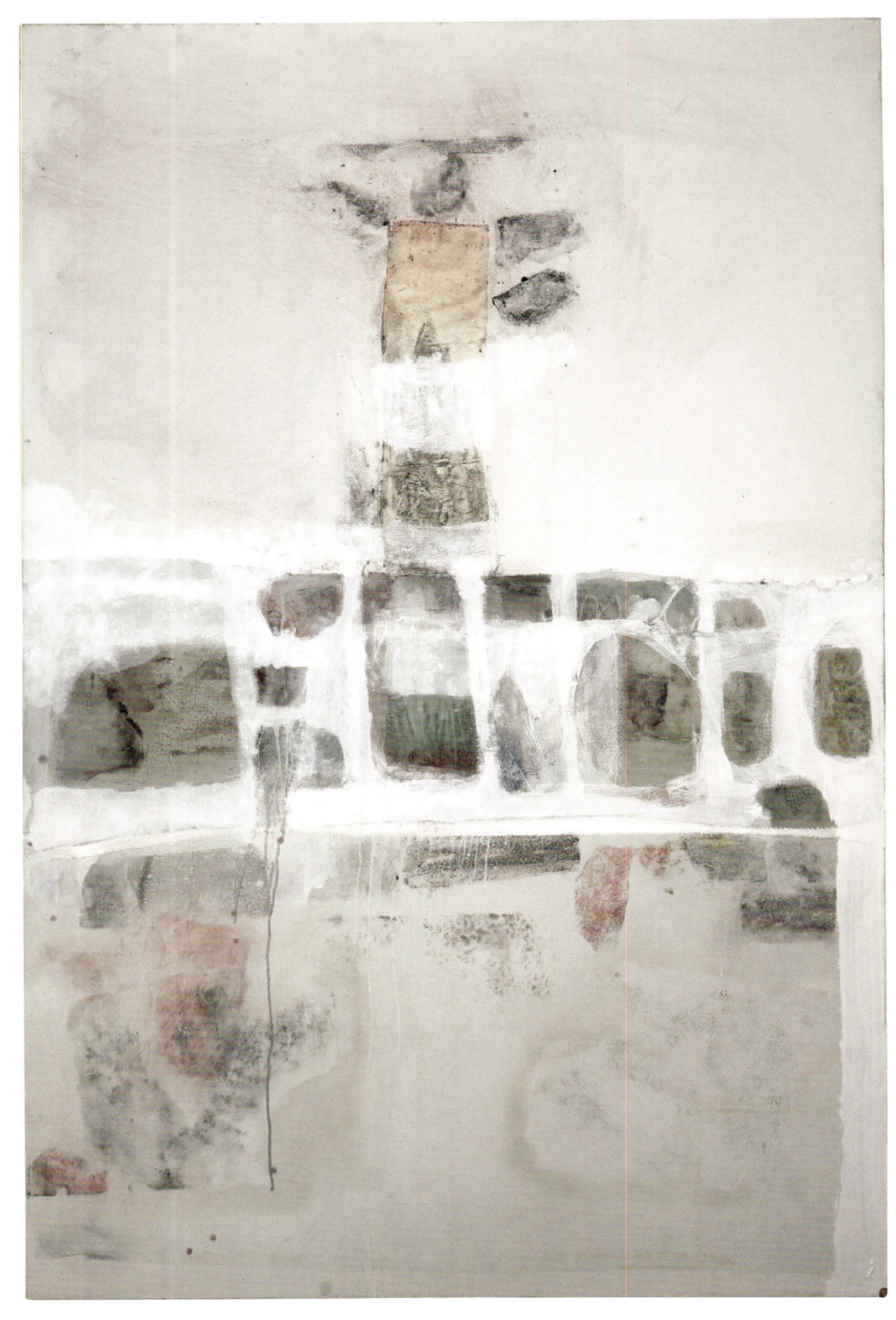

Exhibit A
72 x 48 inches
Mixed Media on Canvas
2011

348

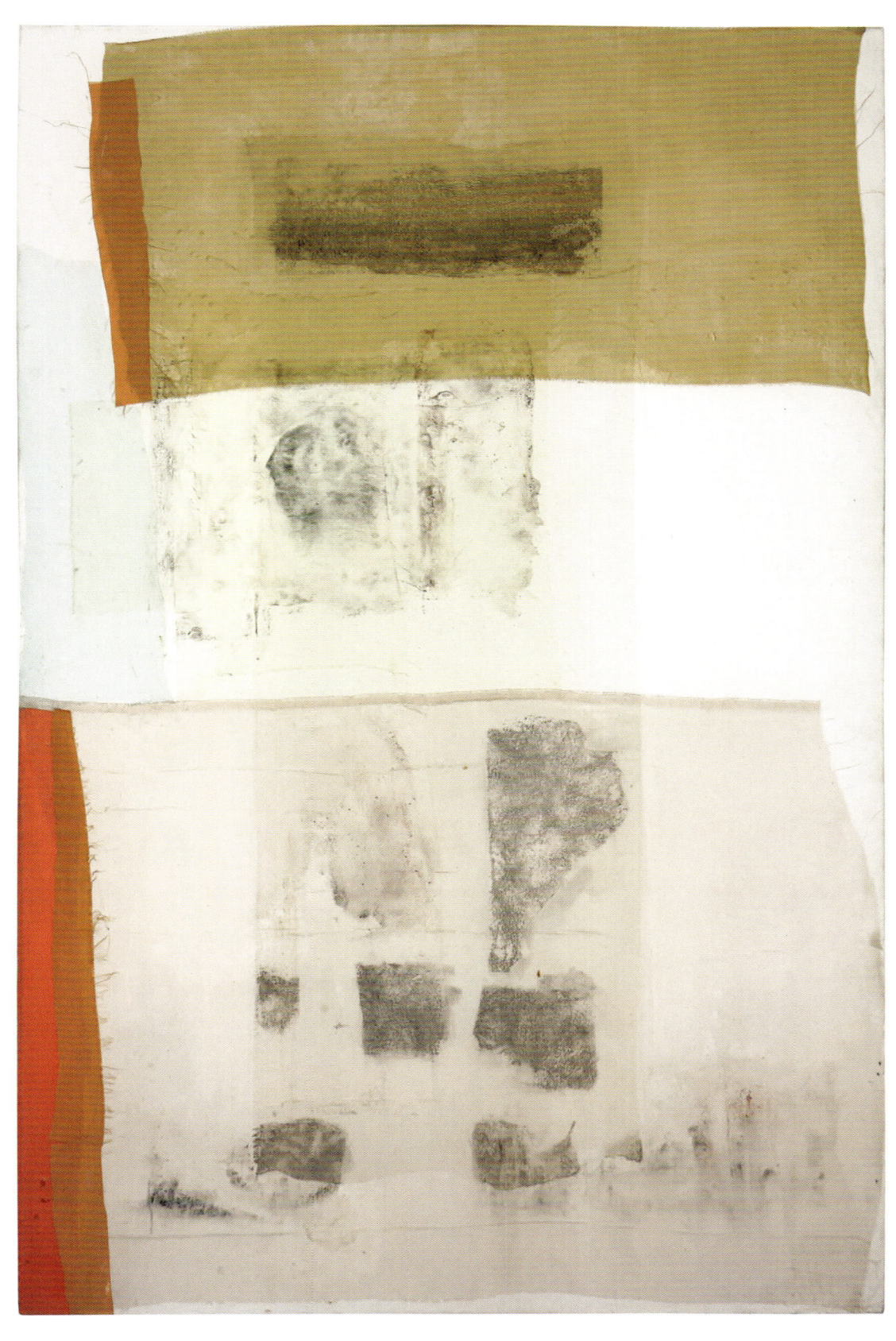

Exhibit B
72 x 48 inches
Mixed Media on Canvas
2011

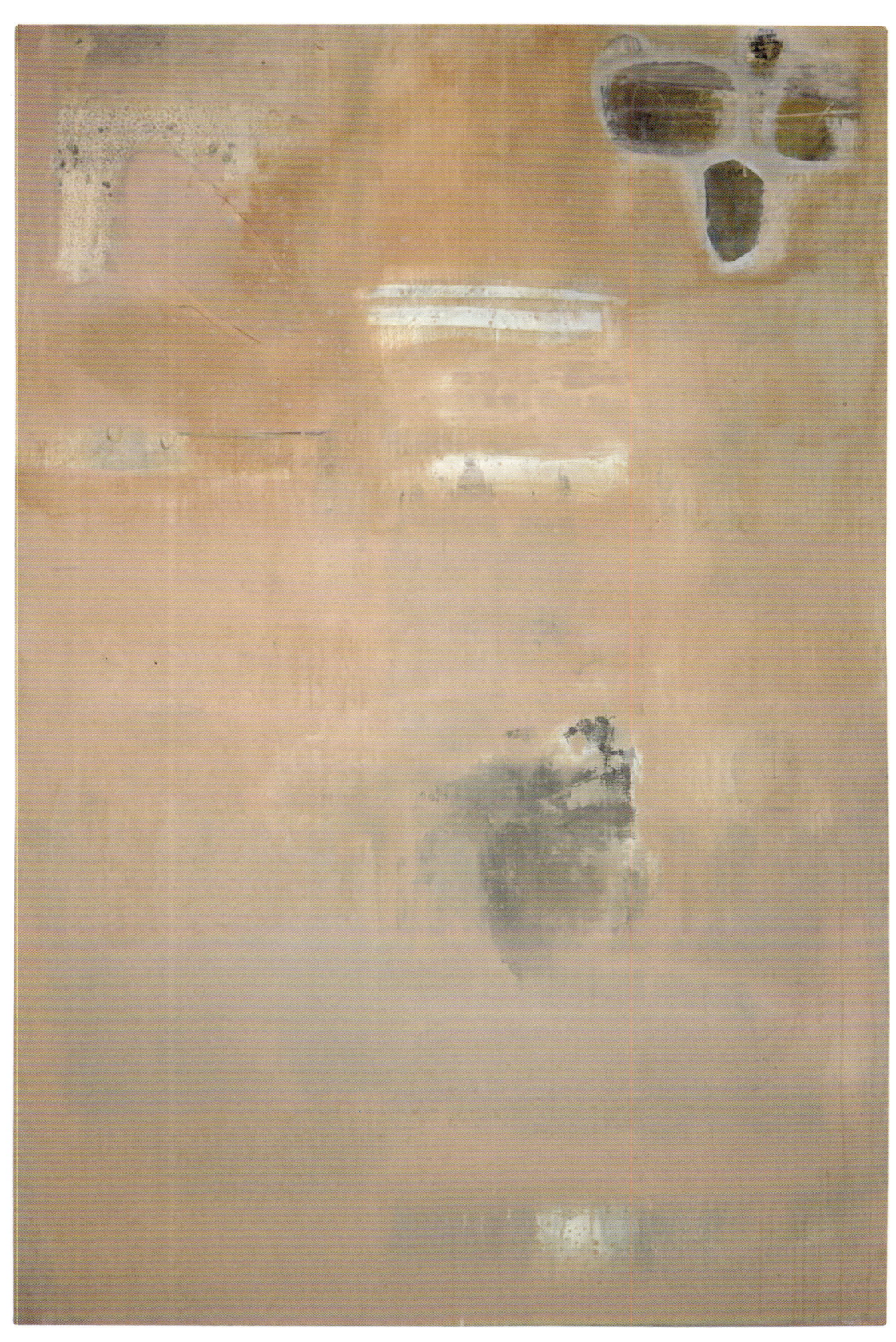

Banquet
72 x 48 inches
Mixed Media on Canvas
2013

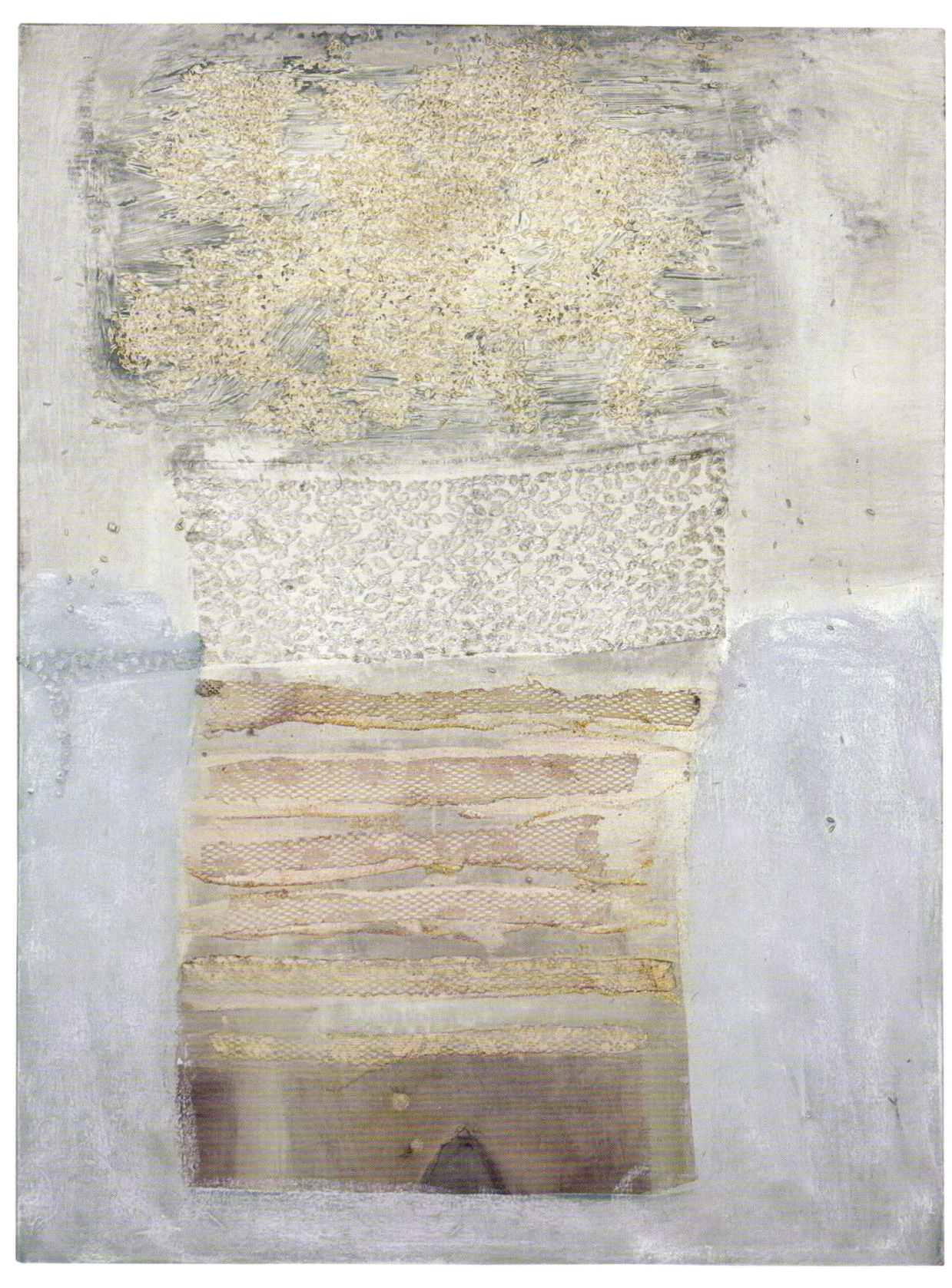

Tidal Page
48 x 36 inches
Mixed Media on Canvas
2011

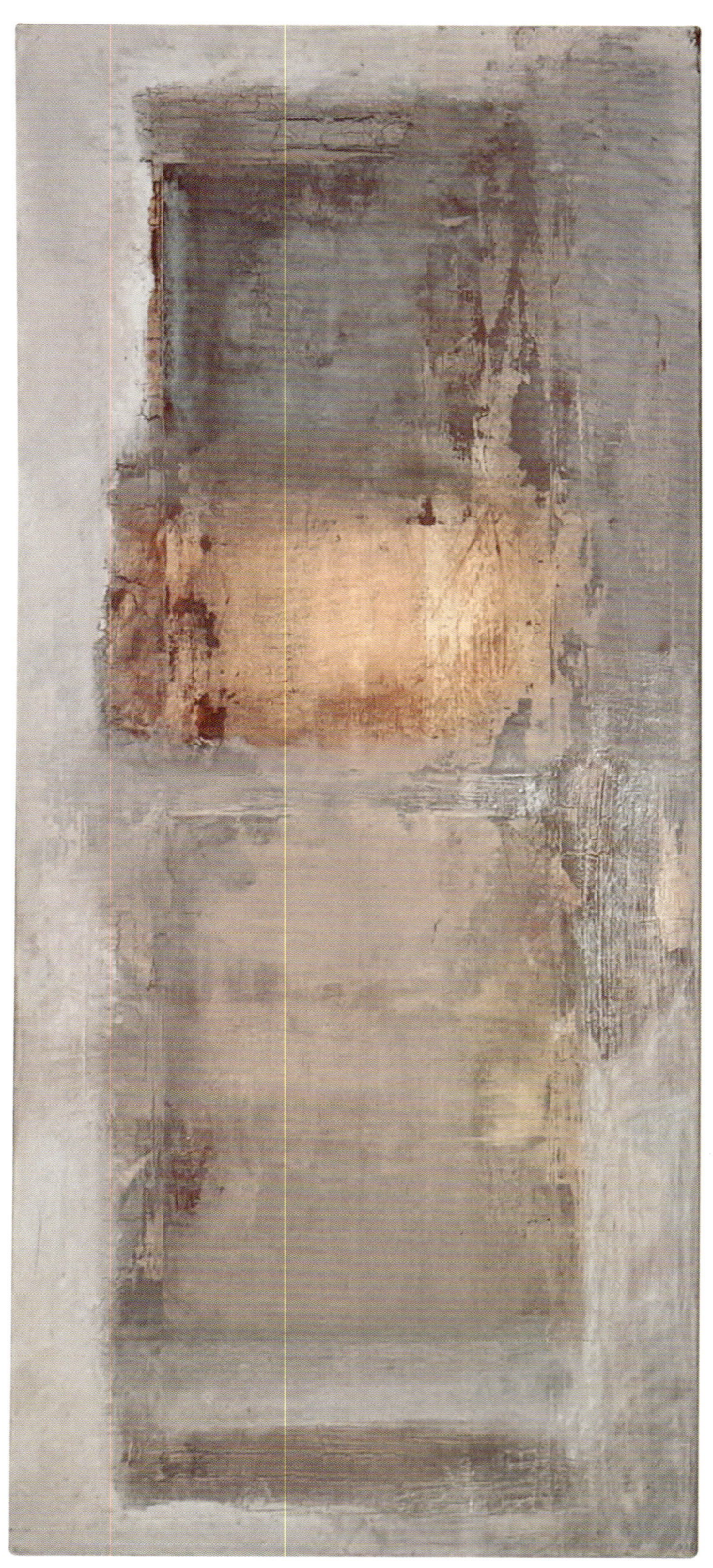
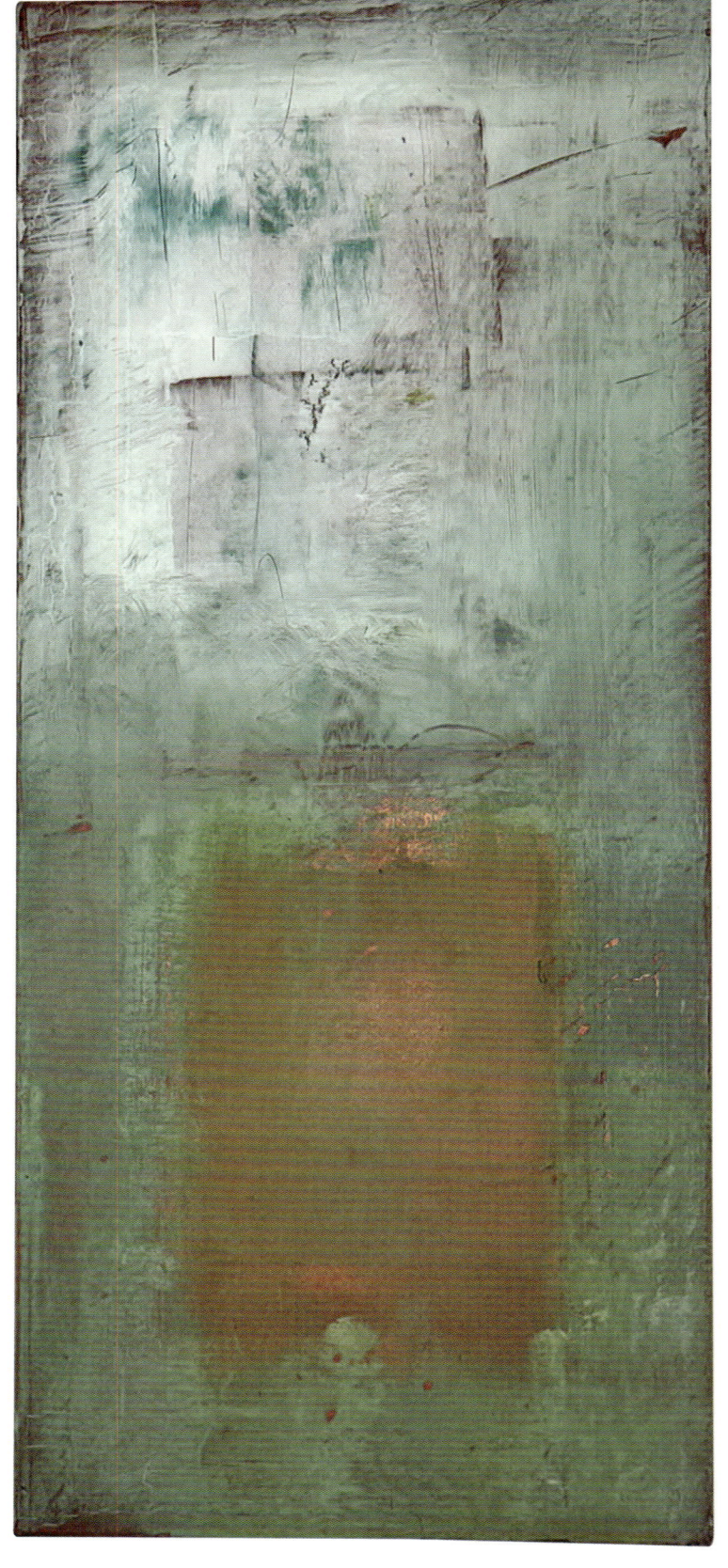

The Fire Escape
40 x 18 inches (Diptych)
Mixed Media on Canvas
2010

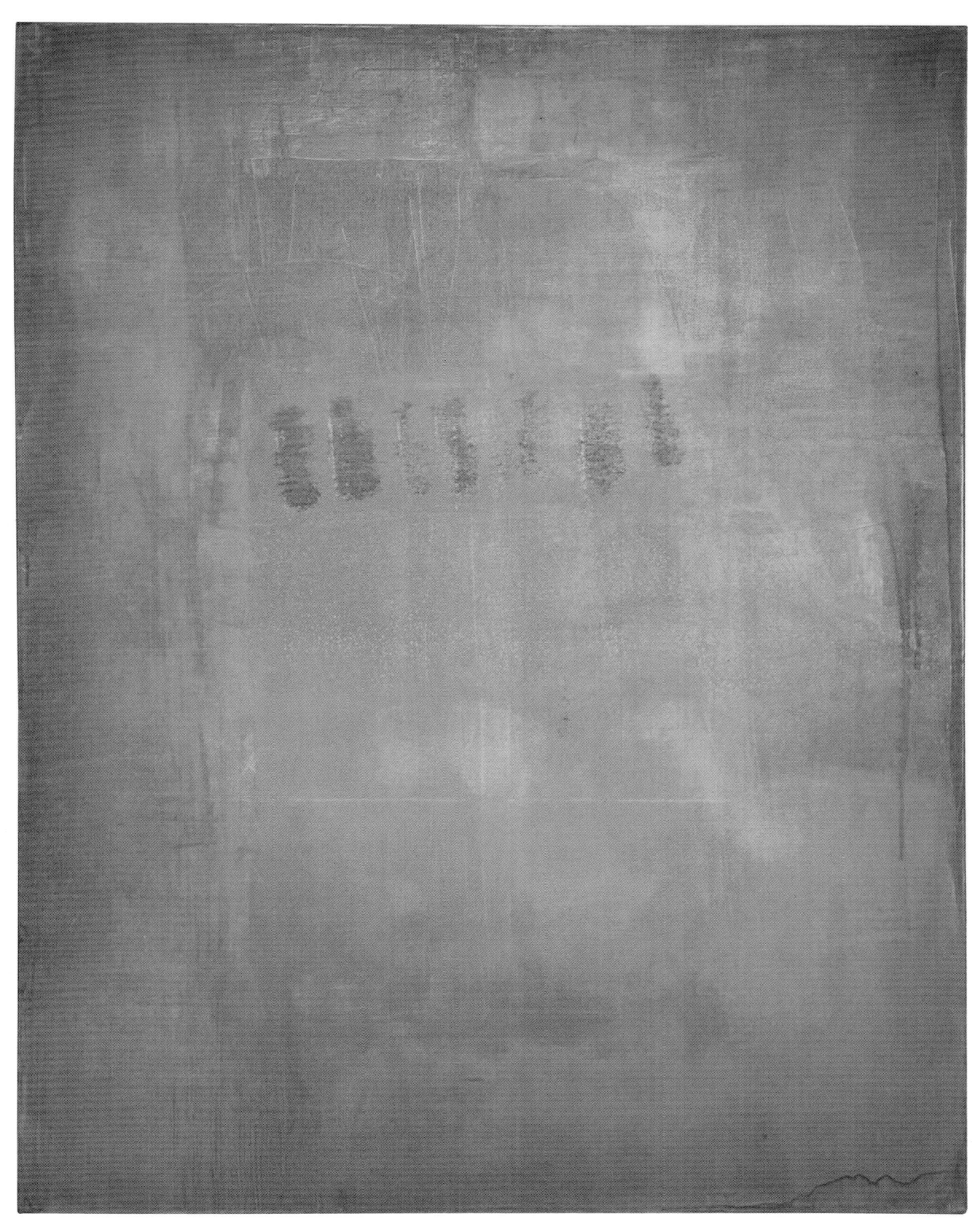

The Saints of Kerosene
60 x 48 inches
Mixed Media on Canvas
2012

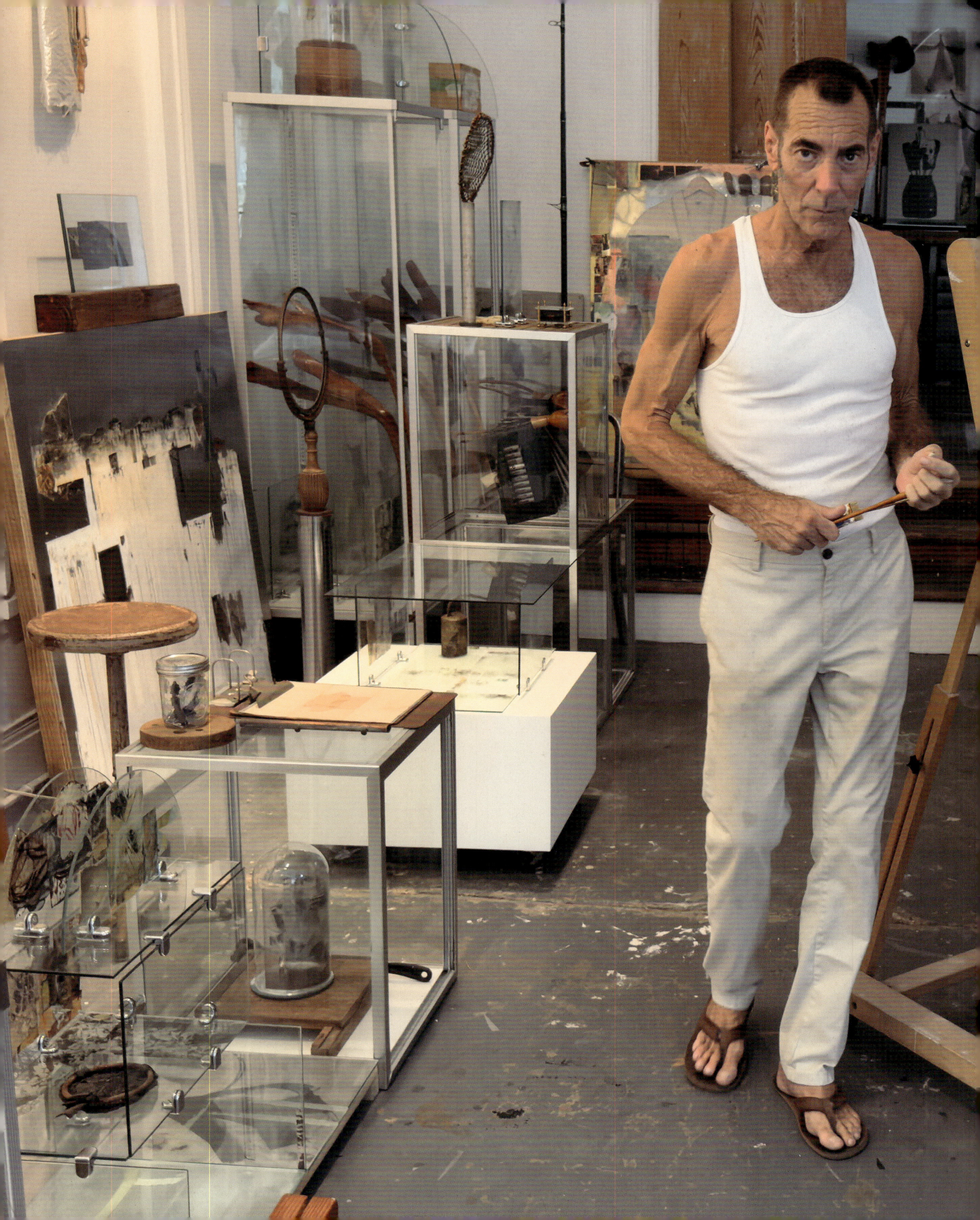

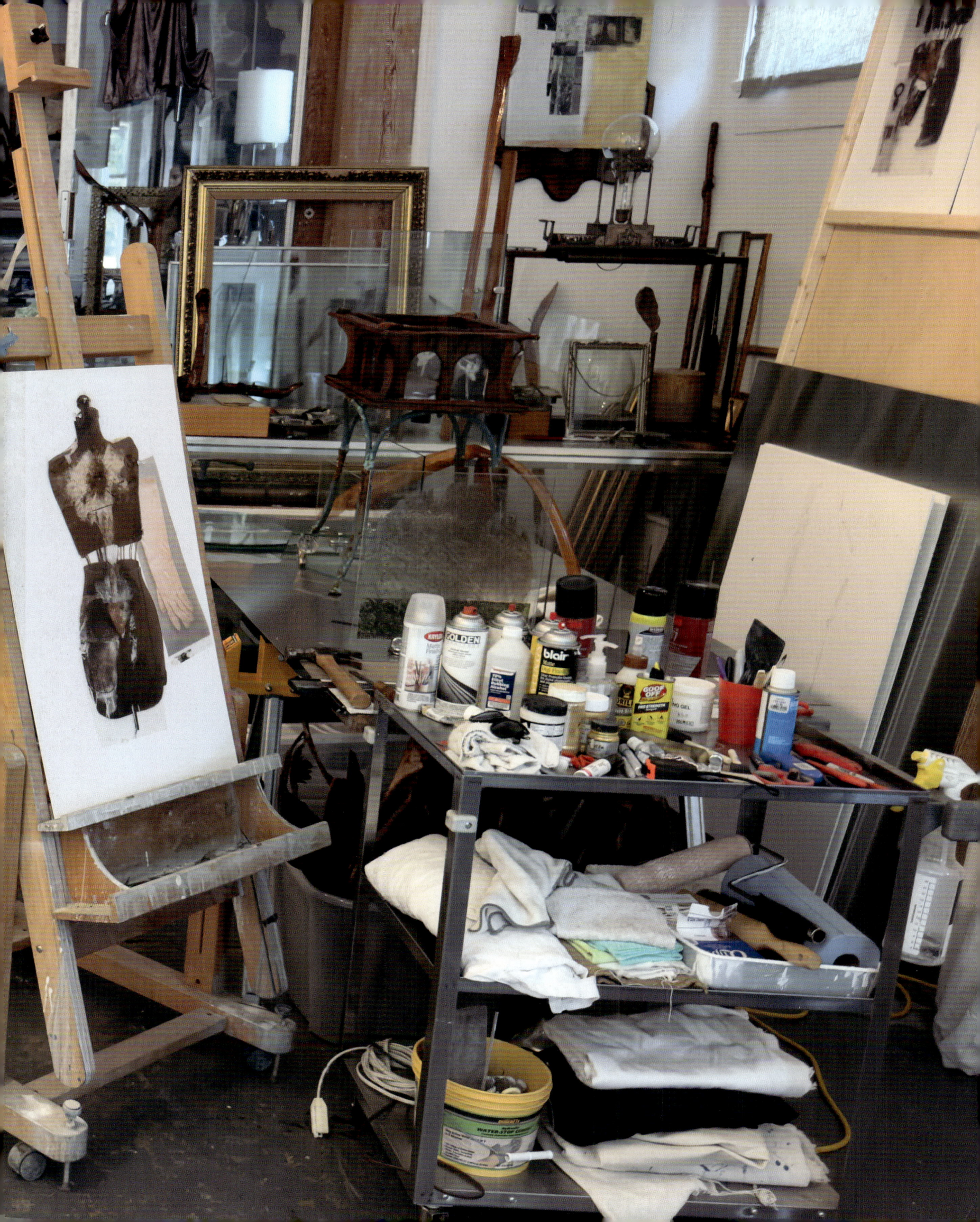

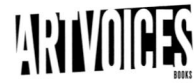

ARTVOICES

BOOKS

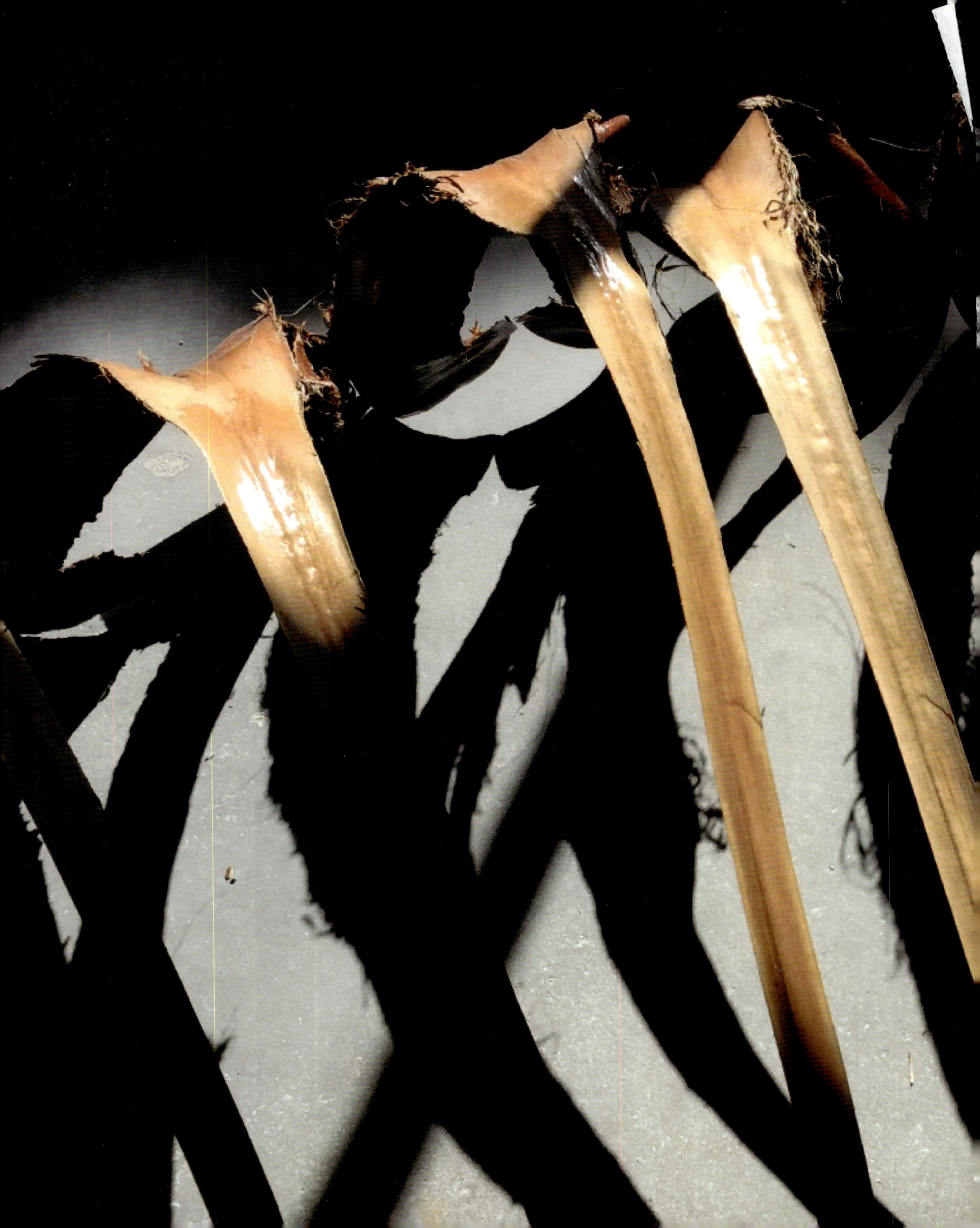